P9-ECI-176

FOODS

Chief Consultants

Joan M. Clement
Professional Caterer and Home Economist
Urbana-Champaign, Illinois

Mary Ann Fugate
Extension Adviser Home Economics, Senior II
Champaign County Cooperative Extension Service
University of Illinois
Urbana-Champaign, Illinois

Consultants

Mamie Hardy
Director, Professional Services
Changing Times Education Service
Arlington, Virginia

Phoebe Rose
Director of Home Economics Education
Houston Public Schools
Houston, Texas

Marilyn L. Steichen
Home Economics Educator
Monte Vista High School
Danville, California

Janet E. Popp Stout
Associate State Supervisor
Home Economics Education
New York State Education Department
Albany, New York

Design, Photography, and Production
Slater Studio, Minneapolis, Minnesota

FOODS

Alice R. Vernon, C.H.E.
Home Economist and Educator
B.S. Foods and Nutrition, University of Illinois
M.Ed University of Illinois

Changing Times Education Service
EMC Publishing
St. Paul, Minnesota

Eileen C. Slater
Editor

Library of Congress Catalog Number: 87-8973

ISBN 0-8219-0298-9

Published by EMC Publishing
300 York Avenue
St. Paul, Minnesota 55101

Printed in the United States of America
0 9 8 7 6 5 4 3 2

Introduction

Foods has been written with you in mind. It is divided into seven sections that guide you through the world of foods and nutrition. Starting with why people make the food choices they do, you'll move on to the basics of good nutrition. Next you'll find a helpful orientation to foods equipment and preparation techniques. In Section 4, you'll be introduced to quick and easy foods that you can fit into your busy schedule and the convenience of the microwave, as well as the time-honored techniques of food preservation. "In the Kitchen," you'll discover nutrition, consumer guidelines, storage tips, and preparation techniques for specific types of food. Planning meals and understanding how to make healthful food choices when eating out are covered in "Let's Eat!" *Foods* concludes with a section on food careers, which includes some handy tips for getting started right now.

Throughout this book, you'll find special features that highlight the importance of related facts and issues pertaining to each chapter's subject matter. These features include:

- *Cooking Hints*—easy-to-follow steps for food preparation.
- *Consumer Guide*—tips for making wise consumer decisions.
- *Creative Tips*—special techniques and gourmet projects that guide you through the "art" of food preparation.
- *So They Say*—current research and news to alert you to what is known "so far" about nutrition.
- *Safety Tips*—"what to do in case of..." and guidelines on how to prevent accidents.
- *Food Facts*—developments and controversies of the food industry.

In addition, you will find tempting recipes throughout *Foods*. A special feature of these recipes is the "Nutrition Bar." This bar is colored to highlight the percentage of the recommended food group serving furnished by one portion of the food product. (See the Basic Four Food Groups on pages 38-41.) The bars can be read as follows:

- Completely colored—one complete serving of the food group.
- Partially colored—a percentage of the food group serving. For instance, if one-half of the square is colored, then one-half of a serving of the food group is offered by that recipe.
- Completely colored plus a number—more than one serving of the food group.
- Gray—no servings in that particular food group.

This informative bar is not a complete listing of the nutrients in the food product, but a handy guide for quickly analyzing the nutritional value of the food product. It's "nutrition at a glance" to help you plan a daily balanced diet—and just one part of the feast of facts you'll find in *Foods*. So dig in and enjoy!

Table of Contents

Section 5 In the Kitchen

Section 6 Let's Eat

Section 7 Off to Work

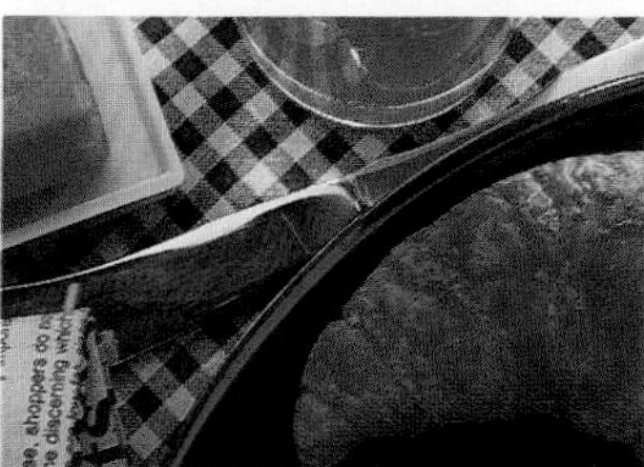

Section 1

The Meaning of Food

Chapter 1: Your World of Food

Why You Eat

Did you have breakfast this morning? If you did, you know you could spend the first part of the day not worrying about grabbing a bite to eat. Without having breakfast, though, you would have a constant reminder of what you missed. Hunger—a powerful reminder. Your stomach would "growl" and you might experience other effects such as a headache. Then as lunchtime grew nearer, you would find it hard to concentrate on anything but the time and how soon you would be able to eat. Now take that feeling and imagine how it would feel if you didn't eat for one day. Then two days. Finally a week. Do you think you would be able to think about anything else but food?

Studies have shown that if food is withheld from people to the point of strong need, the urge to obtain food overrules all else. People will forget about their other needs because of their desire to eat. Eating is a basic survival instinct.

If this were how you were going to spend your spring break what would you take along to eat? For 55 days in the early spring, five men and one woman struggled over the frozen Arctic Ocean in their attempt to reach the top of the world—the North Pole. On the good days, the temperature would reach -20°F. On bad days it dropped to -70°F and the slightest wind could freeze tears in their eyes. Those were the conditions facing the Steger International Polar Expedition as they traveled 1000 miles by dog sled to the North Pole without supplies or assistance from the outside world.

In order to survive those cold, rugged conditions, the five men and one woman required a very special diet to give them the energy they needed. Their diet was designed to give them between 6000 and 8000 calories daily. (An office worker needs only 2000.) However, because they had to carry all of their own supplies, they had to watch the weight of the food they took along. Breakfast was usually oatmeal. Lunch consisted of prepacked energy bars that were eaten on the trail. Dinner was a stew of pemmican, egg noodles, butter, cheese, and a fortified soup mix. Pemmican is a concentrated food that was used by North American Indians. The pemmican recipe used for the Steger Expedition was 20 pounds of dried ground red meat, 6 pounds of dried ground liver, 25 pounds of rendered fat, 6 pounds of whole wheat meal, 3 pounds of wheat germ, 3 cups of molasses, and 2 ounces of rose hip powder. The ingredients were formed into large blocks and then cut into 1-pound bars. That's not exactly most people's idea of a good meal. However, it fulfilled the team's needs of a high-

Special circumstances require special foods. On a polar expedition, these people chose a diet high in calories to give them the energy they needed.

energy food that was easy to carry. It was what they needed to survive.

Obviously you are aware that you need food, but why do you eat the foods you do? Your food choices are based on needs and wants other than basic survival. What are those influences? The remainder of this chapter will help you understand why you choose the foods you do.

As you read this book, you will learn about **nutrition** (the science of how your body uses food) and **nutrients** (the chemicals in food that your body needs). Many of your food choices then will be based on this information. However, there are many other influences on your food choices.

Why Do You Like Certain Foods?

Your feelings about food—where do they come from? Everyone likes some foods and dislikes others. You already may have experienced the frustration of trying to get a group of friends to select a party menu they all like. Or what about those times a group of you disagreed on where to eat because of strong differences in food preferences. More bluntly, what one person "loved" another "hated."

Food likes and dislikes are created by all your past experiences, the people around you, and several other influences. Pleasurable experiences, such as enjoying hot sliced turkey at happy family get-togethers, can create strong feelings for certain foods. Your feelings about foods are not always pleasant ones, though. How would you feel about hot dogs if you became ill shortly after eating one at the beach? Past experiences strongly influence how you will feel about foods in the future. Every individual has associations with food that are affected by lifestyle, emotions, and values.

The people around you—your family, friends, neighbors, and groups you join—contribute to your feelings and choices regarding foods. Other influences on your choices include the region of the country in which you live or have lived, ethnic customs, and religious customs.

The People Around You

Food is more than a means to satisfy your hunger. If that were all it meant to you, you would eat the first thing in sight. However, food choices also offer a sense of belonging or companionship with others. Have you ever tried a particular food because someone you know likes that food? Maybe you go out for chicken because all of your friends do even though you would rather have a pizza.

Perhaps as a small child your parents gave you carrots seasoned with dill and now you wouldn't think of eating carrots any other way. Have you avoided some foods just because they are not served in your home? Don't let the people around you be the only influence. You could be limiting your diet nutritionally and limiting the fun of trying new foods. Learn to choose foods based not only on your own likes and dislikes but on sound nutrition guidelines. You'll learn all about those in Chapters 3 and 4.

Regional Foods

Perhaps you've traveled from one part of the country to another and noticed how favorite foods can change in just a few miles. Even with sophisticated communications and transportation systems, certain areas of the country develop food specialties, known as **regional foods.** Regional specialities often develop from local crops and products and ethnic groups who have settled in the area. A southern breakfast, for example, is likely to include grits and smoked, sugar-cured ham with red-eyed gravy. Those foods are not common or favored a hundred miles north. Coastal areas feature raw oysters, a delicacy not always appreciated in areas where fresh seafood is not available.

In the southwest and California, the closeness of Mexico and the large numbers of Mexicans living in that part of the country have long made authentic Mexican foods a familiar favorite. Florida is currently developing a Cuban **cuisine** (kwi-zin) thanks to the more recent influx of individuals from Cuba.

Alaska

You could have smelled a "sourdough" coming your way during the gold-rush days. Sourdoughs, as the trappers and gold rushers were often called, carried their pots of sourdough starter on their bodies to keep the bacterial dough "starter" alive in the harsh winters. The characteristic odor was unmistakable—and also unavoidable. Besides sourdough breads and pancakes, Alaska has long reveled in a wealth of sea treasures such as baked-king salmon, king-crab salad, whale steaks, and Arctic char. You still will find mooseburgers and ptarmigan (a wild game bird) pie, cranberry catsup, and fiddlehead ferns served in that awe-inspiring area.

Hawaii

Many tourists waste their time saying "Pooey to Poi," a seemingly tasteless, sticky paste made from the starchy vegetable, taro. They forget to rave about the other food wonders of beautiful Hawaii. Naturally ripened exotic fruits such as mangoes, pineapples, guavas, papayas, coconuts, and bananas are like presents from paradise. Traditional main course meats feature pit-roasted chicken and pigs. The emerald sea contributes unusual fish steaks

Like the rich tropical foliage of the Hawaiian islands, this lush fruit echoes the abundance of exotic produce and balmy weather of the Tropics. Supermarkets now carry many of these formerly rare fruits.

such as mahi mahi and bonita that taste and chew differently from any mainland fish. Raw fish marinated in citrus juice and other flavors to "cook" it offers a uniquely Hawaiian experience. Natural desserts include macadamia nuts and the little known kukui nuts. The delicately flavored guava sherbet is an island memory worth recreating at home.

California

The fresh fruit and vegetable produce of California are unrivaled. So are the healthful recipes and food combinations that the health-conscious Californians have made well known. Many food favorites such as frozen yogurts, granola, colorful avocado salads, and whole-grain or vegetable pastas have become classic cuisine throughout the United States. Artichokes are grown almost exclusively in California. In some of the local restaurants near the fields in the San Joaquin Valley, you can order artichoke omelet, pie, muffins, and pickles. "Trend-setting," "healthful," and "creative" will long describe the regional foods for California—even though the latest specialties may change.

Washington and Oregon

Apples, pears, and peaches flourish in the fertile valleys of these two states, and the wealth of recipes featuring the local produce could fill books. Perhaps most unique is the apple candy. Starring attractions for these states are the seacoast catches that become salmon steaks, kippered salmon, and canned salmon for exporting all over the world. If you caught a salmon in these areas, you could have it canned right there to take home with you. Halibut, trout, dungeness crabs, razor clams, and tiny Olympia oysters also are regional favorites.

The Mountain States—
Idaho, Nevada, Utah, Wyoming, Montana, Colorado

The cities of these regions take pride in "showing off" the prizes of the wilderness. Wild-game dishes such as braised moose, venison, and elk steaks abound just as the game itself does. A family of trout—rainbow, steelhead, and cutthroat—beckon the fishing enthusiast and eaters alike. Varieties of bass, crappie, char, and perch species lend further sporting excitement to the area. Camping and just plain picnicking partner perfectly with campfire cooking for all of the regional specialties. Wild mountain berries, huckleberries and elderberries, and dandelion greens are utilized for beverages, vegetables, breads, and salads.

The Southwest—
Arizona, New Mexico, Texas

If you stand still long enough in the Southwest, rumor has it you just might be barbecued! Everything tastes better to Southwesterners with a tangy and sometimes spicy barbecue sauce. The "Tex-Mex" regional foods stamp traditional Mexican dishes such as tacos, wheat tortillas, tamale pie, chili con carne, and chiles rellenos with a Texas touch. Wild brush honey, agarita jelly, mustang-grape pie, and pinon nuts are other local favorites.

The Plains States—
North Dakota, South Dakota, Nebraska, Kansas, Oklahoma

Pheasants in the Dakotas are roasted, braised, and fried for a wild-game dish that nourished the pioneers and "savors on the pal-

No one can coach as much flavor out of a barbecued meat as a Texan can. This taste treat is still copied nationwide, including the Texas toast!

ate" of today's natives. Nebraska beef is broiled rare at home and shipped out for gourmet steak treats all over the country. Prevalent throughout these states is the ancestry of the early Scandinavian, Bohemian, and Russian settlers. Fine breads and pastries still echo the look and taste of the "old country." Oklahoma favors the southern style of cooking and local game such as fried squirrel and rabbit.

The Midwest—
Minnesota, Iowa, Missouri, Michigan, Illinois, Wisconsin, Indiana, Ohio

You can find a wide variety of ethnic influences in the larger midwestern cities such as Chicago, St. Louis, Milwaukee, and Cincinnati, but a majority relates back to German heritage. Persimmon pudding showcases a unique flavor of the Midwest, and corn is featured in homestyle cooking in dishes such as scalloped corn and roasted ears. Catfish comes from the rivers, but the Great Lakes' area features trout, bass, and perch. The Friday night fish fry with crisp cornmeal batter is a favorite with crunchy cole slaw and fries. The Midwestern Indian tribes have contributed their fried breads and wild rice to regional favorites. Wild rice grown exclusively by Indians on reservation land in Minnesota is marketed throughout the U.S. as a gourmet treat especially valued with game dishes.

The New England States—
Maine, Vermont, New Hampshire, Massachusetts, Connecticut

Historical New England sports saltwater fare that is world famous. The Maine lobster's delectable sweet flavor is legendary throughout many parts of the world! The traditional seaside clambake combines much of the regional bounty. For a clambake, a hole is dug in the beach and rocks are added which are then heated by a large fire. After the fire dies down, lobster, rock seaweed (for steam and flavor), whole potatoes, roasting ears of corn, clams, and mussels are layered on the heated rocks and covered with a canvas for several hours to steam through. The rest is legendary taste history—local eating lore at its best! Other well-known and lesser known regional specialties include maple syrup, maple sugar candies, wild blueberries with cream and brown sugar, brown bread, and clam chowder.

The Mid-Atlantic—
Pennsylvania, New Jersey, New York, Maryland, Delaware, Rhode Island

You could find any kind of food and cooking in the world in New York City, but the seafood throughout this region of the country is probably the most representational of the area. Outstanding tender cherrystone and littleneck clams and Chincoteague oysters are prized by natives and visitors alike. Maryland is noted for a terrapin which is eaten several ways. New Jersey's beefsteak tomatoes and Delaware's mushroom farms are regional specialties that are shipped country-wide. All across the waterfront areas in this region, you can stop and enjoy fresh seafood in the shell by the bucketful on oilcloth picnic tables with informal gusto.

The Pennsylvania Dutch have shared their unique culture and beliefs with the world through their down-home cooking that features the range of the flavors from sweet to sour in every meal. Vinegar pie is a fun example of their resourcefulness.

The South—
Kentucky, Virginia, West Virginia, North Carolina, South Carolina, Georgia, Alabama, Mississippi, Arkansas, Louisiana, Tennessee

You will find that the gracious hospitality of the South extends to its many fine foods and specialties. Many Southerners are just as dedicated to keeping their unique style of cooking flourishing and appreciated as they are to eating it. Truly, southern cooking and eating is a lifestyle in itself. Grits for breakfast—even to a newcomer—soon change from a rather tasteless white cooked meal to a "must have" with the morning eggs and bacon. The old traditional southern biscuit is called a beaten biscuit that is worked and kneaded until it is hard and almost crisp like a cracker. It's a priceless skill that few people can master outside of the South. Greens are stewed for hours with smoked salt pork, bacon, or ham. Southern fried chicken is smothered by cooking in a pan with the lid on for a tender "fall off the bones" dish that has to be experienced to understand. Baking skills have been treasured for centuries and fine cakes are still a source of pride for the baker. Fruit ambrosia is savored for the nectar. It is served with the salty Smithfield cured ham and beaten biscuits in an envied traditional dinner.

Louisiana with its Creole and Cajun cooking is a completely different world of culinary pleasures. Many of the specialties take advantage of the close waterfront and fresh fish. Red snapper blackened in a burned butter is considered a height of skill and good eating. Hot pepper sauces spice up long-simmered legumes and rice dishes. **Jambalaya,** a diverse stew of ham, sausage, chicken, shrimp, and oysters, is seasoned and thickened with gumbo (okra). (See the photograph in Chapter 6.) The chickory-flavored dark coffee and the sugared beignuts (a fried pastry) sold on the streets and in special coffeehouses say "New Orleans" to some people as much as the lacy iron balconies of Bourbon Street.

Florida

You will look overhead at the Spanish moss around the Suwannee River in northern Florida and feel that you are still in the Deep South. Even the signs of local barbecue and boiled peanuts in the shells depict typical southern food, but soon the tropical look and the citrus mania creeps into the landscape.

The Atlantic coast of New England nets many fresh seafood treats. Broiled cod and tart coleslaw are a traditional combination for everyday fare.

The tiny Key lime tree originally from Key West, Florida, furnishes the tart, high-pectin lime that gives the real regional Key lime pie its unique flavor and texture. The rest of the U.S. has to be content with regular limes.

Orange marmalade and fresh citrus juices in various mixtures with piles of fresh fruit beside the road signal the fruit grove country. Avocados, lemons as large as grapefruit, kumquats, mangoes, papayas, and guavas grow in the yards and are marketed commercially as well.

Equally pervasive for the Florida cuisine is the fresh fish—both freshwater and saltwater or brackish water, which is a mixture of the two with the tides. Mangrove snappers perk up skillet frying and the big Florida red fish bakes into a moist feast with seasoned stuffing. The southern coast displays stone crab eateries and wharfside sales.

Florida Crackers, as natives pridefully call themselves, can point out a wealth of greens and produce in the swamplike forests. Hearts of palm, ferns, swamp cabbage, and other natural plants make wonderful eating around the campfire or in a fancy restaurant. Shrimp recipes abound, but none surpass the steamed-in-the-shell seafood houses that serve tart horseradish, tomato sauce spiking a crisp cracker along with the tender, fresh shrimp.

Key West originally contributed the famed Key lime pie to the scene, but the pie is now available throughout Florida. The high pectin content of the tiny acidic Key limes worked together to make a luscious, cooled custard pie of sugar, eggs, and lime juice topped by unsweetened sour cream. Now many restaurants serve an adapted version made with evaporated milk and lime juice with whipped cream. Conch (a large seashell mollusk) soup and salad with green turtle meat and soup also spotlight the unique Key West regional foods.

Ethnic Foods

Think about the foods you've had today. Why did you choose them? Think about the social influences of your family, friends, and neighbors. How does their input join with the cultural influences of recent immigrants and the past pioneers who settled this land to affect what you chose to eat.

Our rich heritage of ethnic and religious customs is reflected in these delicately designed eggs. Boiling in water with red onion skins coats the eggs with a unique reddish color that is scratched into intricate designs.

The gradual combination of all the cultural traditions from both the past and the present has created our unique American culture in which food plays an important part. Within that American culture are many ethnic foods that originated in other countries or from cultural traditions.

Even within the same city, certain areas feature different ethnic foods that echo the neighborhood's cultural and regional backgrounds. A city with a variety of ethnic groups might feature areas with aromatic hickory smoked barbecue, while a few blocks away the streets could be lined with Oriental restaurants with such delicacies as egg rolls, fried rice, and **sushi** (specially seasoned rice usually served with raw fish).

Cultural and Religious Customs

Family religious beliefs often directly influence what and even when you choose to eat. Perhaps most widely known is the former direction for Roman Catholics not to eat meat on Fridays during **Lent** (the six-weeks just before Easter). Although this practice is optional for individuals now, many religious customs still have influence.

Lent (the 40 weekdays between Ash Wednesday and Easter) was a strict time of fasting for the Roman Catholic Church members. During Lent it was dictated in rigid detail just what practitioners could and could not eat. The Vatican Council changed those centuries of customs in 1965. Now there are only two prescribed fasting days of the year, Ash Wednesday and Good Friday. On Fridays during Lent, the nonuse of meat now is voluntary and prescribed by the individual's conscience. Still old customs hang on—especially in the ethnic neighborhoods. Within the framework of the church, there are many ethnic practices that are celebrated each year.

The Slavic neighborhoods continue an ancient celebration called Swieconka—the blessing of foods. Part of that celebration includes elaborate feasts preceding the fasts of certain foods. The forbidden foods are put in elaborate forms and blessed for all to enjoy prior to the fast. One of the most charming traditions is the blessing of eggs, the sign of hope and resurrection. Because of the special meaning, the eggs to be blessed are decorated with symbols of Easter. Often they were boiled in red onion skins for a rich color and fine artistic lines and designs are scratched through the color. Children's Easter baskets owe their origin to this custom and the later blessing of children and their Easter baskets of candy and eggs.

In the Orthodox Jewish faith, it is considered vital to carefully follow the biblical **edicts** (laws) of the Old Testament which forbid the eating of pork in any form. Serving both meat and dairy foods at the same meal is also forbidden. Special processing in small plants and having a rabbi inspect the foods makes it possible for families to be able to comply with those edicts in modern markets by purchasing kosher food. (**Kosher food** is ritually fit according to Jewish law.) Often the family's influence is so strong, the food customs are followed even if the individual discontinues practicing the religion.

During the 1960s, the so-called flower-children generation tuned in to the peaceful philosophies of the Hindu religion. This included the doctrine of not eating meat. This practice fell into step with another trend—eating foods in their natural state or with less processing and cutting back on red meats. The new eating patterns of emphasizing fresh fruits and vegetables and substituting whole grains, nuts, and **tofu** (soybean curd) for red meats led to the creation of many so-called health-food stores. That trend has continued to grow, resulting in whole-grain products and more foods in their natural state being available in most supermarkets.

Many people also grow their own food in order to follow this healthful lifestyle. The gardens range from large country plots to container-growing for apartment dwellers.

What Else Affects Your Food Choices?

Other people and your past are not the only influences on the foods you choose to eat. Today's technology, your own resources, and even advertising all play a part in what you'll have for lunch today. The millions of dollars that advertisers spend convincing you to choose their product brings them even more money back when you buy their products.

Availability

Several factors control the availability of foods. Just a few years ago, the number one factor controlling when you could eat certain foods was the season. Fried chicken, which requires young tender fowl, could only be served in the summer because young chickens were raised just in warm weather. Today, poultry industries grow young chickens economically all year in large, heated buildings.

Fresh sweet corn and tomatoes could only be enjoyed from local fields during a few short weeks of each year's growing season. Now the high technology of refrigerated cars and efficient transportation and storage systems make fresh produce available year around. New produce specialties from all over the world such as the star fruit or jicama (hic-a-ma) have been introduced to produce departments at reasonable and competitive prices.

Technology of Preservation and Storage

The technology of freezing has made practically any food available in any season. Home-cooked flavor is ready in minutes, while fresh produce flavor is almost unchanged after weeks of storage. Our transportation systems enable

The need to satisfy traditional appetites with lower cholesterol foods has brought foods like tofu out of the unusual health food category and into the supermarket and many homes.

the rapid and economical distribution of those products to your local stores. This is a convenience most people now take for granted, but is a relatively recent situation.

Resources

It certainly doesn't matter what you decide to eat if you do not have the resources. Yearning for a $15 lobster dinner when you have 50 cents obviously makes the lobster unavailable, even if you are on the seacoast next to the restaurant. Also not available for you would be a roast turkey dinner at home when you only have 10 minutes to grab a bite to eat. Many of your food choices depend on your resources.

Resources are things or people who can help you. These include time, money, skills, energy, and information.

Time

Time—your time—makes a big difference in what food choices are available to you and your family. If you have the time to spend on food preparation, you can plan ahead and arrange for more variety to increase your choices. A few hours shopping, preparing, and freezing lunches over the weekend or some evening could increase your variety, provide more zestful nutrition, and save you money. Hurried mornings often mean a lunch of purchased fast-food or snacks from the coin machines.

Money

The amount of money available for food budgets affects what and how much food is eaten. Most people have limited budgets. Therefore, making wise, informed consumer decisions is invaluable in obtaining the healthful food needed.

Skill

Your ability to prepare meals influences your food choices. Of course, by learning new skills you can increase the variety of foods available to you. That can have immediate and tasty rewards. Also it has financial rewards. By preparing foods yourself, you do not pay the extra costs of having others do the work.

Information

Information is the key to making the most of all your available resources. In order to shop wisely, you need to know about the nutritive value of the food before you can decide if it is a good buy. Price, or a reduction in price, is not the only factor that determines a good value. Learning food skills and finding out where to obtain information about foods skills will increase your options all of your life. Classes in school or evening programs, books, and commercial pamphlets from grocery stores and food companies are a few of the information sources available.

A visit to your County Cooperative Extension Office will open up a whole world of free and inexpensive publications on practically every subject pertaining to food preparation, nutrition, and health. The county agent also is available to answer your questions in person or by telephone. Personal computer programs and video tapes have emerged on the market and in libraries for your use in acquiring food information and skills.

Combining Resources

All the resources that make food available to you work together. For instance, if you have the time, you can develop your cooking skills so you can prepare nutritious meals without purchasing pre-prepared foods. Then you'll save money you would spend on prepared foods. It is up to you to manage your resources to fit your lifestyle and still meet your food needs.

Advertising and Current Food Trends

In the 1950s consumer magazines featured advertisements showing a mother, father, their two children, and the family dog gathered around the living room fireplace grilling large steaks. Open a magazine now and chances are you'll see a young, single adult eating a fresh lettuce salad topped with alfalfa sprouts, grated cheese, tomatoes, and popcorn shrimp. Just as families have changed since the '50s, so have food choices. And many of the food choices are reflected in and influenced by advertising.

People are more health-conscious today—and they owe much of their newfound concern to advertising. That is one of the benefits of ads. They can teach you about new findings in the foods and nutrition field. For example, think of the cereal commercials that say you need to eat more fiber to help prevent colon cancer. Advertisements can help you make wise food choices.

Advertising also can make you want to buy foods that are not wise choices. In recent years, parents have been concerned about the advertising during Saturday morning cartoons. Many of the ads promote cereals that are high in sugar. The ads are so appealing to the children that they plead with their parents to buy the cereal.

Advertising can influence you, too. Have you ever purchased a food because you liked the advertising? Were you pleased or unhappy with your decision? Advertising can be a benefit to you if you use it to gather information about products and base your decisions on sound nutrition guidelines. Learn to avoid the pitfalls of being carried away by the glitter and glamour of a product that doesn't fit into your budget—nutritionally or economically.

How Food Is Used

For most people, it is natural that the foods they enjoy best are those they're familiar with. Learning to try new foods is a skill some people must work to acquire. But by doing so, they will open a whole new world of pleasurable experiences and healthful nutrition.

Mexican foods and favorite taste combinations have influenced eating preferences in the United States. Colorful tomato sauce with tangy olives spice up the fish in this Mexican and U.S. popular dish.

A nation's well-known foods often tie-in both special holidays and celebrations. This nutritious Russian Easter bread is a delicious holiday event in itself, but its true significance is its symbolism of the religious holiday. Sometimes the symbolism celebrates a season or date. Can you think of any U.S. foods that traditionally are part of celebrations or events?

You are raised being pampered by your "favorite" foods. Family members who return home after an absence are often greeted with their favorite food—reinforcing the welcoming love with the reassurance of familiar food. A large baking company alluded to this with the slogan "nothing says loving like something from the oven!" It creates a powerful combination: the emotional association of past good times and a remembered favorite food.

Celebrations and Events

Festivals, holidays, and special occasions are usually celebrated with special foods. There's nothing quite so festive as gathering to enjoy delicious treats. Harvests are traditionally celebrated with a feast of the newly gathered crop. The work stops and differences are put aside as everyone enjoys the festivities. Birthdays for all ages have traditionally been observed with a personalized cake. The Easter ham and challah (a bread for Jewish holidays) are other examples of "traditional holiday fare." The food industry is well aware of the powerful connection between holidays and eating special foods. Food store ads are full of the traditional favorites offered at special prices to convince shoppers to buy everything in their store for the holidays.

The sharing of food is also an expression of friendship and caring. Traditionally, throughout the world lovingly prepared food is shared as solace to grieving friends and family after a funeral. When guests visit someone's home, food and drink are offered as symbols of welcoming hospitality. Even at business meetings, the refreshment break is considered crucial to establish the most successful interaction of the participants.

Food itself or the manner in which it is presented can help a person achieve status. Expressing your creativity through food preparation can evoke much admiration from friends and family—or possibly lead to a job! Even the restaurants you eat in can lend a certain distinction. Restaurants also follow the latest food trends so that eating at the newest "in" place is a source of pride for some people. Price is not necessarily the standard for making a place prestigious. The place people want to try could be the new Japanese sushi bar, the sidewalk cafe featuring sorbet (sor-bay) (French frozen fruit juice), or the new fast-food place in town.

Making Decisions

How many decisions do you make in a day? Can you count them? Probably not. "Deciding" seems to be an automatic and unthinking process. Or is it? Just as your past experiences, the people around you, your own likes and dislikes, and other influences make a difference in why, what, and even when you select foods, the same factors also influence any decision you make.

Does this mean past happenings and present circumstances rule your life, or you have no control over your own choices or behavior? How sad it would be if you learned that you needed a balance of protein, vitamins, minerals, and energy at noon but were powerless to switch from a lunch routine of French fries and soft drink to a cheese-and-broccoli-topped potato and glass of milk just because your friends did not switch. As strong as influences such as friends and habit are, you can take charge of your life and health.

You know you ponder over major problems or dilemmas. What type of career you want, if you should buy a car, whether to work after graduation or get further education are examples of decisions that you would expect to require some planning and deliberation. Decision-making is a skill that you can develop and improve.

There is no mystery to developing decision-making skills. It is a simple six-step process:

1. Describe the situation or problem.
2. Determine your goals.
3. Investigate your resources.
4. Decide
5. Do it!
6. Look back. Did it work? Would you do anything differently next time?

Let's go over the steps as they relate to a situation over which you could have control.

1. Describe the problem. Perhaps a "problem" in your life might be a daily hectic morning with everyone urging you to hurry—and a parent telling you to eat breakfast. You never seem to have enough time, though, so you leave feeling hungry, disgruntled, and misunderstood.

What do you do now? Decide which is the problem: the anxious parent, your long hair that takes too long to dry, your ride or bus leaving too early, the inconvenient kind of food available for a morning meal, not getting up early enough, or your brother or sister taking too long in the bathroom? Perhaps all of these are contributing to the situation, but your responsibility is to determine the basic problem before you can take action. In this case, leaving home in an unhappy state not fully prepared to face a challenging day is the problem. Obviously, more than one factor is contributing to that situation, so it is time to move to Step 2.

2. Determine your goals. What is most important to you? What are you trying to accomplish? You've decided it would be heavenly to leave for school or work each day feeling good physically and in a happy mood equipped to accomplish "whatever."

You have learned that eating something to give you energy and nutrition helps you feel and perform better. That means having breakfast becomes a goal. Real-life problems are seldom solved in one step and you do not usually have control over all situations. To reach your goals, you might decide you need to somehow get ready quicker and still have time to eat before leaving. To accomplish those goals, it is time to consider Step 3.

3. Investigate your resources. Time, skills, money, available materials or equipment, and information are the resources you either have or need. You are lacking time. You know you could get up earlier, but you would rather try another solution. You like sleeping. To "get ready quicker," you know you could shorten the time needed to dry your hair by buying your own hairdryer for your long hair instead of waiting to borrow your brother's dryer. Another choice would be to cut your hair into that new shorter style you've been admiring. Both cost money. The new hairdryer costs $12.95 on sale, while a new hairstyle and permanent might be around $50. You have $15. You don't have the resource or "authority" to limit your sister/brother's time in the bathroom or to get first use of the shared hairdryer. That means those are not solutions to saving time.

Even with those changes, you still won't have time to sit down to a traditional hot breakfast. Experience has shown you that the quick pickup energy from the soft drink and candy bar grabbed at school doesn't last the morning. Besides, your skin doesn't seem to be as attractive and your clothes seem to fit a little snugger because of those extra calories.

Part of your resources are the sources of information that are available to you. For example, nutrition information and food preparation examples from classes, TV, and magazines might create ideas for you. Your need now is for information about a quicker breakfast that is healthful.

You remember one of your favorite magazines had an article on quick breakfasts that included new ideas for "morning food." Because the article related the vitamin, mineral, and calorie (energy value) content in the recipe ideas, you decide it is worth considering.

Some of the appealing ideas from the magazine include these easy, "take-along" or eat at home quick breakfasts:

- A shake made from milk, frozen orange juice, and ice cream to take along or sip at home with some whole-wheat toast.
- A toasted peanut-butter sandwich with fruit, raisins, or jelly.
- A piece of frozen or leftover pizza heated in a toaster oven or microwave.
- A carton of yogurt with a small bag of granola to sprinkle over it.

Other resources you can use are your own skills. In this case, your food preparation skills might still be quite limited, but you do know how to make toast. Mixing a milkshake in either a blender, mixer, or by hand is an easy skill to learn now if you don't already know how. Therefore, all of the food ideas are possibilities that would both save time and provide significant energy and nutrient power for your day. Now, it's time to decide.

4. Decide. Several decisions are involved in solving the "hectic morning rush problem." You have determined that fixing your hair takes too long and that you just don't have time to sit down and eat a breakfast at home.

You decide to keep your present long hair, but buy your own hairdryer. This will help you have some time to grab a quick breakfast snack to take with you in the morning.

Now you need to decide which of the quick breakfast ideas fits your lifestyle and taste. Since you like peanut butter, pizza, milkshakes, and yogurt, all the foods are possibilities. You decide to start out trying all of them on different days, depending on what is available. (Check the supply on hand the night before to avoid a "mad search" in the morning.)

5. Do it! It's now time to "do it"! You start out with the easiest, the snack you are most used to fixing yourself. This is the toasted peanut-butter, whole-wheat sandwich with jelly. You do it and walk out the door on time leaving an "amazed" family, feeling good about yourself, and feeling in charge instead of feeling "pushed." Did it work? You are ready for the final step of the decision-making process.

6. Looking back. You are pleased with how much time the dryer saved you in fixing your hair. You are still considering a further change in your hairstyle, but first you need to save the money. That decision worked for you.

The unusual "quick breakfast" tasted surprisingly good, but you forgot to include a drink, so you got pretty thirsty during the ride to school. You decide to do something different the next day by taking the milkshake or yogurt on the mornings when a drink isn't convenient to take along. You also consider waiting to eat your snack until you can buy a carton of milk at school. Another alternative is to take a Thermos or have small cartons of milk or juice to take from home.

Now you have discovered that the decision-making process is indeed a never-ending story. It is one that continually evolves as you shape your actions to fulfill your needs in order to take charge of your own life and health.

Toasted Peanut-Butter Sandwich with Fruit (raisins or jelly)

Traditional	Ingredients	Metric
2 slices	Whole wheat or enriched white bread	2 slices
2 Tbsp.	Peanut butter	30 mL
1 small	Banana and/or 2 Tbsp. (30 mL) raisins	1 small

(optional—2 Tbsp. (30 mL) dried apples or chopped peanuts, 1 Tbsp. (15 mL) jelly)

Directions

1. Toast the bread.
2. Spread on your favorite peanut butter.
3. Add the "special" fruit ingredients of your choice.
4. Top the spread piece of bread with the second piece of bread as a convenient "lid" for easier carrying. (An open-faced sandwich is great for saving the calories of a second piece of bread, but is difficult to package for a portable snack.)

Note: Be certain to buy peanut butter; peanut spreads contain more oil and less peanuts, so therefore offer less protein for the same money and calories.

Hint: If you don't have a toaster, or just want to try something different, melt 1 tablespoon (15 mL) of margarine in a skillet and grill the sandwich on both sides for a crispy hot treat!

Protein Grain Milk F & V

2x 2x

One-Piece Pizza

Ingredients: 1 piece 4 to 5-inch (10 to 13 cm) wedge uncooked frozen or leftover pizza Any extra toppings you might like to add: bacon, sausage, green pepper, tomatoes, extra cheese. (Ideas limited only by your imagination and what's in your refrigerator.)

Directions

1. Cut a 4- to 5-inch (10 to 13 cm) wedge from a frozen pizza or cut a 4- to 5-inch (10 to 13 cm) wedge from a leftover* pizza.
2. Add any toppings you might want.
3. Bake the cut wedge of the frozen pizza about 6 minutes in a preheated 425°F (220°C) oven or regular oven. Reheat the leftover pizza until cheese is melted, about 3 minutes in the preheated toaster oven.

*(Be certain the pizza has been stored in the refrigerator or freezer until needed.)

Microwave Directions

1. Follow steps 1 and 2 above.
2. Microwave on High about 3 minutes. Note: The crust will not be crisp. Reheat leftover pizza about 1 minute.

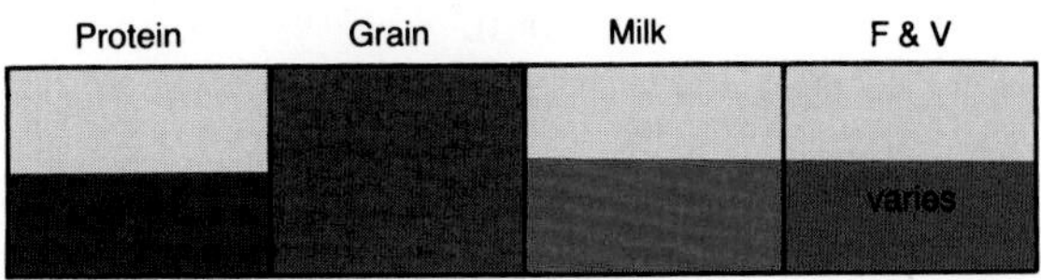

A Juice Freeze for Breakfast

Traditional	Ingredients	Metric
1 cup	Vanilla ice cream	250 mL
¼ cup	Frozen orange juice concentrate (grape, cranberry, or apple juice concentrate could also be used variety)	50 mL

Directions

1. Mix by hand, blender, or mixer the above ingredients just until creamy in texture, but still thick and icy.

2. Eat immediately or store in freezer for no longer than one hour (if mixture refreezes too hard to eat, break up and stir again to a creamy texture.)

Protein	Grain	Milk	F & V

Dotted Yogurt

Traditional	Ingredients	Metric
½ pint	Yogurt, flavor of your choice	250 mL
¼ cup	Granola	50 mL

Directions

1. Pack the granola into a plastic bag or wrap in wax paper for carrying until needed.

2. When ready to eat, sprinkle a spoonful at a time of the granola on top of the yogurt and enjoy the contrast of the smooth yogurt and the crunchy granola.

Protein	Grain	Milk	F & V

Vocabulary Review

Nutrition
Nutrients
Regional foods
Cuisine
Sushi
Lent
Edicts
Kosher food
Tofu
Resources

Questions for Review

1. What creates the strongest desire to eat? Why?

2. What happens to people's desires for things such as stylish clothes, cars, and social fun when they are in a severe need for food (such as near starvation)? Have you ever experienced giving up an opportunity for something you really wanted to do because you were too hungry and decided to eat instead?

3. Why do you think you have different food likes than some of your friends or family? Give some examples of foods you like and try to remember some of the reasons—besides tasting good—that you like them.

4. What are at least three things that help to create food likes and dislikes. Give examples.

5. What are some ways that people around you can influence how you feel about food?

6. What are some of your area's special foods that might not be appreciated in another part of the country? Why are those foods favorites in your area?

7. Name a few areas of the United States and describe some of the favorite regional foods for each? Why do regional foods become favorites to that area?

8. What influence does the ethnic background of people in an area have on that area's favorite foods? Does the ethnic influence always spread to the whole area or region? Explain.

9. Do religious customs ever affect food preferences? Explain and give examples.

10. How have the transportation and marketing technology of today affected the way people eat today?

11. How do resources such as time and money make a difference in the food you choose to eat?

12. Can skills in food preparation, planning, and shopping influence what you eat? Explain how with an example for each.

13. Can advertising provide both beneficial and wasteful influences upon your eating and buying habits? How can you tell the difference between useful information and motivating information that isn't helpful for wise choices?

14. What are some special events that you celebrate with special foods? Do the traditional foods of those events help make the event more festive and special? Describe an example.

15. Are you aware of all the decisions that you make? Why?

16. How do each of the following factors influence the decisions you make: past experiences, the people around you, your own likes and dislikes, and other influences such as advertising? (Give an example for each factor.)

17. Does a factor that might influence your decisions also control your decisions? Give an example to explain your answer.

18. Is it possible for people to improve their decision-making skills? How?

19. What are the six steps to developing decision-making skills?

Things to Do

1. The opinion of your friends is one of the social influences that helps to determine the food that you like. Set up your own experiment to test this idea. Arrange to offer a new food such as carrot cookies or a vegetable dip to a group of at least 4 or 5 friends or relatives. (Pick something you think everyone would ordinarily like.) Clue in all but two people to act very negative about the food with "put down" comments like "Do you really expect me to eat that?" and "Oh yuk, that looks terrible!" See if the two unsuspecting people want to even try the food. Chances are they won't be wild about a perfectly good food just because of the reaction of their friends. Record all the remarks and report on the results. What do you predict will happen? What do you think would happen if everyone raved about a new, and somewhat "questionable tasting" new food? Would people be swayed to like it?

2. Pick a region of the U.S. that interests you. Look up that region in the library for a detailed report on the types of food favored in the area and why they are available. Plan a complete regional meal. Pick some of the foods that are less familiar to you and prepare them. Did you like them right away or do you feel like they would taste better after they became familiar to you? What are some of your regional foods that might seem "different" in other areas?

3. Imagine that you won three meals of your dreams all prepared and paid for. Write down what you would choose. Could you arrange for the same meals yourself? What factors would limit making the same "dream foods" a reality for you? Would money, preparation skills, time, and information about where they are available affect what you can realistically choose to eat? Explain.

4. Imagine you are living in a medium-sized town sometime before freezers and refrigerated transportation systems were available for meats, seafood, and fresh produce. How would meals differ from your choices today? Plan a day's meals for that past time and another day's meals for today.

International Taste Test

Not all "melting pots" are on top of the stove. Cooking in the United States "melts" numerous international cuisines into a global foods tour of the world. Our national enthusiasm for international cooking can be traced back to the influx of new citizens and visitors from other lands as well as travelers who bring back treasured culinary "discoveries."

Learning about food customs of other countries reveals much about the history, climate, and geography of a region, as well as the lifestyles, religions, and traditions. This knowledge of cultural similarities and differences also can help to promote understanding between peoples.

The current popularity of international foods has created a tremendous increase in the number of restaurants featuring foreign foods. Even fast-food chains have climbed on the bandwagon to meet the growing demand for exotic foreign foods. Rapid acceptance of formerly "foreign foods" has actually created some new American favorites. The taco, Swiss cheese fondue, pizza, gyros, and croissant are a few examples of "imported" foods that have become honorary American food "citizens."

A world tour of foods within the United States might include the following countries, foods, and customs.

Mexico

Although there are at least 20 different cuisines in Mexico, an ideal Mexican meal would begin with appetizers served with hot tortillas, soup, and then rice or spaghetti as a separate course. The main dish is meat or fish with a sauce and more warm tortillas, sometimes followed by beans. Tortilla chips are seldom eaten by themselves, but are sometimes used to scoop up food such as refried beans. Although Mexican foods often carry the reputation of being fiery hot with spices, a noted Mexican cuisine authority praises good Mexican sauces as ones in which ". . . the flavors are complex, but they don't burn your mouth out!"

South America

You would have difficulty locating any restaurants in the U.S. that specialize in South American foods. Most of the restaurants feature foods from Latin America. Argentina, Brazil, Chile, Colombia, and Peru differ in cuisines mostly because of the influence of the original settlers and foods introduced into the area from other lands at that time.

Argentina does, however, stand out for its fondness of beef. The fame of the Argentine cowboy of the Pampas is close to that of our rugged frontier cowboys. Steak is eaten at any time and enjoyed with gusto.

Brazil is notably influenced by the Portuguese settlers in language and food.

Caribbean Islands

Can you picture yourself on a small island in the Bahamas enjoying the beach and pounding surf surrounded with baskets of inexpensive fresh fruit and a sandwich? Good luck if you do. A more accurate picture would be one small orange with a price tag of several dollars and a hamburger for $7.50! The small islands do not have a wide selection of foods. They are too small or rocky to grow their own, so everything has to be shipped in. This definitely does effect the dietary habits of the islanders. Luckily, the ocean is always near for a ready source of seafood.

Larger islands have the wider offerings of crops and fresh produce. There is an abundance of tropical fruits and **plantain,** a starchy fruit that resembles a banana in looks, but is hard and starchy like a potato. You can cook them anyway you can cook a potato.

Food Facts

"Daily bread" to Mexicans is the unleavened tortilla. Starting with either corn or wheat, the grain is ground often by hand in a stone mortar called a *metate.* The roller, called a *metlalpil,* looks like a handleless stone rolling pin. The ground corn is called *masa.* The ground grain is mixed with water and rolled into a round pancake that is served many ways. When wrapped around a filling, the tortilla becomes and enchilada or burrito. Deep fried, the tortilla turns into the crisp base for a tostado. Folded in half around a filling and fried, it becomes a quesadilla.

Cuba

Tropical weather, an abundant supply of fresh seafood, and a terrain that allows raising small crops and livestock lend to Cuba a varied and colorful food supply. Rice and black beans are the staples that mix with a multitude of island foods for everyday fare. A typical meal might consist of rice, a bean and meat dish, and tomatoes.

Great Britain

You can group the European countries as neighbors with temperate climates, but they have many variations in food preferences, customs, and serving styles. Great Britain is fortunate to have an ample supply of beef, mutton, and pork. You would notice that the preferred cooking methods are quite simple, with boiled meat being very popular. The British seacoasts contribute popular seafoods that have become quite well known through the traditional **fish and chips** served wrapped in newspapers (Recently, for health reasons, newspapers were banned as wrapping for food. The Britons were so nostalgic about their fish and chips wrapped in newsprint that a special food wrap was created with a newspaper print design to appease the public.)

Britons hang on to their traditions, and food is no exception. Steak and kidney pie, Yorkshire pudding (a soggy popover cooked in the meat drippings), and **trifle** (a rich dessert of leftover cake, fruit, and pudding) probably will

Subtle spicy flavors characterize this Cuban classic—chicken picadillo pie.

remain classic favorites as long as there is a Great Britain. Another proper British favorite is cheddar cheese which originated in the village of Cheddar in the 16th century.

Tea is the traditional beverage, and it is served faithfully every afternoon. High tea with the tiny fancy sandwiches and pastries is offered in the fancier restaurants and for special occasions in the home.

France

The French differ from the Britons in the way they take pride in fussing over their food preparation. Even the **provincial** (country) cooking often simmers carefully selected local fresh foods and aromatic herbs with enthusiasm and pride. The French cuisine evolved historically from the days of the French aristocrats (upper class) who competed amongst themselves with their fancy master chefs. The chefs continually created elegant foods and sauces such as souffles, croissants, French pastries (petit fours, napoleons, and more), sorbets, and Hollandaise sauce.

The more earthy country cooking varies according to the province just as our States feature regional specialties. Generally, the hearty soup, fresh crusty bread, local specialty cheeses, and long-simmered one-dish meals are mouth-

Food Facts

Burritos (meaning "little donkeys" in Spanish) are soft tortillas wrapped around refried beans and seasoned meat. They can be "finger food" or served on a plate as a main dish, usually with shredded lettuce and a red pepper sauce.

watering without the elegant sauces and delicate pastries.

Fresh fruit and vegetables are valued and prepared with care. An elegant French dessert, though simple in preparation, would be an assortment of cheeses and fruit. Different regions have developed their own unique specialty cheeses—some from centuries old methods and recipes. The soft Brie cheese is a special treat

Refried Beans

Traditional	Ingredients	Metric
2 cups	Water	500 mL
8 oz.	Dried pinto beans (about 1¼ cups)	250 g
1 medium	Onion, chopped	1 medium
1 clove	Garlic, chopped	1 clove
1 tsp.	Salt	5 mL
3 Tbsp.	Melted bacon fat, melted lard, or vegetable oil	45 mL

Directions

1. Heat water, beans, onion, and garlic to boiling in pan.
2. Boil for approximately 2 minutes.
3. Remove from heat and cover.
4. Let stand at least 1 hour
5. Add just enough water to cover beans; add salt. Heat to boiling.
6. Reduce heat and cover.
7. Simmer for about 1½ hours (stir occasionally and add water as needed to keep beans covered.)
8. Mash beans and stir in fat.

Convenience Method

Use one can (about 16 oz. size) of purchased refried beans. Heat.

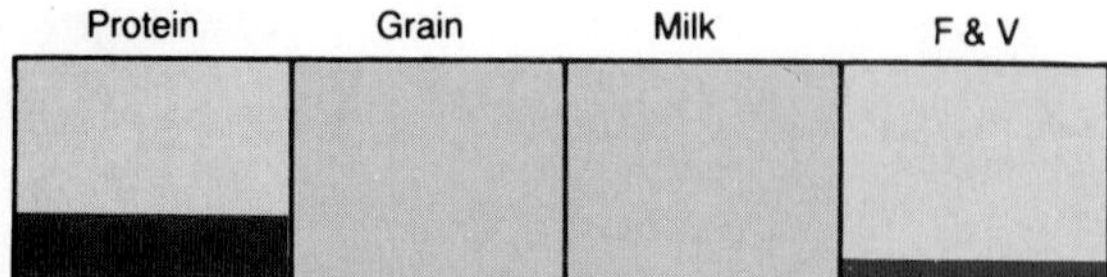

anytime, but especially for dessert. Dark roasted coffee called French roast is the favored wake-up or breaktime beverage.

Germany

You may have heard travelers newly home from Germany complaining about their expanded waistlines from the hearty meat and potatoes food fare they simply could not resist. German cuisine is not only hearty and robust in rich foods, but the customs call for large servings. Potatoes and vegetables are often incorporated into one-dish simmered meals. The unique taste of the foods comes from the German's fondness for the sweet-sour or pickled flavors. Classic dishes such as sauerbraten and sauerkraut call for long soaking in a vinegar-sugar mixture for the unique flavoring and preserving.

Many of the dishes combine fruits and meats. Stewed fruits are cooked with the meat, similar to the way Americans prepare pot roast with vegetables. Black rye and other regional specialty breads live up to Germany's fame for fine breads and complement the robust stew dishes perfectly.

The German Christmas bread (**stollen**) is rich with candied fruits and nuts. Desserts are also generous and often contain fruits. The Black Forest of Germany has inspired many a dessert creation. The name usually refers to a chocolate cake or torte with a sauce of dark sweet cherries, whipped cream, and slivers of almonds.

Switzerland

Can you picture the scenic Swiss countryside? If so, you can see why goats, dairy cows, and a few chickens are about all the steep hilly pastures and high summer grazing areas can support. Dairy products such as Swiss cheese and rich creamy Swiss chocolate are among the most memorable of the food products.

Soviet Union

Peasant food, scorned by the early aristocrats before the revolution, form the hearty base of Russian meals. The dark breads are made from assorted whole grains that bake into heavy moist breads with crisp crusts. Soups are meals in themselves with filling vegetables, sausages, and meats added. If you were asked to name one Russian food, you probably would remember the name borsch, even if you did not know what it was. **Borsch** is a colorful soup made from beets and often served with sour cream topping.

Easter is celebrated as the beginning of spring and has its own decorated and flavorful breads—often with added dried fruits. A tart apricot pudding (kissel) is considered the national dessert of the Soviet Union.

Scandinavia

The Scandinavian countries also enjoy the bounty of their seacoasts, but feature the salted and cured fish more as a course in itself or as flavoring in other dishes. Much of the area is mountainous, so pastureland is scarce. The expense of fresh meat makes it a rare delicacy. Cheese and sliced sausages mostly replace fresh meat in the meals. Reindeer are eaten in Lapland, but much of that meat is also cured into sausages and assorted cold meats.

Denmark, Finland, Norway, and Sweden started the **smorgasbord,** an elaborate food buffet that is so popular in the U.S.A. it has become an accepted word in our language. The beautiful breads of these Scandinavian countries feature elaborate braids in an assortment of rye and white flours. The exotic spices, saffron and cardamon, give many of the breads their unique taste. Traditional shapes are often prepared to help celebrate holidays such as Christmas and the end of the long, dark winter days and nights.

German Apple Pancake

Yield: 6 servings

Traditional	**Ingredients**	**Metric**
3 medium	Golden Delicious apples, peeled and cored	3 medium
2 tsp.	Lemon juice	10 mL
	Vegetable cooking spray	
2 tsp.	Unsalted margarine	10 mL
2	Eggs, lightly beaten	2
½ cup	Skim milk	125 mL
½ cup	All-purpose flour	125 mL
1 tsp.	Vanilla extract	5 mL
½ tsp.	Lemon rind, grated	3 mL
⅛ tsp.	Ground cinnamon	0.5 mL
1 Tbsp.	Powdered sugar, sifted	15 mL

Directions

1. Cut each apple into 16 pieces. Combine apples and lemon juice in a small bowl, tossing well.
2. Coat a large skillet with cooking spray; add apples. Cover and cook over low heat 5 minutes or until apples are tender. Uncover and cook 2 minutes or until lightly browned; set aside, and keep warm.
3. Place margarine in a 10-inch (25 cm) cast-iron skillet coated with cooking spray. Bake at 425°F (220°C) for 4 minutes or until margarine melts and skillet is hot
4. Combine eggs, milk, flour, vanilla, lemon rind, and cinnamon in a medium bowl. Beat at medium speed of an electric mixer until smooth. Pour immediately into hot skillet. Bake at 425°F (220°C) for 12 to 15 minutes.
5. Remove from oven; top with apple slices, and sprinkle with powdered sugar. Cut into six equal wedges. Serve immediately.

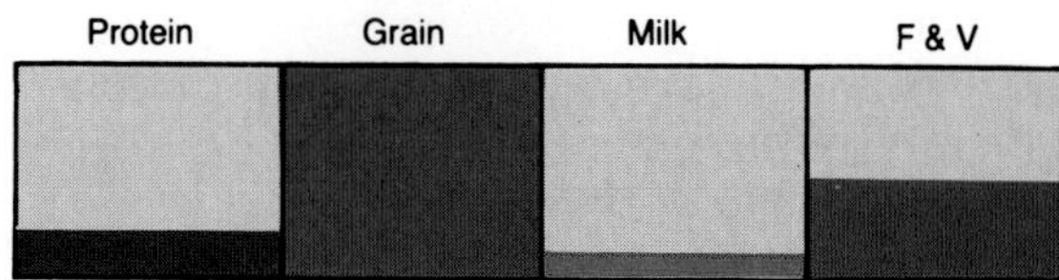

When time is available, a new taste sensation worth mastering is the Spanish tortilla (omelet), which is like a fried egg pie.

Italy

Pizza did indeed come from Italy. In recent years the pizza places in the U.S. outnumber the hamburger restaurants in popularity, but pizza's origin dates back to Naples around the year 1000. Then it was known as *picea*—a circle of dough with spices and herbs. Pizza as we know it now was created in the late 1880s when a shop owner created the Italian flag for the Queen, using red tomato, green basil, and white mozzarella cheese. Outstanding pasta typifies the cuisine. See Chapter 13 for more history and description of the true Italian pasta.

Italian omelets are called frittatas and are eaten cold or hot. The egg-vegetable mixture is browned in a skillet, then finished under a broiler.

Refreshing flavored Italian ices are sold by vendors on the streets as snacks or served after elegant meals. Historically, Italians were important in the development of ice cream also. The well-known spumoni flavor of ice cream has become a world-wide favorite.

The dry hard cheeses of Italy present pungent characteristic flavors that are musts. They are grated onto many national dishes such as pasta and pizza. The soft ricotta cheese is exactly the opposite—soft, mild, and a main part of dishes such as lasagna.

Spain

Countries in the Mediterranean are famed for their use of olive oils in foods and for cooking. Kitchens around the countryside do not feature elaborate stoves. Most of the cooking is done over a burner or charcoal cooker. Since fuel is limited, you will find an abundance of one-dish meals featuring the catch from the sea, rice, chicken, and sausages. Fresh meat is used when it is available. Garlic is treated as a food itself as well as a flavoring and is used widely. Tomatoes in all forms help to flavor and color the variety of dishes. Sun-dried tomatoes provide a flavorful winter addition to dishes. The Spanish omelet, called a *tortilla* (no resemblance to the Mexican bread!), can contain potatoes and other vegetables and meat. It resembles a pie and is cut in wedges to serve.

Greece

Greek marketplaces feature their own form of "fast foods." Vendors walk around with their own portable food service selling to customers and shopkeepers. Comparable to the hot dog vendor or hamburger stand in the United States is the gyros vendor. The gyros is a spicy ground lamb mixture that is pressed into a long column and roasted slowly on a turning vertical spit. (The spices act to both flavor and preserve the meat.) The huge piece of meat is kept warm on a revolving spit or carried by the vender to the hungry marketgoers. Each serving is sliced thinly and piled onto a pita (Greek "pocket bread") with sliced onions and a cucumber, sour cream sauce. This pungent treat has become a familiar sight in ethnic restaurants and some supermarkets throughout the U.S.

Filo (also spelled phyllo) are the paper-thin pastry sheets used throughout the Middle East. They are incorporated in many Greek national dishes from appetizers to main courses to desserts. Perhaps the most popular is **baklava,** the many layered filo, honey-lemon, and walnut pastry. A hearty main dish made with filo leaves

Spanish Crullers

Yield: 24 crullers

Traditional	Ingredients	Metric
1 cup	Water	250 mL
½ cup	Margarine or butter	125 mL
¼ tsp.	Salt	1 mL
1 cup	All-purpose flour	250 mL
3	Eggs	3
¼ cup	Sugar	50 mL
¼ tsp.	Cinnamon, ground	1 mL

Directions

1. Heat oil (1 to 1½ inches [2.5 to 2.67 cm]) to 360°F (185°C).
2. Heat water, margarine, and salt to rolling boil in 3-quart (3 L) saucepan.
3. Stir in flour.
4. Stir vigorously over low heat until mixture forms a ball, about 1 minute.
5. Remove from heat.
6. Beat in eggs all at once.
7. Continue beating until smooth.
8. Spoon mixture into decorators' tube with large star tip.
9. Squeeze 4-inch (10-cm) strips of dough into hot oil.
10. Fry 3 or 4 strips at a time until golden brown, turning once, about 2 minutes each side.
11. Drain on paper towels.
12. Mix sugar and cinnamon.
13. Roll crullers in sugar mixture.

Microwave Directions

Changes

Decrease water to ¾ cup (175 mL)

½ cup (125 mL) margarine or butter, diced

1. Follow step 1 above.
2. In a 2-quart (2 L) microwave-safe casserole, microwave water, diced margarine, and salt on High for 3½ minutes, or until boiling.
3. Stir in flour vigorously until mixture forms a ball.
4. Beat in eggs all at once.
5. Continue beating until smooth.
6. Proceed as directed in step 8.

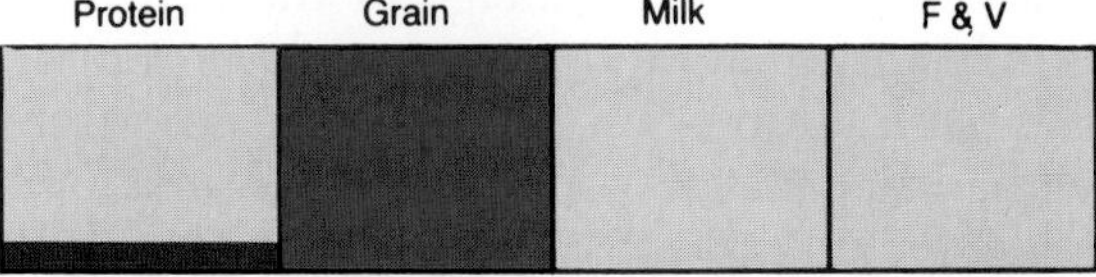

India's version of stuffed fried pastries is samosas. Pastry dough is folded around a spicy filling and fried in hot oil. A mild yogurt dip is often served with this hot food.

is spanokopita, a spinach-cheese pie. Because goats and sheep thrive on the rugged terrain of Greece, many of the foods incorporate both meats and special goat cheeses. The cheeses range from the semisoft and salty feta to the hard kasseri used for the spectacular flaming cheese appetizer, saganaki.

Sweet desserts follow the tangy spicy foods. The desserts take advantage of the many-sun dried fruits such as dates and apricots. Centuries old traditions link the treasured rose scent with eating flavors, making rose water a favored flavor for foods and desserts.

Africa

If you traveled throughout Africa, you would feel as if you were still in the Middle East until after you crossed the Sahara Desert. What we often consider as the more typical African cuisines start south of the desert. The extremes from tropical rain forests to dry, rocky mountainsides make it difficult to generalize about African foods. Other countries such as England, Holland, and France who originally established colonies in Africa also influence the foods close to their settlements.

East African people have difficulty finding grass for grazing animals, so cattle, sheep, and even goats are highly prized. One tribe counts cattle as money and uses them for dowry for daughters. The cows are not eaten, but used for milk and nutritious blood. A vein in the neck is carefully cut and bled (much as we would milk a cow) into warm milk for a nutritious meal that is extremely important for that area's balanced diet. The foods are spiced heavily and grain products are important. The Middle Eastern influence shows in the popularity of the curry for spice. Fish are available in some areas.

As you traveled west, you would find an increase in produce such as cassava, **yams** (much like our sweet potatoes), corn, black beans, peanuts, and even some tropical fruits such as bananas and coconuts. Cassava, a tuber, is ground into flour for baking and thickening. Fish are eaten often and chickens can be raised for food.

The best of all grazing croplands are located in the southern part of Africa. It is interesting to note that the centuries of reliable foods and good nutrition are considered to be the main reasons so many world-famous athletes have come from the southern part of the continent. The diet benefits from the relatively inexpensive and easy-to-raise fruits, vegetables, grains, and meats. Convenient seacoasts also furnish a wealth of seafood that increases the food choices even more.

India

You probably have heard of the "sacred cows" associated with the Hindu religion in India. To eat one is forbidden. However, milk and milk products are eaten often. Many Indians are vegetarians for religious reasons and from custom. Meat is scarce in this highly populated country. Indians avoid a deficiency of protein through the combination of other foods such as **dal** (a lentil dish) that is served at every meal. It can be made with farina, dried beans, split peas, or other lentils. This lentil dish combined with the other staple, rice,

African Sweet Potato Salad

Yield: 6 servings

Traditional	Ingredients	Metric
4 medium (about 1½ lbs.)	Sweet potatoes	4 medium (about 750 g)
¼ cup	Peanut or vegetable oil	50 mL
2 Tbsp.	Lemon juice	30 mL
½ tsp.	Salt	3 mL
¼ tsp.	Pepper	1 mL
1 medium	Green pepper, chopped	1 medium
1 small	Onion, chopped	1 small
1 stalk	Celery, chopped	1 stalk
	Parsley	

Directions

1. Heat enough salted water to cover potatoes (½ tsp. [3 mL] to 1 cup [250 mL] water) to boiling.
2. Add potatoes.
3. Heat to boiling; reduce heat.
4. Cover and cook until tender, 30 to 35 minutes; drain.
5. Cool potatoes; slip off skins.
6. Cube potatoes; place in glass or plastic bowl.
7. Mix oil, lemon juice, salt, and pepper; pour over potatoes.
8. Cover and refrigerate at least 4 hours.
9. Stir in green pepper, onion, and celery. Garnish with parsley.

Protein	Grain	Milk	F & V
			3¼x

makes a complete protein. Those who do eat beef in their diet also consider eating lamb, chicken, goat, and seafood.

Americans are used to cooking whole foods in ovens for relatively long periods of time, but the scarce fuel supply in India makes this an impossibility. One baked potato could use up a family's month supply of fuel. Indians compensate for the lack of fuel by cutting foods into small pieces that cook quickly. Often foods are soaked or marinated before cooking. This also helps to shorten the cooking time.

Most breads (called pooris and chappatis) are flat and are fried or grilled in skillets over tiny cooking fires. They are made fresh daily and offered at every meal. Often the flat breads are used as the eating utensil to scoop up the steaming food from the family-style serving dishes in the center of the table.

You would find Indian foods very spicy and sweet. Curd (what we call yogurt) is served often as a cool salad with the spicy foods. Indian cuisine calls for a pleasing balance of flavors and textures—smooth, crisp, sweet, sour, and spicy. What we call curry is a mixture of spices that the Indians mix themselves and call masala. Each household maintains its own supply.

Far East

Have you ever eaten chop suey in a Chinese restaurant with splintery bamboo chopsticks and ended the meal with a fun but tasteless fortune cookie? If so, wipe that image from your mind. It was not an authentic experience into the delicate and highly specialized cuisines of the Orient. Beauty and the aesthetics of design, texture, and taste all enter into the presentation of Oriental foods and beverage. Graceful planning and preparation do not necessarily mean elegance.

Cooking in the Orient also has been limited by the extreme scarcity of fuel. Centuries ago, that problem was managed by the careful—almost ceremonious—preparation of small pieces of vegetables, meat, and fish that would cook in seconds in the hot wok or over steam in the Mongolian hot pot. Stir-frying is a quick cooking method that heats foods but doesn't destroy the color and crisp texture of the vegetables. (See Chapter 6.)

Rice, the mainstay for all diets and all regions of the Orient, is the side dish or base of most prepared foods. Rice is considered such a staff of life that leaving a single uneaten grain in the rice bowl is regarded as bad manners. Short, medium, and long-grain rice exist and are favored for different recipes and in different regions.

Noodles are macaroni products that have been eaten in the Far East since 5000 B.C. according to some records. They vary widely and range from wide, flat noodles (chow fun) to translucent noodles (bai fun) that look like stiff fishing line.

The lack of beef and other meats is not missed due to the soybean product tofu, a bean curd resembling a hunk of cheese. Tofu contains high-quality protein with little or no cholesterol. These qualities have led to a high popularity for tofu in the U.S. Tofu can adapt to most any flavor combination and Oriental cooking method. It can even be eaten raw.

Dairy products are not a part of the Oriental diet, but soybean milk is a nutritious substitute for cow's milk. Soybean sprouts are tasty as a vegetable.

Soups such as egg-drop, wonton, and bird's nest are uniquely part of the cuisine and a mystery to most Americans who wonder how Orientals can eat them with chopsticks. Some porcelain spoons are available, but most Orientals tip the bowl, stir the liquid in a circular motion, and kind of move it with the solids into the mouth. It's similar to creating a small whirlpool. Much slurping and sipping is quite accepted. Americans are sometimes told by other cultures that they miss half the pleasure of eating by not showing their enjoyment with smacking the lips and other gustful noises of eating good food.

Unusual vegetables used in Oriental foods include bokchoy, celery cabbage, garland chrysanthemum, bean sprouts, snow peas with edible pods, ginger root, soybeans in pods, corinander, white radish, yard-long green beans, sponge gourd, butter melon, fuzzy melon, winter melon, bamboo shoots, water chestnuts, lotus root, and seaweed.

China

Have you ever wondered what the difference was when an Oriental restaurant advertises food as Cantonese style, Hunan, or Szechuan? Four regional styles of cooking exist in China that are distinctly different.

Shanghai style is probably well characterized by the hearty casserole type of mixtures with gravy that is served in many of the older Chinese restaurants in the United States. Soy sauce dominates as the usual seasoning.

Szechuan and **Hunan** styles are attractive foods that send many an unaware tourist gasping for water! The hot pepper and generous use of fresh ginger make the foods quite hot.

Cantonese style cooking is popular in the United States Oriental restaurants. The colorful, crisp cooked foods served in the delicate sauces have a universal appeal.

Peking style food preparation can be quite tricky. Imperial court chefs developed strict rules of preparation and cooking.

Japan

Seafood abounds in Japan. You will find it fried, steamed, baked in paper, and prepared for eating raw. **Sukiyaki,** meat and vegetable dishes, prepared in a wok are popular. The tempura foods are crispy fried after dipping in a light batter and may be any type of seafood, meat, or vegetable.

Stir-fry dishes, favored in the Orient, are also now popular in the United States. Americanized versions may substitute local vegetables for Oriental specialties.

Your Chance to Explore

Foods around the world do just that—they keep going around the world. You can sample most any cuisine of the world in restaurants right here in our own country and our influences reach most any place you might visit. An issue of *U.S. News & World Report* magazine quoted a Russian TV announcer commenting about a film being aired on Russian TV. He said, "Maybe there is something we can learn from this." What were they watching? A film of Big Macs on the grill and smiling patrons at a New York McDonald's. How true that old saying, "What goes around comes around!"

Egg-Drop Soup (Tan Hua T'ang)

Yield: 6 servings
(about ¾ cup [175 mL] each)

Traditional	**Ingredients**	**Metric**
5 cups	Water	1.25 L
1 Tbsp. plus 2 tsp.	Instant chicken bouillon	25 mL
½ tsp.	Salt	3 mL
½ tsp.	Monosodium glutamate (optional)	3 mL
3 Tbsp.	Cold water	45 mL
1 Tbsp. plus 1 tsp.	Cornstarch	23 mL
1	Egg, slightly beaten	1
2	Scallions or green onions (with tops), diagonally sliced	2

Directions

1. Heat 5 cups (1.25 L) water, the bouillon, salt and monosodium glutamate to boiling in 2-quart (2 L) saucepan.
2. Mix 3 tablespoons (45 mL) water and the cornstarch; stir gradually into broth.
3. Boil and stir 1 minute.
4. Slowly pour egg into broth, stirring constantly with fork, to form shreds of egg.
5. Remove from heat; stir slowly one or twice.
6. Garnish each serving with scallions.

Protein	Grain	Milk	F & V

Vocabulary Review

Tortilla
Trifle
Provincial
Stollen
Borsch
Sukiyaki
Smorgasbord

Questions for Review

1. The popularity of international foods in this country is usually attributed to what?
2. What can you learn about other countries through the study of the area's food customs?
3. Why do you think there are so many restaurants featuring international foods in this country? What are some international eating places or international feature foods in your area?
4. What are some of the favorite American foods that used to be considered "foreign foods?" Several were listed in this chapter, but what are some other examples?
5. What food serves as the Mexican bread? How is it made? What are the ways that this food product is eaten?
6. What nutritious mix of foods are the main staples of the Cuban diet?
7. Describe some of the traditional British foods that are well-known as old-time favorites?
8. What are the two main types of French cuisine? Why is one type elegant and complicated while the other is rather wholesome and earthy?
9. What type of seasoning is responsible for the unique flavor of many German dishes? Name some of the classic dishes incorporating this unique flavor.
10. Describe the so-called peasant foods that form the base of Russian meals.
11. What geographical features of Switzerland make it ideal for dairy products and the making of its famous cheeses?
12. What spices give many Scandinavian breads their unique flavors? Why are the seasonal celebrations with special festive breads so important to the morale of most Scandinavians?
13. Describe some characteristic cheeses of Italy. For what types of food dishes are they used?
14. How do Spanish people use olive oil in cooking?
15. What is a gyro? How is it usually served? Why is lamb eaten frequently in Greece?
16. Why is it difficult to generalize about the characteristics of African food?
17. Why is a lentil dish, such as the popular dal, so important to balance the diet in India?
18. Why do Oriental and Indian cuisines call for foods to be cut into small pieces before cooking?
19. Describe the process of stir-frying food.
20. What are the four regional styles of cooking that exist in China? Describe each one.

Things to Do

1. Select a recipe representing another country from this book and make it for the class to try. Read about the country of origin in this book and from sources in the library. Report to the class geographical and social influences that helped to make the dish typical of the country.
2. Demonstrate a stir-fry dish in a wok or an electric skillet for the class. See Chapter 6 in this book for a description of stir-frying.
3. Invite a local chef from an international restaurant in your area to demonstrate an international specialty.
4. Use the local telephone book and newspaper ads to compile a list of international restaurants in your area. Make a list of featured foods in ads from "American" restaurants that could be considered of foreign origin. Report on the American "melting-pot" of international cuisines in your area.

Section 2

Nutrition for Healthful Living

3 The Value Of Good Nutrition

A Riddle for You . . .

What new science makes headlines with "lifesaving" information everyday?

You would have great difficulty finding a magazine or newspaper for the general public that did not feature some claim for a "breakthrough" in the mysteries of this relatively new science. This science is so young, there is a constant call for new research to discover the answers so vital to humans.

Hint . . . It is thousands of years younger than the beginning of modern medicine.

Hint . . . The first discovery that led to the beginning of this science occurred centuries after the prophets first predicted the flight to the moon.

Hint . . . People already had mastered amazing techniques in metallurgy (the science of the study of metals) before this science was even named or discovered.

Hint . . . This science is relatively so new, much of the knowledge is still limited to facts about what can be demonstrated to be "true." Often the why is still an unknown that is under intense investigation!

So, what is the answer? Nutrition. Yes, nutrition is the young science that still holds so many unanswered questions.

In this era of high technology, people have learned to design and send a ship with people to the moon, substitute artificial organs in humans and animals, implant natural body parts, manufacture fibers and fabrics of incredible strength and beauty, and transmit radio and video signals around the earth and into space. The list is almost endless and absolutely awesome. What humans cannot do is recreate or even identify all the nutrients that we eat in our everyday foods, such as an apple or a glass of milk. Scientists still have not discovered all the nutrients that are working together to make the body function properly.

The discovery of the first vitamin didn't occur until the early 1900s. People almost flew in airplanes before they knew enough to eat fruit to prevent the killer disease, **scurvy,** or to leave some bran covering on their rice to prevent the dreaded disease, **beriberi.** You may remember the colorful stories from grade school of how sailors who ate limes on long ocean trips didn't get the dreaded scurvy. Those who did not eat the fruit were stricken with the disease. Perhaps you remember the story of the doctor who discovered that the chickens eating the thrown-out rice with the bran hulls were healthy, while the cared-for chickens fed the prized, polished white rice sickened and died. Exciting discover-

ies followed as he reasoned that perhaps the polished rice was not good for the children either. It all sounds so simple to us now, but the whole idea of nutrients in foods was unheard of then.

Familiarity has almost moved nutrition into the class of being "taken for granted." In the words of one teenager, "Vitamins? Oh, yes, I know all about those. We had them in grade school." Fascinating isn't it how some people think they know all about something that the nutrition scientists, who have spent their lives studying, have not yet been able to answer? Can you imagine yourself refusing to look at any sweaters in new styles or revolutionary colors, saying "No, thank you, I had a sweater in grade school? Discovering new styles and fabrics that suit your needs takes an open mind and constant exploration of the media and store windows for what's new and right for you. Discovering what's new in nutrition that's right for you also requires your constant exploration and a questioning attitude.

In this section, you will have the opportunity to explore the latest discoveries and the questions that are being researched worldwide by scientists, nutritionists, and doctors. You can research your own best health guidelines from the very latest findings. At the same time, you

Daily Food Guide

Milk Group

Foods

Milk, yogurt, cheese, pudding, cottage cheese, ice cream

This group supplies:

calcium, riboflavin, protein

Daily needs	**Servings**
Children	3
Teenagers	4
Adults	2
Pregnant Women	4
Breast-feeding Women	4

A serving is:

1 cup (250 mL) milk
1 cup (250 mL) yogurt
1 oz. (1 1/2 slices) cheese
1 cup (250 mL) pudding
2 cups (500 mL) cottage cheese
1 cup (250 mL) ice cream

can learn about the current controversies that often splash across the headlines in conflicting statements. You will learn reliable sources for checking out information for accuracy. The science of nutrition can be confusing, controversial, complicated, and fascinating.

Good News

The good news is that good daily nutrition for you can be as simple as following a Daily Food Guide developed by the U.S. Department of Agriculture. By following this guide, you can be assured of receiving the nutrients your body needs.

What scientists do know is that over 50 different nutrients are needed to maintain and build the body. All 50 of those nutrients are found in the natural foods you can eat everyday. Natural foods are foods that occur in nature, not manufactured or highly refined by humans. Those 50 nutrients are distributed in different foods. No one food contains all of the needed nutrients. The nutrients are classified as water, protein, carbohydrate, fat, vitamins, and minerals. (Fiber often is discussed as if it were a separate nutrient, but it is a kind of a carbohy-

Meat, Poultry, Fish, and Beans Group

Foods
Meat, fish, poultry, eggs, cheese, dried peas or beans, peanuts, peanut butter
This group supplies:
protein, niacin, iron, thiamin

Daily needs	**Servings**
Children	2
Teenagers	2
Adults	2
Pregnant Women	3
Breast-feeding Women	2

A serving is:
2 oz. (63 g) cooked, lean meat, fish, poultry
2 eggs
2 oz. (63 g) cheese
1 cup (250 mL) dried peas or beans
4 Tbsp. (100 mL) peanut butter

drate.) Some foods are better sources for various nutrients than others.

To make it easier for you to select a healthy and balanced diet, the foods have been divided into four basic groups according to the key nutrients they contain, plus one group of foods that is to be limited or avoided. These divisions are known as the Basic Food Groups. (See the photographs on pages 38 - 41 that illustrate the foods in each group and how many servings of each you need.) Each food group supplies you with a different combination of the main nutrients you need. The numbers and sizes of servings recommended from each group are calculated to supply you with the nutrients you need without too many calories. The nutrition bar used in this book is based upon the recommendations for the average needs of the teenaged male for the key nutrients because males require slightly higher amounts of some of the key nutrients.

What science does not know is what other essential nutrients or substances have yet to be

Fruit-Vegetable Group

Foods

Juice, cooked vegetables or fruits, raw vegetables or fruits

This group supplies:

Vitamin A, vitamin C

Daily needs	**Servings**
Children	4
Teenagers	4
Adults	4
Pregnant Women	4
Breast-feeding Women	4

A serving is:

½ cup (125 mL) juice
½ cup (125 mL) cooked vegetable or fruit
1 cup (250 mL) raw vegetable or fruit
1 medium apple, banana, or orange
½ grapefruit
¼ cantaloupe

Note: Dark green, leafy or orange vegetables and fruit are recommended three or four times a week for vitamin A. Citrus fruits are recommended daily for vitamin C.

discovered in foods. Those unknowns might work alone, in connection with other nutrients, or enable other nutrients to work. The only way you can be certain to get all the identified 50 nutrients and the unknown nutrients is to eat a variety of foods from each of the four basic food groups each day.

Grain Group

Foods
Whole-grain or enriched bread, ready-to-eat cereal, cooked cereal, pasta, rice, grits, oatmeal
This group supplies:
Carbohydrate, thiamin, iron, niacin

Daily needs	Servings
Children	4
Teenagers	4
Adults	4
Pregnant Women	4
Breast-feeding Women	4

A serving is:
1 slice bread
1 cup (250 mL) ready-to-eat cereal
½ cup (125 mL) cooked cereal
½ cup (125 mL) pasta
½ cup (125 mL) rice
½ cup (125 mL) grits

Other Foods *(not shown)*

Foods
Butter, margarine, sugar, dressing, jelly, mayonnaise, soft drinks, pie, layer cake, corn chips, pretzels, gravy, candy, sweet rolls
This group supplies:
These foods contain fats and calories. Those nutrients are available from foods in the other food groups. As such, foods in this food group are not a necessary part of your daily food plan.
Daily needs:
There are no recommended servings for food in this category.
A serving is:
1 tsp. (5 mL) butter, margarine
1 tsp. (5 mL) sugar
1 Tbsp. (15 mL) dressing, jelly, mayonnaise
1 cup (250 mL) soft drink
1/6 of a 9" (22 cm) pie
1/16 of a 9" (22 cm) layer cake

The News About Nutrients

Nutrients are chemical substances obtained from food during digestion that work together to supply you with energy, to build and maintain body cells, and to regulate body processes. ("Guide to Wise Food Choices." 1984 edition, National Dairy Council.)

The nutrients that actually provide the energy are protein, fats, and carbohydrates. Water, vitamins, and minerals work together with the other nutrients to help release the energy, but do not actually provide energy directly. A **calorie** is the unit of measure used to calculate how much energy is provided by each food.

Water

Water is the most abundant substance in your body. It is easy to forget, but vital to all the chemical reactions that take place in your body. Your skin needs water from the inside and the outside of your body to remain attractive and supple. Perhaps you can remember a time when your lips cracked or hands became rough and sore after exposure to a dry wind in either summer or winter? That was a good example of an outside element removing water from the skin. It helps to remind us how important water is to the health of the skin.

Water, The Body's Transportation System

Water transports the nutrients you eat to the cells where the nutrients are used. After the body uses nutrients, the leftover waste products must be removed from the cells. That is a job for water, too. Water carries the wastes to the intestines where they can be conveniently removed from the body.

Life-Saving Assignments

Water alone will maintain your life longer than food alone. Your body cannot regulate its temperature without an adequate supply of water. Only oxygen is more important than water in maintaining life in the human body. Some foods are high in water content, but they do not replace the need for drinking fluids. Have you passed by any good drinking fountains lately?

Protein

Protein is the basic building material for all the body cells. You cannot grow or replace body cells without it. Protein also forms enzymes. **Enzymes** are substances that start or encourage the chemical reactions in your body. Your hormones also are made of protein. Even a vital part of your red and white blood cells and antibodies are made of protein. When your diet does not supply enough carbohydrates or fat for energy, your body can break down proteins to meet your energy needs.

Protein is the second most abundant material in your body. Can you imagine trying to live without being able to build, maintain, or regulate your body? Obviously, protein is essential to begin a life and to continue living after that life has begun.

Proteins are not all the same structure. They are made from different combinations of at least 22 amino acids. You might picture in your mind 22 colors of plastic building blocks as amino acids. In fact, amino acids are often referred to as the building blocks of protein. Those blocks fit together into different sizes and shapes to make various structures representing proteins. You can imagine that the resulting protein structures could vary greatly. These different proteins also vary in their quality for use by the human body. **Complete proteins** are high-quality substances that supply the indispensable amino acids in the right proportions for your body to use. Complete proteins come from animal food sources. Foods from plant sources usually supply **incomplete proteins** that lack all the essential amino acids or a sufficient amount of the amino acids to supply the body's needs.

However, you can cash in on the inexpensive

Complete proteins are available from meats. Remember, too, that combining plant proteins can supply the right amount of amino acids.

protein provided by foods from plant sources by learning how to combine foods in order to create a complete protein structure. Some plant proteins provide certain amino acids, while other plant proteins provide different amino acids. By using those building blocks in the right combinations, you end up with a complete-protein structure. Some cultures and countries survive without meat protein. They do so by following the practice of compatible plant foods. The Cuban's national dish of beans and rice is a tasty example. Rice and dried beans is just one of the mixtures that supplies the right combination of amino acids to form a complete, high-quality protein. Other combinations might be dried beans and whole wheat, dried beans and corn, or peanuts and whole wheat. That certainly does raise the peanut butter sandwich made with whole-wheat bread to a high rating as a "main dish" possibility. Combining a plant protein with a small amount of protein from an animal source is yet another way to meet your body's need for protein—and at reduced cost.

So They Say

Caffeine: The Pros

Caffeine may make you breathe a little easier . . . after about three cups.

Medical researchers say that 600 milligrams of caffeine make breathing muscles stronger and breathing more fluid. In one study, the researchers tried to imitate the effects of lung disease on the breathing muscles of 12 participants. A heavy load was placed on their breathing muscles. The researchers found that caffeine eased their breathing and made the work seem less of an effort.

Some researchers suggest that athletes might perform better from using caffeine—but the jury is still out on that. The Food and Drug Administration (FDA) lists caffeine as "generally regarded as safe." For the average person, though, there are more risks than benefits. Caffeine has been associated with heart disease and sleeplessness.

Caffeine: The Cons

Two recent studies link caffeine to heart disease, but don't put down your coffee cup too fast.

One study found that "heavy" coffee drinkers were 2½ times more likely to have heart disease than nonusers. The other study found that among heavy coffee drinkers, there was a 70 percent increase in heart disease.

More research needs to be done. Factors such as personality, lifestyle, job stress, and diet might also explain heart trouble.

It is estimated that 80 percent of Americans drink coffee each day.

Fats

You could easily forget that fats are valuable, necessary nutrients when you hear the cautions about restricting the use of fats. Fats suffer from a "bad reputation" because the Dietary Guidelines (see page 63) restrict their use. In addition, fats have the highest energy value (calories) and possibly contribute to a high cholesterol blood level. Although those factors are mostly true, to give in to the temptation of eliminating fats from the diet would be extremely harmful to your health.

Fats are essential for good health and proper body functioning. Without fats, your body could not absorb fat-soluble vitamins (vitamins A, D, E, and K). Without fats, even if you ate foods high in those vitamins, you would be deficient because your body could not use them. Fats help you to prevent hunger from returning too soon after eating. Fat acts as a cushion for your vital body organs and as insulation to protect you from temperature changes. Not the least of its functions is the attractive shape fat gives to the human body.

Butter, lard, margarine, and oils are all fats. Other foods that contain a high percentage of fats include mayonnaise, salad dressings, bacon, peanut butter, and deep-fried, batter-coated foods. Fats are also in such food as red meats, poultry skin, egg yolks, and nuts.

See Chapter 4 for specific information reagarding the relationship of fats and cholesterol.

Carbohydrates

Carbohydrates are the starches, sugars, and fiber in foods that are formed by the elements carbon, hydrogen, and oxygen. The simple forms of carbohydrates are sugars. The more complicated arrangements of the three basic elements form **starches,** known as complex carbohydrates. Most carbohydrates come from plant sources, but some dairy products contain lactose, a milk sugar.

Carbohydrates are essential nutrients that many people mistakenly think can be safely

Scientists have discovered that oat bran fiber has special nutritional benefits for lowering the blood cholesterol level in some people.

Oat Bran Muffins

Yield: 1 dozen

Traditional	Ingredients	Metric
2½ cups	Unprocessed oat bran	625 mL
½ cup	Raisins	125 mL
1 tbsp.	Firmly packed brown sugar	15 mL
1 tbsp.	Baking powder	15 mL
⅛ tsp.	Salt	0.5 mL
½ cup	Chunky unsweetened applesauce	125 mL
1 cup	Skim milk	250 mL
½ cup	Egg substitute or 2 eggs, lightly beaten	125 mL
1 tbsp.	Corn oil	15 mL
	Vegetable cooking spray	

Directions

1. Combine the oat bran, raisins, brown sugar, baking powder, and salt in a large bowl. Make a well in the center of the mixture.
2. Combine the applesauce, milk, egg substitute or eggs, and oil. Stir well.
3. Add the applesauce mixture to the dry ingredients, pouring the liquid into the well. Stir until the dry ingredients are just moistened
4. Coat the muffin pans with cooking spray or line with paper baking cups.
5. Spoon the batter into the pans, filling them three-fourths full.
6. Bake at 425°F (220°C) for 20 minutes or until golden brown.

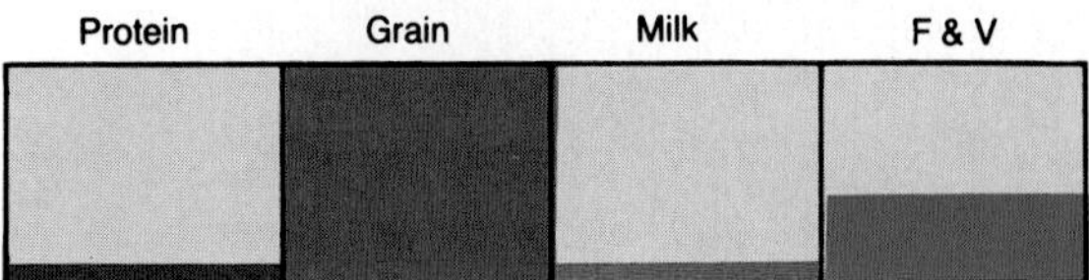

So They Say

Dateline . . . University of Kentucky Medical Center. Dr. James Anderson discovered about 10 years ago that diets high in water-soluble fiber helped diabetics. Recently, he has found that the same high water-soluble-fiber diet tends to lower the blood cholesterol rating. When he fed 100 grams of oat bran daily to persons being tested, their blood cholesterol levels were reduced by more than 10 percent in just 10 days. Stay tuned for further developments.

eliminated from a healthy diet. Starchy foods are often wrongly considered to be fattening, low nutrient foods. Some carbohydrates do provide a high amount of calories in relation to their nutrient content. The difference between the "good guys and the bad guys" is the difference between the simple and complex carbohydrates. Simple carbohydrates (sugar) and highly refined carbohydrates (nonenriched, bleached flours or pastas) supply a high proportion of calories compared to their other nutrient contribution. You could eliminate sugar, cakes, and pastry and still be healthy. On the other hand, foods that are high in complex carbohydrates supply much-needed vitamins, minerals, energy, and fiber. They also help your body make efficient use of protein and utilize fats for energy. Natural foods that are high in complex carbohydrates, such as potatoes and whole grains, are low in calories compared to the essential nutrients they contain.

Yesterday's Roughage Makes News as Fiber

Today's nutrition-conscious people have rediscovered the importance of fiber in the diet. Just a few short years ago, fiber was valued for its "roughage" that helped prevent constipation. The "apple a day keeps the doctor away" grew out of the high fiber content and laxative effect that apples had for many people. Awakened to the pleasures of whole-grain tastes and textures, people have developed a new appreciation for the health qualities of these high-fiber foods.

Wheat bran and most whole-grain products contain fiber that is not digested by the body. The bulk or roughage from that fiber helps to push wastes through the body. There is also some evidence that a high fiber diet decreases the risk of intestinal cancer.

Researchers have recently discovered that oat products, unpeeled fruit, vegetables, and legumes contain a water-soluble fiber that actually helps to lower blood cholesterol levels. The water-soluble fiber lowers the cholesterol by taking with it the bile salts from the intestines as the fiber is eliminated from the body. The bile salts are forms of cholesterol, so the loss affects the blood cholesterol level. This is new research, so the full impact of lowering the blood cholesterol upon lessening the risk of heart disease is not yet known.

Vitamins—A Life Support

You probably have heard about vitamins all your life, but you might be amazed to discover what a tiny amount is needed to support the life in a human body. That tiny amount, however, can mean the difference between a zestful life and death.

Vitamins are organic substances needed by the body in very small amounts to assist chemical reactions in the body. They do not give you energy, but they help the body to use the energy from carbohydrates, fats, and proteins.

There are many vitamins that have been identified, but all fit into two categories—water soluble and fat soluble. These terms refer to whether a vitamin dissolves in water or fat. Knowing this can help you select the best food preparation methods to preserve nutrients and understand how the body stores the vitamin.

The **water-soluble vitamins** are the B vitamins and vitamin C. Extra amounts of the water-soluble vitamins are not stored in the body. Your body uses what it needs and flushes out the extra amounts of the water-soluble vitamins from the body in urine or other body wastes. Massive doses of certain water-soluble vitamins that exceed the body's needs can cause kidney problems, nerve damage, and other health complications.

The **fat-soluble vitamins** include vitamins A, D, E, and K. When you consume extra fat-soluble vitamins, they are stored in the fatty parts of the body. This includes brain tissue. If massive amounts of concentrated fat-soluble vitamins in pills or other supplements are consumed, they can accumulate and cause severe illness and damage to the body. Overdoses of vitamins are not likely from eating any natural food, but can occur from massive doses of vitamin pills, other supplements, and shots. You definitely can get too much of a "good thing" when it comes to vitamins.

Vitamin A

Vitamin A is the only vitamin you can actually see evidence of in food. You often can judge the richness of the amount of vitamin A by the color of the food. The yellow pigment, carotene, in food is made into vitamin A in the body. When you see yellow and deep orange-yellow coloring in foods, you can bet the vitamin A potential is there. Carrots, pumpkins, apricots, nectarines, corn, butter, cheddar cheese, and egg yolk are examples of foods colored by carotene. The yellow-colored foods are the easiest to identify, but often the coloring is hidden by green chlorophyll in foods such as spinach, broccoli, asparagus, and dark green lettuce. Even the rich red of the tomato starts with the yellow pigment. Carotene is turned

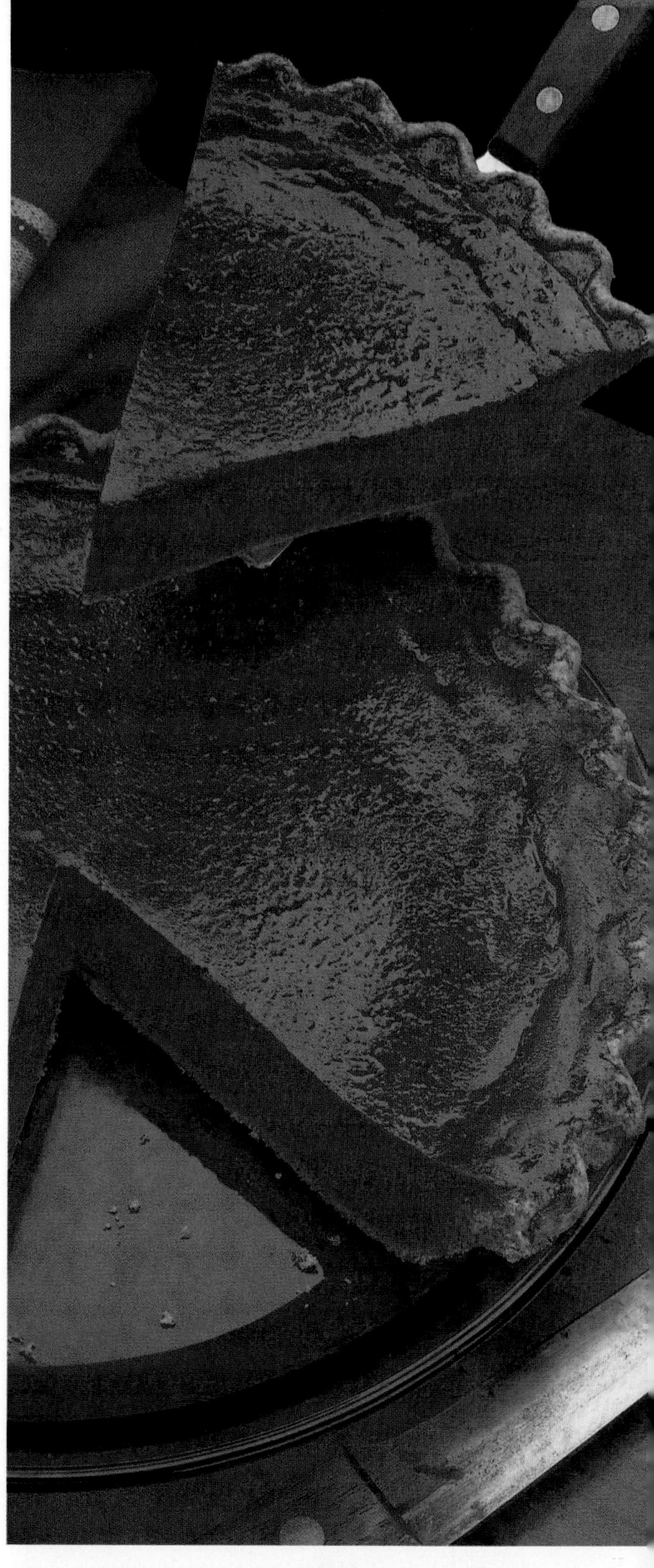

You can have your dessert and your vitamins, too! Pumpkin pie is a rich source of vitamin A. Would the color of pumpkins give you a clue as to the vitamin content?

into the vitamin A in the body, so it is known as a provitamin. **Provitamins** are substances your body can turn into a vitamin. When vitamin A occurs in foods in its true vitamin form, it is colorless, as in fish oil.

Food Facts

What's in a name? Vitamins were first named by the letters of the alphabet in the general order of their discovery. As the chemical composition for each vitamin was determined, a scientific name was assigned for each vitamin. The correct names of the vitamins (chemicals) are:

Vitamin A . . . Retinol
Vitamin B . . . Niacin
Vitamin B_1 . . . Thiamin
Vitamin B_2 . . . Riboflavin
Vitamin B_6 . . . Pyridoxine
Vitamin B_{12} . . . Cobalamins
B Vitamin . . . Panothenic acid
B Vitamin . . . Biotin
B Vitamin . . . Folic acid
Vitamin C . . . Ascorbic acid
Vitamin D . . . Calciferol
Vitamin E . . . Tocopherols
Vitamin K . . . K. (The initial for the German spelling of coagulation.)

Discussing individual vitamins can be as complicated as the highest level of biochemistry, but a few simple facts can help to clarify why they are so important and how to make certain they are in your diet. Refer to the individual vitamin sections in this chapter for more specific information.

What It Does For You

Vitamin A is necessary for good vision at night. You need it for smooth, attractive skin and shiny, resilient hair. The mucous linings of your mouth, nose, throat, and digestive tract are kept moist and resistant to infections with enough vitamin A. It promotes growth and the development of the bones and teeth. Moderate amounts of extra vitamin A that are eaten can be safely stored in the liver for use when less than the needed amount is eaten. It is a myth, however, that extra amounts of vitamin A will give the body additional help. Your body needs about 5000 International Units (IU) daily. Any more than that will simply be stored until needed another day. Much more than that can become toxic to the body. Anything over 50,000 IU can be hazardous to the body.

The U. S. Recommended Daily Allowance (U.S. RDA) of vitamin A is measured in IUs because it is available directly as vitamin A and as a provitamin in the form of carotene. The units measure the vitamin "potential" of a food.

Too much vitamin A may result in headaches, nausea, and extreme irritability. Sometimes the skin turns yellow and dry with extreme itchiness.

Too little vitamin A may result in rough skin that gets infected easily and eyes sensitive to light. One severe symptom can be night blindness.

Vitamin A is easy to obtain from everyday foods that are inexpensive and convenient to buy. The concentrated amounts that occur in food would seem to eliminate the need to even consider taking vitamin pills for this nutrient. You could obtain over a 2-day's supply of this vitamin by eating 3/4 cup (175 mL) of cooked carrots or a 9-day's supply of the vitamin by eating less than 3 oz. (86 g) of beef liver. Vitamin A is a fat-soluble vitamin that is stored in the body, so you don't need to eat an excellent source of it every day.

Vitamin D

You will hear the important message from nutritionists that you can get all the vitamins you need from natural foods without taking any vitamin supplements or pills. There is an exception to that guideline. The sunshine vitamin, vitamin D, is not likely to be available in natural foods unless they are fortified. Before the days of fortifying food, sunshine triggered the production of most of the vitamin D in the human body. A provitamin on the surface of the skin is converted to vitamin D in the body by the ultraviolet rays of the sun.

People who did not have the opportunity to experience direct sunlight on their skin used to suffer from a lack of vitamin D. The federal government corrected that situation by directing the fortification of milk with vitamin D. Milk was chosen because it is a food most everyone uses, so it would reach the most people. Milk also is rich in calcium and phosphorus. Those are the two minerals that work well with vitamin D in building and maintaining strong bones. The only food that is naturally rich in vitamin D is fish liver oil—not exactly an everyday food for many people.

What It Does For You

You need vitamin D to absorb calcium from the intestine and to maintain normal calcium and phosphorus metabolism in the body. Too little vitamin D causes rickets, bowed legs, a deformed spine, and sometimes stunted growth in children. Adults need the vitamin to maintain healthy bones and teeth. Some scientists believe that a lack of vitamin D and calcium is involved in the weakening of bones in the elderly. This condition is called **osteoporosis.** See page 54. The U.S. RDA for vitamin D is 400 IUs from birth to young adulthood. Following the guidelines of the Basic Food Groups for four servings from the Dairy Food group (using fortified milk) will easily meet that requirement. Note: The four servings a day applies to teenagers. Children need three servings; adults, two.

Too much vitamin D can be hazardous to your health since this fat-soluble vitamin is stored in the body. Nausea, weakness, excessive urination, and serious hypertension are some of the side effects of an unsafe amount of stored vitamin D. Too much vitamin D also causes calcification of soft tissues. You will find that reading the label for vitamin D fortification is important to prevent an overdose—especially in young children. Margarines, fruit drinks, breakfast foods, and even candy are sometimes fortified with vitamin D. One serving of some of the sweetened flavored milks can provide up to 150 IUs of vitamin D. Three to four times the U.S. RDA (400 IU) for vitamin D is considered hazardous to your health by some experts. Others suggest you might tolerate 10 times the U.S. RDA. Either amount would be possible to eat through fortified foods, so caution is suggested.

Vitamin E

You can watch the magazines for the latest fads in foods and vitamins. They come and go out of style just like clothing styles. About 10 years ago, enthusiastic believers were preaching that taking vitamin E supplements was the answer to sterility, pregnancy problems, and even muscular dystrophy. The truth is that vitamin E deficiency in the United States is practically nonexistent because vitamin E is so plentiful in a variety of foods. Milk, green leafy vegetables, egg yolk, vegetable oils, whole-grain cereals, and liver are extremely rich in this nutrient. Your body can store this fat-soluble vitamin in the muscle and fat tissues.

What It Does for You

The primary job of vitamin E in the body is to prevent oxygen in the body from destroying fatty substances, such as vitamin A and fatty acids. It is such an effective preservative (antioxidant), you will find that it is added to catfood to prevent the polyunsaturated fish oils from spoiling.

Lack of this vitamin in humans is so rare it is necessary to refer to experiments with deprived rats for any deficiency symptoms. Rats that have been completely deprived of this vitamin show heart and reproductive abnormalities. Too much vitamin E can cause blurred vision, nausea, dizziness, and extreme fatigue.

Vitamin K

Vitamin K was named for the German word "koagulation" which means the clotting of blood. This vitamin must be present for the body to stop bleeding. A very small amount of vitamin K can mean the difference between bleeding to death or efficient clotting of the blood. You probably have not heard much about "eating your vitamin K" because it is made by your body. Bacteria that live in the intestinal tract manufacture the amount of the vitamin that is needed by the body. Vitamin K also is found in green leafy vegetables, cauliflower, potatoes, and liver. The vitamin works for your health by assisting the liver in forming prothrombin, a necessary factor in the formation of blood clots.

Food Facts

The myth of organic vitamins. You could "myth" the whole idea of what a vitamin is if you "buy" the advertisements that so-called organic vitamins are superior to synthetic vitamins. You have learned that vitamins are organic substances necessary in small amounts in the diet for normal growth, maintenance of the body, and chemical reactions in the human body. Vitamins are organic chemical compounds that are made of different structures of the basic elements carbon, hydrogen, oxygen, and sometimes nitrogen. The term "organic" in this case refers to a carbon compound, not the source of the vitamin. There is absolutely no difference between a synthetic vitamin manufactured from the chemical elements and a so-called organic vitamin manufactured with the same chemical elements from plant and animal sources (organic).

The so-called organic and synthetic vitamins are identical, but the prices are not. Organic vitamins are much more expensive to manufacture. It is not unusual to have the same dosages of "organic" vitamins cost 10 times as much as the synthetic variety. By law, for both types of vitamins, the generic brand vitamin is identical to the high-priced brand-name products. Only the appearance, form, and coatings can be different.

B Vitamin Group

Scientists thought they were discovering one vitamin when the first B vitamin was isolated. That vitamin became the vitamin B complex when more water-soluble vitamins of a similar composition were discovered. There are now considered to be about nine vitamins in this group, but three are better known than the rest. Thiamin (B_1), riboflavin (B_2), and niacin have been found to be lacking in the diets of some population groups of the U.S in the past. You might want to give the "big three of the Bs" your special attention in selecting foods for a healthy diet. You can depend upon getting good amounts of the B vitamins from animal products, such as pork, fish, poultry, beef, milk, and eggs. Organ meats are concentrated sources for the B vitamins. Plant sources of vitamin-B-rich foods are enriched breads and cereals, whole grains, dried beans and peas, peanuts, fresh peas, and dark green leafy vegetables. Niacin is not present in milk, but the body converts the amino acid tryptophan in milk into niacin.

The drama of the dreaded diseases caused by long-term deprivation of the B vitamins is not considered a problem in the United States. Those diseases, beriberi, pellagra, and pernicious anemia, mostly occur in countries where a variety of food is not available. In an area where corn is the only grain in the diet, pellegra might occur from a lack of niacin. Such countries also usually lack dairy foods due to the absence of whole grains to feed the animals. The

A lively green spinach salad becomes a one-dish meal with the surprise of pork added. Flavorful pork adds a rich source of B vitamins to this dish.

lack of milk and milk products removes the chance of obtaining niacin from the tryptophan from milk.

What They Do For You

The B vitamins contribute to the body's inner workings in several specific ways.

Thiamin (B_1)

Thiamin is crucial as a coenzyme in the process of getting oxygen to the body tissues. It also assists the body in using carbohydrates for energy. This vitamin helps in the building of ribose, a sugar that is part of the RNA. Through these functions, thiamin indirectly promotes good appetite and a healthy central nervous system.

Riboflavin (B_2)

The work of riboflavin as a coenzyme in helping to carry hydrogen to the cells is so basic that the vitamin can be found in almost any tissue in the body. This vitamin is essential for healthy skin. It also helps you see well in bright light.

Niacin

Niacin provides the "tools" for the body to utilize carbohydrates and to synthesize human fat. It is essential in the chemical reactions of taking apart and fitting together the hydrogen and oxygen atoms of the body cells. It also nurtures a normal appetite by assisting the maintenance of a healthy digestive system.

Other B Vitamins

Other B vitamins are present naturally in the food from which you obtain the "big three" of the B vitamins. If your diet is planned to obtain your requirements for the "big three," you will also be likely to get the small amounts of the other needed B complex vitamins.

Recent research has been done to determine if vitamin B_6 might be helpful for treating premenstral syndrom (PMS) in women. Those studies have not supported this treatment. What has been established, however, is that taking vitamin B_6 in extra dosages can cause severe nerve damage. For some women, that damage is probably permanent. Contrary to what was formerly believed, the body can suffer damage when excess amounts of water-soluble vitamins are taken.

Vitamin C

The advertising world of the last decade has created the image of vitamin C as the cure-all miracle vitamin. Most colorful labels in the drink and cereal sections of supermarkets splash banners proclaiming "vitamin C." There has never been any evidence that the U.S. diet needed such a "bandwagon" approach to the fortification of foods with vitamin C. Even before all the fortification, only a few problems casued by a lack of vitamin C showed up.

The controversy over massive doses of vitamin C for special curing powers of the common cold has triggered years of intensive research on the subject. There is still no conclusive evidence that those extra-large doses will either prevent or cure the common cold. Recent studies have shown that there might be a benefit from vitamin C because it is a weak antihistamine that counteracts histamines produced by a cold virus. That might relieve the symptoms of the cold virus, but does nothing to destroy the virus itself. An extra glass of orange juice or two would answer that need.

There is evidence, however, that shows potential harm to your body and the delicate balance of nutrients in the body by taking massive doses of vitamin C. Your body is not equipped to store the water-soluble vitamin. Any amount that you don't use each day should be excreted in the urine. Your kidneys can suffer from processing the unused vitamin. Also, the digestive tract can be thrown out of balance by the massive addition of this ascorbic acid.

You probably are fond of many of the foods that are high in vitamin C. Most fruits and vegetables are good sources of this nutrient. Citrus fruits, such as oranges, grapefruit, and lemons, are outstanding sources. Vegetables that rate high in this nutrient include broccoli, tomatoes, and most greens. All of those foods are delicious when eaten raw. You probably want to eat these foods uncooked whenever possible. Remember, vitamin C is easily destroyed or lost by high temperatures and soaking in liquids. If you do cook these foods, be sure to not overcook them.

What It Does For You

Vitamin C, ascorbic acid, has long been appreciated for its role in forming the "glue" that helps to hold the body cells together. That "glue" is collagen, the connective tissues that bind your body cells together. Obviously, that is a basic need to help wounds and bones to heal. It also aids in helping to maintain the elasticity and strength of your blood vessels. Some dentists and doctors recommend that patients consume vitamin-C-rich foods prior to dental work or surgery. The long-term vitamin C deficiency disease, scurvy, can cause thickened skin and internal bleeding under the skin and between the joints. If unchecked, the disease can kill. A controlled experiment in England with human volunteers showed that the body has a wide tolerance to this disease. It took five months with no vitamin C for any symptoms to appear and a small amount cured the problems.

A short-term deficiency of vitamin C might cause bleeding of the gums as an early symptom, but it is unlikely in the U.S.

Minerals

Minerals are similar to vitamins in that they are substances needed by the body in very small amounts for chemical processes. They, too, do not supply energy. Unlike vitamins, minerals are more than bystanders promoting chemical changes in the body. They become part of the structure of the body in bones, tissues, and fluids.

The two most abundant minerals in the body are calcium and phosphorus. Potassium, magnesium, and sodium are the other minerals used by the body in a significant quantity. The remaining minerals are vitally important, but only required in small amounts, so they are called **trace minerals.** The trace minerals are plentiful in food, so they are rarely needed to be considered separately for a healthy diet. The exceptions are iron and iodine. These nutrients often require special dietary planning, so in this book they are discussed separately from the other trace minerals. The trace minerals are

What star nutrient do these fresh fruits and vegetables have in common? Answer: vitamin C.

listed to help you evaluate the sensational headlines that hit the media stressing the need for some new mineral. If you are eating foods that give you the other minerals and vitamins, you are receiving enough of the trace minerals without any special worry. You can, however, harm yourself by taking excessive amounts of them. You also can create a deficiency of a trace mineral by taking massive amounts of vitamins. Massive amounts of vitamin C may cause a deficiency of copper. That is just one more reason to select a varied diet. If you do, you can read the following list, then relax and forget these minerals. Copper, cobalt, selenium, manganese, zinc, molybdenum, silicon chromium, cadmium.

Calcium and Phosphorus

Although 99 percent of the body's calcium is used in bone and teeth structure, the remaining 1 percent is crucial to the operation of the body. If calcium were not present, the nerves would "short circuit" and send out uncontrollable impulses. Calcium also plays a part in the clotting of blood to stop bleeding. It works in close teamwork with phosphorus in the body. Most of the sources for calcium are also good for phosphorus. The highest amounts of these two minerals are found in milk, cheese, yogurt, and canned fish eaten with the bones. Other excellent sources are leafy green vegetables and some fortified foods. Phosphorus is also found in egg yolks, meats, fish, poultry, and whole-grain products.

The body uses the calcium and phosphorus that it needs. Extra amounts of the minerals are stored in the bones as a reserve supply. If more calcium is needed than has been eaten, certain parts of the bone ends give up the mineral for other uses in the body.

Lack of calcium in the American diet is a primary nutritional concern. Unlike phosphorus which is plentiful in meats and cereals, calcium is often lacking in diets. To compound the problem, certain groups have an increased need for calcium. Pregnant women, growing adolescents, and breast-feeding women are groups who temporarily need extra calcium. Recent research also has uncovered the crucial need for women and elderly people to keep up their calcium intake.

You gain in bone mineralization up to about age 35. At that time of peak bone strength, the mineral content of bones begin to decrease in density. If your bone condition is less than the

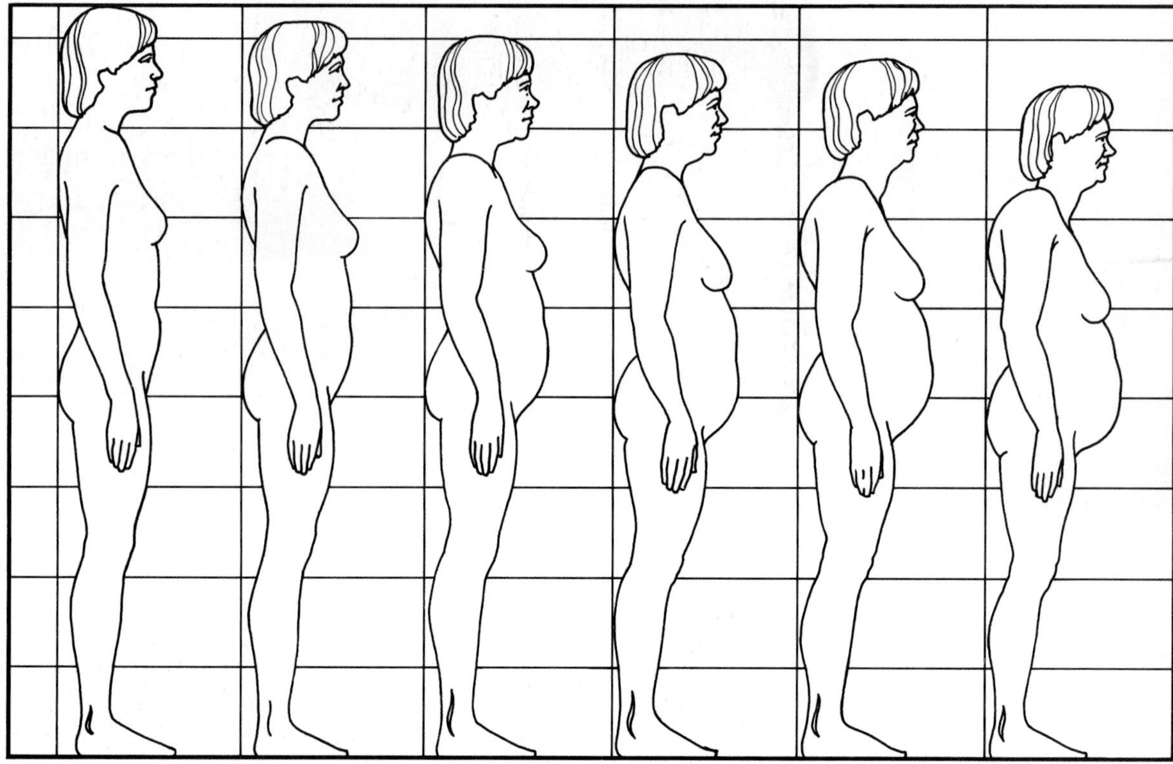

One glance at these silhouettes ought to make a calcium fan out of anyone—especially women!

best when you are 35, you could be headed for trouble in terms of later bone fractures and diseases such as osteoporosis.

Osteoporosis

Calcium deficiency can lead to the development of osteoporosis, a condition in which calcium has been removed from the bones to maintain the mineral's level in the blood. Over time, this results in thin, fragile bones that are dangerously porous. The resulting "settling" of the bones can result in a "dowager's hump" and a loss of height and mobility. Bones can be fractured from even a minor blow.

The disease and complications from the disease are the 12th leading cause of death in this country. There is no cure for this disease, but an adequate calcium intake might help to prevent it. Weight-bearing exercise is also important to maintain the bone's density.

Who Gets It?

People who have eaten less calcium than their bodies need are at high risk for developing osteoporosis. There are also several genetic and environmental factors that contribute to a person's risk level. Women are at a greater risk of getting this disease. Women have less bone density than men and lose it more rapidly after menopause. They usually are less active physically, which contributes to the loss of calcium from bones. Other factors include a family history of the disease, a small-boned frame, an Oriental or European heritage, early menopause, no pregnancies (for women), cigarette smoking, and excessive consumption of alcohol.

Adolescence, a time of rapid bone growth, already calls for an adequate supply of calcium. Not getting enough calcium in the diet at that age doubles the risks of:

1. Not getting full-growth potential.

2. Increasing a person's chances of developing osteoporosis in later years.

The average teen's diet of choosing carbonated beverages over milk drinks also increases the risks. The phosphorus-rich soda might cause another problem. Evidence is being developed that a high phosphorus intake in relation to a low amount of calcium can actually interfere with the absorption of the calcium that is consumed. Further complications develop with the chronic dieting habit of many teenage girls who often omit dairy products in the dangerous search for supposedly low-calorie foods.

Food Facts

Calcium quickies. Yogurt is an ideal calcium loaded snack for mealtime food. It's so portable in its original package that it's great for quick trips. The low-fat content answers the guideline for a low-cholestrol and low-calorie treat. Even the flavor is zesty and will combine well with sweet dessert like combinations or more hearty entrees.

Prevention

You have to start early to prevent osteoporosis. At about age 20, the bones stop developing length and start "filling in." Ages 20 to 35 are the critical years to maintain your calcium intake in order to ensure a large deposit in the bone for withdrawals. Exercise teamed with an adequate calcium intake stimulates healthy bone formation both before and after age 35.

Calcium Thiefs

You actually can eat the right amount of calcium and then defeat your efforts by the effect of other substances in your diet. If eaten out of proportion, the following substances can rob you of your needed calcium.

- **Protein.** Too much protein may encourage the body to excrete more calcium in the urine.
- **Fiber.** A high amount of fiber can decrease the available calcium by holding onto it and preventing absorption. The laxative effect of the fiber also can hurry food through the body giving the calcium less time to be absorbed. This is not a concern for Americans who follow a varied diet.
- **Phosphorus.** Consuming a lot of soft drinks that contain high amounts of phosphorus or any low-calcium high phosphorus diet can contribute to bone deterioration. It is not understood how excessive amounts of phosphorus interfere with the absorption of calcium in people, but current animal studies indicate this is true. Human studies don't support this if the phosphorus comes from meat and milk. No human research using soft drinks as the source of phosphorus has been done. Phosphorus and calcium work together as a team when the proportions of calcium are high enough. Doctors recommend a ratio of equal parts or twice as much calcium as phosphorus.
- **Caffeine.** People who drink four or more cups of coffee a day have lost more calcium than noncoffee drinkers. The same is true of other drinks containing caffeine. Those trips to the bathroom lose more than time for the caffeine consumer.

Exercise

Inactivity for anyone increases the loss of calcium from the bones. Even astronauts in the peak of physical condition suffer from calcium loss to the bones after being weightless and inactive in space. Effective exercise must supply weight-bearing stress for all parts of the body. Walking or jogging does not help the bones in the upper parts of the body. Carrying weights while jogging or walking helps work the upper body. Swimming is excellent for flexibility, but does not produce enough stress on the long bones to develop them. Swimming is, however, good therapy for people with osteoporosis because it does not place stress on their weakened bones.

Veggie Yogurt Dip

Mix plain yogurt with cottage cheese, a squeeze of lemon, fresh herbs, and a touch of seasoned salt. Whirl in the blender or mash with a fork. Serve with the crispest of veggies, such as carrot coins, broccoli trees, whole green beans, and green pepper strips.

For a texture contrast, toast whole-wheat strips in the oven until crisp. Sprinkle with grated Parmesan cheese and herbs. Serve with your yogurt dip. This combination also packs for a lunch treat, or keeps well in the refrigerator for emergency munchies.

Fruit Honey Yogurt Dip

Dips are usually considered a before-meal treat. Why limit this fun way to eat before lunch or dinner? Linger over dessert or satisfy your sweet tooth with this dip!

Combine plain or flavored yogurt with frozen, unsweetened raspberries or strawberries. (You may want to push the raspberries through a sieve first to remove some of the seeds.) If you started with plain yogurt, you may want to add honey until the taste suits you. You can use a blender, food processor, or armpower and a fork.

Place the fruit mixture in a pretty glass container on a larger plate. Surround the mixture with cut slices of bananas, pineapple chunks, and apples. Fill small bowls with granola, chopped nuts, and coconut. Use long wooden skewers or toothpicks to dip the smaller pieces of fruit into the yogurt and then into any of the "crunches" you have provided.

Iron

Iron shortages in the diet are a concern in this country. Diets of toddlers, teenagers, and women up to age 50 have been found to contain much less than the recommended amount of iron. Iron forms the hemoglobin in the blood that carries oxygen to the cells.

Iron is best obtained from meat sources such as beef, poultry, and fish because the body absorbs it well. Iron from plant sources is not as readily used by the body. New evidence shows that eating iron-rich plant foods with food rich in vitamin C increases the amount of iron the body can absorb. Iron also seems to be absorbed better when the foods from plant sources are eaten at a meal with meat or fish.

Infants past six months of age but still relying on milk for most of their calories can hardly meet their iron requirements. This is one of those rare occasions when a person may not be able to obtain enough of a nutrient from food. Doctors usually prescribe an iron-enriched formula, use of an iron-rich infant cereal, or supplements for infants. Doctors also routinely prescribe iron supplements for pregnant and nursing mothers, although they may not always be needed.

People eating less iron than they need usually develop **anemia.** This condition is diagnosed by a blood test and is far too common. Severely anemic people are pale, excessively tired, and extremely weak. The mild anemia that is more typical does not usually produce noticeable symptoms, but can be diagnosed with a blood test.

Too much iron can be toxic. The liver and body tissues are damaged by too much iron. Toddlers eating all of their iron supplements are a common and tragic source of infant poisonings.

This is yet another case where you definitely can get too much of a good thing. Treat all supplements with respect.

Magnesium, Sodium, Chlorine, and Potassium

Magnesium, sodium, chlorine, and potassium are seldom lacking in healthy people. If you are getting other essential nutrients, you also will be getting enough of these minerals that are required in very tiny amounts.

Magnesium is deposited in the body's skeleton. It is involved in basic cell processes for energy use and the handling of other nutrients. Alcoholics and drug addicts who sacrifice food for drugs often exhibit muscle tremor and shaking from magnesium deficiency.

Potassium, sodium, and chlorine work together as salts to maintain the electrolyte balance of fluids in the body. These are the salts you taste in your perspiration. The body protects itself from losing too much salt during times of heavy sweating by decreasing the salt concentration. If a person does lose too many body salts, fainting and vomiting may occur.

One of the latest guidelines for healthful diets recommends limiting your intake of sodium. Some people do not easily eliminate excess sodium well. The amount of fluid that is required and held by the body to dilute the sodium to the right concentration can cause a swelling that increases the blood pressure. High blood pressure is a definite health hazard.

Lean red meats excel as a source of iron.

RDAs: Recommended Dietary Allowances

One of the most reliable sources for the amount of each nutrient healthy people should be eating to meet their body's requirements is the Recommended Dietary Allowances, (RDA). The RDAs are based on reliable scientific information about human nutrient requirements from the Food and Nutrition Board of the National Academy of Sciences-National Research Council. Using the expertise of nutrition specialists and scientists, the National Academy issues what are known as Recommended Dietary Allowances for people from birth through adulthood. Its recommendations are based on an extensive reveiw of current research and knowledge in the nutrition field.

The RDAs are very complicated. The **U.S.RDAs** (United States Recommended Daily Allowances) are a simplified set of the nutrition information to make it easier to use. In addition to providing nutritional guidelines, the U.S.RDAs are used for **nutrition labeling.** Consumers used to have little guidance for the nutritional content of the foods they bought. Labels were only to highlight the brand names and content until a decade ago. Now, the FDA requires food processors that make nutritional claims to include nutritional labeling to help consumers compare nutrient content of different brands and forms of food. For the consumer who is trying to make sensible food choices, these labels are one of the most readily available sources for nutrient content.

Nutritional labeling appears on about half of the packaged food sales in the United States. The labeling is required for companies who make any kind of nutritional or diet claim for their product and on any product that is enriched. Other manufacturers choose to include the information on a voluntary basis.

The label includes two important areas of information for the consumer. The first area shows the number of calories in a specified serving of a food. Also, the amounts of the protein, carbohydrate, and fat are expressed in

Food Facts

The Food and Nutrition Board of the National Academy of Sciences plans on updating the RDAs according to the latest research finding every four to five years. The most recent set of RDAs was scheduled to be released in mid-1985, but was delayed for another five years. The Board disagreed with the research committee's recommendations that would drop RDA levels for some vitamins. The researchers and the Board hit a scientific difference of opinion that could not be resolved. Consequently, the report will not be released. The next recommendation is due in 1990. . . . Stay tuned.

grams. (Remember, there are 28 grams to an ounce.) The other area is headed "Percentage of Recommended Daily Allowances (U.S. RDA)." That section gives the percentage of the U.S. RDA of the essential vitamins and minerals that are contained in a serving.

Digesting Nutrients

You know that when TV and movie critics call a show "absorbing" they are promising you the chance of being completely held and made a part of the action! The exciting prospect of your attention not being lost or distracted leaves little doubt that you will benefit from such entertainment. You also can be certain that you will benefit from nutrients that are not lost but are absorbed by your body. How does your body make use of all of the countless nutrients you get in your food? Obviously something happens to the foods you eat. Has the pizza you ate last night turned into energy to keep you going or build new cells? Or is that orange juice you drank for breakfast already helping your body to fight off an infection?

In order for your body to use nutrients, they must be changed from a solid to a liquid form. That liquid form is then carried by the bloodstream to your cells. This mechanical and chemical transformation is called **digestion.** You could easily take the smooth workings of digestion for granted. In fact, most thoughts turn to digestion only upon the rare occasions when it isn't working smoothly. The efficient process of digestion includes the interaction amongst several organs: the mouth, esophagus, stomach, small intestine, liver, and large intestine.

The Beginnings

Digestion starts in the mouth—almost before the food gets there! The very smell or sight of appealing food starts the "mouth-watering" reaction that means you are actually preparing to digest food with saliva. Chewing your food is a mechanical process that physically breaks down the food into small pieces. This process is aided by the chemical action of saliva. The saliva is produced by three types of salivary glands. Saliva moistens the food and also starts the digestive action on the starches in food.

Automatically, you swallow causing the food to move into the **esophagus.** This is a muscular tube that connects the mouth to the stomach. The food in the esophagus does not drop straight down the tube. It is carried along by muscle contractions called **peristalsis.**

From the esophagus, the food enters the stomach through an opening called a sphincter. The sphincter is a muscular opening that carefully times its actions so that food moves into the stomach but not back out of the stomach into the esophagus. The stomach produces gastric juices that chemically change the food from solid into liquid form. This liquid is called **chyme.** Different foods pass through the stomach in different lengths of time. Water moves through first. Carbohydrates pass through

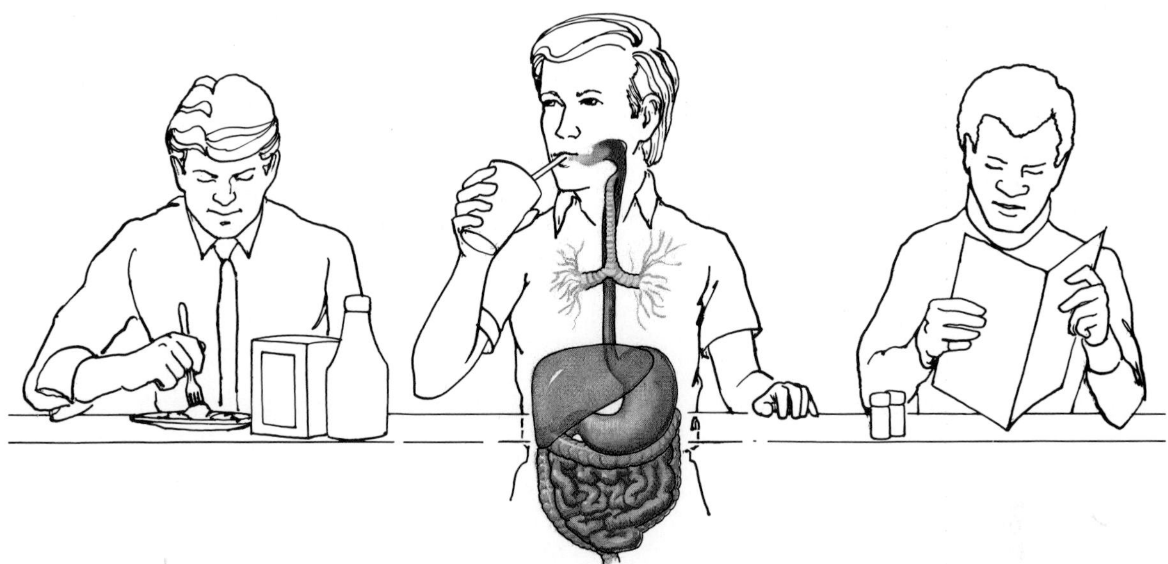

The digestive system breaks food down into the nutrients your body needs.

next, followed by proteins. Fats remain in the stomach the longest. A well-balanced meal will move through the stomach in approximately four hours.

The next digestive organ, into which the chyme passes, is the small intestine. In the small intestine, digestion is completed by enzymes from the intestine, chemicals from the pancreas, and bile from the liver. The nutrients are chemically changed into forms the body can readily use. Proteins are broken down into amino acids. Carbohydrates are turned into simple sugars. Fats become fatty acids and glycerol. All these substances can be absorbed directly into the bloodstream!

After the food is digested (converted into a form that can be absorbed by the blood) it is absorbed into the bloodstream where it can be used by your body's cells. Undigested products, wastes, and bacteria move into the large intestine to be eliminated as feces. Solid wastes are eliminated through the rectum. Water is absorbed from the large intestine and moved to the kidneys to be eliminated as urine.

Absorbing Nutrients

Absorption of food occurs in the small intestine. There is no absorption from the stomach—and only water and some inorganic salts are absorbed from the large intestine.

The inside of the small intestine is covered with tiny, hairlike projections called **villi.** They line the intestine and give it a velvety appearance. As peristaltic waves move the chyme through the small intestine, the villi absorb the nutrients.

Nutrients that are ready to be used by the body are transported by the bloodstream to body cells. The other nutrients that still need processing to be used by your body travel to the liver. In the liver, the final conversion of nutrients takes place. The nutrients are changed into glucose, the body's fuel. When the glucose enters the bloodstream, it is taken to the cells where it is used. Glucose that is not needed immediately is stored as glycogen. Some of that glycogen is stored in muscles. The liver changes glycogen back to glucose when the body needs it for energy. Energy potential is also stored in the body as fat in individual cells and special cells (adipose cells) that can enlarge to hold large amounts of fats. These cells are the ones that form the cushions of fat to protect inner organs and insulate the body.

Keeping the Fires Burning

All of your body processes need a constant supply of oxygen to ignite food into energy. The oxygen may come from the air that you breathe, but the blood has to carry the oxygen from the lungs to the cells.

Blood is pumped by your heart through blood vessels. The bloodstream carries nutrients, water, and oxygen to your body cells. At the cells, the blood picks up waste products for its return trip through your system. It's a continuous process that is fueled by the nutrients in the food you eat.

Vocabulary Review

Scurvy	Complete proteins	Provitamins
Beriberi	Incomplete proteins	Osteoporosis
Nutrients	Starches	Trace minerals
Calorie	Vitamins	Anemia
Protein	Water-soluble vitamins	Nutrition labeling
Enzymes	Fat-soluble vitamins	

Questions for Review

1. Nutrients are divided into several classifications for easy identification. What are they?
2. What are the Basic Four Food Groups?
3. Why are the Basic Four Food Groups organized into those particular groupings? What does each of the groups have in common? What is the fifth group? Why is it not a neccessary part of the daily diet?
4. Which nutrients actually provide energy?
5. Why is water an essential nutrient?
6. What are the building blocks of protein called? Why are they referred to as building blocks?
7. Why is fiber an important part of our diets?
8. Give examples of water-soluble vitamins and explain what happens if the body takes in more than it needs.
9. Give examples of fat-soluble vitamins and explain what happens if the body takes in more than it needs for immediate use.
10. What are two factors that destroy vitamin C?
11. How do minerals assist the body? In what way do minerals work in the body that differs greatly from vitamins?
12. What are the two most abundant minerals in the body?
13. What are trace minerals?
14. What factors contribute to the chances of developing osteoporosis?
15. What are some substances that can affect the amount of calcium absorbed by the body?
16. Why is milk fortified with vitamin D?
17. What are some factors that affect the amount of iron absorbed in the body?
18. Why is nutritional labeling helpful?
19. What two important areas of information are included on a nutritional label?

20. Is there any basic difference between organic and synthetic vitamins? Is one kind better than the other? How do the costs usually compare?

21. Why is digestion important to your getting all the nutrients you need? Give an example.

22. Briefly outline what happens to food when you eat it— in relation to the digestion process.

Things to Do

1. Plan a day's meals without meat that combine incomplete proteins to make complete proteins.

2. Find current articles on the importance of fiber. Do they all agree? Do some of the articles seem to exaggerate the benefits of fiber? What makes you come to your decisions about the articles? Make a poster or give an oral report on your findings.

3. Give examples of foods high in water-soluble fiber. Think of creative ways to incorporate them into your diet. Write a week's plan to incorporate water-soluble-fiber foods into your diet.

4. What is meant by the terms "good carbohydrates" and "bad carbohydrates"? Give specific good examples of each kind. Why are some carbohydrates rated as undesirable or "bad"?

5. Visit a health food store and record the prices of organic vitamins. Compare these prices with synthetic vitamins of the same strength. Note any "special claims" made for the organic vitamins just because they are organic. Evaluate those claims. Are they accurate? Do they seem to exaggerate? What conclusions can you make from your investigation?

6. Read the nutritional labels of food products in your home. Become aware of what the labels are telling you. What did you learn?

7. Using the reference charts in this chapter, look up the following nutrients: vitamin A, vitamin D, vitamin E, vitamin K, thiamin, riboflavin, niacin, vitamin C, calcium, phosphorus, and iron. For each, list good food sources, what it does in the body, and some problems that might develop from too much or too little of this nutrient in the body.

100% PURE
JUICE

4 Food and Fitness

Connecting Fitness and Nutrition

Nothing is more closely interlocked with your well-being and ability to perform physically than good nutrition. Eating the right foods helps you maintain desirable body weight, stay physically fit, and establish optimum nerve-muscle reflexes. You, as a unique individual with special needs and abilities, have to shape your own lifestyle to fit your body type and goals. The delicate balance of energy taken into the body through food and energy spent from the body through exercise and internal body activity determines your weight and well-being. Your daily choices of food and activity will either balance or "tip the scales." Are you prepared to make those lasting decisions?

This chapter discusses the latest research findings for both exercise and the selection of the right food to help you make the fitness and nutrition connection.

Researchers have uncovered much of what works for health, body maintenance, energy, and well-being. By following the seven dietary guidelines for healthy Americans published jointly by the United States Department of Agriculture and the Department of Health and Human Services, you're doing your best toward creating a healthy lifestyle. It is up to you to learn how to stay tuned in to further developments in this new science. Your county extension office is one place to learn the latest information. You are lucky. For now, you can select your own healthy diet simply by following these seven guidelines.

The Seven Dietary Guidelines

- Eat a Variety of Foods
- Maintain Desirable Weight
- Avoid Too Much Fat, Saturated Fat, and Cholesterol
- Eat Foods with Adequate Starch and Fiber
- Avoid Too Much Sugar
- Avoid Too Much Sodium
- If You Drink Alcoholic Beverages, Do So in Moderation

Please Note: The guidelines do not apply to people who need special diets because of diseases or conditions that interfere with normal nutritional requirements. These people may need special instructions from registered dietitians and consultation with their own physicians.

Eat a Variety of Foods

How would you like it if you found out that you had to eat the same four foods over and over all your life in order to stay healthy? Even a favorite treat would seem less tasty after a few days. Luckily you are not limited to a few foods. The number one dietary guideline stresses variety for nutritious eating. That recommended variety assures you of a lifelong opportunity to select from many flavorful and interesting foods.

"Weight" No Longer

If you are overweight, decide to do something about it now! The dietary guidelines spell it out clearly with their directions to "Maintain Desirable Weight."

You will notice that the key word is "maintain." It is not enough to lose weight if you allow it to creep back up on the scales and all over you. The yo-yo effect of continually going up and down in weight can be harmful to your health.

If you have too much fat in relation to the amount of muscle mass, you are increasing the risk of getting high blood pressure, high blood fats (triglycerides) and cholesterol, heart disease, strokes, diabetes, certain cancers, and many other types of ill health.

Things to Avoid in Any Diet

The nutrient fat is the most concentrated source of food energy. A gram of fat supplies about 9 calories compared with about 4 calories per gram of protein or carbohydrate. **Cholesterol** is a fat-like substance found in the body cells of humans and animals. Cholesterol is needed to form hormones, cell membranes, and other vital body substances. The body is able to make all the cholesterol it needs, so cholesterol is not a necessary part of the diet.

Fatty acids are basic chemical units of fat. They are either saturated, unsaturated, or polyunsaturated. All dietary fats are made up of mixtures of the fatty acid types. Some foods are higher in **saturated fats.** Beef, lamb, pork, egg yolks, whole milk, butter, and lard fall into this category. Lean meat, fish, poultry, soft margarines, and vegetable oils are higher in **polyunsaturated fats.**

Avoid too much fat, saturated fat, and foods high in cholesterol. The dietary guidelines are based on the studies that show the increased risk of having a heart attack if you have a high blood cholesterol level. American customs have long featured foods and food-cooking methods that have a high level of fat—especially the undesired saturated fat. Potatoes french fried in animal lard, fried chicken, apple pie with rich flaky crust that is high in saturated fat, gourmet dark chocolate ice cream, and lobster dripping in melted butter are a few of the favorite foods that illustrate this nation's love affair with the rich taste of fatty foods. Some countries, such as Japan, have a noticeably lower rate of heart attacks, which is attributed to their different diets.

Eating extra saturated fat, foods with high levels of cholesterol, and extra calories will increase the blood cholesterol level in many people. Saturated fat seems to raise the cholesterol level the most. There are many factors that influence who gets high blood cholesterol. Heredity, the individual's use of cholesterol in the body, stress, and even exercise are all factors.

The mystery of the blood cholesterol level has been deepened over the years by the way some people can eat foods high in saturated fats and cholesterol and never seem to raise their blood cholesterol level. Some people seem to have high blood cholesterol level regardless of what they do or don't eat. Whatever the controversy, the evidence remains that it makes sense for the U.S. population as a whole to reduce daily consumption of all fats—particularly saturated fats.

The dietary guidelines do not suggest eliminating any one food from the diet. Many foods that contain fat and cholesterol also provide high-quality protein and many essential vitamins and minerals. Eat those foods in moder-

Tuna—a fish rich in Omega-3 fish oil—makes a healthy and tasty meal. Perhaps tuna lunches like this one might help you prevent heart disease someday.

ation. American diets have averaged 40 percent of their total calories as fat. It is suggested that fat be limited to no more than 30 percent of the total diet. Furthermore, limit the saturated fatty acids to about a third of the total fat.

Sweet Tooth

Do you feel a little defensive when you buy a king-size chocolate bar in front of friends? You may find yourself "explaining" why you "deserve" such a treat with statements like, "Hey, I've been studying hard for hours. I deserve this," or "I haven't had any candy for weeks. It's O.K." It seems to be expected that anyone eating a rich candy will be "teased" by others—regardless of how thin the eater might be. The point is that everyone seems to know that high-sugar foods should be avoided, but consider that it is O.K. to "earn" the privilege of splurging calories on this treat. In fact, it is often expected and accepted for people to pamper themselves with a reward of sugar treats. It's almost like the fantasy dream of the Sugarplum fairy soothing all fears with her goodness.

While it is true that high-sugar foods contain large amount of calories, that is not the number one reason for the dietary guidelines to urge Americans to avoid too much sugar. The significant health problem that results from eating too much sugar is tooth decay. The risk of dental decay is exaggerated more by the number of times you eat sugar than by the total amount of sugar eaten. It takes just a trace of sugar sticking to your teeth to ferment and provide the perfect food for the bacteria living in your mouth. These bacteria thrive and multiply forming huge colonies of soft **plaque** on your teeth. The "stuff" you feel on the surface of your teeth is actually a living colony of billions of bacteria. The bacteria give off an acid that

So They Say

Can fish oil help people avoid heart disease? Exciting research that is still in progress is showing a relationship between a certain oil and reduced chances of heart disease. Omega-3 oil, found in some fish and marine animals, may protect against heart disease in three major ways:

1. Omega-3 oil seems to make platelets—important clotting factors in the blood—less sticky. The blood is therefore more fluid, which means it is less likely to clot inside the body.

2. Omega-3 appears to lower blood fat levels thus decreasing the likelihood of atherosclerosis, the build up of fatty deposits in the arteries.

3. Fish or fish oil in the diet may favorably change the balance of fats and cholesterol in the blood.

The evidence of tests on seamen in the Netherlands in a 20-year study indicates that eating fish regularly may be good for the heart. The results conclude that "as little as one or two fish dishes a week may be of preventive value in heart disease." Scientists also have been studying societies of people who include fish as a main part of their diet. This includes Innuits (natives of Alaska and Greenland) and the fishing people of Japan. The studies have found that these people show little evidence of heart disease and have lower levels of blood cholesterol. Perhaps the most dramatic indication is that when patients with high blood cholesterol were given large doses of Omega-3 fish oil, their total cholesterol blood level went down.

Stay tuned for more of the answers that are only beginning to come in.

eats through your tooth enamel causing decay. The stickier the sugar food, the worse it is for your teeth. Both starches and sugar cause problems when eaten between meals, but the simple sugars are the most harmful. Thus, frequent in-between-meal snacks of foods such as candies, cakes, pastries, dried fruits, and soft drinks can cause more decay than eating large amounts less often.

It is almost impossible to avoid all sugar in the diet. Sugar is already in most foods. However, you can avoid eating the sugars and foods high in sugar. Another important defense is brushing your teeth after eating sugar foods. When that is not possible, rinse your mouth out with water.

People on weight-reducing diets and the elderly who have less of a need for energy foods both still have the same need for nutrients. Spending their calories on sugars and high-sugar foods creates the risk of not getting all the nutrients they need without going over their calorie allotment.

Please Don't Pass the Salt

The snack counter has taken on a new look since research has shown that too much sodium is harmful. Bags of chips are often described colorfully as "lite-salt" or "no-salt" for the many who wish to cut down on their intake of sodium chloride (table salt).

Sodium is a major risk for persons who have high blood pressure. Other factors contribute to high blood pressure, but sodium is one of the causes that can be controlled. There is still no way to predict who might develop high blood pressure, but certain groups of the population, such as blacks, seem to be more prone to develop the disease. Avoiding too much sodium can help to prevent high blood pressure from developing.

You can cut down your sodium intake by using less table salt, not adding salt during cooking unless absolutely necessary, reading food labels for "hidden" sodium content, and cutting back on foods high in sodium. Foods that are extremely high in sodium content in-

Adding herbs to a dish is a zestful way to add flavor without adding sodium.

clude soy sauce, steak sauce, catsup, pickles, olives, sauerkraut, canned soups, canned vegetables, and some cheeses like feta (Greek goat's milk cheese used on salads).

It takes time to get used to the flavor of foods without the overall presence of salt. You only realize how much you have begun to depend on the salt flavor after you have cut back and then taste a salty food that didn't used to seem salty. For instance, after going without salt on a special diet, many people report finding fast-food hamburgers too salty for their taste. Prior to their diet change, they used to add "extra" salt to the burgers! You will be amazed how much more of the natural flavor of food like vegetables and meat you can taste after you become accustomed to no added salt.

Have you ever tasted pizza that seemed bland and tasteless until you added the "Italian seasonings"? Those spices and herbs added flavor and zest to a familiar product. You can do the same with tasty vegetables or meat. Try experimenting with the old familiar flavors like parsley, oregano, dill, and mint on new foods. When you discover the subtle flavorings that are available, you can try less familiar flavors like anise, rosemary, thyme, fennel, and bouquet garni (see page 68). Dried herbs are available in the spice section in the supermarket. They represent a whole new world in eating and food preparation. With no added calories, you can completely change an ordinary food into a gourmet production. Fresh herbs are available in the produce department and at farmers' markets during the summer. You can grow your own, too. In the winter, you can grow herbs in pots to add a fresh taste to your meals and a fresh, living color to your home.

Creative Tips

A popular collection of herb flavors favored for steeping in stews and soups is called a bouquet garni. It traditionally combines the flavors of the herbs thyme, parsley, and bay leaves. Some people add a peppercorn or two and rosemary. The idea is to blend an interesting mixture of flavors that enchance the taste of the main dish you are preparing—not to overwhelm it.

To prepare a traditional bouquet garni, use one of the following three methods:

1. Gather a sprig of fresh thyme, parsley, and a bay leaf and tie the stems together with a string. Leave a "long handle" of string to lift the bouquet garni in and out of the food. You can even tie the end to a pot handle to avoid fishing it out.

2. If you use dried herbs, measure about 1/4 teaspoon (1 mL) of each herb onto a square of thin cotton or cheesecloth. A piece about 3 inches (7.5 cm) square will work fine.

3. Cut a 3-inch (7.5 cm) section off a leek (a long, straight green onion that easily peels off in layers. See Chapter 11). Peel off the largest two or three sections. Measure the dried or chopped fresh herbs onto one of the sections. Cover with the second section and reinforce with the third section of the leek. Tie tightly with a string, leaving a long end for handling. The wonderful mellow flavor of the leek combines with the herbs for a refreshing, natural bouquet garni.

Any handmade bouquet garni makes an appreciated gift for someone you know who appreciates fine foods and flavors.

Avoiding Alcoholic Beverages

The dietary guidelines advise that if an adult drinks alcoholic beverages, he or she do so in moderation. Alcoholic beverages are amazingly high in calories and have almost no nutrients. They are second only to fats in calorie count. Anyone who needs to cut back on their calories can hardly afford to spend them on alcoholic beverages. The elderly would have great difficulty consuming alcohol and still be able to get their vital nutrients without going over their calorie limits.

Heavy drinkers frequently develop nutritional deficiencies from the effects of the alcohol on the body's absorption processes and from the danger of neglecting to eat. Alcohol irritates the lining of the stomach and small intestine. The irritation impairs the absorption of nutrients, particulary thiamin. A deficiency of vitamin B can cause such symptoms as weakness, numbness, partial paralysis of fingers and toes, and even slow motor reflexes. If the person stops drinking, these are usually reversible with a balanced diet and possibly a doctor's prescription for vitamin B supplements.

Pregnant women should refrain from the use of alcohol. Alcohol is known to cause birth defects, but to what degree is unknown. Low birth rate, reduced growth rate, birth defects, and mental retardation may result from a pregnant woman drinking alcohol.

How Fit Are You?

Jump into the food and fitness partnership with your eyes open. You are fortunate to be living in an exciting age of breakthroughs in the nutrition and exercise "connection." Fitness calls for physical activity powered by appropriate nutrition for everyone. No longer can people hide behind their thinness as an excuse for not needing exercise. Those who feel they are too fat can "go public" with lots of company as Americans hit the exercise trail. The aerobics break has begun to replace the coffee break with combined exercise-social sessions for many busy students, workers, and homemakers. Exercise is no longer optional for anyone who cares about his or her health. Now it is a must!

Wherever you measure up on the fitness ruler, you will benefit from establishing lifelong patterns that repeat wise choices of nutritious foods and adequate exercise.

Value Your Energy!

Have you ever completely relaxed in bed without moving for a period of time? Did you feel like your body was resting and not using any energy? You may have stopped conscious physical activity, but your heart kept on beating and your lungs continued to take in air. Those internal functions require a constant supply of energy. Your body needs energy to keep you alive as much as you need energy to dance the night away. You can't live without eating to supply your body with energy. That energy is measured in calories. A **calorie** is the amount of heat energy needed to raise the temperature of 1 kilogram (about 4 cups) of water 1°C (1.8°F). Fats, carbohydrates, and proteins all contain calories your body can use for energy. If your body's stores of fat are low (a condition near starvation), it gets energy by breaking down muscle tissue. That is a hazardous situation for the body. Value and respect the need for calories (energy), but also "count" their value in terms of how many calories are present in relation to the nutritive value of the foods you choose.

How Much Is Enough?

The number of calories you need depends on your age, weight, sex, health, and physical activities. The rate at which you personally burn up calories while your body is at rest for basic body processes (breathing, pumping of your heart, etc.) is called your **basal metabolism.** The basal metabolism is measured by the energy your body burns while it is resting. That rate is higher in people with more muscle mass. The rate goes down when the muscle is lost from inactivity. The muscle mass also decreases naturally as you age if you do not compensate by increasing your activity and decreasing the number of calories you eat.

The link between your fitness, food, and health chain is exercise. Find "your way" and make it a habit.

Persons who are taller need more energy to move their bigger bodies than shorter, smaller framed people do. With all factors such as age, health, and size being equal, you can consume more calories without gaining weight if you are in good physical condition than if you are in poor physical condition. Exercise helps you control calories by burning calories during the activity and also by increasing your muscle mass. Muscle tissue burns an increased number of calories. The result of increasing your muscle tissue is that you can actually eat slightly more calories without gaining weight. Regular exercise also helps to control your appetite. Contrary to the myth that exercise will make you feel hungrier, exercise develops your appetite thermostat. When you are inactive, that "appetite thermostat" seems to turn off. You feel hungry without reason and there is no healthy limit to how much you feel like eating. With a regular exercise program, you tend to eat just

Food Facts

Starting in mid-1986, the FDA required that nutritional labeling list the sodium amount of the food. Also, the following terms for sodium content were standardized:

- Sodium-free. Less than 5 milligrams per serving
- Very low sodium. 35 milligrams per serving
- Low sodium. 140 milligrams or less per serving
- Reduced sodium. Sodium content has been reduced by 75 percent compared to the product it is replacing.
- Unsalted, no salt added, without added salt. Salt has not been added as it usually would be during processing.

enough to supply your needs for energy. Physical fitness helps keep you healthy and also helps you lose or control your weight.

Constantly losing and gaining weight through fasting or feasting also can defeat your attempts to lose weight by confusing your basal metabolism rate (BMR). Your BMR trys to adjust the rate your body burns energy. Have you ever wondered why some people can survive for weeks without food when you feel faint and headachy after just a few extra hours with no nourishment? The reason people can survive long fasts without dying from starvation is that the body slows down the BMR and other processes. That means the body needs less food to function. You can defeat your efforts to lose weight by constantly dieting over a period of time because that registers with your body as a signal to lower the amount of food you need. Exercise is a way to counteract that effect.

Variety—The Key To Exercise and Nutrition

You have seen how important a variety of foods is to balancing your food intake. Your body also needs a variety of types of exercises for personal fitness. There are three types of exercise to condition your body. All workout sessions should include gentle stretches as part of the warm-up and a slow-down, cool-down activity at the end.

Flexibility exercises relieve tension and stretch muscles and connective ligaments. Hold a stretch for a short time—do not bounce. Bouncing to stretch a muscle farther can result in an injury.

Strength exercises develop stronger muscles. You have several options for strengthening exercises. Calisthenics and various weight training methods develop strength in muscles. You will want to seek skilled coaching before starting weight training. Breathing is particularly important. Breathing out whenever you lift or push is vitally important to prevent straining your heart with increased blood pressure.

Aerobic exercise elevates the heart rate through sustained, vigorous activity that elevates the heart rate to a target heart rate. This is combined with proper breathing for maximum oxygen. Activities such as brisk walking, dancing, running, and swimming can be aerobic exercise.

You also can attend an organized aerobics class through places such as school, the YMCA or YWCA, a community center or a health club. Evaluate your instructor carefully. Current studies show that "easier is better." When the exercise trend started, classes pushed that you had to "hurt" to progress. That theory has changed. To help prevent injuries from aerobic dancing, work out only on floors that have a "giving" surface. Many injuries can result from repeated exercising on concrete or tile floors.

Calories Used During Physical Activities		
Activity	*Calories Used per Hour*	
	Male	*Female*
Resting in bed	70	58
Sitting at a desk	90	74
Standing quietly	113	94
Dressing	118	97
Walking	120	99
Walking fast (4 miles an hour [mph])	360	298
Doing calisthenics	300	248
Cycling	360	298
Tennis	420	348
Jogging (5 mph)	480	398
Aerobic dancing	480	398
Basketball	540	447
Running (7 mph)	720	596
Handball	720	596
Swimming (2 mph)	720	596
Cross-country skiing (fast pace)	720	596

Weigh Your Best Weight

Have you "weighed" your feelings about your own weight? Are your emotional responses to the figure in the mirror balanced by the facts about your body type? Are you one of those people who say automatically, "I wish I could lose 10 pounds" without any thought about what your body needs to weigh. Body weight is the measure by which most people evaluate their eating. Check the table on page 72 for the appropriate weight for your height, age, body type, and sex. Use the figure that matches your type of body frame. The lower figure in each range applies to a person with a small frame, and the higher figure applies to a person with a large frame.

Weight alone, however, is not an adequate measurement of your body. Some people in good physical condition weigh more than the average figures in the chart because of muscle tissue weight. The real danger to your health is when you are lugging around extra weight in fat. You can help figure out how fat you are by pinching a fold of skin from the back of your upper arm. If the loose part is more than 1 inch thick (2.5 cm), you have too much fat in proportion to the amount of muscle tissue.

Realize, though, it is normal and healthful to have some body fat. It is also normal for women to have more body fat than men. Unfortunately, some teens, especially girls, go to extremes to try to reduce body weight or body fat. The result can be loss of menustruation and

Height and Weight

MEN					WOMEN				
Height Feet	Height Inches	Small Frame	Medium Frame	Large Frame	Height Feet	Height Inches	Small Frame	Medium Frame	Large Frame
5	2	128-134	131-141	138-150	4	10	102-111	109-121	118-131
5	3	130-136	133-143	140-153	4	11	103-113	111-123	120-134
5	4	132-138	135-145	142-156	5	0	104-115	113-126	123-137
5	5	134-140	137-148	144-160	5	1	106-118	115-129	125-140
5	6	136-142	139-151	146-164	5	2	108-121	118-132	128-143
5	7	138-145	142-154	149-168	5	3	111-124	121-135	131-147
5	8	140-148	145-157	152-172	5	4	114-127	124-138	134-151
5	9	142-151	148-160	155-176	5	5	117-130	127-141	137-155
5	10	144-154	151-163	158-180	5	6	120-133	130-144	140-159
5	11	146-157	154-166	161-184	5	7	123-136	133-147	143-163
6	0	149-160	157-170	164-188	5	8	126-139	136-150	146-167
6	1	152-164	160-174	168-192	5	9	129-142	139-153	149-170
6	2	155-168	164-178	172-197	5	10	132-145	142-156	152-173
6	3	158-172	167-182	176-202	5	11	135-148	145-159	155-176
6	4	162-176	171-187	181-207	6	0	138-151	148-162	158-179

harmful changes in hormone levels. Moderation is important! If your weight checks out O.K., but you still don't think you look or feel your best, it might be time to make the fitness connection.

The fit of last year's favorite jeans also influences your opinion of your body. Your weight might be the same, but maybe now the fit looks more like a sausage than a lean green bean. More important than weight to your health and appearance is the amount of lean body mass relative to the fat. Even when your weight remains the same, your body composition can change progressively throughout your life. Controlling your body composition, not just reducing weight, should be the goal of any diet or weight control program.

Controlling Body Fat

Do you remember hearing someone take a passing bag of potato chips or candy and grab a handful saying, "I really shouldn't, but thanks!" Perhaps you've ordered at your favorite fast foods restaurant and had the person taking your order ask, "Do you want fries with your order?" Many people shrug and say something like, "Sure, why not." That is why restaurant workers are trained to suggest tempting foods. Indeed there probably is no reason "why not" if you have not developed an eating strategy that includes planning ahead. You can strengthen your willpower by deciding ahead of the tempting moment what you are going to do.

Controlling your body fat and staying fit takes a lifestyle plan. The food diet part of that plan calls for thinking ahead about what you can eat each day so you don't gain weight but still get the nutrients you need. Not many people have the time or willpower to figure out on the spot each "yes" or "no" decision about food they are offered. To do so, you would have to calculate the calories and other nutrients in what you had already eaten that day and what you were likely to eat later. Then you could decide about the present choice. Rather than that, consider your lifestyle and plan for those possibilities ahead of the time. You also can balance your diet by the week. If one day is likely to mean a high expenditure of calories, plan for it by eating less calories the day before or after. Remember, however, the other nutrient needs remain the same.

Losing Fat

The only way to lose weight is to take in fewer calories than you burn. The two ways to do that are to eat fewer calories or to burn off more calories through physical activity. If you just eat fewer calories, you could be thin but not fit. Just trying to exercise enough to burn up excess fat is extremely time consuming and hard work. Most people give up. Combining the two methods works the best and is the best for you.

A good weight loss plan offers you appealing food choices that fit your lifestyle and contain all the vitamins, minerals, protein, fat, carbohydrates and water you need, but fewer calories than you have been eating. A steady loss of 1 to 2 pounds (0.5 to 1 kg) a week toward your goal is generally safe. The first weight loss includes a loss of water, so it takes a long-term reduction and consistent nutritious eating and exercise for true fat loss. To lose that weight, you need to cut about 500 calories a day.

Safe Loss

You simply cannot expect to lose in a few weeks what it has taken you months or even years to accumulate. Crash diets that starve you, but seem to help you lose lots of weight quickly will not work out in the long run. On severe or fad diets you are destined to "crash" and fail. The records show that most people who lose a large amount of weight quickly just gain it back when they stop the diet and resume their lifestyle. There also are some harmful side effects of starvation diets that injure your

You'll want to reach for these attractive snacks—and you can! The low-calorie and high-nutrient content will reward you with guiltless snacking.

health. There have even been reported cases of sudden deaths from such inadequate diets. Diets containing fewer than 800 calories may be hazardous and should be followed only under medical supervision. Some dieters have developed kidney stones, disturbing psychological changes, and other complications while on such diets.

Deadly Thinness

Just as dangerous as being overweight is **anorexia nervosa.** Anorexia nervosa is an eating disorder that causes people to continue dieting to a point of not eating at all. They starve themselves. Anorexics fear being fat and see themselves as being obese no matter how thin they actually are. If they are not treated, anorexics become seriously ill and can die. Anorexia nervosa usually affects young women.

Other dangerous practices to lose weight are forcing vomiting and using laxatives. This type of eating disorder is known as **bulimia.** Frequent vomiting and purging can cause chemical imbalances which cause the heart to beat irregularly or even stop completely! The extreme acidity of vomit also erodes the tooth enamel at an alarming rate.

Both types of eating illnesses require medical treatment. The patients need help with emotional problems to help them overcome these illnesses. If left untreated, these people can starve themselves to death.

The Painless Way to Diet

To lose weight safely, use the following guidelines.

• Make a diet diary. Keep a record for two weekdays and one weekend day. Record what,

Chocolate-Almond Fluff

Yield: 6 servings

Traditional	Ingredients	Metric
1 envelope	Unflavored gelatin	1 envelope
2 cups	Skim milk	500 mL
¼ cup plus 2 Tbsp.	Sugar	80 mL
¼ cup	Dutch process or unsweetened cocoa	50 mL
½ tsp.	Almond extract	3 mL
1 Tbsp.	Sliced almonds, toasted	15 mL

Directions

1. Soften gelatin in milk in a small saucepan; let stand 1 minute.
2. Add sugar and cocoa; cook over low heat, stirring constantly, 5 minutes or until gelatin dissolves.
3. Transfer to a large bowl; stir in almond flavoring.
4. Cover and chill until consistency of unbeaten egg white.
5. Place bowl in a larger bowl of ice water; beat at high speed of an electric mixer until chocolate mixture is light and fluffy (about 5 minutes).
6. Spoon evenly into dessert dishes; chill thoroughly. Garnish with almonds.

Microwave Directions

1. In a glass bowl, soften gelatin in milk, let stand 1 minute.
2. Stir in sugar and cocoa. Microwave, uncovered, on High for 3 minutes, or until gelatin dissolves, stirring constantly.
3. Proceed as directed in steps 3 - 6.

To toast almonds: Place almonds on a paper towel. Microwave on High for 30 seconds, or until toasted.

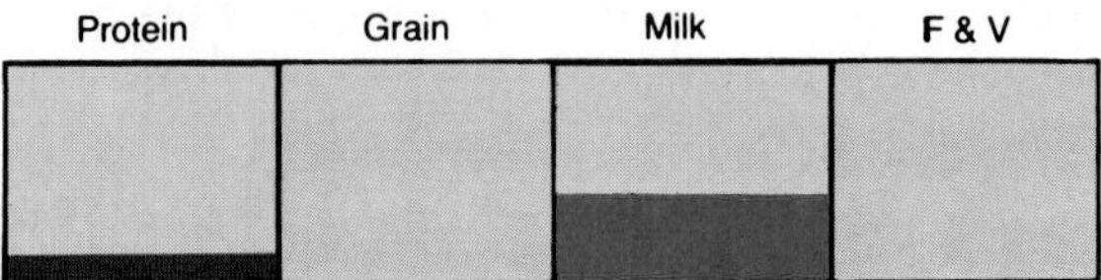

Dieting does not have to mean depriving yourself of desserts. This chocolate almond fluff recipe is tasty and low in calories.

how much, where, and when you eat. These are important clues as to why you are eating. Do you see any pattern? When you come home from school do you immediately have several cookies? When you are unhappy, do you reach for the bag of potato chips? Use your "research" to see when you are eating.

• Instead of trying to eliminate all those extra snacks right away, help yourself ease into new patterns by planning low-calorie snacks ahead of time. There's no need to memorize a calorie chart to select snacks. Select from juicy fruits and crisp, raw vegetables. Puffed or airy grain products such as unbuttered popcorn are low in calories, too.

• Count your calories twice. Count on your calories to give you needed energy. Then recount them in terms of the nutrient value.

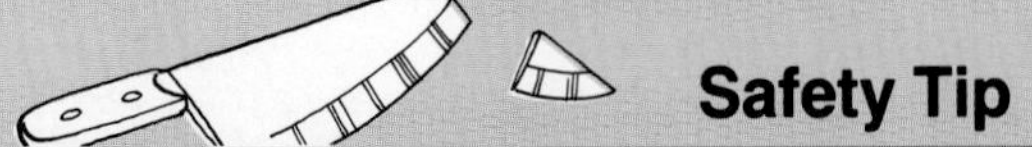

Safety Tip

If you try to meet your nutrient needs through supplements or pills, you would be missing the unknown substances that are in food. Scientists are also just beginning to find out about the interactions of nutrients. Some of the latest research shows that you can actually create an imbalance of one nutrient by taking too much of another one. Even with all the research that has been done in nutrition, it still is dangerous to play around with "mother nature"!

Make your calories count by balancing them with a healthy vitamin, mineral, carbohydrate, protein, and fat content. The interaction between nutrients means you cannot leave any of them out of your diet. The "unknown" nutrients in food make it necessary for you to obtain the known nutrients from a variety of foods. Remember, scientists only know what combinations of food will maintain your health. They do not know everything that is in that food.

• Eat regular meals. Skipping a meal is not a healthy or effective way to cut down on calories. It is likely to lead to unplanned snacking on calorie-expensive foods.

• Each of your three meals should include a part of the day's servings from the high protein group because the slower digesting proteins help hold off hunger pangs. Invest your calories in the Basic Four Groups and make certain that investment is protected by also having the recommended number of servings from each group. Remember to choose a variety of foods

Making New Lifestyles Stick

You already have taken the most important step toward sticking to your diet lifestyle. Planning meals and snacks that are practical for your schedule and habits gives the plan a push toward success. Studies have shown that it takes about three weeks to establish new behavior patterns, so stick with your plan for that time. It will become more natural for you. Watch for pitfalls at parties and restaurants, too. Chapter 20 has do's and don'ts to help you sail through the temptations when eating out.

Your attitude toward your lifestyle of health, food, exercise, and daily activities can make the difference between success and failure. Once you really decide that you want to be fit and are sold on the benefits of feeling and looking good, you can do it.

Adding Weight

You can watch most any ad on TV and notice that our society tends to idealize the long, lean look in men and women. Society has improved its standards some. Just a few years ago, the look was even more exaggerated—the emaciated look was "in." You actually had to be half-starved and somewhat unhealthy to be in style. Luckily, people came to their senses and realized that young people were harming themselves rather than staying healthy and fit. Today the lean look in ads is not the starved look, but the fit look. Still, anyone who is extra thin tends to be admired and envied by others. Thinness below the recommended weight on the charts is O.K. if that person is also healthy. Signs of underweight include poorly developed muscles and sagging posture. The lack of fat layers means no reserve supply of energy and insulation. Consequently, if you are underweight, you will notice that you tire more easily than friends and probably are more susceptible to feeling chilled. Feeling cross and nervous are other signs of nonfit underweight.

To gain weight, you can follow the opposite guidelines of the overweight person's diet. That is, choose the higher calorie foods from the Four Basic Food Groups. For instance, have a milkshake with your dinner rather than a glass of low-fat milk. You'll still be getting a needed serving from the milk group, plus those extra calories you need. Because many of the foods in the Fats-Sweets group contain not only a lot of calories but undesirables such as sodium and sugar, avoid those foods. Stick with the Basic Four.

You will need to remember three meals a day, but you might want to add a few heartier snacks to spread your calories and eating over the day.

Athletics and Nutrition

Bang! The starting gun goes off. The race begins. . . . Have you ever run in a competitive race or played ball on a team? Tingling excitement and the pounding of your heart tell you it is time to rely on your training and "give it your best." However, you can't give it your best performance unless proper nutrition was a part of your training program. Without proper nourishment, accomplishments achieved by physical conditioning and expert coaching can be limited.

The nutrients you've learned about in Chapter 3 are teammates that work together to provide good nutrition. Just as each team member carries out different tasks during a game, each nutrient performs specific functions in your body. A lack of just one nutrient is a disadvantage to your body, just as losing a player to the penalty box is to a hockey team. Studies suggest that these nutrients should be supplied by each meal in correct amounts and proportions for peak body condition.

Special Nutrient Needs

The increased physical activity of athletes increases some food needs. If you participate in athletics, you will require more energy, water, and possibly salt (sodium chloride). An athletic teenage boy may need 5000 calories a day compared with the 3000 calories required daily by his nonathletic friends. A teenage girl athlete may need 3000 calories a day compared with the 2000 calories required daily by her nonathletic friends. You can fill this increased energy need by taking extra servings of food from all Four Basic Food Groups (particularly starchy foods).

Athletes need to take care to obtain the energy and nutrients needed for training and competition.

Salt and water lost through sweating are not as easily replaced, especially if water intake is restricted during meets and practice sessions. Low water intake during strenuous exercise leads to dehydration. This causes fatigue and heat stroke. Water should never be restricted during training sessions. However, if you drink too much water too quickly during strenuous activity, you might bring on the unpleasant "waterlogged" condition. Take smaller amounts of water frequently before, during, and after the activity to prevent becoming waterlogged.

Commercial sports drinks may contain too much sugar and salt. These drinks should be diluted by one-half with pure water before use. A diluted mixture is a good way to supply water as well as salt to an athlete who has been sweating heavily.

Salt needs also can be met by increased use of seasonings on foods. The use of salt tablets is not recommended.

Iron deficiency can be a problem with some teenage women athletes, particularly during menstruation, and for athletes on diets. Studies show that some highly trained athletes are likely to have lower levels of iron in their blood than sedentary individuals. It might be wise for all athletes to have a doctor check the level of iron in their blood. Only a doctor should prescribe an iron supplement and only then after a clinical examination.

Diet Hints For Athletes

At one time it was believed that muscle-building exercise greatly increased the need for extra protein in the diet. This idea led to the development of special high-protein meals and drinks for athletes. Nutritionists now agree, however, that your protein needs for muscle development as an athlete are not significantly greater than the needs of your nonathletic friends. These slightly increased protein needs can be met quite easily without using protein supplements or consuming high-protein diets. Increasing basic foods to meet your increased energy needs will supply more than enough protein. Eating high-protein diets may prove harmful. It may lead to loss of appetite, diarrhea, dehydration, and undue stress on the kidneys. Extra protein is also expensive.

Opinions vary about whether athletes need vitamin or mineral supplements. While the athlete needs more vitamins to utilize the extra calories needed for increased physical activity, if he or she gets the extra calories from nutritious foods, the extra vitamins will be supplied also. Most nutritionists think that increased physical activity does not increase the body's need for vitamins. Excessive amounts of some vitamins (especially vitamins A and D) taken as supplements over a period of time have proved harmful. Depend upon a well-balanced diet to safely supply all your vitamin needs.

Some think that the mineral potassium should be added to the athlete's diet. Potassium-rich foods such as oranges, bananas, and baked potatoes will supply adequate potassium. Supplements are not necessary.

A practice called **carbohydrate loading** is practiced by mature athletes who participate in endurance events such as long-distance running and swimming. A high-protein, high-fat, low-carbohydrate diet is eaten for a few days while the athlete exercises strenuously. This depletes glycogen, a carbohydate, stored in the body. After the depletion phase and just a few days before the event, a very high carbohydrate diet is followed and the athlete exercises very little. This eating routine increases the body's stores of glycogen in liver and muscle tissue. That makes more carbohydrates available for muscle energy during endurance events. But this practice is not considered safe or effective for young athletes.

Carbohydrate loading should not be confused with a diet high in carbohydrates which is recommended for all athletes, including the teenager. Carbohydrate loading has not been thoroughly tested for the rapidly growing high school athlete. The disadvantages may outweigh the advantages. The effects on immature muscles are unknown. The practice may not increase endurance as it does with adult athletes. Most high school events are not of sufficient duration to exhaust the athlete's normal levels of muscle glycogen. Furthermore, during the high-protein, high-fat phase of carbohydrate loading, performance is decreased and the athlete may feel exhausted. During the final phase, water is retained and weight is increased. Young athletes can safely ensure themselves of adequate glycogen stores by eating more starchy foods (pancakes, rice, and noodles, for example) and reducing exercise the last 24 to 48 hours before the event.

Some athletes may need to lose excess fat to make a special weight category. This practice, though, has been shown to limit performance. Moderate weight reduction with an adequate supply of vitamins, protein, and minerals over an extended period of time may be acceptable. Severe weight reduction or restriction of normal weight is not recommended. Starvation and dehydration during growth retards muscle development. Scientific studies show that per-

A carbohydrate-rich meal eaten three hours before the game digests well yet provides energy for competition.

formance is reduced when athletes who are in shape lose more than three percent of their body weight within a short period of time. Muscle is lost and strength is reduced.

Even more important, weight reduction may permanently stunt growth and muscle development. Lost muscle growth will not be restored later.

To Eat or Not to Eat. . . Before the Game!

You can eat before the game, but generally not later than three hours before the contest. Your digestive processes may be slowed down by your keyed-up emotional state. To combat this condition, eat an easily digestible meal. This means a meal high in carbohydrates. Avoid foods that contain substantial amounts of fats or oils. Fats are more slowly digested than other nutrients.

Some athletes like poached eggs, toast, and juice as a light pregame meal. Others drink liquid meals before games. These meals are convenient, particularly if you have to travel to a meet. Also the nutrients in these meals pass through the stomach rapidly and are quickly digested. However, liquid meals should be limited to pregame use. When used regularly, they are not a good substitute for solid foods.

Food Facts

Liquid pregame meals eaten at least three hours prior to competition can be an acceptable alternative to solid food before a competitive event. Liquid meals need to be part of a varied, balanced diet. They will not replace the needed nutrition of following the recommended Basic Four Food Group servings day in and day out.

Daily Fare for the Athlete

Breakfast is especially important because you need food to start the day. Your body begins the day in a low-energy, fasted condition. Teens who eat breakfast score higher on physical-fitness tests. Breakfast can be made up of any combination of foods from the Basic Four Food Groups. Spaghetti and meatballs, together with an orange and a glass of milk, is a nutritionally adequate meal for any time of the day—even breakfast.

To meet increased energy needs, most teen athletes require more than the minimum number of servings listed in the Daily Food Guide. For example, an athletic teenage girl may consume five servings of milk, three servings of meat, five servings of fruits and vegetables, and six servings of breads and cereals daily. Commonly eaten foods that are in the fifth or other food group such as butter, margarine, sugar, fats, jellies, and unenriched cereal products provide energy and some nutrients, but should be used with discretion. Get your energy from foods that supply needed nutrients. Make the Basic Four Food Groups the basis of your training table.

Special Needs for Special Times—Pregnancy

You don't have to be a woman to share in the special time when a baby is expected. Family and friends can help a mother-to-be ensure the baby's healthy development and arrival. The special needs for that time center around helping the mother get rest, exercise, and the nutrients the baby needs.

What's Right When?

The importance of diet for the development of a healthy baby cannot be overemphasized. Even what an expectant mother eats from the very first day of pregnancy can make a difference in the baby's development. Just days after conception, blood vessels and blood pools form in the unborn baby. Adequate protein, iron, and vitamin C are essential nutrients at this time—even before the woman is likely to know that she is pregnant.

Twenty-one days old and the baby's heart and brain begin to develop. Protein has to be there to build the new tissue. At the same time, the eyes begin forming. Vitamin A is necessary for healthy eyes.

At four weeks, the ears and nose form. Protein, riboflavin, and niacin are crucial for those formations. At eight weeks, the skeleton begins to form. Calcium, protein, vitamin D, and phosphorus must be available or the growth cannot take place.

What many people do not realize is that the baby's growth cannot delay until the nutrients are available. If the mother's blood does not transport the nutrients at the proper time and in the correct amounts, the **fetus** (unborn baby) will never reach full growth in height, weight, and body development. Brain cells, for example, develop the most rapidly in the last two months of pregnancy. If the fetus doesn't receive the right nutrients during that time, the brain may never develop to its full size and maturity.

"Balance" is the key to athletic success in selecting winning, healthful meals as well as performing a sport. High-carbohydrate dishes not too heavy on protein have been found to help performance.

Liquid Pregame Meal

Traditional	Ingredients	Metric
½ cup	Water	125 mL
½ cup	Nonfat dry milk	125 mL
¼ cup	Sugar	50 mL
3 cups	Skim milk	750 mL
1 tsp.	Cherry or vanilla flavoring	5 mL

Directions

1. Mix all ingredients together with a whisk or blender. Chill.

2. Transfer the mixture to a vacuum bottle for a portable pregame meal to be eaten on the road.

3. Eat at least three hours before competition.

Protein	Grain	Milk	F & V
		3½x	

Daily Nutrition Guide

Food Group	*Servings Needed Per Day*
Milk	
1st trimester (adult)	3 or more
1st trimester (teenager)	4 or more
2nd and 3rd trimester (adult)	4 or more
2nd and 3rd trimester (teenager)	5 or more
Meat or Meat Equivalent	3 or more
Breads and Cereals	4 or more
Fruits and Vegetables	4 or more total
Rich in vitamin C	1 to 2
Rich in folic acid	1 to 2
General	1 to 2
Fats and Oils	1 to 2 tablespoons as needed for calories
Sugars and Sweets	As needed for calories

A poorly nourished mother is more apt to have a premature baby. Her body is not strong enough to take the full stress of pregnancy. A premature baby has less chance of surviving and developing.

Studies have shown that weight gain is important to the baby's development. Pregnant women need to gain 24 pounds. If the mother was underweight when she got pregnant, she will need to gain more than 24 pounds. On the other hand, if she was overweight she still needs to gain the full 24 pounds. Dieting must wait until after the baby is born. Gaining 24 pounds is not enough alone, it must be 24 pounds from nutritious foods.

Weight gain should be steady throughout pregnancy. A sudden weight jump needs to be reported to the doctor immediately. After the delivery, the mother can safely return to her prepregnancy weight within 3 to 6 months.

Nutrient Needs

You will notice that selecting a healthy diet for pregnancy sounds very familiar. The basic guidelines are the same as for anyone. Selecting a wide range of foods from the Basic Four Food Group guidelines is the answer. The servings of some of the groups, however, are increased for pregnancy. The nutrient needs almost double when eating for two, but the calories increase relatively little. You can see that every morsel of food must count for nutrients. Refer to the Daily Nutrition Guide on this page for specific guidelines.

By following the guidelines, nutrient needs could all be satisfied except for iron. It is impossible to get the amount of iron needed during pregnancy from food alone. Sometimes calcium and folacin supplements are also prescribed by the doctor for the mother-to-be. A pregnant woman should never take any nutritional supplement unless it is prescribed by a doctor. Too much vitamin A and vitamin D in particular can be dangerous.

Substances to Avoid

Tobacco is harmful to the unborn child. Tar, nicotine, and carbon monoxide affect fetal development in several ways. Their use can result in depriving the fetus of adequate nutrients and oxygen. The effect of smoking on the baby is immediate. For example, the fetus practices some breathing motions while in the womb. If the mother smokes just two cigarettes a day, the baby slows down those movements immediately.

Alcohol is another substance to avoid. It goes right through the placenta to the unborn baby. No amount is actually proven safe.

Drugs can go right through the placenta to the unborn baby. Most birth defects are caused during the first 12 weeks of pregnancy when the arms, legs, and internal organs are forming. Even harmless nonprescription drugs taken by the mother could interfere with the baby's development. Drugs can harm the baby later on in pregnancy, too. For instance, aspirin can disrupt the fetus's blood-clotting mechanisms. Some drugs cross the placenta to the baby while others don't. Let the doctor make the decision about what is safe.

Caffeine has long been considered a harmless stimulant. Only recently has it been rightfully identified as a drug that could be risky to the baby. Studies have shown that consuming large amounts increase the risk of birth defects. The effects of a small amount is unknown, but would you want to take a chance?

Feeding the Baby

If you have ever been around babies during the first year of their life, you probably noticed that they grow and develop incredibly fast. The first year is the fastest growth time in a human's life. Good nutrition during that time forms the cornerstone for the potential brain growth and health for the coming lifetime.

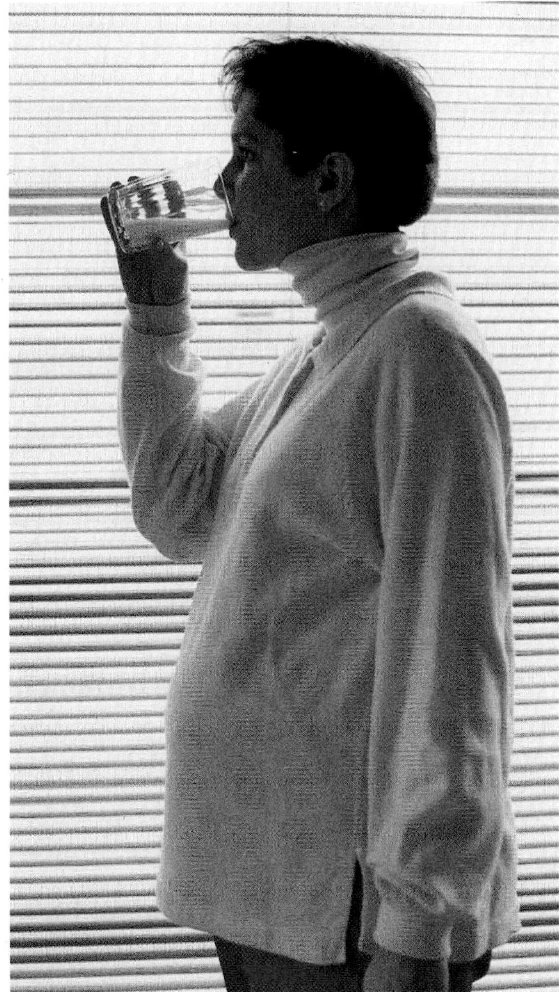

Pregnancy is a time for special reflections about the future event and present preparations. What are some special needs for this time?

Good nutrition is more than just providing the baby with the proper nutrients. The feeding patterns during the first year of life will influence children's eating habits for the rest of their lives.

Breastmilk or infant formula (not cow's milk) is the only food a baby needs or can tolerate for the first few months. Breastmilk is considered the best food for a baby, but infant formulas are made to resemble breastmilk as closely as possible.

Food Facts

The urge to eat inedible things like clay, dirt, laundry starch, or paper is a condition that some pregnant women develop. This is called *pica*. A doctor can help with treating this condition. Besides making the mother feel silly, the pica substitutes worthless stuff for other food that she should be eating. Sound nutrition will help to make a healthy baby and a special time for the mother more enjoyable.

Advantages of Breast-Feeding

There is a special "bonding" between mother and child during breast-feeding that promotes a tender mother-to-infant interaction and affection. Feeding time also can be a special time for mothers who bottle-feed their baby, but special cuddling and care must be taken to do so.

No one can argue with the advantage of having an instant supply of the perfect nutritional milk that is just the right temperature, sterile, and leaves no bottles to wash! Breastmilk has everything a baby needs to grow and develop in just the right amounts, except possibly for vitamin D. (The evidence is still inconclusive on vitamin D.) Breastmilk is also easier for a baby to digest than infant formula. Breast-fed babies are less likely to have food allergies or respiratory and intestinal infections. Breastmilk contains antibodies and other substances that help the baby's immunity. Breast-fed babies also may have fewer skin problems such as diaper rash and eczema. The sucking exercise from breast-feeding puts the infant's mouth in the right position to promote good dental arches, palates, and other later facial features. A bottle does not have the same advantage.

Nutritional Needs

Even after the baby is born, a breast-feeding mother is still eating for two. She also needs extra energy as well as a double share of nutrients. A nutritious diet is essential for the health of both the nursing mother and the baby. Remember, vitamin and mineral supplements need to be treated like prescription drugs. A woman should use them only if the doctor prescribes them. Too many can be harmful or even lethal.

Lots of fluids, at least eight to ten cups per day, are needed for the production of breastmilk. Milk, water, juice, soups, and decaffeinated coffee and tea are beneficial fluids. Caffeine drinks actually decrease fluids from the body due to its diuretic action.

When the new mother is nursing, her food needs increase in some groups and decrease in others. Follow the chart for a Daily Food Guide to a healthy mother and baby.

Bottle Feeding

Do you think you could feed a baby a bottle? It may look simple, but good information for bottle feeding is just as important as accurate facts for breast-feeding. Once you are aware of a few simple facts, bottle feeding is not difficult.

Sterilizing

You may have noticed the elaborate-looking utensils and appliances in the baby departments that are used for sterilizing bottles and formula. This process of sterilizing used to be an absolute must for all baby feedings before premixed formula and sources of safe drinking water were available. That daily drudgery can be eliminated from most new mothers' routines if they can meet the following conditions:

- Clean surroundings are available in which to prepare the bottles.
- An approved water source is available. (Local and state authorities will test well water that is not covered by a city water source.)
- The prepared formula is used immediately after opening.

Daily Food Guide

Food Group	*Number of servings per day*	*Equivalents of one serving*
Milk	4 to 5	1 cup (8 oz.) milk (whole, 2%, skim, and nonfat dry); 2 ounces of cheese (could count as a "meat" instead); 1½ cups cottage cheese; 1 cup yogurt, pudding, or custard
Meat	3	2 to 3 ounces cooked lean meat; 2 eggs; ¼ cup or 4 tablespoons peanut butter; 1 cup dried beans, peas, or lentils
Fruits and Vegetables Vitamin C	1	1 citrus fruit or ½ cup citrus fruit juice; ¾ cup strawberries; ½ cup broccoli, cabbage, green peppers, or tomatoes
Fruits and Vegetables Vitamin A	several times every week	½ cup carrots, broccoli, Brussel sprouts, cabbage, greens, spinach, green peppers, sweet potatoes, or asparagus; 2 halves dried apricots; ½ cup cantaloupe
Other Fruits and Vegetables	2	1 medium size pear; ½ cup vegetables
Breads and Cereals	4 to 6	1 slice bread or dinner roll; ¾ cup dry cereal or ½ cup cooked cereal; ½ cup cooked rice, spaghetti, noodles, or other pasta

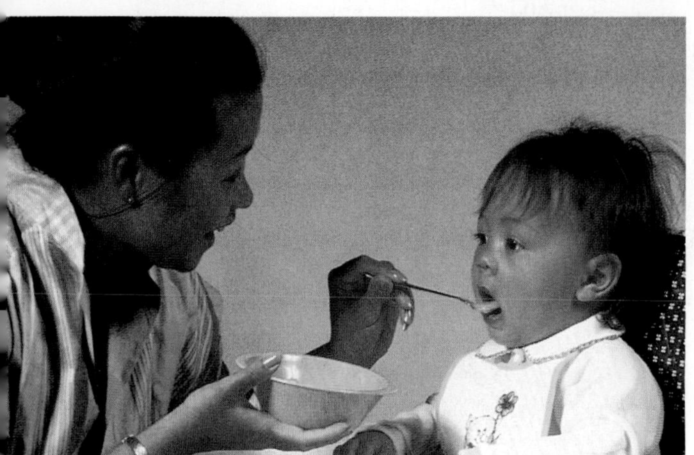

Mealtime can be a special time if it is not rushed.

Food Facts

Any medication the mother takes should be discussed with the doctor. There are some medications that should not be taken while breast-feeding. Medications known to be harmful to the baby are oral contraceptives, anticancer drugs, and radioactive compounds in therapeutic doses. Mothers need to avoid taking any over-the-counter medication, and that includes aspirin, without checking with their doctor.

Alcohol and other mood-modifying drugs are undoubtedly harmful for the baby in any amount. It has been shown that the active compound of marijuana (THC) transfers to the mother's milk. Alcohol, too, will get into the mother's milk. No amount of alcohol has been determined a "safe" amount. You can see that if a new mother is not willing to go without alcohol or other drugs, she should not nurse her baby.

The burden of sterilizing may be removed, but sanitation is still very important in preparing baby's food. Wash all equipment and utensils in hot, soapy water. Rinse in hot, running water and let the utensils dry in the air. Your kitchen counter and sink need cleaning also. Wash your hands both before and after handling foods. Clean your fingernails. If you have an infected finger or hangnail, wear a bandage over it when preparing the baby's (and family's) meal.

When to Feed the Baby

You might agree that these are luckier times to be a baby than a couple of decades ago when it was considered harmful to feed a baby more often than every three or four hours. One of the most pleasant changes for the baby is the agreement that it is best to feed an infant when he or she gets hungry. That sounds so logical and simple to us, but mothers and families used to have to suffer through long hours of crying hungry babies if it was not the correct time for a feeding!

"On demand" feeding is now considered better for a growing infant than strictly scheduled feedings. Just as you differ from those around you in when you get hungry, babies also differ in their food needs. Some infants will wait hours before signaling their hunger. Others need to eat smaller and more frequent amounts to feel satisfied. The result has been a more peaceful household and happier babies and mothers.

How to Feed the Baby

Most formula can be fed cold right from the refrigerator or at room temperature from a newly opened can of formula. But many infants do seem to prefer it warmed. Warm the bottle of formula in a pan of warm water or on low in the microwave. (Remember, don't put metal cans in a microwave.) Shake the formula slightly to distribute the warm formula. Shake a small amount on the inside of your wrist to test the temperature. The temperature should feel slightly warm to the skin. Testing is vital. Too high a temperature can burn the baby's mouth and throat. Be especially careful when heating the formula in the microwave. It can get very hot.

Any baby needs to feel the warmth and security of another body while feeding. Soft talking and cooing will cement the bond of affection and communication.

The baby knows when he or she has had enough. Turning the head away and general restlessness tell you when it is time to stop feeding. Do not leave the leftover formula in the bottle. Bacteria grow quickly in the warm milk. Rinse the nipple and bottle immediately in cool water.

Feeding a baby can be anyone's pleasure when the bottle is prepared safely, held correctly, and given with gentle talk and cuddling.

Problems to Avoid

Those pretty bottles of sweetened gelatin water for infants can create ugly dental decay in a short time. Never use any liquid in a bottle other than milk, formula, or unsweetened water.

Have you noticed cute little animal toys that have a holder on them to prop a bottle for a baby too young to hold its own bottle. Cute, maybe, but propping a bottle in a baby's mouth at any age causes serious problems. Bottle mouth syndrome is a disease that develops in babies who have had their bottle propped. A bedtime bottle that is propped leaves milk in the baby's mouth all night. The milk coats the teeth night after night forming the perfect environment for thriving colonies of bacteria. A typical result from night propping could be all the upper teeth rotted out to the gumline. Painful and expensive fillings have to be inserted into the gums. Even then the jaw might develop deformed and the later teeth come in crooked. Proof of what the long contact with milk does to the teeth is shown by the lower teeth that remain healthy. The lower teeth are covered by the tongue and rinsed by the saliva.

To safely feed a baby before bed, give the baby unsweetened water to drink. A pacifier also helps to quiet a restless baby trying to fall asleep.

Food Facts

Commercial infant formulas are made as much like breastmilk as possible. Formulas supply the same quality and quantity of proteins, carbohydrates, vitamins, and minerals as breastmilk.

A trip down the aisle of the baby food section at the supermarket can be most confusing. The choices for formulas range from powdered to liquid forms with different variations of enrichment and packaging. Formulas can be purchased at most any food store, corner convenience store, and drug store. Generally formula is less expensive at discount stores and large supermarkets.

Commercial formulas are dated to show how long the formula can be stored. Once a can is opened, the remaining contents should be covered, and put into the refrigerator immediately. If it is not used by the next day, it should be thrown away.

You can make baby food at the table from the family's meal if you avoid salt, heavy spices, and sugar.

Starting Solids

Fun pictures of messy babies smearing food all over themselves create the expectation for the days of spooning gooey applesauce into the baby. Studies have shown, however, that solid foods have been started too soon in the past and some problems may result. The American Academy of Pediatrics recommends that it is best to wait at least three months before introducing solids and even better to wait four to six months. This differs from the accepted "picture" of parenting, but is the recommended way.

Feeding Successfully

It might be tempting to try a whole supermarket of food choices for babies when they start on solids. However, to watch for allergy reactions, only one new food should be introduced at a time. Limit your testing to two to three new foods a week. Any rash, fussiness, diarrhea, or other symptoms may indicate an allergy. Stop using the food. If you try the food again and the same condition comes back, discontinue that food for several months. Babies often have temporary allergies that they "grow out of." Remember to tell your baby's doctor.

Never feed directly from the jar. Place a small amount of food on a plate or bowl and feed from there. This keeps the baby's saliva out of the food supply where it will spoil quickly. If there is any food left in the jar, it can be saved one day. After that, discard it. Placing food on a plate also lets you inspect for any foreign material that might have gotten in the jar or can, such as broken glass, screws, or insects. Rare as those occurrences are, it is a wise precaution to be safe rather than sorry.

Overfeeding

Smiles from the roly-poly baby in many ads and movies keep alive the myth that a fat baby is a healthy baby. Fat babies have several strikes against them for childhood and adulthood health. A fat baby is more likely to become a fat adult. The answer is simple. Don't stuff the baby. Let babies indicate when they are full.

Be certain tears are from hunger before you feed a crying toddler. Check the diaper, any "would-be" injuries, and review when and what the child ate last before rushing to stuff in food. That way you can help the child develop a healthy and realistic appetite.

Baby-Made Chaos

What fun is ahead for everyone when the baby starts shoving the food back. The rest of the great texture experience follows as food is rubbed in the hair, ears, and dropped carefully over the side of the high chair. Relax and enjoy the process. It is truly a once in a lifetime experience.

Plan ahead for chaos. Spread out newspapers or spread a piece of plastic on the floor. Strip the baby down to the diaper (in warm weather) for easy cleanups. Just remember to clean the tray everytime and the chair often.

Mealtime should be a series of wonderful sharing times all through life. Enjoy the baby and that special mealtime with calmness and enthusiasm. It's catching!

Patience, a sense of humor, and gentle guidance can be your most successful clues to feeding a baby.

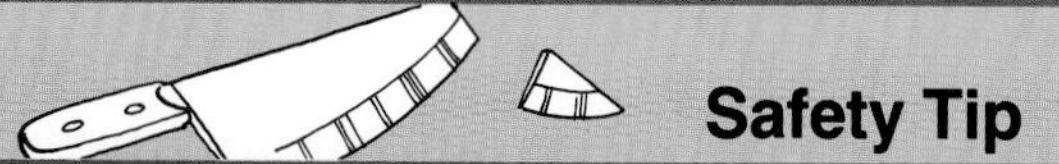

Safety Tip

You are feeding a child, and you suddenly notice tiny pieces of glass in the food. What do you do?

First, stop feeding the child. Do not panic. The mucous present in a child's throat coats sharp edges making internal damage less likely. If there are no cuts in or near the child's mouth, chances are there's no problem. But don't take the chance. Call a doctor right away. Follow his or her directions.

Spoon the food back into the jar and call the manager of the grocery store where you purchased the item. You probably will need to tell the manager your name, address, telephone number, and the approximate date you purchased the food. The manager will know who to contact from there.

When you are shopping for baby food, take extra care to inspect the jars carefully. Do not buy any baby food item with a broken seal. Do not buy any baby food item even if there is only a slight chip on the rim of the jar. If you notice any signs of tampering, talk with the store manager.

Whole-Wheat Pasta

Traditional	Ingredients	Metric
1 Tbsp.	Olive oil	15 mL
4 oz.	Whole-wheat spaghetti	125 g
1 Tbsp.	Margarine or butter	15 mL
	Grated cheese*	
	Fresh basil, chopped, when available	
	Tomatoes, chopped	

Directions

1. Add olive oil to water for cooking spaghetti and bring to a boil. Follow package directions for cooking the whole-wheat spaghetti. Note: Whole-wheat pasta cooks faster than regular pasta and falls apart if overcooked.
2. When the pasta is cooked, drain but do not rinse.
3. Put pasta on a heated plate and toss with the margarine or butter. Sprinkle with grated cheese of your choice. Add chopped basil and tomatoes for a colorful and nutritious garnish.

* Parmesan, romano, or mozarella cheese are good choices.

Protein	Grain	Milk	F & V

Vocabulary Review

Cholesterol
Saturated fats
Polyunsaturated fats
Plaque
Calorie
Basal metabolism
Aerobic exercise
Anorexia nervosa
Bulimia
Carbohydrate loading
Fetus

Questions for Review

1. What are some of the health risks associated with obesity?
2. Rate fat, carbohydrates and proteins in order of the highest number of calories per gram to the lowest number.
3. What factors influence the blood cholesterol level?
4. Would it seem wise to limit the use of saturated fat? Why?
5. What significant health problem can result from eating too much sugar?
6. What do the following standardized terms mean in relation to sodium content: sodium-free, very low sodium, low sodium, and reduced sodium?
7. Why do heavy drinkers of alcoholic beverages frequently develop nutritional deficiencies?
8. Why is controlling your body composition just as important as reducing your weight?
9. What determines the number of calories you need per day?
10. Constantly losing and gaining weight can hurt your attempts to lose weight. Why?
11. What is the difference between anorexia nervosa and bulemia?
12. What is a reliable and healthful guide to follow for planning calorie-controlled meals.
13. What are some special eating needs of someone in an athletic training program?
14. Why is it so important for a pregnant woman to eat a balanced, nutrient-rich diet?
15. What are some advantages and disadvantages of breast-feeding?
16. How do infant formulas compare nutritionally with breastmilk?
17. What determines when solids are introduced into a baby's diet? Why should only one new food be introduced at a time?
18. Is it possible to overfeed a baby? Why could that be unhealthy for the baby?
19. What foods from the family's meals might be considered O.K. for a baby or young child?

Things to Do

1. Interview your school coach about what foods to eat before an athletic event. Plan a complex carbohydrate pregame meal that someone could eat on the way to a competitive event.

2. Divide into groups. Discuss ways sugar can prevent you from getting the nutrition you need. Make a bulletin board demonstrating "sweet goodies" vs. "good eats" that are healthful.

3. Visit a supermarket dairy case. Hunt for products that have packages making claims for unsaturated fats. Read the nutrition label (when available) for the type of fats or oils in the product.

4. Explain why sugar can cause tooth decay.

5. Prepare a hot vegetable such as green beans or a baked potato using no salt. Divide the vegetable into four dishes and season one each way: a salt substitute (such as potassium chloride), lemon juice, an herb mixture, and nothing. Have a taste test.

6. Describe the three types of exercise needed to condition your body.

7. Keep a 24-hour food diary for two weekdays and one weekend day to become aware of what you are eating.

Section 3

The Foods Dictionary

EKCO
1/4 TEASPOON

The Right Tool for the Job

Have you ever started a project, maybe baking a spice cake, only to discover you didn't have a needed utensil, such as the right size baking pan? The resulting product was a miserable failure. It looked more like a pancake when baked in the too large pan.

Having the right tools is as important to product quality and working efficiency in food preparation as it is in building a house. In both instances, it is possible to throw something together quickly with the wrong tools, but it requires more time and effort and the end result can be miserable. Sometimes using the wrong tools even results in accidents. Have you ever tried to peel a potato with a large butcher knife? The chances of cutting yourself in the process were great, and the peeled vegetable looked more like an angular hexagon than an oval potato. You also probably wasted quite a bit of the vegetable and nutrients with the peeling. A small paring knife, however, would have been safer, quicker, and allowed you to cut closer to the contours of the potato.

Using the appropriate tools, called **utensils,** for kitchen tasks can sometimes be just as crucial to food preparation as having the right ingredients. The right utensils for the job can affect your safety and the quality of the food product, as well as your convenience by making a task easier. This does not mean you need fancy expensive utensils for successful food preparation. Contrary to many colorful advertising claims, it is not necessary to have all the latest utensils and appliances to prepare delicious and attractive food.

Modern small electric appliances have revolutionized food preparation, but often you can eliminate them and still prepare wonderful meals and refreshments. Not many electric mixers are taken camping, yet you might remember meals or snacks from such occasions as very special treats. On the other hand, you could not accomplish much in the kitchen without reliable knives, containers for consistent measuring of food, cookware, and some kind of protection to remove hot pans from the oven and stove.

Currently in this country there is a kitchen "craze" for expensive, specialized tools for every conceivable food preparation. It is fun to read the colorful gourmet catalogs or to browse the stylish kitchenware departments and shops, but not everyone has to have special tongs for escargot (edible French snails considered by some to be a gourmet delicacy) or the latest electric pasta maker. The extreme of

Consumer Guide

Factors to consider in evaluating kitchen tools and appliances:

- **Does it work well?**
- **Does it perform more than one task?**
- **Does it duplicate the tasks of another utensil you already have?**
- **Is it appropriate for the quantity of food you usually prepare?**
- **Is it for a good preparation method that you use?**
- **Is there storage space for it?**
- **Is it too costly considering how seldom you'll use it?**
- **If it is electric, does it really need to be electric? Does it have the Underwriters' Laboratories Seal of Approval? This seal means the appliance has been tested and is safe to use.**

buying the newest tool for seldom-performed tasks is a fad that is more of a hobby than a true need for furnishing the kitchen with basic tools.

Beginning cooks can start with a few basic pieces of equipment and then add others as their needs change and grow. Sources for those beginning utensils could include garage sales, extras from relatives and friends, discount stores, and secondhand or resale shops as well as regular retail stores. You also can improvise measurers from containers or equipment that you already have. For example, it is possible to use a glass peanut butter jar for a measuring cup. (See Chapter 6.)

In this chapter, you will be able to familiarize yourself with the basic types of utensils and how to use them. It is up to you to choose the ones for your own kitchen that fit your lifestyle, food preparation preferences, and pocketbook.

A Word about "The Word"

Exactly what *word* you choose to call a utensil can be important. Names assigned to utensils vary in different families, localities, and businesses, but there is a general **nomenclature** (name or designation) that is recognized throughout the food professions. In order to work in a group situation such as a fast-foods kitchen, a group cookout, or in a home economics lab, it is helpful for everyone to use the same words to identify tools. Imagine the potential for confusion when the cook at the skillet hurriedly calls for a spatula because the pancakes are about to burn and the helper gets a plastic scraper. What the cook wanted was the metal turner. A rubber scraper, turner, and spatula are often referred to as a spatula. None of the names is basically wrong, but a variety of terms for the same tool simply does not communicate to a group of people. You will find the names listed in this chapter used consistently throughout the recipes and instructions in this book. This will help you in food preparation and communicating with others.

Measuring Equipment

Recipes are reproduced successfully only if the same amount of each ingredient is used every time. You will learn more about why the right proportions are so important in the following chapters on individual food preparation. To accurately measure any ingredient, you will need the proper utensil and the proper technique. Being consistent with your proportions is what repeats a successful product.

Measuring Spoons

Small amounts of dry, solid, and liquid ingredients are measured in standardized sets of spoons. A basic set usually includes four spoons: ¼ teaspoon, ½ teaspoon, 1 teaspoon, and 1 tablespoon. The metric measures include 1 mL, 2 mL, 5 mL, 15 mL, and 25 mL sizes.

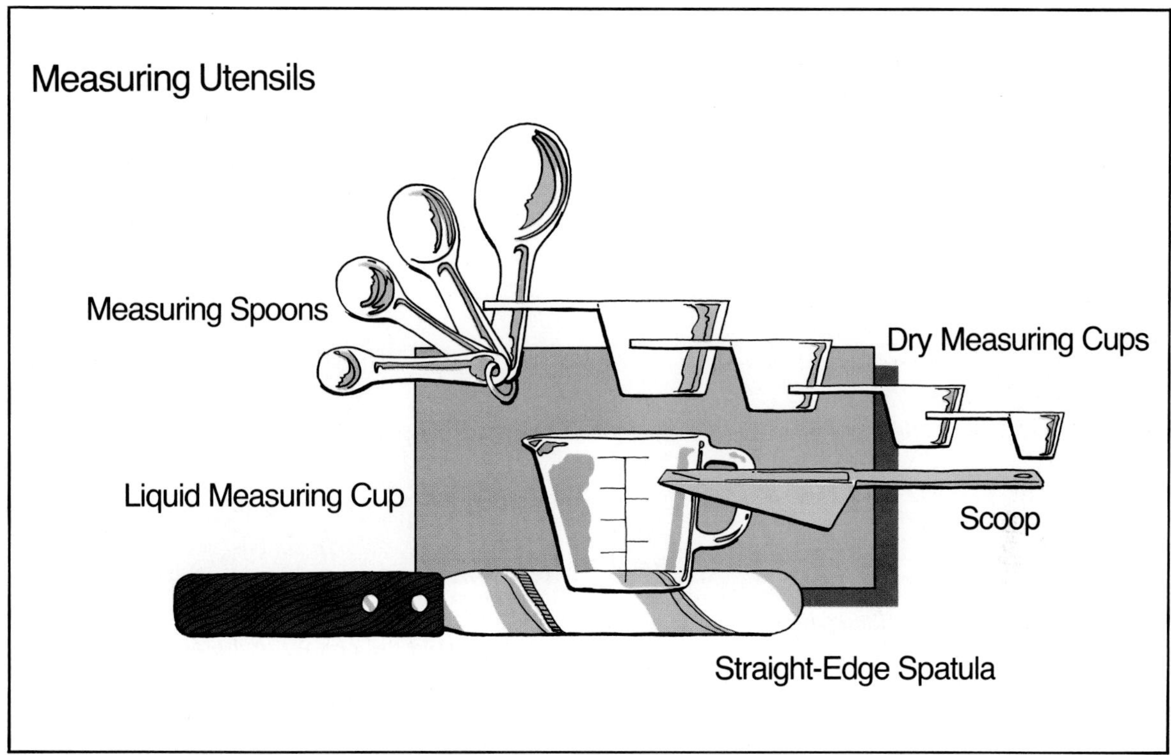

Measuring accurately requires dry and liquid types of utensils.

Dry Measuring Cups

Larger amounts of solid ingredients, such as flour, sugar, salt, butter, margarine, or shortening, are measured in a set of dry measuring cups. Dry measuring cups are used to measure nonliquid ingredients. The set includes ¼ cup, ⅓ cup, ½ cup, and 1 cup. The metric measures are 50 mL, 125 mL, and 250 mL. If you designate another container for a measuring cup in your kitchen, remember to use the same one each time for consistency.

Liquid Measuring Cup

A liquid measuring cup has a pouring spout and extra space above the last marked measure. The volume measurements are marked on the side of the cup and may be in customary, metric, or both measurements. A liquid measuring cup is easier to use if it has a handle. It also needs to be clear so you can read the volume measurements through the side at eye level. In addition to liquid ingredients, you can measure fats and oils with a liquid measuring cup.

Measuring Partners

Scoop

This small container with a handle and flat sides dips dry ingredients from storage to the measuring cup or mixing bowl.

Straight-Edge Spatula

This is a straight-edge spatula that looks similar to a wide-blade knife. This type of metal spatula has a dull, straight-edge flexible blade and is used to level ingredients in measuring. It is also the best tool for spreading soft fillings or icing cakes.

A straight-edge spatula levels dry ingredients accurately. Be careful when handling the cup so the ingredients do not pack down.

Read the markings for liquid measuring so that your eye is on the same level as the surface of the liquid. Do not try to hold the cup up to the eye—you can't tell when it is level. Notice how looking down at the cup gives an inaccurate reading of the measurement.

Another handy use for this utensil is to lift off rolls or cookies from baking sheets or to loosen baked products from the edge of the pan.

Measuring Techniques

Dry Ingredients

To measure dry ingredients:

1. Scoop or spoon the ingredient lightly into a measuring cup of the correct size until it is slightly mounded on top.
2. Be careful not to shake the cup because you don't want to pack down the ingredients. Tap once lightly on top of the cup with a knife to settle any airholes.
3. Level off the top of the measuring cup with the straight-edge spatula or knife. Scrape the extra ingredients onto wax paper or an extra bowl, not into the mixing bowl you are using for the recipe. The extra amount might change the proportion of the ingredient and ruin your finished product.

Flour is usually sifted before measuring for an accurate measurement. The exception would be the treated flours that do not require sifting. They will be labeled "no sift flour" on the package. These flours require special recipes.

If no sifter is available, a strainer and wooden spoon can substitute. Working over a bowl, clean paper, or a dry towel, scoop the flour into the strainer and scrape or shake through the flour.

Whole-grain flours are often too coarse to go through the sifter, but should be fluffed by scooping up several cupfuls and letting the flour fall back into the container. This helps counteract the settling that takes place when any flour stands in the container for a period of time. Packed flour does not measure accurately.

To evenly mix dry ingredients such as flour, salt, spices, and baking powder after they are accurately measured, scoop them into the sifter or strainer and shake directly into a bowl or onto clean paper. Save the combination until the recipe calls for the "dry ingredients."

You can measure solids by the water displacement method. Fill the cup with water and then pour off the amount that you want to measure (left). Add the solid ingredient until the water returns to the top measure.

Special Measuring Techniques

Brown sugar requires special packing into the measuring cup. Pack it solidly with a spoon, then invert the cup. The sugar will fall out and hold the shape of the cup. It's much like making sand castles!

Powdered sugar (also called confectioner's sugar) requires fluffing or "unpacking" for an accurate measurement. Powdered sugar also tends to form lumps. For both reasons, it is wise to shake or scrape powdered sugar through a strainer or sieve before using. Do not use a flour sifter for powdered sugar. The sugar sticks to the screen and interferes with sifting action.

Liquid Ingredients

To measure liquid ingredients:

1. Place the clear measuring cup on a level surface.
2. Pour in the liquid ingredient to the mark for the measurement needed.
3. Look at the liquid at eye level. Usually this means leaning over to counter height to check the mark and liquid level. Looking down from above gives an inaccurate reading. It is also inaccurate to try to hold the cup up to eye level for a reading. Remember, being even the tiniest amount "off" the required measurement can often ruin your finished product!

Fats and Oils

Measure oils the same way you measure liquid ingredients. Measure solid fats by the **water displacement method** or with a measuring cup. To use the water-displacement method:

1. Using a liquid measuring cup, fill it with cool water.
2. Pour off the exact amount that you want to measure of solid fat. For instance, if you want ⅓ cup (75 mL) fat, pour off ⅓ cup (75 mL) of water.
3. Spoon the shortening or solid fat into the measured water until it raises the water level to

the full 1 cup mark. You have displaced the exact amount that you wanted to measure, so the solid fat is the right measurement.

4. Remove the fat and use in recipe.

To use a dry measuring cup:

1. Spoon the solid fat or shortening into a dry measuring cup.

2. Use a wooden spoon or broad mixing spoon to pack the shortening down into the cup removing any air spaces.

3. Heap extra shortening on the top, much like packing an ice cream cone.

4. Level the top with a straight spatula or knife. (Hint: Turn the cup upside down and hold it under hot running water for a few seconds and the shortening will slip out cleanly and in one piece. Keep one hand under the cup to catch the shortening in case it starts to slip out. You wouldn't want your work to go down the drain!)

Measure stick butter and margarine by cutting through the markings on the outside wrapping for the amount that you need.

Cutting and Shaping Tools

The clues to successful and safe cutting of foods are using a sharp knife and selecting the appropriate type and size of knife for the job. Strange as it may seem, dull knives cause more accidents. This is because sharp tools cut easily and dull knives sometimes need to be forced through the food giving the user less control and sometimes a painful surprise. Knives perform many different tasks in food preparation, so selecting a variety of knives can be quite helpful. Just a few basic choices, however, make a good beginning to build upon as you become more experienced in the kitchen. Through experience you can determine which cutting tools are right for your needs.

Paring Knife

The smallest of the knife family is used for scraping, paring, and cutting most small foods.

Utility Knife

Named for the general usefulness or "utility" of this narrow blade, a utility knife can be used for cutting, slicing and small boning tasks.

French Knife or Chef's Knife

This is one of the most useful knives in food preparation once you develop the very special skill of using its triangular blade for slicing, chopping, and dicing. Properly used, its speed can match electrical chopping appliances and result in more attractive and uniform pieces.

Butcher Knife

The wider blade near the point dates back to an era when a strong blade was needed for "butchering" the livestock on farms. Now the butcher knife is used for dividing large cuts of meat, melons, or vegetables.

Bread Knife

This long, thin blade is usually serrated to saw through a crust, bread, or cake without mashing the soft inside dough.

Boning Knife

Sharply pointed to slip in close to the bone, this knife eases the job of boning and cutting up meat and poultry.

Slicing Knife

Larger than the utility knife, this long, narrow blade slices meats, poultry, fruits, and vegetables.

Carving Knife

A large knife to accommodate roasts, this slicer often comes in a set with a matching fork to hold a large piece of meat. Sometimes the set is attractively designed for carving meat at the dinner table.

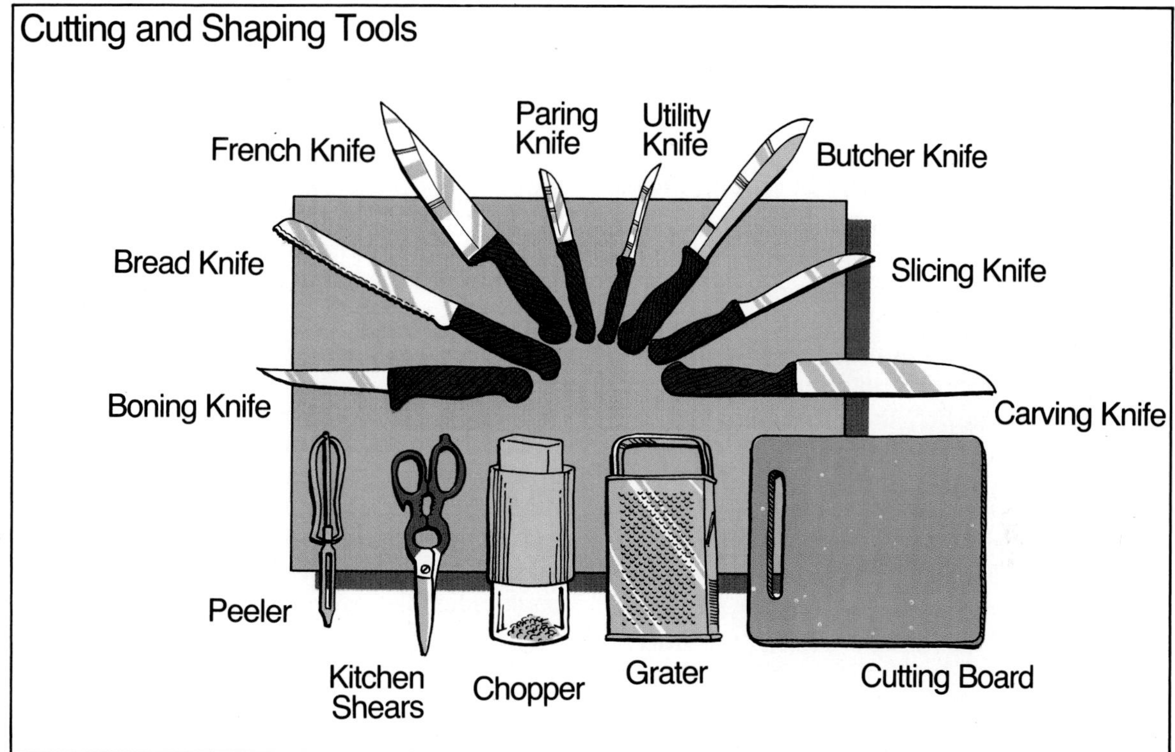

A knife is not just a knife—the above shapes are designed to best perform certain jobs safely and easily.

Small Chopper, Mincer, or Dicer

Small dicing tools are sold in a multitude of designs and sizes. Most have specialized uses, such as dicing onions in a covered container to avoid the fumes, mincing parsley, or chopping nuts. The cost and efficiency of such tools also varies, but generally, skilled use of the French knife or kitchen shears could easily replace these accessories in most kitchens.

Peeler

Several styles of the double-bladed peeler that swivels to cut close to the fruit or vegetable are on the market. Choose the style that is most comfortable for you. The super thin peeling job from this utensil saves nutrients, prepares an attractive product, and can create many attractive, healthful garnishes for food dishes.

Kitchen Shears

These "designed for the kitchen" shears need to be rustproof and heavyduty for cutting fresh greens, fruit stems, pastries, and doughs. Some models separate into two parts for easier cleaning. Regular scissors could be set aside for kitchen use, but special care must be taken to dry and oil them or they will rust and corrode.

Grater

Graters are also available in a number of forms, but basically supply several different size blades for grating, shredding, or slicing vegetables, fruits, and cheese. A nonrusting stainless steel is a desirable material.

Knife Sharpener

Often called a sharpening steel, this metal rod is used to keep knife blades sharp.

Consumer Guide

The best knives are made of tempered steel (steel subjected to a high heat process at the foundry). Tempered-steel knives hold the sharp cutting edge better than other knives. They often are coated with stainless steel to prevent rusting. However, an all stainless steel blade does not hold a sharp cutting edge. Look for a knife blade that is marked "tempered" or "vanadium steel."

Knives should not soak in hot water. Both the handle and the sharpness are damaged by high heat in soaking or the dishwasher. Also, you could seriously cut yourself by reaching into soapy dishwater and grabbing the knife blade rather than the handle.

The best handles feel comfortable in your hand and feature a long shank. The shank is the part of the blade that fits into the handle. Good quality knives have at least two rivets fastening the shank to the handle.

Price does not determine the quality of a good knife. Look for the properties just listed in determining a good buy.

Cutting Board

Using a cutting board is basic to safe and efficient use of knives in the kitchen. The so-called board does not have to be made of wood just as long as it protects the countertop. Cutting "boards" range from an invisible clear plastic to the extremely decorative inlaid woods. Your choice of a cutting board is best determined by its size, shape, and ease in cleaning, not the decoration.

Food Movers

Wooden Spoon

Because wood is a poor heat conductor, a wooden spoon allows you to stir hot foods without burning your fingers. Because bacteria can hide and multiply in the porous wood surface, careful cleaning in hot, sudsy water is required.

Turner

The angled heatproof flat surface of the metal turner lifts, turns, and serves food. Sometimes the surface is slotted to allow fats or liquids to drain. Grilled foods such as pancakes, hamburgers, chops or baked foods such as cookies handle easily with a turner.

Ladle

The large angled bowl of the ladle pours liquid ingredients or serves prepared foods like soup, stew, sauces, or drinks.

Utility Forks

These kitchen forks are used for holding and lifting food. They have a strong handle and often are heat resistant.

Tongs

Use tongs for moving, turning, lifting, or serving foods. The advantage of tongs is that the food is not pierced, allowing juices to stay inside the food.

Baster

Use a **baster** to pour juices or liquid over cooking foods to prevent drying of the surface and to lend flavor and sometimes texture. A baster is also handy for removing or saving liquids.

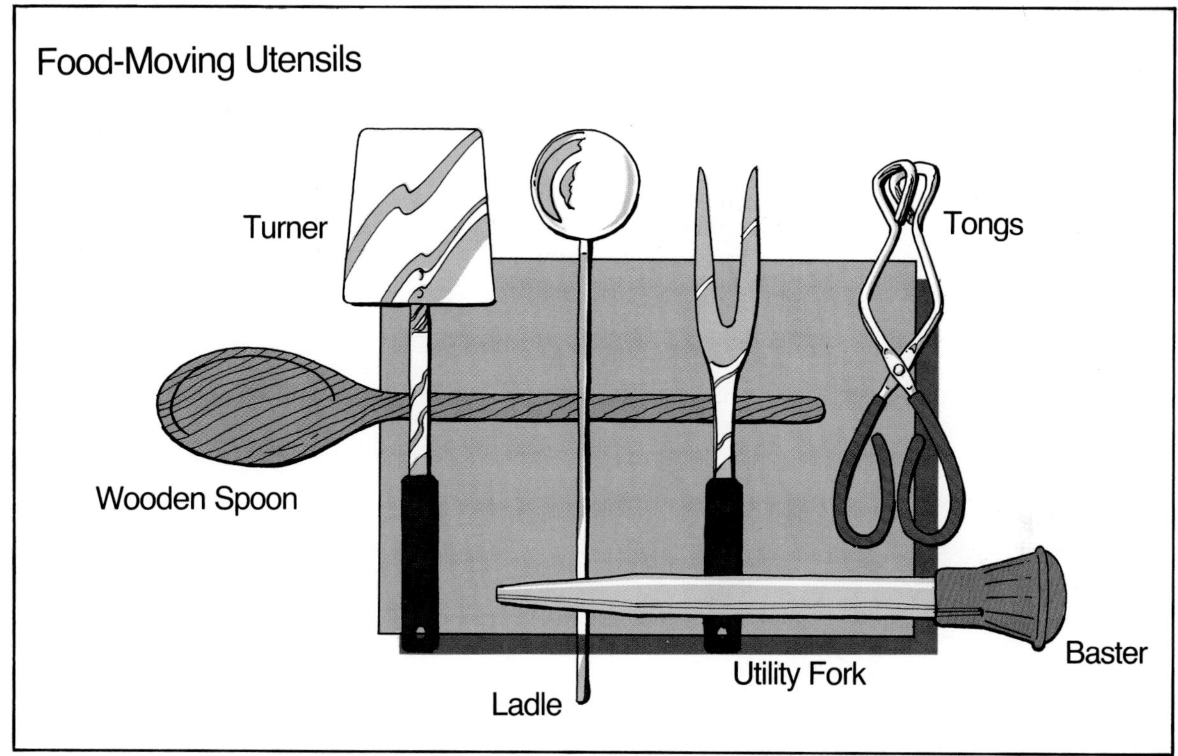

Preparing foods often means having to move it around for mixing, turning, and serving with specialized tools like the familiar ones here.

Mixing Tools

How many recipes have you read that the directions started with, "Mix the ingredients. . . "? Chances are that most recipes have mixing steps somewhere in the instructions, because that's what most cooking is—combining ingredients! To mix and then to hold those mixtures, there are a few tools that help to make your food products a success.

Mixing Bowls

Mixing bowls usually come in graduated sets that nest for storage. They are made of glass, stainless steel, copper, pottery, and both hard and soft plastics. Some sets come with half a dozen bowls and range from the very small to a large 12-quart (12 L) size.

When working with eggs, avoid plastic bowls which tend to absorb oils and interfere with beating egg whites to large volume. Avoid, too, any bowls made of aluminum. They turn egg whites dark. Glass or metal mixing bowls are better for beating egg whites.

Rubber Scraper

The **rubber scraper** is unmatched for removing food from curved sides of bowls, spoons, and pans. It is also an effective tool to use for folding in ingredients with beaten egg whites. When using a rubber or plastic scraper with egg whites, scrub the blade in hot sudsy water first. The rubber or plastic sometimes absorbs oils which would interfere with beating egg whites to a large volume. The rubber scraper is sometimes confused with a spatula, so it is worthwhile keeping the terms separate.

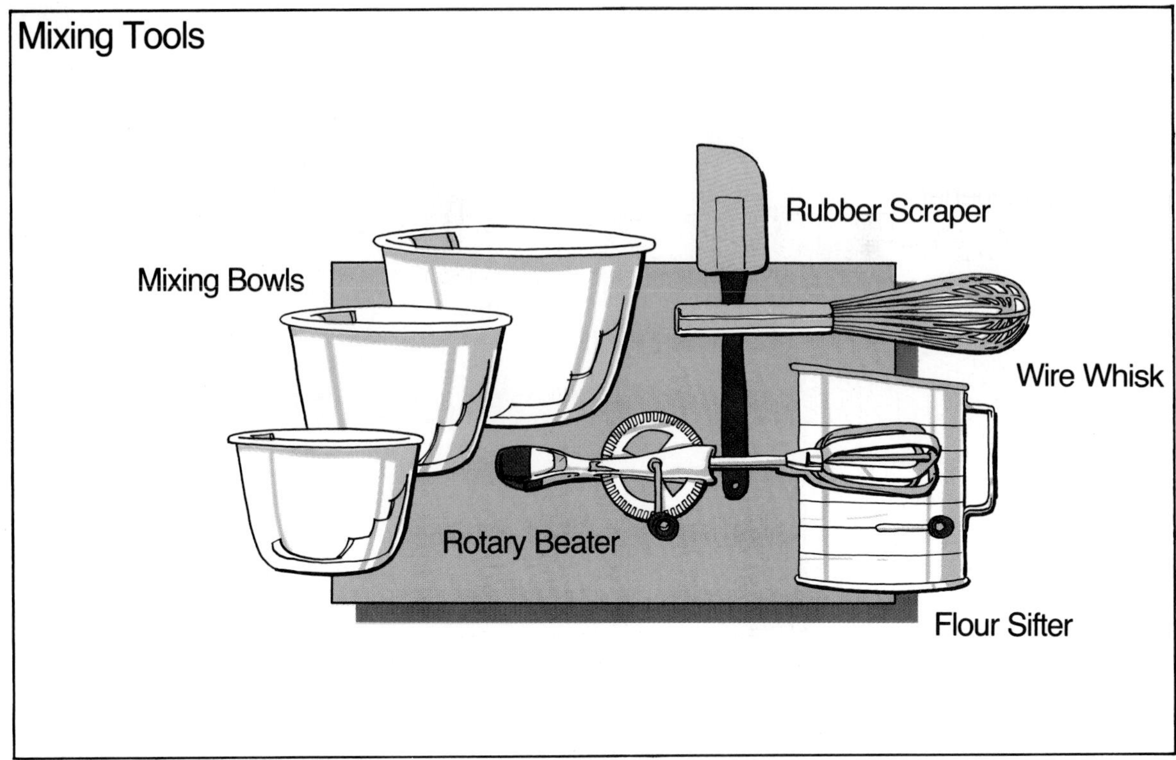

Mixing foods and ingredients can be simple when you have the right tools.

Rotary Beater

Before electric mixers, rotary beaters were the convenience tool for beating ingredients. Even today they are easy to use for small projects.

Wire Whisk

This wire tool is lightweight and easy to handle for hand mixing and beating. The wires bend to one side for easy cleaning or emptying of batter.

Flour Sifter

A **flour sifter** is used to add air to dry ingredients and mix ingredients. Many recipes using flour require that the flour be sifted before measuring. See "Measuring Techniques."

Kitchen Accessories

Can Opener

For opening cans, there is no convenient substitute for the can opener. Models range from the small clip-on variety to the decorative or electric ones. A worthwhile model is the low-friction variety with ball bearings to ease hand turning. (This is the hand-operated model that was developed by NASA for the astronauts to use easily in space.) Look for a model that also has a bottle opener and you can eliminate purchasing another tool for the kitchen.

Bottle Openers

The bottle opener is the safest way to remove tops from glass bottles without chipping the glass or hurting your fingers.

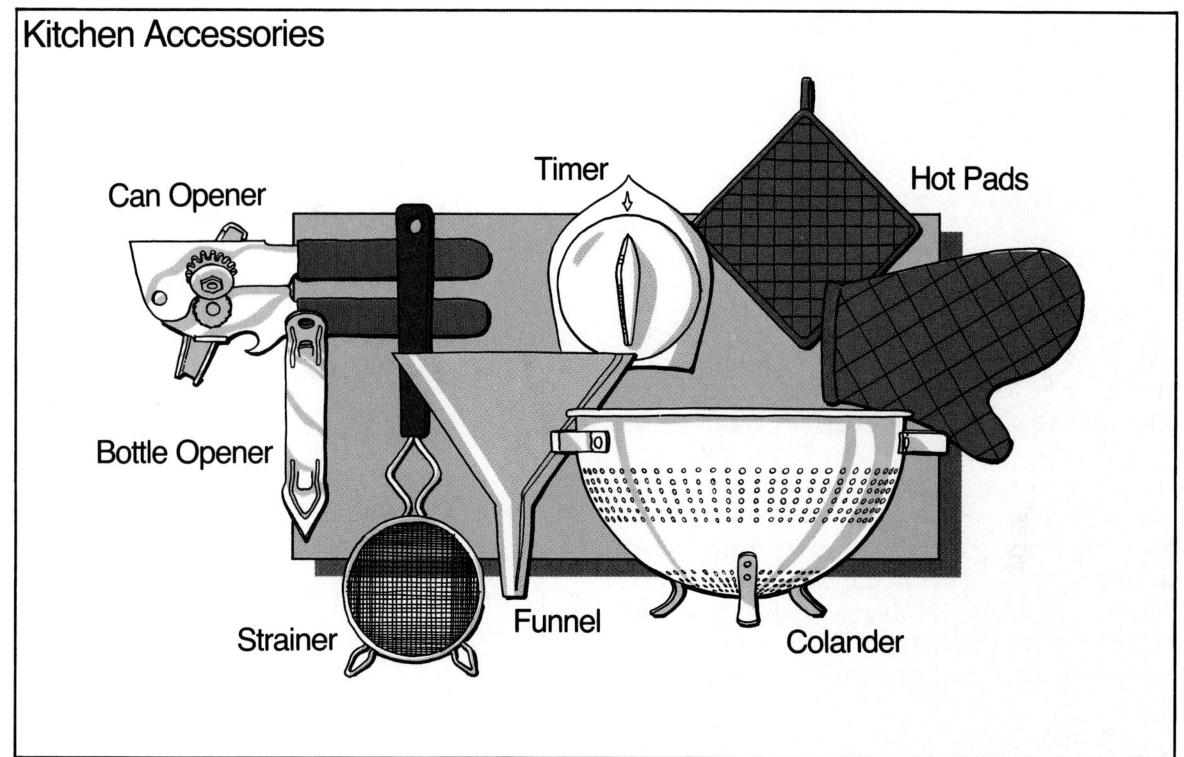

Additional good ideas to the "mixers" and the "movers" in the kitchen include countless accessories. A few of the more basic accessories are pictured here.

Strainer

A **strainer** separates solid food or food particles from juices or other liquids, such as seeds from blackberries or cooked tomatoes. A strainer also can be used with sauces to reduce the size of any particles or lumps. A flexible rubber scraper could be used to facilitate moving the food through the small holes of the screen.

Colander

Larger than the strainer, the colander is used to drain liquids from food. Spaghetti and other pasta are often poured from the cooking pot into a colander to drain prior to serving. Foods may be washed by placing them in the colander and running water over them. Colanders are made of aluminum or pottery.

Timer

Setting a timer helps you concentrate on other tasks while waiting for foods to cook or reminds you to start a food preparation. The buzzer or bell rings when the chosen time passes. New digital models allow you to set more than one alarm setting at the same time. Many kitchen ranges with clocks also include timers.

Funnel

A funnel can be found in many sizes and with various size spouts. For canning, the wide-mouth funnel facilitates pouring the prepared food quickly and cleanly into canning jars. The narrow-spout funnel is used to fill bottles or other small mouth containers with liquid.

Hot Pads or Oven Mitts

Heavy layers of quilted cloth in a pad shape or the complete mitt help to protect the hands from heated pans, baking sheets, and hot handles. These can be made from old towels or other heavy materials.

Cooking Utensils

Different types of utensils for cooking (commonly called **cookware**) are used on top of the stove, in the oven, under a broiler, and in the microwave oven. Not all cookware can be called "pots and pans" anymore. Although some types of cookware are made of traditional metal for quick and even heat conduction, microwave cookware can be glass, special heat-resistant plastic, or even paper containers. (See Chapter 8 for more on microwave cooking.) Thanks to space-age technology, new nonstick surface finishes ease cleaning and food preparation. New ceramic-type materials can be used on top of the range as well as in the oven and are often attractive additions to the table. Refer to the "Cookware Materials" chart at the end of this section for a handy buying guide.

With all the choices available, selecting cookware can become confusing. Large sets of pans usually are not a necessary purchase. Remember, you will need to store your purchases after you buy them! Top-performing cookware is usually worth paying more for, but large complete sets sometimes contain items you will not need or use. Remember, garage sales are a great place to pick up good buys in cookware if you know what to look for!

Skillets

Skillets (or frying pans) require a heavy, flat bottom cooking surface with a relatively low side. Frying, sautéing, and panbroiling food needs a surface that actually touches the food to brown it. Available in several sizes, purchase the size that corresponds to the number of servings you need to prepare. A lid does not always come with the skillet, but other pan lids in the same size can double for use with the skillet to help hold in heat and spatters of grease.

Saucepans and Pots

The common **pan** with one long handle and a lid is usually classified as a saucepan, while a **pot** has two handles, one on either side, and a lid. Both are available in a variety of sizes. When you buy a matched set of cookware, the saucepan and pot sizes offered are usually 1 qt. (1 L), 1½ qt. (1½ L), 2 qt. (2 L), and 3 qt. (3 L). Saucepans and pots are manufactured in many materials that conduct heat.

Double Boiler

A **double boiler** is a set of two saucepans that stack one on top of the other to protect delicate foods from burning or scorching from too high a temperature. The top pan holds the melting or cooking food over the steam formed by the boiling water in the lower pan.

Dutch Oven

An extra heavy pot with a lid, the **Dutch oven** combines the cooking principles of an oven and stove-top cooking. The heavy pot holds in the heated air like a miniature oven, while the direct heat of the burner heats liquid for simmering or steaming the food. Sometimes a Dutch oven is covered with coals in an open fire or suspended in a fireplace for a long-simmered treat such as stew or chili.

Soup Kettle

A large pot with a lid, a soup kettle is useful for simmering stews, soups, and miscellaneous treats like corn on the cob, lobster, and large whole vegetables.

A few basic types of cookware such as a skillet, pan, and kettle allow you to perform most kinds of dry and moist cooking methods.

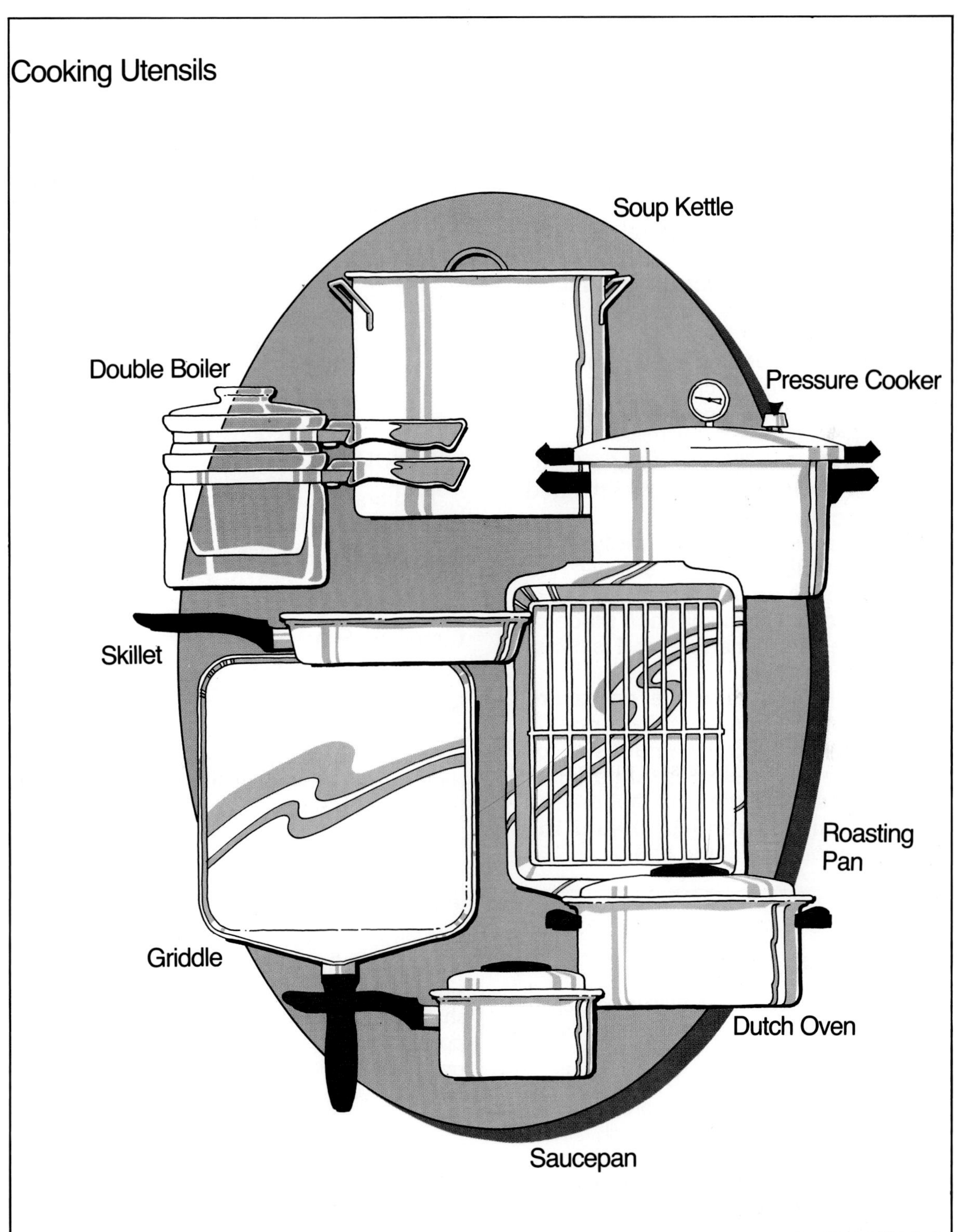
Cooking Utensils
Soup Kettle
Double Boiler
Pressure Cooker
Skillet
Roasting
Pan
Griddle
Dutch Oven
Saucepan

Consumer Guide

Use these factors to help you evaluate saucepans and pots for range-top cooking:

- **Is the cookware heavy or strong enough to last without getting bent out of shape?**
- **Is the bottom flat for maximum heat contact?**
- **Is the pan or pot made out of a material that conducts heat well and evenly (refer to the chart, Appendix).**
- **Is it made in one piece with no seams?**
- **Are the handles made of a heat-resistant material and firmly attached to the cookware?**
- **Does the utensil rest firmly when empty or does it tip over easily?**
- **Does the lid fit snugly?**
- **Is the lid handle or knob made of a heat-resistant material and is it fastened securely?**
- **Could you take the cookware right from the freezer to the range?**
- **Is the pan or pot the right size for the burner on an electric range? Heat escapes around utensils that are too small. On gas ranges, adjust the flame to the size of the pan.**

Pressure Cooker

The **pressure cooker** is a heavy saucepan or pot that is built to hold in steam until the pressure raises the temperature above 212°F (100°C). This causes foods to cook quicker and helps prevent nutrient loss. A pressure cooker is a valuable cooking aid in high altitudes where the lower atmospheric pressure allows water to boil at a lower temperature and therefore causes foods to cook quite slowly. A pressure cooker corrects that condition.

Griddle

A griddle supplies a hot, flat surface ideal for cooking thin hamburgers, pancakes, French toast, eggs, and sandwiches. Most popular has been the grilled cheese sandwich.

Oven Cookware

Cake Pans

Different sizes and shapes of cake pans are available in aluminum, stainless steel, and glass with a variety of plain or nonstick finishes.

Pie Pan

Traditionally, a pie pan is a round flat pan of aluminum, stainless steel, ceramic, or glass to bake pies and quiches (egg dishes baked in piecrusts).

Cookie Sheet

This flat sheet of aluminum or stainless steel is used to bake cookies, crusty breads, or other foods that need good circulation of the heated oven air to bake evenly. Nonstick surfaces help prevent cookies and other foods from sticking, but the dark finishes tend to overbrown the bottom of most foods.

Jelly Roll Pan

A cross between a cake pan and the cookie sheet, the jelly-roll pan has 1 inch (2.5 cm) sides all around for baking bar cookies and shallow sheet cakes that need some side support. It is often used for cookies, but tends to overbrown the bottom of the food.

Cooking in the oven presents the challenge of providing cookware in a variety of shapes from flat cookie sheets to narrow tube pans.

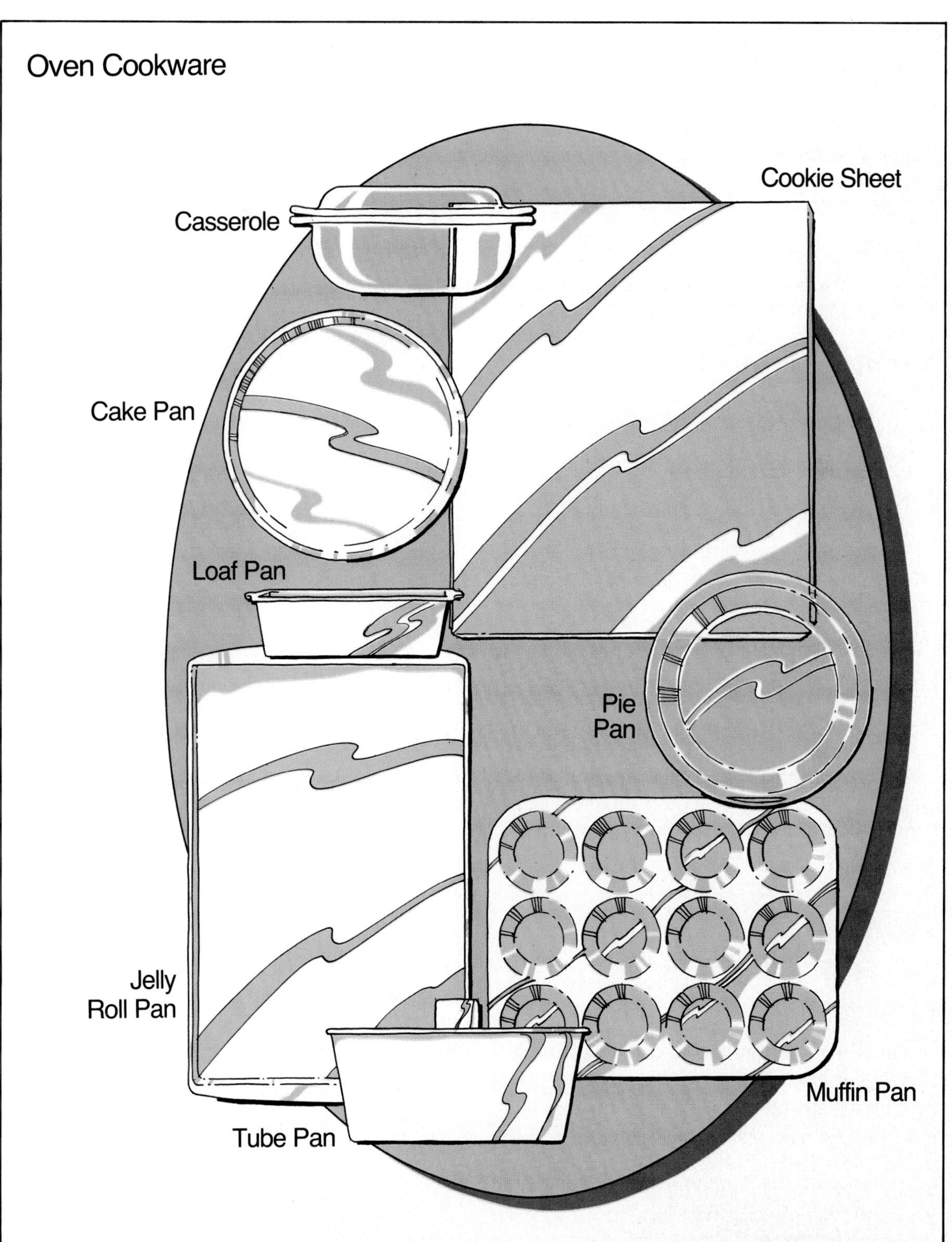
Oven Cookware
Cookie Sheet
Casserole
Cake Pan
Loaf Pan
Pie
Pan
Jelly
Roll Pan
Muffin Pan
Tube Pan

Casseroles

A casserole is a covered baking container designed to be taken directly from the oven to the table. Casseroles are available in a variety of sizes and materials.

Loaf Pan

A narrow pan, the loaf pan (often called a bread pan) is used for baking yeast breads, quick breads, and various meatloaves.

Muffin Pan

Individual compartments of the muffin pan evenly bake muffins, cupcakes, rolls, individual meatloaves, and other creative products.

Oven Roasting Pan and Rack

A large, flat pan with a rack to hold roasts and fowl over the drippings while roasting.

Tube Pan

Often called an angel food or sponge cake pan, this pan allows tender batters to hold to the narrow sides while the product becomes firm during the baking process. Cakes that rise from the tiny air bubbles beaten in during mixing would collapse in an ordinary cake pan before they could bake to a firm product.

Baking Accessories

Rolling Pin

This long cylinder made of wood, marble, metal, or even hollow glass filled with a weighted material is used to roll out dough. Usually the rolling pin has two handles, but not always. Rolling pins come with various finishes or coverings to discourage sticking. Most commonly used is a knitted cotton cover which holds extra flour to prevent sticking.

Pastry Blender

Equipped with bladelike slots or wires, the **pastry blender** actually cuts through chunks of shortening and flour in a bowl until they are blended correctly for a flaky pastry. (See Chapter 6.)

Pastry Brush

A heat-tolerant bristle brush is used to coat pastry and breads with melted butter, beaten egg glaze, or icing.

Hot Pads

Hot pads mentioned earlier are also a vital part of baking equipment. No part of a pan from the oven (except a microwave) is cool enough to handle.

Wire Rack

Wire cooling racks allow baked products to cool without getting soggy and limp. Cookies, cakes, and breads may be transferred directly from the hot pan to the cooling racks.

Pastry Board

This large square "board" of plastic, wood, or marble is used for rolling out and cutting doughs, pastry, biscuits, or cookies. Flour is rolled into the surface, or a pastry cloth of heavy canvas may be used over the board to prevent dough from sticking and to hold the extra flour.

Biscuit or Cookie Cutters

These shaped cutters of plastic or metal are used to cut out biscuits and cookies before baking. Cutters also can be used for baked cakes, breads, vegetable and fruit as garnishes, and small sandwiches.

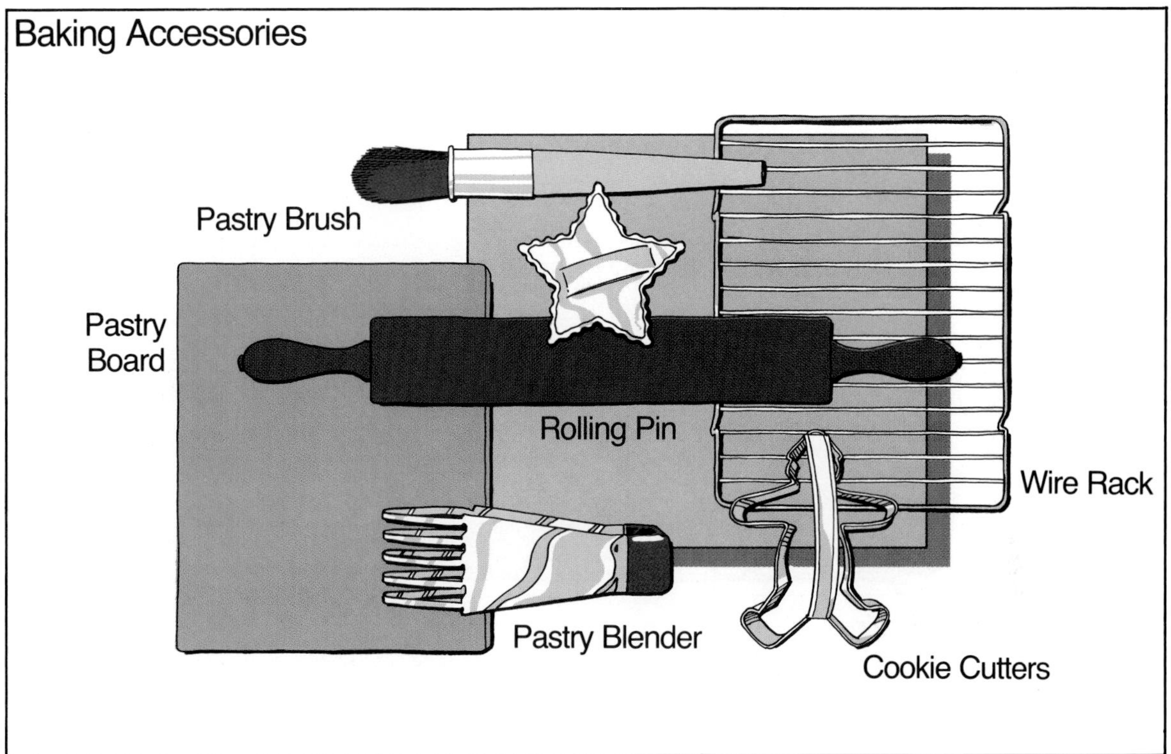

Although you can accomplish wonders with a basic knife and spoon, the above baking accessories are "marvels" at simplifying baking steps for pie crusts, pastries, and cookies.

Cleaning Accessories

You will be more inclined to want to cook another time if you do not have a mountain of unwashed utensils and dirty counters when you finish making a product. Cleaning up as you prepare foods takes seconds and can become an automatic part of the preparation process. Anyway, it's a terrific habit to encourage!

Although fancy dishwashing utensils and dish towels are not essential, some equipment is necessary for this important task. The following items are worthwhile to have.

Dishcloth

You can convert any soft piece of natural fiber such as cotton or linen into a dishcloth. They also can be purchased inexpensively.

Some people prefer using a sponge for dishwashing. Sponges are available in assorted sizes and shapes. Ones with a scouring pad on one side are particularly handy.

Both the dishcloth and sponge are useful for washing dishes and for cleaning counters.

Towels

It is most important to have two towels for the kitchen: one to dry dishes and utensils and one to dry your hands. Look for towels that contain at least 50 percent cotton or linen fiber. Natural fibers are the most absorbent materials. Some of the synthetic fibers do not hold any water at all.

Scouring Pads

Baked on food and discolored spots on metal are easy to scrub away with the help of a scouring pad. They also help to save your fingernails. Some shiny cookware and stove sur-

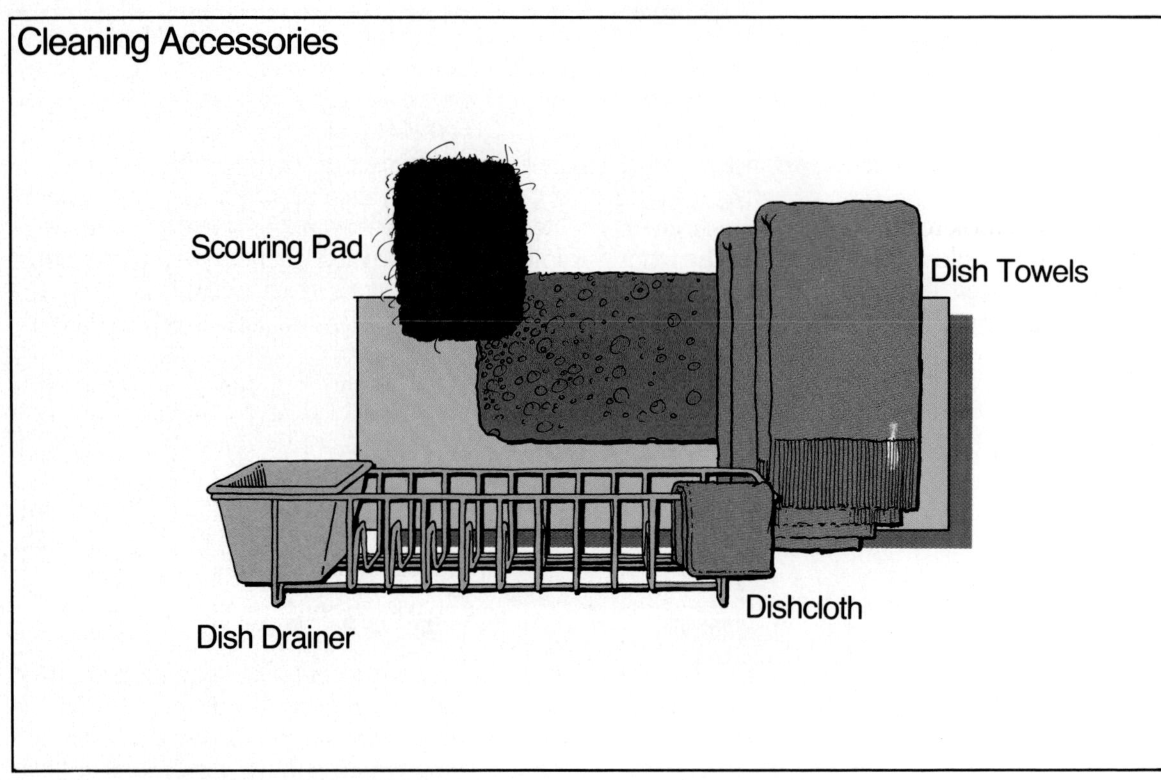

Clean, fresh dishwashing aids can help make this necessary activity easier and healthier.

faces would scratch if steel wool was used on them. Read their use and care manuals if you are in doubt.

Dish Drainer

An inexpensive dish drainer helps to drain and air dry utensils and dishes. It also helps prevent breakage.

Choosing Major Appliances

There is no doubt: purchasing major kitchen appliances represents a big financial investment. Before you set out to purchase major appliances, think about the following.

Your Family

Do you live in a household of five people? Are you living alone? Single persons may find it more economical to purchase a compact and portable refrigerator. A 5-person household, however, might better use a two-door refrigerator.

Your Budget

Although major kitchen appliances are expensive, it is almost unheard of to purchase a refrigerator or stove at the full retail price. Watch newspaper ads and circulars for department store sales. Another place to look for appliances is a warehouse or liquidation business. Bargains may also be had through newspaper "Moving Sale" ads.

Don't forget, too, that the cost of an appliance does not end with its purchase. You will need to pay the utility costs to keep the appliance running and any repair costs that might occur if the appliance does not work. One way to judge the cost of operating the appliance is to look for the **EnergyGuide** label. This is a bright yellow label pasted on the front of large appliances. It gives the total dollar estimate for running the appliance for one year. Also listed on the EnergyGuide label are comparison costs for different models of the same appliance.

To protect yourself against high repair costs, check on the warranty of an appliance. A **warranty** is a guarantee by the manufacturer to repair the appliance or parts of the appliance for a specified length of time. Not all manufacturers offer the same warranties, so read each one carefully. You will find that some are full warranties and some are limited warranties. A **full warranty** covers all the parts and labor for a certain time. There are limits to the coverage of a **limited warranty.** Not all the parts or maybe the labor costs will not be covered. Also check on the service offered by the store. Will they work on the appliance or do you need to take it to a service center? Will they come to your home for repairs? Do you need to take the appliance into the store? All of these factors will affect your long-term enjoyment of the appliance.

Your Space

Of course, you must be certain the doors in your home or apartment are wide enough to accommodate the size of the appliance you want to purchase. Will the appliance fit the area you want to put it in? Is there enough space to allow for ventilation and possible servicing?

Your Needs

Quality is an important consideration when purchasing a major kitchen appliance. You want the best possible buy for your dollar, yet it doesn't follow that the more expensive an appliance, the higher the quality. Name-brand appliances are of high quality. They have name recognition as well as a stream of satisfied customers in their favor.

House brand (or store brand) appliances are good buys because the appliances are manufactured by a brand-name company and then sold under a private label. It pays to research consumer publications to find out about the retailer's private label appliance and the manufacturer's other products.

Realize that convenience and additional special features on appliances cost money. Ask yourself if the convenience or extra features will be used often enough to justify the extra expense. Do you really need an ice and water dispenser in the door of a refrigerator? One interesting high-tech refrigerator feature is called a "door open" symbol. It glows when any door has been left open, and after three minutes, makes a beeping sound. You might find it useful to write a list of features that you need to have on appliances, and those you would like to have. Then compare the costs.

Certification by an appliance industry organization is another sign of a quality appliance. Electrical appliances should have the **Underwriters' Laboratory** seal. Gas appliances should have the **American Gas Association's** (AGA) seal. Appliances carrying these seals have met the appropriate safety requirements.

Major Appliances

Of course, kitchens include a range and refrigerator, but the types vary considerably. Also, some kitchens are equipped with other large appliances.

Range

A range is a necessary kitchen appliance for cooking foods. There are a variety of styles and options from which to choose. The two basic types are gas ranges and electric ranges. Many times the gas range versus electric range deci-

Safety Tip

Exercise caution in the kitchen by following these kitchen safety tips:

- **Avoid wearing clothing items with long, loose-fitting sleeves. They are more apt to catch on fire than clothing with short sleeves. Also, you can get burned if your sleeves catch on a pot handle and overturn hot food.**
- **Make sure that flammable and combustible items are stored away from the range and oven.**
- **If you have curtains that could accidentally brush against a heat source, either shorten the curtains or remove them.**
- **Know if your kitchen ventilation system or range exhaust is working properly. Use it while you are cooking.**
- **Don't keep dish towels hanging on an oven handle. If towels are located close to a burner, you should find another place for them.**

sion is based on personal preference or what type your family uses. The type of fuel hookup in your home may be the final deciding factor.

Ranges have burners or cooking elements on the surface of the range and an oven. The oven is used for baking, roasting, and broiling. Some newer types of electric ranges have smooth glass ceramic surfaces rather than heating coils. Another type of electric range is the induction range that heats the cooking utensil which in turns heats the food.

Refrigerator

Refrigerators are important appliances because they keep food cold and prevent spoilage. Several styles (one door, two door, and compact-portable) and features are available.

The model determines the amount of defrosting a refrigerator requires. Manually defrosting refrigerators are the least expensive to purchase and operate. You should defrost this type of refrigerator about every two weeks. Never allow frost to accumulate to more than 1/2 inch (1.3 cm). Too much frost can cause the refrigerator to break down.Only the freezer on an automatic defrost refrigerator will require defrosting.

Frostless refrigerators require no defrosting at all. Both the automatic defrost and frostless models cost more to purchase and operate.

Microwave Oven

Changes in today's lifestyle have made microwave ovens very popular appliances. Microwaves with a variety of cooking options and control devices are available. The reduction in cooking time is a great advantage to owning a microwave. In Chapter 8, you will find information on the proper microwave cookware and utensils and cooking procedures.

Dishwasher

An automatic dishwasher saves time and energy for large households. Single people living alone may find it a luxury.

There are two models. The built-in model fits between two cabinets. Because it has more insulation than the portable model, it operates more quietly. The portable model is rolled to the sink before use and can be stored anywhere.

For maximum efficiency, run the dishwasher when it is full and use an automatic dishwashing detergent. Some items that should not be washed in a dishwasher include plastic utensils if they are not heat-resistant and heirloom china.

Garbage Disposal

A garbage disposal allows you the convenience of getting rid of food garbage by simply putting it down the disposal. Two models are available: batch feed and continuous feed. In

Don't forget that part of the price of an appliance is the utility cost! EnergyGuide labels can help you find the most economical unit.

the batch-feed model, a small amount of food is sent down the disposal. The grinding action starts when the lid is placed over the opening and turned. This model is ideal in households with children. With the continuous feed model, you need only to turn on the switch and push food into the disposal continuously.

You need to be sure that no cutlery or other utensils are in the sink before starting the disposal.

Before purchasing a garbage disposal, ask yourself: do I really need one? Are there other ways of disposing garbage that are readily available within my community? (Some communities forbid garbage disposals. To be safe, check before buying.)

Small Equipment

Some kitchens are loaded with small electric appliances. As with other expensive purchases, be sure you will use the product enough to warrant spending the money. Don't forget, too, that all those appliances have to be stored somewhere. Do you have the counterspace? If you need to store an appliance in a cabinet, how often will you go to the trouble of getting it out to use it? The decision-making process you read about in Chapter 1 is useful at times when major purchases are being considered.

Food Processor

It kneads, it mixes, it slices, it shreds, it grates, it chops, its beats, it blends, it purees. The food processor has become an important piece of kitchen equipment because it can do a number of time-consuming kitchen tasks quickly and easily.

Blender

Blenders can chop, shred, grind, puree, and liquefy foods. You can use a blender to prepare nutritious homemade baby foods, beverages, dips, and soft meals. The blender's surgical steel blades should be cleaned after each use.

Safety Tip

What's slimy green, hides in your refrigerator, and is scarier than your worst nightmare?

It's mold, and, unfortunately, most of us have experienced the refrigerator variety. Mold spores are everywhere, even in the air.

If you store leftovers in small, plastic margarine containers only to return to them a few days later, you have probably seen the surface mold invasion. So what can you do?

First, if you are serious about it, you'll find the time to work some house-cleaning into your schedule. Clean your refrigerator with 1 tablespoon (15 mL) of baking soda dissolved in 1 quart (1 L) of water. Rinse the refrigerator with clear water, then dry it. This routine will prevent mold spores from building up and shortening the life of other foods.

If you see a spot of mold on a block of cheese or hard salami, all is not lost. You may be able to save the food product if you cut off at least 1 inch (2.5 cm) all around and below the spot of mold. Keep the knife out of the mold itself. Forget about saving mold-infected cheese slices, yogurt, cottage cheese, soft cheeses, cream, or sour cream.

Toss out moldy jams and jellies. You just can't tell how deep the mold's roots have grown.

You will be able to cut off mold spots on the surface of firm vegetables and fruits (pears, apples, peppers, cabbage). But throw out soft vegetables, such as tomatoes and cucumbers, if you see signs of mold.

The same rule applies to moldy bread products. Toss out moldy buns, pastry, cake, rice, beans, and peanut butter. Natural foods are at a particularly high risk because they are processed without preservatives.

Always discard food that is heavily covered with mold. Don't rely on the sniff test to tell you what food is bad or good—unless you're looking for respiratory troubles!

Check all the food products you buy especially packaged foods and fresh fruits and vegetables. If you see signs of mold, particularly around the stem area, call the store manager.

Perhaps the most effective way to prevent mold growth on food items is to buy smaller amounts of food and to use them quickly.

Mixer

Used for mixing, beating, stirring, whipping, and blending, these often-used kitchen appliances come in two models: standard and hand. Standard mixers are suitable for heavy-duty baking needs. They may come equipped with a dough hook, food chopper, and juicer. Smaller, handheld mixers are lighter than the standard variety, but they are not as versatile.

Slow Cooker

Popularly used for stews and soups, slow cookers have a low and a high setting. They cook foods very slowly over a period of hours. This quality makes them popular with working people who can fill the slow cooker in the morning and arrive home in the evening to a cooked meal. Slow cookers come with their own recipe books. Follow them for best results.

Toaster

Most Europeans would not think of "burning" their bread in the morning, but many people on this continent enjoy a couple of slices of toast for breakfast. Toasters come in two-slice and four-slice models. The two-slice models usually cost less and are sufficient for small families or single persons. If you choose a toaster with wide wells, you will be able to toast more than bread.

Another type of toaster that does more than just toast is the toaster-oven. This small appliance can toast bread, English muffins, and irregular-shaped breads. In addition, it can top-brown foods and even bake or roast. A toaster oven is ideal for small families and single people because it saves heating up a large oven to prepare small servings.

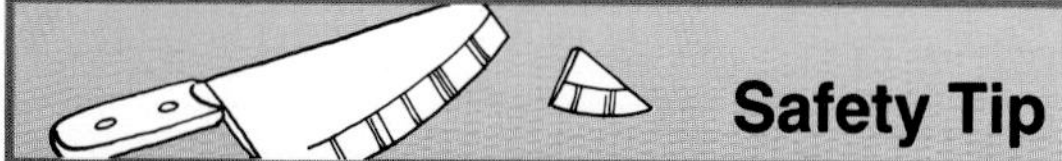

Safety Tip

Here are some measures you can take for poison prevention in the kitchen:

- **Don't keep household products — cleanser, ammonia, furniture polish—under the sink.**
- **Keep medicines off the kitchen counter.**
- **Household cleaners should be out of reach and stored in proper containers. Keep lids on tight!**
- **Know the location of the nearest poison center. Keep their telephone number near your phone in case of an emergency.**

Pasta Maker

Making your own fresh pasta is a popular culinary activity, and pasta is good for you as well! Pasta makers reduce the time spent in the kitchen mixing and kneading dough. A selection of discs that produce different types of pasta is usually available.

Kitchen Work Triangle

Imagine you are designing your own kitchen. You know that you'll need a space for a refrigerator, range, and sink, and a space for meal preparation. Now take a look at your design. Most likely you can observe an imaginary triangle running from the refrigerator to the range to the sink. This imaginary triangle is called the **work triangle** because it parallels the flow of activity in a kitchen. Think of the flow of activity in this manner. First, food is taken from the refrigerator and brought to the sink to be cleaned. Second, the food is taken from the sink to the range for cooking. Finally, after the meal, leftovers are returned to the refrigerator. Ideally, the distance walked between the refrigerator, sink, and range should not be greater than 21 feet (7 m). If the work triangle is larger than this, more personal energy will be required to complete a task.

There are five different work triangle plans commonly used in most kitchens.

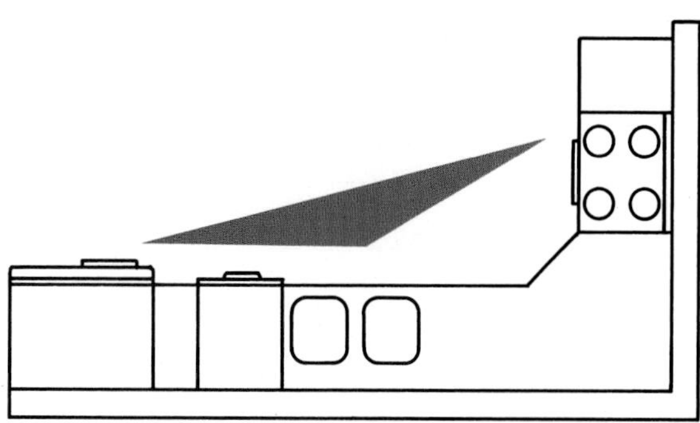

- **L-shaped kitchens** look just like their name sounds, in an "L." The cabinets and appliances are on the two walls that form the "L." This is a good plan that avoids the problems of the corridor and one-wall kitchens.

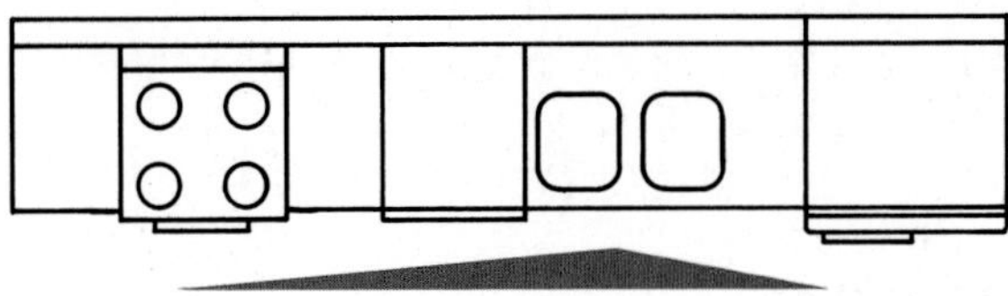

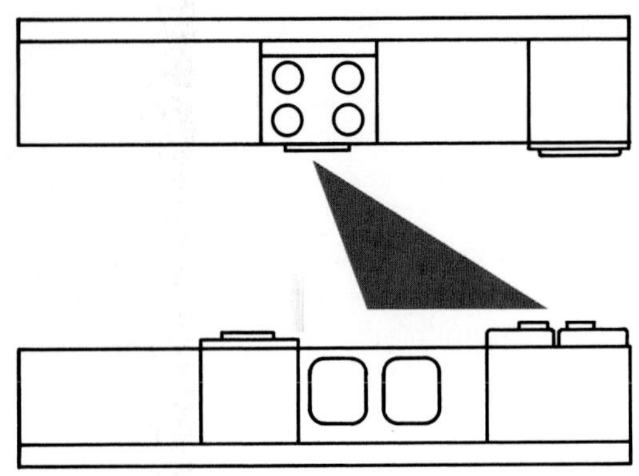

• **One-wall kitchen** plan has the refrigerator, range, and sink all along one wall. This is not a very efficient plan. If the distance between each unit is large enough to allow for enough counter space, then the walking distance is too great. If, however, the walking distance is cut down to something manageable, the amount of counter space suffers. This type of kitchen plan is a good space saver in small homes and many apartments.

• **Corridor kitchens** are designed with the refrigerator, range, and sink on two facing walls. This can be a very efficient plan allowing for enough counter space and little walking distance. One disadvantage arises if there is a door at either end of the kitchen. Then through the middle of the work triangle is the traffic pattern (the path people take through a room). Having people walk through the kitchen during meal preparation times can be a bother and a danger if you were to spill hot food on someone.

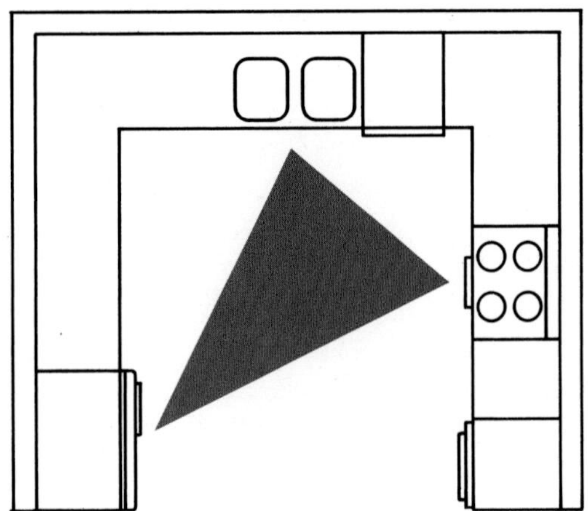

• **U-shaped kitchens** are in the shape of a "U." Usually one appliance is on each wall of the "U." This is a very efficient plan that gives a large amount of counter space, a short walking distance, and no traffic pattern passing through the work triangle.

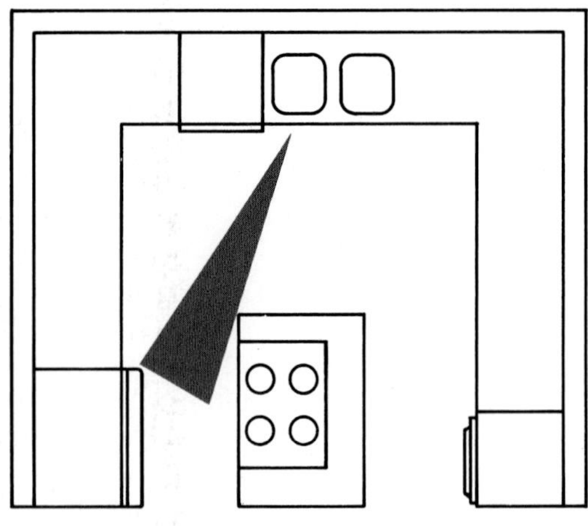

• **Island kitchens** are not found only in ocean homes. They are so called because they have a freestanding counter in the middle of the work triangle. This is a good design in large kitchens because it cuts down on the walking distance between counters.

Vocabulary Review

Utensils
Nomenclature
Water displacement method
Rubber scraper
Flour sifter
Strainer
Cookware
Pan
Pot
Double boiler
Dutch oven
Pressure cooker
Pastry blender
Energy Guide label
Warranty
Full warranty
Limited warranty
House brand
Underwriters' Laboratory seal
American Gas Association's seal
Work triangle

Questions for Review

1. Why is it important to use appropriate utensils in food preparation?
2. What are some basic items needed in the kitchen? Why?
3. What are some factors to consider when evaluating kitchen tools and appliances?
4. Why is it helpful to know general nomenclature for utensils?
5. Why are different types of measuring cups used for dry and wet ingredients?
6. What method is used to measure dry ingredients? Wet ingredients?
7. What two methods can be used to measure solid fat?
8. What features are important when purchasing a knife?
9. What are some things to consider when selecting a knife to use for a specific food preparation task?

Things to Do

1. Brown sugar and powdered sugar have special measuring techniques. Measure ½ cup (125 mL) of each.
2. Measure ⅓ cup (75 mL) shortening by the water displacement method and ⅓ cup (75 mL) shortening using a dry measuring cup. Which method do you prefer?
3. Accurately measure 1 cup (250 mL) of flour as directed in this chapter. Inaccurately measure a second cup of flour. Weigh each cup of flour on a piece of waxed paper. Compare weights.
4. Familiarize yourself with your laboratory kitchen. Can you identify everything?
5. Familiarize yourself with your kitchen at home to see what kind of utensils are available. Do you have everything you need? What changes would you make?
6. Become informed about the best choice of cookware materials. Visit the housewares section of a deparment store to see what kinds of selections they have available. What would you purchase first if your were setting up your own kitchen?

CHIUSURA DI GARANZIA
CONTAINS
NO CHOLESTEROL
COLD PRESSED
100% PURE
MADE IN U.S.A.
BRAND

Getting Directions

If you were to go to another country, you would expect to learn some of the language. Even if you were to travel to another part of this country, you would learn the directions on how to get there before leaving.

Now you are ready to venture into a closer area that has its own unique language and directions—the kitchen. Your kitchen roadmap of where you are going and how to accomplish what you want is the recipe. A **recipe** is a set of reliable instructions for making a food dish from specific ingredients. Recipes have their own unique language and methods. Once you learn the language and how to follow the directions, you will be able to figure out any recipe, as well as develop your own creations. Using a recipe is much like following a map and then exploring the territory.

The Great Motivator!

There's nothing quite like a luscious-sounding recipe with or without a tempting picture to inspire you to create a mouth-watering food product. Recipes are powerful motivators and reading them is a popular pastime in this country. The numerous and colorful food features in the Sunday newspaper capture many an "armchair chef's" attention.

Perhaps you have noticed that most of your favorite specialty magazines, from autos to fashions, feature a section on foods and innovative recipe ideas. Food sells! Manufacturers take advantage of that market appeal by including recipes with appliances as well as on food packages. Large companies employ home economists to develop and test their product recipes and to develop new products. Food stores sell their products through helpful demonstrations and pamphlets featuring recipes. That same market appeal guarantees cookbooks their place among the number one sellers each year. Recipes surround you throughout many seemingly unrelated interests. Where to find a recipe doesn't seem to be a challenge, but how do you know if it is a reliable recipe without costly errors in time, money, and self-confidence?

Will It Work?

Has a colorful food photo ever made your mouth water to the point you decided to try the recipe by its appearance alone? Then, unfortunately, all your work and expense disappointed you with an unimpressive result. The directions may have left out an important step such as bringing egg whites to room temperature before beating. Perhaps the proportions of flour in a cake or cookie could have been too high or too low, causing the product to be rather tasteless or a collapsed failure. You can learn to recognize some faulty recipes through acquired food skills and knowledge, but while you are still learning, the best guide to proven tested recipes is through reliable sources.

Reliable Recipes

Reach for the familiar basic cookbook as the best starting source for your recipe collection of favorites. Remember, the classic names became familiar because they earned their reputation. New flashy specialty cookbooks can be limited in subjects covered and might omit important background instructions for the less experienced cook. It would be easy to invest in a dozen new specialty cookbooks and still not have a good recipe for an everyday favorite, but a basic complete cookbook provides guidelines for almost any type of food preparation.

The "tried and true" food favorites from relatives and friends are traditional sources of "good" recipes, but only if the directions and ingredients are complete. Study the recipe format shown on page 123 and remember to ask for any of the missing information. Have you ever heard anyone say, "I tried your recipe for that marvelous___, but somehow it just didn't taste the same"? The reply might have been "Oh, I guess I forgot to tell you about. . . ."

No one source will furnish all the recipes you might like to have and try. Collecting your own personal file of ideas and examples can be a rewarding and valuable activity to enjoy for a lifetime of changing needs.

Recipes

What does a recipe include?

1. Name of product.
2. Number of servings in recipe. Do you need to change the amount to suit the number of people to be served?
3. Cookware and needed size. Check beforehand to see if you have the appropriate utensil.
4. Oven temperature. Do you need to preheat the oven so it will be ready for baking the food once it is mixed? Starting to bake at the correct temperature can be crucial for leavened products.
5. A complete list of ingredients and their amounts in order of use. There's no sense in starting if you don't have what it takes or its substitute. The amounts (measurements) might be listed in the metric system or in both metric and traditional form. See page 126 for the conversion chart for metric units.
6. Step-by-step instructions.
7. Cooking time and temperature setting. The time is often accompanied by some clue to determine when the product is ready. Some examples might be ". . . until golden brown and translucent," or ". . . until center bounces back when pressed with finger."
8. Serving or "presentation" instructions. These are listed when they are appropriate for the product.

Various Recipes Forms

How a recipe is written, the format, varies in different publications. Some list the ingredients within the directions, while others separate the ingredients from the instructions. One format combines the whole recipe into one paragraph. The format example just illustrated is the easiest to follow and the most widely used in cookbooks.

Become familiar with the basic parts of a good recipe and you'll be able to recognize reliable instructions as well as to follow a recipe more successfully.

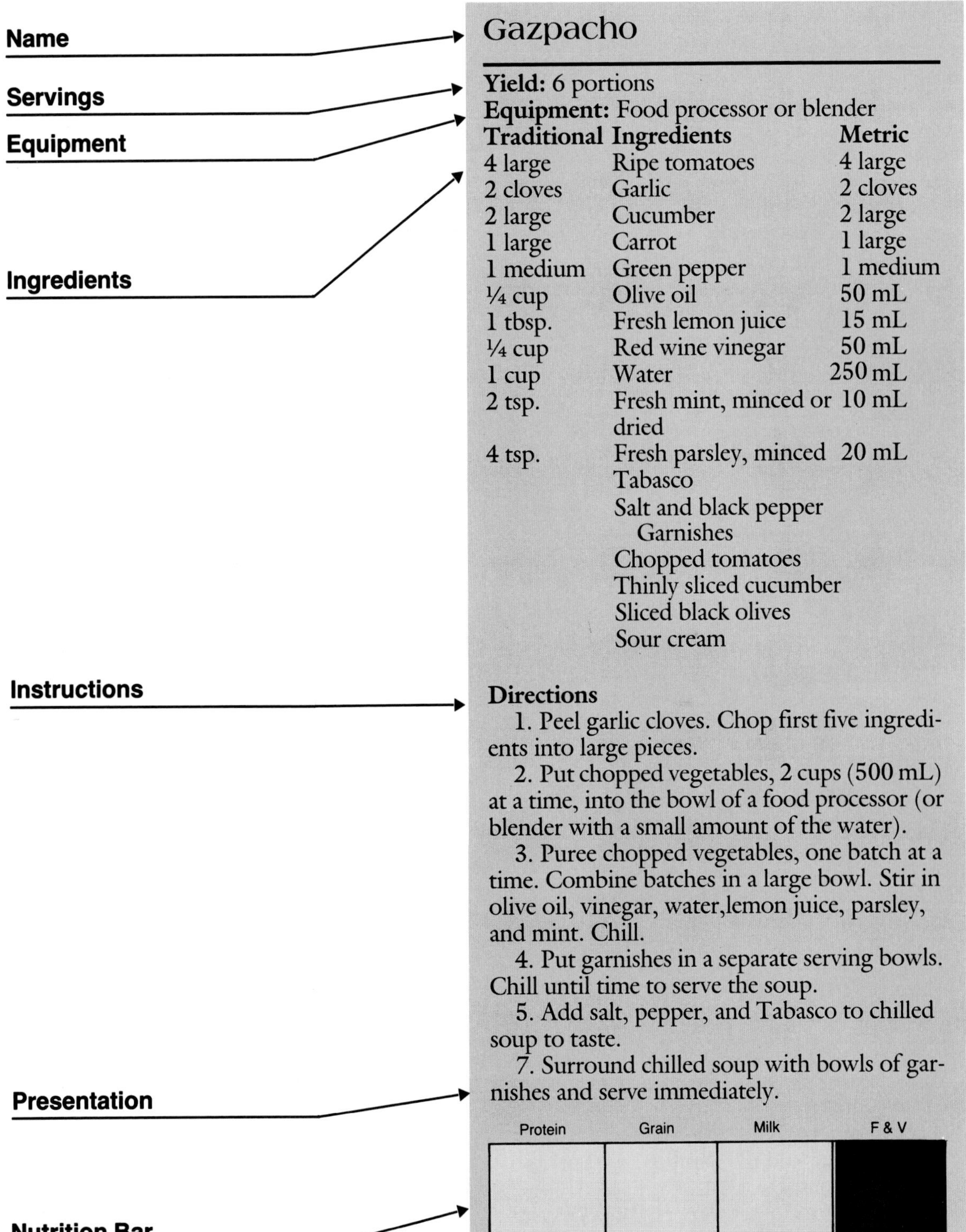
Name
Servings
Equipment
Ingredients
Instructions
Presentation
Nutrition Bar
Gazpacho
Yield: 6 portions
Equipment: Food processor or blender
Traditional Ingredients Metric
4 large Ripe tomatoes 4 large
2 cloves Garlic 2 cloves
2 large Cucumber 2 large
1 large Carrot 1 large
1 medium Green pepper 1 medium
¼ cup Olive oil 50 mL
1 tbsp. Fresh lemon juice 15 mL
¼ cup Red wine vinegar 50 mL
1 cup Water 250 mL
2 tsp. Fresh mint, minced or dried 10 mL
4 tsp. Fresh parsley, minced 20 mL
Tabasco
Salt and black pepper
Garnishes
Chopped tomatoes
Thinly sliced cucumber
Sliced black olives
Sour cream
Directions
1. Peel garlic cloves. Chop first five ingredients into large pieces.
2. Put chopped vegetables, 2 cups (500 mL) at a time, into the bowl of a food processor (or blender with a small amount of the water).
3. Puree chopped vegetables, one batch at a time. Combine batches in a large bowl. Stir in olive oil, vinegar, water,lemon juice, parsley, and mint. Chill.
4. Put garnishes in a separate serving bowls. Chill until time to serve the soup.
5. Add salt, pepper, and Tabasco to chilled soup to taste.
7. Surround chilled soup with bowls of garnishes and serve immediately.
Protein
Grain
Milk
F & V

Turning Good Intentions into Action

How do you get started? There are a few preliminary steps to following a recipe that can make the difference between happy success and discouraging failure. These steps will soon become automatic with more experience.

Before starting a recipe, be certain that you:

1. Read the recipe all the way through!
2. Be sure you have all the ingredients and utensils listed.
3. Decide upon any suitable ingredient or cookware substitution you might need to make. (See the Ingredient Substitution chart in the Appendix.)
4. Perform any of the preliminary steps listed. Examples might be scalding milk, heating water, melting chocolate, chopping, slicing, peeling, or chilling ingredients.
5. Assemble all the ingredients and equipment within reach of your working space.
6. Familiarize yourself with all the terms and methods in the recipe. (See "Food Preparation Terms" on pages 129-130.)
7. Measure carefully and consistently. See Chapter 5.
8. Follow the directions.
9. Enjoy the results and evaluate the product for anything you would like to do differently next time, or decide if you even want there to be a "next time." Make notes.

Jambalaya

Yield: 4 portions
Equipment: 4 quart (4 L) heavy pot

Traditional	Ingredients	Metric
½ cup	Onion, chopped	125 mL
⅓ cup	Green pepper, chopped	75 mL
1 cup	Celery, chopped	250 mL
3 Tbsp.	Olive oil	45 mL
1½ cups	Long-grain rice	375 mL
3 cups	Chicken or fish stock	750 mL
½ tsp.	White pepper	3 mL
¼ tsp.	Cayenne pepper	1 mL
1	Bay leaf	1
2 cups	Canned tomatoes, undrained	500 mL
¾ cup	Cooked ham, chopped	175 mL
1 lb.	Shelled raw shrimp, or 2 cans shrimp	500 g
½ cup	Cooked chicken, shredded	125 mL
1 cup	Raw fish, cut in 1-inch pieces optional	500 mL
1 Tbsp.	Fresh or dried basil	15 mL
½ tsp.	Filé gumbo	3 mL

Directions

1. Heat the olive oil in heavy pot.
2. Sauté onion until golden brown. Stir in the celery and rice.
3. Add the stock, salt, black pepper, cayenne pepper, bay leaf, and filé gumbo. Simmer, covered, for 10 minutes.
4. Add chopped green pepper, tomatoes and juice to the pot. Simmer covered, for 5 minutes.
5. Add the ham, shrimps, chicken, and fish. Stir gently.
6. Cover and cook over low heat until the rice is tender (about 10 minutes).
7. Transfer jambalaya to a warmed serving dish and add basil. Place hot sauce by jambalaya for individuals to add if desired for a true Cajun flavor.

Tempting colorful photos of food help you to imagine the flavor and texture of a recipe you are considering. Have you ever been disappointed when a resulting product did not match the picture? How can you predict whether a recipe will work?

Making Recipes Work

Following the directions of a recipe is important to success. Equally important are performing all the steps and measuring correctly. And how can you be sure of success if you want to alter the recipe? Measuring is how!

Why Measure?

Standard measuring cups and spoons are used as the basis for the proportions given in modern recipes. The test kitchens of companies that develop products and recipes as well as cookbook authors try to achieve consistent products using standard measuring equipment.

If the measuring utensils you use are not the standard type described in Chapter 5, then you will need to make corrections. Compare the volume of your utensils to the standard and adjust any recipes accordingly. For example, if you are using a coffee cup or mug, the amount of liquid could range from 6 to 10 fluid ounces (180 to 300 mL). The standard cup holds 8 fluid ounces (250 mL), so you would have to add an extra 2 ounces (60 mL) to the small coffee cup and remove 2 ounces (60 mL) from the mug to successfully make the recipe. Using the standard measurers is simpler whenever possible and leaves less possibilities for error or wasted time and money.

Consumer Guide

Looking through this book and at the foods in the supermarket, have you noticed abbreviations such as mL, g, and cm? These symbols are used in the metric system. Most measurements in the U.S. are based on the traditional measurements that include teaspoons, cups, pounds, etc. Now, U.S. companies are including metric measurements on their products.

What is the metric system? The metric system is based on multiples of 10, which means it works like a decimal system. By moving the decimal point, small units change to large units and large units change to small. Our money system is based on this type of system. For example, one dollar is written as $1.00. Move that decimal point one space to the left, and you have ten cents, $.10. One cent is written as $.01.

The metric system has basic units for weight, volume, size, and temperature. The following chart will help you understand these metric units.

Metrics

What Are You Measuring?	Unit	Symbol
Weight of ingredients	gram	g
Volume of ingredients	liter	L
Length, width, and depth	meter	m
Temperature	° Celsius	°C

The metric system uses prefixes to show smaller or larger amounts of these basic units.

Prefix	Amount	Symbol
milli	1/1000	m
centi	1/100	c
kilo	1000	k

The prefixes are combined with the metric units to denote the amount or size. For instance, a centimeter is 1/100 of a meter. A kilogram is 1000 grams. The symbol for the prefix is used with the unit for an abbreviated form of the term. Centimeter becomes cm. Milliliter is mL. Kilogram is kg.

Ingredient Substitutions

Every once in awhile you'll get caught. You'll be already preparing a food only to discover you don't have one of the ingredients. What do you do? Give up on the project? Take the time to go to the store? Find the closest neighbor? Those are options, but you also can look around your own kitchen for substitutions. Not all ingredients can be substituted, but the list in the Appendix shows you which ones are the most successful. You need to realize, though, that recipes are developed with specific ingredients to give them a desired taste or texture. By changing the ingredients, you will change the final product.

Salads and other food mixtures are easy to increase or decrease to fit the size of the group. Why can you "stretch" a salad easily?

Room for One More?

Changing the size of a recipe requires careful attention to small details. Have you ever decided to bake a cake for just yourself and a friend, so you didn't want to bake a large one? After using just half of the required ingredients of the recipe or mix, you baked the batter in the pan called for in the instructions. To your dismay, the result was not moist, light, and fluffy, but dry, flat, and slightly burned. Successful changing of a recipe's size depends on the type of recipe, the equipment involved, and corrected timing.

Baked Products

Baked products that depend upon rising in the oven for a fluffy texture—most breads, cookies, and cakes—need the same proportions of ingredients as in the original amounts listed in the recipe. You cannot increase or decrease one ingredient and still produce the expected

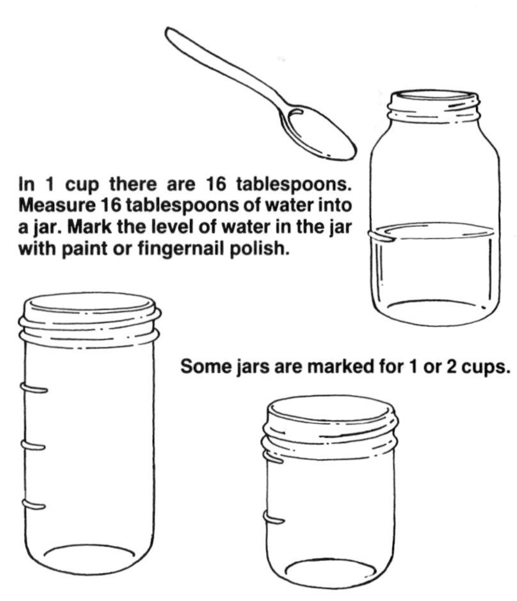

You can use a jar as a measuring cup. Mark the level of 1 cup (250 mL) for accurate measurements.

product. (This does not apply to flavoring ingredients like extracts or nuts.) You might enjoy the pudding-like dessert that resulted when you increased the milk and eggs without increasing the baking powder and flour, but it certainly was not the expected birthday cake.

Unless the recipe breaks easily into an exact half or thirds, you are risking failure to try to decrease the amount. You can, however, double most baked product recipes successfully. Be sure you also increase the size of the baking pans or split the batter between two pans. All of these principles apply to prepackaged mixes as well as making the product from scratch.

Food Mixtures

Recipes for various mixtures of foods such as casseroles, soups, stews, sauces, salads, and desserts can be increased or decreased without affecting the product's quality. The baking time involved should be increased or decreased also. The size of cookware required will change to a smaller size for the decreased recipe and a larger size for the increased recipe.

Meat Roasts

Although you can usually increase the size of your roast, as long as it still fits into your oven, cutting down servings to two or three may result in a dry, tough piece of meat. For two or three servings, try cooking another cut of meat using a different method, maybe panbroiling. You may roast an acceptable size of meat and plan to use the uneaten part for a lunch or another meal. (For food safety, however, refrigerate leftover meat immediately.

Increasing and Decreasing Measurements

Perhaps you can automatically double a recipe by multiplying every ingredient times two in your head, but when you need to decrease a recipe to one third the amount, or one fourth, you must know how measurements are related or their equivalents. See the chart (Appendix) for common equivalent measurements for food. A few minutes spent learning the basic equivalents will save you time and effort in food preparation whether you are working with convenience foods, commercial mixes, or recipes made from scratch.

Correcting for High-Altitude

The chances are that the area in which you live is located at an altitude below 3,000 feet (915 m), because the majority of the populated areas in the United States are at that or even lower altitudes. For that reason, recipes are developed for the atmospheric conditions at that altitude. People who live in areas of the country with higher altitudes adjust food preparation methods and recipes to counteract the effect of the thinner air and lower pressure which causes water to boil and evaporate at a lower temperature. Every 500-foot (153 m) increase in altitude causes water to boil at a 1°F lower (0.5°C) temperature. Although water boils at a lower temperature, foods cook more slowly because they are not cooking at as high a temperature. That would be like turning down the heat on your burner permanently and having to cook everything on low heat. Food does not cook as fast at a lower temperature, so at higher altitudes cooking times have to be increased.

On the other hand, leavened products that are baked in the oven rise faster because of the lower air pressure. To counteract this, any leavening agents (yeast, baking powder, soda) are decreased slightly and the liquids are increased. In addition to those modifications, the oven temperature is usually increased. It often takes "trial and error" to adjust the modifications for a specific area to determine the appropriate amount of increase or decrease in ingredients and temperature settings. You can contact your local county extension service for help.

Mixing ingredients by beating them with an electric or hand rotary beater is an efficient method for combining and incorporating air into the mixture.

Breading ingredients by dipping the food into a liquid or beaten egg and then into a flour or crumb mixture provides the base for a crisp, cooked crust.

Food Preparation Terms

baste: to moisten meat or other foods with a liquid while cooking to add flavor and to prevent drying of the surface. Usually meat drippings, melted fat, sauces, fruit juices, or syrups are used. Handy tools include baster or brush.

beat: to make a mixture smooth or to incorporate air into a mixture using a circular motion. Tools include a mixing spoon, wire whisk, rotary beater, electric mixer.

blanch: to dip a food in boiling water or steam for a short time. Blanching is used to soften skin for easy removal (such as on a tomato or peach) or to treat fresh foods before freezing to stop the enzyme action that would deteriorate the food during storage in the freezer.

blend: to mix two or more ingredients until thoroughly combined.

braise: to cook meat or poultry slowly in a covered utensil with some liquid.

bread: to cover a food with fine crumbs. Food can be dipped first in a liquid or milk-and-egg mixture to help crumbs adhere to the surface.

brown: to turn food's surface brown through applied heat from frying, broiling, or baking.

brush: to spread a coating of sauce, fat, or glaze on the surface of a food with a brush, soft cloth, or paper towel.

caramelize: to heat sugar or a food with a high concentration of sugar slowly until it turns brown and develops the characteristic caramel flavor.

chill: to remove the heat from a food by placing it in a refrigerator until it is cold throughout.

chop: to cut food into small, uniform pieces. Tools include a knife, French knife, food chopper.

coat: to cover a food with another ingredient such as flour, cornmeal, bread crumbs, or sugar by dipping, rolling, or shaking the food in a paper bag with the other ingredient.

cool: to let heated food stand at room temperature until it reaches room temperature.

core: to remove the central portion of seeds and/or hard materials from fruits and vegetables.

cream: to work one or more foods until soft and smooth with a spoon rubbing against the side of a bowl or by using a rotary beater.

cube: to cut into small squares—usually about ½-inch (1.25 cm) cubes.

cut in: to distribute small pieces of fat evenly throughout dry ingredients using a pastry blender or two crossed table knives in a scissors-like motion.

dice: to cut into small cubes—smaller than

those for instruction "to cube." Tools include French knife.

dilute: to add water to another liquid.

dissolve: to mix a solid ingredient such as a sugar with a liquid until they form a solution.

dot: to place small pieces of an ingredient over a surface.

drain: to separate a liquid from a food. Tools include a strainer, colander.

dredge: to coat a food with a dry ingredient such as flour.

dust: to lightly sprinkle a coating of dry particles such as flour or sugar.

flake: to separate layered sections of a food, such as cooked fish.

flour: to dust the surface lightly with flour.

flute: to decorate the edge of a food such as the edge of a pie crust pastry, with a wavey shape.

fold in: to combine two ingredients or mixtures by gently cutting down through a mixture around the bottom, back up to the surface, and across the top in an up-and-down circular motion that does not leave the mixture until it is well blended. Tools include a scraper or large wooden spoon.

fricassee: to cook by braising when referring to fowl, veal or rabbit.

garnish: to add another touch of food to a prepared food for decorating with color, texture, or contrast.

glaze: to coat with a thin syrup.

grate: to rub food through the cutting blades of a grater to make various sizes of small pieces.

grease: to rub a surface with fat or oil.

knead: to manipulate dough with the hands by pressing with the palms and folding until the dough becomes smooth and elastic.

marinate: to let stand in a specified mixture for a specified length of time for flavor and/or tenderizing.

melt: to convert a solid to a liquid with heat.

mince: to cut food into very small pieces. Tools include a French knife, knife, chopper, or scissors.

mix: to combine two or more ingredients. Tools include a mixing spoon, wire whisk, rotary beater, electric mixer.

mold: to shape a food. Tools include hands or shaped mold.

pare: to cut off the thinnest possible layer of peel. Tools include paring knife or vegetable peeler.

peel: to pull off the rind or outer covering of an orange, banana, pomegranate, etc.

pit: to remove seeds from fruits.

puree: to force food through a fine strainer to make a pulp. Tools include a strainer, blender, or food processor.

reconstitute: to add water to a concentrated food to return it to its original state, as in frozen juices.

reduce: to cook a liquid food product such as a sauce or a liquid until enough moisture evaporates to concentrate the remaining sauce or liquid.

rehydrate: to soak or cook dried food in liquid to replace the water removed in drying.

scald: to heat a liquid just to the simmering point. Milk is scalded for several cooking preparations by heating until bubbles form around the edge of the cookware.

score: to make very straight cuts in the surface of a food, usually in parallel lines. Ham and bread dough are often scored on the surface. A knife is the tool used.

scrape: to remove a small amount of the outside surface by rubbing the surface with a knife.

sear: to brown a meat surface quickly with high heat.

shred: to tear or cut food into thin strips.

sift: to force a dry ingredient through a fine sieve. Tools include sifter, strainer.

skim: to remove a film from the surface of a liquid such as fat from syrup or foam from hot jelly. Tools include slotted spoon, skimmer.

steep: to let stand in hot liquid below the boiling point to extract flavor and color.

stir: to mix ingredients using a circular motion.

toast: to brown in a toaster or oven.

toss: to tumble ingredients lightly. Tools include fork and spoon used together.

whip: to beat rapidly to incorporate air to increase volume and fluffiness. Tools include wire whisk, rotary beater, electric mixer.

You can chop small amounts of food faster than a food processor when you acquire the skill of using a French knife. Hold the point down with your fingertips of one hand and rock the knife over the pile of food. Scrape the pile back together with the blade and chop again until the pieces are as small as you need. This is an ideal way to chop herbs.

Large pieces of fat or shortening can be blended into flour by cutting the fat using a chopping motion with a pastry blender or two knives in a scissor-like motion. Keeping half of the pieces about the size of a pea allows for flakiness in a baked product such as pie crust. The other half of the mixture can be cut into the texture of coarse cornmeal.

You can use your fingers to flute (shape) the edge of a pie crust into an attractive scalloped pattern.

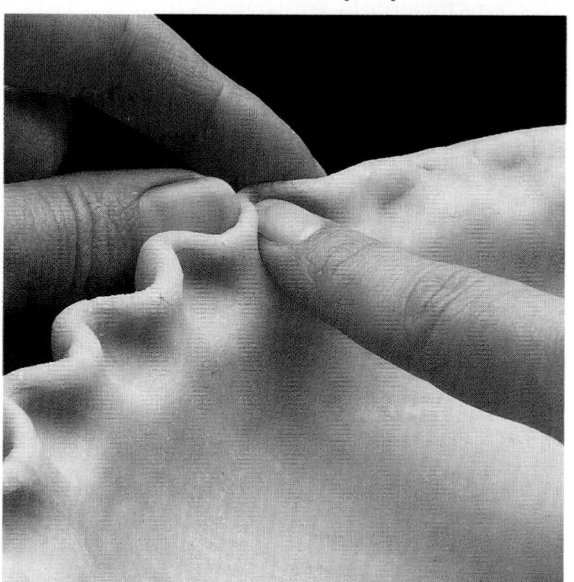

The vegetable peeler saves more vegetable than paring with a knife.

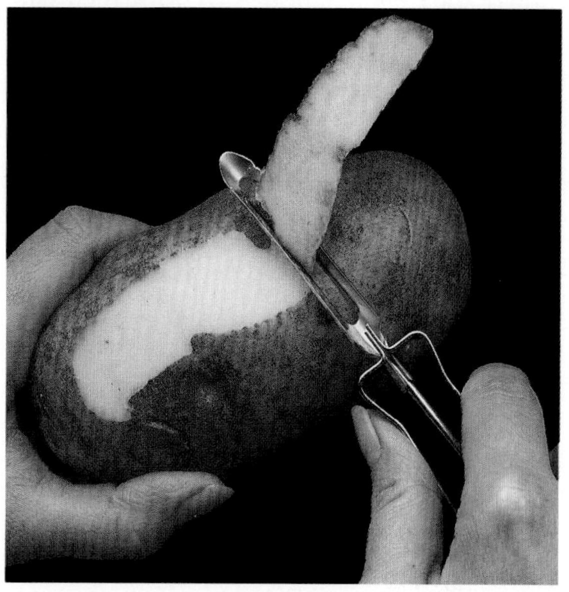

Scoring the top of bread dough before baking gives it an attractive appearance and helps it rise more evenly.

Flour is sifted to fluff up the particles after they have settled in the container. By sifting each time you measure flour, you get more consistent measurements.

Cooking Methods

Many foods require cooking—the application of some form of heat—to ensure their safety, tenderness, and variety and to bring out the flavor. Choosing the method of cooking is based upon a principle of cooking for that particular food, personal preference, available equipment, and time. Guidelines for cooking specific foods will be discussed in Chapters 10 through 18. Generally, however, cooking methods can be classified into four basic types:

1. Cooking in liquid
2. Cooking with a moist heat
3. Cooking in fat
4. Cooking with dry heat

Cooking in Liquid

Methods of cooking in liquid include boiling, simmering, poaching, and stewing.

Boiling

Boiling is the highest temperature water can reach with simple application of heat. Water boils at 212°F (100°C) at the average sea level. The temperature of that water will never rise above the 212°F (100°C), regardless of how long or hard you boil it. (Adding another substance such as sugar to water to form solutions can raise the boiling temperature.) A rapid boiling creates a vigorous bubbling action, while a slow, rolling boil creates less movement of the liquid.

When cooking pieces of food at a fast boil, they collide and break up. Tender foods such as fruits, fish, and most vegetables tend to break apart, overcook, and lose shape, color, flavor, and important nutrients during boiling. Of all the cooking methods, prolonged fast boiling is responsible for the most destruction of vitamins and loss of minerals from the food. Some of the losses from boiling food are due to the evaporation of water which takes nutrients and moisture away from the food.

High heat also toughens proteins. Foods high in protein such as eggs, poultry, and meat also toughen with the prolonged high heat involved in boiling.

Stewing

When foods are stewed, they are cooked at the same temperature as simmering, but in a larger amount of liquid. Stewing is a long, slow process that is ideal for tenderizing less tender cuts of meat and poultry. Potatoes and other starchy vegetables are added to thicken the liquid. The final mixture resembles a very hearty soup.

To stew, add the unheated liquid, meat or poultry, vegetables, dried beans or peas, and seasonings to a heavy pan with a tight-fitting lid. Bring it to a slow simmer and cook until the ingredients are completely tender.

Simmering

Simmering food involves cooking food in liquid that never reaches the boiling stage, about 186° to 200°F (90°C). Compared to boiling, simmering is a peaceful, less violent motion of the water. When a food is cooked by simmering, the pieces move gently around in the liquid because the bubbles rise slowly but do not break the surface. The temperature is hot enough to cook, but fewer nutrients are lost through physical breakup of the food, high heat, and evaporation.

Poaching

Poaching foods involves cooking foods at the same temperature as simmering, but in a small amount of liquid so that the food stays in its original shape. To poach, bring the liquid to

Stewing foods is a long, slow cooking method of simmering food in liquid. It brings out the flavor of individual foods for a delicious, hearty mixture, such as this steaming meat and vegetable stew.

the simmering point and gently place the food in the liquid. Cook until the food reaches the desired stage of softness, but still holds its shape. Food also can be placed in the cold liquid and slowly brought to a simmer. Some foods are so delicate it is wise to use a porous material (such as cheesecloth) to hold the food while putting the food in and out of the water.

Moist-Heat Cooking

Like cooking in liquid, moist-heat cooking involves liquid, just not as much liquid. The various methods of moist-heat cooking utilize a pan with a tight-fitting lid and a little liquid. Moist-heat cooking is another excellent way to prepare less tender cuts of meat and poultry. In addition to preparing meats and poultry with these methods, vegetables and fish can be turned into tender, succulent dishes by braising or steaming.

The types of moist-heat cooking include braising and steaming.

Braising

To braise meat and poultry, choose a pan that just fits the amount of food to be cooked. The right size pan allows the liquid that condenses on the inside of the lid to fall back on the food. This is what makes braising an excellent cooking technique.

The meat or poultry is first browned in a small amount of heated fat. The food is then added to the pot along with seasonings and approximately 1/2 cup (125 mL) liquid. It is simmered over low heat until the meat or poultry is tender. Large, cut pieces of vegetables can be added during the last 15 minutes of cooking to make a tasty meal.

Steaming

When food is cooked by steaming, it does not actually touch the water. Rather it is held up out of the simmering water with a steaming rack or colander, and the steam cooks the food. Steaming is well suited to tender fish, poultry, and meat. It is especially ideal for vegetables because the water-soluble nutrients are not lost in the simmering water.

To steam foods, place the food on the steaming rack or in the colander. Lower the rack or colander into the pan and add the liquid. The liquid may be water, milk, juice, or a seasoned bouillon. Cover the pan with a tight-fitting lid or aluminum foil. Bring the liquid to a simmer. Cook only until the food is tender. Do not overcook. Steamed vegetables retain their bright color and are not waterlogged.

Cooking in Fat

People sometimes think that cooking in fat is not healthy because of the cholesterol in fat and the extra calories. With the use of polyunsaturated vegetable oils in cooking, the concern over cholesterol and saturated fats is reduced. Also, cooking in fat can mean cooking in a little or a lot of fat, so extra calories can be avoided. In fact, stir-frying is one method of cooking in fat—and it's one that health-conscious cooks enjoy.

Because fat reaches a higher temperature than water, foods cooked in fat become crisper. Some people feel this makes the food more flavorful. Cooking in fat is a full-flavored way to prepare meats, eggs, poultry, fish, vegetables, and even fruits. The methods of cooking in fat include panfrying (often called sautéing), deep-fat frying, and stir-frying.

Panfrying

Panfrying or sautéing is the "classic" way of cooking eggs, chicken, and fish. Fried chicken is a favorite in many families and almost everyone has had a sunny-side-up egg fried in butter. Panfrying meat is a simple preparation and an easy way to prepare the American favorite—the hamburger.

To panfry chicken and fish, the food is often first coated with a batter and crumbs to create a crispy crust. Eggs are panfried without a coating, and meat usually is, too. Sometimes meat

Tempura, a popular Japanese dish, is prepared by dipping the food in a light batter and then frying until crispy.

is coated before frying and then is called chicken-fried steak.

Using a frypan, heat a small amount of fat until it is melted but not bubbling. The melted fat should cover the bottom of the skillet. Because you are cooking protein foods, use low heat. This also will prevent the fat from getting too hot and burning.

Slip the food into the pan, being careful not to burn yourself with spattering grease. Fish, poultry, and meat are browned on one side and then turned over and cooked until done. Eggs are fried on one side only unless you want them "over easy," in which case they are turned gently so the yolk does not break.

Deep-Fat Frying

Deep-fat frying requires enough fat to completely cover the food being cooked. The fat must be heated to a temperature high enough to quickly cook the food without causing it to soak up the fat. If the temperature is too high, it will overcook the food on the outside before the inside has a chance to completely cook. Very high temperatures can ignite the fat. If the fat reaches a high enough temperature to smoke, the fat breaks down and develops an acrid flavor that ruins the food and the oil.

This cooking method can pose several problems in the kitchen. Care must be taken to avoid spattering grease and starting a grease fire or burning yourself with the hot grease. A large, heavy pot that is steady on the stove top will help prevent the dangerous situation of overturning the pot. If a fire does occur, smother it with a lid or another pan to remove the oxygen. You also can use a fire extinguisher. Never use water. It scatters the fire and makes it worse.

French fries are a longtime popular deep-fat fried food. Now, in recent years, other vegetables such as zucchini, onions, mushrooms, and carrots are being served deep-fried and finding wide acceptance. Deep-fat fried seafood is another favorite.

To deep-fat fry foods, use a deep pot and fill it about halfway with fat or oil. Using a thermometer, bring the fat to the temperature listed in the recipe you are using. Add the food carefully with tongs or a long-handled slotted spoon. When the food is cooked, remove it from the fat with tongs or a slotted spoon. Drain off excess fat by placing the food on a paper towel.

Stir-Frying

Stir-frying is commonly used in China and Japan. It is popular there because the food cooks quickly, which means little of the scarce fuel is needed. Stir-frying has become popular in America now because it allows time-conscious cooks to prepare meals in a hurry. In addition, stir-frying is the way to enjoy vegetables and other foods at their crispy best. Very little fat or oil is used, and the quick cooking brings out the natural, flavorful goodness of foods.

Quick cooking in a small amount of fat requires a very hot pan with a wide cooking surface. The Chinese pan called a **wok** is best for stir-frying, but a frypan will also work. The wok features high sides and a rounded bottom. They are useful for holding cooked foods away from the hottest part of the wok while the other foods finish cooking.

Foods to be stir-fried are cut into small pieces to allow them to cook quickly. The preparation time of cutting the foods actually takes longer than the cooking time. Once the food is cut up, a small amount of oil is heated in the frypan or wok. The foods that will take the longest to cook are added first. The other foods are then added. The foods are gently tossed or stirred to keep them from sticking. Vegetables are cooked only until slightly tender. Properly cooked vegetables still retain their "crunch."

Cooking with Dry Heat

Do you live in an area of the country that is dry or humid? If you have experienced both types of climates, you know the difference between cooking with moist heat and cooking with dry heat. When you cook with moist heat, the food is steamed by the heated water. With dry heat cooking, no liquid is used and the food cooks only with its own moisture or juices. The methods of dry heat cooking include baking or roasting and grilling or broiling.

Baking or Roasting

Baking and roasting both refer to the same method of cooking food in an oven. The technical difference in the words relates to the type of food being cooked. Meats and poultry are roasted. Breads, cakes, pies, vegetables, fish, and fruits are baked.

Roasting is a word that has changed in meaning during this country's history. Historically, roasting referred to cooking food in front of a heat source with free air circulation on all sides—much like roasting a hot dog on a stick. The meat often was skewered on a spit and turned occasionally to ensure even cooking. Today, food cooked in an oven is referred to as "roasted." Even though oven roasting uses dry heat, there is more moisture in a closed oven than with an open-heat source. That is why foods cooked outdoors seem to taste better and crisper—they are! Even so, meats and poultry roasted in an oven can produce taste-tempting delights. Because no fat or liquid is used, roasting is a method suitable only for tender cuts of meat and poultry.

Recipes often require your knowing many different cooking terms. Read through the recipe for this spicy burrito. Can you find at least 10 of the terms that call for "learning the language" of the kitchen?

Spicy Sausage Burritos

Yield: 8 burritos

Traditional	**Ingredients**	**Metric**
16-oz. can	Refried beans*	500 g
1 lb.	Bulk pork sausage	500 g
1 medium	Tomato, coarsely chopped	1 medium
1 Tbsp.	Chili powder	15 mL
1 Tbsp.	Vinegar	15 mL
1 clove	Garlic, finely chopped	1 clove
½ tsp.	Salt	3 mL
¼ tsp.	Ground cinnamon	1 mL
8 10-inch	Flour tortillas	8 25 cm
1 cup	Monterey Jack cheese, shredded	250 mL

Directions

1. Heat refried beans. Cook and stir pork sausage in 10-inch (25 cm) skillet until light brown; drain.

2. Stir in tomato, chili powder, vinegar, garlic, salt, and cinnamon. Heat to boiling; reduce heat.

3. Simmer uncovered, stirring occasionally, until thickened, about 10 minutes.

4. Soften tortillas one at a time in ungreased hot skillet, about 30 seconds on each side.

5. Spread about ⅓ cup (75 mL) refried beans over each hot tortilla.

6. Spoon about ¼ cup (50 mL) sausage mixture onto center of tortilla. Fold slices over and roll from bottom.

7. Place seam sides down in ungreased jelly roll pan, 15½ x 1 inch (39 x 2.5 cm). Cook uncovered in 350°F (175°C) oven until hot, about 20 minutes.

* You can use the recipe in Chapter 2.

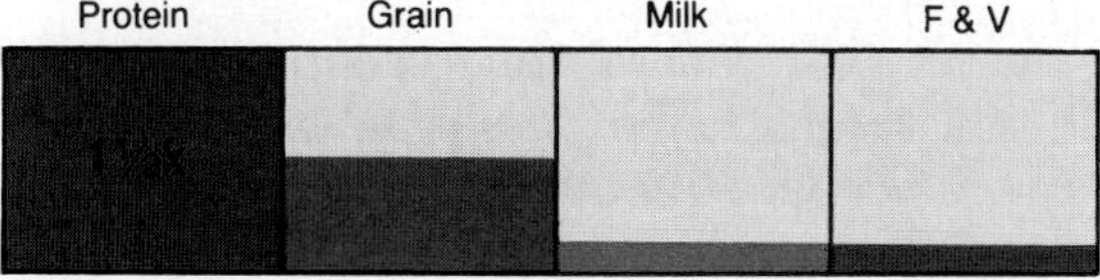

Safety Tip

Grilling foods outdoors requires a few safety precautions. Do not wear loose clothing that may catch fire. Do not put the grill indoors or in an enclosed area such as a garage. The fumes can be very harmful.

If a fire should start in the grill from fat falling on the coals, douse the flames with water. Try not to get your food all wet in the process.

In the oven, place the food on the broiler pan. For grilling, the food may be placed directly on the grill, except for tender fish which may break apart and fall on the coals. In that case, place the fish on foil. Foods without much fat, such as fish, fruits, and poultry, can be lightly brushed with oil before broiling or grilling.

To broil, preheat the broiler. To grill, have the coals white hot. Because the temperature of the heat cannot be controlled with this method of cooking, the way you control the cooking of foods is to vary the distance the food is from the heat. Thicker pieces of food are placed farther from the heat source. Thin foods that will cook quickly are placed closer.

To roast meat and poultry, place the food in a shallow baking pan without a lid. Using a lid would cause moisture from the food to condense and create steam. That would then make it moist-heat cooking. Recipes specify how long to cook meat or poultry according to the weight.

Broiling or Grilling

Broiling and grilling also refer to the same type of cooking. The terms differ according to where the cooking is done. If you prepare food in your kitchen under the broiler in your oven, the food is broiled. If you cook outside on the grill, the food is grilled. Once again, use only tender cuts of meat or poultry, fish, vegetables, and fruits.

Learning the Fine Points of Cooking

As simple as a recipe's easy-to-follow instructions may look, experience will show you that there is no substitute for understanding why ingredients combine or cook the way they do. Have you ever tried to beat cold egg whites or to whip warm whipping cream? See Chapter 12 for the reasons those methods don't work well.

Food preparation is based on scientific principles that can help you to predict whether a recipe will work. In the following food preparation chapters, you will learn the why behind food preparation methods while you learn how to prepare various food products.

Vocabulary Review

Recipe
Boil
Stew
Simmer
Poach
Braise
Steam
Pan fry
Deep-fat fry
Stir-fry
Wok
Bake
Roast
Broil
Grill

Questions for Review

1. What is the first step before you start making a recipe?
2. What are the important considerations when increasing or decreasing the recipe size?
3. Why is it important to be consistent in measuring ingredients?
4. If you do not have standardized measuring utensils, how can you adapt your equipment to get standard measurements?
5. What modifications are needed when cooking at higher altitudes?
6. How do you decide what cooking methods to use when preparing foods?
7. Describe the following methods and give examples of an appropriate food to be prepared by each method.

a. cooking in liquid
b. cooking with moist heat
c. cooking with fat
d. cooking with dry heat

Things to Do

1. Collect recipes from magazines, newspapers, friends, and other sources and analyze them. Are they well written?
2. You are going on a camping trip and will not have standard measuring equipment. Make a set of measuring devices from items that would be available on the camping trip.
3. Divide into groups. Each group bakes a cake as follows:

a. Make a standard recipe.
b. Divide the recipe in half.
c. Double the recipe.

Compare the results and discuss what adjustments were needed in ingredients, cookware, and baking time.

Section 4

Foods: Now and Then

7 Quick And Easy Foods

Easy Does It

Nothing says "Home Sweet Home" quite like the rich aroma of freshly prepared foods wafting from the kitchen. However, times have changed and the amount of free time most people have has also changed. What remains the same is your pleasant satisfaction from creating a terrific fresh food that brings grateful raves from your friends or family. You probably have discovered by now, however, that freshly baked aromas do not have to come from long hours in the kitchen. You can plan more variety and satisfaction into meals by taking advantage of convenience foods in many different ways. Sometimes you will be showing the best judgment by not choosing to make food products from scratch.

Taking Shortcuts

You can battle a lack of time and still create interesting foods by taking shortcuts using convenience foods in your cooking. Foods that have been partially or completely prepared offer a convenience to you.

Perhaps the first convenience food was the invention of baking powder for the "convenience" of the baker in the late 1800s. Next probably was the ready-to-eat food from cans followed by boxed cake mixes. All of those foods are so commonplace to you now, you probably don't even think of them as any special help. However, they seemed like little miracles to the homemaker when each was first introduced.

Convenience foods are now so plentiful in the supermarkets, it is almost difficult to find any food that has not had some "helpful" preparation on its way to you. Even a head of lettuce has been stripped of its damaged outer leaves and washed!

Cost of Convenience

You may have been saved some of the work, but someone had to complete the labor involved in preparing convenience foods. Labor costs money, and you pay the extra price for that service when you buy the product.

The custom packaging that catches your eye in the supermarket adds to the cost of convenience foods, too. Advertising, to let you know the product exists and to motivate you to use it, also costs money. That is why **generic products,** products with no brand-name identity, cost less than name-brand products. There is no advertising costs added on to the product.

Realize, though, that when thousands of packages of an advertised convenience food are sold, the service and advertising costs are spread out over those millions of dollars. Therefore the cost to you may be small. However, you need to be aware of what you are paying for. You might be buying a "service" that you really don't need or that is not worth the extra price.

You also might be happily surprised to find that sometimes purchasing the ingredients separately costs more than the convenience product. Cakes mixes usually cost less than making the product from the individual ingredients. **Unit pricing,** pricing that figures the cost per ounce, item, or other package size, helps you to compare the cost of different-sized items or different brands. Some stores help you by posting the unit price on the shelves near the products. Be aware and you will not have to beware of convenience costs.

Using Convenience Foods

Have you ever wanted to make a favorite recipe for a meal or treat, but gave up the idea because you didn't have the time? By taking advantage of convenience foods for some of the ingredients in a recipe, you can be the cook you want to be. For example, a favorite casserole might call for fresh chopped carrots, potatoes, and small onions. You can use frozen mixed whole vegetables from the bag.

That was a simple solution, but what if you wanted to make a Black Forest Cake recipe (such as the one on page 150), but didn't have the time or the individual ingredients? You could "shortcut" by using a chocolate cake mix and cherry pie filling with prewhipped frozen whipped topping that you have on hand. If the pie filling on hand turned out to be apple, you may want to substitute the apple for the cherry or even change the flavor of the cake mix. If it turns out well, you would have discovered the trick of using a recipe for an "inspiration" to create and substitute from convenience foods on hand. Planning meals sometimes means making plans quickly to adapt to the time on hand. Even so, it is still planning and planning takes skill and practice. You will learn more about meal planning in Chapter 19.

Handy Convenience Products

Its good sense to keep some convenience foods on hand for emergencies, such as friends dropping by around dinner, or to have for the times you "feel" like cooking "up a storm." The following are some basic cabinet-stocking suggestions.

Cake and quick bread mixes can be combined with canned pie fillings, applesauce, and fresh fruits for original and nutritious quick treats. You can use the time saved for decoratively shaping the cakes or adding personalized toppings on healthful muffins.

Grated cheese is a real timesaver and adds a colorful, nutritious touch to salads, vegetables, casseroles, and many other dishes. Frozen and canned fruits and vegetables can help you meet your need for a balanced daily diet. They are also very useful for the occasions when unexpected guests drop in around dinnertime. Of course, fresh fruits and vegetables just washed and served as snacks or part of a meal make some of the best "convenience foods." In Chapters 10-18, you will learn other helpful hints on making convenience foods of your own to keep on hand.

Fresh baked bread with no additives like "grandma used to make" can come from a boxed mix or frozen dough already shaped into loaves. These breads smell divine and can be "doctored" to turn into garlic, herb, cheese, cinnamon, or honey bread with a few flicks of the wrist when you sprinkle on the added ingredients before baking. The dough can be shaped to look festive. You can create eye-catching centerpieces that can be eaten later, but provide a creative holder for fruit, soup in a bowl, or crackers. What are some other ideas? See page 151 for some of the other quick-shaping ideas you might try with frozen breads.

Add up the prices for the individual ingredients of a box mix like these brownies with cream cheese added. Cake-type mixes are often one convenience food that costs less than regular recipes.

New Trends in Convenience Foods

Do you ever have a tight schedule when you can't work in dinner with the family, but would love to have a complete hot meal? One of the newest trends in convenience foods is the "gourmet" type complete meals of high-quality foods and recipes. Some are quite expensive compared to the TV dinners of the last few decades. However, they are less expensive than eating out. A few even include stylish baking-serving dishes. Companies are introducing complete lines of these dinners with a dozen or more different menus from which to choose. Seven minutes in the microwave or 50 minutes in the oven and you have a decent, balanced meal!

The other half of that trend is the slim-line or low-calorie version of the meals. These convenience foods supposedly offer a meal for less than 300 calories. Consumer research has shown that some of these offerings are slightly more than 300 calories, but the most significant finding is related to serving sizes. Basically, smaller portions of the low-calorie dinners are given, but the price is the same as for the regular meals. They are usually lower calorie because the serving size is smaller. You are

Take advantage of convenience products such as frozen dough to create quick fancy breads and gourmet decorative accents.

paying more because you are getting less. The same was noted for other low-calorie prepared foods in the frozen foods line. You can see that the best practice for getting a good buy is to read the label and to compare values for size and nutrient content.

The convenient, easy-to-use packaging and serving containers with portioned food helps to give you ideas about making your own instant gourmet meals. Why not save the containers, or use plastic plates and make your own dinners when you prepare a regular meal? Make an extra portion or two, wrap it tightly with clear freezer wrap, and put it in the freezer. You can stack several of these meals for easy retrieval and identification. Create your own convenience!

Labels: Your Guide to Good Value

Some of the best advertising that gives you good information are the labels of food products. By carefully reading labels, you can be assured of what you are purchasing. You will know what the ingredients in the product are, the contents or weight of the food, how to store the food, and who manufactures the product. What's on a label?

• Ingredients. The label on food products lists the ingredients in the food. If more than one ingredient is used, the ingredient present in the greatest amount is listed first. This is very helpful when you are determining the nutrient content of a food. For instance, if sugar is listed first on the label, you know the food contains more sugar than anything else. Would that food be a healthful choice based on what you know about the U.S.RDA? Some products, such as catsup, do not have to include a list of ingredients. Why? Because of a regulation of the Food and Drug Administration (FDA). The FDA has established certain ingredients that can be used in common foods. This is known as a **standard of identity.**

• Net weight or contents. Have you ever purchased a large bag of potato chips or cookies only to be surprised by how few were actually in the package? Would another package possibly have contained more? Reading the label to find out the net weight or contents of the package is the way to compare the actual amount of food you are getting in each brand of a product. Unit pricing allows you to compare the price differences of products so you can find the better buy.

• Storage directions. Foods that need to be kept in the refrigerator or freezer are so labeled. These perishable foods that spoil easily require proper storage. Labels on canned foods or foods that do not spoil quickly do not need to have storage instructions.

• Other information. Food labels also may tell you how to prepare a convenience food. Cooking times or special microwave instructions may be included. Foods that are inspected and graded by the USDA are so noted on the packaging.

Gourmet-type prepared frozen foods have improved since their introduction. Different brands of this type of product vary greatly in quality and price, so compare, or try freezing your own!

Consumer Protection

What's to prevent a food manufacturer from falsely advertising its product or mislabeling it? Laws. The FDA is the government agency that checks the accuracy of food labels and makes sure the manufacturers include the required information. The Federal Trade Commission (FTC) is a government agency that is responsible for false advertising claims made by any company. The FTC is the agency that receives complaints from consumer groups interested in guarding against false advertising. Because of FTC's actions on certain ads, many claims have been modified or toned down.

To prevent problems in labeling, the FDA has developed a set of guidelines for labeling. They include the following:

- Labels need to be educational.
- Claims that are made need to backed up with research.
- No single food can be emphasized as the "cure-all" for health problems and dietary needs. A balanced diet must be encouraged.

You can help advertisers present the type of labeling you want and need by carefully reading the labels. If you find statements you feel are untrue or find labels that do not include all the necessary information, contact the FTC or your local consumer action groups. The government has provided you the right to truth in advertising. You can take advantage of this service by responsibly reading and using the information given by manufacturers.

Nutritional Labeling

Foods that are enriched or fortified are subject to additional labeling laws. These laws also apply to foods about which the manufacturer makes nutritional claims. Some manufacturers provide nutrition labels even though they are

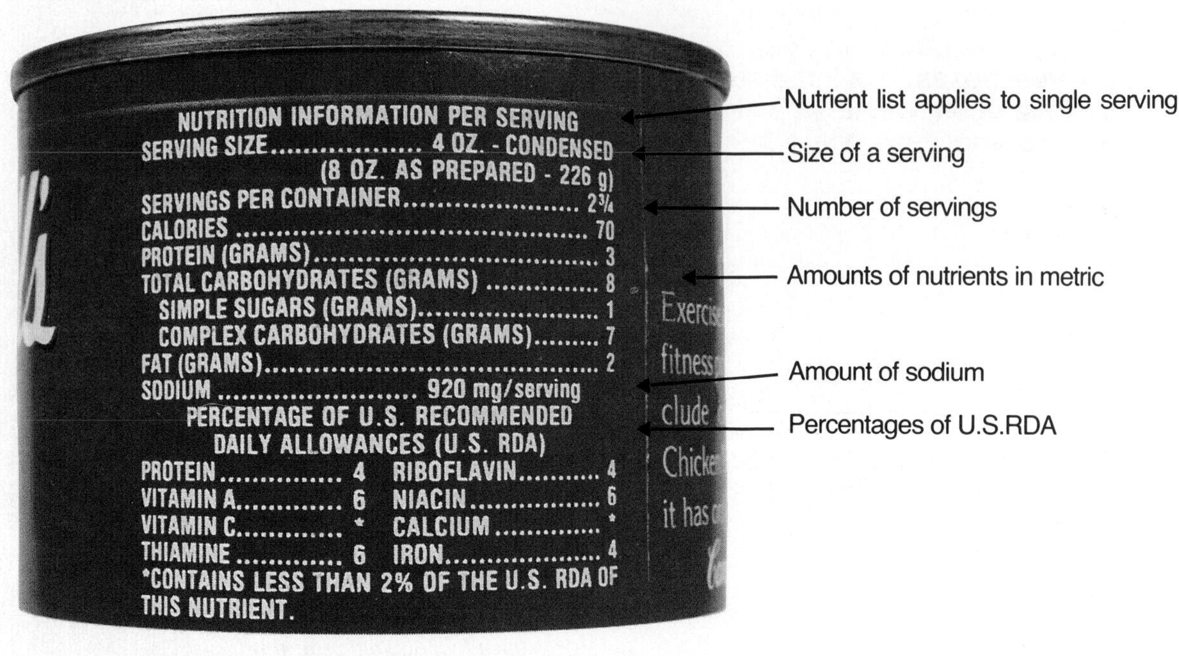

Take your glasses to the grocery store—an amazing amount of help is on the nutrition label.

not required by law to do so. **Nutritional labels** must include the following:

- The serving size of the food product and the number of servings per package or container.
- The amount of calories, protein, carbohydrates, and fats in a serving. The listing for proteins, carbohydrates, and fats is given in grams.
- The percentage of the U.S.RDA included in the food for protein, vitamin A, vitamin C, thiamin, riboflavin, niacin, iron, and calcium. Other nutrients may be listed, but they are not required by law.
- The amount of sodium is listed in milligrams. This information also is based on the size of one serving.

Nutritional labeling is a great benefit to people who are closely watching their intake of such ingredients as sodium. By reading the label, they can choose the product with the least amount of sodium. Can nutrition labels be helpful to others, too? Certainly. By looking at the nutritional content of a food, you can decide how to get the most nutrition value for your food dollar. Instead of risking the purchase of a relatively expensive high-calorie, low nutrient food, you can inform yourself on the spot by reading the label. That pays off in your grocery bill and can mean a balanced budget as well as a balanced diet.

Safety Tip

What's in a package? Product packaging is not just designing a label for a new pasta sauce or artwork for cereal boxes. The Food and Drug Administration wants to make sure the food and over-the-counter drug items you purchase are free from tampering.

The development of tamper-proof packaging alternatives was a result of several deaths in the Chicago area. Seven people had taken over-the-counter capsules that had been poisoned with cyanide. The food and drug industry wanted to reassure the American public that it would be very hard to tamper with a product without the customer noticing. Thus, many different types of packaging were introduced.

Some packaging methods include:

- Bubble Packs—For products protected by bubble packs, both the product and the container are encased in plastic and then mounted on a display card. You must tear or break the plastic in order to remove the product. Some vitamins are sold in bubble packs.
- Strip Packs—Individual dosages of capsules or tablets are sealed in foil or clear plastic. You must break open the individual compartment to get the product.
- Film Wrappers—A transparent film is wrapped around a product. Some brands of bacon are protected by film wrappers. This not only secures the item, but allows you to determine the quality of the product.

No packaging method is completely tamper-proof. Therefore there are steps you can take:

- Food items in cans that are dented or bulging spell disaster. Pay attention to the condition of the can you plan to purchase. Never purchase any item in a dented or bulging container. Check the seals of boxed or bagged items such as cereals and cookies. If a seal is broken, do not purchase the product.
- Check produce and meat or poultry items for loose plastic wrappings. Make sure the plastic is securely wrapped around the food item.
- Train yourself to become observant. Do not purchase anything that has been punctured or otherwise disturbed.

What should you do if you notice a product that has been tampered with in some way? Notify the store manager immediately. The manager will be able to contact the proper authorities regarding the possibility of tampering, and you will be doing yourself and others a good public service!

Black Forest Cherry Cake

Traditional	Ingredients	Metric
2¼ cups	All-purpose flour or cake flour	550 mL
1⅔ cups	Sugar	400 mL
⅔ cup	Cocoa	150 mL
1¼ tsp.	Baking soda	6 mL
1 tsp.	Salt	5 mL
¼ tsp.	Baking powder	1 mL
1¼ cups	Water	300 mL
¾ cup	Shortening	175 mL
2	Eggs	2
1 tsp.	Vanilla	5 mL
	Cherry Filling (see recipe)	
1 bar (4 oz.)	Sweet cooking chocolate	125 g
2 cups	Whipping cream, chilled	500 mL
¼ cup	Sugar	50 mL
	Maraschino cherries	

Directions

1. Heat oven to 350°F (175°C). Generously grease and flour two 9-inch (23-cm) or three 8-inch (20-cm) round layer pans.

2. Beat flour, 1⅔ cups (400 mL) sugar, the cocoa, baking soda, salt, baking powder, water, shortening, eggs, and vanilla in large mixer bowl on low speed, scraping bowl constantly, for 30 seconds. Beat on high speed, scraping bowl occasionally, 3 minutes. Pour batter into pans.

3. Bake until wooden pick inserted in center comes out clean, 30 to 35 minutes. Cool 5 minutes; remove from pans. Cool on wire racks.

4. Prepare Cherry Filling. (See recipe.)

5. With a vegetable parer or thin, sharp knife, slice across chocolate bar with long strokes to form 12 to 14 chocolate curls for garnishing cake. For best results, let chocolate stand in warm place 10 to 15 minutes before slicing. Refrigerate curls until ready to use.

6. Place one cake layer upside down on serving plate.

7. Beat whipping cream and ¼ cup (50 mL) sugar in chilled bowl until stiff peaks form.

8. Spread bottom layer with about two-thirds of the Cherry Filling and 1 cup (250 mL) of the whipped cream. Place other cake layer top side up on the whipped cream. Spread with remaining Cherry Filling.

9. Frost the side and top of cake with the remaining whipped cream.

10. If desired, coarsely shred enough remaining chocolate to measure ½ cup (125 mL). Gently press shredded chocolate onto the sides of the cake. Garnish the top of the cake with chocolate curls and maraschino cherries. Refrigerate until serving time.

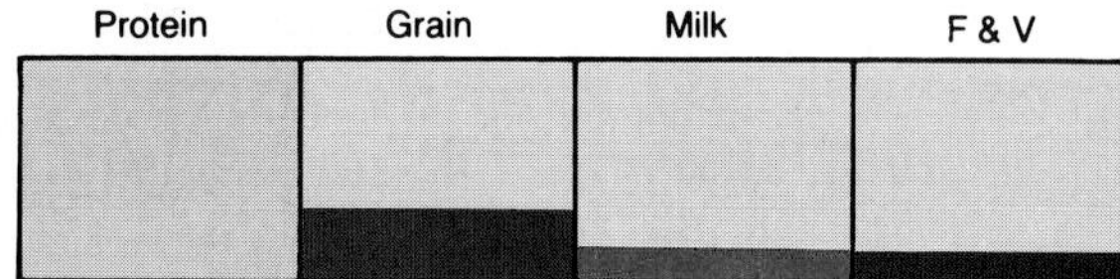

Cherry Filling

Yield: 8, ½ cup (125 mL) servings

Traditional	Ingredients	Metric
½ cup	Sugar	125 mL
3 Tbsp.	Cornstarch	45 mL
1 can (16 oz.)	Pitted red tart cherries*, well-drained (reserve liquid)	500 g
	Few drops red food color (optional)	

Directions

1. Mix sugar and cornstarch in 1-quart (1 L) saucepan.

2. Add enough water to reserved liquid to measure ¾ cup (175 mL); stir into sugar mixture.

3. Cook, stirring constantly, until mixture thickens and boils. Boil and stir 1 minute.

4. Stir in food color.

5. Cut cherries into halves; stir into filling. Refrigerate until completely chilled.

* 1 can (16 oz. [500 g]) pitted dark sweet cherries can be substituted for the red tart cherries and the maraschino cherry garnish; decrease sugar to 2 tablespoons (30 mL).

Protein Grain Milk F & V

Apple Cinnamon Rolls

Traditional	Ingredients	Metric
1 loaf	Frozen whole-wheat bread dough	1 loaf
6 tbsp.	Butter	90 mL
1 tsp.	Cinnamon	5 mL
¼ cup	Honey	50 mL
1 cup	Sliced apple with skin	250 mL

Directions

1. Thaw the bread dough, about 2 hours.
2. Flatten the dough by gently pulling it into a rectangle about ½ inch (1.3 cm) thick.
3. Spread the butter on the rectangle
4. Add the honey and cinnamon on top of the butter.
5. Spread the apple slices evenly over the dough.
6. Roll up the rectangle, starting at a long side.
7. Cut 1 inch (2.5 cm) slices off the long roll and put in a greased or sprayed baking pan.
8. Let rise over the warm stove top while the oven heats to 375°F (190°C).
9. Bake for 20 to 25 minutes.
10. Turn out on a plate and enjoy while warm. Save the cool rolls for lunch or snacks.

Note: You can use many different fillings instead of the apples. Try shredded cheese and chopped nuts, or use a pie filling. You might even want to make it a one-dish meal by adding chopped meat, vegetables, and cheese. What combinations would you like?

Protein Grain Milk F & V

Bread Wreath

Traditional	Ingredients	Metric
2 loaves	White frozen bread dough	2 loaves
	Nonstick spray coating	
1	Egg	1

Directions

1. Thaw the dough.
2. Cut the dough lengthwise into halves, then into fourths, so you end up with eight strips.
3. Working on a sprayed or greased sheet, braid three of the strips. When you come to the end, use three more strips. Shape the long, braided chain into a wreath.
4. Roll the extra strips into a long, thin ribbon. Tie them into a bow and attach over the seam of the start of the braiding.
5. Let rise in a warm place on top of the stove while the oven is heating to 375°F (190°C). Bake when the dough has risen to almost double its size.
6. Bake for about 25 minutes.
7. Remove and brush with a beaten egg. Return to the oven for 5 minutes for a glorious shiny golden glaze.
8. Serve or use as a centerpiece or as a gift.

Note: You can leave off the bow and use the shaped wreath any time of the year or use just one loaf and make a straight braid.

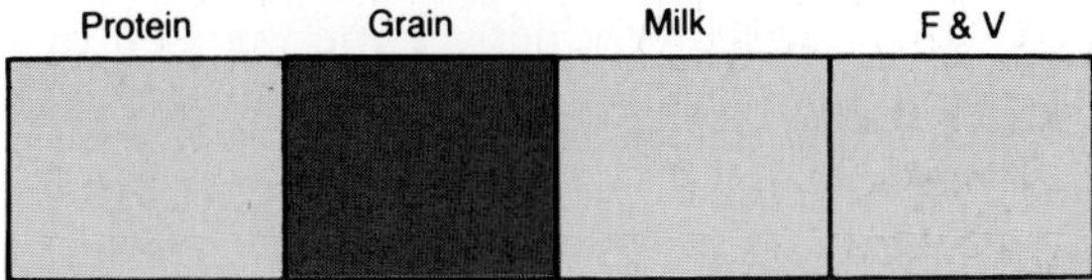

Vocabulary Review

Generic products Standard of identity Nutritional labeling
Unit pricing

Questions for Review

1. What are convenience foods?
2. Describe the historical development of some of the early convenience foods.
3. What are the services you might be paying extra for in partially prepared or prepared food?
4. What are some occasions that often occur when home-prepared food would be welcome, but there isn't enough time? What are some ways you could use convenience foods to allow you to do the cooking?
5. What are some convenience products that might be handy to have for emergencies, such as friends dropping by or a needed quick meal to meet a schedule change? Describe how you might use those products to help solve your needs.
6. How can you use convenience products to develop your own creativity in preparing foods? Give an example.
7. What are some examples of how you can make a chosen recipe in less time by substituting convenience products for ingredients?
8. Labels on food products can provide excellent nutritional and buying information. How can you tell the difference between misleading advertising and factual information?
9. Why do some product's labels *not* have to include a list of ingredients? Give some examples.
10. What information is usually included on a food label?
11. Which ingredient would be listed first on a label for the following foods: A macaroni and cheese mix–macaroni or cheese? Frozen spaghetti and meatballs–spaghetti or meatballs? Could you answer that question without knowing which there was more of, cheese or macaroni, or spaghetti or meat? Why?
12. How does unit pricing help the consumer to find the best buy?
13. Which government agency checks the accuracy of food labels and also makes certain all the required information is included?
14. Which government agency is responsible for false advertising claims made by any company?
15. What are the three FDA guidelines for labeling?
16. Which foods qualify for additional labeling laws?
17. Manufacturers who make nutritional claims for their product are required to supply what type of label?
18. What information is required on all nutritional labels?
19. Are nutritional labels limited to the foods that are required to use them?
20. Why might a consumer be interested in the amount of sodium in a food serving?

Things to Do

1. Select a favorite recipe for a product "made from scratch" that could be made using one or more convenience products. Time yourself making the recipe in the traditional manner using the individual ingredients. Also, time yourself making the recipe, substituting the convenience prod-

uct (or products) for the regular ingredients. What was the savings in time and effort? How did the quality of the two products compare? What was the difference in cost between the two products? What would you conclude from your experience?

2. Select a recipe for yeast bread. Make a loaf using the regular ingredients from scratch. Buy a mix for making yeast bread and make a loaf following the directions on the package. Purchase frozen bread dough and make a loaf from the frozen product. You may make all of the products yourself, or divide the class into teams. Time the products so that they are ready to eat at the same time. Compare the three breads for taste, quality, appearance, texture, and overall quality. Compare the time needed to prepare each of the types of bread. Compare the cost of making each loaf of bread. Rate your products for time, quality, and cost. What are your conclusions about which product you would make again and when?

3. Thaw several loaves of frozen dough. Shape into some creative shapes of your own or copy the suggestions in this chapter. Would you be likely to have the time to make the more time-consuming shapes if you used dough made from scratch? Would you be more likely to be able to experiment creatively by using a convenience product such as bread dough? What are other convenience products that lend themselves to creative and novelty food preparation?

4. Select cans of food from the store shelves that have nutritional labels on them. Select other cans of the same foods that do not have nutritional labeling. Compare them for general information content. Which type of labeling would help you more if you were trying to maintain or lose weight? Explain. Which type of labeling would help you more if you were trying to restrict the use of sodium (salt) in your diet? Why? What are some of the other uses for the nutritional labels that would be helpful to you or your family? Compare the prices. Did the nutritional labeling for the same type of foods cost any more? (Be certain that the products are the same quality and type.)

5. Plan a day's food that supplies 1800 calories for a teenage girl. Be sure to include all of the suggested servings of the Basic Four Food Groups. Select foods from the store shelves that will supply servings that supply the approximate 1800 calories for the day's diet. Which type of labeling made such planning possible? How could you find the information for products that did not have nutritional labels? Which process made it simpler and more accurate for the consumer? Why?

6. List some ways that nutritional labeling might help the consumer to check the nutritional content of a diet that is planned using the Basic Four Food groups as the only guideline. Is it possible to eat all the required servings from the food groups and still not get all of the recommended percentage of each essential nutrient? What are two ways you can help ensure getting all the nutrients you need, but still take advantage of the convenient food group guidelines?

7. Compare cereal boxes for product titles. Why are some products titled supplements instead of cereals? Find two examples of breakfast supplements.

8. Compare cereal labels for sugar content. What does it mean when sugar is listed first in the ingredient contents? How do the cereals with the highest amounts of sugar compare in price to cereals that are not sweetened? What do you think about cereals that taste like chocolate chip cookies or sweetened fruits? What suggestions might you make in a day's eating if the breakfast included a high-sugar cereal?

9. Select several nutritional labels that you considered useful and well designed. Write those companies thanking them for "caring enough" to go to the extra effort and expense of using nutritional information. Explain to the company why you thought their label was well designed. Why do you think it might be worth the time and effort involved for consumers to write to food companies about what is helpful and valuable?

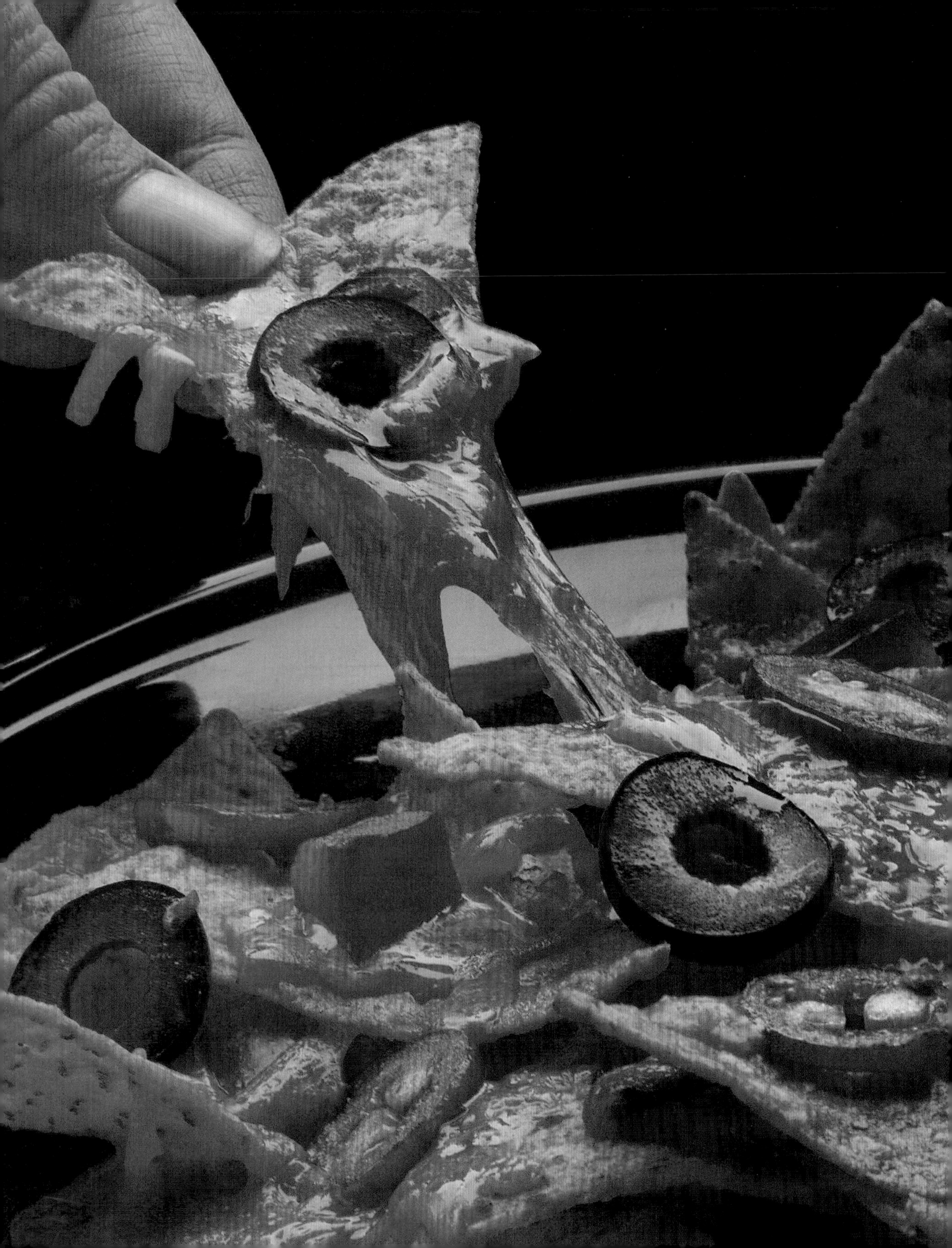

How Do Microwaves Work?

Next time you're listening to your radio, stop and think about how your favorite tunes reach you. A radio station creates radio waves, then broadcasts or sends the waves through the air. When your radio is turned on, it receives those waves and converts them into sound.

A microwave oven works very similarly to a radio station. Instead of sending waves out over a great distance, with a microwave it all happens inside the metal box. The microwave oven is simply a metal box containing a type of miniature, self-contained radio broadcasting system. When the microwave oven is turned on, a **magnetron tube** sends or broadcasts the microwaves through the wave tube guide into the range cavity.

Just as your radio receives or "absorbs" sound waves from a radio station, microwave energy is absorbed by materials. Rather than producing sound, though, **microwaves** produce friction in food molecules. The microwave's friction, rubbing together of molecules, creates heat. In foods, the increase in temperature is rapid and makes it possible to cook foods quickly.

Not all materials absorb microwave energy. Metallic materials, such as oven walls, grids, and screens, largely reflect microwave energy. Glass and many nonmetallic wrapping materials allow microwaves to pass through them. These properties affect which materials can be used in microwaves. You will learn more about this in the section Utensils.

Microwave Safety

Some people are concerned about the safety of microwave ranges. They are fearful of radiation. Microwave ranges will not make food and other materials radioactive. Microwaves are a *non*ionizing form of radiation. Ionizing radiation is radiant energy that can cause molecular changes. X-rays and gamma rays are two forms of the ionizing radiation and should not be confused with the nonionizing form used to create microwaves.

However, you should not be exposed even to the radiation microwaves produce, so safety standards have been established for microwave ranges.

The Food and Drug Administration is the U.S. government agency that monitors the safety of microwave ovens. Government regulations require that there be two safety interlocks on the door so the microwave cannot be operated when the door is open. There have been no documented cases of radiation injury related to microwave appliances when they have been used according to manufacturer's directions. Improper care, such as allowing grease to build up around a door seal, and damage to the door have been identified as causes of leakage on a small scale.

Another safety feature to check on microwaves (as with all appliances) is the Underwriters' Laboratory (UL) Seal of Approval. This seal indicates that an electrical appliance has passed certain tests for fire casualty and electrical safety. Check to be sure your microwave oven has the UL Seal.

Utensils

One of the special features of microwave ovens is the type of cooking utensils they use. Because not every material absorbs microwaves, you can use some things in a microwave oven that you wouldn't use in a conventional oven. For instance, in a microwave oven, you can heat foods on paper plates and use paper towels, too. Imagine what could happen if you did that in a conventional oven set at 425°F (220°C).

An ideal microwave utensil transmits microwave energy. It does not reflect or absorb the microwaves. By transmitting the energy, the utensil helps the food heat, but does not heat up itself. Utensils that are "safe" to use in the microwave oven only become hot when the food being cooked in it transfers heat or steam back to the utensil. Then, it may be necessary to use pot holders to remove the dish from the microwave oven.

Many manufacturers label their products "microwave safe" or "suitable for microwaving." If you want to use a utensil that is not so labeled, test it first.

To test a utensil for microwave cooking, place the empty utensil and a glass cup with 1/2 to 1 cup (125 to 250 mL) of water in the microwave. Microwave on high for 1 minute. Feel the utensil. If the utensil is cool to the touch, it has transmitted the microwave energy and is safe for use in the microwave oven. If the utensil is warm or hot, it has absorbed some of the microwaves and would not be a microwave safe utensil.

Glass materials that are safe for microwave cooking are heatproof glass, ceramic, glass ceramic, and some china, and pottery or earthenware. Fine china, lead crystal, any glass utensil trimmed or decorated with metal, and any glass or ceramic utensils that have metal reinforced handles are unsuitable. The metal will reflect the microwaves and damage the oven.

A wide variety of plastic materials can be used in the microwave oven. High-temperature plastics, dishwasher-safe plastic, styrofoam, plastic wraps, and boil-in-the-bag plastics as well as roasting or cooking bags can all be used in the oven, depending upon the intended use.

Foods with a high fat or sugar content require that a thermo or high-temperature plastic be used. For example, if bacon were cooked in a styrofoam container, the hot fat from the bacon would melt the styrofoam. The hot fat could also melt or distort softer plastics such as food storage containers. However, a bacon rack that is designed for use in the microwave oven is made to withstand the high temperatures.

Metal utensils should not be used in the microwave. Use of metals can cause arcing, a sparking or lightning-like effect which can damage the oven. In addition, metal utensils prevent the food from absorbing the microwaves and cooking time is greatly increased. As the microwaves are not absorbed by the food being heated, they go back to the magnetron tube and over a period of time will cause the tube to become weaker and weaker. This will result in longer and longer cooking times.

There are a few exceptions to the rule about metals. Some metals can be safely used in the microwave if directions are carefully followed. Aluminum foil can be used for shielding.The aluminum foil is used to shield or protect food from beginning to cook during a defrost cycle. Foil can also prevent overcooking an area such as a leg or wing tip of a chicken. There should

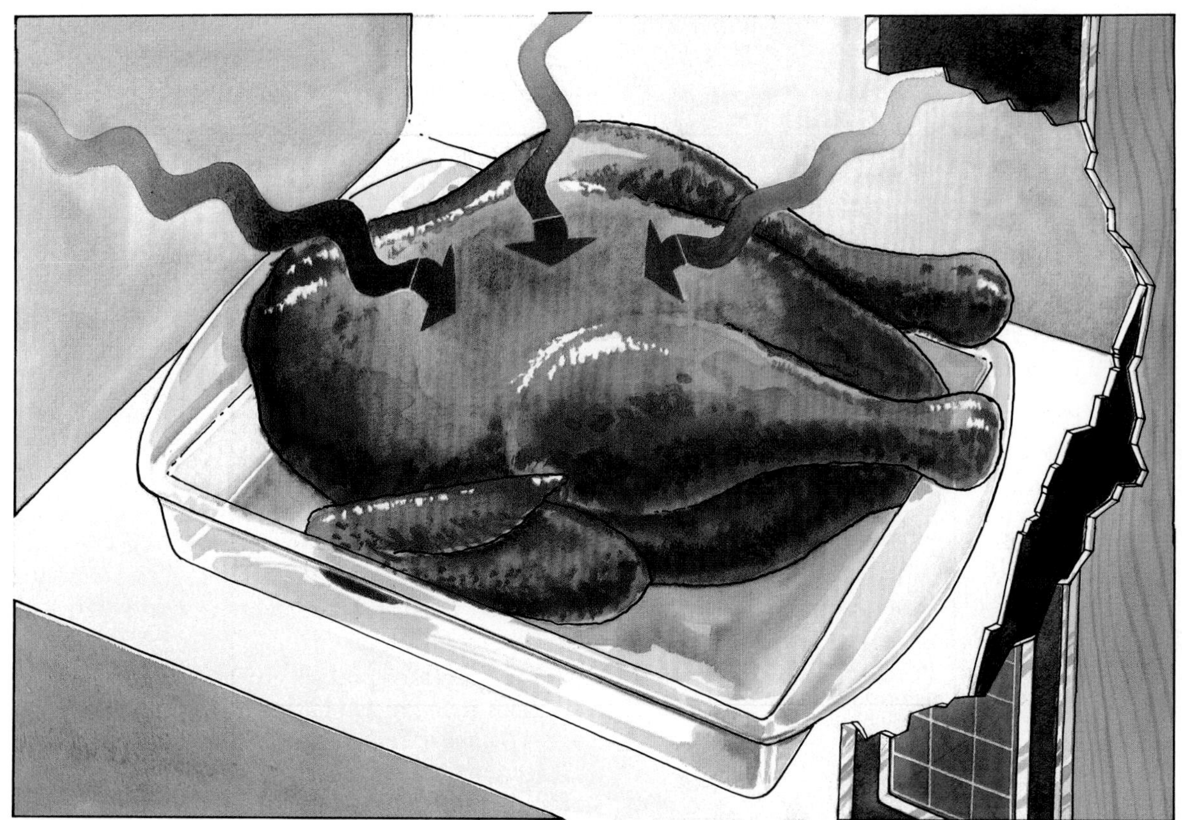

Like rubbing your palms together, microwaves rub molecules together creating heat.

always be more food area exposed than area covered by the foil. Also, be sure the foil does not come close to or touch oven/range walls or arcing will occur.

Some TV dinner or convenience food trays can be used if they are not so large that they come close to oven walls. Again it is important to be sure there is enough food present to absorb energy. Since the energy will not pass through the aluminum tray, uneven cooking will take place because the food is being heated from the top and not from all sides.

Paper products are ideal for use in the microwave oven. Paper plates, napkins, towels, cups, and wax paper all can be used. White rather than colored paper products should be used because the dye might color the food. Foods that are in the microwave for a short period of time work well with paper products. If high fat content foods are cooked, such as bacon, watch the food carefully in order to be sure the fat does not become too hot and cause the paper to ignite.

There are many grades of plastic wrap. Some brands are heavy enough to withstand the high temperatures of cooking foods, and other brands will tear or even melt at high temperatures. Manufacturers usually label those products that are safe for use.

The ideal shape of the utensils used in microwave ovens is a round shape and a ring/donut shape. Since microwaves penetrate all sides of foods to a depth up to 1½ inches (3.8 cm), these shapes give the fastest, most even cooking results. Square corners receive more energy because there are more exposed surfaces to attract the microwave energy. This causes the corners to overcook.

Paper towels can be used to absorb extra moisture from a heating food, such as bread.

Features of Microwave Ovens

When you're cooking with a conventional oven, you select a temperature setting to achieve the desired results. With a microwave oven, you can control the results with the **power setting.** Most microwave ovens are equipped with at least full power (100 percent) and defrost power (30 percent or 50 percent). Microwaves are also available with variable power settings. The power range or percentage refers to the length of time the magnetron tube is engaged. For example, cooking at 70 percent power means the magnetron tube is cycling on and off so that microwave energy is generated 70 percent of the time.

To determine how many power levels you might need in a microwave oven it is important to think about how you will use the appliance. If you will use a microwave to defrost frozen foods and reheat leftovers most of the time, a number of power levels will not be required. If the microwave oven will be used for a wide variety of food preparation, more power levels will be beneficial.

Wattage levels of a microwave oven also will affect the speed of cooking in a microwave. The higher the wattage output, the more microwaves and the faster the food will cook. The wattage output can be found on the identification plate usually located on the back of the appliance. If the oven cavity size is small, often a lower wattage (400-500 watts) will be found. Ovens with a larger cavity have a higher wattage (600-700 watts).

Some models have a browning element in the top of the microwave. The element is used before or after the microwave cooking, but not at the same time. The same effect can be achieved by using a broiler in a conventional oven.

Temperature probes are one of the sensing devices that are available with some models of microwave ovens. The temperature probe is placed in a food item and senses when the food's interior reaches a preselected temperature. The temperature probe is especially useful for meat cookery.

Another sensing device is a humidity sensor that senses moisture emitted by the food being cooked. Once moisture is detected by the microwave sensing device, the food continues to cook for a time that has been programmed into the microwave based upon codes for a variety of foods.

Cooking by weight is also a feature that is available on some recent models. A built-in scale in the floor of the oven weighs the food. After you program the cooking level, the cooking time will be calculated according to the weight of the food.

Turntables in microwave ovens rotate food during cooking. This helps to cook the food evenly without having to turn the dish by hand.

Many of the top-of-the-line microwave ovens offer a memory. This control allows the microwave oven to be programmed to remember to perform several functions in a series. A memory control is helpful when defrosting and then cooking an item, or cooking an item that requires several power levels. However, before purchasing a microwave oven with a memory, you should ask yourself how often you would use this feature before paying more for it.

Microwave/convection oven combinations utilize the speed of microwave with the good browning results of convection cooking. (**Convection cooking** involves the use of a fan to help evenly distribute heated air.) With this type of appliance, cooking can be done by microwaves alone, by convection alone, or by a combination of the two methods.

As with any appliance, extra features on a microwave oven mean extra costs. Before paying for a top-of-the- line model, consider how much you will use all the features. Are they worth the price?

Factors that Affect Microwave Cooking

Starting temperature, density, size or shape, and the amount of the food all affect the cooking times. This is true with both microwave and conventional methods of cooking. However, it is often more noticeable when cooking in the microwave because of the faster speed at which foods cook.

The higher the starting temperature of a food, the faster the food will cook. The colder the starting temperature of a food, the longer it takes to cook. For example, refrigerated or frozen food will take a few minutes longer to cook than the same food at room temperature.

Although foods may be the same size, foods of different densities will cook at different rates of speed. The density of a food determines how microwaves will be absorbed, thus affecting the cooking time. Dense foods such as a potato or meat will cook slower than a porous food such as cake because the depth of microwave penetration will not be as great with the denser foods. Because of less resistance, microwaves can penetrate less dense foods much easier.

The size and shape of foods also have an effect on microwave cooking. Small items cook faster than large items. The microwave is not quite 5 inches (12.7 cm) in length and as the waves enter the food they give up their energy as heat. Small items such as baked potatoes heat well. Large items such as a turkey or roast absorb the microwave energy before it reaches the center. In this case the roast or turkey must finish cooking by conduction. Conduction is the transfer of heat from one part to another.

Paper towels can also be used to add moisture to cooking foods such as vegetables. To add moisture, soak the towel in water before covering the food.

Regular shapes heat more uniformly. The thinner, narrower parts of irregular shapes, such as the wings of a whole chicken, tend to cook more quickly than the thicker parts. Care must be taken to shield the thinner areas with small pieces of aluminum foil to produce desired uniform cooking. As mentioned earlier, the ideal shape for microwave cooking is a round shape or a ring/donut shape since microwaves penetrate all sides of foods to a depth up to 1 ½ inches (3.8 cm). These shapes give the fastest, most even cooking results.

As the quantity, volume, amount, size, or thickness of the food increases, so does the

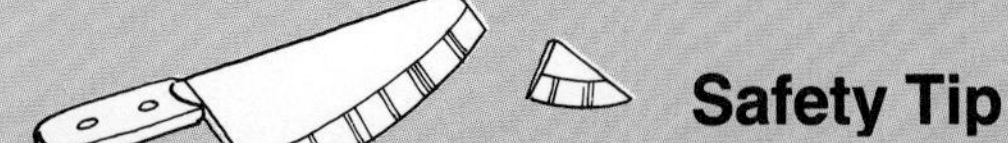

Safety Tip

Caution: Steam quickly builds up during microwave cooking so use care when removing the utensil lid or plastic wrap to prevent steam burns. Remove the lid by tilting it away from you. Pull up plastic wrap on the side away from you. Do not reach across the steam.

Wax paper will form a loose seal that allows steam to escape. Wax paper can also be used to cover foods that tend to spatter.

Paper towels also are used to loosely cover foods that spatter. Since paper towels absorb moisture, they are often used to wrap breads or other baked goods to prevent the food from becoming soggy. When snack foods such as potato chips and pretzels become soggy, they often can be refreshed by placing them on a paper towel for a short time in the microwave. This will help to draw moisture out and away from the food.

cooking time. It does not matter whether it is one potato vs. five potatoes or a small potato vs. a large potato. If the quantity is increased, the cooking time will be increased.

Increasing the cooking time is necessary as the quantity of food is increased because at full power the oven is producing the same amount of energy at all times. It is not possible to increase the amount of energy coming into the microwave oven/range. However, it is not a rule that cooking time is doubled when the amount of food is doubled. Cooking times will vary. Recipes will give you guidelines on these differences. Just as all the factors just discussed affect cooking time, the type of food will also affect it. Fatty or bony foods cook faster than meaty foods of the same weight. For example fatty ground beef cooks faster than lean ground beef. Liquid foods may heat faster than chunks of food in a mixture such as stew. Light airy foods cook faster than heavy, thick, or dense foods. Foods with high sugar or fat content will cook faster than foods with less sugar or fat. This is because microwaves are absorbed quickly by fats and sugars.

Microwave Cooking Techniques

Covering

Covering foods cooked in the microwave oven is a useful technique. Recipes usually will indicate when and what type of cover should be used. There are five reasons for covering foods while cooking in the microwave oven. They are:

1. To retain steam for more even and faster heating.
2. To help tenderize tough meats or rehydrate dried foods.
3. To keep foods moist.
4. To prevent spattering of foods.
5. To absorb extra moisture and prevent food from becoming soggy.

Different types of coverings are used for different purposes. A utensil lid or plastic wrap will help to hold in steam that can tenderize and speed cooking. If a cooking utensil does not have its own lid, use plastic wrap. Turn back one corner of the wrap to form a vent to allow steam to escape.

Turning

Recipe directions often call for the food being cooked in the microwave to be stirred. Stirring will help to shorten the cooking time while promoting even heating. Because the microwaves penetrate the food from all sides and the heat works toward the center, it is most effective if the food is stirred from the outside to the center of the dish to help equalize the temperature.

Turning or rotating food as it cooks is a technique used for foods that cannot be stirred or rearranged. Turning or rotating a food, such as a cake, during the microwaving process will help to promote even cooking.

Turning food over helps evenly heat large dense foods such as roasts, turkey, or whole vegetables. When large foods are placed in the microwave oven, they usually cook more on the top since the top is nearer to the microwave source. Turning the food over allows for more even cooking.

Arranging

Arranging foods in the microwave oven in a ring also will promote even cooking. When baking more than two baked potatoes, arrange them in a triangle or circular shape. Also arrange unevenly shaped foods with the thicker parts to the outside. Placing the thicker parts to the outside allows them to receive more microwave energy while preventing the thinner areas in the center from overcooking.

Uneven or irregular-shaped foods often require shielding from microwave energy to have a quality end product. A small strip of aluminum foil will "shield" a bony chicken wing or tip of a roast to prevent that portion from drying out during the microwaving process.

Standing Time

Standing time is especially important when cooking large quantities. **Standing time** simply allows microwaved foods to finish cooking by internal heat after they are removed from the oven. It is helpful to cover the food with aluminum foil during the standing time to prevent the surface from cooling too rapidly.

These foods would not take the same amount of time to cook in the microwave oven. Why? Hint: The potatoes are different sizes, the fresh and frozen broccoli bunches are different temperatures, and the meats vary in fat content.

You only need to add a small amount of moisture to cook vegetables or fruits in the microwave oven.

Advantages and Disadvantages of Microwave Cooking

There are advantages and disadvantages to microwave cooking. Learning how to make full use of the advantages and avoid the disadvantages helps you avoid cooking disappointments.

One advantage is that the foods cook rapidly in a microwave oven. Remember a microwave cooks many foods in approximately ¼ to ⅓ of the time required to cook the foods by a conventional method. There is no preheating with a microwave oven and this also saves both time and energy.

With a microwave oven it is possible to defrost foods in a matter of minutes. Microwave defrosting is a unique benefit, as no other appliance can do it as efficiently or effectively. However, when defrosting meats, cook them at once and do not allow them to stand in the microwave after defrosting. Food-borne illness could develop if the food is not handled properly.

One of the greatest advantages is that the nutritional value of foods cooked in a microwave is generally equal to or higher than the same foods cooked conventionally. One factor contributing to the higher nutritional value is that vegetables in particular are cooked with little or no water and in a very short period of time. This eliminates the loss of vitamins and minerals in the liquid. In addition, many foods cooked in the microwave do not need fat or butter added to them when cooking. This enables a food to have less calories. For example, eggs can be scrambled in the microwave oven without adding fat in the form of butter or margarine.

Another advantage of microwave cooking is that it is cool. No amount of heat is added to the home. Foods cooked in a microwave oven get hot. Yet in most cases the oven and the cooking utensil remain cool. Unlike a conventional oven, you can open the door of a microwave oven to check cooking without having hot air escape into the kitchen.

Reheating foods in a microwave is another advantage of microwave cooking. Leftovers become planned-overs and help to stretch today's food dollar. Reheating food also enables family members to eat at different times and still have a safe, nutritious meal.

Microwave cooking can be energy efficient. A microwave oven will draw less energy than a conventional oven or range. The current used for most microwaves is 115 or 120 volts, while an electric range uses 240 volts. Also the shorter cooking time required for foods cooked in a microwave saves energy.

With today's hectic family schedule, one last feature is a real advantage to many people. Microwave ovens are easy to clean. Many utensils used in the microwave oven stay cool, thus not baking food particles on them. Also, you often can prepare, cook, and serve a food in the same utensil, saving extra cleanup time. If foods spill over in the microwave, the food does not become as baked on as it would in a conventional oven because of the shorter cooking time. Often all that is required to clean a microwave is a damp cloth.

As with all things, the microwave oven is not perfect. A disadvantage is that egg-leavened products such as chiffon or angel food cakes, cream puffs, and popovers cannot be baked in a microwave oven. Microwave energy tends to "rubberize" chiffons or angel food cakes. Also no crust is formed on the cream puffs or popovers during microwave cooking to hold up the light, airy structure.

Deep fat fried and fried foods cannot be cooked in a microwave. The temperature of the fat cannot be adequately controlled in a microwave oven. In addition, glass and plastic microwave utensils are not designed to withstand high frying temperatures.

Also eggs in shells cannot be cooked in the microwave oven. The steam builds up within the shell and causes the egg to burst. If an egg is cooked out of the shell, the membrane on the yolk should be pierced in order for it not to burst.

Another disadvantage is that quantity cooking works poorly in a microwave. As stated earlier, the amount of food affects the cooking time. Cooking times increase and the microwaves do not penetrate into the food more than 1½ inches (3.8 cm). Thus the foods would not cook evenly or would take as long or longer than cooking the foods conventionally. In addition, some conventional cooking utensils, such as metal, cannot be used for microwave cooking. Thus new utensils may need to be purchased.

Microwave ovens are usually placed on the countertop and in some instances are built into cupboard space. While they are movable, they usually are too large and heavy to move frequently. To some people, especially those with small kitchens, the loss of counter space required for a work area is a disadvantage.

Converting Recipes for Microwave Cooking

Although there are many microwave recipes available, you may have some conventional favorites you want to use. Once you are familiar

Place unevenly shaped foods with the smaller parts toward the center in a circular pattern.

with using the microwave for cooking, you may find you can adapt some of those favorite recipes for microwave cooking. A set of hard-and-fast rules for converting recipes is impossible to develop. However, you can follow those general guidelines.

First, pick a conventional recipe and find one similar to it in your microwave cookbook. Note the technique and recommended time. Determine whether or not both recipes have the same basic ingredients. Compare the two recipes to see if the quantities are similar. If they are, the time and techniques will be much the same. If one is larger, the time should be adjusted accordingly. Remember, factors such as volume, density, and starting temperature of food affect cooking time.

A general guideline is that foods cooked in the microwave take about one-fourth the time of conventional oven cooking. A casserole that requires 1 hour conventionally will cook in 15 minutes in the microwave. Foods cooked conventionally on the surface of the range will often require more than the one-fourth microwave time guide. Sometimes it will be identical with the conventional cooking time. You may prefer to continue to cook these foods conventionally and use the microwave for the remain-

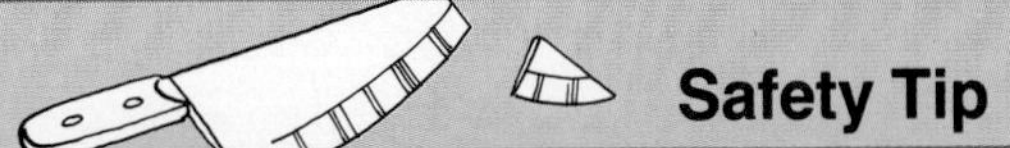

Safety Tip

Attention microwave oven users . . . take care when you are heating water in a microwave oven. The water can reach temperatures far beyond the boiling point. You may meet with a nasty surprise when you go for your coffee cup! If the water spills, you may get burned. The water can boil over if you add instant coffee or cocoa. Manufacturers of microwaves suggest you break the water's surface tension by stirring the liquid before placing it in the microwave. If you do this, the liquid will boil as it should.

der of the meal. Rice and noodles are examples of foods requiring the same cooking time.

Conventional cooking temperatures have a tendency to dry foods during cooking. A larger amount of moisture is usually included in the recipe to prevent a dry, tough cooked food. With microwave cooking, the chemical properties of foods change more rapidly and less moisture is needed. To compensate, a smaller amount of moisture may be added when preparing the recipe for microwave cooking. Reduce the moisture content by one-fourth. If the recipe calls for 1 cup (250 mL) of water, reduce it to 3/4 cup (175 mL). For example, a casserole may call for 1 can of soup and 1 can of water. For microwave cooking, add 1 can of soup and 3/4 can of water.

Select a microwave power level similar to the temperature used in your conventional recipe. If your recipe suggests baking at a moderate temperature, select a moderate or medium power level.

Always remember to allow for standing time as a part of the total cooking time. Overcooked foods in the microwave dehydrate and toughen and there is no way of restoring the food when this occurs. Always undercook, especially when you are experimenting!

You may have to experiment with your favorite conventional recipe more than once before you achieve the best results. Make a note of your changes so you will remember the next time. Above all, try many of your favorites. You may find the food even better because of the advantages of microwave cooking.

How and What to Cook in Your Microwave Oven

Many of the same principles that apply to conventional cooking also apply to microwave cooking. If a food requires a short cooking time conventionally, it will require even a shorter cooking time when cooked in the microwave oven. Likewise if a food requires a longer cooking time conventionally, it will require a longer cooking time in the microwave. It is important to remember that successes and failures can be had with microwave cookery just as with conventional cooking.

Cooking Meats with a Microwave Oven

If meats and other protein foods are cooked too fast, they will toughen. Since microwaving is fast cooking, most techniques for meat cooking relate to speed control. It is best if the cooking process is as quick as possible without causing the meat to toughen.

Most of us use for everyday meals less tender cuts of meat that require long, slow simmering to become tender. Often when we first hear of microwave cooking speed, we imagine forktender Swiss steak in minutes or a simmered, savory pot roast in half the time. Unfortunately, these meats are considered less tender, and the only way to achieve the forktender, savory flavor is through slow, moist cooking. While this can be accomplished in the microwave oven (especially with the lower power

You can make a crisp chicken or meat dish in the microwave by adding the dry texture with a crumb coating of bread, cracker, or cereal pieces. This Company Chicken recipe features a crushed cornflake topping that crunches in the mouth like a deep-fat fried batter.

Company Chicken

Yield: 6 servings
Equipment: 9 x 12 inch (23 x 30 cm) baking dish

Traditional	Ingredients	Metric
3 large	Chicken breasts, skinned, boned, and halved lengthwise	3 large
6 thin slices	Boiled ham	6 thin slices
6 small slices	Mozzarella cheese	6 small slices
1 medium	Tomato, seeded and chopped	1 medium
½ tsp.	Dry sage	5 mL
½ cup	Cornflake crumbs	125 mL
2 Tbsp.	Grated Parmesan cheese	30 mL
2 tbsp.	Snipped parsley	30 mL
¼ cup	Butter or margarine, melted	50 mL

Microwave Directions

1. Place chicken bone side up on a cutting board.
2. Place a piece of clear plastic wrap over it and working from the center out, pound lightly with a meat mallet until each piece measures 5 x 5 inches (12.5 x 12.5 cm).
3. Remove the wrap and place a ham slice and cheese slice on each cutlet, cutting to fit.
4. Mix the tomato and sage and top each piece with some of the mixture.
5. Tuck in the sides of the chicken and roll up jelly-roll style, pressing to seal well. (It may be necessary to use toothpicks to hold it in place.)
6. Combine crumbs, Parmesan cheese, and parsley. Dip chicken into the butter or margarine, then roll in the crumb mixture.
7. Place in a shallow glass baking pan. Bake 10 to 12 minutes on high in the microwave.
8. Let stand 5 to 6 minutes.

Note: This recipe is good served with rice. Cook rice according to package directions.

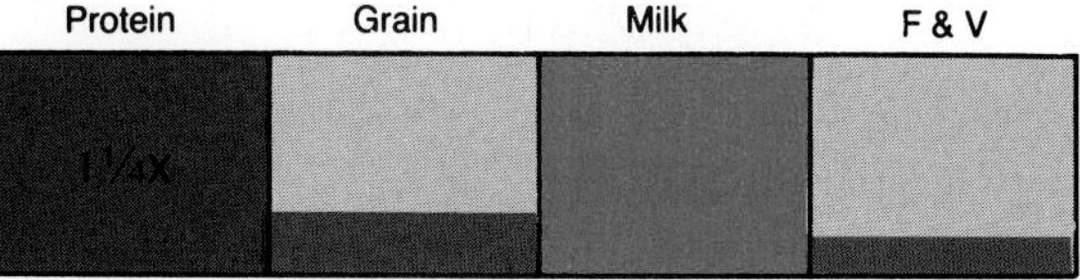

settings available on many ovens today), the time will be quite similar to conventional methods. You may have tried some microwave recipes in which these cuts were quickly cooked using full power. The meat is fully cooked, but it requires a lot of chewing because the connective tissue, has toughened from the fast cooking. The connective tissue which is common in all less tender cuts needs a long, slow simmering time in order to soften.

More tender cuts of meat, on the other hand, can be prepared quite successfully with fast microwave cooking. Tender beef cuts include rib and T-bone steaks and standing or rolled rib roast. You may be used to eating steaks which are nicely browned on the outside. Since very short time is required to cook steaks, they do not brown adequately with just microwave cooking. Additional browning from a skillet, broiler, or grill may be used before microwave cooking. A browning dish is another possibility. A rib roast is in the oven longer, so it will brown quite nicely, making it one of the more successful roasts for microwave cooking. However, it is one of the more expensive meats.

Usually, meats microwaved longer than 10 minutes will start to brown. The longer the microwave time and the more fat on the meat, the more browning. Sometimes products or glazes are added to help foods to look browner. For instance, a honey-soy sauce mixture is used with a pork roast or a barbecue sauce is often used for ribs.

When cooking larger cuts of meat, the microwaves must have an opportunity to evenly cook all parts. Usually a roast is 4 to 5 inches (10 to 12.7 cm) high and the top portion tends to attract the microwaves. The upper portion of the roast will cook so quickly that it may overcook before the underside reaches the desired doneness. Turning the roast over once or twice during the cooking time gives a more evenly cooked product.

Also, microwaves penetrate only the outer 1 to 1 1/2 inches (2.5 to 3.8 cm) of the meat. If a roast is 3 or 4 inches (7.6 to 10 cm) thick, the inside cooks only as the heat builds up in the outer 1 1/2 inches (3.8 cm) and is then conducted toward the center. This is why a roast cooks best when microwaved about two-thirds of the time, is covered and allowed to stand, and then microwaved again. In actual meal preparation, the standing time for the meat can be used to microwave the potatoes or vegetables. Although the meat reaches the desired temperature more slowly and evenly, the total meal preparation time is the same as if the roast were cooked all at once before the other foods.

Another way to slow the cooking is to lower the power setting. This is similar to a standing time except that the oven automatically spaces the standing time between cooking periods. If your oven has a lower power setting, even if it is only a defrost button, you will find it convenient when cooking meats.

A third method of slowing cooking is to add a sauce or other ingredients to the meat. The more food in the dish, the less concentrated the microwaves are in the meat and the more slowly the meat cooks. These mixtures should be stirred and rearranged to insure even cooking.

Many roasts are not perfectly symmetrical, and smaller ends will cook more quickly than larger portions. If a roast is unevenly shaped, pieces of foil can be used to shield smaller areas during the first half of the cooking time. Or, if a high area on the roast is cooking too fast, a small piece of foil can be placed firmly over the area to shield it from additional cooking. When using foil for this purpose, be sure the portion of meat exposed to cooking is much greater than the amount of foil.

Browning in the microwave is more a steam-type process than the crisp-type browning associated with a conventional oven. If you still prefer the crisp-type browning, you can complete your roast in the oven. This same combination technique can also be used with the barbecue grill.

Microwaving Fruits and Vegetables

Microwaving fruits and vegetables uses the same technique as microwaving other foods.

Cooking Hints

Microwaving Meats

1. Cook fresh or completely thawed meat.
2. Season meat to taste after cooking—salt dries out the surface.
3. Place meat, fat side down on a roasting rack.
4. Cover tender meats with plastic wrap or waxed paper. Tuck it beneath edges of roasting rack.
5. For medium tender meats, place 1/2 cup (125 mL) water in the bottom of the roasting pan or cover the meat with sauce. You also can cover the meat with plastic wrap or waxed paper.
6. Less tender meats can be placed in cooking bag.
7. Cook on "1st setting" for one-half of the cooking time.
8. Turn meat, fat side up.
9. Cook on "2nd setting" for remaining time. Check for doneness.
10. Use a microwave thermometer during cooking for accuracy in doneness.
11. Let the meat stand, covered with foil (shiny side in) about 10 minutes before serving.
12. The temperature will rise about 15 degrees during the standing time.

Microwaving Fish

1. Use a shallow dish.
2. Cover with plastic wrap or lid.
3. Cook fish on high or full power.
4. Don't overcook!
5. Cover the dish with plastic wrap during standing time.

Microwaving Poultry

1. Cook completely thawed or fresh poultry.
2. Season before cooking.
3. Arrange the pieces skin side up and with the thick edges toward the outside of the dish.
4. Cook most whole poultry uncovered.
5. Use foil to cover portions that appear to cook quickly or dry out.
6. During cooking and standing time, cover dish containing turkey or chicken pieces that have no crumb coating or sauce.
7. Turn poultry weighing 10 pounds (5 kg) or less once during cooking. Turn poultry weighing over 10 lbs. (5 kg) three times.
8. The thermometer should read 170°F (77°C) when a whole bird comes from the oven.
9. Poultry skin can be crisped by placing under a conventional broiler.
10. Standing time is essential:
- whole birds or pieces totaling 10 lbs. (5 kg) or less should stand for 5 to 10 minutes
- whole birds or pieces totaling over 10 lbs. (5 kg) stand for 10 to 15 minutes
- internal temperature will rise 10 to 15°F

11. Cover whole birds with foil. Cover cutup birds with a utensil lid, plastic wrap, or waxed paper.

Keep in mind that standing time is most important. However, it is often neglected when cooking fruits and vegetables. If the food is not done to your taste after standing, you can always microwave it longer. Any fruit, such as apples, cherries, peaches, or rhubarb, that is cooked conventionally can be cooked in a microwave. Many fruits cooked in the microwave are combined with other ingredients to make a dessert of one type or another. When preparing such a dish, follow the recipe. Frozen fruits also are available in many forms and often are defrosted in the microwave. It is best to defrost pieces of fruit only until a few pieces feel warm. During the standing time, the fruit will finish defrosting.

Vegetables cooked in the microwave are very easy to prepare and offer a wide variety to family meals. Fresh, frozen, or canned vegetables retain their attractive color, flavor, and natural texture when cooked in the microwave oven. When cooked in the microwave, very little water is added to vegetables. You only need enough to produce steam. This is very beneficial because water-soluble nutrients are not discarded in the cooking liquid.

Fresh vegetables cooked in the microwave oven need to have added only 2 tablespoons to 1/4 cup (30 to 50 mL) of water. More water increases the cooking time and decreases flavor and nutritional value.

Vegetables should be covered tightly with a lid or plastic wrap when they are cooked. Whole vegetables cooked in their skin, such as potatoes, do not need to be covered. However the skin should be pierced several times to allow excess steam to escape.

Fresh and frozen vegetables are cooked at full power. They should be arranged so that stems or stalks are toward the outside of the container as they take longer to cook. Frozen vegetables should not be thawed before cooking. If the frozen vegetables come in a box, they can be cooked in their carton. Remove the waxed paper wrapper. The ice in the package provides sufficient moisture for cooking. Vegetables that are frozen in cooking pouches also can be cooked in the microwave. Before cooking, pierce a hole in the pouch to allow steam to escape. It is helpful to flex the pouch midway through the cooking to help distribute the heat.

Home-canned vegetables should be cooked conventionally and not in the microwave. It is important to boil home- canned vegetables for 10 to 15 minutes to kill all harmful microorganisms. If vegetables are cooked this long in the microwave they will be very overcooked.

Cooking Cheese, Milk, and Egg Products with a Microwave Oven

Cheese, milk, and egg products often use the same basic principles of cooking in the microwave as they do conventionally. In order not to toughen the protein in them, a lower temperature for a longer period of time is preferred.

Cheese should be cooked on lower power setting to avoid separation and toughening. Cook most cheese products at a 60 to 70 percent power level. Some products such as cheese fondues often are cooked on a 50 percent power level to insure a smooth, creamy consistency. When combining cheese with other ingredients, the mixture should be stirred briskly every minute to keep the product from separating.

Cheesecakes and custard pie fillings should be cooked on a low power setting. If cooked on too high a power setting, they will become tough on the outside before setting in the center.

Cooking eggs in the microwave oven illustrates one difference between conventional and microwave cooking. An egg that is poached in a conventional manner cooks first in the white portion, just as it does when hard cooked. The opposite is true of eggs cooked in the microwave oven. Because an egg yolk contains more fat than the white, it attracts more energy and cooks first. An egg that is microwaved until the white is set will be overcooked. Standing time is important to obtain a well-cooked egg.

When the egg is scrambled, it is still best to allow for a standing time. This still helps avoid overcooking the egg. Remember, an egg cannot be cooked in its shell as the steam will build up inside and cause the egg to burst. Also, do not cook or poach a whole egg without first piercing the yolk.

Microwaving Cereal, Pasta, and Baked Products

Cereal products, pasta, and a wide variety of baked products can all be prepared with much success in a microwave. Hot cereals are simple to microwave and can help to solve a common early morning problem. This is especially true if different family members eat different cereals for breakfast or eat at different times. The cere-

Chewy microwave granola bars are a quick, nutritious answer to the question, "What's for dessert?"

al can be prepared right in the cereal bowl. The water and cereal can be placed in the bowl and microwaved 1 to 3 minutes. One caution is to use a bowl that allows enough room for the cereal to increase in volume or it will boil over.

Rice is easy to prepare in the microwave. Rice expands two to three times in volume, so use a glass dish that's big enough to hold both rice and water! Stir the uncooked rice into the water and cover with a glass lid or plastic wrap. Microwave on defrost or a low setting. Let the rice stand 5 minutes, covered before serving so it absorbs all the moisture. Converted rice can be substituted for long-grain white rice, but it will require a longer cooking time. Quick-cooking rice is cooked much as it is conventionally. You bring the water to a boil using high power and then add the rice.

Pasta products such as macaroni and noodles should be cooked covered with water so they tenderize completely. Use a large casserole or bowl so that the water will be deep enough to cover the pasta. First bring the water, butter or cooking oil, and seasoning to a full, rolling boil. Stir in the pasta. While pasta cooks very well in the microwave, it takes about the same length of time to cook as if it is cooked conventionally. You may find it best to cook other foods in your microwave oven and cook the pasta conventionally. Pasta will cook in casseroles without precooking. Lasagna is one dish that can be easily prepared in a microwave.

Most bar cookies, quick breads and cakes cook quite well in the microwave oven except they do not brown. To disguise that fact, use toppings, frostings, nuts, or spices. Baked products will rise higher and bake much faster in the microwave than they do conventionally. Baked products have a more moist appearance cooked in a microwave than if cooked conventionally. Because baked products don't dry out as much in the microwave, the amount of liquid in a conventional recipe needs to be decreased. The results are not as satisfactory, when microwaving drop cookies. There is little time saved and the cookies do not cook evenly. It is possible to have a cookie that is both raw and scorched. The best way to make cookies in the microwave oven is to make a bar cookie. A bar cookie recipe usually is cooked first at 60 to 70 percent power to blend the shortening and sugar and then is finished on 30 to 50 percent power so the dense center of the mixture cooks through without overcooking in spots.

Microwaved cakes are more moist, more tender, and have a greater volume than cakes baked conventionally. Because the microwave oven does not bake by a conventional hot air method, microwave baked cakes do not have a browned crust. Tube cakes bake most evenly because of a microwave oven's cooking pattern. Remember, a circular container works better than a square or rectangular container. As a microwave cake rises higher than a conventional cake, only fill the dish half full of batter. The remaining batter can be used to make cupcakes. Layer cakes are generally baked one layer at a time to insure even baking of all the layers.

To judge doneness in microwave baked cakes, use the standard toothpick test. Also, if a cake begins to pull away from the sides of the pan, it is done. Avoid overcooking. Do not wait until the surface is totally dry. Allow 3 to 5 minutes standing time.

Quick breads bake on the same principles as cakes. Remember that whole-wheat flour will not only add color to the quick bread or other baked product, but may also increase the nutritional value of the product.

Vocabulary Review

Magnetron tube
Microwaves
Power setting
Convection cooking
Standing time

Questions for Review

1. How is heat created in foods in a microwave oven?
2. Improper care of your microwave can cause leakage of microwaves. Give two examples of poor care practices.
3. List several materials that would make ideal microwave utensils?
4. What is likely to happen if you use a utensil that reflects microwaves?
5. In the microwave oven, why will uneven cooking occur when preparing TV dinners in aluminum trays if there is not enough food in proportion to the tray size?
6. What is the ideal shape for microwave cookware? Why?
7. Define power range or percentage.
8. What are the factors that affect how fast food will cook in the microwave oven?
9. Give five reasons for covering food while cooking in the microwave oven.
10. Describe the effect of covering food with plastic wrap while cooking it in the microwave oven.
11. What techniques help slow the cooking of meat so that it will cook more evenly?
12. Why do cheese, egg, and milk products need to be cooked at a lower power setting in the microwave oven?
13. Why is it dangerous to cook home-canned vegetables in the microwave oven?
14. Why do you stop cooking foods before they are done when using a microwave oven?
15. When converting conventional recipes for microwave cooking, why do you need to reduce the moisture content?

Things to Do

1. Test a utensil to see if it is microwave-safe. Explain why it is or is not.

2. From your kitchen cupboards and drawers, find three utensils that are appropriate for cooking in a microwave oven and three utensils that are not appropriate. Explain the reasons for your choices.

3. Make three ground meat patties of equal weight. Shape one of the patties in a square, one in a round shape, and one in a donut shape. Cook in the microwave. Compare your results. Which shape cooked the best? Why?

4. Convert one of your favorite conventional recipes into a microwave recipe. Test your conversion by making the recipe. Is there anything you would do differently next time? How long did it take to make the microwave recipe? How does that compare to the conventional time? What are the guidelines to follow when converting a conventional recipe for microwave cooking?

5. Make your favorite cake recipe conventionally and in the microwave. Compare the results. What are the differences?

6. Collect materials describing several different microwave ovens. Compare the features and costs. What features would be nice to have? Which features do you need to have? Which model would you buy and why?

Kerr
MASON

9 Preserving Foods at Home

Garden Fresh Foods

Today you don't neeed to have a green thumb to have fresh produce. You may be one of the many who enjoys gardening, but even if you're not, you can purchase fresh produce at a farmers' market, produce market, or a grocery store. In addition, many localities have places where you can go and pick your own fruits and vegetables. Besides getting fresh foods, picking your own has the added benefit of being outdoors to enjoy the summer or fall air.

Regardless of how you get your fresh produce, you will often have more than you can use at one time. Freezing, canning, or drying the fruits, vegetables, and herbs can hold the freshness for use during the winter. These prepared foods also can be given as gifts to family and friends throughout the year.

Food is preserved to prevent it from spoiling. Several factors cause spoilage in food kept at room temperature. The action of enzymes in food causes undesirable changes in flavor, texture, and odor. The action of air accelerates decay, causes discoloration, ruins the flavor, fades the aroma, and changes the texture. Bacteria, molds, and yeasts also cause decay. Also, eating spoiled foods can make you sick—sometimes very sick. Spoilage can be prevented, however, or at least slowed drastically, by freezing, canning, and drying foods.

Freezing Foods

Freezing food preserves the texture, flavor, appearance, and nutritive value of fresh products and prevents the food from spoiling. Freezing is the easiest and quickest method of food preservation. Freezing is easier than canning, although it involves more than just putting the food into the freezer. Don't take shortcuts in the recommended procedures or you'll be unhappy with the results.

Improperly frozen food results in a loss of nutrition, texture, and flavor. However, there is no danger from botulism toxin poisoning in frozen foods. (**Botulism** is a food poisoning that can result in death.) The conditions under which frozen foods are handled and stored are not favorable to the production of botulism toxin. No case of botulism from frozen food has ever been reported.

Small amounts of foods can be frozen at a time. Unlike canning, you do not need enough food to fill a canner. Also, freezing does not require a large block of time. From the start to finish, most foods can be frozen in less than one hour. Canning may take several hours to complete the task.

Freezing foods is inexpensive. You do not need special equipment to prepare the foods for freezing and the storage containers are reusable, so there is only a small one-time cost.

Cooking Hints

Freeze fruits and vegetables as soon as they are packed. Put no more unfrozen food into a freezer than will freeze within 24 hours. Usually this will be about 2 to 3 pounds (5 to 7.5 kg) of food to each cubic foot of the freezer's capacity. Overloading slows down the rate of freezing and, if foods freeze too slowly, they may lose their quality or spoil.

Foods should be stored at 0°F (-18°C) or below. At higher temperatures, foods lose quality much faster. Moist fruits and vegetables maintain high quality for 8 to 12 months at 0°F (-18°C) or below. Citrus fruits and citrus juices can be stored for 4 to 6 months. Longer storage will not make foods unfit for use, but may impair quality.

The largest cost is the freezer or the refrigerator-freezer in which the food is stored. The cost of owning and operating a home freezer varies with the rate of turnover of foods, electricity used, and costs of repairs, as well as the original cost of the appliance. You have to ask yourself, "How much will I use the freezer and what will it cost me?"

Freezing preserves the nutritive value of fruits and vegetables better than other home methods of food preservation. The nutrient content of frozen foods depends upon food selection, proper handling, freezing methods, and storage temperatures. If food stands at room temperature before freezing, it may lose certain vitamins. Underblanching or overblanching of vegetables also will result in a loss of vitamins. Still more vitamins are lost if the freezer is maintained above the recommended temperature of 0°F (-18°C). Vitamin C is the most vulnerable.

Storage Containers

Packaging is very important in freezing to insure that the quality of food is maintained. Proper packaging keeps food from drying out and losing its color, flavor, and texture. A vacuum seal is not necessary, but the package must be airtight. Freezer wrappings or containers should be moisture- and vapor-proof, durable, and able to withstand temperatures below freezing without cracking or breaking.

You cannot expect perfect results if you use ordinary foil, waxed paper, or thin plastic wrap.

Rigid containers made of aluminum, glass, plastic, or heavily waxed cardboard are suitable containers for freezing foods. Rigid containers hold their shape, stand upright, and stack well. Be sure they have tight-fitting lids. Glass freezing jars are acceptable. They should be tapered and with a wide mouth. Canning-freezing jars are best because they withstand both extreme cold and heat. Handle glass carefully. Rough handling or sudden changes in temperature can break the glass.

Although the initial cost is more, reusable rigid containers are the most economical in the long run. With proper care, they can be used over and over again. Before each use, just be sure they are thoroughly cleaned and the lids still fit tightly.

Nonrigid containers such as heavy plastic bags and sheets of moisture-and-vapor-resistant plastics are suitable for dry-packed vegetables and fruits. Bags and sheets are used with or without outer cardboard cartons to protect against tearing. Bags without a protective carton are difficult to stack. The freezer sheets may be used for wrapping such foods as corn on the cob or asparagus. When using the sheets, use "drugstore" or "butcher wrap" to make the package airtight.

Heat-in-pouch bags also can be used for freezing foods. They are very easy and convenient to use because they also can be used for heating the food. These bags are great for freezing individual servings for persons in the family who are on a special diet or for people who live

Successful freezing means careful preparation. After foods are blanched, chilled, and drained, they are packaged for storage.

alone. Heat-in-pouch bags are more expensive than the other type of containers and are not reusable.

Freezing Vegetables

Most vegetables suitable for cooking are suitable for freezing. For example, green beans and corn are usually cooked before serving and freeze well. Lettuce and radishes are usually served uncooked and do not freeze well. However, remember that freezing cannot improve the initial quality of a vegetable. It only preserves the quality and nutrients already present and prevents spoilage. For that reason, choose young, tender vegetables. Immature vegetables will lack flavor. Overmature vegetables will taste flat and be tough or soft and mushy. If you grow vegetables, harvest early in the morning before they have absorbed heat from the sun.

When you are ready to freeze the vegetables, sort them according to size and maturity. This helps insure more even cooking. Wash vegetables thoroughly, whether they are to be pared or not, because dirt contains some of the bacteria that are hardest to kill. Wash small lots at a time under running water. Do not let foods soak or they will lose flavor and nutrients. However, if you have insects in vegetables such as broccoli, brussel sprouts, or cauliflower, soak the vegetables in a solution of ¼ cup (50 mL) of salt per gallon (4 L) of water for half an hour. Rinse and drain well.

Blanching vegetables (scalding) is absolutely necessary. There is a reason for blanching home-frozen vegetables.

Blanching vegetables before freezing inactivates protein substances called **enzymes** that are present in food in very small quantities. During freezing and storage, these enzymes cause changes in vegetables' texture, flavor, and odor such as those associated with ripening. The scalding process simply heats the vegetables long enough to stop the action of the enzymes, but not long enough to cook the vegetables. Do not omit blanching and expect high-quality frozen vegetables. Vegetables that are not blanched will be inferior in quality and taste.

A blanching kettle and a strainer or cheesecloth is used to hold the vegetables in boiling water during the blanching process. Most vegetables are cut into small pieces and require about 3 minutes in the boiling water. It is best to work with a small amount of food at a time, about 1 to 2 pounds (2.5 to 5 kg) per gallon (4 L) of boiling water. Timing for the blanching is started immediately after the vegetables are placed in the boiling water. Do not wait for the water to return to a boil. Keep the kettle covered during the blanching process. The blanching water may be used several times.

Steam blanching is an alternative to water blanching. Only a small amount of water is used and the vegetables are held in a basket above the boiling water in a covered kettle.

A microwave oven may also be used for blanching some vegetables. With steam and microwave blanching, the heat distribution often is uneven. Therefore the water blanching method is generally preferred.

Cool blanched vegetables as quickly as possible to prevent overprocessing. The cooling step is especially important if you are to have high-quality frozen vegetables. Frozen vegetables can become mushy and watery from overblanching or too little cooling and draining.

To cool the vegetables, place them in a large quantity of cold water with ice cubes added. Add extra ice cubes as the water starts to warm up. You also can cool them under cold running water. Chill until the vegetables feel cool to the touch. Chilling takes about as long as the blanching process. Drain the cooled vegetables well, removing as much water from the surface as possible. Leaving too much water causes the formation of more and larger ice crystals, which can ruin the texture of the food.

Package the foods immediately after draining. Do not add salt. Rigid containers or bags may be used for vegetables. Tray freezing also can be done with vegetables. Spread the cooled blanched vegetables in a single layer on a tray or shallow pan. Cover the tray and put it in the freezer until just the outside of the vegetables are frozen. Then pack the pieces in airtight containers. With tray freezing, the vegetables will not stick together, and you can easily take out as many or as few as are needed. This method is especially good for cut green beans, peas, cut corn, or small mixed vegetables.

Freezing Fruits

As with vegetables, most fruits suitable for cooking are suitable for freezing. Apples, apricots, cherries, berries, rhubarb, and peaches are the most common fruits frozen. Select good quality, fresh, firm, ripe fruit for freezing. If the fruit is underripe, it may become bitter or sour during freezing and freezer storage.

Pick berries when ripe and freeze them as soon after picking as you can. Some fruits—apples, peaches and pears—may need to ripen further after harvesting. But take care that they don't get too ripe. Frozen fruit prepared from overripe fruit will lack flavor and have a mushy texture.

Wash small quantities of fruit gently in cold water. Do not permit fruit to stand in water for any length of time since it will become watersoaked and the flavor and nutrients will leak out. Drain fruit well and blot with a paper towel. Remove all extra moisture to avoid the formation of ice crystals on the surface of the fruit. Peel, pit, cut, crush, or puree the fruit according to the intended use of the food.

Light-colored fruits such as apples, peaches, pears, apricots, and nectarines turn dark from exposure to air. To prevent this, treat the fruit with an **antioxidant. Ascorbic acid** is the antioxidant most commonly used to keep the fruit from darkening. It is safest and most effective. Ascorbic acid is available in powered or tablet form in most drug stores. Commercial products that contain a mixture of ascorbic acid and sugar with other ingredients are available

Frozen strawberries let you enjoy their juicy goodness all year long.

Chapter 9
Preserving Foods at Home

in most supermarkets. Lemon juice can also be used because it contains ascorbic acid, but it is not as effective as pure ascorbic acid. It adds its own flavor to the food, too.

Most fruits have a better flavor, color, and texture if packed in sugar or syrup. The intended use of the fruit determines the method chosen. A sugar pack is recommended for juicy fruits such as strawberries. The sugar draws the juice out of the fruit, and with some stirring a syrup is formed. Syrup made from sugar and water is used to cover less juicy fruits. One cup (250 mL) sugar to 4 cups (1 L) water is recommended for freezing most fruits. Syrups containing less sugar are sometimes used for mild-flavored fruits, while syrups with more sugar are used for very sour fruits. For each pint of fruit, ½ to ⅔ cup (125 to 150 mL) of syrup is used.

Pectin is now being used to prepare syrups for freezing berries, cherries, and peaches. With pectin, less sugar is needed and the fresh-fruit flavor, color, and texture are retained. Pectin syrups are prepared as follows. Combine one box of powered pectin with 1 cup (250 mL) of water in a saucepan and stir. Bring to a boil and boil 1 minute. Stir in ½ cup (125 mL) sugar and dissolve. Remove from the heat and add cold water to make 2 cups (500 mL) of syrup. Chill. Put the cleaned and prepared fruit in a 6-quart (1½ L) bowl. Add enough pectin syrup to glaze the fruit with a thin film, about 2 to 3 tablespoons (30 to 45 mL) per pint (500 mL). Gently fold the fruit into the mixture to coat each piece with the syrup. Package and seal promptly.

Fruits that have tough, waxy skins may be frozen satisfactorily without sweeteners. These fruits include blueberries, currants, gooseberries, cherries, rhubarb, cranberries, and raspberries. They can be frozen in a solid pack in a freezer container or in a loose pack. For a loose pack, spread the fruit on a cookie sheet or tray, cover, and put in the freezer until the outside of the fruit is solid. Pack in freezer bags, label, and return to the freezer.

Some artificial sweeteners can be used when freezing fruit especially if the fruit is to be kept for only 3 to 6 months. Other sweeteners may cause a bitter flavor after the fruit has been frozen. Follow the manufacturer's directions when using an artificial sweetener.

Fruits may also be frozen unsweetened in a liquid pack. Pack the pieces in their own juice, water, or crushed fruit. A small crumpled piece of wax paper or parchment paper placed on top of the fruit helps keep it pressed down in the liquid once the container has been sealed. The paper should loosely fill the headspace area. Do not use aluminum foil since acid in the fruit can form holes in the foil and tiny pieces of foil may drop onto the food.

Thawed frozen fruit is best if it is served when only a few ice crystals remain. If thawed completely, the fruit will become mushy. Thaw fruit in the refrigerator in the closed container. It takes 12 hours per pint (500 mL). If you need to shorten thawing time, run cold water over the container or defrost in the microwave. Remember, when you serve the fruit, serve the juice, too. It contains some of the vitamin C drained out of the fruit.

Canning Foods

When you can fruits and vegetables, you heat them hot enough and long enough to destroy spoilage organisms. This processing also stops the action of enzymes. Processing is done in either a steam-pressure canner or a boiling-waterbath canner. The kind of canner used depends on the kind of food being canned.

Canners

For all common vegetables except tomatoes, use a steam-pressure canner. Why use a pressure canner? It is the only safe method for processing low-acid foods such as vegetables, meat, poultry, and fish. Why? Because heat-resistant spores of bacteria called *Clostridium botulinum* can grow in these foods and produce a deadly **toxin** (poison). The effects of the toxin when it enters our body is botulism food poisoning.

Botulism is a potential problem in canned

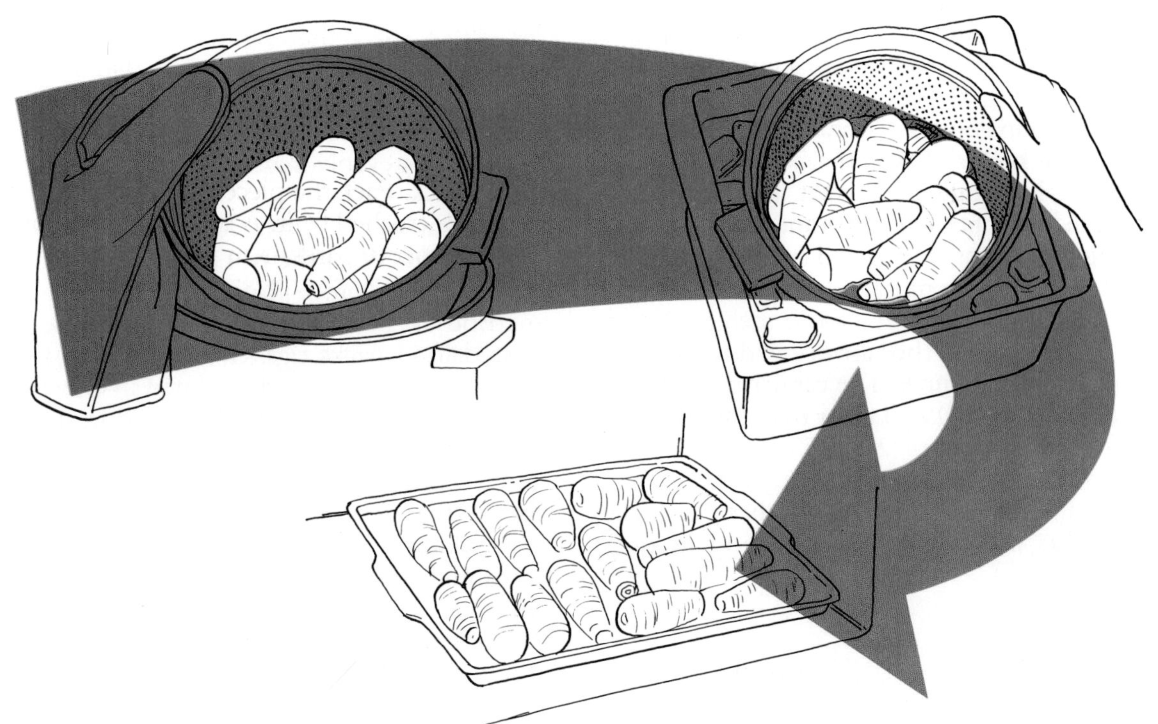

To freeze cleaned vegetables, quickly blanch them in hot water to stop the enzyme action, cool them immediately in icewater, and then spread on a tray for freezing. Pack them in storage containers after they're frozen.

foods because the bacteria cannot tolerate air. The spores only grow where there is no air. Canning creates an ideal place for the bacteria to grow because the canning process drives the air out of the jars. Then, if there is not enough salt or acid to keep the bacteria from growing, it will produce its deadly toxins in the jar. In a pressure canner at 10 pounds pressure, the temperature of the steam is 240°F (115°C). This is high enough to kill the *Clostridium botulinum* organism in a relatively short time. Processing food in a boiling-waterbath canner, even for several hours, is not safe for low-acid foods.

A **pressure canner** is a large heavy kettle with a lid that can be locked on to make it steamtight. It is equipped with a gauge or regulator for measuring pressure, a vent or petcock for exhausting air, a pressure plug for safety, and a rubber gasket for preventing steam from escaping between the lid and the pan rim. The canner also must contain a rack to hold the jars off the bottom.

There are two types of gauges used on pressure canners—a dial gauge and a weighted gauge. The dial gauge is most commonly thought of with the pressure canner. It is attached to the cover and has a meter for reading the internal pressure. This type of gauge must be tested for accuracy every year before the canning season and during the season if used frequently. Dial gauges are tested with a special thermometer or a special gauge. Contact your local Cooperative Extension Service office for information about testing the gauge.

The weighted gauges (more accurately described as a pressure regulator) maintain the pressure at a set maximum, rather than simply indicating the pressure. This pressure regulator does not have any moving parts or springs, so there is nothing to wear out or get brittle with use.

A **boiling-waterbath** canner is used for processing canned acid foods. These include fruits and fruit products, pickles, relishes, tomatoes, jams, and jellies. Acid foods are those that contain enough natural acid to have a pH of 4.6 or below. A waterbath canner is a large kettle with a tight-fitting lid. Jars of food are covered with boiling water and kept at boiling temperature for a specified length of time. A waterbath canner must have a metal or wooden rack to hold the jars at least ½ inch (1.25 cm) off the bottom so they are not in direct contact with the heat source. The canner should be at least 4 inches (10 cm) taller than the jars to allow for 1 to 2 inches (2.5 to 5 cm) of water covering the jars plus a 2 inch (5 cm) space for hard boiling. You will need a canner about 12 inches (30 cm) deep for processing food in quart (liter) jars.

Containers for Canning

Use only standard, glass canning jars for home canning. They are tempered to withstand high temperature and pressure. It is not recommended to use commercial packer jars such as coffee or mayonnaise jars. These are not tempered and may break during processing. Also, the sealing edge on packer jars is not perfectly level nor as thick as standard canning jars. Although the canning lid and screw band may appear to fit right, these jars are not made exactly like canning jars, so they often fail to seal.

The most reliable lids for home canning are the two-piece metal, self-sealing type. The metal disk, called the **flat,** has a sealing compound around the edge. This sealing edge is shaped to prevent the lid from slipping on the jar. The ring band or screw band holds the flat in place on the jar during processing and until the vacuum in the jars seals the lid tightly.

Canning Low-Acid Foods

Most vegetables that are good when cooked are suitable for canning. But some kinds of vegetables, for example, cauliflower and broccoli, are better frozen than canned. Before canning, wash vegetables thoroughly in cold running water. Sort the vegetables according to size and maturity. Vegetables of similar size and maturity will cook evenly, resulting in a uniform product.

Vegetables can be placed into the jars either hot or cold. With the **hot pack method,** you heat the food before placing it in the jars. This method is generally preferred because the heated food packs tighter and requires fewer jars. Generally the food is heated in water and the water is then used as the liquid in the jars when processing the food.

The **cold pack method** is acceptable for vegetables that become too fragile to handle after precooking. Uncooked food is packed in the jars and then covered with hot liquid. After filling a jar with the uncooked food and liquid, use a plastic knife or narrow spatula to get out trapped air bubbles.

Headspace must be left between the food and the top of the jar to allow the liquid to boil freely without spilling. If jars are filled too full, liquid will be lost during processing. This could keep the lids from sealing. The recommended headspace is usually ½ inch (1.25 cm), but corn, lima beans, and peas need 1 inch (2.5 cm) because they expand during processing.

Make sure the rim of the jar is clean, put on the flat, and then put on the ring band. Place the jars in the canner. Do not put the jars on the bottom of the canner. First put in a cooking rack and then the jars.

To can low-acid foods: 1. Fill the canning jars and then insert a long utensil down the side of a jar to release trapped air bubbles. 2. Food expands during the canning process, so leave 1 inch of space between the food level and the top of the jar. 3. Process the food in a pressure canner. Follow specific recipe guidelines for the proper timing.

Place the steam-pressure canner on the burner and add at least 2 to 3 inches (5 to 7.5 cm) of boiling water. The water level should not be over the tops of the jars.

Place the cover on the canner and fasten securely. Turn the heat on high and watch for steam to come out of the petcock. This procedure is often referred to as "exhausting the canner." Once there is a good steady steam whistling from the petcock, let the steam escape for 10 minutes. During this step, air is driven out of the canner and replaced by steam. This step is necessary to ensure correct processing.

After 10 minutes, close the petcock or place the weighted gauge on the canner lid. Let the pressure rise rapidly. When it gets to about 10 pounds or when the weighted gauge starts to rock, turn the heat down. Start counting the processing time when the pressure reaches the 10 pounds. Keep an eye on the pressure for the whole processing time. Processing times vary for different foods and at different altitudes. For exact directions, refer to *Home and Garden Bulletin No. 8* by the U.S. Department of Agriculture or contact your County Cooperative Extension Service.

At the end of the processing time, turn off the heat. Let the pressure drop naturally. Don't try to make it drop faster by opening the petcock, removing weighted gauge, or by running cold water over the canner. The sudden change in pressure will draw liquid out of the jars.

When the pressure has dropped to 0 or when the pressure plug has dropped, wait 2 to 3 minutes before opening the petcock or removing the weighted gauge. Do not take the cover off first. Always tip the cover away from you to avoid burning yourself with steam.

Canning Acid Foods

Mold and yeast spores can grow in an acid environment. However, heating jars of acid food in a boiling-waterbath canner for a specified length of time will kill these microorganisms. Bacterial spoilage from organisms such as *Clostridum botulinum* is not a threat since they do not grow in an acid environment.

As with vegetables for steam-pressure canning, acid foods can be placed in the jars either hot or cold. The hot pack method is also generally preferred for the boiling-waterbath method because the food packs tighter. Also if the product is thick such as applesauce and tomato sauce, the hot pack method enables the product to heat more evenly and insures a safer product.

The same procedures are followed when filling jars with acid foods as with low-acid vegetables. The only difference is if the food is processed for only 15 minutes or less, the jars must be sterilized. To sterilize jars, cover them with water and boil for 15 minutes. Keep them hot until they are filled.

To process acid foods in a boiling-waterbath canner, put the filled glass jars into the canner containing hot or boiling water. For cold pack, have the water in the canner hot but not boiling. For hot pack, have the water at boiling temperature. Add boiling water, if needed, to bring the water 1 to 2 inches (2.5 to 5 cm) over the tops of the jars. Be careful not to pour boiling water directly on the glass jars.

Put the cover on the canner. When the water in the canner comes to a rolling boil, start to count processing time. Boil gently and steadily for the recommended time. Add boiling water during processing if needed to keep the containers covered.

For exact directions for processing fruits, tomatoes, pickles, or jams and jellies as well as the processing times and adjustments for altitude, refer to *Home and Garden Bulletin No. 8* by the U.S. Department of Agriculture or contact your County Cooperative Extension Service.

Remove the jars from the canner immediately when the processing time is up. Let them cool on a rack, a board, or on several layers of towels away from cold drafts to keep them from breaking from a sudden change in temperature. The jars will seal as they sit. You will usually, but not always, hear the lids click when they seal.

After processing any canned food, leave the

jars undisturbed for at least 12 hours. Then check to see that they have sealed. The center of the lid will be down or stay down when pressed lightly.

Unscrew the metal ring bands and remove them. If the bands are stuck on from food or syrup that might have leaked out of the jars during canning, hold a hot, damp cloth around the top of the jar for about a minute to help loosen the band. Label the jars with the name of the food and the date canned.

Storing Canned Foods

Canned food should be stored in a cool, dark, dry place. Even foods that are properly processed will lose some of the nutritive value in a short period of time. The process is accelerated if the food is stored at temperatures about 50°F (10°C). Conversely, canned food should not be stored where it might be subject to freezing, since the food can expand and break the seal. Plan to use the canned foods within a year.

When using home-canned vegetables, it is recommended they be boiled for 10 minutes in a covered pan. Corn and spinach should be boiled for 20 minutes.

Drying of Foods

Drying is the oldest method of preserving food. The early American settlers dried foods such as corn, apple slices, currants, grapes, and meat. Compared with other methods, drying is quite simple and inexpensive. Dried foods keep well because the moisture content is so low that spoilage organisms cannot grow.

Drying will never replace canning and freezing because those two methods do a better job of retaining the taste, appearance, and nutritive value of fresh food. However, drying is an ex-

Rediscover the prized flavor of dried fruit that yesteryear's pioneers treasured for eating and cooking. Drying fruit concentrates the sugars of the whole fruit into a high-energy and high-flavor snack or mealtime food.

cellent way to preserve foods that adds variety to meals and provides delicious, nutritious snacks.

Recommended methods of canning and freezing have been determined by research and widespread experience. Home drying does not have firmly established procedures. Food can be dried by the sun if the air is hot and dry enough or in an oven or food dryer if the climate is humid.

For a good-quality product, vegetables and fruits must be prepared for drying as soon as possible after harvesting. They should be blanched, cooled, and laid out to dry without delay. Foods should be dried rapidly, but not so fast that the outside becomes hard before the moisture inside has a chance to evaporate.

Drying must not be interrupted. Once you start drying the food, don't let it cool down in order to start drying again later. Mold and other spoilage organisms can grow on partly dried food.

During the first part of the drying process, the air temperature can be as high as 150°F (65°C). So that the moisture can evaporate quickly from the food. Because food loses heat during rapid evaporation, the air temperature can be high without increasing the temperature of the food. As soon as the outside begins to feel dry and the rate of evaporation slows down, the food warms up. The air temperature must then be reduced to below 150°F (65°C).

Drying food evenly takes a little extra effort and attention. Stirring the pieces of food frequently and shifting the racks in the oven or dryer are essential because heat is not the same in all parts of an appliance. For the best results, spread thin layers of uniformly sized pieces of food on the drying racks.

Dried fruits are a good source of energy because they contain concentrated fruit sugars. The drying process, however, destroys some of the vitamins present in fruits. Dried vegetables are a good source of minerals and the B vitamins. Both fruits and vegetables provide useful amounts of the fiber you need.

Many kinds of fresh fruits, vegetables, herbs, meat, and fish can be dried. If you have never tried drying food before, it is a good idea to experiment first by drying a small quantity in the oven. This way you can see if you like the taste and texture of dried food. At the same time you can become familiar with the drying process.

Detailed directions for drying foods can be found in *Home and Garden Bulletin No. 217* by the U.S. Department of Agriculture or contact your County Cooperative Extension Service.

Foods that Turn into Poison

Are you flirting with food poison? Do you thaw meat at room temperature, or use canned foods that leak or bulge? Do you store foods near cleaning supplies or in cabinets where water pipes or drains pass through? Do you let foods sit out on the counter? If you answered yes to any one of the above questions, you are flirting with food poison.

There are many government, state, and local agencies that regulate the food you purchase to insure it is safe. A study at Colorado State University found 41,000 federal and state regulations related to hamburger. These regulations touched on everything—grazing practices of cattle, conditions in slaughterhouses, and methods used to process meat for sale to supermarkets, restaurants, and fast-food outlets.

Other studies have found that the occurrence of food-related illness is largely the result of carelessness or lack of knowledge about the proper handling of food on the part of the food preparer. The application of simple storage, food preparation, and sanitation practices will help stop food related illness in the home.

Four organisms are the sources of most food poisoning cases:

- Staphylococcus aureus.
- Salmonella, which includes a large group of bacteria lumped under this general category.
- Clostridium perfringens.
- Clostridium botulinum.

Proper food handling helps prevent food poisoning.

Staphylococcus Aureus

Under the microscope, these bacteria appear as small, sphere-shaped organisms in pairs or short chains. Sometimes they appear in irregular grapelike clusters. They occur normally on the skin and in the nasal passages of humans and animals. The organisms can be expelled into the air in drops of moisture during breathing, talking, coughing, and sneezing.

This species of bacteria does not form spores. **Spores** are the inactive stage of bacteria. They are resistant to heat, cold, and drying. In the laboratory, cultures of Staphylococcus aureus bacteria have lived for many months at room temperature or under refrigeration. When cultures were dried on fiber, paper, and cloth or held in dried food, the bacteria survived many months also.

This bacteria in food does not cause food poisoning. But when the bacteria are allowed to multiply in foods, they produce a toxin which is the agent that causes illness in humans. The bacteria are killed by heat—even as low as 140°F (60°C) maintained for 10 minutes. However, the toxin produced by the bacteria is highly resistant to heat, cold, and chemicals. Freezing, refrigeration, or heating foods at temperatures required for serving does not reduce the toxin significantly. The more toxin ingested, the greater the reaction by the body. The disease is rarely fatal.

This type of bacteria is introduced into the food during preparation, particularly by the food handler. If the food is allowed to stand at room temperatures for two hours or more, the bacteria begin to multiply. As the bacteria grow, they may produce toxin. Moist meat dishes and starchy foods provide an excellent medium for growth and are frequent sources of food poisoning. Types of foods in this class are eclairs, cream puffs, cake fillings, potato salads, and meat salads. Sliced meat, such as roast beef and particularly ham, are often involved. Usually these foods are served without reheating, and unless they are served soon after cooking or refrigerated or frozen promptly, they become "incubators" for bacteria and the resultant toxin. The bacteria do not change the looks, taste, or odor of the food.

When food contaminated with a significant amount of toxin is eaten, the person usually experiences a sudden and violent onset of nausea, vomiting, and diarrhea within two to four hours. Abdominal cramps are common. Depending on the severity of reaction, the symptoms may last in varying degrees for one to two days.

Preventing food poisoning from Staphylococcus aureus is based on the following principles:

1. Practicing personal cleanliness habits and using clean facilities and utensils when preparing food.

2. Using sufficient heat to destroy the bacteria during cooking.

3. Immediately refrigerating or freezing foods to retard the growth of bacteria.

Salmonella

Salmonella is a general term applied to a group of about 2000 closely related types of bacteria that cause food poisoning in humans. Under the microscope, all these types appear as short, thin rods. The bacteria do not form spores.

Salmonella bacteria occur frequently in the intestinal tracts of humans and animals. The organisms are found in raw meats, poultry, eggs, milk, fish, and products made from them. Other sources of the organisms are food handlers and pets, including turtles, birds, fish, dogs, and cats. Insects and rodents are also sources of the bacteria. Food contaminated by salmonella bacteria does not change in taste, odor, or flavor, so the presence of the organisms is not apparent.

The disease caused by salmonella bacteria is called **salmonellosis.** If food containing salmonella bacteria is eaten, the organisms multiply rapidly in the intestine, causing a headache, diarrhea, abdominal discomfort, and, occasionally, vomiting. These symptoms appear within 24 hours after eating contaminated food. Most people recover in two to four days. Children under four, elderly people, and people already weakened by disease sometimes become seriously ill. Death from the disease may occur.

Preventing food poisoning from salmonella is based on four principles:

1. Cooking foods thoroughly and serving them hot.

2. Preventing recontamination of foods through cleanliness and use of sanitary utensils.

3. Prompt cooling or freezing of foods after preparation to retard the growth of all bacteria.

4. Full reheating of stored foods to destroy bacteria.

Clostridium Perfringens

Under the microscope, these bacteria appear as short, plump organisms, occurring singly or in pairs. The bacteria commonly inhabit the in-

After cutting up raw poultry, thoroughly wash the cutting board to prevent Clostridium perfringens.

testinal tracts of humans and other warm-blooded animals. The organism produces spores which are resistant to heat, cold, and drying.

The spores appear virtually everywhere—in sewage, soil, dust, and food. To produce the active form of these bacteria, the spores require warmth and certain anaerobic conditions (without air). In their active stage, these bacteria multiply profusely at 60° to 120°F (16° to 50°C). This form is killed by temperatures of 150°F (65°C) or above or are reduced in numbers in stored foods when the temperature is 40°F (4°C) or lower. However, the spores can survive temperatures of 212°F (100°C) for 1 hour or more.

Food poisoning from this bacteria is associated with meat, poultry, and other high-protein foods that have been improperly cooked or stored. Risk of food poisoning in such instances occurs when large amounts of food are held in containers on steam tables as in restaurants and institutions. An anaerobic condition is produced in meat when air is eliminated by heating. This allows surviving spores to germinate and multiply rapidly in warm foods. Large numbers of this bacterium result in food poisoning.

Symptoms of perfringens poisoning will begin in 8 to 24 hours when food containing large numbers of the bacteria are eaten. Signs of the disease include diarrhea and gas pains, all usually subsiding in 24 hours. Nausea and vomiting rarely occur. This disease is rarely fatal.

These bacteria are so widespread that it is impossible to reduce their incidence. Consequently, either the spore form or the bacteria form should be assumed to be present in foods.

Preventing food poisoning from Clostridium perfringens is based on three principles:

1. Cooking high-protein foods (meat and poultry particularly) well enough to kill the organisms.

2. Keeping foods hot—above 140°F (60°C)—until eaten.

3. Promptly refrigerating foods in shallow containers for quick cooling.

4. Washing thoroughly all cutting surfaces (especially wooden cutting boards) and utensils.

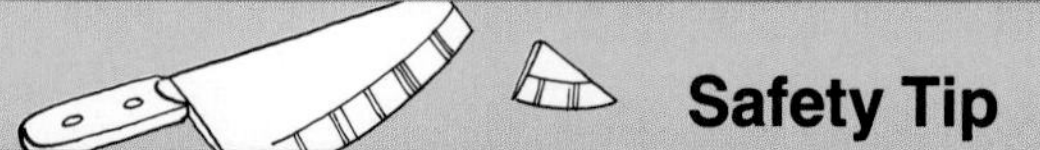

Safety Tip

Do you know what to do if you or a friend should swallow something poisonous? For instance, if you have food poisoning, drink water and then induce vomiting. If someone ingests gasoline, have him or her drink water or milk, but do not induce vomiting. Always call a doctor or your nearest poison center in an emergency. Keep the emergency number and the numbers of the police, poison control center, and hospital near your phone.

Poison Swallowed	*What to Drink*	*Induce Vomiting?*
Cosmetics	Water	Yes
Medicines	Water	Yes
Insect and Rat Poisons	Water	Yes
Food Poisoning	Water	Yes
Gasoline and Petroleum Products	Water or Milk	No
Acids and Alkali	Water or Milk	No
Household Cleaners, Polishes, or Paints	Water or Milk	No
Plants	Water	Yes

Clostridium Botulinum

Under the microscope, these bacteria appear as rod-shaped organisms occurring singly or in short chains. The bacteria form spores that occur throughout the environment—in soil, water, and on produce and other foods. The spores are harmless unless triggered to divide by certain conditions, such as an anaerobic condition. Anaerobic conditions occur in the deeper parts of food products even when the products are exposed to the air.

When the bacteria are in a low-acid food, they multiply and produce a toxin that is responsible for the disease called botulism. The disease is rare, but often fatal. Even small amounts of toxin can be fatal if ingested. Eating improperly canned foods is a major cause of botulism. Since 1925, fewer than 10 deaths have been reported caused by food canned commercially, while about 700 deaths have occurred from eating home-canned foods.

Boiling high-acid foods, such as tomatoes and fruits, will destroy the bacteria. Spores may survive, but they are unable to germinate and grow in high-acid canned foods. Higher temperatures, attained only by pressure cooking, are required to kill the spores in low-acid foods. Low-acid foods include meat, poultry, fish, vegetables, and some fruits. As the bacteria multiply and produce the toxin, they also produce variable amounts of gas. Some strains produce a foul odor, while other strains do not.

When the toxin is ingested, signs of botulism usually occur in 18 to 36 hours, but may appear in a few hours or as long as 8 days. Symptoms of botulism include general weakness, constipation, some headache followed by double vision, impaired speech, and difficulty in chewing and swallowing. The disease frequently results in death within 3 to 7 days unless treatment is initiated promptly at the onset of symptoms.

Prevention of botulism is based on five principles:

1. In canning foods of low acidity such as beans and carrots, use pressure cookers and

cook long enough with high enough temperature and pressure to destroy the spores.

2. In canning of foods of high acidity (tomatoes, for example), cook at boiling temperatures in strict accordance with canning instructions to kill the bacteria, yeasts, and molds. Spores cannot grow in high acid foods.

3. Avoid tasting or eating canned foods from containers showing the following defects: leaking, bulging, or severely damaged cans; cracked jars; or jars with loose or bulging lids.

4. Avoid tasting any canned foods that spurt liquid when the container is opened or any canned food that has an abnormal odor or appearance.

5. Boil low-acid, canned foods for 10 minutes prior to serving.

Protecting Yourself

How can you guard against food contamination? Beginning now, make it a habit to follow these safety rules.

1. Clean your hands before and after handling raw foods. Thoroughly wash all cutting surfaces and utensils after each use.

2. Put perishable and frozen foods in the refrigerator as soon as you get home from shopping.

3. If you prepare foods ahead of time, put them in the refrigerator until you're ready to serve them.

4. Don't leave leftover foods on the table. Store them in the refrigerator promptly.

5. Keep your refrigerator at 40°F (4°C) or below.

6. Don't let frozen foods thaw at room temperature. Defrost them in the refrigerator.

7. Cool foods promptly in small quantities and shallow layers so that the temperature of the food is brought down to refrigerator temperature in 2 to 3 hours.

8. When cooking meats, use a meat thermometer to make sure the interior part of the

Don't take a chance with home-canned foods. Boil low-acid canned foods for 10 minutes to prevent botulism.

meat is cooked thoroughly. For example, that is at least 175° to 185°F (79° to 85°C) for poultry, 160°F (71°C) for fresh pork.

9. If you do home canning, use the boiling waterbath method only for acid foods, including jams, jellies and pickles. Use the pressure canner (at 10 pounds pressure) for all low acid foods.

10. If you find a jar or can in which food does not look or smell right, determine the cause of spoilage, such as an unsealed jar. If the cause cannot be determined, destroy the entire lot. Do not taste the food. It could be fatal.

11. Keep hot foods hot and cold foods cold until it is time to eat.

12. Be careful handling pets in the home. Pet feeding dishes, toys, or bedding should not be allowed in the kitchen or near any items which come in contact with the family's food or with utensils or working surfaces used in the preparation of food.

Other Food Poisons

The food poisons that have been discussed have all related to the safe handling of foods. There are two common foods that at certain times can be poisonous. They are rhubarb and potatoes.

Rhubarb leaves contain oxalic acid and should never be eaten. After a frost, the oxalic acid will migrate from the leaf blades to the stalk. Therefore, the stalk should not be used but should be discarded.

Potatoes sometimes will have a green color. This green color, seen just beneath the skin, indicates the presence of chlorophyll. Greening in potatoes is undesirable because of its association with a bitter taste and the possibility of the presence of solanine. Solanine is a poisonous substance and its presence in increased amounts in the potato is considered to be a health hazard.

Vocabulary Review

Botulism
Blanching
Enzymes
Antioxidant
Ascorbic acid
Pectin
Toxin
Pressure canner
Boiling-waterbath canner
Hot pack method
Cold pack method
Spores
Salmonella
Salmonellosis

Questions for Review

1. Why do you need to can, freeze, or dry foods to preserve them?
2. What are some ways you can prevent the loss of vitamins in the preparation and storage of frozen foods?
3. What types of packaging are suitable for freezing foods?
4. Why is it desirable to freeze foods soon after harvesting or purchasing them?
5. What is the purpose of blanching vegetables before freezing them?
6. Name four steps to follow when freezing vegetables.
7. Does freezing improve the quality of underripe or overripe food?
8. What determines whether you add sugar to fruit before freezing it?
9. Give examples of low-acid foods and explain why they require special care in preserving.
10. Give examples of an acid food and explain any difference that might be involved in canning.
11. How is *Clostridium botulinum* killed? Why isn't it a threat in an acid environment?
12. What containers should be used for canning?
13. What determines whether the hot pack or cold pack method should be used when canning vegetables?

14. Why does drying a food preserve it?

15. Why are dried foods a good source of energy?

16. What could a bulging can of food mean? Would the food in a damaged or bulging can be safe to test by tasting?

17. Why is it necessary to return prepared foods such as roasted turkey, sour cream dip, and creamed corn to the refrigerator immediately after serving? Is a party dip that was left out overnight safe to eat the next day?

18. Describe the conditions which promote the production of toxins by bacteria in foods.

19. Why is it important to wash your hands, countertop, or cutting board after handling raw poultry and before preparing other foods?

20. Are the following foods safe to eat?

a. unheated home-canned green beans right out of the jar.

b. potato salad left on a picnic table for four hours.

c. hard-cooked eggs eaten three hours after an egg hunt.

How could each of these three foods be handled to ensure their safe eating?

Things to Do

1. Freeze one type of fruit such as peaches using a sugar pack, syrup pack, pectin syrup pack, and one with no sugar or syrup. Compare the end products for color, texture, and flavor.

2. Give examples of low-acid foods and explain how to can them.

3. Give examples of acid foods and explain how to can them.

4. Visit the natural foods section of a grocery store to see what types of dried foods are available. If possible, purchase some to sample.

5. Compare the cost of freezing, canning, and drying food items such as apples, peas, peaches, or beans. Consider the equipment costs and time involved.

6. Can a food and use the USDA *Home and Garden Bulletin No. 8* on canning as a reference.

7. Dry sliced apples or bananas in the oven and use the USDA *Home and Garden Bulletin No. 217* as a reference.

8. Call to arrange a visit to talk to the manager of your favorite fast-foods restaurant about food safety procedures. Ask about food storage, preparation, and safe holding times and temperatures for prepared foods. Share what you find out with the class.

9. Plan and make a poster for the classroom about foods that turn into poison and how to prevent problems.

10. Using a thermometer, check the temperature of your refrigerator on different shelves. Do the temperatures vary? Are some locations cooler than others? Where would you store milk, meat, or other foods that spoil quickly in your refrigerator?

Section 5
In The Kitchen

Wanted, Four Servings a Day!

Fresh fruits and vegetables that at one time graced only the tables of the very rich are now commonplace. Sixty years ago, an orange was a once-a-year treasure to stuff in a Christmas stocking. Now cool, tangy orange juice starts the morning for millions of Americans—and at a price most people can afford.

The 20th century has seen a miraculous growth of our agricultural bounty in both quantity and variety. Fruits and vegetables have been developed that are beyond the wildest dreams of our ancestors. Those varieties are grown all year long not just to be deliciously nutritious, but to be shipped over long distances and arrive fresh and beautiful.

Tantalizing, colorful fruits have had magical attraction for most people almost "since time began." Even everyday expressions link fruit with rewards, "good" behavior, and prosperity. "The apple of his/her eye," "the fruits of labor," "a fruitful day," and "their words never bore fruit" are phrases that link our high regard for fruit to behaviors and help advertisers sell their products through name and association. One of the most powerful sales boosts for cereals is to feature juicy red strawberries or freshly sliced bananas on the package.

Nutritive Notes

What's really nice about all this fruit fame is that fruit deserves its good reputation! The rainbow of flavorful fruits available to you supplies precious nutrients and pleasurable eating. The fruit portion of the Fruits and Vegetables category in the Basic Foods Group supplies the key nutrients vitamins A and C. These two vitamins are vital for night vision, to fight infections, and to heal injuries. Fruits are the best source of easily destroyed vitamin C and a good source of the more stable vitamin A. Citrus fruits are almost legendary as the number one source of vitamin C. Vitamin A is plentiful in commonly eaten fruits such as peaches, apricots, cantaloupes, and watermelons.

You can generally rate fruit for its vitamin A content by the depth of its color. The deeper yellow to red colors indicate a larger amount of the plant pigment called **carotene.** This pigment is converted by the body into vitamin A. Besides being important for good vision, vitamin A is needed for growth, healthy hair, and a clear skin. One of the first visible symptoms of a diet without enough vitamin A is coarse, dry hair that doesn't grow.

Fruit also contains important minerals, water, and carbohydrates. Bananas stand out from other food for providing potassium. The

You can take advantage of foods' natural packaging for portable snacks and lunches. Take along an unpeeled whole fruit for nutritious eating.

relatively high iron content of dried fruits, such as raisins and apricots, make them valuable for everyone, and virtually "lifesavers" for the vegetarians who omit iron-rich meats from their diets. Another mineral that various fruits such as oranges and tomatoes supply in significant amounts is calcium.

Fruits contain cellulose that supplies useful fiber to the diet. Fiber is not digested and used as a nutrient by the body, but that is what makes it vital to your well-being. Strange as it may sound, your body uses fiber by not using it! The fiber provides needed bulk that combines with the toxic waste products in the intestines and helps to move them out of the body. During the past few decades, the function of fiber in the diet was neglected as the proportion of highly refined, processed foods increased drastically. Research linking the lack of fiber in the diet to the incidence of intestinal cancer caused everyone to take a slight step "back" to revive the use of whole-grain products and eat more fiber-rich fruits and vegetables.

Although fruit is relatively high in sugar content, the calorie count is low compared to other sweets and desserts. Fruits are delectable and satisfying as snacks, desserts, and as taste-tempting, nutritious additions to other foods and recipes.

Four servings from the fruit and vegetable group is the suggested guideline for a balanced diet.

You will need to choose foods from the other food groups for protein and some fat, which fruit generally lacks. Remember, too, a balanced diet comes from choosing the recommended servings from the other three basic food groups.

Pleading the Case for Natural Foods!

Fruit comes in its own natural packaging. The skin miraculously protects the softer fruit, seeds, and nutrients from spoilage, invasion of insects, and the weather's elements for various periods of time. Some skins on fruits are nutritious to eat, while others are always discarded. (Be sure to wash fruit before eating to remove dirt and insecticides.)

Every time you cut a food and expose more surface, you are providing more avenues of escape for the enclosed nutrients to dissolve, evaporate, destruct in the light, or break down in heat. Any processing of fruit that cuts it into pieces, removes the outer covering, or exposes it to heat, cold, moisture, or drying also will remove or destroy some of the nutritive value. It is for that reason that you would be wise to eat fruit in its natural state, or its most natural state possible, whenever you can.

For example, if you are planning how to fix fresh pears for dessert, remember that a fresh cut juicy pear half attractively arranged on a plate would have more fresh flavor and nutrients than a cut up cooked or canned pear. When purchasing a fruit snack, a whole apple or orange would have more of the original nutrients than a so-called natural dried fruit roll, which is also very high in sugar content. Processed and cooked fruits can be marvelous foods that retain many of their important nutrients. But whenever you can, make the choice to eat fruit in its natural state. You can't lose—it's a winning decision.

Selecting Fresh Fruit

Have you ever purchased fruit only to be disappointed by a tasteless, underripe product or one that was too ripe to enjoy? Whether you are in the **produce department** (the area of a store that has fresh fruits and vegetables) or shopping the local farmers' market, there are certain guidelines that will help you avoid being disappointed by an underripe, overripe, or spoiled fruit. You can judge fruit by sight, sound, smell, and feel. When confronted by piles of fruit or bags of prepackaged items, look, feel, smell, and listen for products that are:

- Deeply developed in their particular color.
- Firm (not mushy or soft in spots).
- Fully developed in their characteristic shape.
- Aromatic. (A ripe pineapple smells like it tastes. Melons similar to cantaloupes have a highly flavored smell.)
- Heavy in your hand. Fruits lose moisture as they are stored. Fresh fruits are likely to be holding more moisture and will therefore be heavier as well as juicier to eat. For example, it's easy to sort oranges and grapefruits for the heavy ones. The difference is obvious.

Melons should sound hollow when thumped with the palm of your hand. Experiment with several melons. When you get your choice home, cut open the melon to check the relationship between the sound and the ripeness. Once you develop this technique, it works well.

Damaged or partly spoiled fruit is not a bargain at any price. Notice how mold is likely to start in the stem area of overripe fruit.

Consumer Guide

Best buys. Fruits may be available the year around, but the prices are lowest during the harvest season when the fruit is most plentiful. If you plan to preserve by canning, freezing, or drying, the harvest season is the best time to buy the fruit. See Chapter 9 for more information about preserving foods.

Some conditions immediately rule out the fruit as an unacceptable choice. Avoid fruits that are withered, mushy, hard, or show mold in the stem area.

Degree of Ripeness

Just how ripe is ripe? The question is a reasonable one. Understanding what "ripe" means will help you judge quality. **Mature** fruit has grown to its full size. **Ripe** is the term used to describe when a piece of fruit is ready to eat. The crispness, firmness, juiciness, and flavor have reached their peak in ripe fruit. **Underripe** fruits might be mature, but have not yet developed the qualities just listed. **Immature** fruits, however will never ripen after they are picked. To tell the difference between immature fruit and underripe mature fruit, compare them to the usual size and color for that kind of fruit. Immature fruits will be noticeably small, hard, and pale in color.

You can keep underripe, but mature fruit at room temperature until it ripens. If you should happen to purchase "green" fruit that never ripens at room temperature, it should be returned to the store. Most produce managers will want to know when you are displeased with a purchase and also will refund the purchase price.

Harvesting

In order to get the mature fruit to the consumer, growers have to judge just the right time to pick the product. Since most fruits continue to ripen after picking, the grower picks the mature fruit when it is underripe to prevent it from overripening or spoiling before it is sold. That is why "locally grown" fruit is considered the top buy. Those growers are closer to the consumer and can take the risk of picking the fruit after it is ripe.

Oranges and grapes must reach maturity before they are picked. They will not ripen after picking. Their keeping qualities, however, allow them to be held and shipped while ripe. Perhaps you have bought an orange that looked green. This coloring does not mean it is underripe. Warm weather and the bright lights in produce departments sometimes cause a "regreening" of oranges which is due to the development of chlorophyll in the skin. It is harmless and does not affect the flavor or quality of the orange.

Packaging Methods

The recent development of an appreciation for natural foods has brought about a new look to the produce department of many supermarkets—the country-market look—featuring self-serve bulk produce. This differs sharply from the sterile prepackaged departments that offered the consumer no choice.

Bulk produce refers to fruits and vegetables that are sold loose (individual pieces in a bin or on a table). Apples, oranges, whole melons, and peaches are examples of fruit likely to be sold loose in the produce department.

Packaged produce is contained in a plastic bag, tray, or box wrapped in plastic. Soft plums, strawberries, blueberries, and cut melons are usually sold in packaged forms.

Unitized produce is sold bunched together with a rubber band or tape. Bananas are often unitized before selling.

There are advantages to these different types of shopping. Buying bulk produce lets you specifically choose each piece of fruit. This allows you to get the best fruit available. You also get just the quantity you want—not too much or too little.

Packaging and unitizing can be a terrific convenience. They are both a time-saving service and a produce-saving protection. Many fruits benefit from the wrappings and the rigid, protective sides of the containers. Choose which type of packaging suits your purpose for a particular fruit and for a particular time.

Pick Your Own Fresh Produce

Have you ever picked your own dew-fresh strawberries on a cool summer morning? Maybe you have seen wonderful pictures of sunny fall days with families selecting a bright orange pumpkin from a whole field for their jack-o-lantern. Now, even city people can harvest their own fresh fruits or vegetables. All across the country, farmers are putting in a new kind of crop—your crop! Acres of strawberries, blueberries, raspberries, oranges, pumpkins, apples, and squash are being planted for the consumer to harvest. Charging by the pound or box, the farmers plant the fields and advertise when the crops are ready to pick. The buyer does the selecting and picking. It's fun and economical. You do the work, but it's all a fun outing. As labor costs continue to rise, watch for this trend of pick your own farming to increase.

Consumer Guide

There are several "new" ways for the shopper to buy ripe, locally grown produce. Revived to fit new times, the farmers' market offers farm-fresh produce, an exciting shopping experience, and usually lower prices. The fun of selecting your own produce can be outweighed by the extra time and inconvenience it causes. However, it also can provide an adventurous outing and magnificent fruit.

Markets across the country represent the local products. Colorful displays and booths offer regional favorites. The southern states sport blackeyed peas, sweet potatoes, and okra, while southwestern states might display cactus leaves, chilis, cilantro, homemade salsa, and more. An eastern tour would include maple syrup, peaches, apples, pears, blueberries, and even a few catches from the sea. San Francisco markets cater to the many Asian and East Indian citizens with sugarcane, bokchoy, daikon, and winter melon.

Even teenagers and youth groups have turned their pleasure garden hobbies into profitable activities. The useful, but limited, farmers' market does not replace the efficient conventional supermarket in supplying food for the whole nation, but it is a charming and enriching addition to food marketing in the United States.

Storing Fresh Fruits

Citrus Fruits

Citrus fruits can be stored for a week or more at room temperature and even longer in the refrigerator. Be certain that the container for room-temperature storage allows for air circulation around the fruits. This retards mold. Citrus fruits are heavy, so the containers should not be too deep. If stacked too deeply, the fruit on the bottom would bruise and spoil under the weight.

Berries and Cherries

Fresh berries and cherries should be refrigerated immediately and used as soon as possible. Using them within one day after purchasing is best. You can store them in the original container if it is the type that allows free circulation of air to retard mold. Do not rinse or remove the stems of berries before storing them. Water washes away soluble vitamins, flavor, and creates a mushy texture. Just before serving, rinse

Food Facts

Irradiation: The Case For

Imagine, food that is free from disease-causing parasites, an increase in the world's food supplies, new markets for American farmers, plus foods that retain freshness for a longer time. Soon these benefits will no longer live only in your imagination as the irradiation food products become commonplace. Irradiation refers to exposing substances to radiant or light energy.

Since many pesticides have been labeled potential health hazards, the food industry has been hard at work testing many different ways to guarantee safe food supplies. Irradiation has been shown to be a very promising alternative. The Food and Drug Administration (FDA) has approved the use of irradiation and carefully monitors the use of irradiation.

Here is how irradiation works. Food products are placed on a conveyor belt that travels through a chamber. On their journey, the food products pass near a specially shielded chamber that houses a radioactive source, usually cobalt. Gamma rays are emitted from this chamber, killing bacteria, yeasts, molds, insects, and other food contaminants.

If you eat irradiated food, will you be exposed to radiation? The National Academy of Sciences says the low intensity level of the irradiation process is not enough to expose you to radiation. It has been said that you run no more risk of exposure to radioactivity through irradiated food than you would from a briefcase passed through an airport's x-ray scanner.

them lightly. Remove the stems and cut berries after rinsing to retain vitamins and flavor.

Bananas

Bananas will ripen fast at room temperature. If you want to store them after they are ripe, put them in the refrigerator. The skin turns dark, but the bananas' flesh stays firm and white.

Melons and Pineapples

Aromatic fruits like melons and pineapples need to be covered tightly with foil or plastic wrap to avoid flavoring other foods. Store them in the refrigerator, preferably in the crisper.

Fruits such as Apples and Peaches

Rinse and pat them dry before storing in the refrigerator. Store them in the refrigerator in the crisper. If there is no room in the crisper, wrap them loosely or put them in a plastic bag with some air holes. Rinsing fresh fruit before eating removes any pesticide residues and any contamination from people and insects during the processing and time at the store.

Cut Fruits

Treat cut surfaces with lemon juice, orange juice, or ascorbic acid crystals to prevent browning from exposure to the air. (This browning is known as oxidation.) Store cut fruit in an airtight container or wrap in plastic wrap or foil before refrigerating.

Underripe Fruits

If you purchase fruit that is underripe, do not refrigerate it. Allow it to ripen at room temperature first. If you want to hurry the process, place the fruit in a brown paper bag with an apple. (The apple is optional, but speeds up the process.) Seal the bag. The gases given off by the fruit hasten the enzymatic action that ripens the fruit.

Selecting Canned Fruits

When you reach for a can of any fruit in the canned foods section, glance around at all the choices you have for that fruit. Canned fruits are packed in three grades of sugar syrup. Your choices of syrups are extra heavy, heavy, or light. The extra heavy grade has the most sugar and calories and is the most expensive. The light syrup is the least sweet, lowest in calories, and generally the least expensive.

Another pack that is even lower in calories than the light syrup is fruit that is canned in water or its own juice. Since no sugar is added, the calorie count is approximately the same as for the fresh fruit. You will notice a mushy texture to waterpack cans of fruit due to the absorption of water by the fruit. This does not occur in a sugar syrup or juice pack.

Fruits are canned whole, halved, sliced, chopped, and in irregular pieces. The whole, fancy packs are the most expensive. The irregular pieces are the least costly. Choose the type that suits your purpose. It would be a waste to buy the more expensive peach halves if you are going to chop them for a salad. On the other hand, you would have a difficult time serving chicken salad stuffed into chopped peaches when the recipe called for attractive peach halves. Read the label to match the product with your needs and budget.

Buying Canned Fruit Juice

Refreshing, realistic fruit pictures on rows of canned drink products often mislead the buyer into choosing a flavored sugar-water product instead of juice. The nutritional content of such

Fruit juices offer a refreshing and nutritious alternative to soft drinks.

Food Facts

Irradiation: The Case Against

The process of irradiation is highly controversial. Within two years, you will notice food products wearing a broken black symbol and geometric design. That is the international symbol for irradiation.

American menus will feature irradiated foods if the food processors and federal officials have their way. The Food and Drug Administration (FDA) has approved irradiation on fruits, vegetables, and fresh pork. An approval for poultry may be the next food product to "go irradiation."

There are many scientific unknowns. Consumers and other critics claim that there haven't been enough tests on the effects of irradiated food on people. Others say that not enough reliable animal studies have been performed. There is also concern over the safety of handling radioactive cobalt which is used in the process of irradiation.

Surveys have shown that most consumers would choose not to buy produce labeled as irradiated. However, under new FDA regulations, the phrase "treated with radiation" will no longer appear on foods. Only the international symbol would remain.

You can make an educated decision regarding irradiation by contacting consumer organizations in your state and the Coalition for Food Irradiation in Washington, DC. The coalition is made up of food processors and retail, consumer, and technical interests. Remember, the final decision is up to you at the grocery store.

a drink is limited to high sugar and sometimes an artificial vitamin additive. The high sugar is not good for your teeth and the single-added vitamin does not supply any of the other vitamins, minerals, and fiber present in real juice. Have you ever noticed a can labeled "contains real apple juice" in large letters, but in the small print you discover the words "fruit drink" and "10% real juice." The trick word is "contains" and the less obvious label, "fruit drink." All of it is perfectly legal, even if it is misleading.

Only products that contain 100 percent fruit juice can be called "fruit juice" on the label. When the product is part juice, the exact percentage must be on the label. It is up to you to react to the important information, not the fruit pictures or the highlighted banners across the corner of the label.

All the information you need is on the label. Take the time to read the label, look for the nutrition information, and buy the product best suited to your needs.

Storing Canned Fruits and Drinks

Sealed canned foods can be kept at room temperature for a year with no deterioration of flavor or texture. After opening the can, treat the food like any other cooked fruit food. Cover and refrigerate. Fruit juices and drinks should be sealed airtight to prevent loss of vitamin C from evaporation.

If a can develops a bulging top, throw it away unopened immediately. Never taste questionable food to see if it tastes all right! Taste is not an indication of safety—and one tiny taste can kill you. Never buy bulging or damaged cans. They indicate extreme danger to your health and life.

Selecting Frozen Fruits

Most fresh fruits available in the produce department at some time during the year are available all year around in frozen form. Freezing preserves the fresh flavor of fruit, but breaks the firmness into a slightly mushy texture.

You can buy fresh fruit frozen in a block of sugar syrup or in individually frozen pieces without added sugar. You can use part or all of the individually frozen fruits instantly, just as you would fresh fruit. You can select the pieces you need and return the rest to the freezer resealed in the bag. The fruit frozen in a syrup block is difficult to divide and must be thawed before using.

Consider using nutritious, frozen berries or fruit slices to top salads, garnish meats, add to muffins and quick bread batter, combine with yogurt for dessert, top ice cream, and decorate cakes. The great taste of fruit in your recipes doesn't need to stop when the growing season does.

You may want to individually freeze fruit yourself. It is quick and simple if you follow the guidelines in Chapter 9.

Selecting Dried Fruits

The concentrated natural sugar in dried fruits and dried fruit mixtures has made them favorites for a sweet, chewy, candylike dessert or snack. This nutritious substitution for the more highly refined "junk foods" and candy has earned dried fruit and fruit rollups (fruit leathers) a place in many vending machines and candy counters. The high concentration of sugar makes any dried fruit product a relatively high calorie snack, but compared to candy, it's a healthy addition to any diet. Dried apples, apricots, dates, prunes, pineapples, and raisins also add wonderful flavors and textures to recipes and quick breads.

The more commonly used dried fruits, such as raisins and apricots, are sold in packages or sealed plastic bags in the baking section or the bulk food section of the supermarket. The specialty dried fruits, such as pineapples and bananas, often are available in bulk form out of bins or combined in prepackaged mixes.

You cannot determine quality of a dried fruit by color. The amount of color retained in the drying process depends upon the addition of a preserving chemical used in the drying process. Naturally sun-dried fruit is very dark with little color left, but it tastes wonderful. Choose dried fruits that bounce back when you squeeze them in your hand.

Fruit Leathers

Next to the candy bars in most stores are the fruit leathers, more commonly known as fruit rollups or fruit taffies. This product is made of any dried fruit or combination of dried fruits and sugar. The fruit content has placed them in the category of health foods for some people, but the high sugar content makes it a fruit-flavored candy.

You can make your own fruit leathers at home and have a nutritious snack that is low on sugar. Your homemade fruit leathers will contain more fruit than the commercial kind—and probably have more flavor. Note: Don't look for bright colors unless you add them artificially.

Directions

1. Select ripe or even overripe fruit. Apricots, apples, grapes, berries, pineapples, oranges, pears, peaches, tomatoes, plums, bananas, and tropical fruits such as mangoes are all suitable.
2. Remove any large seeds
3. Cut the fruit into chunks suitable for the blender or food processor.
4. For bananas and light-colored and yellow-colored fruit mixtures, add 1 tablespoon (15 mL) lemon juice to prevent discoloration.
5. Blend the fruit into a thick puree.
6. Measure the fruit puree. Add 2 tablespoons (30 mL) of sugar per 1 quart (1 L) of fruit.
7. Line a jelly roll pan with wax paper.
8. Pour the puree onto paper in the pan to about ¼ inch (0.6 cm) deep. Coat the pan

evenly by tilting the tray. The mixture will move slowly, but have patience and do not try to "smooth" it with a spatula.

Drying

1. Place the pan in an oven set at the lowest setting 140°F (60°C). Prop the door open so there is a space of about 2 inches (5 cm). If the lowest setting on your oven is 200°F (93°C), prop the door open 3 inches (7.5 cm). Use an oven thermometer to be safe.
2. Let the fruit leather dry about 4 to 5 hours. You can speed the drying by pointing an electric fan toward the oven. The increased air flow speeds the drying.
3. Test for dryness by peeling the fruit from the waxed paper. If it feels sticky, but peels off the paper, it is done. Do not remove it from the paper.
4. Store the fruit leather rolled up stuck to the paper in an airtight container for 3 weeks at room temperature, for several weeks in the refrigerator, or for years in the freezer.

Adapted from the Cooperative Extension Service, University of California, Berkeley, California 94720, Leaflet 2785 "Drying Foods at Home." Reprinted July 1978. Page 7.

Storing Dried Fruit

Unopened packages of dried fruit may be stored on a shelf in a dry, cool place. Dried fruits purchased from the bin can be stored for a couple of weeks in a sealed plastic bag or other airtight container at room temperature. Dried fruits retain their flavor the longest in the refrigerator or freezer.

Presenting Fruits

Have you ever had hungry friends or family sitting at the table eagerly waiting you to present your mouth-watering creation. There is that wonderful moment when you and your guests can appreciate the total picture of your efforts. The color, arrangement on the plate, contrast of textures, the aroma, and sometimes even the sound all add to the presentation of the food. With most foods, making them look and taste good takes time and effort, but fruit has it "all together" naturally. The best advice for serving fruit is to leave it alone. Cut or shape it just enough to make the eating easier, but try not to lose the identity of the fruit itself.

Take advantage of the natural beauty and appeal of fruit to make edible containers for other fruits and foods. You'll enjoy making inexpensive creations out of everyday ingredients to add a festive touch to meals and parties. Use fruit and fruit creations for table decor that can be eaten or saved for another time. Some basic ideas to "start you thinking" might include a:

- Hollowed-out apple holding tuna salad.
- Fresh or canned pear half covered by grape halves stuck on with softened ricotta cheese. A dark spinach leaf completes the picture.
- Jack-o-lantern apple with added raisins, carrot, and celery features.
- Baskets made out of an orange with a spinach handle and filled with orange and avocado salad.
- Pineapple quarters filled with fresh fruit topped by a baked meringue topping.
- Fresh or canned peach half with hot chicken salad.
- Watermelon punch bowl to serve a nutritious fruit punch.

Purees

A fruit puree is a thick liquid form of the whole fruit. When you force a soft peach or raspberry through a sieve, the resulting seedless fruit sauce is a **puree**. You also can puree fruit in an electric blender or a food processor. Since the seeds cannot be removed from some berries before processing, you may need to strain the liquid fruit. The luscious puree has all the fresh flavor of the fruit in a sauce that's ready and waiting to make a fruit soup or cheesecake or turn other fruits, custard, waffles, and ice

This recipe creates a new taste twist to fruit and vegetable combinations.

Crunchy Grapefruit Salad

Yield: 4 servings

Traditional	Ingredients	Metric
1 head	Boston lettuce or iceberg lettuce	1 head
1	Sectioned grapefruit or oranges	1
4 Tbsp.	Leaves from watercress and chopped stems	60 mL
4 Tbsp.	Sesame paste	60 mL
1 tsp.	Lemon juice	5 mL
1 tsp. to 1 Tbsp.	Oil	5 mL to 60 mL
Dash	Soy sauce	Dash

Directions

1. Wash and drain the lettuce. Shred the iceberg lettuce or carefully tear the Boston lettuce. Arrange on four plates.
2. Arrange the grapefruit or orange segments on the lettuce.
3. Make a dressing by mixing together the sesame paste, lemon juice, and soy sauce. Add oil to achieve the desired consistency.
4. Spoon the dressing over the salad.
5. Garnish with watercress leaves and chopped stems to taste.

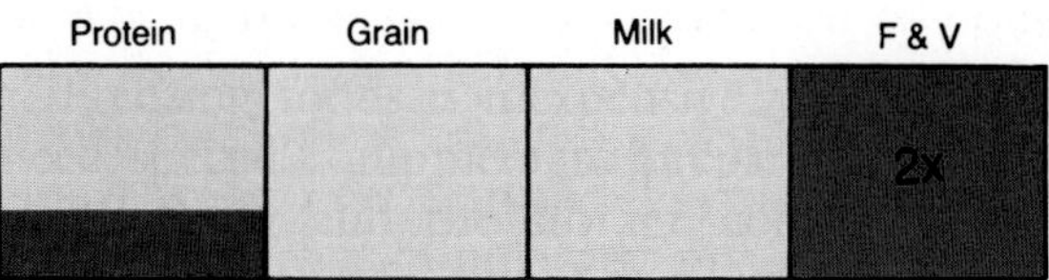

cream into irresistible treats. You also can freeze the puree for a dessert that is tops in nutrition and low in calories. That now popular dessert is called **sorbet** (sor-bay).

Purees are easy to make from fresh or cooked fruit. Choose a fruit that is soft enough to go through a blender or sieve.

Directions

1. Wash the fruit carefully and remove any discolored or spoiled parts. Peel it if the fruit has a rind or heavy peel.
2. Place a small amount of the fruit in the blender or food processor and blend. If a blender is not available, force the fruit through a sieve. Scrape the fruit with a large wooden or metal spoon to work it through the sieve.
3. Strain the liquid into a bowl to remove any seeds or stringy fiber materials. You also can use a food mill. A strainer is easier for berries, and the food mill is better for tree fruits such as pears, apricots, cherries, and peaches.
4. Cover and refrigerate the puree until ready to use.

Cooking Fruits

While most fruits taste great in their natural state, there are a few fruits that should be cooked before eating. Rhubarb, gooseberries, citron (a lemonlike fruit, its peel is usually candied), and plaintains (a hard-fleshed bananalike tropical fruit) are all examples of cooking fruits.

Before cooking a fruit, make sure of your choices. Melons are never cooked, while berries add a special flavor to baked products and make wonderful jellies and jams. Apples are tasty fresh or cooked, but you need to select the right type of apple for cooking or you will be disappointed in the results.

The red delicious apple is better eaten raw. It goes to mush very fast and does not hold its shape during cooking. Choose a Jonathan or Rome Beauty apple for cooking and baking.

As a rule, fruits are only cooked to add variety and different flavor combinations. Fruits can

Gingered Pear Sorbet

Yield: 6 servings

Traditional	**Ingredients**	**Metric**
1 can (29 oz.)	Pear halves, drained (reserve syrup)	906 g
¼ cup	Sugar	50 mL
2 tbsp.	Lemon juice	30 mL
1 to 1½ tsp.	Finely chopped crystallized ginger or 1/8 tsp. (0.5 mL) ground ginger	5 to 8 mL

Directions

1. Heat 1 cup (250 mL) of the reserved syrup and the sugar to boiling, stirring constantly; remove from heat. Cool.
2. Place pears, half at a time, in blender container; cover and puree until uniform consistency.
3. Mix syrup, pure, lemon juice, and ginger; pour into ice cube tray. Freeze until partially frozen, 1 to 1½ hours.
4. Pour into blender; blend on medium speed until smooth and fluffy.
5. Return to ice cube tray. Freeze until firm, about 3 hours.
6. Let stand at room temperature about 10 minutes before serving.

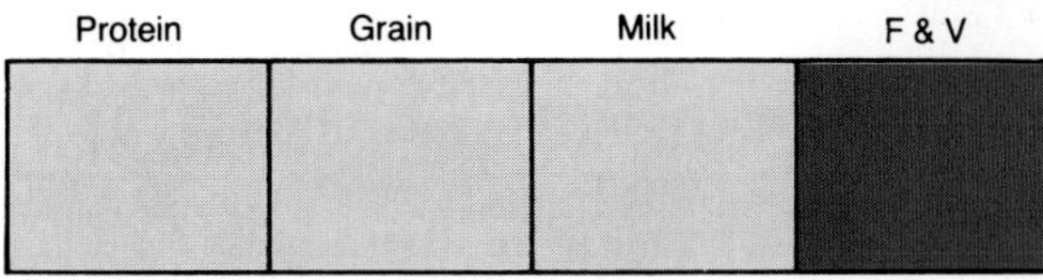

You can enjoy your favorite fresh-fruit tastes deliciously concentrated in a healthy, icy treat called a "sorbet."

be cooked by the same methods as other foods—simmered, stewed, poached, baked, broiled, or fried. Their high moisture content also qualifies them for some spectacular results in the microwave oven.

The introduction of heat in cooking changes the appearance, nutrient content, texture, and flavor of fruit. The heat turns the water in fruit to steam, which swells the fruit and softens the fiber. This process makes the fruits easier to digest and slightly mushy in texture. Choose a cooking method that maintains the shape and color of the fruit and saves as many nutrients as possible. Cooking the whole, unpeeled fruit for a short time at the lowest heat possible and using a small amount of liquid retains the most nutrients.

Cooking Fruits with Added Liquids

One of the most popular cooked fruit dishes from early childhood is applesauce. This versatile sauce is an excellent example of simmering fruit until it has completely lost its characteristic shape, color, and texture. Still, the mellow fruity flavor blends and complements most meals from breakfast through dinner. Home preparation of this favorite preserves a bountiful supply of the fruit until the next crop.

To make a fruit sauce such as applesauce, cook the cored fruit in a small amount of water until soft, then add the sugar. When you cook the fruit with water before adding the sugar, the fruit will lose its firm shape and make a soft sauce. This is because the apple absorbs the water which then swells and softens the fiber, breaking down the firmness. Water always goes through cell membranes toward the most concentrated solution. When the fruit has the most concentrated solution of sugar in its cells, water is drawn into the cells to dilute the solution. Adding sugar before cooking interferes with this process because then there is a more concentrated solution of sugar in the cooking liquid surrounding the fruit. The water in the fruit cells leaves the fruit to go into the cooking syrup. This causes the fruit to lose water not absorb it. This concept is important to remember when cooking dried fruits.

In order for dried fruits to absorb all the liquid they need in order to soften, they must simmer in water first before any sugar is added. Serve the tender, cooked dried fruit with the cooking liquid to retain the flavor and nutrients dissolved during cooking.

If you want a fresh fruit to hold its shape this technique is helpful. Add the sugar to the liquid when you first start cooking. A delicious poached pear is beautiful when it keeps its shape, so add the sugar syrup at the beginning of the cooking period.

Baked Fruits

Baking fruits creates a flavorful and attractive addition to any meal. Individual fruits in their skins are naturals for baking. The smooth, edible skin holds in the moisture as it turns to steam in a hot oven. The slow, gentle steaming from inside the fruit cooks it throughout—and the skin holds the fruit's shape. In some cases the steam builds up enough pressure to burst the skin. To prevent that, core the fruit or peel a strip from the middle. This is usually necessary with apples.

Fruit also can be baked in containers or foil to hold in the moisture. Fragrant spices and flavor-enhancing sugars can be added to the fruit before baking to help it hold its shape and taste terrific.

Fruit also is baked with the other ingredients of many baked products. The American apple pie is legendary, and right behind it are blueberry muffins. What are favorite baked fruit foods in your home?

Broiling Fruits

Broiling fruits gives them a delightful appearance and caramelized flavor in surprisingly little time. Broiling cooks the surface of the fruit and heats it through without destroying the fresh flavor. This cooking method adds a quick new look and taste to canned fruits also. Fruits that can be broiled successfully include

Who says vegetables and fruits should not be mixed together? Surprise your taste buds with this tingling combination of oranges and tomatoes in a hot or cold soup.

apples, apricots, peaches, plums, oranges, grapefruits, pineapples, and bananas.

Directions

1. Cut 1/2 inch (1.25 cm) thick slices, or halve the fruit. Remove the core.
2. Brush lightly with melted butter to prevent the fruit from drying under the broiler. This also stops the discoloring of light-colored fruits such as apples and bananas.
3. Add a flavor enhancer of your choice. Options could include grated nutmeg, ground ginger, cinnamon.
4. If broiling apple slices, brush them with syrup. Sugar or syrup is not necessary for flavor on most other sweet fruit, but adds an attractive caramelized appearance.
5. Place the prepared fruit on shallow pan or flameproof dish. Place about 4 inches (10 cm) below a moderate broiler heat source.
6. Broil until golden brown. This takes about 5 minutes.
7. Serve immediately.

Frying Fruits

Only fruits that have a firm structure such as apples, peaches, pineapples, bananas, or citrus fruits that are held together with membranes can be fried (sautéed) successfully.

Directions

1. Melt butter in a skillet. Clarified butter is best because there is no danger of it burning before the fruit is done. (For directions on clarifying butter, see page 362.)

2. Place the fruit slices in the hot butter.

3. Sprinkle brown sugar with cinnamon over the fruit.

4. Brown the slices on both sides. This takes 1½ minutes for most fruits. Double the time for pineapple and bananas.

5. Remove carefully with a turner and serve immediately.

Microwave Cooking Fruits

Baked apples in 10 minutes! The wonders of the microwave sometimes seem too good to be true for anyone with little time. See Chapter 8 for hints on cooking fruits in the microwave.

Vocabulary for Review

Carotene
Produce department
Mature
Ripe
Underripe
Immature
Bulk produce
Packaged produce
Unitized produce
Puree

Questions for Review

1. Discuss the importance of fruits in the diet.
2. How many servings of fruits and vegetables are recommended for your age group per day?
3. What are some guidelines to follow when selecting fresh fruit?
4. What is the difference between underripe and immature fruits?
5. Describe some advantages for each of the following ways you can buy fruit: bulk, prepackaged, and unitized.
6. What would you do to help cut pieces of fruit to stay light and not turn dark from oxidation? Why does it work?
7. Describe some types of canned fruit from which you can select at the store.
8. When is the best time to buy a particular fresh fruit?
9. What are some of the types of frozen fruit you can buy or freeze yourself? Name some uses for two types.

Things to Do

1. Visit a grocery store and select fresh fruit based on your knowledge of high-quality produce.
2. Cut an apple in half. Brush one half with lemon juice, orange juice, or ascorbic acid crystals. Set aside both pieces for ½ hour. Explain the difference.
3. Ripen an underripe fruit. Place the fruit in a brown paper bag with an apple. Seal the bag. Explain the reaction that occurs. What would happen if you had refrigerated the apple first?
4. As a class, make your own fruit leather from your favorite fruit.
5. Be creative—plan some new ideas for serving fruit attractively.
6. Some fruits can be broiled or fried, which ones? Choose one and experiment.
7. Plan an outing to a local farmer's market or "pick your own garden." Compare prices and quality with that of your local grocery store.
8. Compare fresh, canned, dried, and frozen fruit for taste, costs, and uses. Discuss the advantages and disadvantages of each.
9. Using the chart in the back of this book, compare the nutrient values of a fruit that is fresh, canned, dried, and frozen. What differences did you notice? Which is the most healthful way to preserve fruits?
10. Look through cookbooks and magazines for some ways to combine fruit with meat, fish, or dairy products for a main dish. What does fruit add to the meal in nutrients, flavor, and looks?

Join the Veggie Revolution

March up to the salad bar of your favorite fast-food restaurant and enlist the help of crisp vegetables such as carrots, sweet peas, tangy tomatoes, and crunchy bean sprouts to win the nutrition battle over empty fast-food calories. Over the past decade, vegetables have replaced the standard "meat and potatoes" as a foundation for many meals. Have you eaten any meals without meat lately? Many health-conscious people have made versatile and satisfying vegetables their main dish for many meals. Vegetarians have given up meat altogether. They find that an all-vegetable diet agrees with their body and other ideals. It is quite a complicated undertaking when vegetarians strive to supply all their nutrition from plant sources alone. However, by combining proteins, it can be done.

The increased use of and the demand for year-around supplies of flavorful, attractive, and fresh vegetables have made it possible for food markets to stock more and better varieties of vegetables than ever before. Choices also exist for the canned, frozen, and dried forms of vegetables.

Customers have developed a "new taste curiosity" that beckons them to buy and try new and specialty produce. Not too long ago, the average customer would react to new items with "what's that?" Now the reaction is more likely to be "what's new?" and "how do I prepare it?" Take command of the following pages about the versatile, nutrition-laden vegetables available to you and you'll soon promote them to a top rank in your daily food habits.

Nutritive Notes

You probably feel you've always known that vegetables are "good for you" and that you "ought to eat them." It's so easy to miss the excitement of "discovery" just because the subject is a familiar one. It is really pretty amazing that vitamins and minerals are the rule, not the exception, in vegetables. The leafy greens, stems, seeds, flowers, roots, and tubers that form the vegetable family supply vitamins A and C in plentiful amounts. These vitamins in turn supply you with smooth skin, beautiful hair, the ability to heal from wounds, and much more! Vegetables also supply other vitamins and minerals. The seed vegetables such as lima beans and peas are excellent for B vitamins. The B vitamins promote healthy and steady nerves as just one of their jobs in the body. Leafy greens contain an outstanding supply of calcium and iron which build and maintain strong bones and red blood. All vegetables contribute fiber to the diet, especially when they are served with their flavorful skins.

The yellow to orange vegetable coloring that highlights produce displays is from the carotene pigment discussed earlier in the fruits chapter. This carotene from vegetables is converted to vitamin A in the body. The deeper the coloring, the higher the content of vitamin A. There is one exception. The deep red of the beet has no yellow in it and is not high in vitamin A. The less commonly eaten leafy green tops of beets, however, are a great source for vitamins C and A and minerals. This is only one example of how the nutrition content can vary in different parts of the same vegetable.

Legumes, dried peas and beans, contain significant amounts of incomplete proteins that can be completed by animal proteins or some combinations of plant foods. When you eat a combination of dried beans and whole wheat, dried beans and corn or rice, or peanuts and whole wheat, the foods combine to form high-quality protein. (High-quality protein supplies the essential amino acids your body needs.)

By carefully planning and studying, it is possible to supply protein needs from plant

Zucchini Stir-Fry

Yield: 4 to 6 servings

Traditional	**Ingredients**	**Metric**
½ cup	Onion, thinly sliced[1]	125 mL
2 medium	Zucchini	2 medium
4 oz.	Quartered, blanched almonds	125 g
4 Tbsp.	Olive oil or other flavored oil such as almond or walnut	60 mL
2 tsp.	Juice from fresh squeezed lemon[2]	10 mL
¼ cup	White wine vinegar	50 mL
¼ tsp.	Salt	1 mL
¼ tsp.	Coarse ground black pepper	1 mL
	Optional Creative Additions	
2 Tbsp.	Chopped parsley	30 mL
To taste	Lemon thyme	To taste

Directions

1. Wash and slice zucchini.
2. Toast almonds using a broiler or in a dry pan moving the almonds quickly like popcorn.
3. Heat oil in a large skillet. After heated, add onions and stir-fry until golden, about 10 minutes.
4. Add the sliced zucchini and stir-fry until tender, about 10 minutes.
5. Add lemon juice and oil.
6. Add almonds, salt, pepper, and herbs (optional). Stir-fry only until heated.

Microwave Directions

1. Wash and slice zucchini.
2. Place almonds on paper towel and microwave on high for 3 minutes or until toasted.
3. In a 2½ qt. (2½ L) microwave-safe casserole, microwave oil and onion on high for 5 minutes or until the onion is tender.
4. Add zucchini and microwave on high for 4 to 5 minutes or until tender, stirring every minute.
5. Add lemon juice, wine vinegar, almonds, salt, pepper, and herbs (optional). Microwave on high for 30 seconds.

[1] For a colorful change, use red onions.
[2] Fresh frozen or canned lemon juice may be substituted.

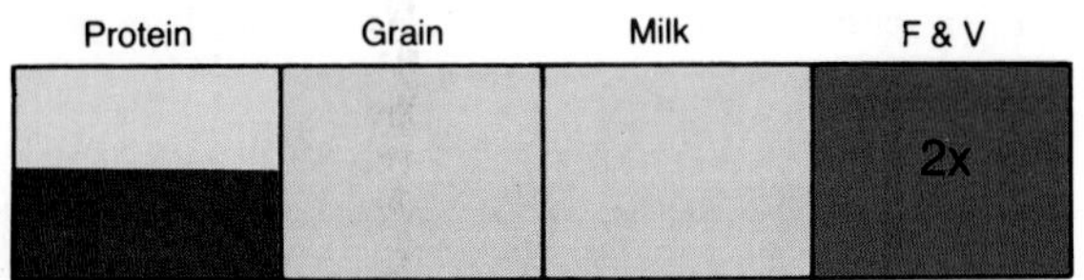

Flavorful peanuts combine with whole-wheat biscuits to make a delicious high-quality protein treat.

Peanut Biscuits

Yield: 2 dozen

Traditional	Ingredients	Metric
2⅓ cups	All-purpose flour	575 mL
¾ cup	Dry roasted peanuts, finely ground	175 mL
1 Tbsp. plus 1 tsp.	Baking powder	20 mL
2 tbsp.	Sugar	30 mL
1 tsp.	Salt	5 mL
¼ cup plus 1 Tbsp.	Shortening	65 mL
1 cup plus 2 Tbsp.	Milk	280mL
	Peanut butter (optional)	
	Grape jelly (optional)	

Directions

1. Sift together flour, ground peanuts, baking powder, sugar, and salt.

2. Cut in shortening until mixture resembles coarse meal.

3. Add milk, stirring with a fork until dry ingredients are moistened.

4. Turn dough out onto a floured surface. Knead 4 to 5 times.

5. Roll dough to ¾-inch (2 cm) thickness; cut with a 2-inch (5 cm) biscuit cutter.

6. Place biscuits on greased baking sheets. Bake at 450°F (230°C) for 12 minutes or until lightly browned. Serve hot with peanut butter and jelly, if desired.

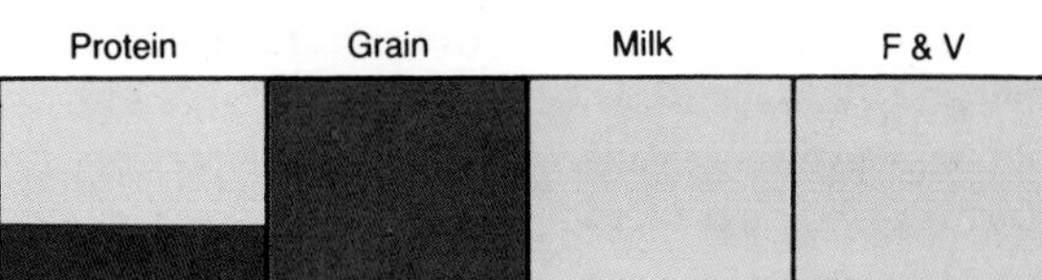

sources. Eating by following the Basic Food Groups as a guide is simpler and safer than trying to compensate for the elimination of one of the food groups from the diet.

Starchy vegetables such as potatoes, corn, peas, and lima beans have a higher calorie count than water-crisp types such as celery, lettuce, tomatoes, or bean sprouts. However, all vegetables are considered low-calorie foods—even lower than fruits. (Fruits have a higher sugar content which increases the calories.)

The valuable nutrients in vegetables will not be able to help you if they wind up going down the drain or disappearing into the air. Food preparation and handling methods determine how much of the nutrient value you actually receive when you eat the vegetables. Your safest choice is to eat your veggies raw whenever it is appropriate. Following simple preparation principles and avoiding any delay between purchasing and eating also will help save the nutrient gifts from the plant kingdom.

Selecting Vegetables

"Beauty is more than skin deep" when it comes to selecting quality vegetables. Appealing colors, shapes, and textures are clues to freshness and nutrient content in fresh produce. Look for produce that is crisp and not wilted or wrinkled. Developed color can mean ripeness as well as a higher nutrient content. Feel for firmness with no soft spots. If a product is not at its peak condition, consider changing your menu plans. Select another vegetable or change to a frozen, canned, or dried form of the product.

Avoid buying any root or tuber that has sprouted. Potatoes that have green areas on their skins must be avoided. The coloring is a poisonous chemical called **solanine** that is caused by sun or light on the potatoes. (If your stored potatoes develop the green skins, cut all of that part away before cooking. Do not try to bake the potato whole. Heat does not destroy the solanine.

Your personal experience in selecting appealing vegetables will teach you which choices provide the taste and texture sensations you want to repeat. From the hustle of the farmers' market to the rewards of the "pick your own" field to the convenience of the displays of the supermarket, you can look forward to a lifetime of versatile vegetable "finds."

Mini-Guide to Freshness

Artichokes

Large unopened flower buds of a plant in the thistle family. Look for a bud that is unopened. Dried, spread leaves mean age. When held in your hand, the artichoke should seem heavy in proportion to its size. Size does not indicate quality. You can select fresh specimens that are 1 inch (2.5 cm) high (bite size to cook whole) or 8- to 10-inch-diameter (20 to 25 cm) globes. Avoid grey-black discoloration, mold, or worm holes.

Asparagus

Tender green stalks that sprout directly out of the ground in spring and early summer. The tips should be closed and firm. Avoid stalks that are ribbed and not round. Look for supplies that have been stored upright in water.

Beans

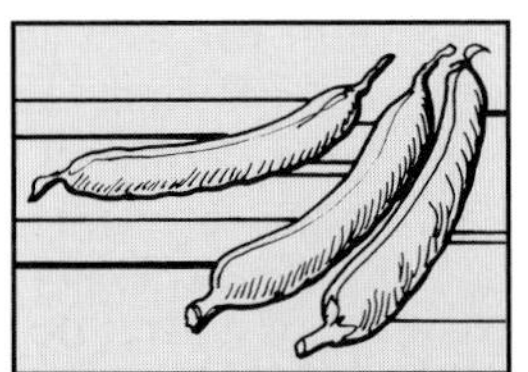

Fresh green and yellow wax beans are immature seeds in tender pods that snap crisply when broken. Avoid wilted or flabby pods. Any blemishes or overdeveloped seeds indicate age and tough fibrous beans.

Beets

Rich red, round, firm tubers with a tiny root. They are often sold with their edible green tops attached. The age of beets can be determined by the condition of the tops when attached. Avoid wilted, flabby beets that will be tough, fibrous, and strong flavored.

Broccoli

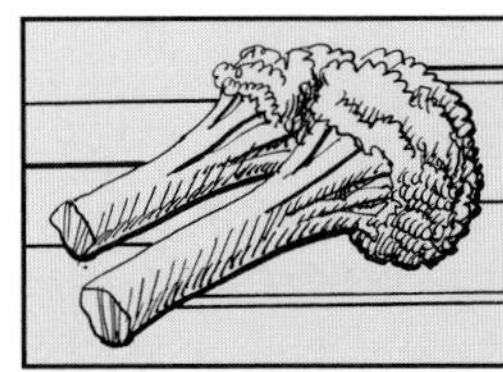

A firm, compact cluster of small flower buds that are tightly closed. When the tiny buds open enough to show yellow flowers, the vegetable is past its peak. Avoid wilted stems, open flowers, or soft slippery spots on the bud clusters.

Brussel Sprouts

Like miniature cabbages. These sprouts should be a bright-green in color with tight-fitting leaves.

Cabbage

A smooth or crinkly leaved, green, round head. It also comes in a deep red color. Cabbage stores well. Look for firm, hard heads that feel heavy for their size. Avoid worm-eaten outer leaves that might indicate inner damage.

Carrots

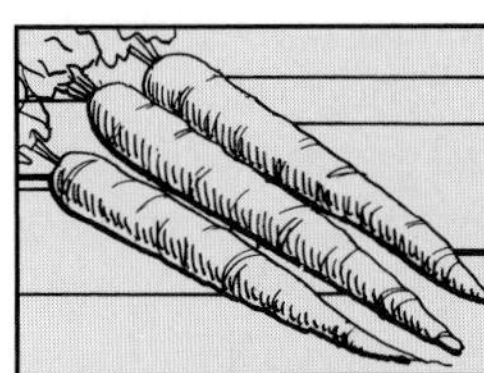

Well-formed, smooth, and firm roots of deep orange color. Avoid roots that are flexible or have a large green "sunburned" areas at the top. Carrots should break crisply.

Cauliflower

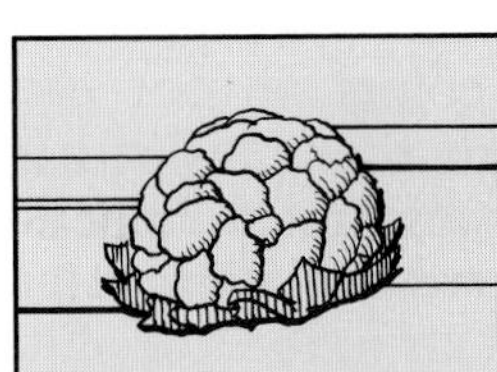

The white edible portion of the plant. Cauliflower has a heavy leaf covering, but most of the leaves are removed before selling. Look for a white to creamy-white, compact head. A slightly granular texture of the head will not hurt the eating quality. Avoid a spreading of the blossom parts, any wilting, or discolored spots.

Celery

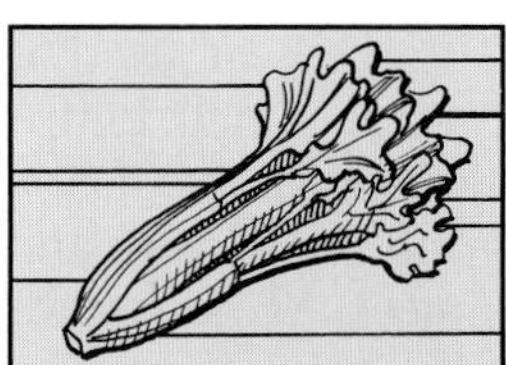

Usually the "Pascal" type which is thick-branched and has green compact stalks. Look for crispness. The leaflets should be fresh with a glossy surface. Avoid wilted celery with pithy, hollow, or discolored centers in the branches.

Chinese Cabbage

Primarily a salad vegetable of crisp, flat stalks that fit into an elongated bunch. Avoid wilted or yellowed parts.

Chicory, Endive, Escarole

All are salad greens that have narrow, notched edges resembling the dandelion leaf. Look for crisp, tender leaves with a good green color in the outer leaves. Avoid leaves which have brownish or yellowish discoloration.

Corn

A sweet corn that is available in yellow or white kernel. New varieties feature a mixture of the colors on one ear. More than any other vegetable, corn must be refrigerated immediately after picking to retard the sugar from turning to starch. This results in the loss of its valued sweet flavor. Look for fresh husks and ears with plump kernels. Avoid ears with underdeveloped kernels, overdeveloped extra large kernels, or kernels that have depressed areas on the outer surface. When punctured with your thumbnail, the kernel should squirt liquid.

Cucumbers

Well-shaped tubes that have many small lumps on their surfaces. Look for good green color and a firm feel. Avoid rounded, overgrown cucumbers that are beginning to turn yellowish. Avoid any withered ends.

Greens

Plants grown for uses as "salad greens," such as spinach, kale, collards, turnip leaves, beet leaves, chard, mustard, chicory, endive, escarole, dandelion, cress, and sorrel. Look for leaves that are tender, fresh, and a good green color. Avoid leaves with coarse fibrous stems and any yellowish-green color. Avoid plants with insects which are hard to rinse off.

Jicama

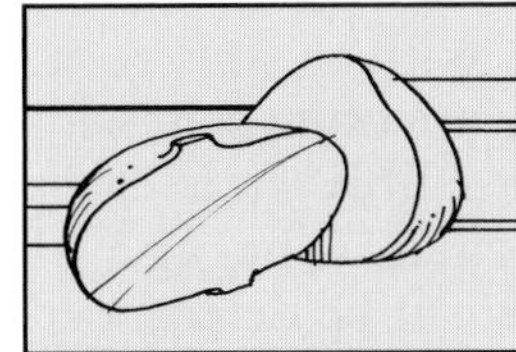

Looks like a small, round potato. It has a bland taste and can be cooked like a potato or added raw to salads for a crunchy taste.

Kohlrabi

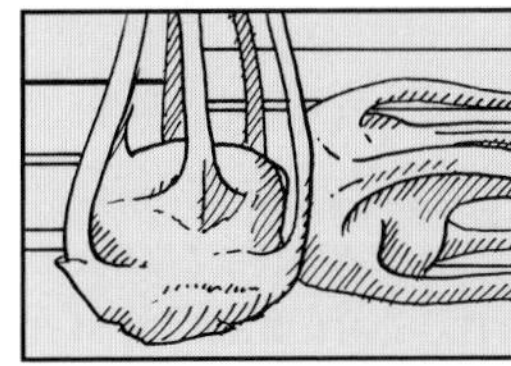

Related to the cabbage family, but is a globe rather than leaves. Look for small, tender globes.

Lettuce

Available in four types: iceberg, butterhead, romaine, and leaf. Iceberg heads are large, round, and solid with little coloring left. Butterhead lettuce includes the Boston and bibb lettuce types that are smaller and darker green than iceberg. This type is also more tender and less crisp in the leaf. Romaine lettuce varieties have elongated crisp leaves that range from white in the stem to dark green in the leaf. Leaf lettuce varieties are loose, broad leaves. They vary in color from light green to green and red. Look for freshness in all lettuce types by the crisp nonwilted leaves.

Melons

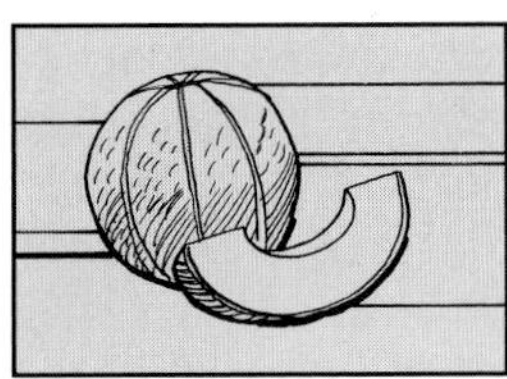

Vegetables by horticultural classification, but are considered as fruits in uses. See Chapter 10 on fruits.

Mushrooms

Fungus growths that have a cap on top and gills underneath the top. The cap is attached to a stem. Look for young mushrooms that are closed around the stem and not discolored.

Okra

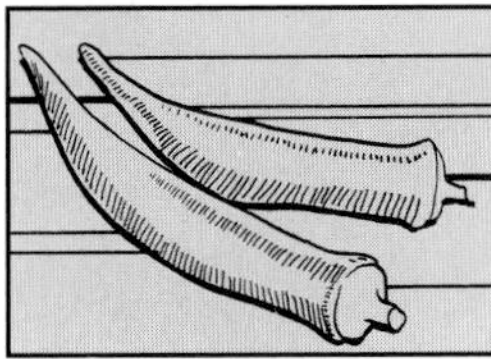

A bright green, immature seed pod that is a traditional favorite in the southern states. Look for tender pods. If you can bend the tip easily, the pod is tender. Avoid tough pods with stiff tips and pale green color.

Onions

Basically of three general classifications. Globe onions with red, yellow or white skins are primarily used for cooking. Granex-Grano are less round and range from the flattened shape to a top-shaped onion. These are mild in flavor and ideal for slicing and eating raw as well as in cooking. The newly popular Vidalia onion from Georgia is of this variety. Spanish onions are generally much larger than other varieties and range from yellow to white. The mild flavor has given them the nickname of "sweet Spanish" and they are ideal for slicing for salads. Look for all onions that are firm and dry with small necks. Avoid onions with wet areas or with fresh sprouts.

Onions (green), Shallots, Leeks

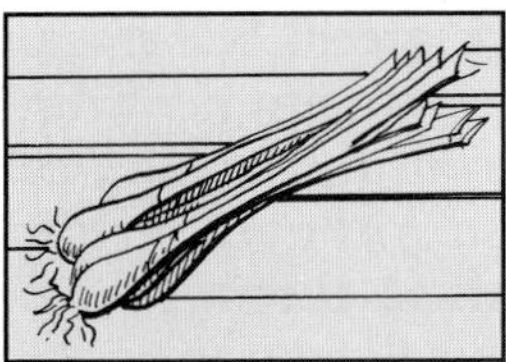

Sometimes called scallions as a group, but differ in use. Green onions are ordinary onions harvested before the bulb is formed. Shallots are similar to green onions in appearance, but never grow a bulb at the base. Leeks are larger than shallots. They grow with a hint of a bulb shape and have broad, flat tops. Look for bunches of these onions that have fresh, crisp, green tops. Avoid yellowing, wilted tops.

Oriental Peapods

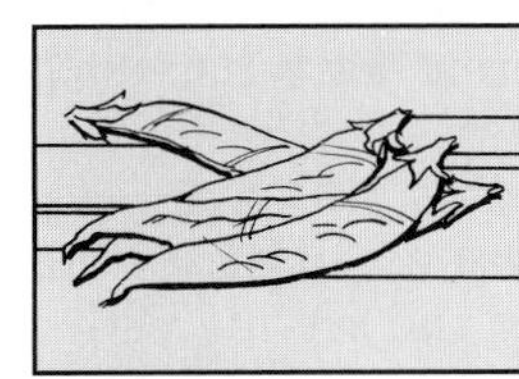

Crisp, tender green pods with immature peas. Look for crisp pods that are bright green in color. Avoid pods with scars and brown spots.

Parsley

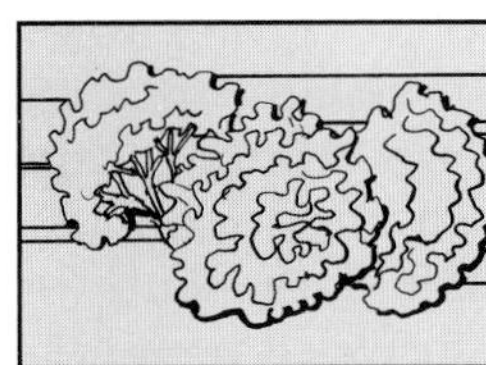

A curly leaf on narrow stems. It is a top vitamin A food which is often wasted as an uneaten garnish. Look for fresh, crisp, bright-green leaves for both the flat-leaf and curled-leaf types.

Parsnips

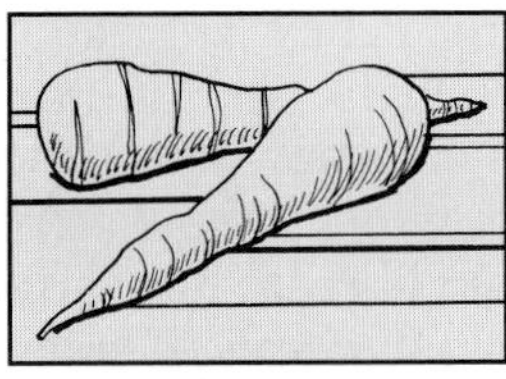

Look like small white carrots. Look for parsnips that are small to medium width and well formed, smooth, firm, and free from decayed spots. Avoid large, coarse roots.

Peppers

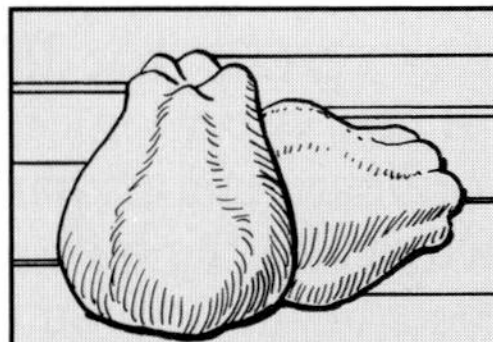

Dark green, bell-shaped sweet peppers. Some areas of the country call these mangoes. (Don't confuse this with the tropical fruit mango.) Look for peppers that are medium to dark green with a glossy sheen and firm walls. Fully mature green peppers of this same type are bright red. Hot red, green and yellow peppers are also available.

Potatoes

Divided into three general groups. "New potatoes" is a term used to describe newly harvested potatoes and freshly dug potatoes which are not quite fully matured. The best use of these thin-skinned potatoes is boiling and serving with a cream sauce. General purpose potatoes are most types offered for sale in the markets including both round and long types. The quality of baking potatoes is determined by the variety and area in which they are grown. The Russet Burbank is the best known of this group. Look for well-shaped, smooth, firm potatoes that are free from blemishes, decay, and sunburn (the green discolored areas which are poisonous). Avoid skinned surfaces and large cuts or bruises. Avoid sprouted or shriveled potatoes.

Radishes

Medium-size, round, firm, crisp vegetables that have a slightly hot flavor. They are eaten raw. Look for plump, firm radishes that are a good red color or a clear white. Avoid very large or soft radishes that are likely to have hollow or pithy centers. Avoid decayed green tops.

Rhubarb

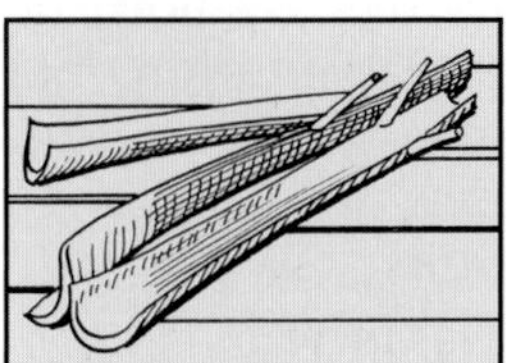

A tart, firm stem that ranges in color from pink to red. It is a highly specialized vegetable used like a fruit for sauces and pies. The season and supply is very limited.

Soybeans (Green)

Special soybeans that are grown to be eaten fresh. Green soybeans feature the same quality protein, vitamins and minerals as processed soybeans. All soybeans lack vitamin C.

Squash (Summer)

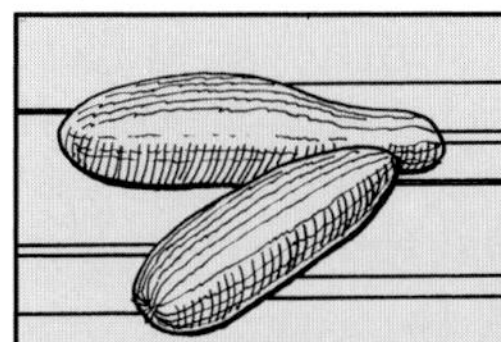

Tender and well-developed shapes that can be harvested while still immature so the entire squash is edible. Summer squash include the crookneck, the large yellow straightneck, the greenish-white pattypan, and the slender green zucchini and Italian marrow. Look for fresh- appearing, well-formed squash that have a glossy skin. Avoid overmature squash which will have a dull skin and a hard, tough surface. Such squash usually have enlarged seeds and dry, stringy flesh.

Squash (Fall and Winter)

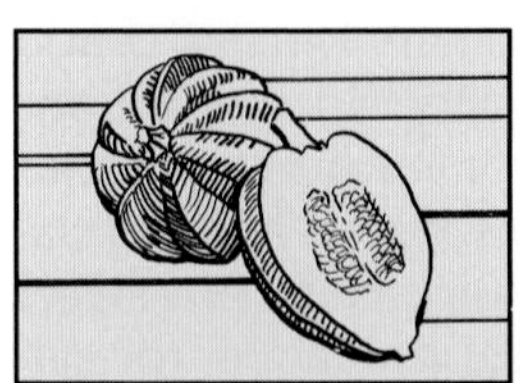

Hard varieties that are harvested only when fully mature. Examples are the acorn, butternut, buttercup, green and blue hubbard, green and gold delicious, and banana squash. Avoid squash with cuts, punctures, sunken spots, moldy spots, or a tender rind.

Sunchokes

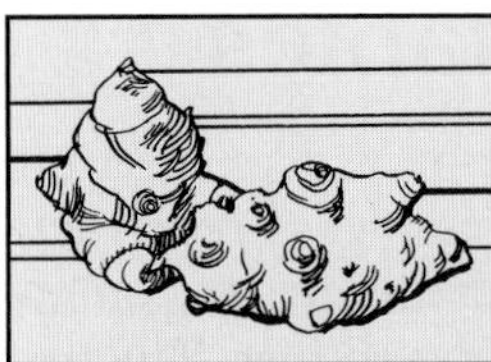

Gnarled, bulblike roots of a prairie sunflower. They were introduced to the Colonists by the Indians. Look for dry, thin-skinned tubers. Avoid any signs of mold or soft spots.

Sweet Potatoes

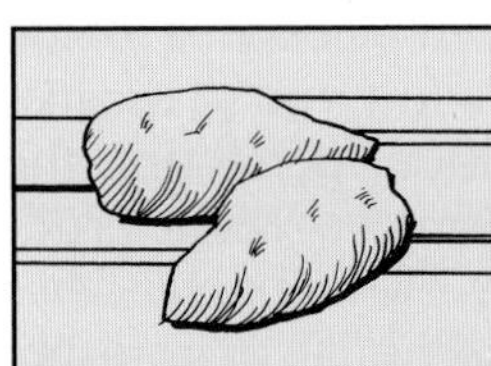

Available in two types. Moist sweet potatoes are sometimes called yams and have an orange-colored flesh. yams Dry sweet potatoes have a pale-colored, dry flesh. Look for well-shaped, firm sweet potatoes with smooth, uniformly colored skins free of decay. Take extra care in selecting sweet potatoes, because they spoil faster than white potatoes. Avoid sweet potatoes with worm holes, cuts, or other injuries that might lead to decay.

Tomatoes

Firm, round and red. Yellow tomatoes are grown in some home gardens. The best flavor comes from locally grown and ripened tomatoes. Look for tomatoes which are well-formed, smooth, trim, and reasonably free from blemishes. Novel varieties sometimes available include cherry, yellow pear-shaped miniature tomatoes, and Italian plum tomatoes. Avoid tomatoes that are mushy, bruised, or sunburned (green or yellow marks around the stem). Also avoid tomatoes with growth cracks around the stem or decayed spots.

Turnips

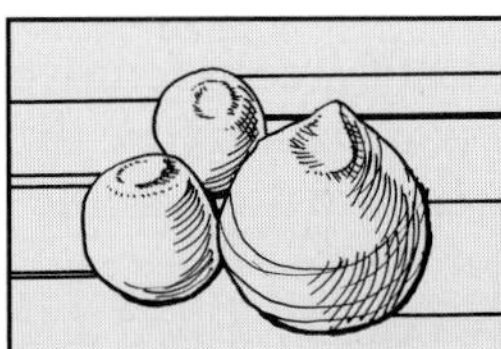

Have white to yellow flesh with a purple top and might be sold with or without the leaf tops. Rutabagas are types of turnips that have a distinct yellow flesh and are larger than turnips. Late winter-storage rutabagas are sometimes coated with a thin layer of paraffin to prevent loss of moisture. These vegetables should be smooth, round, and firm. Avoid large turnips with too many leaf scars around the top and obvious fibrous roots. Avoid skin punctures, deep cuts, or decay.

Watercress

A small, round-leafed plant that grows naturally along the banks of freshwater streams and ponds. It is prized for salads and garnishes because of its spicy hot flavor. Look for crisp, green leaves. Avoid bunches with yellow, wilted, or decayed leaves.

Storage of Fresh Vegetables

Vegetables will continue to ripen at room temperature, so the ideal storage slows down these changes. Refrigeration helps to deactivate the enzyme action that softens the produce. When vegetables are purchased or picked from the garden, clean off any soil, rinse and dry the vegetables, and store them in plastic bags or the crisper drawer of the refrigerator.

Lettuce should be washed, drained, and stored in bags, a plastic box, or wrapped in wax paper in the crisper. If the lettuce is still holding water, pack paper towels in between the layers of leaves and place it all in a plastic bag or crisper. The towels will absorb the extra moisture and help to prevent spoilage.

Root vegetables can be stored from one to several weeks. Do not store root vegetables with their tops because the leafy greens remove moisture from the roots. If you want to use the tops from beets or turnips, remove them immediately and store separately.

Parsley stays crisp for a week if washed and placed in a glass jar with lid or a plastic bag or box.

Potatoes and sweet potatoes should be stored in a cool, dry, dark area. Remove them from any plastic wrapping and place in any airy rack or basket. Refrigerating potatoes turns the starch into sugar which affects the flavor and texture unfavorably. One reason potatoes turn dark after cooking is that they have been too cold or stored in the refrigerator.

Onions also should be stored in a cool, dry area. Do not store them next to potatoes. The combination of the two foods is detrimental to both. The onions absorb moisture from the potatoes, which encourages mold growth. The potatoes sprout faster next to the moist spoiling onions. Onions should be removed from any plastic wrapping and stored in a basket or an open weave bag that allows air to circulate.

Winter squash can be stored in a cool, dry place. Summer squash needs to be refrigerated.

Selecting Canned Vegetables

The convenience of canned vegetables for planned and "spur of the moment" meals is valuable for saving refrigerator room for perishable items. Canned vegetables also serve as needed ingredients for many recipes.

Canned vegetables come in different qualities, sizes, and cuts to suit many purposes. Buy the quality that you need for the job.

Cans should be stored in a dry, cool area. They can be kept for up to a year without any deterioration in quality.

Selecting and Storing Frozen Vegetables

Frozen vegetables taste more like the fresh product than canned vegetables. Frozen and fresh produce also are closer in nutrient content than the processed canned product is. Whether commercially frozen or home frozen, the nutrient content of the vegetable depends upon the period of storage time and the handling conditions of the product from the field to the freezer.

Frozen vegetables are available in block frozen units or individual frozen pieces in a plastic bag. The individual pieces allow you to use just the amount you need without defrosting the whole package. New tempting vegetable products are marketed regularly. A recent trend has been to package ethnic, traditional, or gourmet combinations together. These innovative products come with or without creative sauces. Remember, though, every time a service is added to a product for you, the price is increased. Before buying some of the new convenience combinations, determine if you might be better off buying the separate packages and making your own combinations. It is usually cheaper—if you have the room in your freezer.

Some packaging includes the cooking container. The "boil-in-the bag" pouches are terrific for saving cleanup time and nutrients. This is one of the less expensive cooking packages, but to determine the real cost to you, compare the unit price to a regular pack.

Dried Beans and Peas

Baked beans have earned their place on many a picnic and potluck dinner table with their rich, appetizing flavor and ease of preparation. You probably have taken them for granted or made them from a canned product. However, the traditional Boston baked beans earned their popular place in history by converting stored dried beans and strong molasses from the winter's supply into a fresh taste treat that sometimes meant the difference between

Can you believe that this pasta salad is actually a nutritious vegetable salad? This low-calorie Spaghetti Squash recipe separates into crisp strands that blend with many flavors—just like pasta does.

survival and starvation in the early Colonies. Dry beans, peas, and lentils still supply inexpensive, nutritious food dishes that are staples throughout the world. These food bargains provide more protein per dollar spent than any other food in the protein group of the Basic Food Groups. The protein from the dried legumes combined with protein from foods of animal origin, rice, or wheat makes a complete high-quality protein. Just 3/4 cup (175 mL) serving of dried beans or peas provides about a third of the recommended iron for an adult male.

Consumer Guide

Buy seasonal plentifuls. Ads in the newspapers and in the foods store broadcast the plentiful supplies of "good buys." Take advantage of the quality and money savings of these special supplies and prices, but do not buy more fresh produce than you can use within a few days.

Consumer Guide

A dull or uneven coloring of the legumes in the package usually indicates a long storage. The extra drying of a stale bean increases the time it takes to cook the product. For a quality product, look for a brightness of color.

Big and little sizes of legumes in the same package will not cook evenly. Look for uniform sizes. Cracked seed coverings, foreign material, and pinholes from insect damage are signs of an undesirable product. Avoid those legumes.

Selecting Legumes

Try to select legumes from packages that offer a transparent "window," are in plastic bags, or are in bulk bins. Inspection of the product is needed for selecting quality, since retail packages of beans, peas, or lentils seldom carry the federal or state grade.

Storage of Legumes

Store legumes in tightly covered containers in a dry, cool place. Don't plan to keep the legumes for more than several months. Do not mix packages bought at different times. The older ones will take longer to cook, while the newer ones are likely to get mushy.

Buying Dried Vegetables

Backpacking and the centennial festivals brought back a renewed interest in dried fresh vegetables. Home drying of small amounts and commercial marketing of bulk dried vegetables have made chives, mushrooms, onions, parsley flakes, potato flakes, carrots, green peppers, and potatoes common ingredients for the kitchen or campfire. The dried vegetables can be used for flavorings and separate servings, or ingredients in soups, stews, or casseroles.

Selecting Dried Vegetables

The small packaged flavorings and dried vegetable bits are usually much more expensive than buying bulk dried vegetables. You can scoop from the bin just the "bulk" that you need. However, the chance for contamination from insects, rodents, and human handling is far greater with bulk items. Carefully inspect the food-handling practices of any store you choose for bulk items. See the "Creative Tips" on page 236 for easy food-drying projects you can do in your own oven or microwave oven.

Serving Vegetables

"I'll bring the potato chips!" Since the "veggie revolution," that offer has often changed to "I'll bring the carrot and celery sticks with a dip." The colorful snack appeal of fresh raw vegetables is limited only by the preparer's imagination.

At the height of their flavor, vitamin and mineral content, and crunchiness, raw vegetables invite instant eating for fun and health.

Preparing Raw Vegetables

Rinse vegetables under running water to remove any soil, bacteria, and pesticide residues. If you plan to eat the skin, it is a good idea to scrub the food with a vegetable brush. Scrape or peel the skin and cut the raw vegetables into sizes and shapes that are easily managed as finger foods. Use your skills for making decorative garnishes, but limit the designs to shapes that encourage eating not just "looking."

Arrange the vegetables on a platter or a container made of a similar food. Contrast shapes, colors, and textures of the vegetables, but arrange your design so that pieces can be removed without spoiling the effect. You want your guests to appreciate the care and time

Colorful veggies beckon the snacker to enjoy crisp, creatively shaped vegetables dipped into a low-calorie cottage cheese and mayonnaise herb mixture.

you've taken to serve them. It is sad if the effort makes guests feel guilty about spoiling the effect. How often have you heard, "It's too pretty to eat!"

Cut vegetables can be stored in a plastic bag or large glass jar of water for days. When you need a snack, lunch food, salad, or quick garnish, just reach in and fetch a crispy, low-calorie treat.

Basic Preparation for Vegetables

The secret to fantastic vegetable flavor, texture, and color is avoiding preparation in advance. No cooking ahead, reheating, or keeping vegetables warm is allowed. Make your motto "from the cooking pot to the table" and

Cooking Hints

If for some reason you do have to keep cooked vegetables warm before serving them, here's a saving tip. Cool the vegetables quickly in ice or cold water. This cooling sets the bright color and saves heat-sensitive nutrients. Drain off the water, cover the vegetables, and hold until needed. To reheat, toss lightly in a small amount of melted butter, or steam them in a colander over simmering water for a few minutes until warm.

the results will become the "hit of the meal" instead of the mushy side dish of "must-have vegetables."

You have learned from other food preparation methods that most vitamins and minerals are lost or destroyed through use of heat, water, and air exposure, or a combination of those factors. That tells you that you are wise in eating all types of produce raw whenever you can. It is possible to minimize the losses through cooking by brief and careful preparation. Follow a few basic rules and you will enjoy vegetables that look and taste terrific—and you'll save the vegetables' precious nutrients as well.

Cooking with Water

Simmering vegetables cooks them effectively because it is quick. You usually will use water for the liquid, but when stocks, juices, or other flavored liquids are available they supply creative alternatives. Do not boil vegetables. You'll cause the loss of nutrients and texture.

Equipment

You will need a pan just big enough to hold the amount of vegetables you plan to cook, a tight-fitting lid, a colander or sieve, and a fork or skewer to test for doneness.

Ingredients

Clean the vegetables. Avoid cutting them too much. You may want to add flavorings such as seasonings, herbs, or lemon juice. The vegetables will be simmered in a small amount of liquid, about ½ cup (125 mL) for four to six servings of vegetables.

Directions

1. Bring the liquid (water, stock, or juice) to a full rolling boil. Add any seasonings desired. Try cooking the vegetables without salt. You can always add the salt, and you might discover a whole new world of natural tastes without it.
2. Add the prepared vegetables to the boiling water. Cover the pan until the water returns to a boil.
3. Reduce the heat to the simmering stage. This lessens the loss of nutrients through evaporation and avoids breaking up food with the tumbling action of the water.
4. Cook until the vegetables are tender (not soft) when pierced with a fork or skewer. Watch carefully. Cooking vegetables takes just a few minutes for pieces and less than you might expect for whole vegetables.
5. Drain the vegetables in a colander or sieve. Keep the liquid for soups, sauces, or cooking liquids. That way you save the flavor and nutrients in the water for another product.
6. Stir in butter and any flavorings. Serve immediately on a warm platter or bowl.

Note: Starchy vegetables absorb more water and require more water for cooking. Cover potatoes, beets, and whole carrots with water to cook. Whenever possible, cook them whole with the skins on. There are concentrated nutrients close to the skin. Be careful when removing them from the water. The skins slip off easily, especially from cooked potatoes.

Steaming

The gentle, moist heat of steam is an excellent way to cook vegetables. A perforated rack is used to hold the produce up out of the water and in the steam bath. With steaming, water-soluble nutrients are saved and the gentle heat destroys fewer heat-sensitive nutrients. Since the food is not immersed in the water, it doesn't become waterlogged. To steam vegetables, place them in the steaming rack in the pan. Add water and cover tightly. Bring the water to a simmer and cook the vegetables just until tender. They should still have their bright color.

Cook by Color

Picture the rainbow of colors at the vegetable stand and divide the produce into color categories. Green, yellow, red, and white form the basic colors. Orange is technically a deep yellow. You can predict the timing and liquids needed for each of the groups by color.

Green vegetables contain chlorophyll, a green pigment that turns khaki color when heated. Have you ever lifted the lid from what had been fresh green broccoli to discover a dingy-colored vegetable? You knew then the broccoli had been overcooked. The process probably took just a few extra minutes, but the results were a disaster. To avoid those problems, cook green vegetables with constant watching. Cook until just barely tender to the fork. Some professional chefs are so careful about discoloring green vegetables they never use lids on pans. They think the hot liquid condensing on the lid drops down and scalds the vegetable causing it to discolor before it is tender. Most nutritionists do not recommend cooking vegetables in an open pot because of the nutrient loss through evaporation.

Another unwise way to save the dark green color is to add soda to the water. The color

Steaming whole or cut vegetables cooks them without destroying the shape, flavor, color, texture, and nutrient content of most vegetables. This colorful artichoke would turn khaki if immersed in boiling water.

stays, but the nutrients go. The soda destroys both vitamins and flavor.

Yellow vegetables get their color from the yellow pigment called carotene, which converts into vitamin A in the body. Carotene is not water soluble or heat sensitive. However, even a stable nutrient such as carotene can be lost if the vegetable is overcooked to the mushy stage when the cell walls are broken down. The carotene is "let out" and escapes with the water. If the water turns yellowish, you know some of the carotene is in the water.

White vegetables stay light and bright until they are overcooked. A pigment called flavones dissolves in the water causing vegetables such as cauliflower and turnips to turn gray or yellow when overcooked.

Red vegetables, such as red cabbage and beets, turn blue to purple in some hard-water areas. A small amount of an acid, such as lemon juice or vinegar, brings out the bright red color.

Baking

Many vegetables are naturals for no-fuss baking. The baked potato with toppings has gained great popularity for being a complete meal or snack. Various squashes and whole onions bake individually also. Other vegetables bake into succulent dishes when combined with sauces, cheeses, and other vegetables. Select individual vegetables for baking with extra care. Avoid hidden bruised spots or injuries that mar the skin. When baking several vegetables, select similar sizes so they require the same amount of baking time.

Equipment

Many times, an oven is all you need for baking. A flat baking pan is a convenience, though, for catching drips and transferring the food in and out of the oven.

Directions

1. Rub a little oil or butter on the skins for crispness.
2. Place potatoes or other whole vegetables in a 400°F (200°C) oven.
3. Bake for half the time (about 30 minutes) and then pierce the skins once or twice to allow steam under pressure to escape without exploding the vegetable. (This step might add to the baking time by allowing some steam to escape, but once you've cleaned up the oven from an exploded vegetable, you will probably consider it worth the time.)
4. Continue baking until the vegetable gives slightly when squeezed with a hot pad. A skewer or fork also could be used, but the hole allows more valuable steam to escape if the product is not done.
5. Remove the vegetable from oven. Slit or pierce potatoes immediately to prevent slowly escaping steam from making the crisp skin soggy.

Roasting

The unbeatable flavor from a vegetable that has been roasted around a cut of meat makes this traditional method worth learning. Roasting vegetables combines panfrying and roasting the vegetable with a meat or other vegetables. (Technically, roasting should be done with the lid on for some steaming effect, but baking for a longer time in low heat also creates the same tenderizing effect.)

Directions

1. Cut potatoes into halves or other vegetables into large pieces. Remember, if you leave the skins on, you'll receive more nutrients from the vegetables. Parboil the vegetables.
2. Melt butter or other fat in an ovenproof dish or pan.
3. Turn the potatoes and vegetables so that all sides are well coated with the butter or fat and slightly browned.
4. Add any herbs or flavorings desired and bake for 20 to 30 minutes or until browned and tender.

Alternative Method

1. Roast the meat until about 45 minutes from being done.

2. Remove the hot pan from the oven and brown the vegetables slightly in the drippings.

3. Continue roasting the meat and vegetables until done. Baste the vegetables with the drippings in the pan occasionally.

Frying Vegetables

French frying refers to deep-fat fried potatoes in most people's minds, but could mean any food cooked in hot, deep fat. Currently, other vegetables are popular dipped into a quick-rising batter and then deep-fat fried. Zucchini, mushrooms, onions, carrots, artichokes, and broccoli are being served in restaurants and homes.

Panfried Vegetables

Panfrying refers to browning food in a small amount of fat and then cooking slowly until the product reaches the right stage of doneness.

Parboiled vegetables work better for panfrying. Raw vegetables take so long to cook that they can scorch or overbrown before they are tender inside. After parboiling the vegetables, fry them in a small amount of fat only until slightly crisp.

Stir-Frying Vegetables

Americans have adopted stir-frying as a quick-fixing way to enjoy vegetables at their best—crisp, colorful, flavorful, and healthful. The new specialty vegetables such as jicama, sunchokes, and kohlrabi are perfect for a quick stir-fry. Throw in a few protein-rich nuts and

Spaghetti Squash Salad

Yield: 12 servings

Traditional	Ingredients	Metric
3 lbs.	Spaghetti squash	1.5 kg.
	Vegetable cooking spray	
1 cup	Onion, thinly sliced	250 mL
1 cup	Carrots, shredded	250 mL
3 tbsp.	Lemon juice	45 mL
2 tbsp.	Golden raisins	30 mL
¼ tsp.	Salt	1 mL

Directions

1. Cut squash in half, and discard seeds. Place squash, cut side down, in a Dutch oven. Add 2 inches of water.

2. Bring water to a boil. Cover, reduce heat, and cook 20 to 25 minutes or until tender.

3. Drain squash, and cool. Using a fork, remove spaghetti-like strands; transfer to a bowl and set aside.

4. Coat a skillet with cooking spray and place over medium heat until hot.

5. Add onion, and cook 10 to 12 minutes or until tender. Remove from heat. Let cool.

6. Combine onion, carrots, lemon juice, raisins, salt, and reserved squash. Toss gently. Cover and refrigerate 2 hours or overnight.

Microwave Directions

1. Wash spaghetti squash and pierce in several places with a fork. Place on a paper towel. Microwave on high for 12 minutes or until squash feels almost tender. Let stand 5 minutes.

2. Cut squash in half and discard seeds. Using a fork, remove spaghetti-like strands. Transfer to a bowl and set aside.

3. In a 1½ qt. (1½L) microwave-safe casserole, microwave onion on high for 3 minutes or until tender.

4. Add carrots, lemon juice, raisins, salt, and reserved squash. Toss gently.

5. Cover and refrigerate for 2 hours or overnight.

Protein	Grain	Milk	F & V

maybe some tofu and you have the health dream of the decade.

The Chinese stir-fry technique combines contrasting textures of crunchy (*tsuei*) with the soft and tender (*nun*). Mild flavors are accented by hot spices for a taste-tempting mixture of numerous ingredients that somehow never lose their individual identity.

The Japanese counterpart to the stir-fry are the teriyaki foods. *Teri* is the term for glaze and *yaki* means broiled. The glazed, broiled food describes perfectly the teriyaki recipes.

All cuisines of the Orient are alike in that they do not use butter or any dairy foods. Those foods simply do not exist in that part of the world. Sesame oil, soy sauce, rice wines, and fish stock are used instead.

Stir-Fry Food Preparation

Stir-frying itself takes only a few minutes to complete. The real preparation time is invested in preparing and cutting the food to be stir-fried.

Divide the ingredients you are using into two groups—the fast-cooking and the slow-cooking. Cut or chop the vegetables and meat into pieces that will cook quickly and lie as flat as possible against the pan (this increases the cooking surface). Slicing on the diagonal cuts across more tough fibers and helps to tenderize the pieces. Stir-fried foods are done when the outside is softened slightly, but the inside is still crisp and warm. Any delay in serving will make the vegetable soft all the way through. That detracts from the pleasure of the true stir-fry meal with contrasting textures.

Directions

1. Add a small amount of oil and heat the skillet or wok. Tilt the pan to coat it evenly with the oil.
2. Add the seasoning ingredients to the oil. Peppers, gingerroot, and garlic are the most common seasonings.
3. Add the ingredient that takes the longest to cook. This will most likely be the meat or tofu. Use a tossing motion to keep the food from sticking. (Stir-frying requires your constant attention from start to finish.)
4. Add the prepared vegetables that take longer to cook, such as carrots, beets, turnips, and potatoes.
5. Just before the longer cooking vegetables are done, add the softer, faster cooking ones, such as zucchini, mushrooms, and pea pods.
6. Add a small amount of liquid, cover, and steam the foods briefly. (Usually, this brief steaming is less than a minute.)
7. Uncover the pan and add final seasonings. This is also the time to add a thickening agent such as cornstarch dissolved in a small amount of water.
8. Toss all the ingredients while the pan is still over the heat to coat the ingredients with the shiny glaze and combine the flavors.
9. Serve immediately with rice or another whole-grain product for enjoyable eating and to complete the nutritional offerings of the meal.

Cooking Canned Vegetables

The process of canning actually cooks the food at the same time. Preparing canned vegetables consists of warming them to serving temperature. Use the liquid in preparation whenever possible to save the flavor and nutrients.

Cooking Frozen Vegetables

Processing frozen vegetables breaks down some of the structure of the cell walls, so they tend to be softer and cook faster. The blanching process used in freezing also slightly precooks the foods.

A good guide in preparing frozen vegetables is to consider it more of a heating process than a cooking one. The companies that freeze foods invest time and money in testing their directions. Follow the product directions for dependable results.

Stir-frying vegetables in a small amount of oil produces a fast but crisp nutritious dish with endless combination possibilities.

Mixed Vegetable Stir-fry

Yield: 6 servings

Traditional	**Ingredients**	**Metric**
1 large	Cucumber, peeled	1 large
1 Tbsp.	Cornstarch	15 mL
2 Tbsp.	Reduced-sodium soy sauce	30 mL
1 tsp.	Peanut oil	5 mL
	Vegetable cooking spray	
1 cup	Carrots, sliced	250 mL
¼ lb.	Fresh mushrooms, quartered	125 g
1 clove	Garlic, minced	1 clove
2 cups	Fresh snow peas	500 mL
½ cup	Water chestnuts, sliced	250 g
⅔ cup	Water	150 mL
½ tsp.	Chicken-flavored bouillon granules	3 mL

Directions

1. Cut cucumber in half lengthwise; remove seeds. Cut cucumber into strips; set aside.
2. Combine cornstarch and soy sauce; set aside.
3. Heat oil in a large skillet or wok coated with cooking spray over medium heat until hot. Add carrot, mushrooms, and garlic. Sauté 3 minutes or until crisp-tender.
4. Push vegetables to side of skillet or wok. Add cucumber, snow peas, and water chestnuts. Cook 3 minutes or until crisp-tender, stirring constantly.
5. Stir in cornstarch mixture, water, and bouillon granules. Bring to a boil, and cook 1 minute or until thickened, stirring constantly.

Protein	Grain	Milk	F & V

Creative Tips

All the previously mentioned methods for preparing vegetables usually start with recipes or a set meal plan. The real challenge to use vegetables sometimes starts when you have assorted "leftovers" that still have value and flavor to offer.

Many recipes that call for pieces of vegetables can make use of leftovers. You also can use them for soups and sauces. Try to think of unique uses and you will find yourself creating new family favorites. Which of the recipes in this book do you think could use leftover vegetables?

Preparing Legumes and Dried Fresh Vegetables

Many legumes need to be soaked before cooking. These soaking periods range from 30 minutes to overnight for different dishes and vegetables. Read the directions with your recipe and on the package of your dried product to plan the most effective preparation.

Microwaving Techniques

Refer to Chapter 8 and the examples given for cooking vegetables in the microwave. Some general helpful guides to cooking vegetables in the microwave are:

- Use smaller amounts of water than for conventional cooking methods.
- Cover the vegetables to prevent drying.
- Watch your product cook. Vegetables often cook so fast that you can ruin the product in seconds.
- Cook pieces that are the same size to assure even cooking of all the parts.
- Often you can cook right in the paper package. Read the package directions.
- Home-canned vegetables are not safe to be cooked in the microwave. The heating is often uneven and won't kill any botulism toxins that might be present. There is no way to test ahead for the toxins.

Herbs, The Fragrant Taste!

The threat of obesity, heart disease, cancer, diabetes, and other diet-related diseases is changing the choice for many Americans from salty, fat-rich, deep-fried foods to fresh, crisp foods with little or no added salt. There is no denying the rich flavor that a crisp, fried crust gives foods, but there are other pleasurable, flavorful additions for food that do not add extra fat or salt to your diet. Aromatic herbs and spices have distinctive flavors that assist the natural taste in vegetables, fruits, milk products, eggs, and meats without masking the food's own unique flavor. You can change plain green beans into a taste sensation by adding fresh or dried dill weed. Basil and oregano—sometimes called the pizza seasonings—give meat, pasta, and salads a wonderful flavor that helps you forget about adding extra salt. Other seasonings also can create a memorable meal out of otherwise ordinary foods.

Once you have experienced the clean, captivating aroma of fresh thyme as it is crushed between your fingers to lightly accent a sizzling roast or the compelling scent of fresh cut basil as the pieces scatter over fresh sliced tomatoes, you will become an avid explorer of the frontier of herbs.

An **herb** is a seed-producing plant that dies back at the end of the growing season. It is valued for its taste, aroma, or medicinal properties. Usually the leaves are used, but some seeds, stems, and blossoms are also tasty and useful. A **spice** is a root, seed, or bark product from a plant grown in a tropical climate. These plants produce a pungent or spicy taste such as cinnamon, nutmeg, or pepper. Most spices taste lively, but not hot to the tongue. Pepper and ginger spices are exceptions that do produce a burning sensation in the mouth.

Mustards are made of the ground-up seeds from an herb plant in the mustard family that are combined with other ingredients to make a condiment for serving or cooking food.

Vinegars are acetic (sour) liquids obtained from the fermentation of liquids containing a small amount of alcohol. Vinegar is terrific for making relishes and other foods. Distilled white vinegar has the least character and color. It is just mildly acetic in flavor. Cider vinegar retains some of the color and flavor of the apples from which it is made. You will discover a whole array of colorful and herb-flavored vinegars in the specialty section of food stores. Those specialty vinegars are often quite expensive when purchased, but can be made at home.

Herb Vinegars at Home

Just pour a favorite vinegar into a clean jar and add a sprig of your favorite fresh herb from the garden, farmers' market, or store. Cap the jar tightly and store it for about one month. This is called steeping. The vinegar also can be heated in the jar in a pan of hot water on the stove until it begins to simmer. Remove from the heat and let it cool slowly before sealing with a lid. You also can heat the vinegar and herb at the lowest power setting for 3 to 5 minutes in the microwave oven.

After steeping, remove the herbs and pour the vinegar into smaller attractive bottles for gifts or the kitchen shelf. A fresh sprig of the herb can be added to help identify the herb fla-

You can make your own herb vinegars to spice up your own cooking or to give as gifts.

vor. These flavored vinegars add new taste dimensions to your kitchen creations and make very personal presents for a small cost in time and money.

Tasty Guidelines for Flavorful Seasoning Combinations

You can relax when it comes time to select which herbs to use with main dishes or vegetables. There are no mistakes, but you will like some better than others. A few simple guidelines are furnished in the Appendix, but you are in charge. You will, however, want to follow these simple practices regarding amounts and methods of using and storing herbs and spices.

- Dried herbs are more concentrated in flavor than fresh herbs. If you are fortunate to have fresh herbs, use three times as much of the fresh as the dried. Because fresh herbs are not always available, recipes give the measurement for dried herbs unless otherwise specified.
- Use dried herbs by crushing or rolling the dried leaves between your fingers just before you measure them for the food. This releases the trapped volatile oils that hold the herb's flavor. In fact, part of the joy of cooking with herbs and spices is enjoying the inviting fragrance as you are preparing the seasonings. If you do not enjoy the specks of the dried herb in your food product, you can tie the dried pieces in a piece of cheesecloth or make a vegetable bouquet garni such as the one on page 68.
- Herbs and spices are available in dried whole forms of the plant such as celery seeds, whole cloves, whole stick cinnamon, dried basil leaves, dried oregano leaves, and dried rosemary leaves. They also come ground in powdered form such as ground cinnamon, cloves, basil, and oregano. The ground form loses its fresh flavor faster, but is often easier to use in recipes.
- Fresh leaves, blossoms, or seeds of herbs can be snipped with scissors. They also can be chopped, torn into the desired sizes, or used whole.
- Spices and herbs eventually lose their flavor and aroma. Buy only small amounts at one time. Store in an airtight container in a cool, dark place or in the freezer. It is ideal to date seasonings to avoid keeping them past their usefulness. When the flavor and aroma are gone, you might as well throw out the seasoning and replace it. Insects also can spoil herbs and spices. The airtight containers are helpful in preventing infestation, but the freezer is a better place for storage.

Food Facts

Can you think of any smell that can make your mouth water with delight as much as a fresh slice of crusty Italian bread browning in a light layer of garlic butter? On the other hand, one blast of the same garlic lingering in the house or on someone's breath is enough to chase away the vampires. The glory of garlic could fill a history book. It was brought to England in 1548 from the Mediterranean. Once shunned by the fastidious Victorians, garlic has now become respectable on every continent—including the United States. Even health claims are made for it, from antibiotic qualities to cholesterol-beating folklore.

You just can't beat garlic's sizzling flavor in hot olive oil combined with Italian tomatoes and oregano. Garlic is best at its freshest. Cook it only a short time. It tends to lose flavor on prolonged cooking. Even more important, never brown or burn garlic. It turns bitter fast. When you can lose your inhibitions about strong smells, you can join the Romans, Indians, Chinese, French, English, and all the Mediterraneans who relish this international herb.

• Seasonings develop flavor as they cook in food, but they also can become too strong and bitter during long high-heat cooking. Don't add the seasoning in long-simmered foods and beverages until the last hour of cooking. Remove the stick cinnamon and cloves from hot drinks after an hour of heating to prevent a bitter flavor from forming. For delicate sauces, add seasonings during the last steps of preparation.

• For seasoning foods before cooking or seasoning cold salad dressings, the herbs and spices need time to flavor the mixture. Prepare cold foods and season several hours ahead of serving or store overnight in the refrigerator before serving for the most evenly flavored mixture.

• Store fresh-picked herbs by rinsing them in cool water and putting the stems in a jar of water. Cover the leaves and jar with a plastic bag and refrigerate for several days. You can store the fresh leaves even longer by placing them in vaporproof bags and freezing them. These leaves will retain the fresh taste, but will be limp and should be chopped before using.

Your Own Private Blend

Specific seasonings blend so well together they are often sold preblended under other names. Pumpkin pie spice is a blend of cinnamon, cloves, and nutmeg. Italian seasoning is a preblended mixture of oregano, basil, and fennel. Remember, anytime you buy a convenience you pay extra for the labor. You can make your own herb and spice blends for use in your own kitchen or to give as gifts. Dried flowers and herbs can be combined for a soothing **potpourri** (a mixture of dried flowers and herbs used for their scent). Perhaps you already have favorite mixtures of cinnamon, spices, and sugar you use for toppings on toast or cookies? You can create great blends from purchased herbs or herbs out of your own garden or window ledge pots.

Herb Teas

Many herbs, fresh or dried, make delicious teas when you steep them in boiling water for three to five minutes in a covered pot. Some herb teas have colorful folklore stories about their healing properties and indeed many of

Creative Tips

Start a year around herb garden. Buy seeds or plants from a local nursery or supermarket of your favorite, easy-to-grow herbs such as parsley, basil, chives, thyme, and rosemary. Gardens flowers, nasturtiums, and violets are also herbs that are edible and tasty. Plant them in 6- to 8-inch (18 to 20 cm) pots. Use gravel or broken pieces of old pots in the bottom for drainage. Fill the pots with potting soil from the supermarket or garden store. Plant seeds or plants according to the instructions on the package.

Place in a sunny window. A southern exposure is the best. Water regularly to keep the soil just moist. In a few weeks to a month, your plants will be sprouting. You can keep them growing as long as you water, feed, and trim them. Using the herb leaves encourages them to be productive.

Potted herbs also make an attractive addition to the kitchen or any room. Just before dinner, wave your hand through them and you'll awaken the room with their wonderful fresh aroma. Herbs were the only room freshener in our ancestors' day. Fresh mints and scented geraniums were often kept in pots in Victorian days to be disturbed occasionally to dispel the musty aroma of the big old houses.

our modern medicines do stem from plant origins. The soothing, relaxing, and refreshing drinks make pleasant substitutes for caffeine drinks. You can find many fascinating books about herbs and herbal teas and their historical uses in any library.

Try making your own teas from purchased dried herbs or your own garden herbs, but always read about any plant you plan to eat before you experiment. Not all plants are edible. Some are poisonous. Develop your creativity using only the many wonderful familiar plants and herbs that are proven safe.

Creative Tips

Drying herbs is a simple project that creates a product with outstanding flavor and color. You can dry your own parsley flakes at a fraction of the cost of commercial packages and the color and flavor will be better. You also can use this method for other green leafy herbs such as mint, basil, thyme, rosemary, savory, or sage. Here's how.

Drying Herbs

Equipment

You will need a wire rack and cotton or paper towels.

Directions

1. Rinse and pat dry the parsley.
2. Spread the parsley on cotton or paper towels laid over the wire rack. (You can use the oven rack or cake cooling racks.)
3. Turn on the oven to its lowest setting, approximately 150°F (65°C). For electric ovens, prop the oven door open 1 inch (2.5 cm) to allow for air circulation. Cover parsley with paper towels to absorb the moisture as the parsley dries.
4. Dry the parsley for about 20 minutes in the oven. Watch closely and move the parsley to dry place on towel as moisture is absorbed. You may want to replace moist towels with dry ones.
5. Remove the parsley when it is dry to the touch but still resilient enough to bend without breaking.
6. Let it cool. Remove the stems. They tend to be bitter.
7. Crumble or chop the parsley and store in glass jar away from the light.

Microwaving Technique

1. Rinse and pat dry the parsley
2. Spread paper towels in the microwave oven.
3. Put 1/4 cup (50 mL) water in a cup in the microwave. Arrange the parsley on the paper towels. Cover with paper towels to absorb the moisture as the parsley dries.
4. Microwave on high for 2 to 4 minutes. Watch closely and move the parsley to a dry place on the towel as moisture is absorbed. You may want to replace moist towels with dry ones.
5. Remove the parsley when it is dry to the touch but still resilient enough to bend without breaking.
6. Let it cool. Remove the stems. They tend to be bitter.
7. Crumble or chop parsley and store in a glass jar away from the light.

Ziti with Herbs and Tofu

Yield: 6 servings
Oven: 350°F (177°C)
Equipment: 2-quart (2 L) casserole, saucepan

Traditional	Ingredients	Metric
½ cup	Chopped onion	125 mL
1 clove	Garlic, minced	1 clove
24 oz. can	Tomato sauce	680 g can
2 Tbsp.	Fresh oregano or 2 tsp. (10 mL) dried oregano	30 mL
2 Tbsp.	Fresh basil or 2 tsp. (10 mL) dried basil	30 mL
8 oz.	Ziti macaroni	227 g
12 oz.	Tofu, drained	340 g
1 large	Egg white	1 large
10-oz. pkg.	Frozen chopped spinach, well drained	283 g
¼ tsp.	Ground nutmeg	1 mL
⅛ tsp.	Ground black pepper	0.5 mL
½ cup	Mozzarella cheese, grated	125 mL

Directions

1. In the saucepan, cook the onion and garlic in olive oil for 2 to 3 minutes over medium-high heat.
2. Add the tomato sauce.
3. Bring to a boil.
4. Add the herbs and immediately reduce heat.
5. Cover and simmer 15 minutes.
6. Cook ziti macaroni according to the package directions.
7. Drain ziti while making tofu mixture.
8. Puree tofu with egg white in food processor or blender.
9. Add nutmeg and pepper and blend.
10. Add cooked ziti to tofu mixture. Blend carefully so as not to break up the ziti.
11. Place one-fourth of the tomato sauce in the bottom of the greased or sprayed casserole.
12. Add one-third of the tofu-ziti mixture, spreading evenly over the casserole with a large spoon.
13. Continue to layer sauce and tofu-ziti mixture, ending with tomato sauce on top.
14. Top with grated cheese.
15. Cover with lid of foil and bake for 25 minutes.
16. Remove cover and bake 5 minutes without the cover.

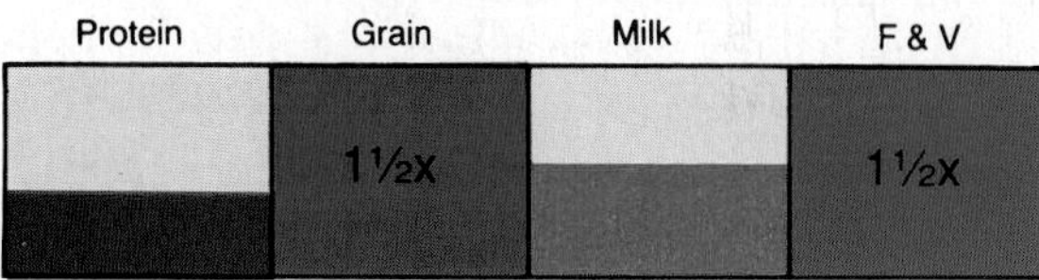

Vocabulary Review

Legumes
Solanine
Herb
Spice
Mustards
Vinegars
Potpourri

Questions for Review

1. Name and describe the six kinds of plants that form the vegetable family.
2. Name two vitamins that most vegetables supply in plentiful amounts. What is at least one benefit that each vitamin provides for your body?
3. What group of vitamins do the seed vegetables, such as peas and lima beans, supply?
4. What does the deep yellow or red color of a vegetable tell you about its vitamin content?
5. What are the guidelines for selecting good quality fresh vegetables?
6. Many vegetables are stored in the refrigerator. Which vegetables do *not* store well in the refrigerator? Why is that true?
7. What nutrients do dried legumes contribute to your diet?
8. Name two foods that can be combined in a meal to give you a high-quality protein. Why does that combination work that way?
9. Name three things to look for in selecting good quality legumes.
10. Describe some package conditions that indicate a poor quality frozen vegetable product.
11. What is the key to successful vegetable preparation? Why is that the case?
12. Describe several steps you can take to help preserve the nutrients in vegetables when cooking.
13. What guidelines should you follow when cooking vegetables in the microwave oven?
14. Vegetables can be grouped into basic color categories of green, yellow, red, and white. Explain the guidelines for cooking each group when cooking by color as suggested in the chapter.
15. Why are so many Americans switching from rich fried foods to crisp foods with no or little added salt? Discuss several of the reasons.
16. What are some of the other flavorful additions for food that can help to substitute for the heavy salt flavor?
17. What is the difference between a spice and an herb?
18. Which spices produce a burning sensation on the tongue?
19. Are dried spices and herbs from the store the only source for dried spices and herbs? Why is it not practical to dry your own spices? Why is it often possible to dry your own herbs?
20. How might you use fresh herbs?
21. What is the general rule to follow when substituting fresh herbs for the measurement of dried herbs listed in a recipe?
22. What are some safety guidelines to follow in making your own herb teas?
23. From what you have learned about the stability of nutrients such as vitamin C and vitamin B complex, do you think that fresh green herbs might be more nutritious than dried herbs?

Things to Do

1. Study the mini-guide to freshness in this chapter. Visit a fresh produce department in a grocery store. Practice identifying the produce and evaluate its condition based on freshness qualities.

2. Dry fresh parsley in a conventional or microwave oven. (See the directions.) Determine the cost of the homemade parsley and compare it with a commercial jar of dried parsley. (Measure your dried parsley vs. the amount in the jar to compare values.) Was there any other difference between your home-dried herb and the commercial one?

3. Look through a cookbook or recipe file to find and list recipes that might make use of leftover vegetables. Do you think you can save money on your grocery bill by using small batches of leftovers in this way?

4. Use combinations of dried legumes and other foods, such as rice, that combine to form a complete protein. Plan an attractive meal that supplies high-quality protein. Plan a similar meal with meat. Calculate the costs of both meals. Which meal costs more? Were they equal in nutritional value?

5. Divide a bunch of broccoli into three equal-size portions. Simmer one just until tender to the fork. Boil another bunch for twice as long. Boil rapidly the last piece four times as long. What happens to the vegetable's color, texture, and flavor of each example. How does this affect your future cooking of vegetables?

6. Look up the history of your favorite herbs or spice flavors in the library. Report in class or write about the colorful histories of the ones you found most interesting. How might you separate "fact from fiction" among the numerous cures and folklore stories about herbs and spices?

7. Dry some flavorful mint leaves and grated orange and lemon peel in a 150°F (66°C) oven or in the air. Make a hot or iced tea from the brew. Experiment until you get a mixture you like. Serve to friends or the class. What suggestions would you have to help someone else develop their own "tea?" Compare the price of your "brew" to the same amount of a commercial herb mint tea. Which was more expensive?

8. Panfry a small fillet of a mild fish. Cut in half. Leave one half free of any seasoning and do not add any salt. Sprinkle the other half with a dried herb such as thyme, dill, or oregano and a sprinkle of lemon juice. Which unsalted fish tasted more acceptable?

9. Plant a pot of herbs in a small container of potting soil and vermiculite. Keep on the window shelf and water when soil gets dry. In 5 to 6 weeks you can have most fresh herbs ready to furnish a continuing supply of tender leaves for flavoring your food.

Perfect? No! Unbeatable? Yes!

What's the one food that comes to your mind as the most perfect of all nature's foods? Chances are that as a small child you heard you would be healthy if you drank your milk. Have you ever been told, "You don't have to finish everything on your plate if you're full, as long as you finish your milk"? Milk is so close to being the perfect food it has long been considered the symbol of healthy eating. In fact, human milk is the perfect food for human infants until age four to six months. After that it does not supply adequate amounts of all the nutrients a person needs. Milk and milk products supply significant amounts of most nutrients, but are lacking in iron, vitamin C, and niacin (one of the B vitamins).

The most refined technological research shows that milk still comes the closest of any natural food to meeting the nutritional needs of humans. Milk's abundance of minerals, vitamins, protein, carbohydrates, fats, and water cannot be matched by any other food. There is no substitute food that equals the amount of calcium supplied by the milk group. As a teenager, you need four servings daily from the milk group. That need can be easy to enjoy because this food group offers such a great variety. Remember, though, it is only from eating a balance of the Four Basic Food Groups that you can receive the right amounts of all the nutrients your body needs.

The term **natural** food in this reference refers to a food that exists in nature; a food that was not invented by people. It does not imply any processing or absence of processing that might have taken place with the natural food. For example milk is often fortified with vitamins A and D, but is still a natural food. Likewise, when the milkfat is removed, the milk is still a natural food. The term "natural food" is not to be confused with the term "in its natural state" which implies no enrichment, fortification, or processing.

Nutritive Notes

Milk provides calcium, phosphorus, protein, riboflavin and other B vitamins, vitamin A, fats, sugar, and water. Although milk is lacking in iron and niacin, other foods can balance that need. Vitamin D, the sunshine vitamin that our bodies actually make from the sun, is usually added to milk to work with the calcium and phosphorus to build and maintain healthy bones and teeth. For year-around strong bones and teeth, look on the milk label for fortification with this valuable nutrient. Milk is tasty

Food Facts

Calcium is found in other foods, but it is extremely difficult to equal the calcium from dairy sources. In order to equal the amount of calcium in 4 cups (1 L) of milk, a person would have to eat:

- **7 cups (1.75 L) of cooked spinach**
- **23 cups (5.75 L) of carrots**
- **32 cups (8 L) of green peas**
- **22 oranges**
- **50 tomatoes**
- **50 slices of whole-wheat bread**

The amount of calcium in the food is not all that is important to you when trying to get calcium from foods other than dairy sources. The body is not able to absorb all forms of calcium. Calcium in dairy products is *bioavailable* (readily absorbed). Calcium in many calcium-rich vegetables, such as spinach, is not used well by the body.

and satisfying by itself and combines beautifully with other foods for an infinite variety of nutritious meals and snacks.

Consumer Milk Choices

Most of the milk and milk products used in this country are produced by cows. A small amount for special diet needs and personal preferences is produced by goats. Other countries must rely upon goats, sheep, buffalo, camels, and reindeer for their milk products due to climate and other geographical conditions.

Milk itself comes in over half a dozen forms. The milk products include luxurious rich ice creams, ice milk, cream, yogurt, and cheese of all textures that range from crisp low fat farmer's cheese to creamy flavored dessert Brie variations. All of them provide the wholesome nutrients of the milk from which they are made.

Milk is available to the consumer in many forms.

Whole milk contains at least 3.25 percent of milkfat. In order to keep the milkfats from separating to a layer on top of the milk, whole milk is usually **homogenized.** This process mixes the tiny milkfat particles uniformly throughout the milk permanently. Perhaps you have seen old collectible milk bottles that used to be delivered to homes. They contained whole milk that divided into a layer of cream on top and the milk underneath. You would have poured off the cream to use on your cereal or for desserts and cooking. The remaining milk was then used for drinking.

Skim milk has less than 0.5 percent of the milkfat left in the milk. When the fat is removed, the fat-soluble vitamins A and D are lost with the milkfat. To compensate for that loss, skim milk is usually fortified with vitamins A and D. (Fortified means vitamins and/or minerals have been added to a food.)

Two percent milk has 2 percent milkfat left in milk. The small amount of fat adds to the flavor, but does not add significantly to the cholesterol or calorie count. It is now a topselling product due to the health benefits for some people of reducing animal fat in their diets. Look on the label. The 2 percent milk should also be fortified with vitamins A and D.

Nonfat dry milk is a dry powdered form of milk that has had the milkfat removed. Read the labels for products that have been fortified with vitamins A and D. The dry milk powder can be used in cooking and baking products just as it is. Water is added to turn the powdered milk into a drink. The taste is usually improved by letting it stand in the refrigerator several hours after mixing with water. Dry milk is a lifesaver for people who do not have access to refrigeration, and a convenience to people who are away from refrigeration for temporary periods of time for pleasure hiking, camping, or scientific expeditions.

Buttermilk used to be the liquid that was

Yogurt has earned its new popularity as a tasty, healthful food. Top your favorite fruits, vegetables, soups, or hot pancakes with the tangy flavor of creamy low-fat yogurt for added calcium without a lot of calories.

leftover after the whole milk was churned into butter. The tangy flavor and different, thick, smooth texture is a favorite treat for many people. Buttermilk is produced today by adding lactic acid to pasteurized skim milk. To simulate the "old time goodness" of country buttermilk, tiny butter particles are sometimes added.

Evaporated milk has had half of the water removed from the milk. The reduced liquid is canned and sterilized, producing a milk that can be stored for long periods without refrigeration. When milk is needed for cooking or drinking, the water can be mixed in again. Evaporated milk also can be used full strength for richness in recipes or as cream on foods.

Sweetened condensed milk has had half of the water milk removed and 40 percent more sugar added. This product caramelizes beautifully and smoothly into wonderful candies. It also is used for making desserts and toppings for desserts.

Goat's milk is available fresh in some areas. When a supply of fresh milk is not convenient, it usually can be purchased in cans. Adults and infants who react allergically to cow's milk can usually digest goat's milk safely.

Flavored milks are manufactured by combining chocolate or fruit syrups to milk to increase the appeal as an all-purpose drink. The extra sugar in flavored milks adds undesirable amounts of sugar to children's diets. Drinking only flavored milks also can overdevelop the taste preference for highly sweetened foods to the point it interferes with the enjoyment of natural flavors.

Yogurt is made from milk that has been treated with a special bacteria that sours the milk for a tasty custard-like texture. It is sold flavored or plain from the dairy case, but also can be frozen for an iced milk dessert treat.

USDA Standards for Milk

All milk transported from state to state for retail sale is Grade A pasteurized milk. Grade A is the highest USDA or State quality rating. Federal regulatory agencies work diligently to enforce the federal laws pertaining to milk and

Food Facts

Can't drink milk? Try yogurt. People who have difficulty digesting milk due to an inability to digest milk sugar usually can digest yogurt. Symptoms of an inability to digest milk include diarrhea and intestinal gas. The problem is caused by the lack of the enzymes (lactase) that digest milk sugar (lactose).

Since it is difficult to obtain enough calcium from nondairy sources, current research indicates that the solution is not to eliminate all dairy products. You can try various dairy products to find what agrees with you. If you have problems with one, try another. Yogurt is well-tolerated by most people who have difficulty digesting regular milk.

milk products. All milk and milk products must be **pasteurized** by a special heat treatment to kill dangerous bacteria that produce disease. Some of these harmful microorganisms cause tuberculosis, diphtheria, scarlet fever, and food poisoning. Federal sanitary regulations and inspections start in the barn and continue through all handling and processing of milk until it reaches the consumer.

A small minority of consumers feel that **raw milk** is more nutritious because it has not gone through the heat of the pasteurization. Drinking raw milk is taking a high risk of contacting one of the previously mentioned diseases. Recently in this country several people died from eating an imported cheese that had been made with raw milk. When the cause was traced, the product was immediately removed from all retail stores, but not before more innocent people were killed. Pasteurization is a silent protector that is so effective in disease prevention it is easy to forget how much it is needed.

Consumer Cream Choices

Cream is the rich part of the milk that contains the fat particles. A cream product must meet minimum federal standards before it can be labeled cream. There are several types of cream available in most supermarkets.

Half-and-half is the lightest cream with 10.5 to 18 percent milkfat dispersed evenly throughout the cream.

Light, or coffee, cream contains 18 to 30 percent cream milkfat.

Light whipping cream contains 30 to 36 percent milkfat.

Heavy whipping cream contains over 36 percent milkfat.

Sour cream contains at least 18 percent milkfat. The smooth, thick product that is now on the market is made by adding lactic acid to "sour" the light cream. Cream that "goes sour" over a period of time in the refrigerator is not considered safe to eat. It has been exposed to the contaminants and molds from the air and other foods around it in storage.

Butter

The butter you buy in the stores today is manufactured from cream with a very high milkfat content. **Butter** is made by churning or agitating cream until the protective coating on fat globules breaks down and the fat particles stick together separating away from the liquid. The remaining liquid is called buttermilk. Salt is usually added to improve the keeping quality and flavor. Unsalted butter is available and preferred by some people. The color of the butter varies according to what the cow has eaten, so the manufacturer adds a fat-soluble color for a consistent appearance of all batches of butter. Most consumers would not find bright orange butter or stark white butter very appealing. The vegetable dyes used are usually beta-carotene from carrots or annatto from the seeds of the tropical tree.

The standard butter stick is 4¾ inches long (12 cm), $1^{5}/_{16}$ inches wide (3.3 cm), and $1^{3}/_{16}$ high (3 cm). It weighs 1/4 lb. (125 g) and measures ½ cup (125 mL) melted.

Nutritive Notes about Butter

Butter is almost all fat with hardly a trace of protein and carbohydrates. However, it is the most easily digested fat. The fats are saturated, which puts them into the highest cholesterol category. The high energy value count is 100 calories per tablespoon (15 mL) as compared to 45 calories for a tablespoon (15 mL) of granulated sugar. Butter does have one redeeming nutritive feature. It is an excellent source of vitamin A.

The relatively high market price teamed with the high cholesterol and high energy value definitely put butter in the luxury class. Use butter with discriminating care for cooking and eating.

Selecting Butter

Butter is available in a wide variety of forms and formulas.

Butter (regular) has had salt added for preservation and flavor. It is packaged in four sticks to the pound (500 g) or solid blocks.

Sweet (unsalted) butter has not had the salt added. It also is packaged in sticks or block forms.

Whipped butter has had air beaten in for an increased volume and easier spreading. It is packaged in sticks and tubs. It can be salted, but is usually unsalted.

Blended butter is a mixture of margarine and butter to contribute the generally preferred flavor of butter to the lower cost of margarine. Read the labels carefully. Blends vary widely from one brand to another. You can blend butter and margarine yourself to suit your own taste and budget.

Margarine is not a dairy product, but it does contain some milk solids. Margarine is used as a substitute for butter on the table, in recipes, and in panfrying. You may have noticed that the two products are so interchangeable, peo-

Cooking Hints

You can make your own tangy, low-calorie sour cream at home in several ways. See the following recipe.

Sour Cream

Method 1

Traditional	Ingredients	Metric
1 tbsp.	Lime or lemon juice	15 mL
1/3 cup	Buttermilk	75 mL
1 cup	Smooth cottage cheese	250 mL

Directions

Mix the lemon juice, buttermilk, and cottage cheese by hand or in blender.

Method 2

Traditional	Ingredients	Metric
1 cup	Evaporated milk, at room temperature	250 mL
1 tbsp.	Vinegar	15 mL

Directions

1. Mix the evaporated milk and vinegar.
2. Let stand until it thickens.

You can prepare you own fresh vegetable dips from homemade or commercial sour cream by adding dried vegetables, drained canned clams or shrimp, fresh or dried herbs, or packaged dry soup mixes. A tablespoon (15 mL) of mayonnaise or salad dressing also adds a little zip and smoothness to the taste.

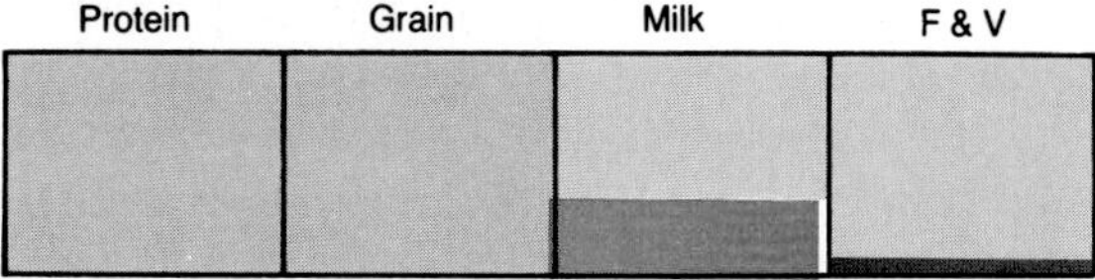

ple still refer to "buttering their bread," even when they know it is margarine. Because of this fact, this section will describe margarine's uses and manufacture.

The minimum fat content for margarine is the same as butter—about 80 percent except for special diet products that are diluted with water. Contrary to butter, many types of fats and oils are used to make margarine. The oils and fats used include corn, soybean, cottonseed, coconut, safflower, oleo, and lard. (Ironically, oleo, the liquid portion of beef fat which gave the name to the original product—oleomargarine—is seldom used now.)

Not all margarine is low in cholesterol. The vegetable oils basically are low in cholesterol, but some of them are also high in saturated fat which is considered unadvisable by the American Heart Association. The vegetable oils made into margarine that are both low in cholesterol and are classified as polyunsaturated are safflower, corn, cottonseed, soybean, and sunflower. Any animal fat such as lard is not advisable for anyone on a low-cholesterol diet. It is important for you to read the labels to determine if the contents match your dietary needs.

Cheese

Say "Cheese!" and everyone smiles. The numerous flavors and textures of cheese offer pleasant eating discoveries for everyone. **Cheese** is a concentrated form of the solid substance in milk. In its simplest form, cheese is made by subjecting milk to various treatments such as heat, motion, enzymes, and bacteria to separate the solid **curd.** Curd is much like curdling milk when you add lemon juice to it or when milk sours naturally. The remaining liquid called **whey** is drained, leaving the solid curd. The handling and processing of the soft curd from that point determines what type of cheese is made. The type of cheese produced also depends upon whether the milk came from cows, goats, or sheep. Imported cheeses from around the world are made from other animals such as reindeer, camel, and buffalo milk.

Basically, all cheese is made one of two ways:

1. **Unripened cheese** is not aged, but sold immediately after being made. It has a higher water content and softer texture. Unripened cheeses are cottage cheese, ricotta cheese, cream cheese, and yo cheese (a soft cream cheese made from yogurt). Unripened cheese with a high moisture content can be called fresh cheese since it is not dried or cured for any period of time. It is made of pasteurized milk and spoils quickly. Even in the refrigerator, it will spoil and sometimes mold within a week.
2. **Ripened cheese** is aged to develop specialized flavors and textures such as cheddar, gouda, colby, swiss, and parmesan. Aged cheese is sometimes called natural cheese.

Because the word "natural" is used in so many different ways to describe various conditions, foods, and nutrients (and, yes, even fertilizers), the terms used for ripened and unripened cheese in this book will be "aged" and "unaged" cheeses. These are also terms that are likely to be used on cheese packaging, so they should be the most helpful.

Processed cheese is a blend of highly flavored, textured aged cheeses and milk or whey to make the cheese easier to spread. These cheeses are sold in jars, slices, and crocks. Another type of processed cheese is called **processed cheese** food. The difference is that in the processed cheese food up to 50 percent of other ingredients such as water, milk, wine, fruits, and nuts can be added. The processed types of cheese are not actually a separate kind of cheese, but combinations or dilutions of already made cheeses.

For a detailed look at cheeses, their flavors, and their uses, see the Appendix.

USDA Cheese Inspection

Most of the USDA inspection stamps and grades for cheese are on the large shipping cartons the store receives. Consequently, the stamps are not in view for the consumer. The important inspections must take place at the production level to protect the consumer.

Eating a cottage cheese salad may not seem like eating a cheese dish, but the creamy curds represent one of the most popular unripened soft cheeses. Other soft cheeses include rich Brie and Camembert that are often eaten with fruit for a dessert.

Unaged Cheese

Unaged cheeses such as cottage cheese and ricotta cheese do not even seem like cheese to many people. These fresh products spoil quickly and must be refrigerated and treated much like the pasteurized milk from which they are made. Unaged cheeses include:

Cottage cheese is the collection of white curds that are not aged or cured. Cottage cheese can be sold dry, with a heavy 4 percent cream, or with a light 2 percent cream added.

Cream cheese is a high-milkfat soft cheese made from cream and milk.

Neufchatel is made like cream cheese, but from milk with a lower milkfat content.

Farmer's cheese is made from skim or part skim milk. It is pressed into a dry, firm cheese that slices. It is a satisfying cheese substitute for persons wanting to cut down on cholesterol in their diet.

Yo cheese is a cream cheese made from yogurt. Its tangy flavor gives it distinctive flavor. This cheese can be made simply at home from yogurt. It is low calorie and low cholesterol, but quite flavorful.

Hard and semi-hard cheeses such as cheddar, gouda, and mozzarella contrast with the soft, creamy Brie which is spread on a cracker or slice of fruit to eat.

Aged Cheese

Aged cheeses (ripened cheeses) are made by adding bacteria, molds, yeasts, or enzymes to milk and then aging it. The aging process can range from two weeks to two years for hard-grating cheeses such as romano and parmesan. The aging also determines the flavor of the cheese. Mild cheeses are aged for a short time, while strong-flavored cheeses age longer.

Frozen Milk Products

"I scream, you scream, we all scream for ice cream!" Nobody really knows when or where it was invented, but Americans claim ice cream as an American tradition. Folklore tells us that Dolly Madison first created an ice cream dish to serve at the White House. History indicates that snow and cream flavored with honey was a special treat as early as the Roman empire. Re-

Baked Brie

The smooth, mild flavor and texture of brie cheese is mouth-watering just before melting temperature. The creamy richness challenges the crisp tangy fruit slices for a pleasurable contrast of tastes and textures. This dessert is nutritious enough for a meal! No empty calories here. Try this surprise for a party table or after-dinner dessert.

Yield: Serves 8

Equipment: Oven-proof plate just large enough to hold the round of brie surrounded by slices of fruit and a knife for cutting and serving. Optional but inexpensive and effective would be a Swedish apple cutter and corer for cutting uniform slices of pears or apples.

Traditional	Ingredients	Metric
1 small round	Brie cheese*	1 small round
½ cup	Slivered almonds	125 mL
	Fresh apples, pears, or a mixture of both	
	Lemon juice to coat the fruit slices	

Directions

* You may have to make arrangements with the cheese department not to precut the wheel into wrapped triangles, but to leave one whole. Brie comes in 7- to 18-inch-diameter (17.5 to 45 cm) rounds. This recipe calls for the smallest one.

1. Preheat the oven to 350°F (175°C).
2. Arrange the almond slices over the top of the cheese.
3. Place the cheese in the center of the plate.
4. Bake it in the oven until the almonds are toasted and the sides of the Brie begin to soften and bulge. You also can test for softness with your finger.
5. While the cheese is heating, core and slice the fruit. Leave the skin on the fruit. Sprinkle with lemon juice to prevent discoloring.
6. Remove cheese and surround the round with the fruit slices.
7. Serve. Cut and spread the soft cheese on the fruit slices similar to how you would use a cracker. Enjoy.

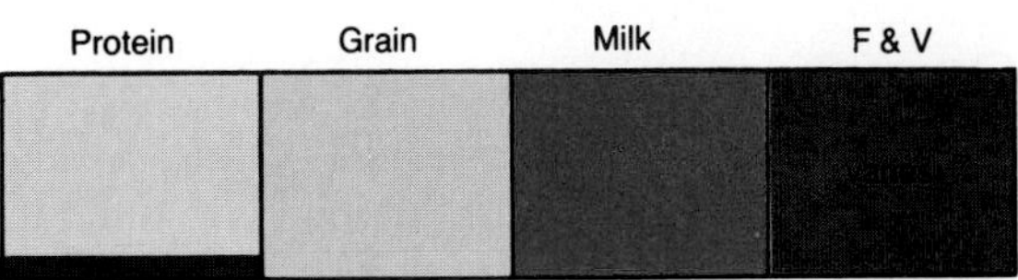

The unique flavor of yogurt makes a tangy frozen dessert that is high in calcium and usually lower in fat than other frozen creams. The low-sugar variety is a low-calorie treat for dieters.

gardless of who was first, Americans enjoy their ice cream now! Today, they consume more than 14.5 gallons (48 L) per person each year!

Frozen dairy products have expanded from the ice cream choice of vanilla or chocolate and, on lucky days, strawberry. Frozen desserts include low-fat ice milks, rich ice cream, frozen custard, frozen yogurt, fruit sherbets, and the nondairy French sorbet.

The federal and state agencies have established categories for standardizing frozen dairy products for easy identification by the consumer. There is no grading system for frozen dairy products.

Commercial Frozen Desserts

Ice cream is made from milk, sugar, flavorings, cream with at least 10 percent milkfat, and usually stabilizers. Some new brands of ice cream claim that no stabilizers, preservatives, or air is incorporated into their old-fashioned products.

Ice milk is frozen from milk, sugar, flavorings, and stabilizers. The federal standard states that it must contain between 2 and 7 percent milkfat. The lower milkfat necessitates a higher proportion of sugar for a smooth product. The higher sugar content makes the calories about equal to the higher milkfat ice cream, but the cost is usually lower.

Frozen custard is an ice cream to which egg yolks have been added for richness.

Frozen yogurt has earned a solid popularity in this health-conscious decade because of its lower fat content and fewer calories. The sweetened and flavored yogurt is frozen and served like ice cream in dishes or cones.

Fruit sherbet contains a small amount of milk, sugar, fruit or juice, stabilizers and sometimes egg white. It is required to contain 1 to 2 percent milkfat.

Ices contain no milk solids, but do have fruit or fruit juice, sugar, and sometimes a stabilizer.

Convenience at the Dairy Counter

Part of the convenience of the dairy foods section of supermarkets and specialty stores is the great variety of products that are ready for the shopper. You can "dine-out" at the dairy section. Individual-size yogurts, milks, flavored milk drinks, and even dips and cheese food are ready for instant eating.

Other forms are ready to use in the kitchen for meal preparation or serving. Whipping cream is available in aerosol cans or blended with stable vegetable nondairy toppings in tubs. Cheese is sliced and packaged for individual servings or wrapped in bulk. Hard cheeses are grated. Some departments make flavored cheeseballs for parties.

Storage of Dairy Products

A breakthrough for the consumer in recent years is having the date after which a product should not be bought visibly printed on the package. Prior to that time, aged cartons could get mixed on the shelves and disturbing surprises could greet the consumer when a carton of milk was indeed spoiled. Thankfully that problem can be avoided now.

Storing Milk and Cream

Bacteria love to feed and grow in room-temperature milk products. Refrigerate milk and cream immediately in their store containers, which are designed for sterile storage. Plan to use the milk and cream products within five days. In warm weather, three days is a safer storage time.

Resist the temptation to save preparation time by leaving the milk or cream carton on the counter after you have measured the needed amount. Return the carton to the refrigerator immediately.

Light destroys the B vitamin riboflavin, so keep the milk carton away from light. If your refrigerator light does not seem to be going off when the door closes, loosen the bulb until the switch can be fixed.

Place milk products away from aromatic foods because the milk products will pick up odors. Keep cartons and packages closed.

Milk can be frozen, but the consistency will change noticeably. Yogurt needs to be stored in the refrigerator. If you carry yogurt with you for snacks or lunch, it should be packed in an insulated container or in a plastic bag with some ice.

Storing Nonfat Dry Milk

Keep nonfat dry milk in an airtight container in a cool, dry area. The dry milk can be kept for months. Once it is made to a liquid, treat it like fresh milk.

Storing Butter

Fresh butter is like a sponge for odd flavors or other foods in the refrigerator. Always keep it wrapped tightly and in a separate compartment whenever possible. Plan to use butter within a week, or store it in the freezer for several months.

Storing Cheese

Both aged and unaged cheese should be tightly covered and refrigerated. The unaged cheeses do not keep as long and should be used within five days. The aged cheeses keep longer than the unaged ones, but vary from the harder cheeses to the softer ones. In general, the harder the cheese, the longer it will store. Soft aged cheeses such as Camembert or Brie continue to ripen and become quite strong.

If surface mold develops on hard aged cheeses such as cheddar or romano, cut it off and use the unaffected cheese. Pieces of dried cheeses that are too hard to eat alone can be grated and used in cooking.

Freezing Cheese

Most any cheese may be saved from spoiling by freezing it. You may not, however, be able to use it in the same serving ways as before it was frozen. Frozen cheese tends to crumble and is hard if not impossible to slice. It is still perfectly acceptable for cooking purposes and eating plain in forms other than slices.

To freeze cheese, wrap it tightly in vaporproof freezer paper. Plan to store cheeses no longer than eight weeks in the freezer. Thaw frozen cheese in the microwave oven on the lowest power setting, or in the refrigerator.

Storing Frozen Dairy Creams

Remind yourself to buy ice cream at the very last minute in the store. Take a cooler if possible to carry ice cream home. In hot weather, this saves product quality, safety, and a drippy mess. Many supermarkets have freezer bags you can use to carry home ice cream.

Check ice cream cartons carefully for signs of former leaks or refreezing in the store and at home. Buy only fresh, firm products.

When serving ice cream, return the carton to the freezer immediately. Melted ice cream that is refrozen—and sometimes more than once—is responsible for many undiagnosed stomachaches or worse. The frozen ice cream in the middle of the carton does not protect the melted portions on the top or around the edges.

It is also an added protection to wrap the ice cream carton with foil or a plastic bag. The added vaporproof wrap keeps moisture in and off-flavors out of the frozen dessert.

You can take advantage of the way freezing makes cheese crumbly upon thawing by using the crumbled cheese for topping salads, casseroles, sandwiches, and soups.

Pick fresh fruit for incredible flavor, top it with nondairy whipped topping, and you will have created a low-calorie and low-cholesterol dessert that is sweetly elegant.

"Mooooove" over High-Cholesterol Milkfat

"Pass the butter please." If you heard that request, you probably would pass the yellow stick or pat of "butter" without questioning whether it was butter from a cow or margarine from a vegetable oil. **Nondairy substitutes** are used so widely, people have the tendency to treat them the same as "the real thing." Do you think the look-alike and taste-alike qualities of nondairy products are meant to deceive or to delight the consumer?

Substituting nondairy products for real milk products usually saves you money, and they are convenient to use. Some nondairy forms do not require refrigeration before or after opening. The less expensive nondairy products often are substituted for dairy butter and cream. Because of the savings and convenience, use of nondairy creams for coffee drinkers has become the rule rather than the exception in most eating places and homes. However, by substituting nondairy products, you lose some nutritional benefits. For instance, nondairy products do not contain any calcium.

There are several reasons though, to use nondairy substitutes. Not everyone can drink milk. Some people are allergic to milk. Others cannot drink milk because they cannot digest the milk sugar called lactose. Still other people are in the high-risk group for having a heart attack. People who have a weight problem, high blood cholesterol level, high blood pressure, or a family history of heart attacks are considered to be in the high-risk group. People identified in this group are advised to eat only foods very

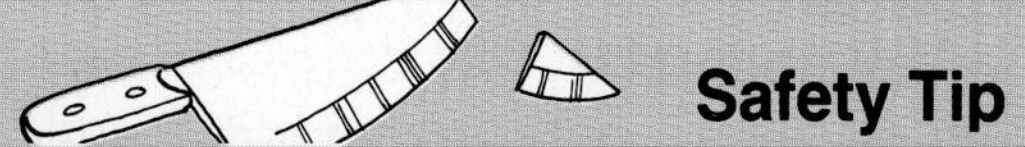

Safety Tip

If you are interested in meeting some of your nutritional needs with a dietary supplement like vitamin-mineral pills do so with the help of a doctor or dietitian (A *dietitian* is a certified specialist in nutrition.) Vitamin and mineral pills should be treated like medicine. An incorrect dosage can harm your health or even cause death.

Products made from coconut oil contain saturated fatty acids, which is unusual for a vegetable oil. The Dietary Guidelines advise avoiding eating too much saturated fat. Read the label of all products and be aware that not all vegetable oils are unsaturated fats.

low in cholesterol and unsaturated fatty acids. Cholesterol-rich foods such as whole milk, cheese, and whole-milk products are traditional favorites in American diets. It can be both unpleasant and difficult to give up familiar tastes and foods completely. Nondairy foods that taste and look like the familiar dairy favorites can be a welcome help to the person on a special diet. But these foods are not restricted to only those people. Such substitutes also can help provide variety, dollar savings, low-calorie choices, and low cholesterol options for everyone.

All of these special nondairy products match special needs. Read the labels to make certain that the product you choose also fits your needs nutritionally.

Whipped Toppings

You don't have to feel guilty about enjoying the rich flavor of whipped topping on your fresh fruit when it's nondairy topping. The vegetable oil product contains nonfat milk solids and sweeteners, but has less calories than whipped cream and little cholesterol. The topping comes already whipped, or in a powder form that you mix with water and whip yourself. There is also a blended product that contains some dairy whipping cream for flavor and smoothness. Read the labels carefully if you are trying to cut down on calories and cholesterol. The blends are higher in both.

Margarine

Margarine made history during World War II when it became the first substitute for the rich milkfat butter. In its first forms, margarine was often sold uncolored with a small packet of vegetable dye. The buyer had to mix the orange dye throughout the messy, oily margarine. At a time when soap was in scarce supply and rationed, the cleanup chore was no small task. The flavor was strong and unmistakable. The first oleomargarine was often called "oleo." Beef fat was the source of the oleo oil. Today this usually has been replaced with vegetable oil. The calories in regular margarine are the same as in butter, but the cholesterol count is much lower.

Diet spreads are margarine products that have been diluted and mixed with water to cut down on oil and calories. These "diet" products do not work for baking and frying because of the water in them.

Imitation Milk

Nondairy milk products must be labeled *imitation* somewhere on the label. The milk substitutes can be made from several different oils such as coconut oil and soybeans. The result is a pleasant-tasting product.

The nutritional content can vary greatly from real milk. Whatever your reason is for choosing the nondairy product, you will need to compensate for the calcium and other nutrients that are lacking in the substitutes by eating other foods that are high in calcium, and vitamins A, D, and B.

Cream Substitutes

Nondairy creams and creamer powders are made of vegetable oils, corn syrup, and sometimes milk solids. They are used as ingredients in instant drink powders such as cocoa and flavored milks. Powdered and liquid nondairy creams are called coffee lighteners by some coffee drinkers.

Nondairy Cheese

Cheese substitutes contain milk solids, but the high cholesterol milkfat is replaced by vegetable oil. These products are similar in look and taste to other processed cheese and cheese foods.

Nondairy Ice Cream

The same creamy, rich flavor of the nondairy toppings and coffee creamers can be captured in frozen desserts for low-cholesterol treats. Read the label to make certain that the vegetable fat used is a low cholesterol and unsaturated oil. Polyunsaturated oils include corn oil, cottonseed oil, safflower oil, sesame oil, soybean oil, and sunflower oil.

Add acid ingredients, like tomatoes, slowly to heated milk to avoid the curdling effect. Have you ever eaten tomato soup that was slightly curdled? The flavor is good, but the appearance is less appetizing.

Preparing Dairy Foods

Milk improves the nutritional and eating qualities of any recipe in which it is an ingredient. Cooking with milk and milk products successfully depends upon remembering that milk contains animal protein. Protein is toughened by high heat, so low temperatures and a brief cooking time are vital.

Principles of Cooking with Milk

Because of the properties of the milk protein, there are four conditions you will want to prevent in your milk dishes.

1. Formation of a scum on top of the milk as it is heated.
2. A rapid boil that spills over the pan.
3. Scorching the product.
4. Curdling or separating.

A skin or **scum** of the milk solids (protein) and fat will form on the surface of milk as it is heated. This rubbery, skinlike covering can be lifted off, but it will just form again and you will have wasted valuable nutrients. The scum will seal the surface and cause steam to buildup underneath until it pushes up and causes the milk to boil over. You can prevent that chain of events by covering the pan when you first heat the milk or stirring the milk as it heats. If a layer of scum does form, beat it back into the liquid and save the nutrients—and the mess of fishing it out.

As the milk heats in the utensil, you will notice that a coating of particles sticks to the hot pan sides and bottom. Because there is milk sugar in those milk solids, any place that overheats will caramelize. Almost immediately the caramelized particles overbrown and scorch, causing the unmistakable burned flavor which penetrates all of the liquid.

Too high a temperature also will cause the milk to separate into liquid and solid lumps. This is a process called **curdling.** Acids such as lemon or tomato juice have the same effect on the milk. (You might remember that adding acid to milk helps to separate out the whey in buttermilk and cheesemaking.) You can prevent milk products from curdling during their preparation. If you think about "sneaking up on the milk" with the acid, you will automatically remember to add ingredients together in this order.

Add the acid ingredient (lemon juice, tomatoes, etc.) very slowly to the larger amount of milk. Stir steadily to distribute the acid ingredient evenly through the milk. The same method works when combining milk with a hot ingredient. Add the hot part slowly and steadily, raising the temperature of the milk evenly throughout. Then you avoid developing a hot section all at once which will curdle. Beating or whipping with a wire whisk also helps to mash the curds back into a smooth mixture.

Milk that has had a thickener such as flour or cornstarch added to it is less likely to curdle. If you add any thickener to the milk before the acid ingredient is added, there will be less chance of curdling. You also can add the thickener to the acid before it goes into the milk.

Use fresh milk for cooking. Milk that has been stored for quite a while becomes less sweet and more acidic. The milk sugar (lactose) begins changing into lactic acid during storage or if the milk has not been kept chilled. Milk with a high acid content will curdle sooner when an acid ingredient is added or when it is heated.

Use low temperatures and cook milk slowly. Stay below 140°F (60°C). If it is not easy to control this exact heat setting on the range burners, use a double boiler. Remember, when you place the hot water in the bottom pan for steaming the top pan, the water should not touch the top pan.

Scalding Milk

You may have noticed directions that called for scalded milk in a recipe. (**Scalded milk** is heated to the point just below boiling.) Scalding milk can shorten the cooking time of some food dishes. Scald milk by heating it to the point where frothy bubbles begin to form around the edge of the pan. This occurs just below boiling, around 180°F (82°C). Watch carefully and immediately remove the milk from the heat when the bubbles appear. If you have a microwave with a thermometer, you can use it to scald the milk.

Cooking Other Milk Products

If you cook with cream, yogurt, cottage cheese, or other milk products, use the same low heat, slow cooking guidelines as for milk.

Whipping Cream

Whipping cream which contains 30 to 40 percent milkfat will expand to double its size when air is incorporated with a rotary beater of wire whisk. The cream must be chilled to beat to a large volume. This is because fat must be cold enough to stay solid and not be oily for the bubbles of air to pile up. If the cream is too warm (above 45°F) (7°C), it will churn to butter quickly.

Do not overbeat any whipping cream. Stop beating as soon as stiff peaks form or it will begin to separate into butter and liquid. A small amount of powdered sugar is excellent to use for flavoring. Also the cornstarch in powdered sugar helps to stabilize the whipped cream.

Whipped cream does not stay for more than an hour before it begins to breakdown. To avoid the hectic and noisy rush of whipping cream just before you need it, prepare it early and freeze it in the shapes you will be needing on waxed paper. When you need the whipped cream to "top" something, just peel off the frozen peak and place it on the food. It will thaw in minutes.

Frozen desserts offer a refreshing variety of ices, sorbets, sherbets, and rich ice cream in a contrasting display of flavors. Which of these tempting treats would you predict to have the lowest amount of cholesterol and the most vitamins? Which ones would contain calcium? Why?

Making Ice Creams and Dairy Desserts

Homemade ice cream made with the rich basic ingredients of your choice can surpass the most expensive **gourmet** (elegant) brand. You can make the most elegant of ice creams and ices with no more equipment than a rotary beater, a shallow metal pan, and the freezer section of a refrigerator! If you want to make larger quantities of ice creams and ices, there are several types of ice cream freezers available.

For a fine, smooth texture in frozen ices and ice creams, the ice crystals need to be very tiny. This is accomplished in two ways:

1. Use ingredients that interfere with the formation of large ice crystals. This would include high-fat creams.

2. Beat the mixture continually or periodically to break down the crystals and to mix in air for lightness.

Frozen ice creams and ices you can create at home include:

Ices

Granitas—a weak-flavored syrup that is frozen and then broken into a coarse icy slush to eat and drink. Coffee, teas, and fruits are favorite flavors for this refresher.

Water ice—a concentrated sugar syrup frozen with a fruit puree and later mixed with beaten egg white.

Sorbet—a fruit puree with sugar syrup that is frozen and then mixed with several beaten egg whites. It is stirred to the finest ice crystals. Frozen desserts that use fresh fruit purees supply fruit flavor in a form that saves much of the vitamin C usually destroyed by a dessert that requires cooking.

Sherbet—a flavored ice like a sorbet, but with some milk or cream added for extra smoothness. It is sometimes referred to as a cream ice. Gelatin may be added for smoothness.

Ice Cream

Ice milk—frozen low-fat milk and flavorings.

Rich ice cream—the most involved to make, and the most luxurious to taste. The base mix is a custard made with cream and eggs to which fruits, nuts, or purees can be added.

Desserts

Mousse—a whipped egg white or cream dessert which can be served chilled or frozen.

Bombe—a molded combination of at least two flavors of ice cream and sherbet.

Ice cream cakes—layered creations of cake and ice creams with sauces and whipped cream frosting.

Baked Alaska—a "show-off" dessert of ice cream surrounded by egg merinque and cake (or pastry) and baked in a hot oven. The merinque and cake act as insulators to prevent the ice cream from melting.

Serving Cheese

Natural or ripened cheese releases its full flavor when it is allowed to come to room temperature before serving. The wide spectrum of cheese color and shapes makes them a natural for appetizing displays with little preparation other than cutting and arranging. Fresh or unripened cheese, such as cottage cheese, should be served chilled or cooked in a recipe.

Cheeses are exciting to serve for snacks or main dishes. Their bland and distinctive flavors combine well with breads, pastas, fruits, vegetables, and just about any food you can recall. You can make beautiful edible displays by hollowing out large cheeses and using them for containers for fresh vegetables, fruits, or other cheeses. Likewise other foods such as cucumbers, tomatoes, or apples can be cored and used to hold cheese or cheese dips. Cheese lends itself to cutting into fancy shapes with cookie cutters or grating onto a hot or cold food for a colorful and flavorful topping.

Some cheeses make the main dish. Cheese fondues, baked Brie for dessert, or pasta and cheese dishes could start a very long list of possibilities.

Cooking Cheese

The principles of cooking protein are very important in cooking high-protein cheese. All you need to do is to melt cheese to bring out the flavor or to combine it with other foods. Some cheeses combine with foods better than others. Cheddar mixes well, while farmers' cheese will maintain its own characteristic texture even when melted with another food. Processed cheeses and cheese foods melt quickly and combine well with other foods. Processed forms of cheese also are less expensive to combine with foods when the cheese's unique texture is not needed.

Some varieties of cheeses are more suitable than others for cooking and melting. Cheddar, mozzarella, and processed cheeses melt nicely into appetizing toppings and fillings.

Microwaving Dairy Products

Milk and milk products are convenient to cook and heat in the microwave, but they need to be watched constantly for signs of boiling over and uneven heating.

Cheese has the tendency to be tough almost as soon as it is melted in the microwave. Cooking it on the low power setting for short periods of time and allowing the hot cheese to set and continue cooking from its own heat helps to prevent tough and greasy qualities.

For recipe ideas and further help with cooking dairy foods in the microwave oven, check Chapter 8.

Vocabulary Review

Natural food
Homogenized milk
Pasteurized
Raw milk
Cream
Curd
Whey
Unaged cheese
Aged cheese
Nondairy substitutes
Dietician
Diet spreads
Scum
Curdling
Gourmet
Scalded Milk

Questions for Review

1. What nutrients are added to fortified skim milk and 2 percent milk? Why are these particular nutrients added to some milk?
2. What is the difference between whole, 2 percent, and skim milk?
3. Describe the following creams: half and half, light, light whipping, heavy whipping, and sour.
4. How is butter produced?
5. What are aged and unaged cheeses? Give examples of each.
6. What are the general guidelines for storing dairy products?
7. Milk contains protein. What principle do you need to remember when cooking milk products?
8. Why must whipped cream be chilled for it to beat to a large volume?
9. How do you insure that ice crystals in frozen ice creams and ices are kept small for a smooth creamy texture?
10. How is buttermilk made?

Things to Do

1. Beat a high fat content cream that is at room temperature until butter forms. Why does butter form when rich cream is beaten? Look up pictures or borrow an antique butter churn and demonstrate how yesteryear's homemaker made her family's butter each day.
2. Visit a grocery store and compare the nutritional labels of margarines and butter. How do they compare in energy value, vitamin A content, salt content, and saturated fat content? Are all the margarines made from unsaturated fats?
3. Organize a taste test panel of classmates or family members. Compare dairy items with their nondairy substitutes. Discuss the similarities and differences.
4. Calculate the calories of each low-calorie version of sour cream mentioned in this chapter. Compare the calories with the same amount of regular sour cream. How do the calories compare between the regular sour cream and the nondairy sour cream products?
5. Make your own buttermilk by adding 1 tablespoon (15 mL) lemon juice to enough skim milk to make 1 cup (250 mL). Let stand 5 minutes. Compare your product with the commercial one.

13
The Bread And Cereal Group

It All Begins With the Grain

When you see appetizing displays of bread, cereals, or pasta, do you think about "how good it is for you," or does an alarm go off in your head warning "calories"? This basic bread and cereal food group actually forms one of the four cornerstones for your balanced diet. Many people mistakenly consider this group of grain products to be extra calories that should be sacrificed for a healthy diet. Have you ever heard someone apologize when they reached for a slice of bread saying, "I really shouldn't, but it looks so good"? Chances are you've heard something similar to that, but have you ever said or overheard someone else say, "Good, this delicious looking piece of whole-wheat bread is perfect for the B vitamins and fiber my body needs today"? Such a statement probably is not a typical thing you or your friends might say, even though it represents the truth. It is sad but true that the last decade of preoccupation with super-slimness often has led to judging foods by calories alone without considering nutrients.

Discover the Nutrient Treasures in Grain

Calories are just a small portion of the nutrients in the bread-cereal food group. Whole grains are rich in carbohydrates, fiber (a form of carbohydrates), iron, and the B vitamins. You can help meet your body's need for these nutrients by eating four servings a day from the bread-cereal food group. That group includes whole grain and enriched or restored breads and cereals. This food group also contains incomplete proteins which form a complete protein when eaten with foods from the milk-cheese group or the meat-poultry-fish-beans group. Remember, a complete protein contains all the essential amino acids required for human growth and maintenance.

When grains are processed by finely grinding or milling, some nutrients are lost in the resulting refined product. The **bran** and **germ** of the grain kernel are the bran germ richest in iron, B vitamins, and fiber. These parts are strained out of the finely ground white flour. Only the **endosperm** which has starch and proteins is used. An endosperm **whole-grain** flour or cereal is not strained, so it retains the nutritious bran and germ. **Processed grains** are enriched, which means the nutrients are added back to the grain. Processed grains also may be fortified with nutrients not naturally found in the grain.

The more nutritious whole-grain flour does not produce as light a fluffy baked product as the refined white flour does. Until recently, the smaller and heavier loaves of whole-wheat bread were less popular than the enriched white bread. The increase in health-conscious consumers has brought about a new appreciation for whole-grain products and the taste of heartier loaves of whole-grain breads. The vitamin and mineral content of whole-grain bread is similar to that of enriched bread, but the remaining bran layers in the whole-grain product leaves a desirable high fiber content. In fact, whole-grain flours, pastas, and breads have become the unofficial trademark of the so-called health food stores and followers.

Why Enrich?

In the 1930s, a nationwide survey exposed alarming nutritional deficiencies among the people in the U.S. This prompted the American Medical Association, the National Research Council, National Academy of Sciences, several departments of the government, and involved food industries to recommend the addition of certain nutrients in specified amounts to foods. As a result, the United States Food and Drug Administration (FDA) set standards for the amounts and specific nutrients that could be used to nutritionally improve common foods manufactured from refined white flour. These standards are based on the Recommended Dietary Food Allowances (RDAs) and are reviewed when any revisions of the RDAs are made. Enriched, restored, and fortified were the terms selected to identify foods that had been nutritionally improved with specified added nutrients.

Enriched cereals and flours have had nutrients replaced according to the recommended amount needed, not just the amount that would be lost in processing. Three B-vitamins—thiamin, niacin, and riboflavin—plus the mineral iron are added to enriched grain products such as breads, rolls, flour, rice, cornmeal, and grits. (Calcium is optional.) These are the nutrients that are naturally present in grains before processing. At least 90 percent of all standard commercial breads are estimated to be enriched.

Restored cereals and flours have had the nutrients that were lost during processing replaced in the same amounts. Restoration is seldom used. The current trend is to add extra nutrients or to use the natural whole-grain product.

Fortified cereals and flours have had one or more nutrients added than naturally existed in the grain before processing.

Consumer Safeguards

Foods with added ingredients must comply with the FDA's labeling regulations by using the preceding terms. The guidelines and rulings of the FDA are designed to prevent random fortification of foods.

Federal regulations require that the food company must add at least 10 percent of the U.S.RDA before the label can list it as a significant nutrient content. When 100 percent of the U.S.RDA is added, the product must be labeled a dietary supplement. Any levels of dietary supplementation that are 150 percent or more of the U.S.RDA designates the product as a **drug** and it must be labeled as such.

Types of Grains

The growing of grains dates back to the earliest agricultural production. Even farmers of ancient times found grains easy to grow, harvest, and store. Grains include wheat, oats, barley, rye, corn, and rice. All grain kernels are basically similar in structure containing a husk, bran layer, endosperm, and germ. Each kernel is a seed capable of reproducing into a new plant.

Uses of Grain

The amazing variety of grain food products ranges from plain breads, cereal, and rice to elaborate pastas, noodles, pastry, and cakes. Because the relatively high fat and high sugar content in pastry and cakes add empty calories and can contribute to other health problems (dental decay and high blood cholesterol), limit your consumption of these foods. Do not rely on them for one of the four recommended servings from the grain products group.

Grain Products

Traveling down the grain-products aisle at the supermarket or exploring the bins of whole grains and grain products at a specialty "health-food store" can be like a tour of world-wide cuisines. Every agricultural area in the world has its favored grain product.

Capellini alla Primavera (Angel's-Hair Pasta with Vegetables)

Yield: 4 portions

Traditional	Ingredients	Metric
2 cloves	Garlic, pressed	2 cloves
2	Carrots, sliced	2
3 large	Tomatoes, chopped	3 large
8 thin	Asparagus spears or celery, sliced diagonally	8 thin
12	Mushrooms, sliced	12
1 small	Zucchini, sliced	1 small
8 Tbsp.	Butter	120 mL
½ cup	Olive oil	125 mL
1 Tbsp.	Green onion, minced	15 mL
2 cups	Cauliflowerets	500 mL
1 tsp.	Dried basil, crumbled	5 mL
⅛ tsp.	Dried oregano, crumbled	0.5 mL
	Salt and black pepper	
1 Tbsp.	Lemon juice	15 mL
1 lb.	Capellini pasta	500 g
1 cup	Parmesan cheese, grated	250 mL

Directions

1. Heat butter and oil in a skillet.
2. Sauté green onion and garlic for 1 minute.
3. Add carrots and cauliflowerets. Sauté for 1 minute.
4. Add tomatoes, asparagus or celery pieces, mushrooms, and zucchini. Stir constantly.
5. Sprinkle in the herbs. Add salt and pepper to taste. Sauté until vegetables are crisp-tender, 3 to 4 minutes.
6. While preparing the vegetables, bring 6 quarts (6 L)water to a boil.
7. Add lemon juice and the capellini pasta to the boiling water. Cook until pasta is firm but tender. This takes about 3 minutes. Do not overcook this delicate pasta.
8. Drain pasta. Transfer to warm dinner plates. Spoon vegetables over pasta and serve at once with grated cheese.

Microwave Directions

1. In a 3½ qt. (3½ L) microwave-safe casserole, microwave butter and oil on high for 1½ minutes or until butter is melted.
2. Add green onion and garlic and microwave on high for 1 minute.
3. Add carrots and cauliflowerets and microwave on high for 30 seconds.
4. Add tomatoes, asparagus or celery pieces, mushrooms, and sliced zucchini. Mix well.
5. Sprinkle in the herbs and add salt and pepper to taste.
6. Microwave on high for 4 to 5 minutes or until vegetables are crisp-tender, stirring frequently.
7. Follow Steps 6-8.

Protein	Grain	Milk	F & V
	3x		4¾x

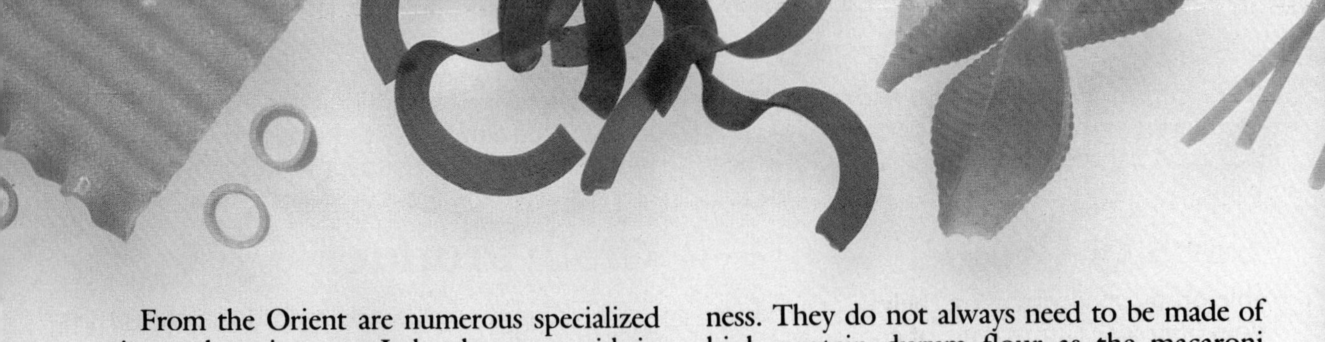

From the Orient are numerous specialized rices and exotic pastas. Italy takes great pride in its durum wheat pastas that are manufactured in a challenging array of shapes and sizes. German pasta features noodles and dumplings, known as "suppeneinlage" or "things to put in soups!" The United States produces excellent pastas and an array of grains that includes rice and wild rice. Russia is famed for its hearty dark rye flours and breads. Do any of those products remind you of food served in your own home? You may not call chicken noodles "suppeneinlage," or buy imported spaghetti from Italy, but food habits and products around the world still supply inspiration for what you buy, eat, and how you prepare it.

Pasta

Pasta is the name of the broad category of ground grain food products that includes all macaroni and noodle products. **Macaroni**-type products are made of super hard durum wheat and water. (Spaghetti, which means "little strings," is a form of macaroni.) The high protein content of the durum wheat flour makes it strong enough to hold its shape, texture, and flavor when cooked. After mixing, the dough is forced through shaped nozzles and dried. Perhaps you played with Play Dough and its Fun Factory making hollow strips and cutting them to desired shapes and sizes. That process is similar to making pasta products.

Noodles are made of flour and water, but also have eggs added for richness and tenderness. They do not always need to be made of high protein durum flour as the macaroni products do.

Types of Pasta

Dried pasta and **fresh pasta** are the two basic types of pasta. Dried pasta keeps for months on the shelf in an airtight container.

Fresh pasta can be made of hard or soft wheat and water, but usually contains eggs. Home preparation of fresh noodles has long been a traditional favorite for many Americans. Making your own hard-wheat pasta is a new trend. The unique appeal of freshly made pasta and the recent surge of interest in food preparation with whole- grain products has created a market for fresh pasta in specialty shops and restaurants.

Vegetable-flavored pastas are now available in a rainbow of colors from many grain-vegetable combinations. Possibly due to the "vegie revolution," you can make or buy pastas with beets, spinach, artichokes, and other flavors in fresh and dried forms.

Whole-grain pasta is made from almost any grain, but falls apart easily during cooking if some of the semolina flour from durum wheat is not included. Whole-wheat, rye, buckwheat, and rice grains are some of the flours used in this new type of pasta that is growing in popularity.

You can purchase dried pasta in many shapes. One cookbook author claims that you could eat pasta every day for a year and not repeat a shape! Not that many shapes are avail-

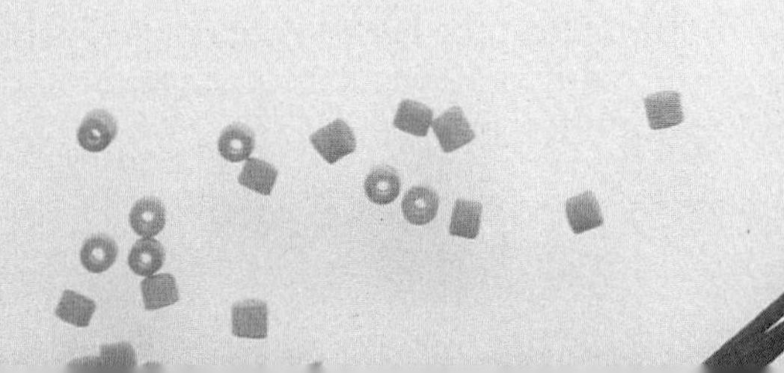

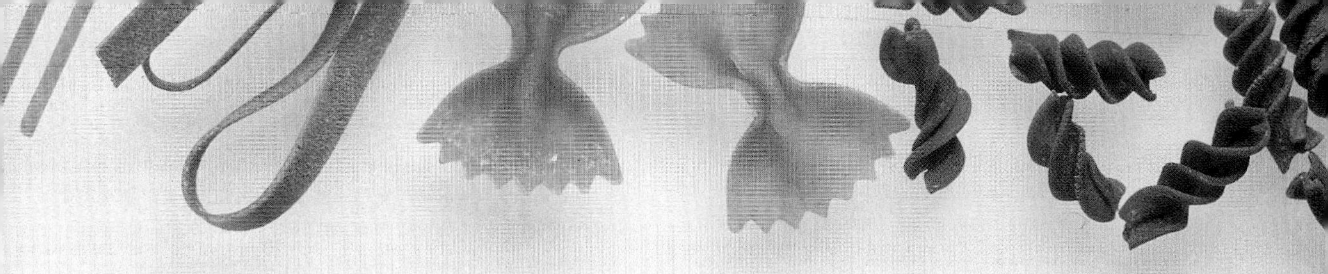

able on most supermarket shelves, but variety does offer an exciting array of choices.

Basically, all the shapes fall under four categories for both macaroni and noodle pastas. Can you match up these four basic shapes with the pictured varieties of pasta?

- Solid, long pasta.
- Flat pasta.
- Decorative pasta.
- Hollow pasta.

The various shapes expand the amazing numbers of ways you can serve pasta. Pasta can be served as side dishes, mixed in with other ingredients, topping food, under food, around food, or as a hearty main dish.

Rice

Rice is one of the world's oldest crops and remains the basic food for millions of people. It was brought to England from Asia during the Crusades centuries ago and has been highly prized worldwide since that time. Rice is not just rice. There are many different types. Many Asians can identify the type of rice, its age, and perhaps the area where it was grown just by sniffing the grains. In the United States, most of the rice used and called for in recipes is the polished, American, long-grain variety. When cooking recipes from other origins, it is worthwhile to expand your experience and try other special rices for their unique flavor, texture, and aroma. Specialty stores and gourmet sections of many supermarkets now offer a wide array of imported rice.

So They Say

The Chinese and Italians both claim to be the originators of pasta. As a point of national pride, Italians say they invented pasta. Evidence points to the Chinese as having had pasta since 1100 B.C. The first undisputed Western reference to noodles is in Jerusalem 400 A.D.

Popular folklore documents that Marco Polo returned from China in 1295 with the first dried pasta. However, pasta was recorded in the estate inventory of an Italian soldier before that date.

By 1400, shopkeepers were already producing commercial dried pasta to sell. It was kneaded by foot. It then was forced through shaping nozzles with pressure powered by two men or a horse.

Young English aristocrats toured Italy in the eighteenth century and returned home showing off their new foreign appetites and fashions. "In the mid-eighteenth century, macaroni referred to an overblown hair style as well as to the dandy wearing it, which may be why Yankee Doodle stuck a feather in his cap and called the effect macaroni." *(Corby Kummer, Atlantic Monthly (Boston, MA) July 1986)*

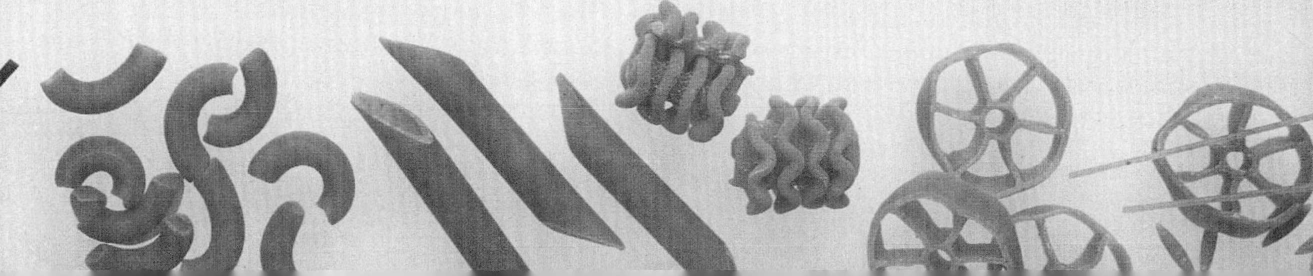

Processing Rice

The long-grain white rice sold most often in this country has had the bran and germ removed in the milling and polishing process. The removal of the germ and dark outer layer removes valuable nutrients, so the rice is enriched to replace those nutrients. The long-grain rice is highly prized for its bright white appearance and the dry, fluffy qualities for eating.

Available Forms of Rice

Milled white rice is most widely used. Look for enriched rice so the nutrients that were lost in polishing and refining are replaced.

Converted rice is partially cooked before the milling process. This enables nutrients from the bran to enter the endosperm before milling, thus saving them. Converted rice is still enriched. The precooking process does not cut down on the cooking time required, but rather increases the time as compared to milled white rice.

Precooked rice, more commonly known as instant rice, is cooked and then dehydrated. The rice then cooks in less than half the time of milled rice. The process is costly and adds to the cost you pay for the rice.

Brown rice still retains most of the bran covering. This bran layer adds to the nutrient content, but makes the rice spoil sooner and take longer to cook. Many people prize brown rice for its natural nutrient content, nutlike flavor, and chewy texture.

Wild rice is actually not a rice, but the seed from a tall water grass that grows naturally around the Great Lakes area. Other areas of the country are also working to develop a wild rice crop. Wild rice is harvested from small boats by knocking the mature seeds into the boat by hand. It is very expensive due to the limited supply and difficulty in harvesting. This highly prized grain has a unique texture and nutlike flavor that has long been used with wild game and fowl dishes.

Cereals

In this country, the "bowl of cereal" says breakfast to most people. Breakfast cereals are made from a wide variety of processed grains. Cereals are made from whole grains, mixed whole grains, whole and enriched grains, and enriched processed grains.

Types of Cereals

Cereals meant to be served hot are available in processed forms that require different amounts of cooking. An old favorite, oatmeal, is now available in three varieties: regular (no precooking), quick cooking (partially precooked), and instant (precooked, add hot water only).

Cereals that are packaged ready to be served are available in a seemingly unending parade of shapes, textures, and flavors. Most of the grains are represented in the manufacturer's race to tempt the consumer with a new "taste sensation." Perhaps you have noticed that when the cereal is not "newer" and "bigger," the extra bonuses of added dried fruit, nuts, or sweets are used to tempt the consumer. Some ready-to-eat cereals of this type have such a high concentration of sugar they qualify more for a candy snack than a breakfast meal.

Cereals offer the nutritious opportunity for enjoying a meal in a bowl if the right choice is made. The protein of the cereal combined with milk, plus fruit on the cereal or a glass of juice can be a helpful start to your day. Read the labels and compare the differences in nutrients such as vitamins and minerals, but don't forget to look for the fiber content.

Have advertisements led you to believe that the word "natural" on a cereal means it is more nutritious? Not so. Compare box labels for yourself. Notice the amount of sugar and calories in relation to the other nutrients involved. The closer sugar appears toward the top of the list, the more sugar there is in that cereal. Check the price. Are you paying for the cute shape of the cereal or for the taste and nutrient content? For a price comparison between two

Hot cereals with fruit are a nutritious way to warm up chilly mornings.

packages of different sizes, compare the price per unit of weight of different cereals. Some stores have small tags on the shelf with this price per unit of weight already figured for you. Learn what you are paying for, and if it is what you really want.

Other Available Forms of Grain

Wheat berries are whole-wheat kernels that have not been milled or processed. They can be kept in a moist place and sprouted for nutritious additions to salads, sandwiches, or baked bread. Wheat berries also are added to some yogurts for a boost in flavor, texture, and nutrition.

Wheat bran is the outer husk of the kernel that is separated by the milling. Its high fiber content is valued healthwise and can be added to cereals or used in cooking. Bran muffins are well-known for their mouth-watering taste and their "good for you" properties.

Wheat germ is the sprouting section of the seed that is a concentrated source of the grain's nutrients, the B vitamins, protein, and fat. You can purchase wheat germ separately to use on foods or in cooking. It has a sweet nutty flavor, but can become rancid soon if not kept in an airtight container in the refrigerator or freezer.

Cracked wheat is the whole kernel that is broken or "cracked" rather than crushed. It adds flavor and texture to baked products in moderate amounts.

Bulgar is precooked wheat in which the content of the kernel has been partially gelatinized, giving it a prized flavor and texture. It is offered in gourmet food sections and restaurants. Most of this product is shipped from the

Middle East where it has been made and used for thousands of years.

Farina is the granulated endosperm that contains no bran and no more than three percent flour. It is most commonly used as a cooked breakfast cereal.

Triticale is a recently developed cross between rye and wheat. It is not as plentiful as wheat, so it tends to be comparatively expensive. The interesting blend of the rye-wheat flavors probably will grow in popularity in the coming years. Still mostly available in the gourmet or health-food sections of stores, it comes in flour, flakes, and the whole berry forms.

Cornmeal is white or yellow corn ground to a coarse powder-like texture. Baked products such as cornbread and tortillas make this product a traditional favorite in North and South American cuisines. Cornmeal is also an old standby for adding crisp texture to breading of fish and other foods for frying. Blue cornmeal from blue corn has long been a favorite of American Indians.

Grits are ground from hulled white corn into coarse particles for cooking. The bland flavor complements many flavorful southern foods and can be eaten alone, in a cheese-flavored casserole, or as a side dish.

Hominy is the kernel of white corn with the bran and germ removed. It is usually sold canned, but is also available dry in some regions. Most of the nutrients are removed from this traditional old food, but it is high in energy value and enjoyed for its unusual bland flavor.

Oats are a versatile grain that can be used as a breakfast cereal or in cooking. You can buy oats processed in regular, quick cooking, and instant forms. Oats are particularly high in a water-soluble fiber, sometimes called the "new fiber." Current research shows that this fiber might prove to be particularly valuable in lowering blood cholesterol.

Barley is a grain that is used mainly in soup, but also adds an interesting, chewy texture to other grain dishes. It can be served alone, similar to a brown or wild rice.

Kasha is coarsely ground buckwheat that has had the bran removed. The nutlike flavor and substantial texture make this an interesting side dish. Kasha is a standard food in the Eastern European countries.

Soybeans might be classified as a vegetable, but they are used in many of the same ways as the classic grains. Soybeans are ground into flour and coarse meals to use in foods and baked products for their nutritive benefits. The dried beans can be cooked and served as a hot cereal or side dish. They are also served as a cereal-like food.

Purchasing Grain Products

Grain products are more widely available in supermarkets and specialty stores than ever before. The health-conscious consumer has created a demand for the supply of these products in a wider variety of types and forms.

If you are purchasing a grain product that is prepackaged, read the label carefully to make certain it is the kind of grain and the type of processing you want to buy. It is easy to compare the nutrient content on prepackaged grain products. Read the labels carefully. Keep in mind that the more processing and preparation done to a product, the more expensive it will be. For instance, ready-to-eat cereals cost more than cereal that needs cooking. You may find the savings in time is worth the higher dollar price. Just be aware of what you are paying for.

Perhaps you enjoy buying grain products in bulk form that you scoop out of the bin. Bulk products are rarely marked in detailed nutrient content. There might be a few signs to highlight the most important nutrients, but you probably will need to rely on a book or composition foods chart such as the one in the Appendix of this book for specific information.

Grain Product Storage

Store grain products in airtight containers in a cool, dry place. Sometimes you can simply reseal the opened package with twist ties, plastic

You can avoid the monotony of the same old grain products by exploring other forms of grains. Including blue corn bread from blue corn and jalapeño peppers would spice up any meal or snack!

Blue Corn Bread

Traditional	Ingredients	Metric
1½ cups	Blue cornmeal	375 mL
2 tsp.	Baking powder	10 mL
3 Tbsp.	Sugar	45 mL
1 large	Egg, beaten	1 large
¾ cup	Milk	175 mL
3 Tbsp.	Bacon fat or margarine	45 mL
1 small can	Green chilies chopped	1 small can

Directions

1. Combine dry ingredients in a mixing bowl. Mix the rest of the ingredients in a separate bowl.

2. Add the liquid mix to the dry ingredients and mix thoroughly.

3. Pour mixture into a greased 9-inch (23 cm) square baking pan. Bake in a preheated oven at 350°F (175°C) for 30 minutes or until a toothpick comes out clean when inserted in the center of the bread.

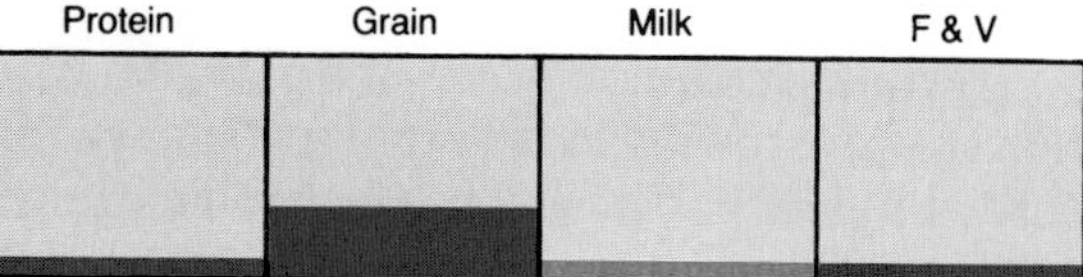

Cooking Hints

Pasta can be frozen for later use if you add 1 to 2 tablespoons (15 to 30 mL) of butter, margarine, or olive oil to keep it from sticking. Thaw and reheat it over steaming water. You can reheat refrigerated pasta the same way.

wrap, foil, or rubber bands. The important point is to keep out air, moisture, and insects.

Whole-grain products should be stored in the refrigerator or freezer to prevent the oils in the kernel's germ from becoming rancid.

Pasta Preparation

Pasta can be served in an endless variety of dishes. Basically, though, the initial preparation is the same no matter if the end result will be a cool, refreshing pasta salad or a steaming hot plate of spaghetti with tomato sauce.

Equipment

The right cooking pot is vital for cooking pasta. You will need a pot that holds at least 6 quarts (6 L) of water, a long-handled spoon or fork, a colander to drain the pasta, and a large, heated bowl for the drained pasta. Note: A wooden spoon is best because it doesn't lower the cooking temperature of the water or burn your hand. The pot must be large enough to allow the pasta to circulate in the water and to prevent the foaming cooking liquid from boiling over.

Amount of Water

To cook pasta, you need a lot of water. You need to have more than enough water to be absorbed by the pasta, which will double in size, and enough water to allow for free circulation of the pasta. That prevents the pasta pieces from sticking to each other. You also will want the water to return to a boil soon after you add the pasta.

For 1 pound (500 g) of pasta, use 1 gallon (4 L) of water. If you are cooking ½ pound (250 g) of pasta, do not decrease the amount of water by half. Use at least 3 quarts of (3 L) of water for ½ pound (250 g) of pasta. If you need to cook more than 1 pound (500 g) of pasta, use two pots.

Cooking the Pasta

1. Bring the water to a rolling boil. (It will come to a boil faster with a lid on.)
2. Instead of salt, try adding 1 tablespoon (15 mL) of lemon juice to the water for flavor.
3. Add 1 tablespoon (15 mL) of oil to the water to keep the water from foaming and boiling over. Olive oil helps add flavor. Some experts also think adding oil helps keep the pasta from sticking together. (Some Italian chefs object to the oil in the cooking water, saying it makes the water absorb unevenly.)
4. Add the pasta to the boiling water all at once. Add long pasta such as spaghetti by gently pressing it in the middle with the fork or spoon until it bends and fits into the pan. Separate any pieces that stick together.
5. Replace the pot lid just until the water returns to a boil. Start timing when the water begins to boil.
6. Remove the cover, keep the water boiling rapidly, and occasionally stir the mixture. It is important to keep the pasta moving to prevent the pieces from sticking together or to the bottom of the pan.
7. Test pastas with egg, such as noodles, after three minutes. Test dried pasta without egg, such as spaghetti, after five minutes. The best way to test spaghetti is to take a strand and bite it. It should be tender yet firm in the center.

Mastering the few simple principles of cooking pastas and rice will put you in command of life-long successes with endless recipe possibilities.

When the pasta is almost done but still just a little firmer than you want it to be, take it off the stove. Pasta continues to cook as it is drained from the heat and steam. If you wait until it is done to take it out of the water, it will be overcooked. Pasta should be cooked until it has water all the way to the center, but should still be firm. "Al dente," firm to the teeth, is an Italian expression referring to how pasta should be cooked.

8. Place the colander securely in the sink and pour the pasta and water into it. Do not rinse it. You will wash away the nutrients.

9. Serve the pasta immediately. Time your meal preparation so the other foods are done at the same time. If you must keep the pasta waiting for other foods, keep it in the colander and place the colander over steaming water.

Cooking Rice

The so-called oriental method for boiling rice helps to preserve the nutrients and needs no special equipment.

Equipment

You will need a large pot that will hold from 6 to 8 cups (1.5 to 1 L) of liquid for four or more portions.

Directions

For white long-grain or short-grain rice use 1 cup (250 mL) with 2 cups (500 mL) of water. For brown rice, use 1 cup (250 mL) with 2½ cups (625 mL) of water.

1. Bring the water to a boil and add rice.

2. If you prefer less sticky rice, add 1 tablespoon oil (15 mL) and 2 tablespoons (30 mL) of lemon juice to the water.

3. Bring the water back to a boil and reduce immediately to a simmer. The heat must be low enough for a simmer or the rice will boil dry and stick or burn!

4. Cover tightly and cook for about 20 minutes, until all the water is absorbed and the rice is tender.

5. Remove the rice from the heat, but allow the pot to remain covered for a few minutes longer. Serve warm.

Rice may be reheated in a colander or strainer over steaming water.

You also can steam, bake, or fry rice. Flavored rices, precooked rices, and exotic rices usually require different cooking methods. Read and follow the directions on the package for the most consistent results.

Cooking Grains

Read and follow package directions for how to cook grains and cereals.

Microwave Cooking

Pasta takes as long to cook in the microwave as it does with a conventional stove because it needs to absorb the water. If you are using a recipe that combines pasta with other foods, cook the pasta by the conventional method. When you attempt to combine other foods with uncooked pasta in the microwave, the other foods usually cook faster than the pasta. The result can be overcooked meat or undercooked pasta.

Vocabulary Review

RDAs
U.S. RDA
Complete protein
Enriched cereals and flours
Restored cereals and flours
Fortified cereals
Al dente
Refined flour
Cake flour
Pastry flour
Whole-grain flour

Questions for Review

1. Why are breads and cereals not extra calories that should be sacrificed for a healthy diet?
2. What is the difference between complex and simple carbohydrates?
3. What are the differences between enriched, fortified, and restored cereals.
4. What type of specialized flour is used in making macaroni products? Why is it important?
5. What are some of the kinds of rice that are available?
6. How do you store grain products to maintain freshness and prevent contamination by rodents and insects?
7. How do you test pasta for doneness?
8. Why would you serve enriched pasta immediately after cooking without rinsing first?
9. What is the history of pasta in the Old World?
10. Grain is available in many different forms. Be able to define the following: wheat berries, wheat bran, wheat germ, cracked wheat, bulgar, farina, triticale, cornmeal, grits, hominy, oats, kasha, and soybeans.

Things to Do

1. Visit a grocery store and make a list of as many variations of pasta as you can. Plan several different meals using those variations.
2. Calculate the cost per serving of milled white rice, converted rice, precooked rice, and brown rice. Compare the nutrients in each. Which would be the best buy for you? Make your choice based on cost, nutrients, and convenience.
3. Compare the cereals you eat at home for nutrient content and price. Are they well balanced for nutrients vs. the amount of sugar?
4. Compare the price per serving of regular, quick and instant oatmeal. Is the time savings worth the higher price per serving of the quick and instant varieties?

Taste Temptations

You can't help but feel rewarded when a sticky lump of dough bakes magically into a fragrant, light golden work of art through your skills and efforts. If you learn the basic principles of baking and master the simple skills, you can delight friends and family the rest of your life with endless creations for everyday and festive celebrations.

Flour Types

The majority of flours are manufactured from wheat. Hard wheat and soft wheat are the two types of wheat used for flour. Breads need hard wheat flour because of the higher quantity of a protein called gluten. **Gluten** gives the dough strength for better volume and texture. A soft wheat flour with a low gluten content is used for products such as cookies, cakes, biscuits, and pastry.

Several types of flours are available to the consumer. They include:

- **All-purpose flour**—a high-protein wheat flour for most baked products from yeast breads to cakes.
- **Bread flour**—flour containing a higher proportion of gluten than all-purpose flour.
- **Cake flour**—a soft winter wheat flour with little protein that produces tender, fine textured cakes.
- **Whole-wheat flour**—contains the bran, endosperm, and germ in the same proportions as in the original wheat kernel.
- **Graham flour**—a coarsely ground whole-wheat flour that may be used interchangeably with other whole-wheat flours.
- **Medium rye flour**—milled from the endosperm of the rye kernel, it is the only other cereal grain which contains gluten. The gluten, however, is weak, so rye flours are usually used with a larger proportion of hard wheat flour.
- **Pumpernickel rye**—a coarser rye flour milled from the whole rye kernel.
- **Self-rising flour**—an all-purpose flour with leavening and salt added. One cup (250 mL) of self-rising flour contains the equivalent of 1½ teaspoons (8 mL) of baking powder and ½ teaspoon (3 mL) of salt.
- **Bleached flour**—flour that has been treated to remove the yellow pigment in the freshly milled flour. The process does not affect the nutritional content or the flavor of the flour and actually makes the gluten more elastic, improving its baking qualities for cakes and breads.

- **Unbleached flour**—a yellowish flour that has not been bleached and tends toward a coarse texture in baked foods.
- **Bromated flour**—a bread flour to which potassium bromate has been added to strengthen the gluten. Flour containing the potassium bromate additive must be labeled. Dough made from untreated flour tends to be soft and sticky.
- **No-sift flour**—a quick-mixing flour in which the particles are crystal shaped and do not pack and settle in the containers. Therefore, this flour does not need sifting before using. This granular flour does not lump in cold liquid.
- **Stone-ground flour**—usually a whole-grain flour that has been ground on a granite stone wheel. The lower heat produced in this slower process is considered beneficial to both the flavor and nutrients.
- **Cracked-wheat flour**—whole-wheat kernels are cracked instead of ground to smaller particles. This process produces a chewy, coarse product that needs to be blended with finer flours for baking.
- **Cornmeal**—coarsely ground corn used for texture in breading fish and meats, frying hushpuppies, and for baking cornbread and tortillas.

Buying Flour

For the best buy economically, buy white flour in the largest quantities you can store and use within six weeks. Buy whole-grain flours in quantities that will be used within a few weeks. The oils in the germ may spoil.

Read the label carefully for the right type of flour for the products you intend to prepare. Also read the label to ensure buying enriched flours.

Check the product carefully for any sign of moths or larvae infestation before storing around other grain products at home. If insects are present when you bring the flour home, return it to the store immediately.

Storing Flour

Store flour in an airtight container in a cool, dry place or in the freezer. Store whole-grain flour in the refrigerator or freezer. Seal the flour in a heavy plastic bag.

Baking Basics

In a heated oven, baked-good products rise from expanding gas bubbles or separate into flaky layers. To accomplish that feat, you need ingredients to form the structure (flour), to mix it together (liquids), to hold it together (eggs), to form the gas bubbles (liquid or leavening agent), to make it tender and sometimes flaky (shortening), and to taste delicious (seasonings and flavorings).

Flour—The Structure

Flour mixes with liquid to form the structure or foundation of the baked product. The gluten can be strengthened by beating or kneading it. Developed gluten gives the flour structure its strength. Think of a fresh stick of chewing gum. It is quite tender and easily tears into pieces, but after it is chewed, the gum stretches and returns to its original shape without tearing. This is similar to the stretching and pounding of dough when it is kneaded. Kneading dough develops the gluten in the flour in much the same way as chewing gum. Kneading the dough stretches it and helps it hold air bubbles.

When you place bread or cake batter in the heat of the oven, the liquid turns to steam or the gas from the leavening agent expands as it heats, making the dough rise. The flour becomes firm and the product takes its final shape.

Liquids

As discussed, liquids help to mix the ingredients, develop the gluten, and start the action for leavening when baking powder, baking soda, or steam is used. Milk and water are the most commonly used liquids in baked prod-

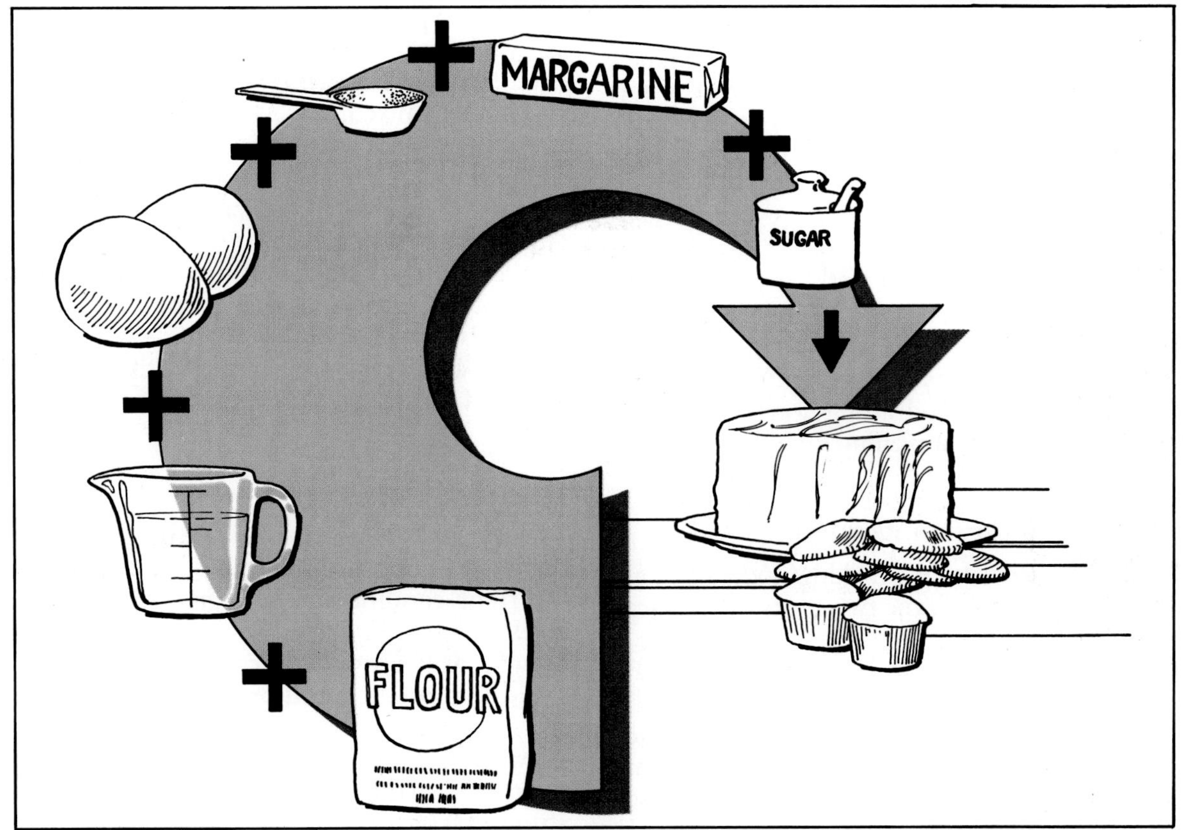

Add up this equation for a successful baking career and instant recognition of a workable recipe.

ucts, but buttermilk, fruit juices, sour cream, and yogurt also work. Milk products and juices add to the flavor and nutritive content of the food.

Eggs

Eggs help bind ingredients together much like a kind of glue. They also trap air bubbles for leavening. The elastic strength of the thick egg whites allows them to stretch and hold a large volume of air when it is beaten into them. Have you ever blown up a balloon? The principle is similar. Anything that thins the viscosity of the egg whites will increase the volume of air they can hold. Room-temperature egg whites are thinner than cold ones, so they will stretch to a higher volume.

Eggs add a rich flavor and tender texture to baked products. See Chapter 18 for how to select and store eggs.

Leavening Agents

The leavening agents are responsible for the rising and the volume of the baked product. These agents are steam, air, the chemicals baking soda and baking powder, or yeast. Leavening agents produce gas bubbles in the dough or batter. The bubbles of air or gas rise and expand, causing the product to rise. If there is a sudden vibration or cold draft on the dough or batter before it has baked into a firm structure, the product could collapse. Then gas escapes and ruins the food.

Steam

A high baking temperature with a product containing a relatively large amount of water will convert the liquid to steam. The steam expands and the product rises. Popovers and cream puffs are leavened by steam.

Air

You incorporate air into a mixture for leavening by physically beating it into the dough or batter. Beating egg whites, batter, fat and sugar (called creaming), and sifting flour are all ways of trapping air for leavening.

Chemical Leavening Agents

Baking powder and baking soda with an acidic ingredient are the two types of chemical leavening agents.

The combination of **baking soda** and an acidic baking soda ingredient will react to form the harmless and tasteless gas, carbon dioxide. When the dough or batter is heated, the carbon dioxide expands and causes the product to rise. A few common acidic ingredients used in recipes with baking soda for leavening are buttermilk, yogurt, sour cream, honey, and molasses. Prior to the first manufactured baking soda in the 1830s, cooks relied mostly on beating air into the batter by hand for leavening. The earlier form of soda, purified potash from wood ashes, was closely related to lye and sometimes imparted an unpleasant flavor to food.

One of the earliest convenience food products, baking powder, was "invented" in the 1880s. It saved labor and introduced the first predictable leavening powder. **Baking powder** is a one-step leavening agent. It is a mixture of baking soda and a powdered acid combined in the right proportions. When liquid is added to the baking powder, it forms carbon dioxide. Three types of baking powder are now available.

- **Tartrate baking powder** combines baking soda, cream of tarter, and tartaric acid. With this type of baking powder, adding liquid sets off an immediate release of the carbon dioxide, making it necessary to bake the batter as soon as it is mixed.
- **Phosphate baking powder** is a slower reacting powder, but will release carbon dioxide before baking if the batter is not baked soon after mixing.
- **Double-acting baking powder** releases most of the carbon dioxide in the heat of the oven. Recipes usually are based on double-acting baking powder unless another type is specified.

Yeast

Yeast is a microscopic plant that feeds on sugar and flour and multiplies quickly under the right conditions. As it grows, the plant gives off carbon dioxide, which leavens the dough. The growth process of the yeast is called fermentation and produces a distinctive aroma and flavor unique to yeast breads. Yeast grows best at room temperature. Temperatures too cool slow the growth rate and high temperatures destroy the plant.

Yeast may be purchased in two forms.

- **Active dry yeast particles** come in packets and may be stored in the cupboard at room temperature. The most common packets contain about 1 tablespoon (15 mL) of dry yeast. You can find the packets near the baking supplies in the supermarket. Check the expiration date before purchasing and again before using.

Dry yeast also is available as a newer fast-rising yeast. This yeast rises in less time than the traditional active dry yeast. Check the package for any directions that might differ from your traditional recipe.

- **Compressed yeast cakes** are available in individually wrapped moist cakes weighing 3/5 oz. (17 g). These moist cakes are purchased from the refrigerator section of the supermar-

Many muffin recipes call for baking soda or baking powder. If these muffins contained buttermilk, would you use baking soda or powder?

ket and must be stored in the refrigerator after purchasing. Check the expiration date before purchasing and again before using.

Fats and Oils

Fats or oils in baked products improve the keeping quality and tenderness of the food. They also contribute a pleasing flavor and taste of richness.

Fats

Several different fats are used in baked products. Each lends its own unique flavor and texture. Preferences for those flavors often originate with the availability of the fat in a particular region or because of cultural customs. Cost also varies for the various fats, so some recipes call for a mixture of types to both save money and still capture some of the flavor and texture of an expensive fat. The different types of fats include the following.

- **Butter** is the fat separated from rich cow's cream. It is high in vitamin A and gives a rich flavor and unique, crisp texture to baked products.
- **Margarine** is a solid vegetable oil formed by a process called hydrogenation. Margarine is packaged like butter and may be substituted in the same measurements. Whipped, soft, liquid, or diet margarines are not all margarine and cannot be substituted in baked products for margarine or butter.
- **Shortening** is a hydrogenated fat made from vegetable oil with no flavor added. Shortening gives volume and a softer texture to baked products.
- **Lard** is fat processed from pork. For products with tender, flaky layers, such as biscuits and pie crust, lard is considered the best. The same qualities make it undesirable for cake baking.

Oils

Oils for cooking are derived from a variety of plant sources. Currently available are corn, soybean, peanut, safflower, olive, sesame, almond, hickory, and walnut oils. The flavor and characteristics of the various oils differ and should not be substituted for another without some experimentation. Olive and sesame oils for example are strong flavors and would dominate most recipes. You can imagine that an olive-flavored cake might not be a nice surprise!

Do not expect to get the same results with oil as with solid fat. They are not interchangeable in recipes.

Buying and Storing Fats and Oils

Select the fat or oil appropriate for the intended use. Read the label for nutritional information such as cholesterol content, any enrichment of nutrients, and price as compared to similar fats and oils of the same volume.

Store solid fats in the refrigerator well wrapped. They absorb flavors from surrounding foods. For long storage periods, keep them in the freezer in their original containers and wrapped in a see-through, freezer-quality covering.

Store oils at room temperature. If your supply will last you more than a month, the oil will keep better in the refrigerator. If refrigerated, allow the oil to come to room temperature before using it in a recipe.

Seasonings and Flavorings

You may enjoy adding various seasonings and flavorings to your baked products. Some of the more common ones include sweeteners, flavor extracts such as vanilla and mint, nuts, chocolate, fruit, and spices. Such additions obviously change the flavor and texture, as well as have other effects.

Sugars and syrups add flavor, promote browning, tenderize gluten, and speed yeast activity. Popular sweeteners include sugar, honey, molasses, corn syrup, and sugar substitutes.

Sugars

Sugar is made from sugarcane or sugar beets. Different types of sugars are suitable for

Popular tasty cookies are made in several different ways and shapes. Cookies don't have to be super sweetened to be good. Oatmeal, fruit, and sesame seeds add flavor and texture to these treats. What else could you add to cookies to increase their nutrients?

different purposes. Granulated sugar or table sugar is good for all purposes. Powdered or confectioner's sugar is used for icings, glazes, and other decoration. Light or dark brown sugar gives a carmelized flavor and dark color.

Honey

Honey is made by bees from flower nectar and varies in color and flavor depending upon the source of the nectar. Honey has more liquid and is sweeter than sugar. Therefore it is not advisable to substitute honey for sugar. Usually it is safe to substitute sugar for honey with the following modification. For each cup of honey called for in the recipe, substitute ¼ cup liquid (50 mL) and 1¼ cups (300 mL) sugar.

Molasses

Molasses is a dark, sticky syrup that is manufactured as a byproduct in sugar refining. The demand for its unique flavor has increased in the last decade because of the growing interest in natural products with less refined sugar. Molasses is less sweet than sugar and combines well with recipes using whole-grain flours. There are several different molasses that vary in flavor and color, but they are essentially used in the same way.

Substituting molasses for sugar in recipes is risky without some experimentation. The equivalent is 1 cup (250 mL) molasses equals ¾ cup (175 mL) of granulated white sugar.

Corn Syrup

Corn syrup is used mostly in cooked frostings and candies. It is a combination of concentrated dextrose (a kind of sugar) and water. Corn syrup makes creamy candy products by preventing sugar crystal formation. Corn syrup should not be substituted for sugar in baking.

Sugar Substitutes

Products featuring noncaloric and low-calorie sugar substitutes are available in liquid, tablet, and crystal forms. The sweetening value varies, and the uses also vary. A few such products claim to be substitutes for sugar in baked products. If you decide to use one of the chemical sweeteners, follow the directions on the package. Do not try to substitute a low-calorie sweetener for sugar for an important occasion without experimenting first. You may not be satisfied with the resulting texture and flavor. Read the label carefully. Some sweeteners, such as aspartame, are affected by heat.

Selecting and Storing Sugars and Syrups

Store sugars and syrups in a tightly covered container in a cool, dry place to keep out moisture and insects. Keep the area around the sugar and the syrup containers absolutely clean to prevent attracting insects.

If the syrup or honey is not to be used within a week after opening, refrigerate. Honey will crystallize at cool temperatures, but can be reconditioned by setting the open container in hot water. You can also microwave it on low power until the crystals are dissolved.

How Heat Bakes

Baking a product with dry oven heat requires the exact temperature specified in the recipe. The cooking occurs when the moisture in the product heats to steam and evaporates in the dry oven air. This leaves a dry surface — a crust. When the temperature of the product continues to rise to that of the oven temperature, browning occurs on the outside first. The product slowly firms to the desired consistency.

When the oven heat is too hot, the surface dries and hardens before allowing the product to rise. As the inside cooks, the surface continues to brown, resulting in a scorched crust. The alternative is an underdone product. Another sign of too high a temperature is a cracked top surface.

When the oven temperature is not hot enough, the dough or batter may dry out before it browns. The product usually collapses when the gluten and starch in the flour are not cooked enough to hold in the gas bubbles for rising.

If an oven is heating unevenly, a cake or loaf of bread placed in the center of the oven will rise and brown unevenly. The oven also needs to be level, or liquid batters will be thinner on the "up" side and cook unevenly.

Baking recipes usually require a preheated oven. Allow the oven to reach the desired temperature before putting in the batter or dough. Preheating time varies with the oven, but can take from 10 to 20 minutes. An oven thermometer can help you check the temperature in your oven if your baking products display any of the symptoms discussed in the preceding paragraphs.

Baking Pans

The right size pans in good condition have a tremendous effect on the success of your product. Too small and the batter or dough overflows. Too large and the batter or dough doesn't rise to the usual height and tends to dry out in the oven. See Chapter 5 for more information on baking pans.

Preparing Baking Pans for the Oven

Most baked product recipes direct you to grease the pan in order to make the removal of the finished product easier. Sometimes there is enough fat in the batter or dough to keep the product from sticking without greasing the pan. You can use shortening, oil, unsalted solid fat, or one of the no-stick spray products to coat the pan. Use your fingers, a paper towel, or brush to cover the entire surface and crevices with the grease. Any small part of food that sticks endangers breaking up the whole product when it is removed.

Recipes for cakes usually require both greasing and flouring the pan for easy removal. Rub or spray the grease on the pan first. Sprin-

The correct oven temperature allowed this cake to bake evenly to a moist, high, and lightly browned product.

Baking in too hot of an oven results in a scorched crust and a product that fails to rise.

When the oven temperature is too low, the baked product, such as this cake, will dry out before it browns.

kle about 2 tablespoons (30 mL) of all-purpose or cake flour around the pan. Holding the pan firmly in one hand, hit the side of the pan to bounce the flour over the bottom, creases, and sides of the pan. When the whole surface is floured, turn the pan upside down and tap the excess flour onto waxed paper or clean bowl to reuse it another time. When the recipe says to line the pan bottom with paper, trace the pan bottom on parchment paper or a heavy grocery sack that has been oiled. (Wax paper will just melt and disintegrate in the high heat.) Cut the shape out and place the paper in the bottom of the greased pan.

Pans for baking angel food and sponge cakes should not be greased. These cakes that have delicate beaten egg whites need to hold onto the narrow walls of the pan while they are rising and the structure is not firm. A slippery side would cause a collapsed product.

Pattern the Pans in the Oven

The heated air in the oven must circulate freely around the baking products for them to cook evenly. You can accomplish this by staggering the pans so that they have the most space between them, yet no pan sits directly above or below another. The pans must not touch each other, the oven walls, or door in order to avoid hot spots where heat collects unevenly. This would cause scorching.

Timing the Baking Process

Resist the temptation to open the door to check the progress of your baking project. Every time you open the oven door, you cool down the oven considerably and slow the cooking time. If the cool air hits the product at a crucial time, it could even result in a collapsed product. The best resistance to peeking is an accurate timer that reminds you exactly when to check for doneness according to the recipe's specific directions. Because oven temperatures vary, set the timer five minutes early for the first check.

Separating the Baking Product from the Pan

Most baked products need to be removed from the pans immediately to prevent sticking and sogginess from condensed steam. The exceptions to that practice are cakes without shortening such as angel food and sponge types, quick breads, and some bar cookies. Allow those products to cool in the pan before removal. Remove yeast bread by placing the pan on its side on a wire cooling rack. If the bread does not pull free easily with a hot pad, loosen it with a straight-edge spatula. Then allow it to cool for a few seconds before easing it out of the pan. Never apply pressure to the loaf while it is still warm. You will mash it.

Remove cakes and quick breads by loosening an edge with a straight-edge spatula. Hold a wire cooling rack on the top of the pan and turn the pan upside down resting on the rack. Lift off the pan, leaving the cake upside down. Quickly and gently place another rack on top of the bottom of the cake and, without squeezing, turn them over so the right side is up again. Carefully remove the top rack and let the cake cool before serving or icing.

Quick Breads

Quick delights for the food fancier and the family on the run are quick breads that only need to rise once—in the oven as they bake! Quick breads use baking powder or baking soda instead of yeast for the leavening agent. This eliminates two extra risings before baking. The quick bread is mixed into a batter and poured into the pan for baking immediately.

Speedy quick breads "rise to almost any occasion" for a tempting array of flavors, shapes, and textures.

Cooking Hints

Oven Time's "Up" When...

...Muffins are lightly browned with rounded tops. (Remove from the pan immediately.)

...Loaf breads are lightly browned with a crack down the center. The bread should be starting to pull away slightly from the sides of the pan. When tapped on top, the bread feels firm. (Follow the individual recipe directions regarding when to remove the bread from the pan.

...The rolled biscuits are lightly browned on top with lighter sides.

...The biscuits have about doubled in size.

Quick Breads—Types and Shapes

Wonderful variety describes the versatility of quick breads. The surprising range of flavors and shapes covers types from pancakes, muffins, and coffeecakes to pumpkin bread and banana bread loaves. All of these can be prepared within an hour's time—a true "quick" bread!

The amount of liquid in the recipe determines the type of batter and eventual shape or type of quick bread you can make. There are two main types of batters:

- **Pour batters** contain enough liquid to be poured. Pour batters contain about equal amounts of flour and water. These are quick breads such as pancakes, waffles, and crepes.
- **Drop batters** have less liquid and need to be spooned into pans. Drop batters contain about twice as much flour as liquid. These quick breads include coffee cakes and fruit breads.

Baking mixtures that have so little liquid they hold a shape without a container or can be shaped by hand are called doughs not batters. **Doughs** contain about one-third as much liquid as flour. Rolled biscuits, cake doughnuts, scones, and some quick coffee cakes are examples of quick breads that are shaped.

Note: Dropped biscuits may be mixed by the biscuit method or the muffin method. The higher amount of liquid makes them a batter instead of a dough. If the muffin method of mixing is used, oil can be substituted for the solid fat. Dropped biscuits made by the muffin-mixing method will not have the same layered, flaky texture that rolled biscuits do.

Quick Bread Preparation Methods

Regardless of which tantalizing quick bread recipe has captured your attention, you will be most pleased with the results when you learn and use the correct preparation methods. Although a quick bread is quick to make, it is equally quick to ruin with the wrong preparation technique. Just a few stirs too many can turn a light, tender, even-textured muffin into a tough, heavy, and tunneled disappointment. There are two methods to mix quick breads—the muffin method and the biscuit method.

Muffin Method

Use the following method for pancakes, muffins, and a variety of quick fruit and nut breads.

1. Measure all ingredients (Refer to Chapter 5 for correct methods.)
2. Sift the premeasured dry ingredients into a bowl. Any dry ingredients that are too large to sift can be stirred into the mixture.
3. Combine room temperature liquid ingredients and melted fat. Stir until blended.
4. Clear a space in the center of the dry ingredients.
5. Pour in all the liquid at one time into the hollowed-out space in the dry ingredients.
6. Stir just enough to barely dampen the dry ingredients. Some flour will still look white and undissolved. Overmixing muffins develops the

Healthful breads make a great addition to your daily food choices.

gluten in the flour causing toughness. Overmixing also results in long, narrow tunnels snaking through the muffins. (Note: Do you wonder why you can beat cake for a long time without getting tunnels? The reason is that the large amount of sugar in cakes actually tenderizes the gluten, preventing the strong, structure needed for breads.)

7. Spoon, without extra stirring, the drop batter into greased and floured muffin tins, loaf pans, or shaped baking pans. The batter should not fill more than two- thirds of the pan to prevent overflowing. For the thinner pour batters, pour the batter in small even amounts onto a hot, greased griddle or skillet. For specialty pancakes, such as waffles, you will need special utensils—a waffle iron. (There are many different types available. Follow the manufacturer's directions for best results.)

When you follow this method, you can turn out the perfect muffin, one that is rounded with a golden-brown, pebbly surface and an evenly textured, tender inside.

Successful Serving

Pancakes should be served hot. Reheating dries and toughens them quickly. Sometimes it is possible to reheat them briefly in the microwave without drying, but the microwaves sometimes make them slightly rubbery or tough. It is most rewarding to simply "cook and serve" the fast-cooking pancake.

Muffins are best served fresh and warm from

Creative Tips

You can make quick breads even more convenient! Make your own mix by combining all the dry ingredients for your favorite recipe, seal it in a heavy plastic bag, and store at room temperature for several weeks or in the refrigerator for several months. Label and date it clearly. When you need a quick, no mess, hot baked bread, put the dry ingredients in a bowl, add the liquid ingredients, and proceed as usual. The quality is the same as your fresh-baked product and the cost is less than conventional mixes from the store. This technique also works well for camping.

the oven. They may be reheated in the oven. Try sealing them in a paper bag and heating in a 400°F (200°C) oven for five minutes. The microwave also works well for muffins. Follow the instructions for the particular microwave.

Loaf breads hold their shape and taste best when allowed to cool before serving. The cooling time assists the blending of the flavors and firms the bread for better slices.

Biscuit Method

The unique feature of a biscuit is the tender, flaky layers that seem to "melt in your mouth! The correct mixing method technique is the "secret" to that feature. The fat is cut into the flour (see page 131) so that many particles of fat are coated with the flour. When the liquid is added all at once, a fork carefully turns the ingredients over to just moisten the flour but not break up the particles of fat. These particles of solid fat melt when the biscuits bake, making a tender, flaky, and layered texture.

Use the following method for biscuits, scones, and short breads.

1. Measure all ingredients correctly. (See Chapter 5.)
2. Sift the premeasured ingredients together into a mixing bowl.
3. Add the fat to the dry ingredients by cutting it into the flour with a pastry blender or two knives. Note: The fat should be cool enough to be firm. The majority of the resulting mixture should look like coarse crumbs with some pieces slightly larger.
4. Add cold milk.
5. Mix with a fork the dry ingredients until just moistened and blended. For rolled biscuits, the dough should pull away from the sides of the bowl when stirred. For drop biscuits, the batter should hold its shape, but it will need scraping from the sides of the bowl.

Kneading Biscuits

1. Gather the mixed biscuit dough together in a ball and place on lightly floured board or pastry canvas. Smooth any extra flour from the board or canvas to one side to add later if the dough sticks. The ideal procedure is to use as little extra flour as possible.
2. Gently fold the dough in half toward you with your fingertips.
3. Give the dough a light push away from you with your palms.
4. Rotate the dough a quarter turn.
5. Repeat the folding, pushing, and turning of the dough (kneading) several times. Knead the dough the number of times specified in your recipe. Overkneaded biscuits will develop too much gluten and become tough.

Rolling Biscuits

1. Lightly roll out the kneaded dough with a floured rolling pin. Remember, until the dough is baked, you are still developing the gluten in the flour whenever you move the dough.

Roll the dough to about ½ inch (1.5 cm) in thickness. Thick biscuits will be crusty on the outside and soft on the inside. Thin biscuits tend to be dry with thick crusts. If you can keep the dough circular in shape, less dough will be wasted in the cutting.

2. Dip a biscuit cutter in flour and cut straight down through the dough. Space the cutter so that you can cut as many biscuits as possible from the first rolling. Rerolling, stretching, and tearing the dough all develop the gluten and make the biscuits tougher.

3. Collect the dough cuttings into a ball, reroll, and cut it again.

4. Move the cut biscuits to an ungreased baking sheet. The high proportion of fat in the dough keeps them from sticking to the sheet. Space the biscuits at least 1 inch (2.5 cm) apart to allow for expansion and oven air circulation.

Shaping Drop Biscuits

The only shaping drop biscuits need is spooning the sticky batter onto the ungreased baking sheet. Like rolled biscuits, they need to be spaced about 1 inch (2.5 cm) apart. Drop biscuits are quick to make and save cleanup time, but definitely have a different texture than the rolled biscuits.

It is easy to add other nutritious ingredients to drop biscuits. You can almost create a "meal in a biscuit" by stirring in some grated cheese and chopped ham or nuts and dried fruit.

Peanut-Butter Banana Muffins

Yield: 16 muffins

Traditional	Ingredients	Metric
1½ cups	All-purpose or unbleached flour	375 mL
¼ cup	Brown sugar, firmly packed	50 mL
1 tbsp.	Baking powder	15 mL
½ tsp.	Salt	3 mL
¾ cup	Skim milk	175 mL
½ cup	Smooth peanut butter	125 mL
⅓ cup	Unsalted margarine, melted	75 mL
2 medium	Bananas, mashed	2 medium
1	Egg	1
	Vegetable cooking spray	

Directions

1. Combine first 4 ingredients in a large bowl, make a well in center of mixture.

2. Combine milk, peanut butter, margarine, banana, and egg in a mixing bowl; beat at medium speed of an electric mixer until smooth.

3. Add to flour mixture, stirring just until moistened.

4. Spoon into muffin pans coated with cooking spray, filling two-thirds full.

5. Bake at 400°F (200°C) for 20 to 25 minutes or until golden brown.

Microwave Directions

Yield: 14 muffins

1. Line microwave-safe muffin pan with two liners each.

2. Combine first 4 ingredients in a large bowl; make a well in the center of the mixture.

3. Microwave margarine on high for 60 seconds, or until melted.

4. Combine milk, peanut butter, margarine, banana, and egg in a bowl; beat at medium speed of an electric mixer until smooth.

5. Add to flour mixture, stirring just until moistened.

6. Fill muffin cups two-thirds full.

7. Microwave on high for 2½ to 3 minutes or until a wooden toothpick inserted in center comes out clean. Rotate pan ½ turn halfway through cooking. Remove outside paper liner from muffins and cool on a wire rack.

Note: The top of the muffins may look moist after the specified cooking time, but this should disappear during the standing time. Do not overbake or the muffins will be tough and dry.

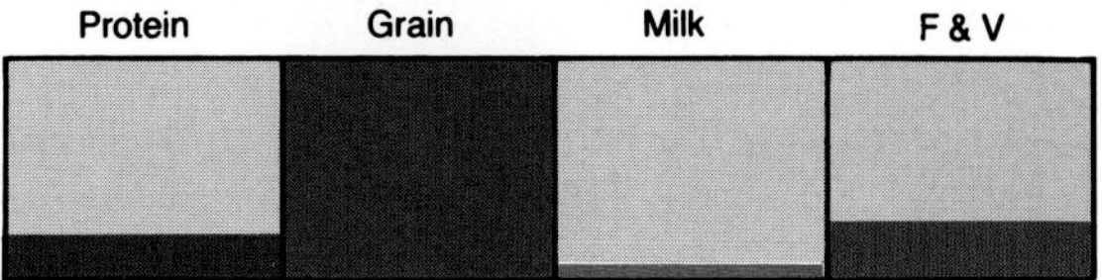

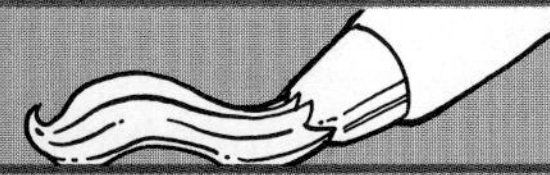

Creative Tips

After you have made several batches of successful biscuits, you will develop a "feel" for the correct time to stop or continue kneading dough. You may develop special preferences for the different flavors and textures of the various solid fats, shortenings, and oils available. Perhaps you might like to develop your own creations. Quick breads are convenient and inexpensive foods to try all those ideas that are uniquely "your own!"

Care and Storage of Quick Breads

Quick breads lose their fresh flavor and moisture quickly at room temperature. For a few days, they can be kept in an airtight container or a moisture-proof wrapping, such as foil or plastic. For longer storage, wrap and store in the freezer soon after baking. Frozen quick breads thaw easily for quick servings at room temperature or in the microwave at the lowest power setting.

Yeast Breads

Throughout history, bread has been the symbol of nourishment. Since ancient times, "breaking bread together" has represented hospitality and good food. Originally, the word "companion" meant "one to share bread with." The tantalizing aroma of baking bread, whether it is on the fireplace hearth of yesteryear or in your own contemporary kitchen, still reassures and soothes. Yeast breads date back to the days of the Egyptian pharaohs, but there is no ancient mystique to mastering the art of bread making with yeast. Basically, five simple ingredients, time for the various risings, and a simple kneading technique are all you need to become a master baker.

Yeast is a living organism that creates a small miracle when it is given a moist, warm place in which to grow and feed. Bread dough is the perfect place. The unique flavor and aroma of bread comes from the yeast as it converts the starch into sugar and releases carbon dioxide causing the dough to rise. Because the yeast tenderizes the gluten, you have to work extra hard to develop that protein for a firm flour structure. Contrary to the principle of gentle handling of quick breads, yeast breads require heavy handling and extensive kneading. This develops the gluten that is essential for the firm structure needed in bread. It's easy. Just relax and enjoy pounding that dough to your heart's content!

There are two basic methods of making yeast bread. The conventional method and the sponge method.

Conventional Method

1. Dissolve the yeast in warm water to start its growth. The right temperature is vital to the success of the bread. Too warm and the yeast is killed. Too cool and it will not grow. See "Food Facts" on page 293.
2. Heat the fat, sugar, and liquid. Note: When milk is used, the recipe may call for it to be scalded.
3. Cool the hot liquid mixture to a warm temperature
4. Add the dissolved yeast to the liquid mixture.
5. Add the flour.
6. Knead the dough and place it in a greased bowl for the first rising.

Master the basics of making yeast breads and you will be able to create rewarding masterpieces or "daily bread" with equal ease.

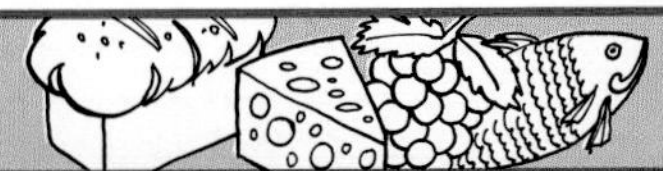

Food Facts

Yeast is the living agent that makes bread rise. It needs food from the other ingredients in the recipe and warm temperatures. The temperature is critical. Too high a temperature will kill the yeast. A temperature too low will slow down or stop the yeast's growth and production of the carbon dioxide that makes the bread rise. The best temperature varies with the method and type of yeast used in the recipe.

- **Fresh cake yeast in liquid—80° to 90°F (27° to 32°C)**
- **Dry yeast sprinkled on liquid—110° to 115°F (43° to 46°C)**
- **Dry yeast first mixed with some or all of the dry ingredients—(other ingredients bring the temperature down.)**

Use a thermometer for the exact temperature. If you have a microwave equipped with a thermometer, you can use it to heat the liquid to the exact temperature. If no thermometer is available, boil 1 cup (250 mL) water and combine with 1 cup (250 mL) ice water. This combination results in an approximate temperature of 105° to 115°F (40° to 46°C), which is right for granulated dry yeast. You should be able to hold your finger in it for the count of 10 without any discomfort. It is more difficult to estimate the lower temperature required for fresh cake yeast. If no thermometer is available, dry yeast is probably a better choice.

Sponge Method

1. Follow the first four steps of the conventional method.
2. Add part of the flour.
3. Allow the mixture to rest until it becomes frothy and bubbly (about 20-25 minutes). This bubbly mixture is called a "sponge."
4. Add the rest of the flour (and eggs if used) to the sponge.
5. Knead the dough and place in a greased bowl for the first rising.

Mixing Methods

There are several helpful techniques to mix the yeast bread ingredients. After all the first dry and liquid ingredients are blended with a small amount of flour, you can use an electric mixer. Add as much of the flour as the mixer can manage, then finish kneading by hand. When using the conventional method of mixing, you also can add ingredients to a food processor. Mix and knead for one minute. Remove the dough and place in a greased bowl for first rising.

Amount of Flour

Yeast bread recipes give a range of flour quantities rather than stating exactly how much to use, as is done for other ingredients. Since flours differ in the amount of liquid they absorb, you need to go by the feel of the dough when it has enough flour. The specific recipe will give you descriptions to guide you, such as "soft dough" or "stiff dough." In general, when the dough stays together in a ball and does not stick to the sides of the bowl, you have added the right amount of flour.

Kneading Yeast Dough

You will find that the freshly mixed ball of yeast bread dough is still sticky and soft. Kneading the dough stretches and strengthens the gluten, building the firm structure to hold in the carbon dioxide gas that the yeast gives off. That structure is then set by baking.

Kneading by hand is stretching and pushing the dough in a rocking rhythm as shown on page 295. The recipe will instruct you how long to continue the kneading process. It is usually about 10 minutes. When the dough is sufficiently kneaded, it will no longer feel

Fold the dough over.

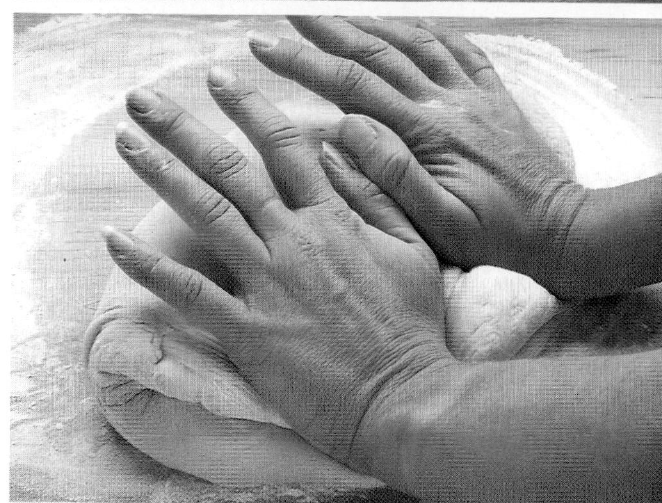

Press the dough with the heel of your hand.

Rotate the dough one quarter turn and repeat folding, pushing, and turning the dough. Refer to your recipe for the kneading time.

Cooking Hints

Rising Facts

• White bread will rise higher and faster than whole-grain breads.

• Slow rising results in a finer textured bread.

• You can interrupt the rising process by placing the partly risen bread in the refrigerator and then continue the faster rising at a warmer temperature later to fit your schedule.

• The more times your bread dough is allowed to rise, the more tender and finer textured it will be.

• If the dough is allowed to rise too much, it will collapse in the high heat of the oven. Instead, punch it down and allow it to rise again to just double its size before baking.

sticky. It will feel smooth and elastic. If it is still sticky, you may add a small amount of flour until the dough feels smooth.

Beginners usually tend to use too much flour on the board or canvas. Try to add as little extra flour as possible.

You can also knead the dough mechanically in a mixer with a dough hook attachment or the food processor. Follow the instructions that come with the appliance.

Ready to "Rise and Shine!"

If you were to immediately bake that smooth ball of dough you just kneaded, it would feel more like a baseball than a light loaf of bread. The next crucial step for breadmaking is the rising. Even though you have already noticed some bubbles forming in the dough as you kneaded it, most of the gas bubbles are formed during the rising periods in a warm, draft-free place. There are at least two rising periods. The dough ball should rise at least once, then the shaped dough rises in the baking pan.

Place the ball of dough in a greased bowl that is twice as large as the dough. Turn the dough so that the top is coated with the fat or oil. Cover the dough with a lightly greased plastic wrap, or place in a large well-greased plastic bag with a closure. (Hint: It is really simple to use a nonstick spray coating on the plastic or directly on the dough surface.)

Batter breads are usually transferred directly to the baking pan to rise. Follow the recipe directions.

Your goal is for the dough to rise to twice its original size. The yeast grows fastest at a warm temperature, but it will also grow in a refrigerator. In a warm place, the first rising averages from 45 minutes to 1 hour. In the refrigerator, it takes hours—even overnight. Yeast grows best at 75° to 85°F (24° to 30°C), which is warmer than the average room temperature. Resist the temptation to place the dough on a radiator or register. The high heat will kill the yeast. Acceptable warm places to raise dough are:

- In a gas oven that has a pilot light. The oven is turned off.
- In an oven that is turned off with a large pan or bowl of hot water on the rack beneath the dough bowl.
- On a rack above a bowl of hot water on the countertop. Drape a clean towel over the setup to hold in the heat.

Risen Enough?

When you think the dough has risen to double its original size, test it by gently pressing with your fingertips. If the dough starts to deflate and collapse, it has overrisen. Punch it down and let it rise again. If the dough retains the dent made by your fingertips, it is ready to shape. If the dent fills up and disappears, the dough should rise longer.

Punching Down

After the dough has passed the "fingertip test" for having doubled in size, punch it down to deflate it. Clench your fist and press your

The peasant shape and French bread shape are two easy ways to mold a loaf of bread.

knuckles into the dough to flatten it completely and remove all gas bubbles. Knead the dough a few times and allow it to "rest" for a few minutes before shaping.

A batter bread is deflated by stirring it down to its original size. It is simply allowed to rise again in the pan and not shaped separately.

Shaping Yeast Doughs

The most common shape for bread is obviously the loaf, but there are many creative ways to shape a "loaf of bread." When the recipe is for more than one loaf of bread, divide the dough into as many equal pieces as the recipe specifies. For the traditional loaf, pat or roll out the dough into a rectangle on a floured surface. One side of the rectangle should be the same length as the pan. Roll up the rectangle and tuck under the ends. Place it with the seam side down in a greased pan. Cover the top with a dry towel and let it rise again before baking in a preheated oven.

If you enjoy the rewards of making your own delicious bread, you might doubly enjoy creating new and different loaf shapes. Some other ways to mold a loaf are:

- **The French bread shape.** Mold a fat oval about 16 inches (40 cm) long. Score the loaf diagonally three times across the top.
- **The round peasant shape.** Mold the dough into a round ball. Place it on a greased baking sheet and flatten the ball of dough. Score a large X in the top.
- **The mushroom shape.** Divide the dough into two balls, making one twice the size of the other. Place the large ball on a greased baking sheet with the small ball on top. Punch your finger down through both balls of dough to hold them together. Cut in 2 inches (5 cm) at regular intervals around both layers.

Baking the Bread

Place the loaf of shaped bread in a preheated 375°F (190°C) oven and bake for 30 to 35 minutes depending upon the size of the loaf. When the crust is golden brown, tap the loaf. A hollow sound means it is done. Turn the pan on its side and remove the bread. Cool the loaf

on a rack, so escaping steam will not make the bottom soggy.

Storing Yeast Breads

Wait until the bread has completely cooled before covering it. Store the bread in a foil or plastic wrap. If you will not use it within two days, keep the bread in the freezer. In hot, humid weather, bread is best stored in the refrigerator to retard molding. The refrigeration does develop a stale flavor in the bread faster than room temperature does, but that is better than mold. The freezer does not seem to develop the same stale quality in breads, but freezing does not give you instant use of the bread.

Microwave Baking

Quick breads bake well in the microwave oven, but they are more compact and do not brown on top. Any type of topping will compensate for any lack of color and can contribute nutrition and flavor to the loaf. See Chapter 8.

Baking yeast breads in the microwave is not usually recommended. Reheating breads and rolls is acceptable and conveniently fast. Follow the oven manufacturer's directions.

Your Just Desserts

Sweets conquer most other flavors in any contest for general popularity. As a child you may have been "bribed" to hold still for a shot at the doctor's office by a sweet reward. A box of candy has been the valentine that is supposed to win "true love." Fancy cakes are presented on birthdays to make the person feel special. You could list numerous examples of how pleasing and rewarding a sweet treat can be. These treats were not a health concern years ago when sugar was laborious to make and sweets were rare. It would have been hard to

For a refreshing dessert, add fresh fruit to a cake such as this frosted meringue with kiwis.

overindulge yourself on candy on the frontier—unless of course you found a honey tree.

Now candy, cakes, cookies, and pies are available at affordable prices wherever you turn. Vending machines beckon where stores are not available. More young people are working and have the available money and freedom to indulge whenever they want to. Studies have shown that all this indulging is not to your best interest for general nutrition health and for preventing tooth decay. It is important that your "just desserts" should be just that. You can work some sugar in your life if you are just (fair) and work in enough opportunities for all the nutrients to get their chance before you crowd in the extra sugar and calories of dessert.

Cookies

A quick treat that is portable and versatile is the inevitable tempting cookie. Cookies can be made a number of different ways and can resemble a healthful whole-grain muffin or concentrated sugarlike candy. Choose your recipe wisely and you can satisfy your sweet tooth and still obtain valuable nutrients. Some types of basic cookie-making methods are:

Bar cookies that are baked in a shallow pan and cut into bars.

Whole-Wheat Bread

Yield: 2 loaves

Traditional	Ingredients	Metric
1 package	Active dry yeast or 1 cake compressed yeast	1 package
¼ cup	Water	50 mL
2½ cups	Hot water	625 mL
½ cup	Brown sugar	125 mL
3 tsp.	Salt	15 mL
¼ cup	Shortening	50 mL
3 cups	Whole-wheat flour, stirred	750 mL
5 cups	All-purposed white flour, sifted	1250 mL

Directions

1. Soften active dry yeast in ¼ cup (50 mL) warm water (110°F [43°C]) or compressed yeast in ¼ cup (50 mL) lukewarm water (85°F [29°C]).
2. Combine hot water, sugar, salt and shortening; cool to lukewarm.
3. Stir in whole-wheat flour and 1 cup (250 mL) of the white flour; beat well. Stir in softened yeast. Add enough of remaining flour to make a moderately stiff dough.
4. Turn out on lightly floured surface; knead until smooth and satiny (10 to 12 minutes).
5. Shape dough in a ball; place in lightly greased bowl; turning once to grease surface.
6. Cover; let rise in warm place until double in size (about 1½ hours).
7. Punch down. Cut into 2 portions; shape each one into a smooth ball. Cover and let rest 10 minutes.
8. Shape in loaves; place in greased loaf dishes. Let rise until double in size (about 1¼ hours).
9. Bake at 375°F (190°C) about 45 minutes. Cover with foil for the last 20 minutes, if necessary.

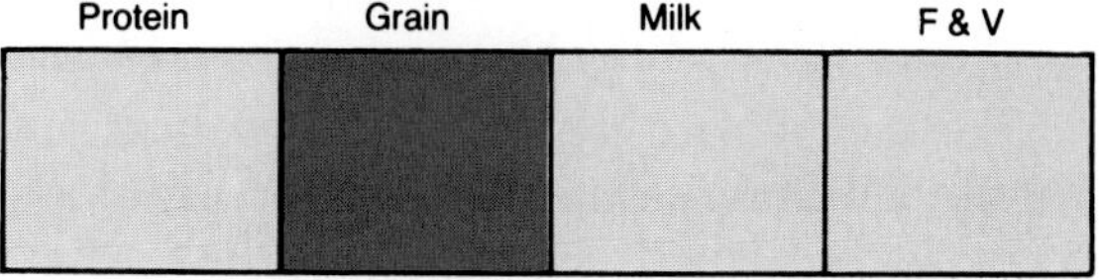

Drop cookies that are mixed and dropped on a cookie sheet.

Molded cookies that are shaped by molds for an attractive pattern.

Press cookies that are pushed through a cookie press to form different shapes.

Refrigerator cookies that are chilled in a roll and sliced to bake.

You can have almost as much fun finding cookie recipes from cookbooks and magazines as you will have making and eating them. Save ideas and make your own collection for those fun occasions that call for a cookie.

There are a few tips that will help to ensure your success in baking cookies of all types.

1. All cookies on a baking pan need to be about the same size. If they're not, they will bake unevenly and you'll have burned cookies and raw dough in the same batch. Besides, evenly shaped and sized cookies on a plate present an attractive offering.

2. Allow space between the cookies for them to expand. Otherwise you could end up with bar cookies that have to be cut into individual pieces. You might want to experiment with one cookie to see how much space works best. Generally, you will need more space between cookies made with baking powder or cookies that have been beaten a long time.

3. Check cookies often. A few seconds can make the difference between perfection and disappointment.

4. Cookie dough that requires shaping by molding, cutting, or forming with a cookie press often need chilling slightly before making.

5. Check the directions for each recipe carefully. Some cookies need to be removed immediately to prevent overbrowning on the hot pan. Others need to cool slightly to "firm-up" before removing.

Chocolate Tips

Treat chocolate gently with low heat and careful blending. Chocolate will separate and look curdled when heated to too high a temperature. It happens suddenly when melting chocolate, so watch carefully. Don't splash water or other liquid into the melting chocolate if you are going to use the melted chocolate in a smooth mixture such as icing or sauce. There are several types of chocolate available. Follow your recipe or your own personal taste for which type to use in your cooking.

Unsweetened chocolate has a strong bitter flavor. It is not for eating straight.

Cocoa results when the fatty cocoa butter is removed and the remaining chocolate is ground into a long-lasting powder. Cocoa keeps longer than smooth chocolates that still have the fatty cocoa butter in it.

Semisweet chocolate has some sugar added. It also can have varying amounts of cocoa butter and flavoring depending whether it is being sold as an eating candy or baking chocolate.

German sweet chocolate has extra sugar added.

Milk chocolate has milk or cream and sugar added. It is sold as an eating chocolate, baking chocolate, and in baking chips. It is reputedly the high fat content of the famed Dutch and Swiss chocolates that give them their luscious creamy flavors.

White chocolate is not chocolate at all, but gives you the same sensation of smoothness and sweetness.

The amount of cocoa butter is what determines the temperature point at which the chocolate "melts" in your mouth. The more cocoa butter, the faster it melts and you can taste it. The cocoa butter is quite expensive and is used liberally in the correct proportions in fancy chocolates.

Cakes

You might say that most cakes are quick breads with more sugar added and sometimes more egg and shortening. Their tender texture comes from the tenderizing action of the high amount of sugar on the flour. The sugar is what allows you to beat cakes for a long time without their getting tough. In general there are three types of cakes.

- Cakes with shortening and a leavening chemical such as baking powder.
- Cakes that have no shortening or baking powder, but use egg whites for leavening, such as angel food cakes.
- Cakes that use beaten egg whites for leavening, but also have egg yolks and shortening folded in.

There are countless delightful versions of cakes. Many are regional or ethnic in origin. Explore your favorite cookbooks to find ones that appeal to you when you feel creative and want to bake a cake "from scratch"! Follow the directions on methods and techniques in the cookbook for the recipes of your choice. Some cake baking tips include the following:

1. The recipe is a result of many tests— follow it. Use the size pan specified in the recipe or be prepared for some surprising results or failures.
2. Check on the cake's progress by looking through the window or waiting to open the oven until the cake is almost done. Cold drafts can cause the delicate structure to collapse because it is not yet set. Sometimes a heavy jar or door slamming can cause a cake to "fall."
3. Feel the top of the cake with your finger. It should spring back if the cake is done. The principles are the same as in checking to see if quick breads are done.
4. Insert a toothpick or skewer, to see if it comes out clean. If no sticky dough is on it, the cake is done.
5. Cool a cake, top down, for a few minutes on a wire rack before removing. Angel food cakes are completely cooled upside down before removing.

Pies and Pastries

Learning to make a good pie crust is a wonderful and worthwhile skill, but you can purchase frozen and premixed ones that are of an acceptable quality. A perfect pastry crust is a delectable treat and can be varied in flavor and texture to suit your purpose if you make it yourself.

Festive occasions call for out-of-the ordinary desserts. Even the preparation time can be special when family members work together.

Pastries are baked flour products that are rolled in layers to make a flaky crust. Puff pastry is made by rolling dough many times as you fold it with layers of butter over and over. The layers separate crisply and lightly when you bake the product. It is an elaborate process, but makes a marvelous product. You also can buy frozen premade puff pastry.

Pie Crust

Whether you use a single crust on the bottom or a top and bottom crust, pies can be sweet or main dish products. To make the usual crust, you combine four basic ingredients— flour, fat, cool water, and salt. If you want to have a richer crust, you can use egg and white sugar. Whole-wheat flour makes a wholesome option to the usual crust.

What type of fat (shortening) you use affects the tenderness, flakiness, and flavor of your crust.

• Lard (an animal fat high in cholesterol) makes the flakiest crust.

• Butter makes a weak crust, but one with a delicious flavor and special crispness. Some people who don't worry about cholesterol combine butter and lard in one crust to obtain the best of both these shortenings.

• Margarine makes a weak, crumbly crust with a good flavor similar to butter crusts.

• Oil can be used, but the crust requires a special method of handling. Refer to the directions on the bottle or look up guidelines in your favorite recipe book.

Basic Tips for Making a Good Pie Crust

1. Handle the dough as little as possible. You want the particles of fat to remain unmelted and distributed in the flour. The heat of your hand will melt the fat particles and that ruins the light, flaky texture of the pastry.
2. Measure the dry ingredients into the bowl and mix well.
3. Cut the cool shortening of your choice into the flour. Use two knives in a crisscross motion or a pastry blender. Mix the flour until the particles are mostly the size of a pea. See the illustration in Chapter 6.
4. Remove one-half of the mixture and set aside. Blend the rest of the flour until it resembles coarse cornmeal in texture.
5. Combine the two mixtures in one bowl.
6. Sprinkle the cool water onto the top of the flour mixture and stir slightly with a fork. Stir until the dough gathers together and seems to "follow" the fork around the bowl.
7. Mound the dough in a ball on wax paper.
8. Twist the paper to cover around the dough and let it "rest" about 10 minutes in the refrigerator. This is an optional step, but helps to cool the fat and distribute the moisture more evenly through the flour.
9. Place the ball on a floured board. Roll to the thickness called for in the recipe. Roll from the center to the outside and keep turning the dough to shape it and prevent it from sticking. Add flour to prevent sticking, but use as little flour as possible. Too much makes a stiff crust.
10. Follow the recipe directions for the type of pan and shaping needed.

The End Result

Enjoy your "just desserts" and earn them by making the whole meal the crowning glory of your creative accomplishments. Take advantage of convenience foods, your new food skills, and nutrition knowledge in planning and preparing healthful, attractive foods.

Carrot Muffins

Yield: 15 muffins

Traditional	Ingredients	Metric
1 cup	All-purpose flour	250 mL
¾ cup	Whole-wheat flour	175 mL
1 tsp.	Baking powder	5 mL
¼ tsp.	Salt	1 mL
½ tsp.	Ground cinnamon	3 mL
¼ tsp.	Ground nutmeg	1 mL
½ tsp.	Maple extract	3 mL
1 cup	Carrots, grated	250 mL
½ cup	Walnuts, chopped	125 mL
2	Eggs, beaten	2
1 cup	Buttermilk	250 mL
⅓ cup	Karo syrup	75 mL
¼ cup	Unsalted margarine, melted	50 mL
	Vegetable cooking spray	

Directions

1. Combine first 6 ingredients in a large bowl; stir in carrot and walnuts. Make a well in center of mixture.
2. Combine eggs, buttermilk, maple extract, Karo syrup, and margarine in a bowl. Add to flour mixture, stirring just until moistened.
3. Spoon batter into muffin pans coated with cooking spray, filling two-thirds full.
4. Bake at 400°F (200°C) for 20 to 25 minutes or until golden brown.

Microwave Directions

Change: add ¼ tsp. (1 mL) baking soda

1. Line microwave-safe muffin pan with two liners each.
2. Combine first 6 ingredients in a large bowl; stir in carrots and walnuts. Make a well in the center of the mixture.
3. Microwave margarine on high for 30 seconds or until melted.
4. Combine eggs, buttermilk, Karo syrup, maple extract, and margarine in bowl.
5. Add to flour mixture, stirring just until moistened.
6. Fill muffin cups two-thirds full.
7. Microwave on high for 2½ to 3 minutes, or until a wooden toothpick inserted in the center comes out clean. Rotate pan ½ turn halfway through cooking. Remove outside paper liner from muffins and cool on a wire rack.

Note: The top of the muffins may look moist after the specified cooking time, but this should disappear during the standing time. Do not overbake, or the muffins will be tough and dry.

Protein	Grain	Milk	F & V

Vocabulary Review

Baking soda
Baking powder
Yeast
Pour batter
Drop batter
Dough
Pastries

Questions for Review

1. What are some basic principles for storing flour?
2. What is the purpose for each of the following in a baked product: flour, liquid, eggs, leavening agents, fats and oils, and seasonings and flavorings?
3. Why should egg whites be at room temperature before beating them?
4. What is a leavening agent? Name several leavening agents used in baked goods.
5. What determines whether baking soda or baking powder will be used in a recipe?
6. What forms of baking powder are available?
7. What must be added to baking powder or baking soda to cause the leavening reaction? Explain.
8. Kneading dough develops the gluten in the flour. How is this helpful?
9. Yeast grows best at room temperature. Why?
10. What kinds of fats are used in baked products?
11. Can sugar, honey, molasses, corn syrups, and sugar substitutes be used interchangeably in recipes? Why or why not?
12. What problems can result when the oven temperature is not exactly what the recipe specifies?
13. What could happen if you opened the oven door in the middle of baking a cake? Why?
14. What are the two main types of quick bread batters?
15. What happens when muffin batter is overmixed? Why?
16. Overkneading biscuits results in a tough products. Why?
17. What are some safe warm places to help bread dough to rise?
18. What are the five different types of cookies? Give examples of each.
19. What determines the temperature at which chocolate melts in your mouth?
20. What are some of the main differences in making a regular cake with baking powder versus an angel food cake?

Things to Do

1. Visit a supermarket and find at least three kinds of flour. Plan an appropriate use and recipe for each. Explain your choices.
2. Look through old magazine ads and articles. Clip out examples of quick breads and yeast breads.
3. List the differences between quick and yeast bread ingredients and the time for preparation.
4. Perform the following test:
   a. Dissolve ⅓ package (or cake) of yeast in cool water.
   b. Dissolve ⅓ package in warm water.
   c. Dissolve ⅓ package in boiling water.
   d. Make a sponge with a small amount of flour with each one as described on page 294.
   Let grow in a warm place for 20 minutes. Did they all grow the same?

5. Make any muffin recipe. Take one-half of batter and put it in muffin pans. Beat remaining batter for 5 minutes put in muffin pans. Bake. Compare the resulting muffins. Cut in half and taste.

The Meat of the Matter

Do you know people who have to trap or shoot their dinner in order to put meat on the table? It has been a long time since the population depended on wildlife as their only source of food. Hunting animals has become a recreational pastime that supplements the food locker. It's unrelated to the fight for survival from starvation. A vast array of meats, poultry, and fish already dressed and skillfully prepared for cooking is available in supermarkets 24 hours a day.

Meat, the "talented star" of most meals, is the key attraction for many menus. If you think of a meal as a beautifully staged event to be presented to friends or family, then certainly it would show off the "star attraction"—the meat roast or main dish. Like the star of a play, the meat dish is usually the most expensive performer. However, its quality and lasting gifts of good nutrition can make the price a good buy.

Meat's Nutrient Gifts

Your approving applause for meat has been demonstrated by the amount of meat the average American eats at home and in restaurants. In just one year, Americans eat over 130 pounds (60 kg) of animal meats. That doesn't even count fish and poultry meats!

Meat has terrific gifts to offer. Besides the enjoyable flavor and a stick-to-the ribs ability to conquer hunger, meat offers complete proteins as well as iron and the B vitamins.

Meat is an excellent source of complete protein. That means it provides all the essential amino acids. Remember, too, that plant foods can supply complete proteins by combining them or by combining a plant protein with a small amount of meat.

Protein

Protein is the substance of which our muscles and body organs are made and is an essential nutrient for all body cells. You have to have protein from food to build and maintain your body tissues. Protein also is used by the body for energy for physical activities and maintaining body temperature. There is no substitute for protein.

Vitamins

Lean meats, such as beef, pork, lamb, and veal, are important sources for the B vitamins—thiamin, riboflavin, and niacin. How you prepare and eat the meat, however, affects whether you are able to save and use those vitamins. Because B vitamins are water soluble, they can escape in the meat juices. You can save those nutrients by eating the juice with the meat, or use the juice for sauces or gravies. Just remember to separate out the fat from the juice drippings before eating them.

Consumer Guide

Have you been confused about the terms "lite," "lean," and "extra lean" used to label meat and poultry products? If so, thank the U.S. Department of Agriculture for putting an end to the confusion.

The terms "lean" and "low fat" now may be used only for those products that contain no more than 10 percent fat. "Extra lean" refers to products that contain no more than 5 percent fat. Also, the actual amount of fat in the product will appear on the product's label. The terms "leaner," "lower fat," "light," and "lite" will be found on products containing at least 25 percent less fat than most comparable products.

Better yet, these comparisons will be explained on the label. If you were shopping for ground beef, for example, the label on a package of "leaner ground beef" might read as follows. "This product contains 20 percent fat, which is one-third less fat than in regular ground beef." (Regular ground beef can contain up to 30 percent fat, according to USDA standards.)

These new guidelines are designed to help you make better informed decisions on the quality of the meat and poultry products that you purchase. Look for them to help you select the products you really want.

Minerals

Meats are an extremely important source for the mineral iron. Vegetarians have a difficult time obtaining all the iron they need from plant sources alone. If you don't eat any meats, you might find that an iron supplement is needed to balance your diet. Meats also supply the minerals copper and phosphorus.

Iron and copper help make and maintain red blood cells. The red blood cells transport oxygen from the lungs to all the body's cells and remove the waste products. When you are not getting enough iron in your diet, your body cannot produce enough red blood cells. This causes the condition known as **anemia.** Anemic people suffer from extreme fatigue and a lowered resistance to disease. The phosphorus in lean meat is needed to build bones and teeth and to aid in the release of food's energy to the body cells.

Although there is usually a layer of fat surrounding most meats and some fat distributed within the meat, the nutrients described in the preceding paragraphs are all in the lean portion of the meats. Animal fat is a saturated fat, which is associated with the condition of a high blood cholesterol level for some people.

The 1985 Dietary Guidelines for Americans issued by the U.S. Department of Agriculture and the U.S. Department of Health and Human Services recommend avoiding too much fat, saturated fat, and cholesterol. What is "too much" varies greatly among individuals. Amounts depend upon a person's heredity and the way her or his body uses cholesterol. The exact relationship between diet and heart disease is not yet known. One point is certain. Statistics prove that individuals living within populations with diets relatively high in fat and cholesterol such as in the U.S. have a greater risk of having heart attacks than individuals within populations that have diets containing less fat. Since the saturated fat in meat contributes only a concentrated supply of energy as well as some flavor and palatability, choosing lean meats and trimming off the excess fat become wise practices.

To avoid saturated meat fat, select leaner cuts of meat. Which of these cuts of pork would have less saturated fat?

Meats make their own unique contribution of nutrients, but it would be wise to note that they do not contribute significant amounts of calcium, vitamin A, and vitamin C. There is no one miracle food. A healthy diet is a varied and balanced diet.

Selecting Meat

Buying meat can take a large chunk from anyone's food budget. Shopping mistakes can be costly and discouraging. Finding out how to choose the right cut of meat for your plans and needs can save you frustration and money.

Cuts of Meat

Some meat cuts are more tender than others. You will need to know how tender a cut of meat is before you can prepare and serve it satisfactorily. Tender cuts of meat can be cooked with dry heat. Less tender cuts of meat require moist heat. This is because less tender cuts contain more connective tissue called **collagen** that only dissolves and becomes tender with moist

Consumer Guide

Meat labels should show . . .
. . . The standard name for the cut. These include chuck, rib, loin, sirloin, round, shoulder, shank, brisket, flank, tip, breast, neck, and jowl.
. . . The cost per pound. Note that this cost per pound is not the same as the cost per serving. Meat containing bones might cost less per pound than a boneless cut, but have fewer servings. To determine the better buy, you must consider the amount of meat available for eating. See the chart on page 312 for specific guidelines.
. . . The net weight. This is what the meat and bone weigh.
. . . The total price of the package. What you will pay.

heat. The more a muscle was used by the animal, the tougher the cut of meat will be. For example, the cuts of meat from the leg areas are likely to be quite developed and therefore require moist heat in cooking. On the other hand, the long lean muscles lining the backbone do very little work and will be tender enough to cook with dry heat.

You can determine and learn the different cuts of meat by studying the charts in the Appendix. It usually isn't necessary to memorize all the names. You can become familiar the basic names and shapes of the standard cuts, the cut bone, and approximately where the cut came from on the animal. These points will guide you in determining whether that piece of meat needs moist or dry heat cooking.

Meat departments usually use a standard labeling system similar to the names in the charts, but occasionally fun titles are "invented" to help sell a cut of meat. There is nothing wrong with a name such as "patio steaks," if it also is identified with a cut that tells you what part of the animal it came from. Patio steaks in this case might be beautiful, inexpensive, lean, thick cuts wrapped in bacon. They might look like something to take home for the charcoal grill, but you would be disappointed if you did. That cut is usually from the relatively less expensive round steak that is quite tough when prepared without moist meat. Ask your meat department assistant for the source of the meat cut if it is not labeled.

Getting a Good Buy

You probably know that you don't "just get good buys"; you make them happen. You can do that by "arming yourself" with information and shopping skills. The responsibility is on your shoulders to make the right decisions amongst the countless choices facing you in the meat department.

Start with the Store

Often, you decide where to shop by how convenient it is to get there. Small convenience stores may seem worth the higher prices you pay for those "emergency" items, but buying cuts of meat calls for careful planning and the selection of a safe, reliable store. You will want to look for:

- a clean store that is convenient in location and hours to your schedule.
- a meat department with a quantity of meats from which to choose.
- a meat department that keeps a person on duty who can answer your questions or get for you the quantity and cuts you need.
- meat cases that are obviously cold and not piled so high that the top meats are out of the chilled area.
- easy to read labels with the price, size, unit pricing, and cut information you need.
- quality meats with the official United States Department of Agriculture stamp on the meat. This stamp signifies that the meat is **wholesome** (free from disease or harmful chemicals). The shield stamped on meat indicates the grade of the meat. See the illustration on page 314.

A classic American favorite, the hamburger, can be combined with textured vegetable protein (TVP) to lower both the amount of saturated animal fat and the total cost of each serving.

Once you have the store or stores selected that meet your requirements, consider the following steps when purchasing meat:

• Check the ads in the newspapers and "in store" special buys. The prices on specials usually are lowered to lure customers away from the competitive stores. If the cuts of meat match your needs, you can save money by planning your meals to take advantage of the special prices.

• Use the least expensive cut that will serve your need. It would be a waste of quality and money to use sirloin steak in chili. On the other hand, it also would be a waste to substitute a cheaper tough cut such as flank steak to make broiled shish kebobs that were too tough to chew.

• Estimate the "real cost" of the meat to you by estimating the price per serving. See again the chart on the next page.

Beef

Meat from cattle over a year old is called beef. Beef is the most popular meat consumed in America. The bright red color usually contrasts vividly with the creamy white fat. The beef cuts are the largest of the meat cuts due to the size of the animal.

Only the rib, loin, and sirloin cuts of beef are generally considered tender. All the other cuts will need moist heat and a longer, slow cooking period.

Ground beef is made from less tender cuts of meat, but cutting meat into small particles qualifies it for tender cooking methods. Remember that the less tender cuts of beef cost less than the tender cuts.

Consumer Guide

These average servings for meat purchases are based on nutritional needs and recommendations, not the "old-fashioned" piled-high quantities so popular a few years ago.

3 ounces (86 g) of lean meat	**1 serving**
1 pound (454 g) lean meat	**4 to 5 small servings. (If served alone, our society is used to a serving that appears larger than 3 ounces [86 g]. When combined in recipes, 3 ounces [86 g] should be satisfactory.)**
1 pound (454 g) hamburger	**3 to 4 servings**
1 pound (454 g) fatty meat or meat with small bones	**2 or 3 servings**
1 pound (454 g) Meat with large bones (spareribs or short ribs)	**1 serving**

Processed Beef

Processed beef means those cuts have been prepared in some way other than just the cutting. The two main forms of processed beef available in the supermarkets are:

- Corned beef made from cuts of cured beef. It is available in cans and refrigerated plastic bags.
- Dried beef (chipped beef) made from cured beef. It is sold dried in refrigerated plastic bags or cans.

Meat Extenders

To stretch the servings of meat and still add protein to the diet, **textured vegetable protein** may be added to hamburger. Made from soybeans, the textured vegetable protein supplies essential amino acids without cholesterol and at a lower cost than meat. The soybean's unique properties allow it to invisibly take on the flavor and texture of the meat when used in the right proportions. For juicy hamburgers with meat extenders, it is important not to overcook them because the extender tends to absorb the meat's juices. This makes the meat taste dry. The addition of textured vegetable protein to ground beef must be clearly marked on the label in the supermarket. Restaurants using a soybean extender in hamburger do not have to label each hamburger, but should indicate on the menu or in advertising if the meat is 100% beef.

Mild-flavored pork blends with seasonings for many types of processed sausages and sausage-like products.

Veal

Veal comes from cattle 3 to 14 weeks old. The delicate pink meat is fine grained without fat or marbling. It has a high proportion of connective tissue.

Pork

Pork is the second most popular meat consumed in America and is gaining in popularity. Pork comes from young hogs (pigs) usually not more than a year old. Before current agricultural technology in animal breeding, pork contained a high proportion of fat. Today's pork is tender and firm with a small amount of fat that is evenly marbled throughout the meat.

The pork industry and the USDA have virtually eliminated a harmful parasite called **trichinosis** from pork. Through rigid inspection procedures at the processing and slaughtering plants and high sanitation practices in the feeding and raising of pigs, this problem is no longer the health threat it once was.

Ham

Ham is cured pork leg or shoulder. It can be processed several different ways with regionally favored flavors. Ham can be purchased fully cooked and ready to eat hot or cold. It is also available uncooked so that it must be heated to a high temperature before eating. Read the label carefully to determine if a ham needs cooking. Curing ham does not make it safe to eat even though it might taste the same as cooked ham.

The shield inspection stamp indicates the grade of the meat.

Bacon

Bacon is usually made from cured pork sides. You can buy it in the following forms:

• Packaged sliced bacon. The heavy rind (pork skin) has been removed and the bacon sliced uniformly into thin or thick slices.

• Slab bacon. Just as it was cut from the pig's side, the slab bacon still has the heavy rind on it. The meat department usually cuts up the slab bacon several different ways for the meat case.

• Canadian-style bacon. This is made from boneless pork loin and is quite lean and tender. Although the price is higher, you get more servings per pound since there is less loss from melted fat. Canadian bacon can be cooked in slices like bacon, or baked whole like a ham.

Sausage

Sausage is different combinations of ground meats and seasonings. The seemingly endless variety of sausages often comes from ethnic and regional customs. Basically, the two categories for the wide variety of sausages are cooked and uncooked.

• Uncooked, or fresh sausage is stuffed into casings, such as hot dogs, or sold in bulk forms as hamburger is. It spoils extremely fast and must be cooked well before it is safe to eat.

• Cooked sausages are cured and precooked before they are sold, so they are safe to eat without further cooking. They are sold in individual casings or sliced. Bologna and hot dogs are popular examples of cooked sausages.

Lamb

Lamb comes from young sheep not more than 14 months old. Mutton is a strong-flavored meat from mature sheep that is seldom found in the supermarkets due to modern taste preferences for milder flavors and tender meat.

Variety Meats

The organs from meat animals are more graciously termed **variety meats.** All variety meats are concentrated sources of nutrients. They include brains, liver, kidney, heart, tongue, sweetbreads, and tripe. Recent research at the University of Illinois has demonstrated that the unusual grainy and sometimes soft textures of the variety meats have a strong influence on consumer taste preferences. Once you train yourself to expect a less "crunchy" texture, variety meats are easier to learn to enjoy.

Processed Meats

Processed meats have been cured or handled in some special way other than just cutting for the meat case. Curing meat is treating it with preserving ingredients such as salt, nitrates, nitrites, sugar, and smoke. These ingredients retard the spoiling process and add their own unique flavors and textures to the meat. Ham, bacon, corned beef, and dried beef are processed meats, as are luncheon meats. Luncheon meats are processed meats from different animal sources. They are shaped and sliced for convenient servings or sandwiches. Although some are available in bulk, uncut forms, the majority are packaged in plastic in the refrigerated meat case of stores.

The Care and Storing of Meat

Fresh Meat

By the time you get refrigerated fresh meat home from the store, it has warmed up. That shortens the time you can store it in your home. It would be ideal if you could carry a cooler with ice to put selected meats in at the store, but that is simply too impractical.

If you plan to store fresh meat longer than a few days, freeze it. Ground and variety meats spoil even faster than whole meats and should be frozen if not used within 48 hours.

Meat should be kept in the coldest part of the refrigerator. If it is wrapped in butcher paper, rewrap it loosely with wax paper or foil. You can store meat in the prepacked plastic wrap, but the store wrap is not sufficient for freezing. For those packages, add an outer layer of freezer wrap or foil. Mark all packages with the date and contents.

Processed Meats

Refrigerate the various processed meats as follows:

- Bacon and sliced luncheon meats are cured and will keep about 2 weeks in the sealed package. Once that seal is broken, use them within 5 days. Otherwise wrap them well and freeze. Freezing cured meats keeps them from spoiling, but it also breaks down the texture and flavors.
- Hams that are cured should be used within 1 week. Canned hams sometimes need to be refrigerated, but can be stored longer before opening. Read the label to find out how to store them. After opening, use within a week. Hams that have been processed with added water change texture and flavor when frozen.
- Cooked, smoked sausages should be used within 4 to 5 days. Slicing creates a surface area for bacteria to attack, so sliced sausages spoil faster. Use them within 2 to 3 days.
- Uncured bacon is simply uncooked pork and should be used within 4 to 7 days.
- Canned meats vary in their storage requirements. Read the label.

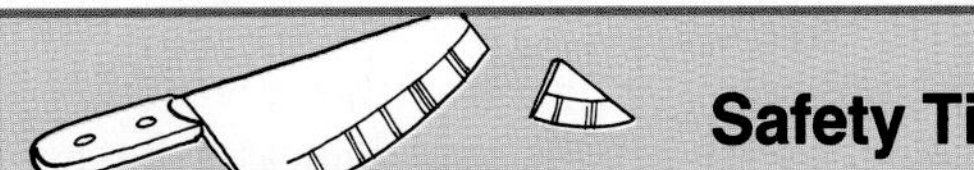

Safety Tip

Meat that has started to spoil will show danger signals even before you notice an odor or off-flavor. First, the color turns gray on the surface, and then throughout the meat. The meat develops an unpleasant odor. You also may notice that the meat surface feels slippery or slimy. Do not taste a suspected food to see if it is spoiled. With some bacteria, even a tiny taste can be dangerous. Besides, the most harmful bacteria can be tasteless and odorless. No food is worth the risk. Throw it away if there is any real doubt.

Defrosting Meat

Resist the temptation to thaw meat on the counter at room temperature. Defrost meat in the refrigerator. Just leave it in its freezer wrap on a dish to catch any juices. If you have to hurry, thaw it in the microwave or try to cook it frozen.

Some people like steaks broiled frozen to avoid overcooking in the middle. Of course, shaping hamburgers and cutting up stew meat is next to impossible frozen. Planning ahead can avoid this problem. Shape fresh ground beef into patties and freeze with pieces of foil or waxed paper in between the patties. You can then take out the number you need. The secret is to plan ahead. Once a meat is defrosted, cook it. Do not refreeze meat without cooking it first. The cooking kills any harmful bacteria that might have formed during the thawing. Refreezing does not!

Principles of Cooking Meat

One of the first steps toward civilization was discovering the joys of cooked meat. The many legends describing that moment all point to the miracle of cooking as a means to preserve meat. Later in history, the killing and roasting of animals began to take on a hospitable and ceremonious nature. To this day, the presentation of the glorious roast sizzling from the oven with juices flowing and aroma alerting the senses makes a meal a "happening"!

You cook meat to make it more tender, improve its flavor, and to destroy harmful organisms. During the cooking process, the meat develops a rich brown color and aroma. The basic principle for cooking meats is that meat is a protein food which is made tough and dry by high heat. Low temperatures will gently coagulate the meat protein and still hold in the juices. Remember that the less tender cuts of meat have more collagen, which requires moisture and heat to dissolve. Moisture, low temperatures, and slow cooking combine to soften collagen and other connective tissues and tenderize the meat.

Methods of Tenderizing Meat

You can tenderize meats by physically breaking or cutting the connective tissues, softening the connective tissue with acidic marinades, or using a commercial enzyme to "digest" the connective tissue in meat.

- Grinding, pounding, and cutting are methods that break or cut the fibers and connective tissues.
- Acids in the form of tomatoes, vinegar, lemon juice, or sour cream will soften the tough tissues. Marinating (soaking) meats in a flavored acid mixture both flavors and tenderizes less tender cuts of meats. This enables them to be cooked by dry heat methods.
- Commercial meat tenderizers sprinkled on tough cuts of meats actually start "digesting" the tough tissues before cooking. You can expect tenderizing with this method to shorten the cooking time by about 25 percent. The protein-digesting enzyme used in these commercial tenderizers is from plant sources such as pineapples, figs, or green papayas.

When Is the Meat Done?

Cooking time and the temperature of the meat clue you in to when the meat is done to the level you desire. In methods such as broiling or braising, when a thermometer is not practical to use, you decide when to remove the meat by its appearance and the cooking time.

Using Temperature for Doneness

A meat thermometer inserted into the thickest part of the meat shows you the internal temperature. Be sure the thermometer is not touching bone or fat. Cookbooks and meat thermometers specify what the internal temperature should be for different kinds of meats.

Most roasts will continue to cook after they have been removed from the oven as they are "resting" before carving. To avoid overcooking, remove the roast shortly before it is done. That should be about 5°F under the desired temperature or five minutes early.

Using Appearance for Doneness

For broiled or braised meats, time them according to size and the type of heat used. Cookbooks list times for different cooking methods. After the required time, cut a small slit in the thickest part of the meat. Red juice in the cut means the meat is rare, while pink to no color

Lean pork combines well with other foods to make popular dishes. By serving an herbal pork chop with steamed vegetables, you can create an attractive, tasty dinner. What other foods could you add to make a complete well-balanced meal?

indicates medium to well done. Use this test sparingly. Every time you pierce the meat, flavorful juices are lost.

Some experienced cooks judge doneness by the reaction of meat when you feel it with your finger. If the meat feels soft and springs back, it is underdone. If the meat feels firm and does not give, it is well done or overdone. Experience will teach you to recognize the degree of doneness you prefer.

Cooking Hints

How done is done? Just how done you want your meat depends upon your own personal preference. Of course, meat should never be cooked to a dry tough stage, but there are four levels of doneness for tender cuts of meat. Generally accepted in homes and restaurants are the terms rare, medium rare, medium, or well done.

- ***Rare*** **refers to meat that is crisp and dark on the outside and red and juicy on the inside. The inside should be warm to the touch, but not actually cooked all the way through.**
- ***Medium rare*** **describes rare meat that is cooked just a bit more on the inside, but still has a red strip of color.**
- ***Medium*** **means the inside is almost all gray, with just a hint of pink in the middle.**
- ***Well-done*** **meat is cooked evenly throughout the whole piece of meat. It tends to be much drier and less tender than the other levels of doneness. Some people think it is a waste to cook any tender cut of meat to the well-done stage because it is so much drier.**

Special Temperature Requirements

Pork should be cooked to 160°F (71°C) to kill any trichina parasites that might be in the meat. This is probably an unnecessary concern because of today's regulations in the pork industry. However, it is still considered by many to be a worthwhile precaution. Besides, the pork meat has more flavor when cooked to a higher heat.

When to Salt Meat

Conscientious cooks love to debate over their charcoal grill about the question of when to salt cooking meat! The choice is yours, but the fact is that salt draws out the juice from the meat. This action both delays browning and dries out the meat sooner. A steak is greatly affected by this drying, but a roast is thick enough that the salt action doesn't penetrate more than about ½ inch (1.3 cm) into the meat.

Starting with Frozen Meat

For those "spur of the moment" times when you can't plan ahead to defrost meat overnight in the refrigerator or defrost it in the microwave oven, you can cook it while it is still frozen. Allow about 50 percent more time to cook meat that is frozen.

Broiling Meat

Broiling (called grilling when done outdoors over charcoal) is a dry-heat method suitable for tender meats, poultry, and fish. The secret to broiling is to use the right thickness of a tender meat cut and the right distance from the broiler rack to the heat source. Steaks and chops should be at least ¾ to 1 inch thick (2 to 2.5 cm) or they will dry out before they are cooked. The distance should range from 3 to 6 inches (7.5 to 15 cm) from the heat source. For a juicy inside and a browned, crisp outside,

Grilling meat brings out a well-developed flavor. What cuts of meat are best for this cooking method?

broil the meat closer to the heat for a short time.

Do not pierce the meat to check doneness. Try the fingertip test or go by the time recommended in a recipe. The time for ¾ to 1 inch thick (2 to 2.5 cm) steaks and chops will vary, but averages from 10 to 20 minutes. Do not overcook!

Other cooking guidelines include:

- For even cooking throughout the piece of meat, move the rack farther from the heat.
- Cook thicker pieces farther from the heat source. Cook thinner pieces faster and closer to the heat source.
- Do not season meats before broiling or grilling. Salt will dry out the meat, while pepper and other spices might burn and turn bitter.
- Turn foods with tongs or two spoons. Piercing meat with a fork allows juices to escape.
- Drier meats may benefit from being brushed with oil before broiling.

Panbroiling Meat

Panbroiling is sometimes called dry frying because you broil the meat in a skillet. A heavy iron skillet is best because it holds the heat so well. Since no fat is added to the pan for this dry-heat method of cooking, only well marbled tender cuts of meat should be used because of their fat content. Chops or steaks need to be at least 3/4 inch thick (2 cm) to avoid drying out.

Directions

1. Preheat the pan. You might oil the surface lightly to seal it and avoid sticking.
2. Do not salt the meat.
3. Cook the meat for a few minutes on each side.
4. Test for doneness by feeling with your fingertip. If in doubt, make a small cut to check the color of the juice. Avoid this method if possible, since cutting the meat allows the loss of valuable, tasty juices.

Frying Meat

Perhaps the easiest, almost no-thinking cooking method for small cuts of meats is frying. Select the frying pan, melt a small amount of fat, and brown thin pieces of tender meat.

Deep-fat frying takes a large deep heavy pot that fits steadily on the burner. The hot fat presents several potentially dangerous situations in the kitchen. Burns from spilled or spattering grease and potential fire from spilled or overheated fat makes deep-fat frying a cooking method to be treated with respect and care.

Deep-fat fried meats are usually breaded with egg and crumbs or a premixed batter before frying.

Roasting Meat

True roasting is a dry-heat method in which all sides of the meat are cooked by hot air. It is not a suitable method for very lean meats or cuts with a lot of connective tissue.

Before roasting, bring the beef, veal, or lamb roast to room temperature. This takes about 2 hours. Pork and variety meats spoil faster and should be roasted without warming. Meats can be seasoned before roasting, but it is generally better not to do it.

Directions

1. Place the meat fat side up on a rack in a shallow baking pan.
2. Insert a meat thermometer so that it is resting in the largest part of the roast, but not touching a bone or fatty part. The bone and fat heat differently than the meat.
3. Place the meat in a preheated oven and note the time, or set a timer. Do not cover the roast or add water to the pan.
4. Remove the roast a few minutes or about 5°F before it is done. Let it "rest" in a warm place for 15 to 20 minutes to firm up for carving. The hot roast also continues to cook during this time. Removing it from the oven early prevents it from getting overdone.

Braising Meat

Braising less tender cuts of meat can turn them into succulent pot roasts, stews, and casseroles. These hearty yet simple dishes can be as elegant as the occasion demands. Perhaps you remember tasting a favorite pot roast after the slow, unhurried cooking with a steaming liquid had developed a flavor like nothing else. When cooked just right, the less tender and more economical cuts of meat often have more flavor.

Chuck, rump, and round roasts are ideal beef candidates for braising. Pork works well for braising also because the long slow cooking is ideal for developing the mild flavor.

In braising, the meat can be placed on a layer of vegetables that act to flavor the steaming liquid. In gourmet terms, this vegetable bed is known as mirepoix. These mushy, overcooked vegetables are usually strained out before the gravy is made.

Braising Equipment

A heavy pot with a tight-fitting lid is essential for braising and pot roasting. It needs to be just large enough to hold the meat. If the pot is much larger, most of the liquid that condenses on the inside of the lid will not fall back over the roast to braise it.

Directions

1. Brown the meat in hot melted fat using the pot or a separate skillet.
2. Add seasoning and 1/2 cup (125 mL) liquid to the meat in the pot. The liquid can be stock, water, or marinade.
3. Cover the pot tightly and cook over low heat on top of the stove or in a 325°F (160°C) oven.
4. Cook about 20 minutes per pound of meat.
5. Check for a falling-apart tenderness with a fork.
6. Remove the meat to a warm plate.
7. Skim the fat from the juices in the pan. Season the juices. If the liquid is thin, you can add 1 teaspoon (5 mL) of cornstarch dissolved in 2 teaspoons (10 mL) of cool water to thicken the sauce.

Meat Marinade

Yield: 6 servings
Oven: 350°F (175°C)
Equipment: 2-quart (2 L) casserole, saucepan

Traditional	Ingredients	Metric
4 Tbsp.	Olive oil*	60 mL
1 clove	Garlic, crushed	1 clove
1	Bay leaf	1
1 small sprig	Fresh thyme (or ¼ tsp. Dried Thyme)	1 small sprig
4 Tbsp.	Lemon juice or tomato juice	60 mL

Directions

1. Blend all ingredients together. Use to marinade meat.
2. For lamb, chicken, or beef, you can substitute these herbs for the thyme: rosemary, fresh parsley, and tarragon.
3. For pork, use sage or savory.
4. For fish, use fresh or dried dill and fresh or dried fennel.

* Regular oil may be substituted for olive oil or soak four olives for several days in a salad oil in the refrigerator.

Cooking Hints

Some fat in a sauce, gravy, or soup adds to the characteristic flavor. However, the excess grease that floats to the top of food is undesirable for the product's quality and your health.

When your recipe directions say, "skim the fat," "degrease the drippings," "blot the excess grease," or even "render the fat," it means remove the extra fat from the product by one of the following simple methods.

Pot Roasting

Pot roasting generally follows the same procedure as braising, but without the base of flavoring vegetables. Use a heavy pot with a tight-fitting lid.

Directions

1. Prepare and brown the meat the same as for braising.
2. Season the meat and add any herbs or spices desired.
3. Pour in 1 to 2 cups (250 to 500 mL) of liquid. Bring to a boil on top of the stove.
4. Cover the pot and cook on top of the burner or in a 325°F (160°C) oven about 20 minutes per pound of meat.
5. About 1 hour before meat is due to be done, add whole onions, carrots, small potatoes, and celery stalks. You also can use other vegetables of your choice such as parsnips or turnips. Unlike in braising, these vegetables are not overcooked and strained out. They are served with the meal.
6. Check the roast quickly about once an hour to add more hot liquid if needed. Add 1/2 cup (125 mL) at a time.

Cooking Stews (Meat in Liquid)

Flavorful stews are made using the same slow cooking method as for braising or pot-roasting. A stew, however, has cut up meat and more liquid. You also do not brown the meat first. Most stew meats have a lot of connective tissue. If you started the stew by high-heat browning the meat, you would toughen the protein to the point where even the stewing process might not tenderize it. Note: If you do use a more tender meat, you can brown the meat to make a darker, rich stew.

Directions

1. Using a heavy pan with a tight-fitting lid, add the unheated liquid to the meat and other ingredients. Add vegetables of your choice, or use any leftovers in the refrigerator. Potatoes and other starchy vegetables will naturally thicken the liquid for a nice gravy.
2. Bring to a slow simmer. Allow to cook for as long as it takes to completely tenderize the meat pieces and produce a rich, meaty gravy.

A slow cooker is a great way to make stews. Put the ingredients in the cooker in the morning and when you arrive home in the evening your meal is done.

Defatting Liquids

Method 1

Holding the corner of a paper towel, place it over the top of the warm liquid. The excess fat floating on top absorbs into the towel. Lift the towel carefully and discard with the unwanted grease. The remaining liquid is ready to use.

Method 2

Float several ice cubes in the liquid. Move them gently around the surface of the liquid or drippings. The fat cools and solidifies around the surface of the ice cubes. Using a skimmer or slotted spoon, skim off the solid fat and discard.

Braising meat requires a heavy pot sized right so that the condensation on the inside of the lid drips back on the meat for flavorful, moist cooking.

Method 3

Chill the liquid in the refrigerator. All the fat in the liquid rises to the top and becomes solid as it cools. Remove the solid fat with your fingers.

Method 4

When there is a large amount of fat in the liquid or drippings, a layer of the liquid fat will rise to the surface. You can see it. Pour the liquid into a clear liquid measuring cup with a pouring spout. Let the layers settle for a few minutes. Carefully and slowly pour the top layer of fat into another container. If you are careful, you will not disturb the bottom layer of liquid. If there are solid bits of food in the liquid, you may choose to pour fat off through a strainer. The liquid that is left is defatted and ready to use.

Microwaving Techniques

Refer to Chapter 8.

Marinated Pork Salad

Yield: 4-6 servings

Traditional	Ingredients	Metric
1 lb.	Pork cutlets or tenderloin	500 g
⅓ cup	Bottled Italian or herb salad dressing	75 mL
6 cups	Romaine lettuce, washed and torn	1500 g
¾ cup	Mayonnaise	175 mL
1 Tbsp.	Lemon juice	15 mL
2 tsp.	Worcestershire sauce	10 mL
3 - 4 drops	Tabasco	3 - 4 drops
½ - 1 cup	Croutons	125 - 250 mL
1 - 2 Tbsp.	Shredded Parmesan cheese	15 - 30 mL
	Freshly ground pepper	

Directions

1. Pound or cut pork ¼ inch (.64 cm) thick.*

2. Put pork into a non-metal bowl; pour Italian dressing over and marinate at least 1 hour, turning once or twice.

3. Combine mayonnaise, lemon juice, Worcester sauce, and Tabasco.

4. Broil or sauté pork, 3 minutes on each side or until done. Cut into ½ inch (1.3 cm) strips.

5. Toss pork, Romaine, croutons, Parmesan cheese, and ground pepper together.

6. Serve topped with a spoonful of mayonnaise dressing.

Note: Cooked pork may be used. Marinate 2 cups (500 mL) cut-up lean pork in Italian dressing for 1 hour.

*Tenderloin cuts easily if partially frozen.

Protein Grain Milk F & V

Vocabulary Review

Anemia	Processed beef	Trichinosis
Collagen	Textured vegetable protein	Ham
Wholesome	Veal	Sausage

Questions for Review

1. About how many pounds of meat does the average American eat per year? Why is this statistic of interest to nutritionists?
2. What are some of the nutrients that meat supplies?
3. What nutrient do you get from eating meat that would be difficult to obtain the recommended daily allowance of from other sources?
4. What does the U.S. Department of Agriculture stamp on meat mean?
5. Name some tender cuts of meat that are suitable for dry-heat cooking methods. Why are those cuts tender?
6. What is the best method for handling and storing fresh meat?
7. What is the safe way to thaw frozen meat?
8. What are some factors to consider in selecting a store to purchase your meats?

9. How can you remove some of the fats and cholesterol from meats?

10. What basic principles need to be remembered when cooking meats?

11. Where do you insert the meat thermometer to test for doneness?

12. What are the guidelines to follow when broiling meat to retain the juiciness and tenderness?

13. What are some danger signs of spoiled meat? Why is it an unsafe practice to taste a meat to test for spoilage?

14. What is the difference between rare, medium-rare, and well-done meat? What meat is unsafe to eat rare?

15. Explain what happens to thin cuts of meat that are salted before being grilled, broiled, or baked? Why doesn't salt affect a large roast the same way it affects a thin cut of meat?

Things to Do

1. Hunt through magazines for ads that mention saturated fats and/or cholesterol in relation to meats. Do all of the ads agree about the pros and cons of eating meat and meat products? From what you have learned in this book, which ads seem more accurate? Why?

2. Draw a rough outline of an animal used for meat. You can illustrate cattle (beef), pigs (pork), or sheep (lamb). Generally point out which parts are cut into the familiar basic cuts, such as ribs, roasts, steaks, ground meat, and specialty cuts.

3. Buy a 5/8-inch (1.6 cm) thick piece of lean round steak with very little marbling. Cut it into four pieces. Pound one with a meat tenderizer (like making your own cube steak). Use a powdered meat tenderizer on one piece following the directions on the label. Do nothing to the remaining two pieces.

A. Panfry in a small amount of fat the pounded, commercially tenderized, and one plain piece of meat for a few minutes on each side. Use low heat and no lid.

B. Panfry the last piece of untreated meat on both sides, but add 1/4 cup (50 mL) of tomato juice or other liquid to the meat. Cover and cook over low heat just until the liquid evaporates.

Time the cooking so all the pieces will be done at about the same time. Taste and compare the pieces for tenderness, flavor, texture, and juiciness. Which pieces were tender? Describe and explain any difference in flavor. How did the textures vary? Which one or ones did you like best? Why? From the results of this test, how would you prepare the same cut of meat another time?

The All-American Birds

Just imagine a steaming, hot, golden turkey surrounded by tart orange halves filled with a jeweled cranberry relish on a beautiful serving platter. Does that suggest anything special to you? Americans have associated the roasting of a fowl, whether it be wild turkey or domesticated chicken, with the celebration of a new happening or a traditional holiday. Even the daily availability of the "Colonel's" southern fried chicken has not detracted from the elegance of a fine bird prepared and served with care. From elegant dining to inexpensive eating, chicken fits the occasion.

You can purchase protein-rich chicken or turkey for a fraction of the cost of the red meats and get a low-cholesterol bonus in the bargain. The old wishful saying "a chicken in the pot every Sunday" has become a reality. What's more, chicken is so versatile and economical, you could serve it every day of the year and never repeat the same recipe.

Nutrient Notes

Poultry belongs to the meat division of the Basic Four Food Groups. This identifies it as both a high-quality and a high-quantity protein food. At the same time, turkey and chicken are relatively low in calories and low in cholesterol. This is especially true of the white meat. The duck and goose contain a higher proportion of fat than any of the other poultry. All poultry are rich in vitamins and minerals.

Meet the Poultry Family

You can get acquainted with the flavors and features of the whole domesticated poultry family from one trip to the supermarket. Most large stores sell chicken, turkey, duck, goose, and specialty chickens such as rich Cornish game hens in the meat department. Their distant cousins from "out-of-town" include specialty game birds such as quail, squabs, doves, pheasant, and wild turkey. These can be ordered frozen through specialty food catalogs.

Forty years ago, Americans ate only about ½ pound (250 g) of chicken a year. Now they consume about 40 pounds (20 kg) a year, and that does not include the other types of poultry.

The mild, adaptable flavor of poultry blends with most foods to create an amazing range of recipes from almost every region of the world. An instant world tour takes you to Mexico for *chicken mole* made with chocolate or northern

India for *tandoori,* a skewered, spiced chicken with yogurt. From France comes *canard a l'orange,* a roast duck with orange sauce. Texas has barbecued chicken, and perhaps your own home offers everyone's favorite, roast turkey with sage dressing.

Chicken

Most meat departments offer chickens packaged whole, cut-up whole, or in quantities of similar pieces such as breasts, wings, thighs, and livers.

Food Facts

Where does the chicken come from? There is a time when the chicken definitely comes first—before the egg! Most chicken farmers do not own their own chickens. They raise them for a large company. The company supplies the farmer with both the baby chickens and the feed to raise them. Only about 1 percent of the 30,000 chicken farmers in the United States own their own chickens. The farmers raise large quantities of the fowl and then sell them back to the company by the pound. Using the new technologies developed by universities and companies, a chicken farmer can raise 150,000 chickens and more a year! A total of approximately 4½ billion broilers a year are raised.

The new chickens, feeds, and raising methods have decreased the time it takes to grow market-size poultry and with less feed, too. In fact, if you grew as fast as the new breeds of chickens do, you would have weighed 349 pounds by the time you were two months old.

Chickens are available fresh-chilled or frozen. **Fresh-chilled** poultry is cooled to a temperature just above the freezing point for the meat. The excess juice around the chicken parts may freeze partially. The extreme low temperature helps to preserve the meat, save juices, and prevent some messy leakings.

Chickens also are used in processed sandwich spreads, luncheon meats, and sausages. You can even purchase convenience forms of chicken preserved by canning and freezing. For example, it is possible to buy frozen diced chicken for use in quick salads and casseroles.

When you buy convenience foods that have been partially or fully prepared for you, the cost will be higher. You are paying for the labor and processing costs. Sometimes the cost of convenience is worth the price, but as a consumer you should be aware of the reasons for the costs. You might decide to buy more of the nonconvenience food and do the preparing yourself. Such decisions need to be based on individual needs and circumstances.

Determine the true cost of fowl by comparing the amount of meat (the part available to eat) with the price. For example, comparing the price of $2.40 for four chicken backs to $3.00 for two boneless chicken breasts could mean first determining the number of servings in each package. Consider that the amount of meat in four chicken backs will barely make one serving. On the other hand, two breasts will divide into three servings. The true cost per serving is $2.40 for the backs and $1.00 for the breasts. In this example, the higher package price for the boneless chicken breast meat really is the least expensive meat due to amount of waste from bone in the backs. The general guidelines for purchasing servings is to buy 1 lb. (500 g) of whole chickens or parts with bones for one serving. For one serving of boneless meat, you will need ½ lb. (250 g).

Turkeys

Turkeys are available in the meat department packaged whole, prestuffed, in boneless rolls, ground, and cut in parts. Processing a large turkey into more usable portions has increased the use of turkey for year-around use. The introduction of the turkey breast for a small roast also created many uses for turkey.

Processed turkey is available in both smoked and cured forms. In recent years, the process for making a product that tastes, feels, and looks just like a pork ham has expanded the turkey market. Hot dogs and luncheon meats that resemble pork and beef products are also being made from turkey. The low-fat and low-cholesterol qualities of the turkey open up food possibilities for persons on special diets.

Allow about 1 lb. (500 g) of whole turkey for a serving. When choosing between turkey sizes, remember that the larger size of any fowl has more servings per pound. This is because there is more meat in proportion to the amount of bones.

Ducks

There is no white meat on ducks. All the meat is dark, tender, juicy, and extremely flavorful.

Ducks have an amazing amount of fat compared to the leaner types of poultry such as turkey and chicken. Because so much more of the duck weight melts away as fat, you get fewer servings per pound of duck. Allow 1½ lbs. (700 g) of duck meat for a serving.

Geese

Geese also are a dark meat and have a high fat content. Plan on the same amount per serving as for ducks.

Grilled Sesame Chicken Breasts

Yield: 4 servings

Traditional	Ingredients	Metric
½ cup	White grape juice	125 mL
¼ cup	Reduced-sodium soy sauce	50 mL
1 Tbsp.	Sesame seeds	15 mL
2 Tbsp.	Vegetable oil	30 mL
¼ tsp.	Garlic powder	1 mL
¼ tsp.	Ground ginger	1 mL
4, 4 oz.	Boneless chicken breast halves, skinned	4, 125 g
2 Tbsp.	Unsalted butter	30 mL

Directions

1. Combine first seven ingredients in a shallow dish; mix well. Add chicken, turning to coat; cover and marinate in the refrigerator for two hours.

2. Remove chicken from marinade, reserving marinade. Melt butter, sauté in skillet 15 minutes, turning and basting frequently with reserved marinade.

Microwave Directions

1. Combine first seven ingredients in a shallow dish; mix well. Add chicken, turning to coat; cover and marinate in the refrigerator for two hours.

2. Place chicken in a 10x7x2 inch (25x18x5 cm) microwave-safe baking dish with thicker pieces toward the outside. Reserve marinade. Cover with waxed paper and microwave on High for 3 minutes.

3. Turn and rearrange chicken pieces. Microwave, covered, on High for 2½ minutes, or until chicken is tender. Brush the chicken every 30 seconds with the reserved marinade.

4. Microwave remaining marinade in a 1-cup (250 mL) glass measure on High for 2½ minutes, or until hot. Serve in a small pitcher.

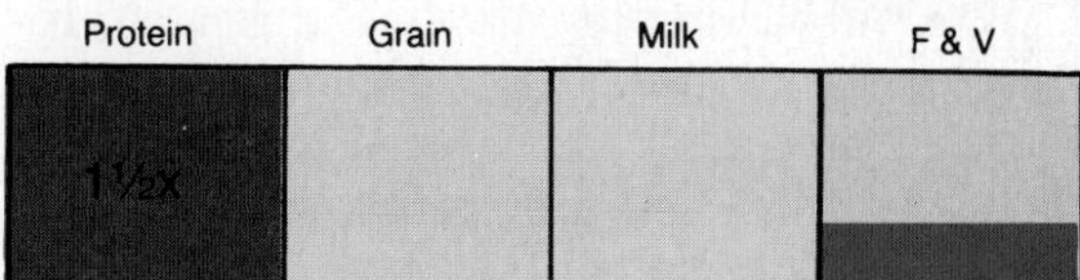

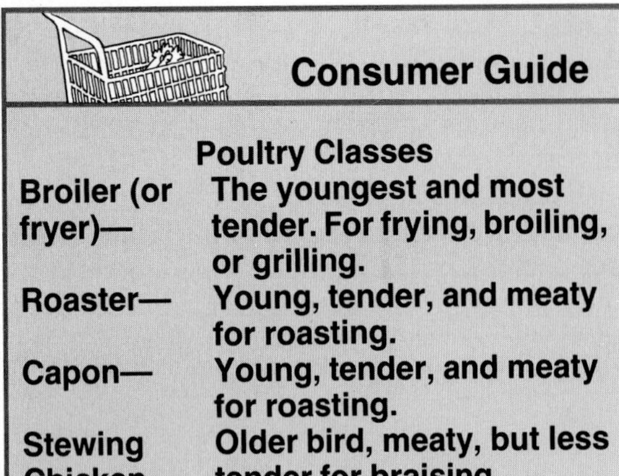

Consumer Guide

Poultry Classes

Broiler (or fryer)—	The youngest and most tender. For frying, broiling, or grilling.
Roaster—	Young, tender, and meaty for roasting.
Capon—	Young, tender, and meaty for roasting.
Stewing Chicken—	Older bird, meaty, but less tender for braising, stewing, or simmering.

Selecting Poultry

USDA Grades

The USDA grades poultry according to its quality and wholesomeness. Grade A identifies a top-quality bird that is meaty. It is good looking with no broken bones, bruises, or pin feathers.

Grade B birds are less meaty and not quite as attractive. This grade usually is not sold directly to consumers, but to food companies for use in foods such as soups and casseroles where the appearance of the bird is not important.

Poultry Classes

Select the poultry that is appropriate for the method you want to use. The USDA wholesomeness and quality inspections do not indicate the poultry's age. The class title on the label does. **Poultry classes** identify the bird by age and weight. The classes include broiler (or fryer), roaster, capon, or stewing chicken. See the chart above.

You will need to buy the class that is appropriate for your needs. The younger the bird, the more tender but less flavorful it will be. The older birds have more fully developed flavor, but are less tender.

A **capon** is the name of a class, but the term represents a type of bird, not the age. Capons are neutered roosters, a treatment that enables them to grow large and meaty but still stay tender.

Storing Poultry

Poultry spoils quickly. Cutup poultry is more perishable than the whole bird because there is more surface area in which bacteria can be introduced and grown. When you bring fresh-chilled poultry home from the store, open the package and rinse the poultry with cool water. Remove the **giblets** (organs) from the cavity of whole birds and save them for making stock. (**Stock** is the flavored liquid used as a base in many recipes and soups.) Pat the poultry dry and wrap it loosely in its original plastic wrapper or wax paper. The air circulation through the loose covering helps retard the growth of some bacteria for one to two days.

To freeze poultry that was purchased unfrozen, remove it from the store package, remove the giblets, rinse the bird, and pat it dry. Cut it into pieces. Wrap it tightly in aluminum foil, plastic freezer wrap, or coated freezer paper. Label it with the date and contents.

Poultry that was purchased frozen can be stored in its original wrapping. You can keep poultry in the freezer several months.

Cool and store turkey and dressing separately before and after cooking. Prestuffed turkeys are available on the market, but generally are not recommended due to the potential for food spoiling. If you do purchase a prestuffed bird, do not thaw it before cooking. Roast it frozen.

Principles of Cooking Poultry

Poultry is basically a high protein food, so you follow the rules for protein cooking. Since protein becomes dry and tough in high temperatures, the first rule is to cook at a low temperature to preserve the tenderness. The second

Turkey luncheon meats offer a healthful alternative for hearty sandwiches.

rule is to use the age of the bird to determine the best method of cooking. Young birds are more tender than older birds. Broil or fry young birds. You can tenderize the older birds with the moist-heat cooking methods, such as braising and stewing.

Poultry must be cooked until well done. The meat is not safe or tasty to eat rare.

Most of the fat that occurs in poultry is located just under the skin, not distributed throughout the meat. For low-fat diets, the skin and thus the fat is always removed before cooking or eating. The meat from the new breeds of fast-growing chickens tend to darken around the bones during cooking. This coloring is harmless, tasteless, and should be ignored. Sometimes fresh poultry that has not been frozen seems to darken less than meat that has been frozen.

You will need to plan ahead to use frozen poultry. Defrost poultry in the refrigerator in the original wrapping. Do not defrost at room temperature. Out of the refrigerator, the bird's skin temperature warms to room temperature. This can encourage the growth of harmful bacteria while the rest of the bird is still thawing. If you have a defrost power setting on your microwave, you can use it to thaw poultry.

Broiling

Young tender chickens and turkeys can be broiled. The young birds range in size as follows:

- Chickens—1½ to 2½ pounds (0.7 kg to 1.1 kg)
- Turkeys—4 to 6 pounds (1.8 to 2.7 kg)

You can cut both turkeys and chickens to the size and shape that suits the recipe you want to use. Cut the birds into halves, quarters, or individual pieces and broil or grill with or without the bones.

Deboning chicken can produce impressive products that are attractive, tasty, and easy to eat. There are several different ways to remove the bones from various parts of poultry. Some of those methods will be discussed in the following discussions on cooking methods.

Marinating broiling chicken and turkey flavors and tenderizes the meat. Soak the meat for 30 minutes to 2 hours in the **marinade** (flavoring and tenderizing liquid). A longer soaking time for tender fryers would result in mushy textured meat. Broil the meat using the marinade for basting during cooking.

Cut-up poultry pieces of duck, goose, and capons can be broiled. The higher fat content in the meat of these birds allows them to be broiled without basting.

Directions

1. Arrange the poultry pieces in a shallow pan. It isn't necessary to use a rack due to the low fat content of the fryers. Fold the wing tips back behind the shoulder or larger bone to prevent the small tip from burning.
2. To help seal in the juices, brush the meat surface with an oil, melted fat, barbecue sauce, or marinade. Place chicken with bone side down about 4 inches (10 cm) from the source of heat. Place turkey with bone side down about 9 inches (23 cm) away from the heat.
3. Turn the pieces at least once during the cooking time to ensure even cooking and browning. Use the tongs to turn the poultry rather than a cooking fork. Piercing the meat with a fork causes juices to be lost.
4. Broiling usually takes from 20 to 30 minutes depending upon the size of the pieces.

Dilled Chicken Pasta Salad

Yield: 8 servings

Traditional	Ingredients	Metric
6 oz.	Seashell pasta, cooked *al dente* without salt or fat	185 g
2 cups	Turkey breast, roasted	500 mL
2 cups	Tomatoes, chopped	500 mL
½ cup	Celery, diced	125 mL
¼ cup	Red onion, minced	50 mL
¼ cup	Fresh parsley, chopped	50 mL
1 tbsp.	Vegetable oil	15 mL
1½ tsp.	Dried whole dillweed	8 mL
1 tbsp. plus 2 tsp.	Red wine vinegar	25 mL
2 tsp.	Parmesan cheese, grated	10 mL
2 cloves	Garlic, minced	2 cloves
½ tsp.	Pepper	3 mL
¼ tsp.	Salt	1 mL

Directions

1. Combine pasta, chicken, tomato, celery, onion, and parsley in a large bowl. Set aside.
2. Combine remaining ingredients in a small bowl. Mix well.
3. Pour dressing over pasta mixture, and toss gently. Cover and chill 1 to 2 hours to blend flavors.

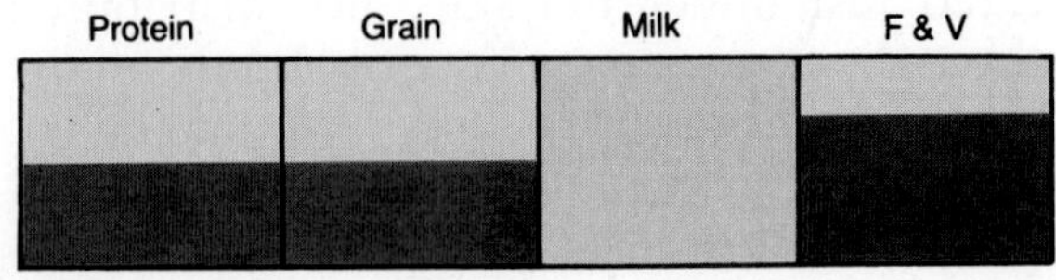

Broil cut-up pieces of turkey for a crunchy, crisp skin contrasting with the tender, moist meat inside.

Roasting

Roasted poultry is a holiday favorite. The low-heat, slow cooking method produces a golden brown bird that is a delight to the senses.

Poultry covered in aluminum foil or plastic cooking bags is not being roasted but steamed. This is true even when you remove the covering for the last 20 minutes to crisp and brown the surface.

Roasted whole poultry can be stuffed with a dressing or stuffing before cooking. Always stuff the bird just before baking. Stuffing a bird the day before and then chilling the whole bird results in a lukewarm stuffing that can harbor and grow harmful bacteria. If you want to save preparation time on the day of the event, you can prepare the dry stuffing and the bird a day ahead. Refrigerate them separately and add the liquid ingredients to the stuffing just before cooking. Stuffing a bird with dressing, vegetables, or fruits adds moisture and flavoring.

Directions

1. If the turkey is frozen, prepare the bird by thawing overnight in the refrigerator. (Very large turkeys may take two nights.) Remove the giblets from the body cavity or under the skin of the neck cavity. Wash the bird in cold running water and pat dry. This is not necessary for fresh-chilled poultry that you have already rinsed.
2. Prepare the stuffing.
3. Pack the neck and body cavities with the moist dressing just before roasting. Loosely pack it because the stuffing will expand during cooking. If the stuffing is warm from the liquid ingredients, cool it in the refigerator before stuffing the bird.
4. Truss the bird (bind the legs and wings) to keep the legs and wings close to the body. (See the illustration on page 335). Trussing keeps the smaller wings and legs from drying and cooking too fast and improves the appearance of the bird.
5. Use a metal or wooden skewer to fasten the neck flap under the body. (Don't forget to remove the skewer before serving.
6. Seal the body cavity over the dressing or other flavoring foods. The proper way to close the body cavity hole is to insert metal skewers across the opening and fasten with string, just as you would lace a shoe. (See the illustration.) If the time or equipment is not available, cover the opening with a piece of aluminum foil.
7. Rub the skin with softened margarine, butter, or fat. If the poultry is quite large, place a triangle of foil loosely over the breast and remove 20 minutes before the cooking time is up. An alternate method is to overlap strips of bacon over the top and thighs. Replace the bacon strips during the roasting time if they become too crisp. Remove the bacon 20 minutes before the bird is done to even the browning on the skin.
8. Insert a meat thermometer into the inside of the thigh muscle or the thickest part of the breast. Do not allow the thermometer tip to touch any bone or fat. (Some turkeys come with a thermometer built into the bird. It pops up when the turkey is done. Such convenience costs more than a plain turkey.)
9. Roast the bird in a preheated 325°F (160°C) oven. Refer to a cookbook for approximate cooking times. Roast poultry is done when the internal temperature at the thigh or breast reaches 185°F (85°C). You also can test for doneness by wiggling the leg to see if it is loose. Inserting a fork into the thigh to see if the juices run clear is yet another test.
10. Allow the bird to "rest" for 15 to 20 minutes to firm-up for easier carving and better flavor.

Roasting Game Birds

Wild game birds are usually less tender than domesticated game birds. Cover the game bird with bacon while cooking and follow the previous instructions for roasting and stuffing.

Frying

Poultry can be fried in the pan or oven. A heavy skillet with high sides and lid and tongs for turning are required.

Directions

1. Coat the surface of the poultry pieces with the batter or breading called for in the recipe.
2. Heat the fat in the skillet. Use enough fat to more than cover the bottom of the skillet.
3. Lower the pieces one at a time into the hot fat. Turn to brown evenly. Cook slowly to avoid an overdone outside or undercooked inside. For very crisp chicken, do not use the lid. Fry for 30 to 45 minutes. For turkey, fry for 45 to 60 minutes. For a medium-crisp crust with moist meat, cover the pan for about 15 minutes after the pieces are browned and uncover for the last 10 minutes. To "smother" the poultry southern style, cover the pan after the pieces are browned and continue cooking at a lowered temperature.

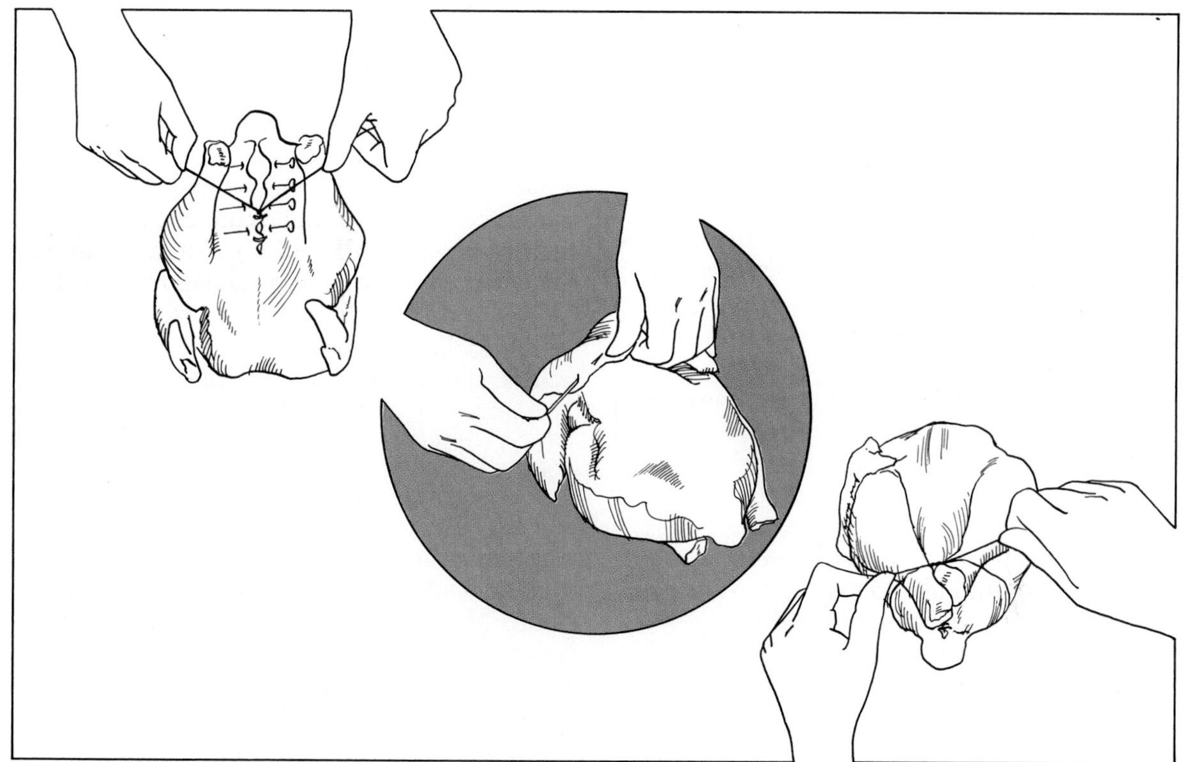

To truss poultry: 1. Use metal skewers to close the body cavity and lace string around the skewers. 2. Insert a skewer through the neck flap to hold it in place. 3. Secure the legs to the tail with a string.

Oven-Frying

Oven-frying creates a crisp fried texture because the cooking fat drains away better. Consequently, this method has become a favorite of cholesterol- and calorie-conscious people. It also frees the cook to do other things during the hour's preparation time. For oven-frying you need a shallow pan large enough to arrange poultry pieces without their touching. You also need tongs and a mixing bowl for the binding liquid and crumb pieces.

Directions

1. Dip poultry pieces into a beaten egg, a milk and egg mixture, fruit juice, or vegetable juice and then coat with a flour-crumb mixture.
2. Brown and bake in a 375°F (190°C) oven or the temperature your recipe specifies for about 50 minutes.

Braising

Braising, a moist-heat method of cooking, tenderizes mature poultry or game that is likely to be less tender. It also works well to develop the desired flavors and texture in younger poultry. Use cut-up or whole birds. Most braising combines quick browning in an open pot with the slow, moist cooking.

Use a heavy pot or skillet with a tight-fitting lid that just fits the amount of poultry to cook.

Directions

1. Brown the meat in a small amount of moderately hot fat. It is optional whether you coat the meat with flour or other crumb mixtures before browning. The browning takes about 10 minutes.
2. Add the liquid. Usually it takes about 1 cup (250 mL) for a 3 pound (1.5 kg) bird.

Creative Tips

Make your own bouquet garni by assembling your favorite fresh or dried herbs for use in soups, stocks, and poaching foods. Use the large outer layer of a clean leek at least 4 inches long (10 cm). Gather the herb selection together and wrap the leek shell around the mixture. Wrap the leek tightly with string or rubber bands. Use it in cooking liquids.

3. Simmer for at least 30 minutes.
4. If you would like to make a "whole meal in a pot," add large, cut pieces of flavorful vegetables of your choice for the last 15 minutes of cooking.

Poaching

The recent surge of interest in gourmet, perfectionist-type cooking has brought the "rediscovery" of a classic cooking method for poultry—poaching. For a couple of generations in America, poached has meant an uninteresting egg cooked in water. Now, cooking magazines and books are praising the tender delicacies created by this gentle cooking method. Some of the most prized hot and cold chicken dishes start with a large bird poached in flavored water. The fattier birds such as duck and goose also poach well. In fact, poaching may be the best way to extract the large amount of fat without drying the meat of a duck or goose.

Directions

1. Rub the whole bird with lemon. (You may also poach whole breasts nicely.)
2. Truss the chicken. (See page 335.) This step is optional, but does contribute to both the looks and quality of the product.
3. Lower the chicken into enough liquid (water or flavored broth) to cover the chicken. Use a large pot with a tight-fitting lid.
4. You can add flavoring vegetables such as carrots, onions, celery, and herbs to the water.
5. Bring the water to a boil and immediately lower the heat to a bare simmering temperature. Poach for about 45 minutes.
6. When the chicken is done, lift it carefully out of the pot with large tongs or two large slotted spoons. Use as your recipe specifies, or use the delicately flavored meat for sandwiches, salads, and hot or cold casseroles.

Stewing

Larger mature birds may be stewed whole or cut up. The long, slow stewing process with vegetables and meats combines the flavors in one thick mixture that resembles a very hearty soup. No thickening agent is added. Starchy vegetables such as potatoes, carrots, beans, and dried peas naturally disintegrate during the long cooking and release their starches to thicken the liquid. Try a variety of flavors. Remember the tastiness of celery leaves, cloves, bay leaves, onions, turnips, and salt. If you plan to use only the cooked chicken, serve the liquid as soup or save the stock to add to other recipes.

Microwave Techniques

See Chapter 8.

Crunchy Hot Chicken Salad

Yield: 6 to 8 servings

Traditional	Ingredients	Metric
3 cups	Poached chicken, diced	750 mL
1 cup	Celery, finely chopped	250 mL
2 tsp.	Onion, chopped	10 mL
½ cup	Almonds, sliced	125 mL
10¾ oz. can	Cream of chicken soup, undiluted	305 g can
½ cups	Cooked rice	375 mL

1 Tbsp.	Lemon juice	15 mL
½ tsp.	Salt	3 mL
¼ tsp.	Pepper	1 mL
¾ cup	Mayonnaise	175 mL
¼ cup	Water	50 mL
3	Hard-cooked eggs, sliced	3
2 cups	Crushed cracker crumbs	500 mL
¾ cup	Monterey Jack cheese, shredded	175 mL

Directions

1. Combine first nine ingredients; toss gently and set aside.
2. Combine mayonnaise and water, beat with a wire whisk until smooth. Pour over chicken mixture; stir well.
3. Add eggs, and toss gently. Spoon into a greased 2-quart (2 L) shallow baking dish; cover and refrigerate 8 hours or overnight.
4. Bake at 450°F (230°C) for 10 to 15 minutes or until thoroughly heated. Sprinkle with cracker crumbs and cheese; bake an additional 5 minutes.

Microwave Directions

1. Combine first nine ingredients; toss gently and set aside.
2. Combine mayonnaise and water; beat with a wire whisk until smooth.
3. Pour over chicken mixture; stir well.
4. Add eggs and toss gently.
5. Spoon into a 2½-quart (2.5 L) microwave-safe casserole, cover and refrigerate 8 hours or overnight.
6. Microwave, covered, on High for 7 to 8 minutes, or until heated through, stirring occasionally.
7. Stir in cheese; sprinkle with cracker crumbs.

Poaching chicken in water or a flavored liquid provides tender and easily skinned meat for recipes such as Crunchy Hot Chicken Salad.

Vocabulary Review

Fresh-chilled poultry
Poultry classes
Deboning
Marinade

Questions for Review

1. What is fresh-chilled poultry?
2. Larger fowl (poultry) has more servings per pound than a smaller bird. Why?
3. The USDA grades poultry according to its quality and wholesomeness. What is the difference between Grades A and B? Does that difference affect the eating quality?
4. Poultry classes identify the bird by age and weight. Name some of the classes by the type of bird. How would you cook each class? Why is the correct cooking method so important for the older classes of birds?
5. How long can fresh poultry be kept safely in the refrigerator?
6. What are the basic principles to consider when cooking poultry?
7. What is the danger involved with stuffing a whole bird hours ahead of cooking it?
8. What are some of the methods that can be used to test for doneness in poultry?
9. A younger bird is more tender and less flavorful than an older bird. Explain why this is true.
10. Why is it advisable not to marinate chicken and turkey longer than 2 hours?
11. Why do you think that the eating of poultry has increased in the last 40 years from about a 1/2 pound (250 g) a year to over 40 pounds a year for chicken alone?
12. Why is it unsafe to eat rare or raw chicken? Why must chicken be cooked until it is still juicy, but well done?
13. Why is it unsafe to thaw frozen chicken at room temperature? What is the correct way to thaw frozen chicken?

Things to Do

1. Bake a whole chicken. Immediately insert a thermometer into the largest part of one leg so that no bone is touching the end of the thermometer. Record the highest final temperature reading. Insert another thermometer into the other hot leg so that it touches the bone. Record the highest final temperature reading. Compare the temperature readings. Why is there a difference?

2. Find some grocery store ads for poultry in a newspaper. Compare the cost of poultry per pound to the cost of another meat. Using the information in the charts in this book, determine the cost per serving for the poultry and the meat. Which meat is the best buy for that day? Also strengthen your decision of the best buy of the day with some nutritional benefits for your decision.

3. Using the charts in the Appendix, determine what size bird (in number of pounds) to buy for serving six people turkey, chicken, and duck.

4. Visit the poultry section of a grocery store. List some of the various forms of chicken that are packaged for you to buy. Are all of the cuts of chicken the same price per pound? Why? Which packaged form of chicken represents the lowest price per pound? How do you decide which form of chicken is the best buy for your intended uses? How do you know which cooking methods are best for the type of chicken you decide to purchase? List the answers to these questions and compare your results with the rest of the class.

5. Look through several newspapers from your area for restaurant ads that feature chicken or other forms of poultry. How many feature chicken that is deep-fat fried? How many feature baked or broiled chicken? Which is the more common way to sell chicken? Why do you think this is the case? Are there other ways of preparing chicken that might be more healthful for most people? Describe a possible chicken item for a menu that is not fried. Explain what nutritional and health benefits it would provide that the fried chicken does not provide.

6. Divide the class into two groups. Have one group prepare deep-fat fried chicken. The other group can prepare an oven-fried chicken that is actually a coated chicken which is baked. Compare the taste, the amount of fat used for each method, and consider any other benefits or drawbacks of each method. Also, which was the most convenient to prepare? All things considered, how would you like your next "fried chicken"?

Fish Facts

You can get "into the swim" of fish and shellfish's new popularity as a delicious health and gourmet food! Because of their low-fat benefits, both fish and shellfish are now in great demand at the local supermarket as well as in restaurants. People have begun discovering the delicate flavors of all sorts of varieties of fish that before now only could have been found near a waterfront area. The increased demand for fish and shellfish and the efficient transportation systems have made possible a fresh fish and seafood department in your local supermarkets. This is true in the very heart of the country as well as on the coasts or Great Lakes.

As different varieties of fish and shellfish have become available, the interest in new and different ways to prepare and serve them has increased. More popular magazines, newspapers, and cookbooks and government department brochures are featuring innovative cooking techniques and nutrition facts for the newly favored food.

Fish

Fish is a general term that describes varieties with fins and a center spine of bones. They are found in fresh water and saltwater. Fresh-water fish that are considered good to eat include catfish, trout, and bass. Other local varieties you might catch in your area could include various sunfish, crappies, and northern pike that usually are not available in stores.

Perhaps you have fished in your area or know someone who has and can think of other types of fresh-water and saltwater treats that are localized to your area.

Shellfish

There are two types of shellfish that are commonly eaten. Those that have hard shells called **mollusks.** These include clams, mussels, oysters, and scallops. Crabs, lobsters, and shrimps belong to the soft-shell type called **crustaceans.** They have movable, brittle shells that resemble a coat of armor. Both kinds of shellfish can be served alone or together for some spectacular results. Just picture in your mind a platter of steaming lobster tails surrounded by hot crispy shrimp and tender poached, buttery scallops in the half-shells. These amazing mouthwatering delicacies are nutritious, easy to prepare, and divine to eat.

Nutritive Notes

The protein in fish and shellfish is a high-quality protein that can supply up to one half of your daily requirement if you eat at least ¼ pound (125 g). Fish also are rich in thiamin, niacin, and riboflavin.

Fish are lower in calories and cholesterol than the red meats. Some fish varieties contain a higher content of fat, significant amounts of vitamins A and D, and are higher in calories than other fish.

Any fish or shellfish from the ocean has an abundance of minerals—especially iodine. When fish are processed with their bones, such as canned salmon or sardines, they become an excellent source of calcium. Other minerals found in both fish and shellfish are iron, phosphorus, potassium, copper, magnesium, and fluoride.

Purchasing Fish and Shellfish

Times have changed drastically since vendors traveled the streets singing, "Cockels and mussels alive, alive, oh." However, the principle of buying fish foods alive or as fresh as possible remains the same. If it is not still alive, you can determine the wholesomeness of fish and shellfish by a stamped inspection rating. The National Marine Fisheries Service, an agency of the U.S. Government, inspects fish and seafood. Inspected products carry a round seal and those that are graded in addition to being inspected will bear a U.S. grade shield.

The pricing of fresh fish is related to the "supply and demand." Some restaurants will not price their fresh fish offerings ahead of time due to the fluctuations in the cost and supply. When you buy fresh fish regularly at the store,

Sweet-and-Sour Fish

Yield: 4 servings

Traditional	Ingredients	Metric
3 Tbsp.	Cornstarch	45 mL
¼ cup	Cold water	50 mL
8 oz. can	Tomato sauce	250 g can
8 oz. can	Pineapple chunks, undrained	250 g can
½ cup	Brown sugar, firmly packed	125 mL
⅓ cup	Red wine vinegar	75 mL
¼ cup	Onion, chopped	50 mL
1 small	Green pepper, cut into ½-inch (1.3 cm) strips	1 small
16 oz. pkg.	Frozen fish fillets, thawed	500 g pkg.

Directions

1. Combine cornstarch and cold water in a 2-quart (2 L) glass measure or deep casserole dish, stirring well to dissolve cornstarch.
2. Add the tomato sauce, pineapple chunks, brown sugar, vinegar, onion, and green pepper; stir well to dissolve the sugar.
3. Microwave at High for 4 minutes, stirring once; then stir well at end of cooking period.
4. Microwave at High for 4 to 6 minutes or until sauce is thickened and bubbly, stirring at 1-minute intervals.
5. Arrange fillets in a 12x8x2-inch (30x20x5 cm) baking dish with thicker portions to outside of dish (thinner portions may overlap, if necessary).
6. Pour sauce evenly over fillets. Cover with waxed paper; microwave at Medium High for 7 to 9 minutes or until fish flakes easily when tested with a fork, giving dish one-half turn during cooking.

Protein	Grain	Milk	F & V
1½x			1¼x

Common fish cuts for consumer sale:

Dressed—
Scales are scraped off, insides are removed, and the head, tail, and fins are cut off. (Head is sometimes left on.)

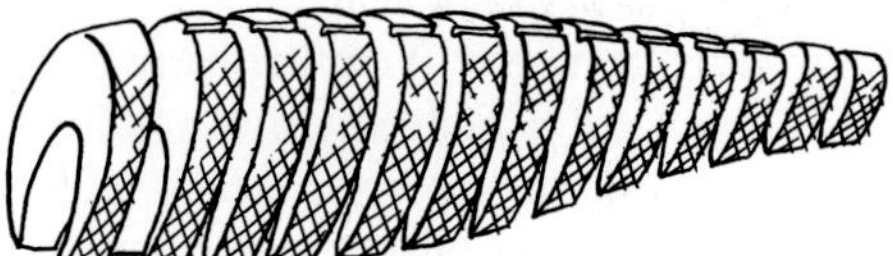

Steaks—
Thick, vertical slices are cut across the edible part of the fish. Steaks include the bone.

Fillets—
The sides of the fish are cut close to the backbone from head to tail. The cut is meant to be boneless, but a few slip by sometimes.

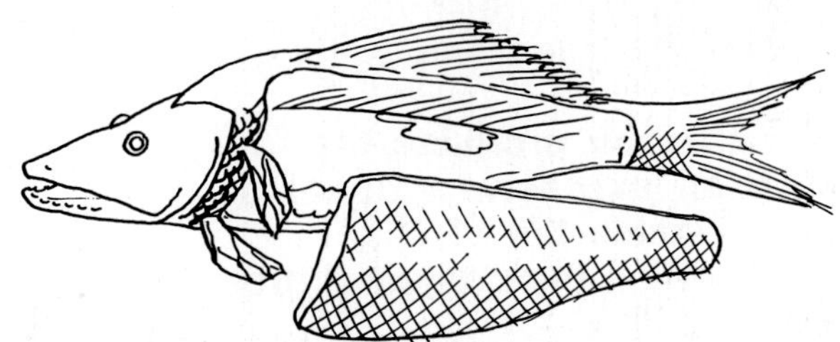

the prices will vary more than for other items. Also the kind of fish available will be based on the "catch of the day." There is a certain charm and nostalgia in the fact that all our technology can still be outsmarted by the elusive schools of fish. You'll also feel the excitement of making a good catch yourself when you find an unusual variety available at the market.

Selecting Fish

After the fish product has been inspected, the proper handling is crucial to maintaining the flavor and safety of the food. It is well worth the time to learn a few tips on picking the freshest fish in the market.

Selecting Shellfish

Fresh clams and oysters can be purchased live in the shell or shucked (removed from the shell). The shells should be tightly shut or close quickly when tapped. The loose shucked clams should have a clean, nonfishy odor and a clear liquid. Avoid buying quantities with visible pieces of broken shells in them. Frozen and canned clams are also available.

Fresh scallops are not available in the shell away from the seacoast, but the shucked scallops are sold both fresh and frozen. Sea scallops can be 2 inches (5 cm) or more in diameter. Bay scallops are sometimes no more than a 1/2 inch (1.25 cm) in diameter. The flesh has a pinkish cast with a small amount of clear liquid. The smell is like the flavor, slightly sweet with very little hint of fish.

Lobsters must be kept alive until they are cooked or cleaned. A dead fresh whole lobster in the shell is not safe to eat, even if it has been kept chilled. Lobsters are sold live from tanks in the markets or restaurants. You can keep a lobster alive chilled on ice for several hours before cooking. The meat is also sold frozen, canned, or precooked and chilled. The African lobster is more like a crab and has most of its

Consumer Guide

Fresh Fish Tips

• Whole fish should have clear, bright eyes

• Touch the flesh with your finger. It should feel firm.

• Of course the fish will smell fish-like, but it should not smell unpleasantly fishy.

• Study the illustration on page 343 for the various ways fish can be cut for cooking.

Frozen Fish Tips

Freezing the fish preserves it, but robs some of the fresh delicate flavor.

• Select frozen products that do not have an excessive amount of frost on, or inside, the package.

• Make certain the product is frozen firm.

• Avoid any discolored packages that appear to have been defrosted and refrozen.

• Avoid any packages with punctures or tears.

meat in the body's tail section. It is sold frozen or canned.

Crabs vary according to the locality from which they are shipped. Soft-shelled crabs have shed their hard shells and are in the process of growing a new one. The Alaskan king crab grows to a size of 3 feet (1 m) in diameter and has long spiderlike legs full of meat similar to that of the lobster. The Florida stone crab has delicate meat in its claws. The claws are covered with a hard, thick shell that breaks like china. It is against the law to kill a stone crab. However, stone crabs do have the ability to regenerate the heavy claws if one is lost, so the trappers tear off one claw and throw back the crab to grow a new one.

Crab meat is sold fresh, cooked in the shell, cooked and frozen, or canned. Live crabs are sold chilled. When you buy live crabs, they should be visibly moving and cooked while still alive. The cooked crab meat is white with streaks of deep pink.

There is a less expensive crab leg product on the market that looks like a cooked crab meat. Actually it is a processed fish product blended with crab. This product is a pleasing substitute for the expensive crab meat.

Shrimp are sold fresh or frozen in many different forms. You can buy fresh shrimp raw or cooked. Fresh shrimp are light gray in color, but turn a bright coral pink when cooked. Shrimp are also available frozen and breaded ready to fry. Some shrimp have a black vein running through the middle of the back. It is not harmful to eat, but it is more pleasant to remove when it is noticeable. The more shelling, cleaning, and preparation of the shellfish, the higher your price will be.

Caring for Your Catch

If you can, use an insulated container to carry home your fresh fish purchases. You will be well rewarded by better flavor and longer keeping times. Leave the fresh fish in the store wrapper and refrigerate as soon as possible. It should be used within a day. Sometimes fresh fish can be kept well for two to three days if you rinse it, rewrap it, and put it back in the coldest part of the refrigerator.

To freeze fresh fish, seal it well in a freezer wrap that is both moisture- and vapor proof. Fish can give an off-flavor to other foods and also can absorb other flavors, so wrap it well. The oily types of fish freeze the best.

Any leftover cooked fish should be covered well and stored in the refrigerator or freezer. Fresh cooked fish should not be stored more than three days in the refrigerator.

Fresh uncooked shellfish can only be kept for a day in the refrigerator. Freeze it in a heavy foil or freezer wrap. If you purchased frozen shrimp, you can store in the original container.

Search for signs of freshness when selecting shellfish. Look for firm, clean meat with unbroken shells that don't smell objectionably "fishy." How would you judge frozen shellfish?

Cooking Fish

Fish and shellfish are naturally tender because there is no connective tissue in most of the edible parts. The high protein content of these tender foods calls for gentle heat and quick cooking. The number one rule for cooking fish of all types is never overcook! Overcooked fish is dry, tough, and rubbery. Some of the cooking methods are slightly unusual and fun. From baking a paper-wrapped fish to stir-frying at the table, preparing fish or seafood can be a festive affair.

The tenderness of fish qualifies them for quick dry-heat cooking methods. Baking, broiling, panfrying, and grilling are ideal if the heat is moderate and the time is short. When cooking whole fish, cut several diagonal slits in the fish on each side. This helps the heat penetrate the fish and prevents it from curling up toward the heat as it cooks. Fish should be cooked to kill any harmful bacteria, but some ethnic recipes use raw fish to create exotic delicacies in design and flavors. **Sushi** is a seasoned rice dish that sometimes features the use of fine slivers of raw fish for adornment and flavor. Making and serving it is an accomplished oriental art. For health reasons, raw fish only should be used when you are absolutely certain of its source and freshness. Therefore, it is not recommended that you use raw fish.

Food Facts

"Farming" doesn't always mean plowing the back 40 acres anymore. Some farmers need their flippers and aqualungs to take care of their crops. Seeding the oceans with mollusks and tending and harvesting the beds is not a new idea, but converting the cornfield into a lake and raising catfish is a new and successful farming technique. You may have purchased one of the new, large, skinned catfish at the market. They are milder, sweeter, and larger than the wild catfish which can be fishy tasting. For an inexpensive price, fish farming offers a superior tasting fish at a controlled regular supply year around.

Broiling

Broiling is especially good for fatty types of fish. It is hard to determine the amount of fat for each species because the fattiness varies by season and the fish's diet. To play it safe, broil all fish as though it were of the lean type. Very thin fillets should be panfried.

Equipment

You will need a shallow pan large enough to hold the fish, a turner, and a basting brush.

Directions

1. Rinse the fish and pat it dry before cooking.
2. Preheat the broiler.
3. Brush the fish with melted butter or an oil to prevent drying. You also can marinate fish before cooking for 20 minutes and baste with the marinade during cooking.
4. If fish fillets have skin on one side, place the skin side down first. Place the fish under the broiler 4 to 5 inches (10 to 12.5 cm) from the heat source.
5. Broil fillets with skin 2 minutes with the skin side down, then turn and broil 3 minutes. Baste each side. Broil fillets without skin the same length of time. Broil fish steaks for 6 to 12 minutes depending upon their thickness. Turn over after half of the cooking time. Broil whole fish for 5 to 15 minutes per side, depending upon the thickness of the fish.
6. Watch carefully and remove the fish with the turner when the meat separates into flakes easily with a fork.

Note: Defrosted fish can be broiled following the same steps except you must use slightly more oil. This is due to the liquid lost in the freezing-thawing process.

Frozen fish can be broiled while still frozen if the pieces are no more than 1 inch (2.5 cm) thick.

Baking

So simple but so impressive is the baked whole fish straight from the oven with a crisp, dry outside and steaming, flaky flesh inside. Fillets and steaks also can be baked. Frozen fish can go directly to the oven, but will take longer to cook.

Equipment

You should use a large shallow ovenproof container. This is an excellent time to use one of the "oven to table" cooking-servers. The cooked fish is difficult to transfer to another serving dish because it breaks up easily.

Directions

1. Oil the baking utensil or spray it with nonstick coating.
2. Brush the fish with butter or oil to prevent it from drying out and to encourage crispness. As an alternative, you can coat the fish

The firm and oilier meat of the salmon makes salmon steaks perfect candidates for dry heat cooking such as broiling.

with a crumb mixture of butter, bread crumbs, egg, and seasonings.

3. Bake the fish uncovered at 350°F (175°C) until done. Fish flakes easily with a fork and bones separate from the flesh when done.

4. Serve with colorful garnish of a complementary food such as lemon wheels or a flavored herb.

Panfrying

Other terms for the method panfry are saute, quick fry, or stir-fry. Sautéing is basic to many French cooking techniques and a standard in any fast-food restaurants for individually prepared portions. The Chinese restaurant's fast food preparation is stir-frying.

Try panfrying a small whole fish, fillets, and steaks. None should be over 1 inch (2.5 cm) thick. For very thin fillets, fry the bare meat with no coating for 2 to 3 minutes. The fish would get overdone waiting for a coating to cook.

Equipment

You will need a heavy skillet, a turner, wax paper or a bowl to hold breading mixture, and tongs to transfer the fish from flour to hot fat in pan.

Directions

1. Rinse and pat dry the fish. Use four fish steaks or eight small fillets to serve six to eight.

2. Spread a seasoned flour mixture on wax paper. Press the fish into the flour mixture and shake off the excess. For a heavier coating, dip the fish in milk first and then the flour mixture.

3. Heat clarified butter in the skillet. (See Chapter 18 for clarified butter recipe.) Panfry the fish in the hot fat for 2 to 3 minutes. Turn and panfry until the fish is golden and just to the flaking stage.

4. Transfer the fish to a heated serving dish. (You can heat the dish in a warm oven or in hot water.

5. Wipe out the skillet with a paper towel. Add the rest of the clarified butter.

6. Heat the butter until it turns golden brown. This happens quickly, so watch intently.

7. Pour the brown butter over the fish in the serving dish. Sprinkle with lemon juice and chopped parsley. You also can season the fish with fennel or dill weed herbs. Serve immediately. Do not try to keep the fish while waiting on the other foods. The fish will dry out.

Note: You can add interesting flavor to fish dishes by pouring a vegetable sauce or adding moist vegetables like tomatoes in the skillet with the frying fish.

Oven-Frying

Oven-frying is a term for baked fish, but the technique is called frying because of the crispy crust that is associated with frying. The high temperature required for oven-frying is needed to brown the crisp coating. That same coating insulates the fish, so that the protein does not overheat and become tough. The high heat and the coating seal the surface of the meat for a steamy moist center with a crisp outside. And it's all without the added fat of frying. The nutritive bonus of less fat and fewer calories has made this method a new popular style.

Equipment

Use a shallow pan, wax paper or a bowl to hold the crumb mixture, and a turner or tongs.

Directions

1. Rinse and pat dry the fish. Use seven to eight fish fillets to serve six to eight people.

2. Dip the fish in milk and then press it into a flour and crumb mixture on wax paper. You will need 1 cup (250 mL) of milk, ½ cup (125 mL) flour, 1 to 2 cups (250 to 500 mL) bread crumbs, and seasonings of your choice.

3. Transfer the fish carefully with tongs or turner to the oiled pan. You also can use a nonstick spray coating.

4. Bake in a preheated oven at 500°F (260°C) until done. Bake about 20 minutes for

Flavorful perch are small fish that work well with a coating of breading which fries or bakes to a crisp outside texture.

thin fillets; 45 minutes to 1 hour for a whole fish.

5. Transfer the fish to a serving plate and garnish with a colorful edible garnish, such as parsley, tomato wedges, or raw broccoli.

Steaming Fish

Steaming is well suited to tender and delicately flavored fish. The fish is cooked by the steam rising from flavored liquid in a container below. The temperature should stay below a rapid boil, about 190° to 200°F (86° to 93°C). This is a highly nutritious cooking method because the relatively low temperature of the food prevents the escape of the nutrients. Fish cooked by this method should be extremely fresh and in good condition.

Equipment

You can invest in special fish steamer pans that are long and narrow to fit a large whole fish or an authentic bamboo steamer to set over a wok. Chances are a home-fashioned steamer will work just as well. Some of the choices might be a stainless-steel basket steamer set in a saucepan, a roasting pan with a cake rack set in the bottom, or even a colander set in a kettle.

Directions

1. Rinse fish and pat dry. Use whole fish, fish steaks, or fish fillets.
2. Sprinkle the fish with lemon juice, gingerroot, or herbs.
3. Place the fish on your steaming rack.
4. Lower the rack into the pan and add the cool court bouillon, milk court bouillon, or salted water. (See the bouillon recipes.)
5. Cover the pan. If your improvised pan has no lid, shape a tight-fitting lid out of aluminum foil.
6. Use only low heat to slowly bring the liquid to a simmer.
7. Cook for the time needed for the fish size. It takes 10 minutes per 1 inch (2.5 cm) of the thickest part of the fish after the liquid begins to simmer.
8. When the fish is done, transfer it to a plate and keep in a warm place.
9. Save the liquid for making a sauce. Reduce the cooking liquid to half its original volume by simmering.
10. Strain the liquid.
11. Stir in 2 tablespoons (30 mL) butter.
12. Serve over the fish. Remember, don't add salt. The seasoning was in the cooking liquid.

Milk Court Bouillon

Traditional	Ingredients	Metric
2 cups	Water	500 mL
1 cup	Milk	250 mL
3 slices	Lemon	3 slices
1 tsp.	Salt	5 mL
5	Peppercorns, crushed	5

Directions

Combine ingredients just prior to poaching fish.

Court Bouilllon

Traditional	Ingredients	Metric
3 cups	Water	750 mL
2 cups	White wine vinegar (use red for strong-flavored fish)	500 mL
2 large	Onions, chopped	2 large
1	Carrot	1
1 large stalk	Celery with leaves	1 large stalk
1	Bouquet garni (usually thyme, parsley, and bay leaf)	1
10	Peppercorns	10
½ tsp.	Salt	3 mL

Directions

Simmer all of the ingredients for 1 hour. Cool and strain. Store in refrigerator to use for poaching fish, chicken, and veal.

Steaming in Paper

Do you know anyone who doesn't like opening a present? This special dish provides guests with a "grand opening" when the fish is done. The fish is wrapped in a butterfly-shaped wrapping of oiled parchment paper or foil, oven baked, and served still in the paper. When the package is opened, the aroma of the herbs, lemon, and delicate fish wafts up and greets the nose with promises of the taste to come.

Equipment

You will need parchment paper, an oiled brown grocery bag, or aluminum foil and a turner.

Turn a simple dish into an artful presentation. Steam a whole fish in a folded covering of paper. Uncover at the table for a dramatic "whoosh" of steam.

Directions

1. Make the paper wrapping by folding the paper or foil in half. Cut into a large heart.
2. Butter the center of the heart-shaped paper.
3. Place the whole or cut fish on the paper. Add lemon slices and herbs on top.
4.Fold the heart shape in half over the fish and fold over the edges twice.
5. Place the fish-filled papers on an oiled pan.
6. Bake in a preheated 375° (190°C) oven for 15 to 30 minutes, depending upon the size of the fish. Remember the rule of 10 minutes per 1 inch (2.5 cm) of fish thickness.
7. Serve the unopened packet of fish on a preheated serving plate with a colorful garnish.

Cooking Shellfish

The richness of shellfish comes from its unique natural flavor and goodness, not from being high in fat or calories. All shellfish share a similar flavor and require similar cooking techniques. The two main rules for buying and serving shellfish are:

1. Buy only the very freshest. Alive is the best!
2. Cook for the shortest time possible.

Never soak delicate seafood in water. The flavor is drained away with the water. Rinse it only lightly, and use as little liquid as possible when cleaning shellfish.

The shellfish may all be cooked by the same methods used for fish. Follow the same princi-

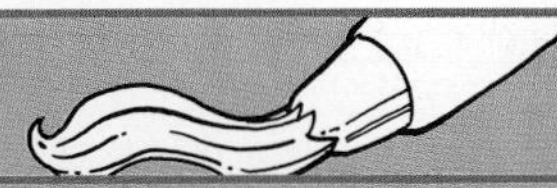

Creative Tips

Just imagine a pat of deliciously flavored herb butter slowly melting over a moist fish fillet, a hot ear of corn, a grilled chicken breast, or a fluffy baked potato. Taking the extra time to add a mellow-flavored butter is a special touch well worth the effort. Flavoring a stick of butter ahead of time and keeping it in the refrigerator until needed to rescue an otherwise ordinary dish is so simple, yet so smart. Technically, these butters with added flavoring are called *compound butters.* They can be used on cold or hot food that would use ordinary butter. By using compound butter, you match up flavors that zing.

ples for the type of product you want to have. For instance, if you want a crispy crust, panfry the seafood. One small difference in serving is that shellfish are served chilled often. Fish (with the exception of salmon) is rarely served chilled. The moist-heat methods of cooking, such as poaching and steaming, are the best to use for shellfish that is to be served cold.

Microwaving Techniques

See Chapter 8.

Compound Butters

Traditional	Ingredients	Metric
1 stick	Butter (unsalted is best)	1 stick
2 tbsp.	Fresh dill weed*	30 mL
4 tsp.	Fresh lemon juice (fresh frozen juice works well)	20 mL
	Salt and pepper to taste	

Equipment

Small mixing bowl, wooden spoon, small knife, and wax paper.

Directions

1. Cut the butter into small pieces and place in a bowl. Let them warm to room temperature.
2. Add the herbs and beat them into the softened butter with a spoon. Beat until the mixture is smooth.
3. Add the lemon juice and seasonings to taste. Mix until smooth.
4. Wet your hands in ice water and roll the mixed butter into a long tube shape.
5. Wrap the roll in wax paper and chill in the refrigerator. After it is chilled and firm in shape, put it in a plastic bag for double protection from off-flavors.

* Alternate flavors for butter include: blue cheese; 2 tbsp. (30 mL) chives; 2 tbsp. (30 mL) fresh chopped mint or dried leaves; juice from 3 garlic cloves; 2 tbsp. (30 mL) currant preserves; 3 tbsp. (45 mL) honey; or 2 tbsp. (30 mL) orange rind.

Vocabulary Review

Fish	Crustaceans	Sushi
Mollusks	Compound butter	Fillet

Questions for Review

1. What are the two classifications of shellfish that are valued for eating? Give examples of each.
2. Name the main nutrients that are found in most fish. Fish is highly valued now for a healthful diet because it does not usually contain a certain substance. What is that substance?
3. Restaurants often wait to price their fresh fish of the day on the menu. Why?
4. What are the main characteristics of freshness in fresh fish?
5. Describe a fresh shellfish, such as shrimp, compared to one that is not fresh. What are the main differences?
6. How do you care for and store fresh fish?
7. What is the most important rule for cooking all types of fish? Why?
8. Why is it a good idea to cut several diagonal slits on each side of a whole fish before cooking?
9. What happens to the delicate flavor when shellfish or fish is soaked in water during cleaning?
10. Why brush fish with melted butter or oil before broiling it?
11. What is the purpose of the crisp coating on oven-fried fish?

Things to Do

1. Find pictures of the following shellfish: soft-shelled crab, Alaskan king crab, Florida stone crab, lobster, African lobster, clams, oysters, sea scallops, bay scallops, and shrimp. Write a brief summary of where each comes from and how to prepare and serve each one.
2. Look through cookbooks, magazines, and newspapers to find recipes featuring new and creative ways to serve fish. Plan several meals around fish that vary greatly in flavor combinations and cooking methods. With such variations possible, would you consider it possible to eat fish several times a week without tiring of it?
3. Read about fish farming methods at the library. Give a short report about the possibilities for fish farming. Are there any fish farms in your area? Could there be? Why is fish farming a helpful addition for the farmer and the consumer?
4. Make a flavored butter with your favorite seasonings or herbs. Conduct a taste test with and without the flavored butter on steamed or broiled fish. What did the small amount of the compound butter add to the fish?

The Good Egg

"Eggs-actly" how important the lonely egg is in food preparation would be hard to define, but the Encyclopedia Britannica comes close. It says, "Considering all factors, eggs rank next after milk in importance and efficiency among foods of animal origin."

In cooking, the egg will leaven, thicken, emulsify, coat, bind, tenderize, flavor, and shape. You can use eggs for appetizers, main dishes, salads, and desserts. They are marvelous in the morning for breakfasts and carry on through the day for lunch, snacks, and dinner. All this plus eggs contain important nutrient contributions to your health.

Nutritive Notes

Eggs supply a variety of vitamins and minerals including vitamin A, the B vitamins, zinc, and iodine. Egg yolks are high in phosphorus, magnesium, and iron. Egg yolks are also high in cholesterol and for that reason the American Heart Association recommends eating no more than three eggs a week.

Eggs are also a source of high-quality protein. For vegetarians who do not eat meat but do eat eggs and milk products, eggs are invaluable in helping them meet their protein needs. Eggs also can help vegetarians obtain the amounts of iron they need.

Some people feel that brown eggs are more nutritional or healthful than white eggs. This is not the case. The color of the eggs depends on the type of chicken that laid the egg. Both types of eggs have the same nutrients.

Egg Uses

You can learn to analyze a recipe by the ingredients and their purposes. Eggs in a recipe have the numerous functions just listed. For instance, in a baked bread, eggs help the product to rise and also tenderize and flavor it, as described in Chapter 14. Some other functions of the egg in food products are:

- Emulsifier. Eggs can help combine two nonmixing ingredients, such as oil and vinegar, by holding them together. Mayonnaise is an emulsion of oil and vinegar held together by the egg.
- Binder. Cookie ingredients are held together by eggs. The small pieces of ground meat in a meatloaf are bound together by the egg.
- Thickener. Soups, sauces, custards, and puddings are thickened by the principle that egg yolks begin to thicken at about 145°F (63°C). When blended over low heat with a

Consumer Guide

The USDA has set a minimum weight per dozen for comparing eggs. The size rating has no relationship to the freshness (quality) rating.

- **Jumbo eggs—30 ounces (850 g) or more**
- **Extra Large—27 to 29 ounces (765 to 822 g)**
- **Large—24 to 26 ounces (680 to 737 g)**
- **Medium—21 to 23 ounces (595 to 652 g)**
- **Small—18 to 20 ounces (510 to 566 g)**

Most recipes give egg requirements based on large eggs. If you are using very small eggs, you probably will need to add an extra egg.

liquid such as milk or soup stock, the egg thickens the mixture. The mixture can be almost solid with a high proportion of eggs, or thinner with less egg.

- Coating. Acting as a binder and a coating, beaten eggs hold breading onto foods to be fried. Have you tried fried zucchini squash appetizers or crispy fried catfish? Chances are they both were dipped in an egg or an egg mixture to hold on the crisp, tasty coating.

What's a Good Egg?

Freshness is the key word. Although an egg just a few hours old is unsurpassed for flavor and performing qualities, it is unlikely the average consumer can obtain such a thing. Supermarkets, however, are reliable sources for acceptably fresh and safe-quality eggs.

You can tell the freshness of an egg in several ways. Hold it up to the light. A freshly laid egg will have a very tiny space of air at one end. As the egg gets older, more moisture evaporates through the shell leaving a larger air hole in one end. This inspection is called **candling,** a term that dates back to the days when the farm family held their eggs in front of a candle to assure their freshness before selling them.

Most eggs on the market come from large poultry farms that have mechanized inspection systems which "candle," and grade eggs. The grade is printed in a shield on the carton. The United States Department of Agriculture (USDA) grading specifications are:

- Grade AA. Eggs of this freshest grade will have yolks that stand up in a semicircle when the egg is cracked open. The white is thick with two distinct layers of thickness. Purchase this super high quality for food preparation that requires the egg to hold its shape. This includes poaching or frying a whole egg. Grade AA quality eggs would not be necessary for making an omelet or cookies.
- Grade A. When you break a Grade A egg, it would spread out a little more than the Grade AA. The white still would be thick and stand up. This grade is high enough to use for poaching or frying eggs.
- Grade B. The yolk and the white of a Grade B egg spread out when the shell is broken. Chances are the yolk would even break open as it spreads. Use Grade B eggs for cooking and baking.

Storing Eggs

Eggs keep better if the air space is always on the top, so eggs should be stored with the pointed end down. Since eggshells are porous, they can absorb off-flavors and odors from other foods. To avoid this, store them in a covered container away from strong-flavored foods such as melons and cheeses. A fun way to take advantage of the porous shell is to store eggs in a plastic bag with fresh herbs or other seasonings. Use those eggs in an omelet and you will have a "head start" on the flavoring.

Light can be harmful to both the freshness and the nutrients of an egg, so eggs should be stored in a cool, dark place. The refrigerator is ideal, but any cool dark place will hold eggs for

Lemon juice accents the smooth, rich flavor of eggs in the traditional Greek Egg and Lemon Soup recipe.

(Egg-and-Lemon Soup) Avgolemeno

Yield: 2 portions

Traditional	Ingredients	Metric
46 oz.	Chicken broth	1.4 kg
⅓ cup	Uncooked regular rice	75 mL
2 large	Eggs, beaten	2 large
3 Tbsp.	Fresh lemon juice	45 mL
	Salt	
2 Tbsp.	Snipped parsley, chives, or mint	30 mL
¼ tsp.	Salt (optional)	1 mL

Directions

1. Heat chicken broth, rice, and salt to boiling in 3-quart (3 L) saucepan, stirring once or twice; reduce heat.
2. Cover and simmer until rice is tender, about 14 minutes.
3. Beat the eggs and lemon juice together. Stir 1 cup of hot broth into the egg mixture to warm it and prevent curdling. Then stir it into broth mixture in saucepan.
4. Cook and stir over low heat until slightly thickened, 2 to 3 minutes. (Do not boil or eggs will curdle.) Garnish each serving with parsley.

Microwave Directions

1. Combine chicken broth and rice in a 2-quart (2 L) microwave-safe casserole. Cover with plastic wrap.
2. Microwave on High for 15 to 17 minutes, or until rice is tender.
3. Meanwhile, beat the egg and lemon juice together and add salt to taste (if broth is salted, omit salt). Stir 1 cup of hot broth into the egg mixture to warm it, (this will prevent the eggs from curdling) then turn it into the rest of the soup.
4. Serve at once.

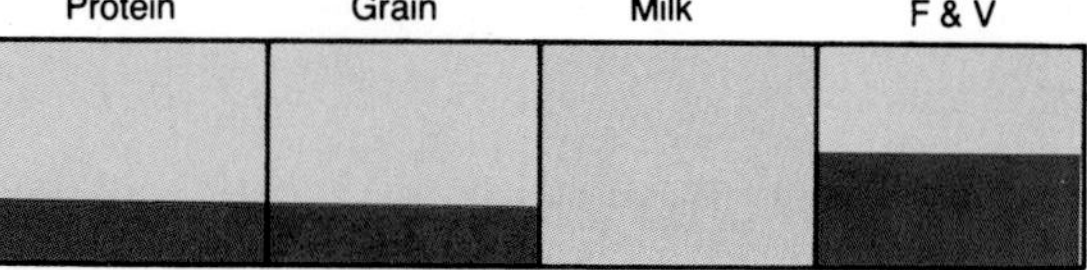

Cooking Hints

Fresh eggs are necessary for poaching, but a handicap for hard cooking eggs. Fresh eggs are difficult to peel when hard cooked. If you need to hard cook eggs but only have access to fresh ones, leave them uncovered at room temperature for a day or two.

several weeks. Cold eggs should be brought to room temperature before cooking in boiling water or the shells will crack.

There is a "bloom" on a fresh egg shell that helps protect their freshness. Do not wash eggs before storing them, but do wash them off just before cracking them open.

Cook any cracked eggs immediately. If they seem to have been cracked open for any period of time, discard them. They could be contaminated and cause food poisoning.

Cooking Eggs

Eggs were among the first foods that led scientists to discover the existence of protein. The word "protein" in some languages is the same as that for egg white. Proteins are heat sensitive and become quite tough under high heat conditions. Eggs, therefore, should be cooked at low temperatures and only until just done. The three parts of an egg—the white, the yolk, and the shell—can all be separated and treated individually or as a whole.

For instance, eggs can be cooked in the shell, out of the shell whole, separated into the yolk alone, or separated into the white alone. For instance, the egg white can be beaten into a foam that has many uses in food preparation.

Eggs Cooked in the Shells

Boiled eggs are misnamed! Eggs should never be boiled. Boiling causes a rubbery, tough egg that is also likely to have a dark line between the yolk and the white. Eggs should be simmered just until cooked to the desired stage. The yolk can be cooked from very soft to hard.

Equipment

You will need a small, deep pan with a well-fitting lid and a slotted tablespoon or wire basket. The spoon or basket is used to lift eggs safely in and out of the water. A timer is helpful, but not necessary if a clock with a second hand is close by. A small pin is necessary, too.

Before cooking, pierce the large end of the egg with a pin to help prevent cracking the shell when it contacts the hot water.

Choice 1

1. Bring enough water to a boil to cover the eggs by at least 1 inch (2.5 cm).
2. Reduce the water temperature to a simmering temperature and lower in the eggs.
3. Start timing. See the chart on page 360.

Choice 2

1. Place the eggs in cold water that covers them by at least 1 inch (2.5 cm).
2. Bring to a boil and reduce the heat to a simmer. Start timing when the water begins to boil.

Peeling Eggs

Peel a hard-cooked egg by cracking the shell with a spoon or gently rolling it in the countertop. Then hold it under cool running water as you peel. Egg whites discolor and toughen in the air, so store the peeled eggs in a bowl of water until you are ready to use them.

Poached Eggs

A plump, perfectly formed poached egg is an attractive sight on a piece of crisp toast or as a garnish for a main dish. You can cook eggs without the support of their shells in water or other tasty liquid such as milk or soup stock. This is known as **poaching.**

A few chops with a knife or pushes through a sieve or pastry bag can turn a plain cooked egg into a protein-rich decorative touch.

Equipment

You can purchase special pans that have individual indentations to form a perfect poached egg circle, but it is not necessary. Any deep narrow saucepan will work nicely. A slotted spoon is important for easing the cooked egg out of the water without breaking it.

Directions

1. Oil or spray the pan with a nonstick coating. Pour in milk, water, or stock and heat to a simmering temperature.
2. Break the egg into a shallow dish.
3. Stir the simmering liquid in a circular motion that creates a small whirlpool action.

Cooking Hints

Cooking timed for eggs in the shell.
Choice 1
Soft cooked—4 minutes (soft yolk, firm white)
Hard cooked—10½ minutes (firm yolk and white)
Choice 2
Soft cooked—3 minutes
Hard cooked—7 minutes

The times listed are a general guide. Experiment for the amount of doneness that suits your personal taste.

After cooking to the desired doneness, pour off the hot water and cover the hot eggs with cold water until they are cool. The rapid cooling releases the gas that sometimes discolors the outside edge of the egg yolk. The rapid cooling also contracts the eggs and makes peeling easier.

4. Slip the egg from the small dish into the top of the "whirlpool" you have just created.
5. The action of the water will hold the egg together while it **coagulates** (thickens) in the simmering water. This should take about 3 to 4 minutes. If you need to poach more than one egg at a time, use a deep skillet and gently slip in the eggs so they do not touch. This is more difficult to hold the eggs together without the whirlpool action, but it does work.
6. Remove the egg gently with the slotted spoon.

Shirred Eggs

Shirred eggs are baked in individual shallow baking dishes. **Shirred** means the eggs are baked. You will need individual small baking dishes or glass custard cups.

Directions

1. Melt 1 to 2 teaspoons (5 to 10 mL) of butter or margarine in the baking dishes.
2. Break one egg into each buttered baking dish. (For larger, shallow baking dishes, use two eggs.)
3. Set the dishes on a baking sheet and bake in a preheated 350°F (175°C) oven for 10 to 12 minutes. If you like a very moist egg, cover the dishes with foil.
4. Add butter or sauce and a colorful garnish to the cooked eggs. Serve in the baking dishes. Don't forget to protect the table top from the hot baking dish.

Fried Eggs

Frying eggs sunny side up is the "classic" way of cooking eggs. As with the other cooking methods, frying an egg requires low heat to avoid rubbery whites and overcooked yolks. A frying pan is needed to fry eggs.

Directions

1. Melt 2 teaspoons (10 mL) butter, margarine, or oil in the skillet until hot, but not "bubbling."
2. Slip the eggs into the moderately hot skillet.
3. Cook for 2 to 3 minutes. To help cook the top of the yolks, cover the skillet with a lid for a few minutes. You also can baste the tops if there is enough fat. Some short-order cooks sprinkle a few drops of water in the skillet and quickly cover the pan to lightly steam the tops. For over-easy eggs, gently turn them over without breaking the yolk. Cook for a very short time.

Scrambled Eggs

The perfect scrambled eggs are light as air and creamy. Anyone can learn to master the few simple guidelines that will prevent scrambled eggs that are dry, stringy, or too moist.

Poached eggs offer a low-calorie breakfast alternative.

Equipment

A heavy frying pan with a nonstick surface is ideal, but a well-greased surface will work. A wooden spoon for stirring, a mixing fork, and a mixing bowl also are needed.

Directions

1. Use cream or milk to thin the eggs. Water will make them too thin and watery. Use about 1 tablespoon (15 mL) liquid for each egg. A handy measuring substitution is to use one half of the egg shell to measure the milk.

2. Break the eggs into the mixing bowl. Beat the liquid and eggs lightly with a fork to blend the whites and yolks.

3. Melt 2 tablespoons (30 mL) of the butter, margarine, or oil in the skillet. Use moderately low heat.

4. Pour the egg mixture into the melted butter and stir slowly with the wooden spoon for a minute. Avoid too much stirring. The eggs should be in fluffy lumps, not evenly mixed. If the mixture seems to be cooking too fast, remove the skillet from the heat for a short time.

5. Before the eggs are completely set, remove the pan from the heat. The eggs will continue to cook. If you leave them on the heat until they reach the desired consistency, they will be overcooked by the time they reach your plate.

Cooking Hints

Some chefs use an extra yolk for every three eggs for an extra rich flavor and creamy texture. Another method is to save some of the liquid to pour on top after the eggs are almost done. This stops the cooking and adds creaminess. You can even add grated cheese for variety.

Cooking Hints

Have you ever tried to heat butter quickly to fry an egg or make popcorn only to find the melted fat smoking before you could even get the food into the skillet? In spite of the flavor and texture butter gives to quick fried (sautéed) foods, it is usually more successful to use an oil that will heat to a higher temperature without scorching. It is extremely difficult to hold butter at just the right temperature to brown foods without scorching.

The presence of a small amount of nonfat milk solids, water, and salt are the factors which make butter so susceptible to undesirable scorching. Salt is added to butter to retard growth of bacteria and to save the flavor. It does not add a noticeable salty flavor, but there is a definite difference in taste between unsalted butter and regular butter with salt. Recipes often list *clarified butter* (unsalted butter) for foods that might scorch easily.

You do not have to purchase unsalted butter from the store. It is simple to remove the salt and other solids from butter yourself by using one of the two following methods.

Clarified Butters

Method 1

1. Melt the butter in a cup over hot water or in the microwave oven.
2. Let the melted butter stand until the solids settle to the bottom of the cup.
3. Pour off the clear liquid butter carefully into another cup.
4. Discard the solids left in the first cup.
5. Use or store the clear liquid, which is now clarified butter.

Method 2

1. Melt the butter in a cup.
2. Let stand until the solids settle to the bottom of the cup.
3. Cool in the refrigerator until solid. The cooled butter will reform into a layer of butter-colored fat with a light film on top and a thicker layer of salty, whitish liquid on the bottom.
4. Wipe off the top film and the bottom layer. The remaining fat is clarified butter.

You may store the clarified butter in the refrigerator for future use, or use it immediately.

Omelets

The **omelet** can be a culinary delight to grace either the dinner table or the wake-up breakfast. The folded omelet most people make is actually a French omelet that is a relatively recent addition to the American scene. Omelets, however, date back thousands of years. Most countries have some sort of omelet dish with regional additions. The Italians savor a "frittata"; the Spanish have their "tortilla." Don't confuse this one with the Mexican quick-bread "tortilla." The Arabic version is an "eggah," while the Persians call their omelet a "kuku." The Basque have a "piperade," and the Chinese the "egg foo yung." Whatever you choose to call it, the egg cookery principles for the perfect omelet are the same. Follow the basic steps for the ideal omelet that is firm on the outside and creamy on the inside.

The maximum size recommended for an omelet serves two people and uses four eggs. If your omelet is any larger, it is too awkward to handle and tends to dry out on the bottom before the top cooks. To serve more than two people, make several small omelets or switch to scrambled eggs which can be fixed in larger amounts.

Equipment

You will need an omelet pan or a frying pan from 10 to 12 inches (25 to 30 cm) in diameter with curved or slanted sides. A frying pan or skillet with straight sides does not allow room for manipulating the omelet. A mixing bowl, a mixing fork, and a turner are necessary, too.

Directions

1. Bring two eggs to room temperature for better texture and a high volume. It takes about an hour for the eggs to warm.
2. Prepare any filling you want to use. Excellent fillings for omelets include sliced or grated cheese, chopped leftover cooked meat or fish, mushrooms, vegetables or even fruits, nuts, or jelly.
3. Break the eggs into the bowl and stir until they are mixed but not frothy.
4. Add 2 tablespoons (30 mL) water and seasonings. Salt, pepper, and herbs and spices you favor are good. Stir with a fork to mix.
5. Heat 1 tablespoon (15 mL) unsalted butter in the pan. Swirl the butter around to coat the pan. You can substitute margarine.
6. When a sprinkle of water sizzles in the butter, pour in the egg mixture all at once.
7. The edges of the mixture should set immediately. With the turner, move the cooked edges toward the center of the pan. Shake the pan gently to free the mixture from sticking to the pan. Continue this gentle rocking motion to keep the omelet, which by now looks somewhat like a sticky pancake, moving freely in the pan.
8. Lift the edge of the omelet with the turner and tilt the pan. This allows the uncooked mixture to run underneath the cooked portion and reach the hot cooking surface of the pan.
9. When all the liquid portion has run underneath, add the filling (if you are using one) over half the surface of the omelet.
10. Tilt the pan away from you and using the turner fold the omelet in half over the filling, if you used one.
11. Slide the omelet onto a warmed serving plate. Add the remaining seasonings or herbs for a garnish. Note: Omelets must be eaten at once. If they are kept hot, they will continue cooking and be tough and dry!

To fold an omelet, tilt the pan and use a turner to move the egg mixture.

Fluffy Omelet

Another wonderful creation that must be served and enjoyed immediately after preparation is the fluffy omelet. This simple, yet delightful creation will make you feel like an accomplished French chef when you present it to your "awed" audience. You create the fluffiness by separating the egg whites from the yolk and beating them to a soft peak volume. See the instructions for beating egg whites on page 365.

Equipment

The necessary equipment includes an omelet pan or skillet with sloping sides, a rotary beater or electric mixer, a rubber spatula, and a turner.

Directions

1. Use three medium eggs for two portions. Bring the eggs to room temperature.

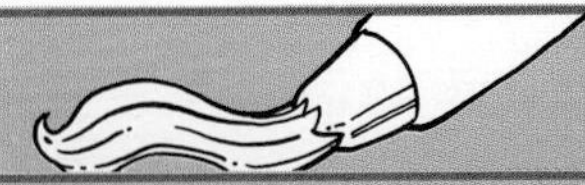

Creative Tips

All the way back to the year 5000 B.C. eggs were colored red to represent the life force. These beautifully colored tokens were given as symbols of love and friendship during festivals celebrating spring. The Polish dye their eggs an elegant mahogany red by simmering them with red onion skins. The skins absorb the natural dye, and it can be scraped off with a knife in intricate designs and patterns. (See photo in Chapter 1.)

2. Preheat the broiler to its highest temperature.
3. Separate the yolks and whites into two bowls. If even the tiniest drop of egg yolk drops into the egg whites, save the eggs for another use and start again with a completely new bowl of egg whites.
4. Add 1 tablespoon (15 mL) tomato juice or lemon juice to egg whites and beat them until they stand in soft peaks.
5. Mix the egg yolks, a pinch of salt, and liquid with the fork.
6. Fold the egg yolk mixture into the beaten whites using a clean rubber spatula or large spoon.
7. Heat butter or margarine in the pan on a stove burner, swirl the pan around to coat the sides. Unsalted butter is preferred.
8. When a sprinkle of water sizzles in the hot butter, add the egg mixture all at once.
9. Cook on the burner until the bottom is set and slightly golden brown.
10. Place the pan under the preheated broiler and cook for 30 seconds to set, but not dry out the top.
11. You can serve the omelet round or flip it in half and place on a warmed plate. You may want to drizzle extra melted butter, a sprinkle of grated cheese, or powdered sugar and fruit over the omelet.

Beating Egg Whites

When you beat egg whites by hand or with an electric mixer, you are whipping air bubbles into the egg whites. The sticky egg white stretches to cover those air bubbles and stick them together. If even one tiny drop of fat or oil gets into that "pile of bubbles," it interferes with the gluing action of the egg white and they collapse. All utensils used for beating egg whites must be freshly washed in hot soapy water and rinsed.

Did you ever wonder why you added a funny white powder called cream of tartar to egg whites before beating them? Tenderizing the egg whites with acidic ingredients before beating helps to thin them and increase their potential volume. Cream of tartar, lemon juice, and tomato juices are ingredients you can use. Also bringing the egg whites to room temperature thins them and helps them stretch to a higher volume.

Use a glass, stainless steel, or copper bowl for beating egg whites. Do not use aluminum. It darkens them. Sometimes you will find a recipe that calls for adding salt to the egg whites, but salt helps break down the foam. Add salt to the other ingredients not the egg whites.

Overbeating

It is easy to overbeat plain egg whites. When the mixture forms stiff peaks, stop beating immediately. Any beating after that stage will just break the air bubbles. The resulting mixture will be dry, lower in volume, and tend to separate into clumps. The overbeaten mixture also does not rise as well in cooked products.

Folding Beaten Egg Whites

Folding in beaten egg whites is a food preparation skill worth developing. Many recipes call for successful folding in of ingredients.

To **fold in** the delicate beaten egg whites without breaking apart all those countless air bubbles, use a gentle up and over motion with a broad spoon or rubber spatula. Turn both the

Three Stages of Beating Egg Whites

• **Foamy egg whites.** The foamy stage is the time shortly after beating when egg whites turn white with some bubbles, but still pour. They still have a liquid consistency.

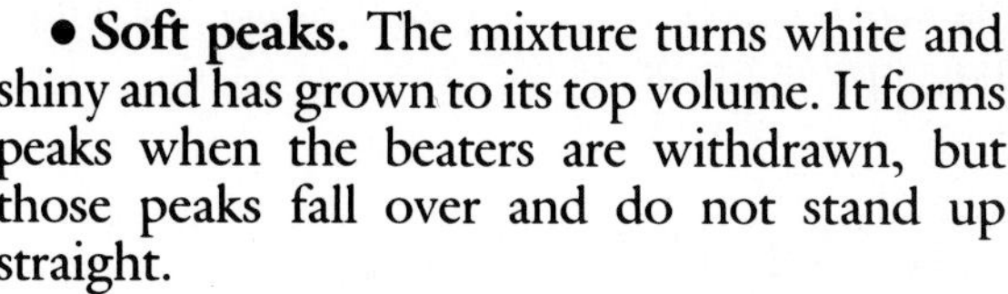

• **Soft peaks.** The mixture turns white and shiny and has grown to its top volume. It forms peaks when the beaters are withdrawn, but those peaks fall over and do not stand up straight.

• **Stiff peaks.** The mixture is white, shiny, and still at the top volume. When the beaters are pulled out, the formed peaks stay standing straight up.

beaten egg whites and solid ingredients into the bowl. Start folding by cutting down through the center of the mixture to the bowl's bottom. Continue back up the side, carrying the ingredients on the spatula. Cut back down through the mixture in a circular folding motion. Cut back into a different location each time until the ingredients are barely blended. Never lift the spatula out of the mixture, keep it down in and next to the ingredients as you fold. Breaking the surface with the spatula releases air and decreases the air volume.

Here's the secret to holding-in all the air bubbles you carefully beat into egg whites while folding them into other ingredients. Never let the spatula break the surface—that lets the air out!

Meringues

A **meringue** is a flavored, candylike beaten egg white mixture that is mixed with lots of sugar and baked. There are two types of meringues. One is a soft baked mixture with less sugar. It is used as a topping on baked desserts. The other is a hard baked mixture that forms cookies or a separate shell to hold fruit and cream desserts.

Both types are easy to make if the weather cooperates. If baked during hot and humid conditions, soft meringues tend to be weepy and separated. Hard meringues stay chewy, sticky, and tough.

For either type of meringue, you need a rotary beater or electric mixer. You can use a wire whisk if you have a strong arm. You also need a large spoon and a glass, stainless steel, ceramic, or copper bowl. (No aluminum please.)

Soft Meringues

1. For soft meringues, you combine 1 egg white with 2 tablespoons (30 mL) sugar. To cover a 9-inch (23 cm) pie usually requires 3 egg whites.

2. After the egg whites are foamy, add sugar slowly and beat until soft peaks form.

3. Spread on a cooled pie or dessert and bake in preheated oven at 350°F (175°C) for 12 to 15 minutes or until peaks are golden brown.

Hint: Meringue placed on a hot pie surface will shrink. Cool the pie first.

Hard Meringues

For hard meringues, use 4 tablespoons (60 mL) sugar to 1 egg white. Many times a flavoring such as mint is added to hard meringues.

Follow this procedure:

1. Beat the egg whites until foamy.

2. Add the sugar and flavoring slowly.

3. Beat the egg whites, sugar, and flavoring until stiff peaks form. Beat until you can no longer feel granules of sugar between your fingers. You cannot overbeat a hard meringue, so this stage may take longer than you expected.

4. Shape the meringue into shells on a greased cookie sheet.

5. Bake in a preheated oven at 225°F (110°C) for 1½ hours or until the shells seem firm.

Baked hard meringue shells welcome the tart addition of any fruit for a melt-in-your-mouth dessert.

6. Allow the shells to dry out in the oven for at least another hour.
7. Cool completely. Store in an airtight container or fill the shells with a dessert mixture.

Microwave Techniques

Refer to the microwave cooking chapter.

Individual Frozen Souffles

Yield: 6 servings

Traditional	Ingredients	Metric	Traditional	Ingredients	Metric
2 Tbsp.	Butter or margarine	30 mL	¼ tsp.	Dry mustard	1 mL
¼ cup	All-purpose flour	50 mL	1 cup	Milk	250 mL
½ tsp.	Salt	3 mL	1½ cups (6 oz.)	Sharp Cheddar cheese, shredded	375 mL
¼ tsp.	Pepper	1 mL	6	Eggs, separated	6

Directions

1. Melt butter in a heavy saucepan over low heat. Blend in flour, salt, pepper, and mustard; cook 1 minute.

2. Gradually add milk; cook over medium heat, stirring constantly, until thickened.

3. Add cheese, stirring until melted; remove from heat, and cool slightly.

4. Beat egg yolks until thick and lemon colored. Add a small amount of cheese sauce to yolks, and mix well; stir yolk mixture into remaining cheese mixture.

5. Beat egg whites until stiff but not dry; fold into cheese mixture. Pour into six buttered 1-cup (250 mL) souffle dishes; cover with plastic wrap and freeze.

6. To bake, place frozen souffles on baking dish. Bake at 350°F (175°C) for 40 minutes or until lightly browned.

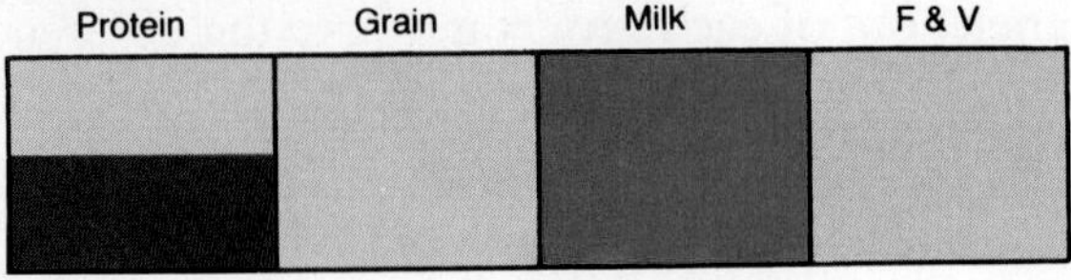

Vocabulary Review

Candling
Poaching
Coagulate
Shirred
Clarified butter
Omelet
Fold in
Meringue

Questions for Review

1. What are some of the functions of eggs in food products? Give several examples.
2. What do you look for to determine the freshness of an egg?
3. What are the USDA grading specifications for eggs?
4. What sizes of eggs can you buy in grocery stores?
5. When recipes include eggs, on what size egg are they based?
6. How do you store eggs to help preserve freshness and flavor?
7. What is the most important principle for successfully cooking eggs?
8. Is "boiled" egg an appropriate name? Why?
9. What is the difference between a poached egg and a shirred egg?
10. What is the consistency of perfect scrambled eggs?
11. What is the maximum number of eggs recommended for making an omelet?
12. What makes a fluffy omelet fluffy?
13. Which acidic ingredients can be used to increase the potential volume of egg whites?
14. What are the three stages of beaten egg whites used in food preparation?
15. What happens when egg whites are overbeaten?
16. Explain why even one small drop of oil or greasy beaters can prevent egg whites from beating to a high volume.
17. What is the difference between a soft meringue and a hard meringue?

Things to Do

1. The USDA has grading specifications for eggs based on how the whites and yolks hold up when the egg is cracked open. Perform your own test using Grade AA, Grade A, and Grade B eggs. Describe the differences in the grading specifications. If you can't find Grade B eggs, let a few sit out at room temperature for a week. Compare them to fresh ones.

2. Experiment with eggs to see how porous they are. Place a few eggs in a plastic bag with fresh herbs or other seasonings. Have a control group of eggs: ones that are left in the carton. Make an omelet out of each group and note the differences.

3. There are three stages of beaten egg whites: foamy, soft peaks, and stiff peaks. Beat two egg whites and note the changes as they reach each stage.

4. Beat two egg whites that are at room temperature, then beat two egg whites while still cold from the refrigerator. What was the difference between the two products? Explain why you think they beat differently.

Section 6

Let's Eat

19 Planning Meals

Planning and Creating Nutritious Meals

What's in a meal? The Japanese might consider specially seasoned rice with an artistic arrangement of slivers of raw seafood and pickled ginger root as an ideal "meal." One region in Switzerland would serve you boiled potatoes spread with Gruyere cheese and topped by dill or sweet pickles. The Aborigines of Australia consider roasted white caterpillars to be a treasured meal. In the United States, a "meal" generally has been accepted as the pattern of eating meat, potatoes or bread, and a vegetable followed by dessert such as apple pie or a hot fudge sundae. Now even that seems to be changing. Throughout the world, no set foods are necessary to "make a meal." So, what's in a meal? What people eat and when they eat depends upon what is available to them and when their lifestyles allow them to prepare and eat the foods that meet their nutritional needs.

Can you imagine telling ranchers or sheep herders that they have to stop at least two times a day to sit down with their families, who are miles away, for a hot cooked meal? They might laugh at you knowing full well that their portable, nutritious, high-energy foods such as beef jerky, hard tack, or cheese and fruit nourish them well in the field. Do you think that the many young people who work after school would agree the only way to get the food they need would be to quit work so that they could sit down to dinner with their families every night? The family meal might be a pleasant luxury and an important time to protect, but necessity has taught working students that they can make other arrangements for eating nutritious meals and still work. There is no one set way that has to be followed to plan your food and meals so that you get the energy, nutrients, pleasing tastes, and social times you and your family need.

Responsibility for Planning

The very freedom of choices in this fast-paced era increases your responsibility for making the right selections. In the past, rigid, old-fashioned meal patterns and routine day-to-day schedules did offer a healthy variety of foods at home and in restaurants. In this age of specialized restaurants, fast-food chains, and eat-on-the-run lifestyles, you can fall into the rut of repeating the same foods over and over without eating the variety of foods that is required to meet your body's needs. The need to be aware of what you are eating, plan for a varied diet, and develop the ability to make meals happen have become crucial survival skills for all individuals and their families.

Did your shopping selections stay within your foods budget? You'll find your answer in the checkout line.

Shopping Plans

Without any food in your home, meal planning is close to impossible. Therefore, one of the first steps is shopping for the food. Today, many teenagers are responsible for stocking their families' refrigerators and cabinets. That calls for careful budgeting and wise shopping practices to get the most nutrition and best buys for your food dollar.

Throughout this book, you have learned wise shopping practices for each of the many types of foods. For instance, you learned that purchasing fresh fruits and vegetables in season is a money saver and offers you the value of good nutrition. When shopping, keep in mind the following and you'll come out ahead on the cash register receipt.

- Unit pricing can help you compare the price difference between two items. By knowing the cost per pound, ounce, etc., you can realize which product offers more for your food dollar.
- Anytime you buy a convenience food or processed food, remember you are paying for the service. Stop to think if you could save money by fixing the food yourself. However, in some cases, the savings in time is worth more than the savings in money.
- Meat purchases add the most to the grocery bill. To cut down the cost, figure the servings per pound. If you buy a less expensive cut of meat that has a lot of bone, you are not getting as many servings as you would from a piece without any bone. Also consider using meat extenders, such as **textured vegetable protein** (TVP) made from soybeans. Using economical TVP increases the number of servings you can get from a pound of ground beef.
- Use food labels to help you make wise selections. Review the section in Chapter 7 on food labels.
- Choose a store that offers the services and prices you want. Types of stores vary in their pricing. **Supermarkets** usually have a wide variety of foods and brands. They may offer specialty areas such as delicatessens and bakeries. **Convenience stores** have a more limited selection and their prices are usually higher than supermarkets. However, they can be handy for picking up a forgotten or last-minute item. **Discount stores** usually have the lowest prices, but they do not offer many services. Often the customers have to bag their own groceries. Some stores sell one type of food with an excellent variety of that food. These **specialty stores** are good places to shop for a special occasion when you want out-of-the-ordinary foods or for a unique gift. Don't forget that farmers' markets and pick-your-own-produce places are fun alternatives to the modern food shopping world—and they can be cost-saving, too.

Ways to Save On the Grocery Bill

Do you read the grocery store ads in your local newspaper? If you've been skipping over them, don't. They can make good reading. By comparing the prices advertised by competing stores, you can find the best buys. Using coupons can save dollars, too. Even more savings are gained by using a store that offers double savings on the coupons.

Before heading off to the store for a carefree

shopping spree, make a list. Check the supplies on hand at your home. What's missing? What's running low? One surefire way to raise your budget is by having to make multiple trips to the store for the week's groceries. Make a list and use it. The less time you are in a store, the less money you will be tempted to spend. Now is also the time to use those store advertisements to plan your shopping around the good deals. Are pork chops on sale this week? If so, try out that new herbed pork chop recipe. Can you buy a larger quantity of a food and make two or three meals from it? For instance, consider how at Thanksgiving the roast turkey not only makes a holiday meal but sandwiches and casseroles after the special day. If you divided the cost of the turkey over all those meals, it is not such an expensive purchase after all. What other foods would be good for several meals?

Comparison shopping is a great way to hold the line on food costs. Reading the stores ads in the newspaper is the way to compare stores, but once you've picked a place to shop, don't stop comparing. In the store, compare one brand with another. Remember, generic brands usually cost less than name brands and may suit your purpose. Compare the different forms of the foods. Are fresh or frozen strawberries the better buy this week? Compare the different qualities of a food. Remember that some foods are graded according to their quality. Choose the quality that you need.

Finally, avoid impulse purchases. Don't be tempted by the colorful labels of foods you don't have on your list. Try to eat before going shopping. That way your growling stomach won't rule your head.

Consumer Guide

Reading between the lines, or rather reading the lines, is a common occurrence in grocery stores. Those parallel lines found on most food items contain a lot of information in electronic code. This code, known as the *Universal Product Code (UPC),* lets a computer system read pricing and product information right from the packaging. The clerk passes the product over a laser beam scanner that "reads" the information. The information is passed to a computer that prints out the name and price of the product on the register receipt. This speeds up the checkout process. An additional advantage is that stores can keep track of the sales of items and reorder before the supplies run out.

Planning the Variety

Fortunes are spent on individual nutrition plans and advice. You are lucky. You already have the valuable basic key to all nutrition planning—the Daily Food Guide. With the assistance of the Basic Food Groups, you can unlock the door to instant variety and balance for your meal planning. You'll even stand a better chance of getting all the nutrients you need by not limiting yourself to a few foods or a few recipes. No one food provides all the nutrients you need. Using the Basic Food Groups as a guide, plan meals that provide variety, balance, and moderation for each day.

Plan a Manageable Meal

Whenever you eat something, whether it is breakfast, a snack, lunch, or dinner, it is a kind of meal. You still need to plan ahead for what and when you will eat and whether it takes any food preparation. If you are planning a meal for yourself and others, you probably will feel the responsibility even more. Managing the many details of getting a meal together involves planning and thinking about a lot of details. By practicing a few simple guidelines, you can de-

Consumer Guide

Are you familiar with open dating and how it can be of value to you? Dates stamped on food packages are called *open dating.* There are four types of open dating:

- **Pack date is the day the food was processed or packaged. Canned foods or other foods with a long shelf life usually have pack dates.**
- **Pull date is the last day a store may sell a food as fresh. This is usually listed as "sell by. . . ."**
- **Expiration date is the last day a product should be used. This is usually listed as "do not use after. . . ."**
- **Freshness date is the last day a food will be at its best quality. This is usually listed as "best if used by. . . ."**

velop management and preparation skills. Those skills will help you turn mealtime into a rewarding experience. Surprisingly, management skills are the same in the kitchen or on the job. When you master the techniques of planning and organizing in the kitchen, you also might be helping yourself for other areas of your life's achievements. Besides, any job well done can help you feel "good" about yourself.

Management Techniques

1. Plan the specific tasks that need to be done. Simple jobs can be planned in your head. Plan the more complex ones on paper.

2. Match the list of jobs with the supplies, equipment, skills, and time needed. If you do not have and cannot get equipment and supplies needed for the planned activity, change the plan to fit what you do have available. If you do not yet know how to do any of the jobs, modify the plan to fit something you can do. For example, when time is short, plan a simple meal.

3. Organize your work area. Clear the area for space to work. Move equipment close to where you will need it. Remember the rule, "point of first use!" Whenever you are faced with decisions regarding where to store a turner, mixing bowl, or mixer, store it by where it is usually used first. You are in more of a "time bind" when preparing food than when putting away the utensils. Have you ever needed to remove a pizza that was beginning to brown in a hot oven only to discover that the hot pads were stored across the room? Another common mistake is to store utensils such as straight spatulas or measuring spoons by the sink or dishwasher, not by where you mix the foods.

4. Practice "one-time handling" whenever possible. Avoid moving objects or projects around to be "done" later. In the office, this is called paper shuffling. Whenever you pick up an object, finish the job then. Chop the onion, carrots, etc., when you first get them out for a recipe. Avoid arranging food to be fixed later and creating piles of dirty dishes to be washed later. Such jobs are small when handled one at a time, but pile up when allowed to accumulate. Have you ever felt challenged and motivated by a stack of dirty dishes? Washing mixing bowls as you first take them to the sink leaves you with a clean kitchen at eating time. Postponing small chores results in a pile of unsightly dirty dishes that you may feel like walking away from later. It is another version of that old adage, "an ounce of prevention is worth a pound of cure."

Rely upon Your Resources

The most efficiently planned meal you can imagine is not going to work if you don't have the resources to make it happen. Remember

What tasks could be done ahead of time to save on final cooking time? (Hint: the vegetables could be prepared and the meat cooked.)

from Chapter 1 that decision-making depends upon investigating your resources. Your resources are time, skills, money, available materials (food supplies on hand in the kitchen), equipment, and information (recipes, food ads, and how to instructions).

Time to Eat

Juggling schedules and available time seems to be the single most determining factor in when meals are eaten and what food is prepared. It is not unusual for everyone in a family to have a job or special activities. If a family has four members, that could be four schedules to juggle into one time slot for a meal together.

Those elaborate preparations that take several hours to prepare might have to wait for holidays and special occasions. But wonderful meals don't have to wait for special days. Simple preparations with short cooking times or advance food preparations necessarily don't mean dull meals. Old favorite recipes also can be converted through use of convenience foods if no one has time to prepare them from scratch.

Everyone in the family can share the responsibility for preparing and serving meals. Breakfasts can be planned so that a family sits together, or individuals can help themselves at different times during the morning. The trick is planning together to have on hand the needed ingredients or prepared foods that meet everyone's schedules and needs. Don't overlook the "portable" breakfast. Breakfast "on the run" can be a satisfying and nourishing treat for children, teenagers, and adults. The long ride to school or work for commuters sometimes provides a more leisurely opportunity to enjoy a nutritious planned breakfast than the get-ready rush at home. (See Chapter 1 for breakfast ideas you can take with you.)

Attractive and tempting foods can be prepared ahead to save on last-minute preparation time.

Skills

Food preparation skills are enjoyable to learn. It is best, however, to develop them when you are not rushed. Plan simple meals that match your level of confidence when time is short. Once you learn the basic principles, such as low heat for protein foods, you can apply the knowledge to lots of different foods without memorizing individual directions. Learn from your successes and mistakes. That old saying, "practice makes perfect" may not be a guarantee of success, but practice makes confidence—for sure!

Have you ever caught yourself remembering difficult and involved directions, but forgetting to do the obvious, like remembering your house key? Reading a recipe all the way through before you start to make it is one of those important but often overlooked steps. Efficiency in meal preparation depends upon simple, important guidelines which include:

1. Read the recipe all the way through before you start combining ingredients.
2. Outline the times involved and the order for preparation steps. Write these down and keep the list nearby so that you can check your progress while you are working. It also helps to keep you from forgetting to serve a prepared food.
3. Lay out the ingredients and equipment before starting.
4. Do all advance preparation steps such as chopping, cooling, warming, and slicing.
5. Overlap preparation steps whenever possible. For example, chop, peel, and measure ingredients while waiting for butter to soften or water to boil. Set the table while foods are baking or heating. Set a timer to remind you about needed cooking steps.

Spicy chile con carne (with meat) and beans is good enough for party food and a wonderful way to combine animal protein with vegetable protein to cut down on costs without sacrificing protein.

Money as a Resource

Food for meals at home and away from home cost most families a large share of their income. To help keep that cost within a reasonable amount, it is useful to establish a weekly or monthly budget. For some families or individuals, it is easiest to figure the budget by each paycheck period. Keep track of what you spend on food items for several paycheck periods. Average the figures. For example, for two paycheck periods, divide the total amount spent on food by two.

How does that figure fit into your total budget? Determine if you are spending the right amount or too much on food. Judge your spending on the amount that you set. To stay within that dollar amount, cut back on high-cost items such as eating out, convenience foods, fresh meats, and of course, junk foods. The good news is that when you discover that you are going to have extra money in the budget, you can treat yourself and family to some of those "luxury" items and feel good about it. Throughout this book, you have learned about foods that supply a high density of nutrients for low cost in money and calories. Apply those buying and food selection hints to stay within your food budget. Your knowledge about nutrition, comparative costs of foods, buying tips, and ways to prepare new and inexpensive foods is now a resource you can rely on for making nutritious decisions and good meals happen.

Plan a Taste-Tempting Meal

Have you ever been "greeted" at the door by drifting aromas of sizzling pizza or the spicy call of cinnamon cookies? When you are hungry, food makes sense. Hunger also makes your senses of smell, sight, sound, feeling, and taste call your attention to the food.

Television and photographs use colorful displays of food with squirting lemons, steaming smoke, and sizzling sound to make you want to eat the food. Some bakeries and restaurants place their exhaust fans to blow tantalizing aromas toward the street to lure people in to eat. In restaurants, food photographs in a menu and the way the food is brought to the table are developed to bring out the best appearance of each item. You can use the same visual cues to make your meals and food arrangements appealing.

Contrast

Use different colors, shapes, and textures of foods together. Picture a soft, red canned tomato next to a rice casserole with a tomato meat sauce on a red plate with a cooked red pepper for a garnish. Everything is about the same color and shape, and all are soft foods. Now change that plate to bright yellow. Use the same white rice with red meat sauce, but add slices of fresh, crisp green peppers for a garnish. Use fresh, sliced tomatoes and add some orange carrot sticks. Basically the menus are the same, but the crisp textures, the different shapes, and the contrasting colors make the second plate exciting and appetizing.

Flavor

Select flavors that stimulate different taste buds in the same meal and everything will actually be tastier. Varying the tastes keeps the flavors sharp. You will want to avoid serving the same food twice in the same meal if possible. Spicy dishes should be the highlight of a plate with mild foods. For instance, serve a Mexican tostado with a spicy hot sauce, crispy corn chips, and smooth, mild refried beans. Can you think of other terrific taste combinations?

Color

Color is very important in taste appeal. Researchers at the University of Illinois used lighting to make food appear unusual colors. Their studies show that the same senses that

Turn ordinary foods into festive treats by adding simple garnishes using thin tomato peels (left), citrus slices (middle), and citrus halves.

make you like a food can make you dislike the food. According to one researcher, "Nobody drools at the sight of blue peas." Can you imagine eating purple mashed potatoes with green butter? Another example of color's effect upon your appetite is the classic demonstration of a white fish fillet with mashed potatoes and white bread on a white plate. Would that make you hungry?

Natural Shapes And Varied Sizes

Food is most attractive in natural, recognizable shapes. It is more pleasant to be able to recognize what you are eating. Food that looks as if it has been "chewed" and molded is simply not as attractive without extensive decorating. Even the decorating can look quite unnatural. Foods on a serving dish or single plate are more inviting when the sizes are varied.

Texture

Sensory-evaluation experts rate the texture and "sound" of food when you bite into it as major factors for liking a food. According to studies, most people would not bother to eat a second corn chip if the first one did not crunch. The look of texture and the contrast of different surfaces of foods makes a more interesting-looking meal. A green, crisp, rough piece of broccoli next to a smooth, browned surface of yellow corn custard looks more appetizing than a piece of rough broccoli next to a pile of whole green beans.

Temperature

A steak should look sizzling hot, while a tall glass of milk looks more appealing with signs of cool condensation running down the glass. Shiny, oily foods are appetizing as long as they look hot. The weather also makes a difference in what we want to eat. Hot soup sales increase on cold winter days, but are seldom in demand on hot summer days.

Meal Patterns

Just a few years ago, any information about meal planning would have included guidelines for a strict three-meals-a-day schedule. A typical day's pattern might be:

Breakfast

- Fruit (usually citrus)
- Main Dish of cereal/eggs or waffles
- Toast and one pat of butter
- Milk and coffee

Lunch

- Main dish featuring a high-protein food (sandwiches, casseroles, hearty soups, or meat salads)
- Vegetable and/or fruit
- Bread with one pat of butter
- Milk
- Coffee or tea

Dinner

- Main dish featuring a piece of fish, meat, poultry, or other complete-protein dish
- Two vegetables
- Salad
- Bread and one pat of butter
- Milk
- Coffee, tea, or juice
- Dessert of fruit, pastry if weight is not a problem

Today, the menu choices are left to you. The guides are there if you want them, but you don't need to follow such a rigid pattern. Breakfast has turned into a flexible meal that is just as likely to include a sandwich as lunch would. Pizza is a nutritious and convenient eye-opener for many.

The perfect dinner is no longer equated with a 16-ounce (500 g) steak with a baked potato and lettuce salad. Poultry and fish dishes are prized by many, and pork is now a lean meat enjoyed by more people. Fresh, crisp cooked vegetables have moved to the spotlight of the meal even replacing the meat in some recipes. Meal planning has never had more opportunities for variety and exciting new flavor combinations. The newly favored styles of cooking such as stir-frying, steaming, and poaching are healthful and flavorful. Snacking between the standard three meals is often the answer to squeezing nutritious foods into a busy lifestyle. Just use your head and the Basic Food Groups and U.S.RDAs as your guides for manageable and healthful meals. (Review Chapters 3 and 4 for nutrition guidelines.)

Serving Beverages

Do you remember, "The pause that refreshes"? For years that was the slogan of one of the world's most successful soft drinks. The slogan may have been replaced, but the need for pauses that refresh the mind and body during the day has not. Breaks might consist of a quick stop at the drinking fountain, an elaborate tea at a local restaurant, coffee at a drive-through restaurant, or a soft drink, carton of milk, or a carbonated bottle of water from a vending machine. Whichever you choose, thirst quenchers help your body. They also can be an enjoyable part of your daily routine and fun times with friends and family. Some choices also can give you valuable nutrients. Milk and fruit juices contain minerals and vitamins and are more readily available in vending machines and fast-foods places than they used to be.

Coffee

Coffee is grown in several locations in the world, but thrives on high mountain locations. Most of the coffee is grown in South America, Hawaii, Africa, and Jamaica. The coffee beans that are used to make coffee are harvested from trees and roasted before being sold to consumers.

Coffee comes in the whole bean form ready for you to grind, or already ground in several

Turn a dull meal on a plate into an adventurous affair by combining interesting flavors and shapes, then serve at sizzling temperature.

Javanese Pork Sate

Yield: 4 servings

Traditional	Ingredients	Metric
1 lb.	Lean boneless pork	500 g
2 Tbsp.	Peanut butter	30 mL
½ cup	Onion, minced	125 mL
1 clove	Garlic	1 clove
2 Tbsp.	Lemon juice	30 mL
2 Tbsp.	Soy sauce	30 mL
1 Tbsp.	Brown sugar	15 mL
1 Tbsp.	Cooking oil	15 mL
Dash	Hot pepper sauce	Dash

Directions

1. Cut pork into ½ inch (1.3 cm) cubes.
2. Blend remaining ingredients together (a blender does this well).
3. Marinate pork in mixture for 10 minutes.
4. Thread pork on skewers (if using bamboo skewers, soak in water one hour to prevent burning).
5. Grill or broil for 10 to 12 minutes, turning occasionally, until done.
6. Serve with hot cooked rice, if desired.

sizes for different types of coffeemakers. Read the label carefully. You will need to buy the grind of coffee that works in your coffeemaker. Coffee is preground for drip, percolator, and automatic drip coffeemakers. (See the section "Coffeemakers.") Instant coffees take no special brewing, so they will not be explained any further in this section.

The canned coffees are already blended for a specific flavor. Buy only what you need for up to a week's time. Coffee loses its flavor quickly—especially after it is ground. Keep it in a dark container tightly closed in a cool place. The freezer is the best place to store coffee, but the refrigerator also works well.

Coffeemakers

Some of the basic types of coffeemakers are:

Drip makers. With drip makers, you put the coffee grounds in a basket and then pour freshly boiled water over them. The brewed coffee slowly drips through to the coffee pot. Some drip makers have a cone with a paper filter that holds the coffee grounds. You slowly pour the boiling water through until all the coffee is made. If you stop, the filter has a tendency to clog.

Percolators. In a percolator the coffee basket that holds the grounds rests on a funnel-like stem. The water is in a pot beneath the basket. When the water in the pot approaches the boiling point, it creates a vacuum that pushes water up the stem and over the coffee. Traveling up the stem cools the water to the correct temperature for the coffee.

Automatic Drip. These electric coffeemakers are made so that all you have to do is to put in the filter, coffee, and water. It brews for the correct time and keeps the brewed coffee warm after it is done.

Coffee Press. With this type of coffeemaker, you put the grounds directly into the pot and then pour the boiling water in with the

Iced tea—a favorite hot-weather refreshment—tastes best when brewed and then cooled with ice.

grounds. A tight-fitting strainer is then pushed down through the grounds and water. This strains out the grounds and hold them on the bottom of the pot.

Espresso maker. The espresso maker of an automatic machine is airtight, like a pressure cooker. It forces the hot water through the grounds under pressure. That extracts more flavor and oils from the grounds. Espresso is much stronger and has a slightly thicker consistency than regular brewed coffee.

Food Facts

You consume caffeine in many of the soft drinks on the market and in coffee, tea, and cocoa. People have been eating and drinking foods with caffeine for thousands of years, but the score on its benefits and harmful effects is not totalled yet. Caffeine is a recognized drug, but until lately its long history of use by people made it appear completely safe. Some of the current concerns link coffee with heart disease. However, the studies conflict in their results. What you can do is to be aware of the caffeine in the food you consume. Read the labels. Many of your favorite beverages are available with the caffeine removed.

Making that Perfect Cup of Coffee

Many social and work situations call for knowing how to make a good cup of coffee. The principles are the same for coffee with caffeine or decaffeinated coffee.

You can help give yourself a headstart on an excellent cup of coffee by always washing the pot with hot sudsy water every time you use it. The oil in coffee coats the pot and turns rancid quickly. That rancid oil ruins the fresh taste of the new brew.

Read the instructions for each coffee pot you use. Directions and measurements vary for different makers. Use the following general guidelines.

- Start with fresh cold water.
- Measure ¾ cup (175 mL) of water for every cup of brewed coffee.
- Measure 2 tablespoons (30 mL) of coffee grounds for each cup of coffee you are making. Hint: If someone prefers weaker coffee, dilute it after the coffee is brewed. You will get better flavor that way.
- Never boil coffee. Water heated to the boiling stage dissolves more tanins from the coffee and releases a bitter flavor.
- Reheat coffee carefully so that it does not boil on top of the stove in a glass pot or in the microwave oven in a glass container. Metal can combine with the coffee to form an off-flavor if coffee stands for a long time in metal or is boiled in a metal container.
- If you want to serve iced coffee, make it ahead and cool it in the refrigerator. You also can make it extra strong and ice it.
- Make only enough coffee to last an hour. Coffee loses its flavor quickly after an hour. If you need more, make more from scratch.

The Art of Making Tea

The gracious serving of a hospitable cup of tea creates a feeling of security whether it is in a proper high tea in England, a formal tea ceremony in the Orient, or a cheery cup in your own warm home. Tea is brewed from the dried leaves of the tea plant from the Orient. There are countless varieties of tea that vary greatly in flavor and color. Some of the most popular teas are blends, such as Earl Grey or English Breakfast tea. Flavored, spiced teas also have become quite popular. True Oriental tea contains caffeine. However tea contains less caffeine than coffee.

Some of the basic types of tea include the following:

Green tea is very light in color and has a distinct flavor. The leaves for green tea are not fermented, but fresh dried.

Black tea is made from leaves that have been fermented to develop a prized rich flavor. It has a full and stronger flavor than teas made from fresh leaves.

The commercial teas that are purchased in tea bags are usually blends of less expensive quality. Tea leaves are graded by size. The orange pekoe that is used widely by the tea companies in the U.S. consists of the smaller leaves, but is a popular flavor.

Making Tea

You can make an elaborate ceremony about preparing the tea, but pouring freshly boiled water over tea leaves or tea bags is the basic step. Be careful to use a ceramic or glass teapot. Metal reacts with the pigments in the tea causing off-flavors and a film that forms over the surface. Steeping the tea while it brews varies according to your preferences, but 3 to 5 minutes is recommended. Use about 1 teaspoon (5 mL) of loose tea per 1 cup (250 mL) of water. Loose tea is supposed to make the best tea, but it is not as convenient as using tea bags. Strain tea made from loose tea or put the tea in a tea ball before adding the water. Serve the hot tea as it comes from the pot. Add lemon, milk, sugar, or honey if you prefer. Stick cinnamon or other spices such as allspice or cloves can be added for a festive touch.

Like coffee, tea also becomes bitter if boiled. Keep tea hot, but if you do reheat it, use the same method as listed for coffee.

Iced tea can be made simply by using double the amount of tea per cup of water and adding ice to cool it. The best iced tea for smooth flavor and clear liquid is made by allowing the tea to steep slowly in the sun. Sun tea is made in a glass jar and set in the sun for a few hours to gently warm up. Strain it and add ice. Cloudy tea is caused by hard water or cooling in the refrigerator. It does not hurt the tea's flavor or drinking qualities.

Nonalcoholic Drinks and Punches

Do you value your personal freedom to make your own choices? As a citizen of this country you can be proud of the continual challenge everyone accepts to ensure personal freedom for individuals! All too often, a common situation that denies equal rights for individual decisions is generally accepted. Have you ever been at a party when no alternative was offered for someone who did not choose to drink alcohol? It happens all the time. Hosts and hostesses forget to provide attractive alternatives. Luckily, as more and more people choose nonalcoholic drinks in this health-conscious era, that situation may not be as common. So if you are having a party, be sure to offer a beverage choice for a healthy life-saving lifestyle.

Nonalcoholic beverages can be just as festive and even tastier and more nutritious than alcoholic drinks. There are many recipes and suggestions available in cookbooks, on TV, and in the newspapers. Collect the ideas so you will be prepared. A tempting example follows. Note: Not using alcohol in these drinks saves about 50 to 100 calories per drink depending on the sweetness of the wine or liquor used in the alcoholic version.

Strawberry Cooler

Yield: 8, ½ cup (125 mL) servings

Traditional	**Ingredients**	**Metric**
1 small can	Frozen limeade	1 small can
10-oz. bag	Frozen strawberries with no added sugar syrup	315 g bag
10-oz. bottle	Club soda	300 mL bottle
1 tray	Ice cubes (cracked) or crushed ice	1 tray

Directions

1. Slightly soften the limeade with a rubber scraper and then blend in the blender.

2. Pour in small amounts of the club soda to keep the mixture moving. Stop the motor often to wipe down the sides with the scraper.

3. When that is all blended, add the individual berries until blended.

4. Add ice cubes until the mixture is the texture of a slushy freeze drink.

5. Serve in pretty glasses with a straw, spoon, and a sprig of mint, if available. A slice of lime or lemon is also attractive slipped over the edge of the glass.

Sitting Down to a Meal

Well, all the meal preparation is done. You can finally sit down and savor your hard work. But, wait, what about setting the table? Just as meal preparation and meals themselves have changed, so have table settings. At one time, families sat down to tables loaded with serving dishes heaped with food (called **family style service**). While that is still a common practice, it is no longer a set way of serving food. Just as often the food may be put on the dinner plates in the kitchen and the pre-served plates then taken to the table. Of course, things go much smoother if the table has been set with the **flatware** or **table service,** (knives, forks, and spoons) and glasses ahead of time to avoid a last minute rush while the food sits getting cold. See the illustration for the standard way to set the table. Customs often vary in different localities.

Table settings are less formal than they used to be. The old rule of always putting on a knife, spoon, and fork whether you used it or not is generally more flexible now. Creative tables are often set with just the piece you need, such as a

This Strawberry Cooler is a tasty, healthful drink alternative for a festive gathering.

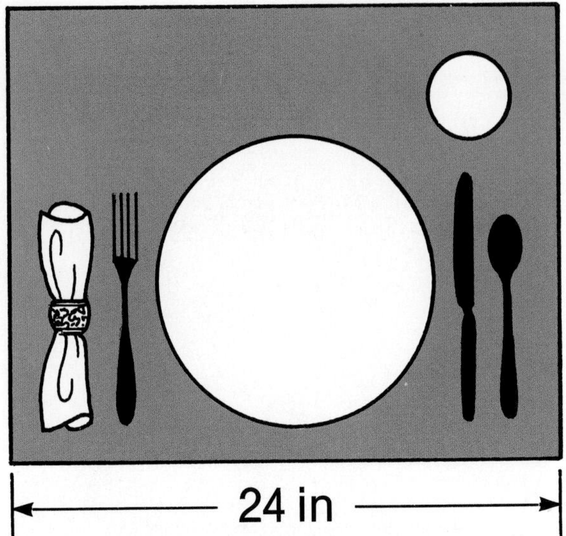

The standard way of setting the table allows 24 inches for each diner's place setting.

soup spoon and knife for a soup and bread meal. Colorful kitchen towels and paper napkins make place mats or napkins. You can add a plant, flowers, or any attractive food for a centerpiece.

There are occasions when more formal table service is used, such as when you dine out. With **formal service,** a table attendant brings the filled plates out from the kitchen and places them before each diner.

If you wish to duplicate formal table service at home for a special occasion, use a tablecloth, cloth napkins if you have them, and your best dinnerware, flatware, and glasses. A colorful centerpiece or candle can create atmosphere or a theme. When serving a salad as a first course, add an extra, smaller fork to the left of the dinner fork. This fork is then used for the salad and is removed with the salad plate before the meal is served. The general idea is to have a separate utensil with which to eat each "course."

Another style of serving food is **buffet service**—one of the first "do it yourself" projects. This is a convenient method for serving large groups of people. The food is placed on a serving table along with the dinnerware, flatware, and glasses. The diners pass by the serving table, pick up a plate, and then fill their plates with the foods of their choice. Beverages may be placed at the end of that serving table, on a separate serving table, or brought to the diners at the eating tables. Place napkins and table service last on the serving table, so the diners' hands are free to serve their food.

Good Manners Consider Others

Whatever type of table service you use, good manners are in order. You may be surprised to know that in other countries, belching at the table is considered good manners and a sign that you like the food. Of course, that is not the case in the United States. The following are some other table manners that are practiced here: The general rule for what makes "good" manners is consideration for others at your table, not fanciful mannerisms.

- Wait for everyone at your table to be served. If you're attending a party or other special occasion, wait for the host or hostess to begin eating before you start. (Sometimes the host or hostess is too busy to begin eating, so he or she will put the fork on the plate as a signal for the guests to "start." In less formal settings, they might say to everyone, "Don't wait for me, please start eating before the food gets cold.")
- Ask to have food passed to you that is out of your reach. Do not lean across other person to grab something you want.
- Don't talk with your mouth full.
- Try to chew with your mouth closed.
- Don't put your elbows on the table. You could interfere with someone else's eating.
- Do not blow on hot food to cool it.
- Put your napkin in your lap. Do not return it to the table until you are finished eating.
- If more than one fork or spoon is included at your table setting, use the outside one first—and work in toward the plate.
- Rest soiled knives, forks, and spoons on the edge of the plate between use, not on the table or in a cup or bowl. (They can be flipped

out or fall and cause an embarassing mess.)

• Speak relatively softly at the table or in a restaurant. It is not considerate of others if your voice drowns out other's chances to visit or enjoy their meals.

• Put butter or jam on your plate first, then butter your bread. Do not butter directly from the stick of butter or margarine.

• Usually it's considered more polite to break a slice of bread or roll in half before buttering or eating it.

• Ask to be excused before leaving the table.

• Don't play with your food. If you don't like a food on your plate, just leave it alone. Don't complain to others about it.

• If you must cough or sneeze, turn your head to the side and cover your mouth. If you must blow your nose, excuse yourself from the table.

• Do not cut up all of your food at once. Cut a bite or two at a time.

• If you spill something, apologize and help clean it up. Don't continue to worry about it.

Good manners are not just to impress your friends. Even when you eat at home with your family, good manners are an important part of good dining.

One of the best parts of any meal can be enjoying the company of others.

The Final Steps

The delight of "doing dishes" is having them done and put away! Even the arrival of the electric dishwasher did not free kitchen users from doing dishes. Preparing dishes for the automatic dishwasher is almost as much work as washing them by hand. You still need to clean off the food and rinse the dishes. Whether doing dishes by hand or machine, you can prevent many cleaning problems by quick steps ahead of time. Follow these tips:

1. Eggs and foods with eggs need to be rinsed immediately in cool water. Hot water cooks on the egg. Dried egg is the base for nature's strongest glue, so don't let egg dry on the utensils.

2. Wash greasy foods and oils with hot, sudsy water. Grease won't dry on plates, so if you are out of hot water wait until some is available. Cool water just doesn't remove grease.

3. Scrape all food off plates immediately. This can be done in a few quick motions when clearing the plates. Remember the "one-time-handling" management guide.

4. Wash dishes as soon as possible.

5. For hand washing, start with the cleanest pieces, such as glasses, then do the flatware, plates, serving pieces, and cookware.

6. Change the washing water as needed when washing by hand. Keep it hot, clear, and sudsy.

7. The hotter the rinsing water, the less drying you will have to do. If you can use almost boiling water (not on soft plasticware), it also will help to kill bacteria.

8. Air drying dishes on a rack is a cleaner method than drying dishes with a used towel. Always try to use a freshly laundered towel each time. Dish towels should be washed in very hot water and preferably separately from the rest of the family laundry.

Vocabulary Review

Textured vegetable protein
Supermarket
Convenience store
Discount store
Specialty store
Universal product code
Point of first use
Meal patterns
Flatware
Table service

Questions for Review

1.What are some of the factors that influence what people choose to eat and when they choose to eat? What are some of those things in your life and background that influence what you eat?

2. What basic guidelines can you use to plan daily meals that provide variety, balance, and moderation? Why is moderation important?

3. Why is it a good idea to check the newspaper before making a shopping list?

4. Which type of store would you choose for the following?

a. The weeks's grocery shopping.
b. A quart of milk.
c. A birthday cake.

5. What are some management techniques that you can use to prepare meals efficiently?

6. Explain "point of first use" and how it might help you in the kitchen.

7. Why is it desirable to avoid accumulating large piles of unwashed dishes and utensils during food preparation?

8. Describe some ideas for using convenience foods to save time in meal preparation. Does the use of convenience foods always add to the cost of a meal? Explain how your ideas for convenience foods did or did not add to the cost of the meal.

9. What are some clues to help you decide if a recipe is a reliable one?

10. After you've selected a recipe, what do you do before you start to make it? Why?

11. What are six visual cues you can use to make your meals more appealing?

12. Why are strict rules for a meal's structure no longer considered necessary or even advisable?

13. Why is it important to not boil coffee?

14. How do you make iced coffee?

15. What is the difference between green tea and black tea?

16. Describe family style service. How does it differ from buffet service?

17. How would you handle each of these mealtime situations when you are eating with others?

a. You would like to have some potatoes, which are at the other end of the table.
b. You want to add to the conversation, but you have just taken a bite of food.
c. You are having a slice of bread and want to butter it.
d. You need to sneeze.
e. You just spilled your glass of milk.

18. How would you wash the breakfast plates after eating "sunny-side up" eggs?

19. Which would you wash first—the glasses or the serving dishes?

20. Why do you need two towels in the kitchen?

Things to Do

1. Look over your kitchen at home. What would you change to make the work area better for you? Why?

2. Suggest ways to plan meals that use food products with short cooking times and foods that can be partly prepared ahead of time.

3. Keep track of what is spent in your household on food a week. Figure a weekly budget and try to use it for one week. Report your successes and problems at the end of the week. How might you change your plan and why?

4. Plan a day's meals that provide the recommended servings for the Four Food Groups. Write the day's food and serving sizes down in an easy-to-follow list. Use the chart in the back of this book for individual nutrient content of the foods in your plan. Do they add up to the individual nutrients you need? Can you find any room for improvement? Remember, the Four Food Groups are organized to help you plan wisely. It takes a variety of choices from the Food Groups to continue to supply you with all your nutrient needs.

5. Look through magazines, newspapers, and books for examples of meals that have a good balance of flavor, colors, shapes, and textures. How does a balance of the contrasts in appearance and tastes affect your feeling about the food? Why?

6. Imagine that you wanted to make the following foods but were missing key ingredients. What could you substitute in the following recipes for the missing ingredient?

a. buttermilk biscuits—buttermilk missing.
b. oatmeal cookies—brown sugar missing.
c. burritos—sour cream missing.

GUEST
0097
DATE
10-4

Eating Out Has Become a Family Affair

Do you like to watch the old classic movies? Think back on the portrayal of the "housewife" (an outdated term that mostly has been replaced with "homemaker." After all, no one is married to a house!). Have you seen portrayed a new bride burning the roast and crying her eyes out as the gallant husband arrives home from work and asks the crucial question, "What's for dinner?" Catastrophe! "Never mind," says the hero husband, "I'll take you *out* for dinner!" Music heralds the ultimate gesture of supreme luxury as the two fade off into the glorious sunset for the rare treat of being waited on and served delicious food by other people.

Today, the old question of "What's for dinner?" is often replaced with "Where shall we eat tonight?" What's more, the person coming home from work is just as likely to be the woman. "Eating out" no longer is limited to an occasion that calls for a whole evening dedicated to being entertained by expensive food and luxurious service.

The relatively recent success of fast-food restaurants and food chains serving instant, appealing, and inexpensive food has helped to revolutionize the way Americans eat. Or maybe this is one of those, "Which came first, the chicken or the egg?" questions. Lifestyles have changed drastically. Busy Americans of all ages work untraditional hours that differ from other family member's schedules. Many wives and mothers work out of the home. Those two changes have created the need and support for 24-hour food service. By eating out together, many families have found they can spend their limited time visiting with each other instead of using that precious time to prepare the food. (Can you think of a way food preparation time also could be time spent together?). Another solution is to buy "take-out" food on the way home. You have learned that there are many ways you can plan and organize to save preparation time and still eat nutritious meals together at home. Eating out, however, remains a convenient alternative that many families, individuals, and students often take advantage of to answer their needs for food and a good time with others.

Eating Out Nutritiously

If you eat out most of the time, you may have difficulty balancing your diet to get the right number of calories and the needed variety of foods within each of the four food groups. There are many types of convenient fast-food restaurants, but all of them tend to offer the

Food Facts

Something is missing from American salad bars . . . and you probably haven't even noticed. It's sulfite-treated vegetables. Sulfites are food preservatives that were used to make lettuce and other raw vegetables look fresh. However, several thousand people were found to be highly allergic to sulfites. Sulfites are suspected in the deaths of at least 13 people, according to the FDA.

Since the chemicals have many uses in the food industry, it is difficult to know when the sulfite level poses a danger to sufferers. The FDA is trying to find a safe minimum and label foods at that minimum. Ten parts per million is the level that shouldn't be exceeded, according to agency recommendations. People's reactions to sulfites vary. The danger can range from hives, to the closing of air passages and shock.

Sulfites occur naturally in many foods, such as shrimp, mushrooms, and fermented foods. They are also used to clean equipment and condition doughs. In fact, sulfites are everywhere. Packaged foods containing sulfites must be labeled, even if the sulfites were added as a baking aid in a biscuit product.

If you are allergic to sulfites, there are some steps you can take to minimize reaction:

. Wash fresh vegetables and fruits carefully before cooking them.

. Avoid potassium bisulfite, potassium metabisulfite, sodium sulfite and bisulfite, sodium metabisulfate, and sulfur dioxide. If you are in doubt about any food product, throw it out.

most universally tempting foods such as deep-fried foods and easy-to-handle sandwiches with generous portions of bread. Think, too, about their other offerings: highly salted and seasoned foods, gooey sweets, salad bars featuring the favored iceberg lettuce (which has almost no nutrients without the outer dark green leaves that are usually thrown away), and starchy vegetables that are relatively high in calories compared to the amount of nutrients, such as beets and corn.

You are usually quite hungry when you place your order at a restaurant. With the stimulating aromas, pictures, tempting variety, and direct sales pitch from the person taking your order, you already have several strikes against you for making practical dietary decisions. Even when you do not order some of the tempting high-calorie extras such as "fries," desserts, or carbonated beverages, the helpers are trained to remind you. Do these questions sound familiar, "Would you like french fries?" and then, "What do you want to drink?" If you ask what the drink choices are, they never seem to mention milk, only the national brands of carbonated beverages that place sells. The technique works to break down that last-minute resistance of many a customer. You can arm yourself with a healthy defense to those "give-ins" at order time. There are some simple practices that can help you eat out nutritiously in a variety of situations and different types of restaurants. These guidelines include controlling your calorie intake as well as getting the nutrients you need.

Nutrition Can Be "In" When You Eat Out!

By using the following guidelines, you can avoid those high-calorie pitfalls of eating out.

1. Make up your mind what you are going to order before you talk to the person taking your order. Stick with your plan. Just because your friend orders a hot-fudge sundae or fries is not an acceptable reason to sacrifice your own intentions.

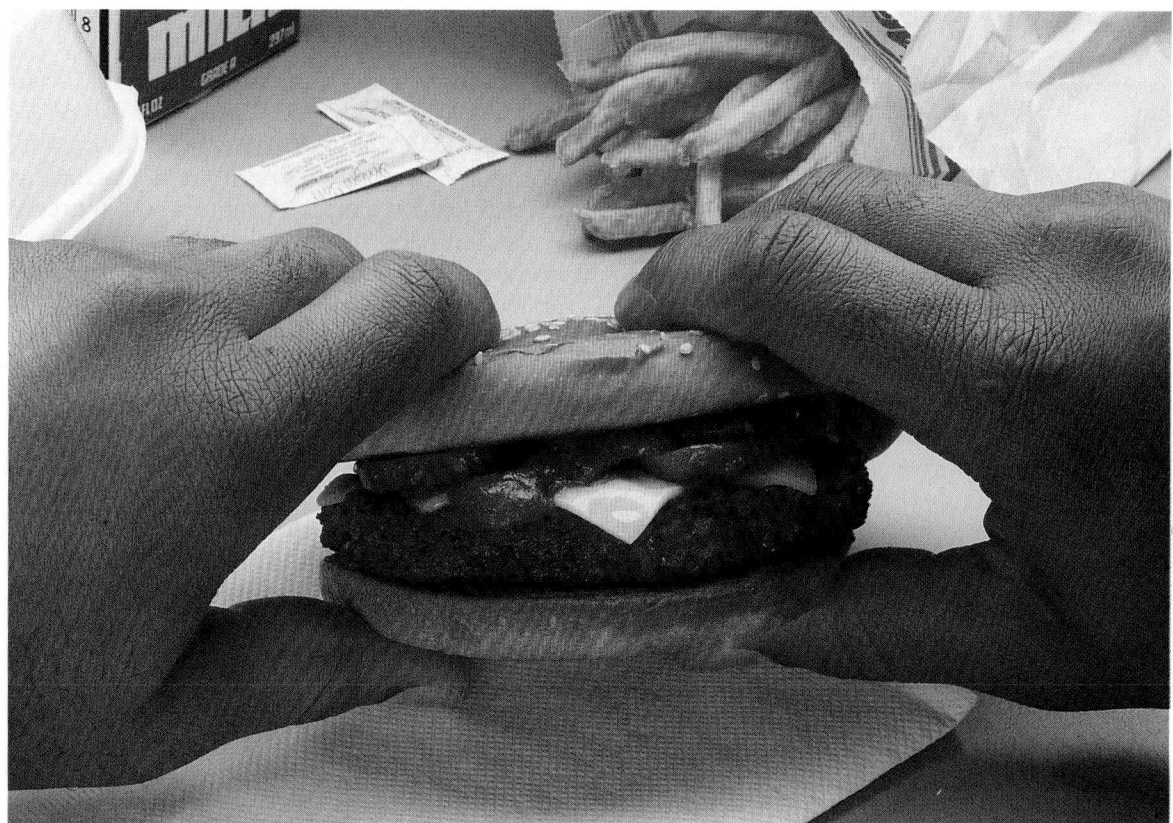

You can ruin a low-calorie meal, such as this broiled-lean hamburger, by adding a rich mushroom gravy sauce. Even "comes with the meal" french fries are a better deal if left uneaten— when extra calories are a problem.

2. Eat at different restaurants. You have learned that it takes a variety of foods from within each of the food groups to obtain all of the nutrients you need. Even when you select nutritious foods such as a lean hamburger with lettuce and tomato or a taco salad, you could be missing the nutrients you need from other foods. Repeating the same foods, even nutritious foods, day after day can create deficiencies of nutrients you need. Restaurants vary their offerings to entice new customers, so eating in a variety of places can add new foods to your choices.

3. Save money and expensive calories by limiting the times you order french fries, desserts, and deep-fried vegetables or meats.

4. Avoid rich gravies, sauces, and salad dressings to cut down on fat and calories. These food items contain high amounts of "hidden" calories and fats. You know you are eating fats when you butter a potato or roll, but such extras as mushroom gravy sauce for hamburgers, cheese sauces for potatoes or other vegetables, mayonnaise-sauces added to famous hamburgers, and mayonnaise-based salad dressings can add calories and a high fat content to the food. The often-used saying, "It is what you put on the potato that makes it high calorie, not the potato itself" also can apply to other foods.

5. Request that your salad be brought without dressing and your food without any sauce that might have been listed. Sometimes you can ask for the sauce, gravy, or dressing in a bowl on the side. Then you can use just a small amount if needed for flavor, and avoid extra calories.

6. Ask if the restaurant has a low-oil or low-

calorie dressing for your salad. If not, ask for separate vinegar and oil. You can apply your own using twice as much vinegar as oil and thereby cut the calories in half.

7. Be aware that a salad bar is not automatically nutritious just because it contains lettuce and other crisp items! You have learned that many nutrients can be lost or destroyed by long-time storage or improper handling. Even a well-stocked nutritious salad bar will not help you if you select items that are low in nutrients. Choose dark green lettuce greens, bright-red tomatoes that look fresh, and bright-looking green peppers. Carrots are a good choice, too, because the vitamin A is not likely to be lost from exposure and storage. Also look for cottage cheese, cheese, sprouts, *fresh* shredded cabbage, fresh melons, berries and other fruits, sesame seeds, sunflower seeds, and whole-wheat bread.

Other foods that contain valuable fiber and trace nutrients but are relatively low in vitamins and minerals include iceberg lettuce, radishes, cucumbers, beets, pale wilted tomatoes, pale chopped celery with no leaves, canned fruits, and fruit cocktails.

High-calorie foods to avoid are commercial puddings, marshmallow canned fruit salads, gelatin, mushrooms, most croutons, soda crackers, corn relish, pickles, and mayonnaise-based salad dressings. Items such as garbanzo beans, kidney beans, turkey, ham, boiled eggs, and bacon are high-protein foods that are also higher in calories than crisp greens and fresh vegetables. However, if you are eating at the salad bar to cut down on calories and to gain a complete meal, it would be valuable to select at least one of these protein foods. When you are eating dinner that contains meat along with the salad bar, you may want to consider the high-calorie content of the preceding items and choose vegetables and fruits instead.

8. Everyone wants to "get what they paid for." Because you feel you have paid for everything on your plate or all you can eat at a buffet, the temptation is to eat more than you really want or need. Remind yourself that it is no bargain to add harmful fat to your body just because you purchased the food. Look at the portions on your plate. Are they larger than you would eat at home? If yes, leave some on the plate or share with someone at your table. You will have made a good buy if you do not overeat just because large amounts of food are available. Don't be shy about asking for a take-home bag if you have a sizable portion that you do not wish to eat. Most restaurants expect this. In fact, many "doggie bags" now say "people bags." Ask to have the take-home meal kept in a cool place if you plan to stay long.

9. Look for the cooking methods that do not use added fat. They are broiling, poaching, steaming, roasting, baking, and stir-frying. Try to avoid looking at the full menu for all the tantalizing descriptions. Order what you know you like, or ask the restaurant personnel to tell you about the foods that are prepared by those methods. Be courteous, but firm, with the person taking your order. Ask if foods have sauces before ordering them. Ask to have a food prepared differently. Fast-food restaurants usually are not prepared to vary food preparation methods, but in a regular restaurant, don't hesitate. For example, you may want preparation such as broiling a meat item even if it is not listed that way on the menu. The worst thing that could happen is that they could say no, they couldn't do it for you.

10. Ask if the restaurant will substitute a green vegetable or a baked potato for french fries. If not, ask for them on a separate plate and give them away to someone else. Once those fries are on your plate, they tend to disappear one by one despite the best of intentions!

11. You can remove hundreds of calories instantly from a meal by simply removing the greasy crisp crust from fried foods. This works well with chicken, fish, and some meats.

You might think that ordering the salad bar is a safe choice for a low-calorie meal. However, one plate pictured has about 1000 calories and few nutrients. The other plate of food contains about half the calories and significant amounts of important nutrients. Can you tell which one is more healthful?

Chapter 20
Out To Eat

Hearty toppings can turn baked potatoes into a variety of nutritous meal possibilities. This is a handy way to use "leftovers," too.

12. Drink water with your meals. Most people tend to order soft drinks when they eat out. Look at your bill the next time you eat out. Beverages add a high proportion of the cost to the meal. Water is a valuable, no-cost nutrient that you are likely to omit when you order a soft drink. Milk is also a nutritious drink with meals.

13. For breakfast, order toast unbuttered with a separate pat of butter. Order eggs poached or soft cooked. If that does not suit you, ask for extra paper napkins and blot the excess fat off your scrambled eggs or omelet. You can remove as many as 50 calories that way.

14. Whenever it is available not fried, order seafood. Seafood is lower in calories than the red meats. Use plain lemon on the seafood and no sauce.

15. Pass up the temptation of munching on the crackers and butter or crackers and cheeses served as appetizers. If you are really hungry, eat a couple of crackers plain and drink a glass of water before the meal.

16. If half portions are available on the menu, order half size. If the full meals with all the courses are going to ruin your diet, consider ordering **a la carte** (each item priced separately).

17. To resist the dessert table, order fresh fruit from the appetizer list.

18. Don't eat any of the harmless-looking tartar sauce served with fish and some cheese dishes. It is mostly mayonnaise and high in calories. Substitute lemon juice.

Answers to Your Concerns

Many of the national restaurant chains care about the nutritional content of their products. They hire home economists, dietitians, and nutrition educators to plan and analyze the company's food choices. The findings are then communicated to the public through programs and publications. You can find examples of nutrient values in some popular fast-foods and fast-food combinations in the following lists. If the items you would like to know about are not listed, ask the manager of your local restaurant. He or she might have information on hand or could order them for you. You may decide it makes you feel confident to buy from a company that seems to care about your nutrition.

Food Fashions

Can you imagine a fashion show where the models display the latest colors, lines, and design of newsy food dishes? Soft French singing might furnish the background music for the narration, "Swallow into fashion this year with the elegant classic, le croissant, rediscovered in America for this season in warm tones of golden brown. Accessorize with a cool butter pat or red sparkling preserves for this year's freshest look!"

Does that sound amusing to you? The average consumer might smile at comparing foods to fashions, but restaurants and food companies will assure you that foods do indeed go in and out of style. You can follow the direction of food trends by new restaurants and products that come on the market. Both are usually a result of trends in American eating preferences, not the start of them. All the various reasons behind food trends are vastly complicated and have been briefly discussed earlier in this book. What is interesting to explore now are some of the recent food fashions you probably will find featured in trendy new restaurants, on menus of established eating places, in specialty food shops, and in supermarkets.

It's considered "new" to eat "old-favorite" foods again! Trendy restaurants are reviving the hearty sloppy joe, macaroni and cheese, and coney dog as a reaction to the now-established gourmet or nouvelle cuisine.

Health-conscious Americans welcomed the success of yesterday's fashion star, the salad bar. Developments from that array of fresh greens and vegetables have spread to an interest in exotic fruits and unusual vegetables. The trend is toward beautiful and sometimes sparing display of unusual greens and rare vegetables, such as the enoki mushrooms and crisp slices of jicama (hic-a-ma). People are looking for—and getting—food choices low in sodium and cholesterol in eating establishments and markets. The choice of white chicken and turkey meat (low cholesterol, low calorie) has greatly increased. The swing has been from crisp, batter-covered fried foods to lean, rare, and sometimes raw meats and vegetables. (The safety of eating raw meats, poultry, and fish is highly questionable due to the possibility of bacteria and parasite contamination which require the high heat of cooking to destroy.)

The emphasis is away from the heaping portions prized in smorgasbords toward smaller portions fixed and arranged elegantly in delicate, low-fat sauces. Sometimes called the **nouvelle cuisine,** the style is a contrast to the fancy rich recipes of the old French haute cuisine that originated centuries ago in the days of the French aristocracy.

Contrasting Trends

Do you ever "reward" yourself for good behavior? Americans feel good about their swing toward more healthful eating and lifestyles. Food fashions reflect that as many people switch to more healthful foods they also tend to "reward" themselves by indulging in extremely rich delicacies, such as designer chocolates; rich, buttery pastries such as the croissant and brioche; and high-butterfat gourmet ice creams. Walk through any large shopping mall and you are likely to see shops dedicated to chocolate delicacies contrasting with health specialty stores displaying items such as low cholesterol safflower oil and tofu. Other offerings might include cookie shops with a vast selection of cookie varieties, coffee cafes with elaborate pastries, and natural-flour muffin shops featuring whole-grain muffins with carrot, squash, fruits, nuts, and cheese ingredients. There is also a trend for fast-food chains that specialize in healthful, low-calorie, low-cholesterol, low-sodium, and low-sugar foods.

Good Nutrition Is Still Up to You!

You are still in charge of your health. All the numerous options that are now available to you to eat at home or "out" in a restaurant make it more important than ever for you to be fortified with information and ambition to make the right choices for your present and future health.

What will the food trends of the future be? With people growing more and more health conscious, trends could lie in the direction of fresh fish prepared in a variety of appealing and flavorful ways. Informed consumers are buying and eating more fresh fish—and the trend is still growing!

Vocabulary Review

Sulfites
A la carte

Questions for Review

1. How have the fast-food type of restaurants affected the way Americans are eating?
2. Has the increased number of working women and mothers made a difference in the numbers of people eating out?
3. What are some ways a family might take advantage of the time they have together while eating out?
4. What are some ways a busy family with different schedules might manage to work in some meals together?
5. What are some of the problems you might experience in trying to get all the nutrients you need if your meals come from vending machines, restaurants, and snack bars all the time?
6. Why is it likely that you might experience difficulty trying to eat a balanced meal at most restaurants and still stay within your calorie (energy) needs?
7. Have you noticed that it is difficult to resist ordering relatively low-nutrient, high-calorie foods such as french fries, fried pies, or hot fudge sundaes even when you have told yourself you weren't going to? What are some practices that might help you stick to your good intentions?
8. What are some marketing techniques used in restaurants and ads to help stimulate your appetite and break down your resistance?
9. List at least six ways you can cut down on calories when you eat at a restaurant.
10. Describe a meal of nutrient-rich selections from a salad bar.
11. Describe a plate filled from a typical salad bar that is low in nutrients, such as minerals, vitamins, and proteins, but high in calories.
12. What are some new foods or food preparations that are currently the latest "fashion" in food trends for your area? Can you remember any foods that used to be more popular than they are now? Why do you think this is the case?
13. Why do you think the main emphasis for serving food has moved away from huge servings of limitless quantity to smaller servings that emphasize the quality and attractiveness of the food?
14. How would you explain the peak of popularity of both rich designer chocolates and wholesome whole-grain muffins at the same point in time?

Things to Do

1. Borrow a collection of restaurant menus. Check them for the following:

a. number of sandwiches or main dishes that are fried.

b. number of sandwich or main dish offerings that are broiled, steamed, or otherwise cooked without the added fat of frying.

c. number of sandwich baskets or plates that offer an alternative to the usual french fries or cole slaw.

d. number of steamed or simmered vegetables that are not deep-fat fried with a batter.

e. a small salad that has vitamin- and mineral-rich ingredients such as carrots, green peppers, broccoli, cauliflower, or dark green lettuce along with the usual light green head lettuce.

What conclusions can you make from your findings?

2. Visit a salad bar at your favorite restaurant. Make a note of all the foods offered. Using the chart in the back of this book and other books, if needed, calculate the nutrients in a plate of your selection. How did your choices rate? Could you improve them? Are some salad bars better nutritionally than others? What information would help you the most in getting the best nutrition for your money at a salad bar?

3. Check out all the places to buy something to eat at your favorite shopping mall. Were there more places that sold candies and dessert-like foods, such as ice cream or rich pastries, or more so-called health-type foods such as whole-wheat baked products, grains, and nuts? For a society that is fitness conscious, do you think there is sometimes too big a gap between the American consumer's good intentions and actual practice? What could be done to help close that gap?

Section 7

Off to Work

21 Careers in The World of Food

How Do You Get into The World of Work?

Remember when people used to ask you, "What do you want to be when you grow up?" Just a few years ago that would have been a sensible question. Jobs and careers remained pretty much the same from the time people looked forward to adulthood to the time they were ready for a career. In today's age of high technological advancements, that often is not true. Complete careers can become obsolete almost overnight when new developments eliminate the need for some skills and generate a market for different requirements. The constant changing of jobs and careers has revolutionized how you plan and prepare for the world of work.

Why Work?

People's needs for working have not changed as much as the work itself has. You will still need an income to purchase food, clothing, housing, and transportation. Your **standard of living** will depend upon the amount of income left over from basic expenses. Those additional funds will provide for education, leisure activities, savings, insurance, and other luxuries that become important to you. The money from a job can buy you those items, but there still are other reasons for working. Your emotional needs for being with other people, feeling challenged, excelling, and believing in something beyond yourself are compelling reasons for you to pursue the career that is right for you.

Not all work ends up being your career. Some jobs are just temporary means to get income for something you want. Carefully chosen jobs can, however, lead to a career. A **career** has traditionally been thought of as a chosen field or profession for which you study and train. Often a career develops from the job you do over a long period of time in a certain field of work.

Another new aspect is that instead of work being something that comes characteristically after education or training is completed, more and more work is being done by young people still getting their education. Between 75 to 85 percent of all students have had some kind of employment experience by the time they leave high school. Planning and preparing for that work experience and the **entry-level job** (beginning job) can help create successful careers. Often those careers can be in the world of food.

For a chance at one of the many exciting careers in foods and nutrition, a student needs to plan ahead for a college education in home economics. Did you know that a home economist or nutritionist needs advanced science and economics courses?

Planning Your Work and Career

In the days of "what do you want to do when you grow up?" deciding exactly what you wanted to do was the major part of career planning. Since a job in today's technology can disappear by the time you are ready for it, the first steps for planning and preparing for a career are to find out what your **aptitudes** (abilities) and interests are. Then it's time to develop more skills through training. You also will increase the choices you have for beginning jobs and an eventual career.

Use Skills to Expand Opportunities

An excellent plan to increase the number of jobs that you might get is to prepare yourself for a group of similar positions in the same area. Have you ever heard the old expression, "Never put all your eggs in the same basket"? If something goes wrong with getting one specific job, having a variety of skills within the field of your choice will allow you to take advantage of other opportunities. Preparing for a group of similar jobs within the same field also allows you to try out various activities to see which ones work best for you. Now that you are beginning to get the feel for what might be involved in planning and preparing for a job, you might consider the many opportunities within the world of food. You already have explored the field of foods and nutrition and developed some skills with foods in reading and working with this book. What did you find out about your interests in foods and nutrition?

The Final Answer

You are the person who is opening the gate to work in the world of food. Do you like helping people to enjoy their food or to have a wonderful time eating out? If you find working and creating with food to be satisfying and challenging and if you find satisfaction working as a reliable team member, you may want to prepare for some of the entry-level positions for working in the world of food.

Looking Ahead to a Career

Basic training and work experience may help to increase your job choices, but further education and professional training can increase your income. Sometimes, too, it will mean an increased satisfaction that you can gain on another job level.

Home economics offers an amazing array of versatile opportunities in foods and nutrition for the management-level jobs for people with college degrees and vocational training. You probably are unaware of the many ways the work of professional home economists touches your life everyday!

Every time you eat a new product at your favorite fast-foods restaurant or buy a new convenience mix at the supermarket, it was most likely developed and tested by a professional home economist. That favorite new kitchen appliance from food processors to microwave ovens was undoubtedly tested and often designed by a home economist. Your favorite commercial on TV featuring delectable steaming food probably was planned and prepared by home economists specially trained in media.

Because home economics touches every phase of your life as well as every phase of food and nutrition, the ways business, government, and food service need a home economist's skills is virtually limited only by the cleverness of the home economist. If you are interested in education beyond high school, you might consider pursuing the following types of careers.

Nutrition educators teach in all types of settings from traditional schools to nontraditional settings such as industry, advertising agencies, social agencies, government, and corporate organizations such as the National Dairy Council and the National Live Stock and Meat Board. There also are many opportunities to work in other countries as a nutrition educator.

Nutritionists and **dietitians** who work in hospitals, clinics, schools, restaurants, industry, and government planning menus and diets. There is a tremendous potential for work in other countries in this much needed field.

Teachers are needed for high school, junior high, community colleges, and universities.

Home economists can work in food related industries for designing, testing, and planning new products.

Home economists find careers in advertising departments of industries or agencies to help plan, design, produce, and market food products and appliances.

Food stylists help set up the format, props, and create the food for photography, television, and publications. This is a highly specialized field which calls for an understanding of the media as well as the science of food preparation and design. Much of the food must be prepared differently than ordinary cooking in order for it to look correct "on-camera." However, an understanding of food preparation principles is also a must. The foods pictured in this book were prepared by a food stylist.

Food stylists need to know both how to prepare foods and how to make them look as attractive and tempting to eat on-camera as they would if you could smell or touch them.

Home economists can work in restaurant management or catering. These jobs for other businesses often trigger the home economist into starting her or his own business or freelancing by catering (planning and serving) special events.

Opportunities For You Now

What do the president of the United States, your best friend, the principal of your high school, the head of the Soviet Union, a member of royalty vacationing on the Riviera, a patient in the hospital, a tour guide in a national park, and a breakdancer on the streets of New York City have in common? You probably guessed. If you said they all have to eat, you're right! Wherever people go or whatever they do, it is necessary to eat and drink. With the majority of time spent working, traveling, and socializing away from home, almost everyone needs some kind of food service. That high demand for some type of food service creates many jobs and opportunities in a wide variety of businesses and locations close to home or wherever you travel. You might want to take advantage of the opportunities of getting into the field of food service, but does it suit you?

The food-service field is one of the largest employers for beginning workers in America. It is also one of the country's largest industries and supplies millions of jobs in entry-level, middle level, and management areas. Perhaps you or some of your friends have already worked in the food service field. Jobs in fast-food restaurants have replaced the newspaper route as the classic money earners for teenagers.

Part-time jobs in the fast-food field can be particularly appropriate for the employee who needs a flexible work schedule that allows for sports practice, rehearsals, and exams. Those entry-level jobs can provide first work experiences that help develop self-reliance, dependability, and a chance for possible promotion

One fast-foods company has stated that it is aware of the responsibility of employing such a large number of this nation's youth, so it tries to maintain the policy of arranging schedules to allow for homework and school activities. It is the students' responsibility, however, to maintain that balance of work and school activities so as to prepare for the future.

What Do Food Service Workers Do?

Before you plunge into an area of work, explore the types of activities you might do. Are they compatible with your likes, dislikes, and abilities?

You can enter food-service work and advance to middle-level jobs doing the following types of tasks.

1. Helping to serve the customer:

- Set tables.
- Take food orders and inform the cooks.
- Serve the food and beverages.
- Pour water, coffee, and clear tables.
- Act as host or hostess to greet customers and seat them.
- Make reservations
- Manage setting and clearing of tables.

2. Helping to prepare the food. Chefs and cooks usually specialize and their careers require vocational training and sometimes advanced degrees from universities.

- Prepare ingredients for the cook, such as slicing meat, cheese, fruits, and vegetables.
- Weigh and measure foods for special diets.
- Prepare leftover foods for storage.
- Operate equipment such as the french fryer, toaster, grill, coffeemaker.
- Set up and restock the salad bar.
- Make recipes as assigned.

3. Assisting with food cleanup, general sanitation, and safety:

- Return soiled dishes to dishwashing area.
- Pretreat and organize soiled dishes for dishwashing.
- Collect the trash and discard soiled disposable dishes.
- Operate garbage disposal and dishwasher.
- Learn and follow health and safety regulations.
- Clean and inspect restrooms.

4. Helping to plan menus and buying supplies:

- Inspect quality and quantity of delivered items.
- Store delivered items.
- Help check menu for color, flavor, and texture.

5. Supervising food service:

- Make arrangements for special promotions and events, such as children's birthday parties and decor for holidays.
- Help plan the number of food portions to be prepared ahead for specific times and schedules.
- Discuss, plan, and communicate employee work schedules.
- Decide on portion sizes (Many "fast-

foods" and prepared frozen foods come divided in portions, so this job often is limited to small, "home-cooking," or gourmet types of restaurants.)

• Plan and maybe prepare specific garnishes for a colorful plate on a cost-effective basis. Determine if the cost of the garnish can be justified with the potential profit from the food sold.

• Write and post (or communicate) work instructions.

If the types of entry-level tasks (like the preceding ones for food-service jobs) coincide with what you can picture yourself doing, it is time to consider some of the advantages and disadvantages of the area of work you are considering entering.

Working students can learn many related skills for food preparation and serving on-the-job.

Advantages of Food Service Jobs

• The industry is still growing. The average American is now eating about half the meals away from home.

• You can choose from a tremendous variety in the kinds and locations of places to work. From hospitals to luxury hotels, the opportunities are there at all job levels.

• You can often be trained on-the-job or seek extra training for a related job once you are hired.

• Advanced training is available through many sources such as some high school home economics classes or work-study programs, technical schools, community colleges, and through the armed forces.

• Working conditions and benefits are being improved. Shorter working hours, flexible scheduling, paid vacation time, low-cost insurance, meals, and uniforms are a few such improvements.

Disadvantages of Food Service Jobs

• The working schedule often uses split-shift hours. That is, you work during the meal-serving times (breakfast, lunch, dinner) with a couple of hours off in between the heavy meal serving hours. For students enrolled in occupational home economics programs, working a split shift allows them the flexibility to work and attend classes.

• Times when you will be needed are the evenings, weekends, and holidays. That often interferes with personal plans.

• Some of the working times are seasonal.

• You usually will need to spend long hours on your feet and work under pressure to "deliver" on-time for meal rushes and customer's preferences.

• You might have to work cheerfully with customers, patients, or fellow workers who are demanding and difficult.

• You can expect the work to require physical strength and stamina.

• Your work area might be hot, crowded, and close to potential danger from burns, cuts, and falls.

Opportunities In Catering

The same versatility and vast need for home economics skills in foods and nutrition also can create special job opportunities for high school students in addition to restaurant work. Catering is one of those opportunities. **Catering** is food prepared by professionals to be served to a group of people at a designated place for a designated fee. You can enter an established catering firm, but as a class or individually you also can cater family get-togethers and other events for a fee. By using the preparation and management skills presented in this book, you will be well-prepared. The following catering information and "how-to" plan represents an idea for a class or individual to tackle.

Health regulations vary in different locations around the country. Before starting any catering project, check your local regulations.

Formerly considered a "service for the wealthy," catering is now in demand for many occasions. Almost everyone has or will attend a catered event on some occasion in her or his life. This growing demand creates many levels of opportunities for employment or "starting your own business."

Catering is used for special reasons—family gatherings; parties; holidays; such memorable occasions as weddings, funerals, anniversaries, bar mitzvahs, graduations; and sports events such as tailgate parties. Catering for businesses includes luncheons, award banquets, dinners, and meeting-break service.

How would you let people know that you are interested in catering for them? How could you communicate your skills to future customers? Would it make sense to gain some experience working for a caterer before you tried small events on your own?

Types of Catering

There are two main types of catering—on-premise and off-premise. **On-premise catering** refers to food prepared and served in the same location to a group of people. **Off-premise catering** is food that is prepared in a kitchen and transported by vehicle to the location where it will be served to a group of people.

Both on-premise and off-premise catering have much in common. Whenever a menu is planned for a potential group, consideration must be given to their ages, the purpose of the get-together, and the duration of the event. Consequently, specific information about dietary restrictions needs to be discussed and taken into consideration in the menu planning.

What to Consider

The initial contact with the customer is important to getting specific information about the catered event. This information, along with the creative food suggestions a caterer has to offer, results in a planned event that will be successful. Details to be decided during the initial meeting with a potential client are:

- Name of client, business, or organization (a billing name and address).
- Type of catering: luncheon, dinner, reception, birthday, picnic.
- Time and date.
- Location of event.
- Purpose of the function.
- Menu.
- Other arrangements such as entertainment, flowers, tables, chairs, tents, and special equipment.
- Payment.

Of all the details, the menu is the most important part of any catered function. The style of serving, how the portions will appear as they are served on plates, and plate garnishes all require some carefully considered presentations to produce a successful function. Room arrangements and the design and traffic flow of the food buffet play a large part in the success of any event. Every step in the serving and eating process has to be anticipated and planned by the caterer. However, the challenge of thinking through the details of each catered event is what makes catering unique and different each time.

Timing of the service schedule involves planning the length of time for each of the menu items to be served. Also included is the time to set up for the catered event, total time to serve, and time to clean up. As a professional caterer, it is occasionally necessary to clean a work area before any preparation begins. Professional caterers always leave a work area clean after the end of a catered event.

The last item of any catered function is the billing. With a pre-established cost it is possible to calculate the costs according to food, labor, and any other special arrangements.

An itemized bill is given or sent to the client specifying terms of payment (such as "pay in full by 30 days"). Copies are retained by the caterer for future use and for tax purposes. Some caterers may require a deposit before the event with the balance due following the function. The method of payment used depends entirely on what the caterer and customer decide on at their initial meeting.

Banana Ice Cream Pie

Yield 2 pies

Traditional	**Ingredients**	**Metric**
5 medium	Bananas	5 medium
2 10 oz. jars	Caramel	2 283 g jars
1 gallon	Vanilla Ice Cream	4 L
2	Graham cracker crusts	2

Directions

1. Soften the ice cream.
2. Mash the bananas in a food processor. Fold the mashed bananas into the softened ice cream.
3. Layer the banana ice cream mixture and the caramel in the graham cracker crust. Layer in this order: ice cream, caramel, ice cream, and caramel. Freeze. Repeat for the second pie.
4. Remove the pie from the freezer and while frozen slice into eight pieces. Return to the freezer and remove ½ hour before serving.

If you are interested in the growing and creative field of catering, ask your teacher about opportunities in your area and special class projects.

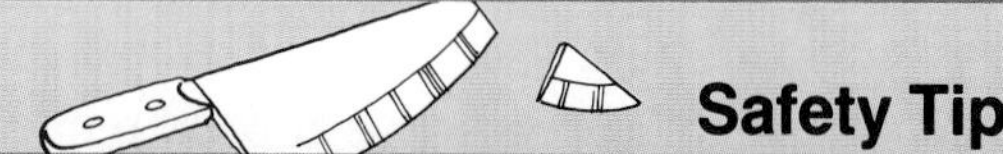

Safety Tip

For off-premise catering there is also transportation to consider along with plans for packing food safely to be transported without spilling. Transporting hot food at temperatures above 140°F (60°C) and cold food below 45°F (7°C) is accomplished with the use of insulated coolers, along with refrigerated vehicles and portable warming units. The importance of keeping the food at safe holding temperatures can protect a professional caterer from an outbreak of a food-borne illness which could result in lawsuits, death, and the closing of the business. A caterer's reputation for high-quality food safely prepared can take years to develop. That should not be risked by one instance of careless food handling. Its a risk no one in food service can afford to take.

Birthday Party

The beginning for anyone interested in catering always starts with the idea of offering food at a planned get-together. You could become a food **entrepreneur** (a self-employed person) by developing your interests into a career. Planning food you could make for many different occasions and parties is a job that leads to a career.

A birthday party is an excellent beginning. Develop a menu for the number of persons who will be attending and consider the age of the guests. The following is the type of basic information needed to prepare for a catered event.

Client:	Mr. and Mrs. David Dudeck Peachtree Lane Oleana, Ohio 46901
Event:	Birthday Party
Time & Day:	7:00 p.m., Wednesday, May 8 Caterers arrive at 5:00 p.m. Guests arrive at 7:00 p.m.
Location:	Dudeck residence. See address above
No. of Guests:	16 youths (15 years old)
Menu:	Homemade Deep Dish Pizza (3 pieces per person) Assorted Fresh Vegetables with Dip Assorted Soft Drinks (3 per person) Banana Caramel Ice Cream Pie (Cut into 8 pieces)

Shopping List

Pepperoni, 1 lb. (500 g)
Pizza Sauce, 1½ qts. (1½ L)
Shredded Mozarella, 1½ lbs.(750 g)
Italian Sausage, 2 lbs. (1 kg)
Fresh Mushrooms, 1½ lbs. (750 g)
Black Olives,(ripe olives), chopped, 3 oz. (94 g)
Green Peppers, 2
Onions, yellow, 2 med.
Pizza Dough Mix, 1 double crust pkg.
Carrots, 1 lb. (500 g)
Celery, ½ lb. (250 g)
Radishes, 1 small package
Sour Cream, 8 oz. (250 g)
Mayonnaise, 8 oz. (250 g)
Ranch Dressing Mix, 1 pkg.
Cauliflower, 1 head
Broccoli, 1 bunch
Graham Cracker Crusts, 2
Vanilla Ice Cream, 1 gallon (4 L)
Caramel, 2 10 oz. jars (315 g)
Bananas, 5 med.
Diet Soft Drinks, 2 2 liter
Regular Soft Drinks, 3 2 liter

Method of Service

1. The day before, assemble two banana caramel pies, using the recipe on page 413. Freeze them. The day of the party, cut each pie into eighths while still frozen using a large knife. Replace in the freezer and remove 30 minutes before serving.

2. Cut all vegetables into bite-size shapes for the vegetable tray and store in plastic bags in the refrigerator. Make the vegetable dip and place in a serving vessel. Cover and store in the refrigerator until ready to serve.

3. Make the pizza dough using package directions one and a half hours before the guests arrive. Let rise. While dough is rising, cut all the toppings for the pizza into thin strips or coin shapes. Tear the sausage into 1 inch (2.5 cm) pieces and place on a baking sheet. Precook in 350°F (175°C) oven for 10 to 15 minutes or until brown and firm with much of the fat cooked out of the meat. Set sausage aside in small bowl. Slice the pepperoni into

Imagine getting paid to plan and prepare creative, fun food and party activities! A catering career may mean long, hard hours, but they can be festive and rewarding in satisfaction and salary. This Banana Ice Cream Pie recipe can be prepared the day before an event to save on last-minute preparation time.

Happy Birthday to you!
Happy Birthday to you!
Happy Birthday to you!
Happy Birthday to you!
Happy Birthday to you!
Happy Birthday to you!

thin, coin shapes. Slice the mushrooms and green peppers into strips along with the onions. Place all ingredients for pizza into individual bowls, along with the shredded cheese and pizza sauce.

4. Before the guests arrive, decoratively arrange the vegetables onto a platter or serving dish lined with a colorful lettuce. Visually imagine a garden of freshly cut vegetables spilling gently over a platter. Nest the bowl of dip somewhere among the bouquet of vegetables for a fresh-looking arrangement.

5. Press the pizza dough into two rectangular 15″x9″x1″ pans. When the guests arrive, let them select the toppings for their portion of pizza. Assemble both pizzas with the sauce first, spreading it all the way to the edge of the dough. Follow with the vegetables and lots of shredded mozarella cheese. Bake at 375°F (190°C) for 12 to 15 minutes or until cheese is melted and slightly browned.

6. While the pizza bakes, offer guests their choice of diet or regular soft drinks. Use plastic glasses.

7. Serve the vegetable tray with napkins. Allow the guests to use their fingers.

8. Cut each pan of pizza into 24 4″x6″ servings and serve directly from pan. Guests will eat from a picnic style plastic plate with a napkin and a stainless steel fork. (Don't forget to remove the pies from the freezer.)

9. Offer seconds of pizza to the guests and when everyone has finished eating, clear all the plates. Serve the banana caramel ice cream pie for dessert with candles, singing "Happy Birthday." Serve ice cream pie in wedges on small dessert plates with forks and fresh napkins.

Two servers are needed to plan, purchase, prepare, serve, and clean up after this party. To figure the cost of the party, figure the time it takes to plan the party, shop for and prepare all items needed, and the cost of those items. After adding up the total time spent in planning, assign an hourly value to that time and multiply it by the number of hours. Add this to the cost of the purchased items to determine the total cost of the party.

What Are Your Fields of Interest?

Now that you have concluded your work with *Foods,* take time to reflect upon your future. Using a blank piece of paper, answer the following questions.

1. List some of your personal interests. (What do you like to do, read, or watch on TV?)
2. What is important to you? (What do you value?)
3. What do you expect to get out of a job now?
4. What would you hope a job could do for you in your future career?
5. List any awards or accomplishments that you are proud of.
6. List any failures such as failing a course, losing a job, or disappointing someone that come to your mind.
7. List two activities you enjoy that could be career related, such as working with people, children, computers, food, equipment, math.
8. List two activities that you dislike that could be career related, such as writing, working alone, budgeting, making change.
9. List your skills, such as developing nutritious dietary plans, shopping, baking, creative cooking, typing, writing, computer programming, or organizing.
10. List three jobs you would be interested in right now.
11. List three careers you would like to work toward.
12. List three careers that your friends suggest that you might consider.

Read through the answers. Does any interest show up more than once? Do your classmates see successes that you might have overlooked? Does what you want in a job coincide with what you are now doing? Will your present schedule of activities lead to what you want to accomplish? Are you getting the training you need for what you want to do in the future? Discuss your findings with others to see if they have ideas you have left out. Outline your immediate plan of action for what you hope to make your career, or one of your future careers. The average person can expect to have about five careers in her or his lifetime as times, needs, and opportunities change.

Professional Organizations

In order to gain more information about home economics careers and scholarships, you may want to write to the following organizations:

- American Home Economics Association (AHEA)
  2010 Massachusetts Avenue, NW
  Washington, DC 20036
  Information is available on the various professional sections: Home Economists in Human Services; Home Economists in Homemaking; Home Economists in Business; Extension; Research; Colleges and Universities; and Elementary, Secondary, and Adult Education
- Home Economists in Business
  5008 Pine Creek Drive, Suite B
  Westerville, OH 43081
- Home Economics Association
  1201 16th Street, NW
  Washington, DC 20036
- American Vocational Association
  1410 King Street
  Alexandria, VA 22344
- American Dietetic Association
  430 N Michigan Avenue
  Chicago, IL 60611
- U.S. Department of Labor, Women's Bureau
  200 Constitution Avenue, NW
  Washington, DC 20219
  (Please send a self-addressed mailing label)

Youth Organizations

- National 4-H Council
  7100 Connecticut Avenue
  Chevy Chase, MD 20815
- Future Homemakers of America
  1910 Association Drive
  Reston, VA 22091
  HERO Chapters, which are part of Future Homemakers of America, help students through grade 12 prepare for jobs and careers in home economics occupations. In addition, members learn life skills, such as decision-making, goal setting, and problem solving.

- Future Homemakers of America
  1910 Assocation Drive
  Reston, VA 22091
  HERO Chapters, which are part of Future Homemakers of America, help students through grade 12 prepare for jobs and careers in home economics occupations. In addition, members learn life skills, such as decision-making, goal setting, and problem solving.

Vocabulary Review

Standard of living
Career
Entry-level job
Aptitude
Catering
On-premise catering
Off-premise catering
Entrepreneur

Questions for Review

1. How does today's constantly changing technological advancements affect how you might plan for a career?
2. How has preparing for a job changed in recent years? Why is that the case?
3. What are the main reasons people need to work? Why have the reasons people need to work not changed as much as the work itself has?
4. What is the difference between a job and a career?
5. Can a temporary job sometimes lead to a career? Explain.
6. Why is work experience helpful to you in getting any kind of job?
7. What is an entry-level job? Give some examples of how an entry-level job might be helpful in eventually leading to a career.
8. Why are finding out your own aptitudes and developing skills through training considered the first steps toward career planning?
9. What are some ways that preparing for a group of related jobs within an area of work can help increase the opportunities available to you?
10. How might training in several related areas of work help you to discover what is right for you?
11. Why does the world of food offer so many different types of opportunities for jobs and careers?
12. What are some of the types of careers available to someone who obtains a degree in home economics?
13. Why is there such a high demand for food service wherever you go?
14. How does the high demand for food service outside of the home create job opportunities? Name a few of the opportunities.
15. Why do you think the food service field is one of the largest employers for beginning workers?
16. Why are food service jobs particularly handy for part-time workers such as students?
17. What are some of the entry-level jobs in the food-service field of work? Which of those jobs could you do now?
18. What are some of the advantages of working in food service? What are some of the disadvantages?
19. What is catering? Why do you think there is an increased demand for catered food service? How might you take advantage of this type of food service for employment?
20. What are the two main types of catering?
21. Discuss three considerations that are important to consider before planning a catered menu. Why are those three items so important?
22. If you are organizing a catered event, what details need to be decided during the initial meeting with a potential client?
23. Why is food safety crucial to any catered event? What increases the risk of food poisoning for a catered event?

Things to Do

1. Invite a professional home economist from a local power company of business to your class to discuss opportunities in the area for home economics related skills and also a home economics career. Explore the possibility of a field trip to the company or an individual interview of the home economist "at work."

2. Invite a dietitian from a local hospital to discuss work opportunities within the field of nutrition. Perhaps a field trip to experience first-hand what a dietitian and other health-care food service workers do could be arranged also.

3. Investigate other home-economics-related careers that might be available in your area, such as a local TV foods show or department store demonstrator. What are some other possibilities?

4. Search through local newspapers for help wanted ads for food-service-related employment. Make a list of entry-level jobs. Which ones could you qualify for? Are there any skills you might develop that would help you be eligible for more jobs? List them and discuss them with our instructor.

5. Visit the school counselor and collect information regarding career opportunities in home economics. List the education requirements and possible vocational training available in your area. Are there some jobs or future careers you might like to pursue? Report to the class your findings.

6. How many catering business are there in your area? Use the Yellow Pages to compile a list of local firms. Invite some speakers to your class to demonstrate some food preparation ideas and to talk about catering careers.

7. Plan an event that you might cater yourself. Follow through with the theme, event, menu and all arrangements. Write up your ideas as shown in this chapter.

Appendix

Recommended Dietary Allowances (RDA)

The Recommended Dietary Allowances (RDA) are designed for the maintenance of good nutrition for practically all healthy people in the U.S. They list the maximum amount of selected nutrients that most healthy people need daily under usual environmental stress. The RDAs are used to plan and evaluate the diets of groups of individuals. Diets should include a variety of common foods so as to provide other nutrients for which human needs have been less well defined.

	Age	Weight		Height		Protein	Fat-Soluble Vitamins			Water-Soluble Vitamins			Minerals		
	(years)	(kg)	(lb)	(cm)	(in)	(g)	Vitamin A (μg R.E.)	Vitamin D (μg)	Vitamin E (mg α T.E.)	Vitamin C (mg)	Thiamine (mg)	Riboflavin (mg)	Calcium (mg)	Phosphorus (mg)	Iron (mg)
Infants	0.0-0.5	6	13	60	24	kgx2.2	420	10	3	35	0.3	0.4	360	240	10
	0.5-1.0	9	20	71	28	kgx2.0	400	10	4	35	0.5	0.6	540	360	15
Children	1-3	13	29	90	35	23	400	10	5	45	0.7	0.8	800	800	15
	4-6	20	44	112	44	30	500	10	6	45	0.9	1.0	800	800	10
	7-10	28	62	132	52	34	700	10	7	45	1.2	1.4	800	800	10
Males	11-14	45	99	157	62	45	1000	10	8	50	1.4	1.6	1,200	1,200	18
	15-18	66	145	176	69	56	1000	10	10	60	1.4	1.7	1,200	1,200	18
	19-22	70	154	177	70	56	1000	7.5	10	60	1.5	1.7	800	800	10
	23-50	70	154	178	70	56	1000	5	10	60	1.4	1.6	800	800	10
	51+	70	154	178	70	56	1000	5	10	60	1.2	1.4	800	800	10
Females	11-14	46	101	157	62	46	800	10	8	50	1.1	1.3	1,200	1,200	18
	15-18	55	120	163	64	46	800	10	8	60	1.1	1.3	1,200	1,200	18
	19-22	55	120	163	64	44	800	7.5	8	60	1.1	1.3	800	800	18
	23-50	55	120	163	64	44	800	5	8	60	1.0	1.2	800	800	18
	51+	55	120	163	64	44	800	5	8	60	1.0	1.2	800	800	10
Pregnant						+30	+200	+5	+2	+20	+0.4	+0.3	+400	+400	18+
Lactating						+20	+400	+5	+3	+40	+0.5	+0.5	+400	+400	18

U.S. Recommended Daily Allowances (U.S. RDA)

Vitamins	Unit of Measurement	Children Under 4	Adults, Children 4 or more	Pregnant or Nursing Women
Vitamin A	IU	2,500	5,000	8,000
Vitamin D	IU	400	—	400
Vitamin E	IU	10	30	30
Vitamin C	mg	40	60	60
Folic acid	mg	.2	.4	.8
Thiamine	mg	.70	1.50	1.70
Riboflavin	mg	.8	1.7	2.0
Niacin	mg	9.0	20.0	20.0
Vitamin B_6	mg	.70	2.00	2.50
Vitamin B_{12}	mcg	3.0	6.0	8.0
Vitamin D	IU	—	400	—
Biotin	mg	.150	.300	.300
Pantothenic acid	mg	5.0	10.0	10.0
MINERALS				
Calcium	g	.800	1.000	1.300
Phosphorus[1]	g	.800	1.000	1.300
Iodine	mcg	70	150	150
Iron	mg	10	18	18
Magnesium	mg	200	400	450
Copper	mg	1.0	2.0	2.0
Zinc	mg	8.0	15.0	15.0

IU = *International Unit*
g = *gram*
mg = *milligram*
mcg = *microgram*

[1]*Optional for pregnant or nursing women. When present, the quantity of phosphorus may not be greater than the quantity of calcium.*

Nutritive Value of Foods

Food	Approximate Measure	Grams	Water (Percent)	Food energy (Calories)	Protein (Grams)	Fat (Grams)	Saturated Fats (Grams)	Unsaturated Fats: Oleic (Grams)	Unsaturated Fats: Linoleic (Grams)	Carbohydrate (Grams)	Calcium (Milligrams)	Phosphorus (Milligrams)	Iron (Milligrams)	Potassium (Milligrams)	Vitamin A value (International units)	Thiamin (Milligrams)	Riboflavin (Milligrams)	Niacin (Milligrams)	Vitamin C (Milligrams)
DAIRY PRODUCTS (CHEESE, CREAM, IMITATION CHEESE, MILK, RELATED PRODUCTS)																			
Cheese:																			
American	1 oz.	28	39	105	6	9	5.6	2.1	.2	Trace	174	211	.1	46	340	.01	.10	Trace	0
Cheddar	1 oz.	28	37	115	7	9	6.1	2.1	.2	Trace	204	145	.2	28	300	.01	.11	Trace	0
Cottage	1 cup	225	79	235	28	10	6.4	2.4	.2	6	135	297	.3	190	370	.05	.37	.3	Trace
Cream	1 oz.	28	54	100	2	10	6.2	2.4	.2	1	23	30	.3	34	400	Trace	.06	Trace	0
Swiss	1 oz.	28	37	105	8	8	5.0	1.7	.2	1	272	171	Trace	31	240	.01	.10	Trace	0
Cream, half and half	1 tbsp.	15	81	20	Trace	2	1.1	.4	Trace	1	16	14	Trace	19	20	.01	.02	Trace	Trace
Cream, sour	1 tbsp.	12	71	25	Trace	3	1.6	.6	.1	1	14	10	Trace	17	90	Trace	.02	Trace	Trace
Milk:																			
Whole (3.3% fat) (with vitamin A added)	1 cup	244	88	150	8	8	5.1	2.1	.2	11	291	228	.1	370	500	.09	.40	.2	2
Lowfat (2%)	1 cup	244	89	120	8	5	2.9	1.2	.1	12	297	232	.1	377	500	.10	.40	.2	2
Nonfat (skim)	1 cup	245	91	85	8	Trace	.3	.1	Trace	12	302	247	.1	406	500	.09	.34	.2	2
Nonfat instant (with vitamin A added)	1 cup	68	4	245	24	Trace	.3	.1	Trace	35	837	670	.2	1,160	1,610	.28	1.19	.6	4
Milk Beverages:																			
Chocolate milk	1 cup	250	82	210	8	8	5.3	2.2	.2	26	280	251	.6	417	300	.09	.41	.3	2
Shake, thick	10.6 oz.	300	72	355	9	8	5.0	2.0	.2	63	396	378	.9	672	260	.14	.67	.4	0
Milk Desserts, frozen:																			
Ice cream	1 cup	133	61	270	5	14	8.9	3.6	.3	32	176	134	.1	257	540	.05	.33	.1	1
Ice milk	1 cup	131	69	185	5	6	3.5	1.4	.1	29	176	129	.1	265	210	.08	.35	.1	1
Sherbet	1 cup	193	66	270	2	4	2.4	1.0	.1	59	103	74	.3	198	190	.03	.09	.1	4
Milk Desserts, other:																			
Custard, baked	1 cup	265	77	305	14	15	6.8	5.4	.7	29	297	310	1.1	387	930	.11	.50	.3	1
Puddings	1 cup	260	66	385	8	12	7.6	3.3	.3	67	250	255	1.3	445	390	.05	.36	.3	1
Yogurt, plain	8 oz.	227	85	145	12	4	2.3	.8	.1	16	415	326	.2	531	150	.10	.49	.3	2
EGGS																			
Fried in butter	1 egg	46	72	85	5	6	2.4	2.2	.6	1	26	80	.9	58	290	.03	.13	Tace	0
Hard-cooked	1 egg	50	75	80	6	6	1.7	2.0	.6	1	28	90	1.0	65	260	.04	.14	Trace	0
Poached	1 egg	50	74	80	6	6	1.7	2.0	.6	1	28	90	1.0	65	260	.04	.13	Trace	0
Scrambled (milk added) in butter	1 egg	64	76	95	6	7	2.8	2.3	.6	1	47	97	.9	85	310	.04	.16	Trace	0
FATS, OILS, RELATED PRODUCTS																			
Butter	1 tbsp.	14	16	100	Trace	12	7.2	2.9	.3	Trace	3	3	Trace	4	430	Trace	Trace	Trace	0
Fats, cooking (vegetable shortening)	1 cup	200	0	1,770	0	200	48.8	88.2	48.4	0	0	0	0	0	–	0	0	0	0
Margarine	1 Tbsp.	14	16	100	Trace	12	2.1	5.3	3.1	Trace	3	3	Trace	4	470	Trace	Trace	Trace	0
Oils, salad or cooking:																			
Corn	1 Tbsp.	14	0	120	0	14	1.7	3.3	7.8	0	0	0	0	0	–	0	0	0	0
Olive	1 Tbsp.	14	0	120	0	14	1.9	9.7	1.1	0	0	0	0	0	–	0	0	0	0
Safflower	1 Tbsp.	14	0	120	0	14	1.3	1.6	10.0	0	0	0	0	0	–	0	0	0	0
Salad Dressings:																			
Blue cheese	1 Tbsp.	15	32	75	1	8	1.6	1.7	3.8	1	12	11	Trace	6	30	Trace	.02	Trace	Trace
French	1 Tbsp.	16	39	65	Trace	6	1.1	1.3	3.2	3	2	2	.1	13	–	–	–	–	–
Italian	1 Tbsp.	15	28	85	Trace	9	1.6	1.9	4.7	1	2	1	Trace	2	Trace	Trace	Trace	Trace	–
Mayonnaise	1 Tbsp.	14	15	100	Trace	11	2.0	2.4	5.6	Trace	3	4	.1	5	40	Trace	.01	Trace	–
Tartar sauce	1 Tbsp.	14	34	75	Trace	8	1.5	1.8	4.1	1	3	4	.1	11	30	Trace	Trace	Trace	Trace

Continued on Next Page

Nutritive Value of Foods (Continued)

Food	Approximate Measure	Grams	Water (Percent)	Food energy (Calories)	Protein (Grams)	Fat (Grams)	Saturated Fats (Grams)	Unsaturated Fats: Oleic (Grams)	Unsaturated Fats: Linoleic (Grams)	Carbohydrate (Grams)	Calcium (Milligrams)	Phosphorus (Milligrams)	Iron (Milligrams)	Potassium (Milligrams)	Vitamin A value (International units)	Thiamin (Milligrams)	Riboflavin (Milligrams)	Niacin (Milligrams)	Vitamin C (Milligrams)
FISH, SHELLFISH, MEAT, POULTRY, RELATED PRODUCTS																			
Fish and Shellfish:																			
Bluefish, baked with butter	3 oz.	85	68	135	22	4	–	–	–	0	25	244	0.6	–	40	0.09	0.08	1.6	–
Clams, raw	3 oz.	85	82	65	11	1	–	–	–	2	59	138	5.2	154	90	.08	.15	1.1	8
Crabmeat, canned	1 cup	135	77	135	24	3	.6	0.4	0.1	1	61	246	1.1	149	–	.11	.11	2.6	–
Fish sticks, breaded, cooked	1 stick	28	66	50	5	3	–	–	–	2	3	47	.1	–	0	.01	.02	.5	–
Haddock, breaded, fried	3 oz.	85	66	140	17	5	1.4	2.2	1.2	5	34	210	1.0	296	–	.03	.06	2.7	–
Ocean perch, breaded, fried	1 fillet		59	195	16	11	2.7	4.4	2.3	6	28	192	1.1	242	–	.10	.10	1.6	–
Oysters, raw	1 cup	240	85	160	20	4	1.3	.2	.1	8	226	343	13.2	290	740	.34	.43	6.0	–
Salmon, pink, canned	3 oz.	85	71	120	17	5	.9	.8	.1	0	167	243	.7	307	60	.03	.16	6.8	–
Sardines, canned	3 oz.	85	62	175	20	9	3.0	2.5	.5	0	372	424	2.5	502	190	.02	.17	4.6	–
Scallops, breaded, fried	6 scallops		60	175	16	8	–	–	–	9	–	–	–	–	–	–	–	–	–
Shrimp, french fried	3 oz.	85	57	190	17	9	2.3	3.7	2.0	9	61	162	1.7	195	–	.03	.07	2.3	–
Tuna, canned in oil	3 oz.	85	61	170	24	7	1.7	1.7	.7	0	7	199	1.6	–	70	.04	.10	10.1	–
Meat and Meat Products:																			
Bacon, crisp	2 slices		8	85	4	8	2.5	3.7	.7	Trace	2	34	.5	35	0	.08	.05	.8	–
Beef, pot roasted	3 oz.	85	53	245	23	16	6.8	6.5	.4	0	10	114	2.9	184	30	.04	.18	3.6	–
Beef roast, oven cooked, relatively fat	3 oz.	85	40	375	17	33	14.0	13.6	.8	0	8	158	2.2	189	70	.05	.13	3.1	–
Beef roast, oven cooked, relatively lean	3 oz.	85	62	165	25	7	2.8	2.7	.2	0	11	208	3.2	279	10	.06	.19	4.5	–
Ground beef, broiled	3 oz.	85	60	185	23	10	4.0	3.9	.3	0	10	196	3.0	261	20	.08	.20	5.1	–
Steak, sirloin	3 oz.	85	44	330	20	27	11.3	11.1	.6	0	9	162	2.5	220	50	.05	.15	4.0	–
Beef and vegetable stew	1 cup	245	82	220	16	11	4.9	4.5	.2	15	29	184	2.9	613	2,400	.15	.17	4.7	17
Chili con carne with beans	1 cup	255	72	340	19	16	7.5	6.8	.3	31	82	321	4.3	594	150	.08	.18	3.3	–
Heart, beef	3 oz.	85	61	160	27	5	1.5	1.1	.6	1	5	154	5.0	197	20	.21	1.04	6.5	1
Lamb chop, broiled	3.1 oz.	89	43	360	18	32	14.8	12.1	1.2	0	8	139	1.0	200	–	.11	.19	4.1	–
Ham, roasted	3 oz.	85	54	245	18	19	6.8	7.9	1.7	0	8	146	2.2	199	0	.40	.15	3.1	–
Pork chop, broiled	2.7 oz.	78	42	305	19	25	8.9	10.4	2.2	0	9	209	2.7	216	0	0.75	0.22	4.5	–
Pork Roast, oven cooked	3 oz.	85	46	310	21	24	8.7	10.2	2.2	0	9	218	2.7	233	0	.78	.22	4.8	–
Bologna	1 slice		56	85	3	8	3.0	3.4	.5	Trace	2	36	.5	65	–	.05	.06	.7	–
Braunschweiger	1 slice		53	90	4	8	2.6	3.4	.8	1	3	69	1.7	–	1,850	.05	.41	2.3	–
Brown and serve	1 link		40	70	3	6	2.3	2.8	.7	Trace	–	–	–	–	–	–	–	–	–
Frankfurter	1 frankfurter		57	170	7	15	5.6	6.5	1.2	1	3	57	.8	–	–	.08	.11	1.4	–
Salami	1 slice		30	45	2	4	1.6	1.6	.1	Trace	1	28	.4	–	–	.04	.03	.5	–
Poultry and Poultry Products:																			
Chicken, breast, fried	2.8 oz.	79	58	160	26	5	1.4	1.8	1.1	1	9	218	1.3	–	70	.04	.17	11.6	–
Chicken, drumstick, fried	1.3 oz.	38	55	90	12	4	1.1	1.3	.9	Trace	6	89	.9	–	50	.03	.15	2.7	–
Chicken a la king	1 cup	245	68	470	27	34	12.7	14.3	3.3	12	127	358	2.5	404	1,130	.10	.42	5.4	12

Nutritive Value of Foods (Continued)

Food	Approximate Measure	Grams	Water (Percent)	Food energy (Calories)	Protein (Grams)	Fat (Grams)	Saturated Fats (Grams)	Unsaturated Fats: Oleic (Grams)	Unsaturated Fats: Linoleic (Grams)	Carbohydrate (Grams)	Calcium (Milligrams)	Phosphorus (Milligrams)	Iron (Milligrams)	Potassium (Milligrams)	Vitamin A value (International units)	Thiamin (Milligrams)	Riboflavin (Milligrams)	Niacin (Milligrams)	Vitamin C (Milligrams)
Turkey roasted:																			
Dark meat, piece 2½ x 1⅝ x ¼ in.	4 pieces	85	61	175	26	7	2.1	1.5	1.5	0	–	–	2.0	338	–	.03	.20	3.6	–
Light meat, piece 4 x 2 x ¼ in.	2 pieces	85	62	150	28	3	.9	.6	.7	0	–	–	1.0	349	–	.04	.12	9.4	–
FRUIT AND FRUIT PRODUCTS																			
Apples, raw, unpeeled	1	138	84	80	Trace	1	–	–	–	20	10	14	.4	152	120	.04	.03	.1	6
Apple juice	1 cup	248	88	120	Trace	Trace	–	–	–	30	15	22	1.5	250	–	.02	.05	.2	2
Applesauce, sweetened	1 cup	255	76	230	1	Trace	–	–	–	61	10	13	1.3	166	100	.05	.03	.1	3
Apricots, raw		107	85	55	1	Trace	–	–	–	14	18	25	.5	301	2,890	.03	.04	.6	11
Avocados, raw	1	216	74	370	5	37	5.5	22.0	3.7	13	22	91	1.3	1,303	630	.24	.43	3.5	30
Banana, without peel	1	119	76	100	1	Trace	–	–	–	26	10	31	.8	440	230	.06	.07	.8	12
Blueberries, raw	1 cup	144	83	90	1	1	–	–	–	22	22	19	1.5	117	150	.04	.09	.7	20
Cantaloupe	½ melon	477	91	80	2	Trace	–	–	–	20	38	44	1.1	682	9,240	.11	.08	1.5	90
Cherries, sweet	10 cherries	68	80	45	1	Trace	–	–	–	12	15	13	.3	129	70	.03	.04	.3	7
Cranberry juice	1 cup	253	83	165	Trace	Trace	–	–	–	42	13	8	.8	25	Trace	.03	.03	.1	81
Dates, whole	10 dates	80	23	220	2	Trace	–	–	–	58	47	50	2.4	518	40	.07	.08	1.8	0
Fruit cocktail, canned	1 cup	255	80	195	1	Trace	–	–	–	50	23	31	1.0	411	360	.05	.03	1.0	5
Grapefruit	½ grapefruit	241	89	45	1	Trace	–	–	–	12	19	19	.5	159	10	.05	.02	.2	44
Grapefruit juice white	1 cup	246	90	95	1	Trace	–	–	–	23	22	37	.5	399	20	10	.05	.5	93
Grapes, seedless	10 grapes	50	81	35	Trace	Trace	–	–	–	9	6	10	.2	87	50	.03	.02	.2	2
Honeydew melon	⅒ melon	477	91	50	1	Trace	–	–	–	11	21	24	.6	374	60	.06	.04	.9	34
Orange, whole	1 orange	131	86	65	1	Trace	–	–	–	16	54	26	.5	263	260	.13	.05	.5	66
Orange juice	1 cup	249	88	110	2	Trace	–	–	–	26	27	42	.5	496	500	.22	.07	1.0	124
Peaches, raw, whole	1 peach	100	89	40	1	Trace	–	–	–	10	9	19	.5	202	1,330	.02	.05	1.0	7
Peaches, canned	1 cup	256	79	200	1	Trace	–	–	–	51	10	31	.8	333	1,100	.03	.05	1.5	8
Pears, raw	1 pear	164	83	100	1	1	–	–	–	25	13	18	.5	213	30	.03	.07	.2	7
Pears, canned	1 cup	255	80	195	1	1	–	–	–	50	13	18	.5	214	10	.03	.05	.3	3
Pineapple, raw	1 cup	155	85	80	1	Trace	–	–	–	21	26	12	.8	226	110	.14	.05	.3	26
Pineapple, crushed	1 cup	255	80	190	1	Trace	–	–	–	49	28	13	.8	245	130	.20	.05	.5	18
Plums, raw	1 plum	66	87	30	Trace	Trace	–	–	–	8	8	12	.3	112	160	.02	.02	.3	4
Prunes, cooked	1 cup	250	66	255	2	1	–	–	–	67	51	79	3.8	695	1,590	.07	.15	1.5	2
Raisins, seedless	1 cup	145	18	420	4	Trace	–	–	–	112	90	146	5.1	1,106	30	.16	.12	.7	1
Raspberries, raw	1 cup	123	84	70	1	1	–	–	–	17	27	27	1.1	207	160	.04	.11	1.1	31
Rhubarb, cooked, added sugar	1 cup	270	63	380	1	Trace	–	–	–	97	211	41	1.6	548	220	.05	.14	.8	16
Strawberries, raw	1 cup	149	90	55	1	1	–	–	–	13	31	31	1.5	244	90	0.04	0.10	0.9	88
Strawberries, frozen	10 oz.	284	71	310	1	1	–	–	–	79	40	48	2.0	318	90	.06	.17	1.4	151
Tangerine, raw	1	86	87	40	1	Trace	–	–	–	10	34	15	.3	108	360	.05	.02	.1	27
Watermelon	1 wedge	926	93	110	2	1	–	–	–	27	30	43	2.1	426	2,510	.13	.13	.9	30
GRAIN PRODUCTS																			
Bagel, egg	1 bagel	55	32	165	6	2	0.5	0.9	0.8	28	9	43	1.2	41	30	.14	.10	1.2	0
Biscuits	1 biscuit	28	27	105	2	5	1.2	2.0	1.2	13	34	49	.4	33	Trace	.08	.08	.7	Trace

Nutritive Value of Foods (Continued)

Food	Approximate Measure	Grams	Water (Percent)	Food energy (Calories)	Protein (Grams)	Fat (Grams)	Saturated Fats (Grams)	Unsaturated Fats: Oleic (Grams)	Unsaturated Fats: Linoleic (Grams)	Carbohydrate (Grams)	Calcium (Milligrams)	Phosphorus (Milligrams)	Iron (Milligrams)	Potassium (Milligrams)	Vitamin A value (International units)	Thiamin (Milligrams)	Riboflavin (Milligrams)	Niacin (Milligrams)	Vitamin C (Milligrams)
Breads:																			
Cracked-wheat	1 slice	25	35	65	2	1	.1	.2	.2	13	22	32	.5	34	Trace	.08	.06	.8	Trace
French or Vienna	1 slice	35	31	100	3	1	.2	.4	.4	19	15	30	.8	32	Trace	.14	.08	1.2	Trace
Italian	1 slice	30	32	85	3	Trace	Trace	Trace	.1	17	5	23	.7	22	0	.12	.07	1.0	0
Rye	1 slice	25	36	60	2	Trace	Trace	Trace	.1	13	19	37	.5	36	0	.07	.05	.7	0
White	1 slice	25	36	70	2	1	.2	.3	.3	13	21	24	.6	26	Trace	.10	.06	.8	Trace
Whole-wheat	1 slice	28	36	65	3	1	.1	.2	.2	14	24	71	.8	72	Trace	.09	.03	.8	Trace
Breakfast Cereals:																			
Hot oatmeal, cooked	1 cup	240	87	130	5	2	.4	.8	.9	23	22	137	1.4	146	0	.19	.05	.2	0
Ready-to-eat—																			
Bran flakes (added sugar, salt, iron, vitamins)	1 cup	35	3	105	4	1	–	–	–	28	19	125	5.6	137	1,540	.46	.52	6.2	0
Corn flakes, sugar coated (added sugar, salt, iron, vitamins)	1 cup	40	2	155	2	Trace	–	–	–	37	1	10	(44)	27	1,760	.53	.50	7.1	21
Oats, puffed (added iron, thiamin, niacin)	1 cup	15	3	100	3	1	–	–	–	19	44	102	4.0	–	1,100	.33	.38	4.4	13
Rice, puffed (added iron, thiamin, niacin)	1 cup	15	4	60	1	Trace	–	–	–	13	3	14	.3	15	0	.07	.01	.7	0
Wheat flakes (added sugar, salt, iron, vitamins)	1 cup	30	4	105	3	Trace	–	–	–	24	12	83	4.8	81	1,320	.40	.45	5.3	16
Cakes (made from mixes with enriched flour):																			
Angelfood	1 piece	53	34	135	3	Trace	–	–	–	32	50	63	.2	32	0	.03	.08	.3	0
Gingerbread	1 piece	63	37	175	2	4	1.1	1.8	1.1	32	57	63	.9	173	Trace	.09	.11	.8	Trace
White with chocolate icing	1 piece	71	21	250	3	8	3.0	2.9	1.2	45	70	127	.7	82	40	.09	.11	.8	Trace
Cookies (made with enriched flour):																			
Brownies with nuts	1 brownie	20	11	85	1	4	.9	1.4	1.3	13	9	27	.4	34	20	.03	.02	.2	Trace
Chocolate chip	4 cookies	42	3	200	2	9	2.8	2.9	2.2	29	16	48	1.0	56	50	.10	.17	.9	Trace
Macaroons	2 cookies	38	4	180	2	9	–	–	–	25	10	32	.3	176	0	.02	.06	.2	0
Crackers:																			
Graham, plain	2 crackers	14	6	55	1	1	.3	.5	.3	10	6	21	.5	55	0	.02	.08	.5	0
Saltines, with enriched flour	4 crackers	11	4	50	1	1	.3	.5	.4	8	2	10	.5	13	0	.05	.05	.4	0
Doughnuts, glazed, made with enriched flour	1 doughnut	50	26	205	3	11	3.3	5.8	3.3	22	16	33	.6	34	25	.10	.10	.8	0
Macaroni, enriched, cooked	1 cup	130	64	190	7	1	–	–	–	39	14	85	1.4	103	0	.23	.13	1.8	0
Muffins, bran, made with enriched flour	1 muffin	40	35	105	3	4	1.2	1.4	.8	17	57	162	1.5	172	90	.07	.10	1.7	Trace

Nutritive Value of Foods (Continued)

Food	Approximate Measure	Grams	Water (Percent)	Food energy (Calories)	Protein (Grams)	Fat (Grams)	Saturated Fats (Grams)	Unsaturated Fats: Oleic (Grams)	Unsaturated Fats: Linoleic (Grams)	Carbohydrate (Grams)	Calcium (Milligrams)	Phosphorus (Milligrams)	Iron (Milligrams)	Potassium (Milligrams)	Vitamin A value (International units)	Thiamin (Milligrams)	Riboflavin (Milligrams)	Niacin (Milligrams)	Vitamin C (Milligrams)
Egg noodles, cooked	1 cup	160	71	200	7	2	–	–	–	37	16	94	1.4	70	110	.22	.13	1.9	0
Pancakes, plain, (made with enriched flour)	1 cake	27	50	60	2	2	.5	.8	.5	9	27	38	.4	33	30	.06	.07	.5	Trace
Pies, (made with enriched flour):																			
Apple	1 sector	135	48	345	3	15	3.9	6.4	3.6	51	11	30	.9	108	40	.15	.11	1.3	2
Pecan	1 sector	118	20	495	6	27	4.0	14.4	6.3	61	55	122	3.7	145	190	.26	.14	1.0	Trace
Pumpkin	1 sector	130	59	275	5	15	5.4	5.4	2.4	32	66	90	1.0	208	3,210	.11	.18	1.0	Trace
Pizza, cheese	1 sector	60	45	145	6	4	1.7	1.5	0.6	22	86	89	1.1	67	230	0.16	0.18	1.6	4
Popcorn, plain	1 cup	6	4	25	1	Trace	Trace	.1	.2	5	1	17	.2	–	–	–	.01	.1	0
Rice, white, enriched, cooked	1 cup	205	73	225	4	Trace	.1	.1	.1	50	21	57	1.8	57	0	.23	.02	2.1	0
Rolls, enriched:																			
Brown and serve	1 roll	26	27	85	2	2	.4	.7	.5	14	20	23	.5	25	Trace	.10	.06	.9	Trace
Frankfurter and hamburger buns	1 roll	40	31	120	3	2	.5	.8	.6	21	30	34	.8	38	Trace	.16	.10	1.3	Trace
Spaghetti, enriched, cooked	1 cup	130	64	190	7	1	–	–	–	39	14	85	1.4	103	0	.23	.13	1.8	0
Spaghetti with meat balls and tomato sauce	1 cup	248	70	330	19	12	3.3	6.3	.9	39	124	236	3.7	665	1,590	.25	.30	4.0	22
Waffles, made with enriched flour	1 waffle		41	210	7	7	2.3	2.8	1.4	28	85	130	1.3	109	250	.17	.23	1.4	Trace
LEGUMES (DRY), NUTS, SEEDS, RELATED PRODUCTS																			
Almonds	1 cup	130	5	775	24	70	5.6	47.7	12.8	25	304	655	6.1	1,005	0	.31	1.20	4.6	Trace
Beans, dry:																			
Navy	1 cup	190	69	225	15	1	–	–	–	40	95	281	5.1	790	0	.27	.13	1.3	0
Lima, cooked	1 cup	190	64	260	16	1	–	–	–	49	55	293	5.9	1,163	–	.25	.11	1.3	–
Blackeye peas, cooked	1 cup	190	80	190	13	1	–	–	–	35	43	238	3.3	573	30	.40	.10	1.0	–
Brazil nuts	1 oz.	28	5	185	4	19	4.8	6.2	7.1	3	53	196	1.0	203	Trace	.27	.03	.5	–
Cashew nuts, roasted	1 cup	140	5	785	24	64	12.9	36.8	10.2	41	53	522	5.3	650	140	.60	.35	2.5	–
Lentils, whole cooked	1 cup	200	72	210	16	Trace	–	–	–	39	50	238	4.2	498	40	.14	.12	1.2	0
Peanuts, roasted in oil, salted	1 cup	144	2	840	37	72	13.7	33.0	20.7	27	107	577	3.0	971	–	.45	.19	24.8	0
Peanut butter	1 Tbsp.	16	2	95	4	8	1.5	3.7	2.3	3	9	61	.3	100	–	.02	.02	2.4	0
Peas, split, dry, cooked	1 cup	200	70	230	16	1	–	–	–	42	22	178	3.4	592	80	.30	.18	1.8	–
Pecans	1 cup	118	3	810	11	84	7.2	30.5	20.0	17	86	341	2.8	712	150	1.01	.15	1.1	2
Pumpkin kernels	1 cup	140	4	775	41	65	11.8	23.5	27.5	21	71	1,602	15.7	1,386	100	.34	.27	3.4	–
Sunflower seeds	1 cup	145	5	810	35	69	8.2	13.7	43.2	29	174	1,214	10.3	1,334	70	2.84	.33	7.8	–
Walnuts	1 cup	120	3	785	26	74	6.3	13.3	45.7	19	Trace	713	7.5	575	380	.28	.14	.9	–
SUGARS AND SWEETS																			
Candy:																			
Caramels	1 oz.	28	8	115	1	3	1.6	1.1	.1	22	42	35	.4	54	Trace	.01	.05	.1	Trace
Chocolate, milk	1 oz.	28	1	145	2	9	5.5	3.0	.3	16	65	65	.3	109	80	.02	.10	.1	Trace
Chocolate-coated peanuts	1 oz.	28	1	160	5	12	4.0	4.7	2.1	11	33	84	.4	143	Trace	.10	.05	2.1	Trace

Nutritive Value of Foods (Continued)

Food	Approximate Measure	Grams	Water (Percent)	Food energy (Calories)	Protein (Grams)	Fat (Grams)	Saturated Fats (Grams)	Unsaturated Fats: Oleic (Grams)	Unsaturated Fats: Linoleic (Grams)	Carbohydrate (Grams)	Calcium (Milligrams)	Phosphorus (Milligrams)	Iron (Milligrams)	Potassium (Milligrams)	Vitamin A value (International units)	Thiamin (Milligrams)	Riboflavin (Milligrams)	Niacin (Milligrams)	Vitamin C (Milligrams)
Honey	1 Tbsp.	21	17	65	Trace	0	0	0	0	17	1	1	.1	11	0	Trace	.01	.1	Trace
Jams and preserves	1 Tbsp.	20	29	55	Trace	Trace	—	—	—	14	4	2	.2	18	Trace	Trace	.01	Trace	Trace
Jellies	1 Tbsp.	18	29	50	Trace	Trace	—	—	—	13	4	1	.3	14	Trace	Trace	.01	Trace	1
Corn Syrup	1 Tbsp.	21	24	60	0	0	0	0	0	15	9	3	.8	1	0	0	0	0	0
Sugars:																			
Brown	1 cup	220	2	820	0	0	0	0	0	212	187	42	7.5	757	0	.02	.07	.4	0
White	1 cup	200	1	770	0	0	0	0	0	199	0	0	.2	6	0	0	0	0	0
Powdered	1 cup	100	1	385	0	0	0	0	0	100	0	0	.1	3	0	0	0	0	0
VEGETABLES AND VEGETABLE PRODUCTS																			
Asparagus, cooked	1 cup	145	94	30	3	Trace	—	—	—	5	30	73	0.9	265	1,310	0.23	0.26	2.0	38
Beans:																			
Lima, cooked	1 cup	170	69	210	13	Trace	—	—	—	40	63	227	4.7	709	400	.16	.09	2.2	22
Green, cooked	1 cup	125	92	30	2	Trace	—	—	—	7	63	46	.8	189	680	.09	.11	.6	15
Yellow or wax, cooked	1 cup	125	93	30	2	Trace	—	—	—	6	63	46	.8	189	290	.09	.11	.6	16
Bean sprouts, raw	1 cup	105	89	35	4	Trace	—	—	—	7	20	67	1.4	234	20	.14	.14	.8	20
Beets, cooked	1 cup	145	91	30	1	Trace	—	—	—	7	14	23	.5	208	20	.03	.04	.3	6
Broccoli, cooked	1 stalk	180	91	45	6	1	—	—	—	8	158	112	1.4	481	4,500	.16	.36	1.4	162
Cabbage, raw	1 cup	70	92	15	1	Trace	—	—	—	4	34	20	0.3	163	90	0.04	0.04	0.2	33
Cabbage, cooked	1 cup	145	94	30	2	Trace	—	—	—	6	64	29	.4	236	190	.06	.06	.4	48
Carrots, raw	1 carrot	72	88	30	1	Trace	—	—	—	7	27	26	.5	246	7,930	.04	.04	.4	6
Carrots, cooked	1 cup	158	91	50	1	Trace	—	—	—	11	51	48	.9	344	16,280	.08	.08	.8	9
Cauliflower, cooked	1 cup	125	91	31	3	Trace	—	—	—	6	29	64	1.3	339	70	.13	.12	.8	90
Celery, raw	1 stalk		94	5	Trace	Trace	—	—	—	2	16	11	.1	136	110	.01	.01	.1	4
Collards, cooked	1 cup	190	90	65	7	1	—	—	—	10	357	99	1.5	498	14,820	.21	.38	2.3	144
Corn, sweet, cooked	1 ear	140	74	70	2	1	—	—	—	16	2	69	.5	151	310	.09	.08	1.1	7
Corn, canned, cream style	1 cup	256	76	210	5	2	—	—	—	51	8	143	1.5	248	840	.08	.13	2.6	13
Cucumber slices	6 or 8 small		95	5	Trace	Trace	—	—	—	1	7	8	.3	45	70	.01	.01	.1	3
Lettuce, butterhead	1 outer or 2 heart leaves	15	95	Trace	Trace	Trace	—	—	—	Trace	5	4	.3	40	150	.01	.01	Trace	1
Mushrooms, raw	1 cup	70	90	20	2	Trace	—	—	—	3	4	81	.6	290	Trace	.07	.32	2.9	2
Onions, raw	1 cup	170	89	65	3	Trace	—	—	—	15	46	61	.9	267	Trace	.05	.07	.3	17
Parsley, raw	1 Tbsp.	4	85	Trace	Trace	Trace	—	—	—	Trace	7	2	.2	25	300	Trace	.01	Trace	6
Parsnips, cooked	1 cup	155	82	100	2	1	—	—	—	23	70	96	.9	587	50	.11	.12	.2	16
Peas, green, cooked	1 cup	160	77	150	8	1	—	—	—	29	44	129	3.2	163	1,170	.15	.10	1.4	14
Peppers, sweet, raw	1 pod		93	15	1	Trace	—	—	—	4	7	16	.5	157	310	.06	.06	.4	94
Potatoes, baked	1 potato		75	145	4	Trace	—	—	—	33	14	101	1.1	782	Trace	.15	.07	2.7	31
Potatoes, boiled	1 potato		83	90	3	Trace	—	—	—	20	8	57	.7	385	Trace	.12	.05	1.6	22
Potatoes, french fried	10 strips		45	135	2	7	1.7	1.2	3.3	18	8	56	.7	427	Trace	.07	.04	1.6	11
Potatoes, mashed, (milk added)	1 cup	210	83	135	4	2	.7	.4	Trace	27	50	103	8	548	40	.17	.11	2.1	21
Potato chips	10 chips		2	115	1	8	2.1	1.4	4.0	10	8	28	.4	226	Trace	.04	.01	1.0	3
Potato salad	1 cup	250	76	250	7	7	2.0	2.7	1.3	41	80	160	1.5	798	350	.20	.18	2.8	28
Pumpkin, canned	1 cup	245	90	80	2	1	—	—	—	19	61	64	1.0	588	15,680	.07	.12	1.5	12
Radishes, raw	4 radishes		95	5	Trace	Trace	—	—	—	1	5	6	.2	58	Trace	.01	.01	.1	5
Sauerkraut, canned	1 cup	235	93	40	2	Trace	—	—	—	9	85	42	1.2	329	120	.07	.09	.5	33
Spinach, raw	1 cup	55	91	15	2	Trace	—	—	—	2	51	28	1.7	259	4,460	.06	.11	.3	28
Spinach, cooked	1 cup	180	92	40	5	1	—	—	—	6	167	68	4.0	583	14,580	.13	.25	.9	50
Squash, summer, cooked	1 cup	210	96	30	2	Trace	—	—	—	7	53	53	.8	296	820	.11	.17	1.7	21

Nutritive Value of Foods (Continued)

Food	Approximate Measure	Grams	Water (Percent)	Food energy (Calories)	Protein (Grams)	Fat (Grams)	Saturated Fats (Grams)	Unsaturated Fats: Oleic (Grams)	Unsaturated Fats: Linoleic (Grams)	Carbohydrate (Grams)	Calcium (Milligrams)	Phosphorus (Milligrams)	Iron (Milligrams)	Potassium (Milligrams)	Vitamin A value (International units)	Thiamin (Milligrams)	Riboflavin (Milligrams)	Niacin (Milligrams)	Vitamin C (Milligrams)
Squash, winter, cooked	1 cup	205	81	130	4	1	–	–	–	32	57	98	1.6	945	8,610	.10	.27	1.4	27
Sweet potatoes, baked	1 potato		64	160	2	1	–	–	–	37	46	66	1.0	342	9,230	.10	.08	.8	25
Tomatoes, raw	1 tomato	135	94	25	1	Trace	–	–	–	6	16	33	.6	300	1,110	.07	.05	.9	28
Tomato juice	1 cup	241	94	45	2	Trace	–	–	–	10	17	44	2.2	552	1,940	.12	.07	1.9	39
Turnips, cooked	1 cup	155	94	30	3	Trace	–	–	–	5	252	49	1.5	–	8,270	.15	.33	.7	68
Vegetables, mixed, frozen, cooked	1 cup	182	83	115	6	1	–	–	–	24	46	115	2.4	348	9,010	.22	.13	2.0	15
MISCELLANEOUS ITEMS																			
Beverages, Carbonated, Sweetened:																			
Carbonated water	12 fl. oz.	366	92	115	0	0	0	0	0	29	–	–	–	–	0	0	0	0	0
Cola type	12 fl. oz.	369	90	145	0	0	0	0	0	37	–	–	–	–	0	0	0	0	0
Fruit-flavored	12 fl. oz.	372	88	170	0	0	0	0	0	45	–	–	–	–	0	0	0	0	0
Gelatin dessert	1 cup	240	84	140	4	0	0	0	0	34	–	–	–	–	–	–	–	–	–
Mustard, yellow	1 tsp.	5	80	5	Trace	Trace	–	–	–	Trace	4	4	.1	7	–	–	–	–	–
Olives, green	4 medium		78	15	Trace	2	.2	1.2	.1	Trace	8	2	.2	7	40	–	–	–	–
Pickles, dill	1 pickle		93	5	Trace	Trace	–	–	–	1	17	14	.7	130	70	Trace	.01	Trace	4
Soups, Canned, Prepared with milk																			
Cream of chicken	1 cup	245	85	180	7	10	4.2	3.6	1.3	15	172	152	0.5	260	610	0.05	0.27	0.7	2
Cream of mushroom	1 cup	245	83	215	7	14	5.4	2.9	4.6	16	191	169	.5	279	250	.05	.34	.7	1
Tomato	1 cup	250	84	175	7	7	3.4	1.7	1.0	23	168	155	.8	418	1,200	.10	.26	1.3	15
Soups, Canned, Prepared with water																			
Beef broth	1 cup	240	96	30	5	0	0	0	0	3	Trace	31	.5	130	Trace	Trace	.02	1.2	–
Beef noodle	1 cup	240	93	65	4	3	.6	.7	.8	7	7	48	1.0	77	50	.05	.07	1.0	Trace
Clam chowder	1 cup	245	92	80	2	3	.5	.4	1.3	12	34	47	1.0	184	880	.02	.02	1.0	–
Cream of chicken	1 cup	240	92	95	3	6	1.6	2.3	1.1	8	24	34	.5	79	410	.02	.05	.5	Trace
Tomato	1 cup	245	91	90	2	3	.5	.5	1.0	16	15	34	.7	230	1,000	.05	.05	1.2	12
Vegetarian	1 cup	245	92	80	2	2	–	–	–	13	20	39	1.0	172	2,940	.05	.05	1.0	–

Source: Adapted from Nutritive Value of Foods, USDA, Home and Garden Bulletin #72.

Cookware Materials

Material	*Heating Capability*	*Cleaning and Care*	*Cost*
Copper	Best conductor, but does not hold heat well because cookware is usually thin.	Easy to clean, but hard to maintain shine if desired.	Expensive.
Iron	Good conductor and holds heat well. Heavy.	Hard to clean and maintain.	Usually inexpensive.
Glass-Ceramic	Conducts and holds heat well. Can develop hot spots and cause scorched spots in food.	Needs soaking to clean.	Moderate.
Stainless Steel	Poor and uneven conductor of heat. Does not hold heat well.	Easy to clean and doesn't rust, corrode, or stain.	Relatively inexpensive.
Stainless Steel over Copper	Combines the best qualities of the heat conduction of copper and the ease of care of stainless steel.	Easy to clean.	Moderate.
Aluminum	Conducts and holds heat well.	Will pit and stain with contact of alkaline foods and water.	Inexpensive to expensive depending upon the way the pan is constructed.
Stainless Steel over Aluminum	Combines the good heat conduction of aluminum with ease of care of the stainless steel.	Easy to clean.	Moderate.
Glass	Poor conductor of heat. Heats unevenly and develops hot spots. Requires special protective trivet to use over a burner.	Chips and breaks easily. Food tends to stick. Hard to clean. Attractive for display and serving food.	Inexpensive.
Enamel Baked on Metal	Conducts heat like the base metal, so varies depending on metal used.	Chips easily. Stains easily. Decorative.	Expensive.
Earthenware-Pottery	Holds heat well, but is limited to oven cooking.	Attractive, but chips and breaks easily. Sometimes difficult to clean.	Inexpensive.

Common Substitutions

Ingredient	Substitution
Arrowroot, 1 tsp.	Flour, 1 tbsp., or Cornstarch, 1½ tsp.
Baking powder, 1 tsp.	Baking soda, ¼ tsp., plus Cream of Tartar, ⅝ tsp. Baking soda, ¼ tsp., plus sour milk, buttermilk, or yogurt, ½ cup (Decrease liquid in recipe by ½ cup)
Butter, 1 cup	Margarine, 1 cup
Dry bread crumbs, ⅓ cup	Bread, 1 slice
Chocolate, unsweetened, 1 oz.	Cocoa, 3 tbsp., plus Butter, 1 tbsp.
Cornstarch, 1 tbsp.	Flour, 2 tbsp., or Quick-cooking tapioca, 4 tbsp.
Cream, sour, 1 cup	Butter, 3 tbsp., plus Sour milk, ⅞ cup
Egg, 1, for baking	Egg yolks, 2, plus Water, 1 tbsp.
Extracts, 1 tsp.	Oil of similar flavor, ¼ tsp.
Flour, cake, 1 cup	All-purpose flour, 1 cup sifted minus 2 tbsp.
Garlic, 1 clove	Garlic powder, ⅛ tsp.
Herbs, fresh, 1 tbsp.	Herbs, dried, 1 tsp.
Honey, 1 cup	Sugar, 1¼ cups, plus Liquid, ¼ cup (Use liquid called for in recipe)
Lemon juice, 1 tsp.	Vinegar, ½ tsp.
Milk, buttermilk, 1 cup	Plain yogurt, 1 cup
Milk, whole, 1 cup	Evaporated milk, ½ cup, plus Water, ½ cup, or Water, 1 cup, plus Butter, 1½ tsp.
Shortening, melted, 1 cup	Cooking oil, 1 cup. (Do not substitute cooking oil if recipe calls for solid shortening)
Shortening, solid, 1 cup	Butter or margarine, 1⅛ cups. (Decrease salt in recipe by ½ tsp.)
Sugar, brown, 1 cup	Granulated sugar, 1 cup

Continued on Next Page

Sugar, white, 1 cup	Honey, 1 cup. (Decrease liquid in recipe by ¼ cup) or Brown sugar, 1 cup, or Confectioner's sugar, 1¾ cups
Tomatoes, 1 cup	Tomato sauce, ½ cup, plus Water, ½ cup
Wine, 1 cup	Water, 13 tbsp., Lemon juice, 3 tbsp., plus Sugar, 1 tbsp.
Yogurt, plain, 1 cup	Buttermilk, 1 cup, or Cottage cheese, 1 cup, or Sour cream, 1 cup

Equivalents

Traditional Measure	*Traditional Equivalent*	*Approx. Metric Equivalent*
⅛ teaspoon		0.5 m
¼ teaspoon		1 mL
½ teaspoon		3 mL
1 teaspoon		5 mL
1 tablespoon	3 teaspoons	15 mL
⅛ cup	2 tablespoons	30 mL
¼ cup	4 tablespoons	50 mL
⅓ cup	5 tablespoons + 1 teaspoon	75 mL
½ cup	8 tablespoons	125 mL
⅔ cup	10 tablespoons + 2 teaspoons	150 mL
¾ cup	12 tablespoons	175 mL
1 cup	16 tablespoons	250 mL
1 pint	2 cups	500 mL
1 quart	2 pints	1000 mL
		1 L
1 gallon	4 quarts	4 L
¼ pound	4 ounces	125 g
Weights		
½ pound	8 ounces	250 g
1 pound	16 ounces	500 g
2 pounds	32 ounces	1000 g (1 kg)
Liquid Measurements		
2 tablespoons	1 fluid ounce	30 mL
¼ cup	2 fluid ounces	50 mL
½ cup	4 fluid ounces	125 mL
¾ cup	6 fluid ounces	175 mL
1 cup	8 fluid ounces	250 mL
1½ cups	12 fluid ounces	375 mL
1 pint	16 fluid ounces	500 mL
1 quart	32 fluid ounces	1000 mL

Vegetable Cooking Times

Watch and test vegetables for color and the right amount of crispness to time their cooking. You also can follow certain guidelines to help you time your other meal preparation duties. These cooking times are guidelines only. Do not leave the vegetable unattended and expect to return after the specified time to a perfectly cooked product. You can think of many factors that will vary the cooking, such as the size, freshness, and cut of the particular vegetable. For instance, you will notice that the cooking time for carrots ranges over 16 minutes. This takes into account the fact that you may be cooking cut up carrots, which would take the shorter time, or whole carrots that require more cooking time. Remember, the following times are only guidelines. Keep a close eye on vegetables while they are cooking to avoid the loss of nutrients and flavor.

Vegetable	*Serving Size Per Person*	*Cooking Method*	*Approximate Cooking Time in Minutes*
Artichoke	One	Steam or simmer	25 to 40
Asparagus	¼ to ½ lb. (125 to 250 mL)	Steam or simmer	4 to 8
Beans (green or wax)	¼ to ½ lb. (125 to 250 mL)	Simmer	8 to 15
Baby Lima Beans	¼ to ½ lb. (125 to 250 mL)	Simmer	10 to 20
Beets	⅓ to ½ lb. (167 to 250 g)	Simmer Steam	35 60
Broccoli*	½ lb. (250 g)	Steam or simmer	10 to 12 (large head) or 4 to 8 (small flowerets or chopped stems)

* Broccoli is easier to cook uniformly if the stems are removed and cooked separately. Separate the heads in uniformly sized bunches to cook or serve raw. Peel the tough layer off the bottom of the stem. If cooked with the stems, cut vertically through the large stalks once or twice to hasten cooking. Place upright in water as you would asparagus.

Continued on Next Page

Brussel Sprouts	¼ to ½ pt. (125 to 250 mL)	Simmer	15
Cabbage*	¼ to ½ lb. (125 to 250 g)	Steam or stir-fry thin wedges or shredded cabbage	3 to 8
Carrots	¼ to ½ lb. (125 to 250 g)	Simmer, steam, or stir-fry	4 to 20
Cauliflower	¼ to ⅓ lb. (125 to 167 g)	Simmer or steam	5 to 20
Corn	1 to 2 ears	Simmer or steam	6 to 10
Eggplant	¼ to ⅓ lb. (125 to 167 g)	Broil Bake	4 on each side 20 (slices) 45 (whole)
Greens	4 times the volume desired after cooking	Steam or stir-fry	3 to 10
Mushrooms	1/4 lb. (125 g)	Steam or broil Sauté	5 to 8 3 to 5
Onions	Sizes vary too much for recommendation	Method of choice	Until tender
Peas	¾ lb. (375 g)	Simmer	8
Pea pods	¼ to ½ lb. (125 to 250 g)	Steam or stir-fry	4
Peppers (green, red, or yellow)	½ to 1 pepper	Simmer	6
Potatoes	¼ to ½ lb. (125 to 250 g)	Simmer or steam Bake	10 to 20 (pieces) 55 (whole)
Spinach	⅓ to ½ lb. (167 to 250 g)	Steam, simmer, or stir-fry	4 to 8

*** To avoid an unpleasant odor when cooking cabbage, never overcook it.**

Continued on Next Page

Squash	⅓ to ½ lb. (167 to 250 g)	Simmer Bake	6 to 15 42 (whole)
Sweet Potatoes	½ to 1 potato	Simmer Bake	35 to 40 (whole) 55
Tomatoes	1	Simmer Broil	3 to 4 5
Turnips	1 medium	Simmer Roast	15 to 20 30

Remember, vegetables are also great when eaten raw. Be sure to wash them thoroughly to remove any dirt and pesticides.

Guide to Herbs and Spices

A skillful cook uses only the amount of seasonings needed to complement the food, not overwhelm it. This herb chart lists some of the more common herbs that you might want to have on hand for some daily uses. These all grow well in the garden or in a pot on the kitchen window for year-around freshness.

Herb	*Qualities*	*Uses*
Basil	Sweetly aromatic, anise-like flavor.	Always good in Italian-tomato dishes, vegetables, cheese-souffle
Bay leaves	One leaf adds strong flavor; remove before serving	Steam with salmon, soups, stews, Italian beef
Chives	Delicate onion flavor	Splendid in sour cream for potatoes, in dips, on seafood salad, egg dishes, fish
Caraway Seed	Distinctive anise-like flavor	Used in rye breads, vegetables, and some ethnic cookies
Dill	Sharply aromatic with mild lemony taste	Salads, cabbage, poached fish, dips, breads, vegetable
(Use the seed or the tiny needle-like leaves called dill weed.)		
Garlic	Stronger than onions; member of the same family	Irreplaceable in Italian tomato dishes, bread, vegetables, and roasts.
Horseradish	Sharp breathtaking flavor that makes the mouth water	Often used alone as a condiment with meats, in seafood sauces, or in prepared sauces
Marjoram	Similar to oregano	Excellent with basil in Italian dishes, chicken soup, veal, lamb, and pot roasts, omelets
Oregano	Similar to marjoram, but stronger	Traditional "pizza" herb, tomato sauces, chicken, eggplant, mushrooms, marinades
Rosemary	Pungent aroma; spicy, bittersweet taste	Any meat roast, some pickles, some stuffings
Sage	Powerfully pungent; slightly bitter aroma	Traditional for stuffings, in cheese dips and cheese breads, beef soups and stews

Continued on Next Page

Tarragon	**Sweet aromatic scent; anise-like flavor**	**In bearnaise sauce, vinaigrette dressing, veal, poached salmon. Wonderful in flavored vinegars for salads**
Thyme	**Penetrating, distinctive taste and smell; very refreshing and pleasant**	**In egg dishes, cheese sauces, meatloaf, stews, stuffings, refreshing and pleasant fish, and clam chowder**

Herb	***Qualities***	***Uses***
Allspice	**A fruity blend of cinnamon, clove, and nutmeg**	**Beverages, baking, toppings, desserts, spiced teas**
Cloves	**Strong, easily recognized flavor and strongly aromatic**	**Desserts, fruits, meat toppings, relishes, beverages**
Ginger	**Peppery; fruity flavor that tingles the tongue. A strong, aromatic flavor**	**Meat glazes, relishes, desserts, baked products**
Mace	**A strong, aromatic flavor**	**Fruit cakes, preserved fruits, some meat toppings**
Mustard	**Hot burning flavor that varies slightly according to country or origin**	**Topping on meats, in sauces, dips, barbecue sauces, vegetable sauces, and with oriental dishes**
Nutmeg	**Festive light taste that blends well with cinnamon and cloves**	**Topping on eggnog and other milk drinks, seasoning for cookies, bake products, baked apples, sweet potatoes; "surprise" ingredient in some popular fried chicken breading**
Poppy Seeds	**Black, chewy seeds that have a mild, but distinct flavor**	**Popular topping on baked breads and desserts; also popular in cakes and puddings; interesting texture to tossed salads**
Pepper	**Hot flavor**	**Vegetables, meat, soup, stew, fish, or dairy food.**
Sesame Seeds	**Oily, chewy seeds with a distinctive flavor**	**Baked products, marinades, toppings for vegetables, meats, fish, and salads**

Guide to Cheeses

Cheese	*Origin*	*Characteristics*	*Serving Suggestions*
Ambrosia	Sweden	Pale yellow, semi-firm, with scattered irregular holes. Mild nut-like flavor.	Appetizers, snacks, dessert.
Bel-Paese	Italy	Semi-soft, creamy yellow interior, smooth texture. Mild, sweet to moderately robust flavor.	On cheese trays, snacks, sandwiches. Topping for casseroles, soups, pizza.
Blue	USA	Milk white, marbeled with blue-green mold; mildly tangy, peppery flavor.	Dips, salads, dressings, cheese tray with fruit and unflavored crackers.
Bonchampe with mushrooms	Germany	Creamy texture; rich, delicate flavor of mushrooms.	Appetizer cheese with toasted rounds or crackers.
Boursin	France	Smooth, white, triple cream, soft cheese; seasoned with garlic, herbs, or cracked pepper.	Spreadable on crackers or bagels. Popular appetizer cheese.
Brick	USA	Creamy yellow, semi-soft texture with tiny holes. Mild to strong flavor depending on age.	Snacks or dark bread sandwiches.
Brie	France	Pale yellow, soft spreadable interior with edible off-white crust; mild to pungent flavor. Plain, with herbs or pepper.	On cheese trays; for dessert with crackers, French bread, fruits.
Brunder Basil	Germany	Pale yellow, semi-soft interior with small irregular holes; burgundy waxed rind. Mild, creamy, naturally smoked.	Snacks, sandwiches, dessert with fruit.
Camembert	France	Smooth, creamy white, runny interior; edible off-white crust. Mild to pungent.	Use as appetizer or dessert cheese with fruit, crackers or French bread.
Cheddar	England	White to orange color; firm to crumbly texture. Mild to sharp flavor depending on age.	On cheese trays; sandwiches, soups, salads, main dishes, sauces, desserts.
Colby	USA	Light yellow to orange, semi-firm. Mild Cheddar-like flavor. Plain, with garlic or caraway.	On cheese trays; snacks, sandwiches, salads, main dishes.

Continued on Next Page

Cheese	*Origin*	*Characteristics*	*Serving Suggestions*
Co-jack	USA	Combination of Colby and Jack cheese. Yellow and white.	On cheese trays; snacks, cheeseburgers, sandwiches, nachos.
Double Gloucester	England	Yellow orange hard cheese; rich, mellow savory flavor.	Sandwiches; after-dinner cheese with fruit.
Edam	Holland	Pale yellow interior with small holes. Red wax coating on exterior. (Brown wax coating on Smoky Edam.) Mild to tangy.	Colorful on cheese trays; for snacks, sauces, desserts.
Feta	Greece	Soft, flaky white cheese from sheep's, goat's, or cow's milk. Rich tangy, salty.	Salads, cooked foods.
Gjetost	Norway	Golden brown color, buttery rich, strong but faintly sweet and caramel-like flavor. Made from goat's milk.	Slice for breakfast, dessert.
Goat's Milk Cheeses (Chevré, Montrachet, Bucheron)	France	Very white; texture ranges from soft, moist, creamy to somewhat dry. Some have bloomy white rinds. Others are coated with vegetable ash, pepper, or herbs. Flavor mild to tangy.	Appetizer or dessert; spreadable on French bread or crackers, with fresh fruits. Used in some cooked foods and salads.
Gorgonzola	Italy	Semi-soft, off-white with blue-green veins of mold. Tangy, piquant flavor similar to blue cheese.	Add to salads, use with fruits.
Gouda	Holland	Firm, yellow to gold interior with a few holes. Flattened rounds, with or without red wax coating. Aged has Cheddar-like flavor. Sometimes smoked.	Cheese trays, snacks, cooked dish es, salads, sandwiches.
Gourmandise	France	A soft, creamy processed cheese spread, flavored with kirsch or nuts.	Appetizers or desserts.
Gruyére	Switzerland	Light yellow, firm interior with a few holes. Mild, but slightly sharper than Swiss.	Cheese trays, sandwiches, fondue, French onion soup.
Liederkranz	USA	Honey colored, runny interior. Rind or crust yellow to golden brown. Mild to pungent flavor; often strong smelling.	Dark breads, pretzels, green onions, radishes.

Continued on Next Page

Cheese	*Origin*	*Characteristics*	*Serving Suggestions*
Limburger	Belgium	Soft, smooth, creamy white interior, yellow brown surface. Strong, robust flavor and odor.	Snacks, dark breads, pretzels.
Parmesan	Italy	Light yellow, brittle, flaky cheese; thin rind, sharp flavor.	Grating cheese for salads, soups, pasta, vegetables, pizza, casseroles.
Pot Cheese	Germany	A cooked cheese curd, smooth, buttery consistency; 99% fat free. Flavorings may be added such as caraway, olives, pimento.	Dips, salads, casseroles, dessert.
Primost	Scandinavian Countries	Light brown caramel color; buttery consistency. Mild, sweet flavor. Usually an acquired taste.	Excellent breakfast cheese, sliced thinly with a cheese plane.
Provolone	Italy	Pale yellow interior, glossy rind. May be in various shapes. Mellow to sharp flavor; sometimes smoked.	Snacks, sandwiches, salads, stuffing for ravioli; grate for main dishes when aged.
Romano	Italy	Very hard, granular texture; sharp, peppery flavor.	Grate on spaghetti, vegetables, salads, soups, casseroles.
Roquefort	France	Blue-veined, white curd cheese made from sheep's milk; crumbly, semi-hard. Sharp, tangy flavor.	Dips, cheese balls, salads, dessert with crackers.
Swiss	Switzerland	Pale yellow interior, yellow, waxed rind. Firm, smooth with large holes. Mild, sweet, nut-like flavor. Also made in other countries under other names.	Cheese-meat trays, sandwiches, salads, Swiss fondue.

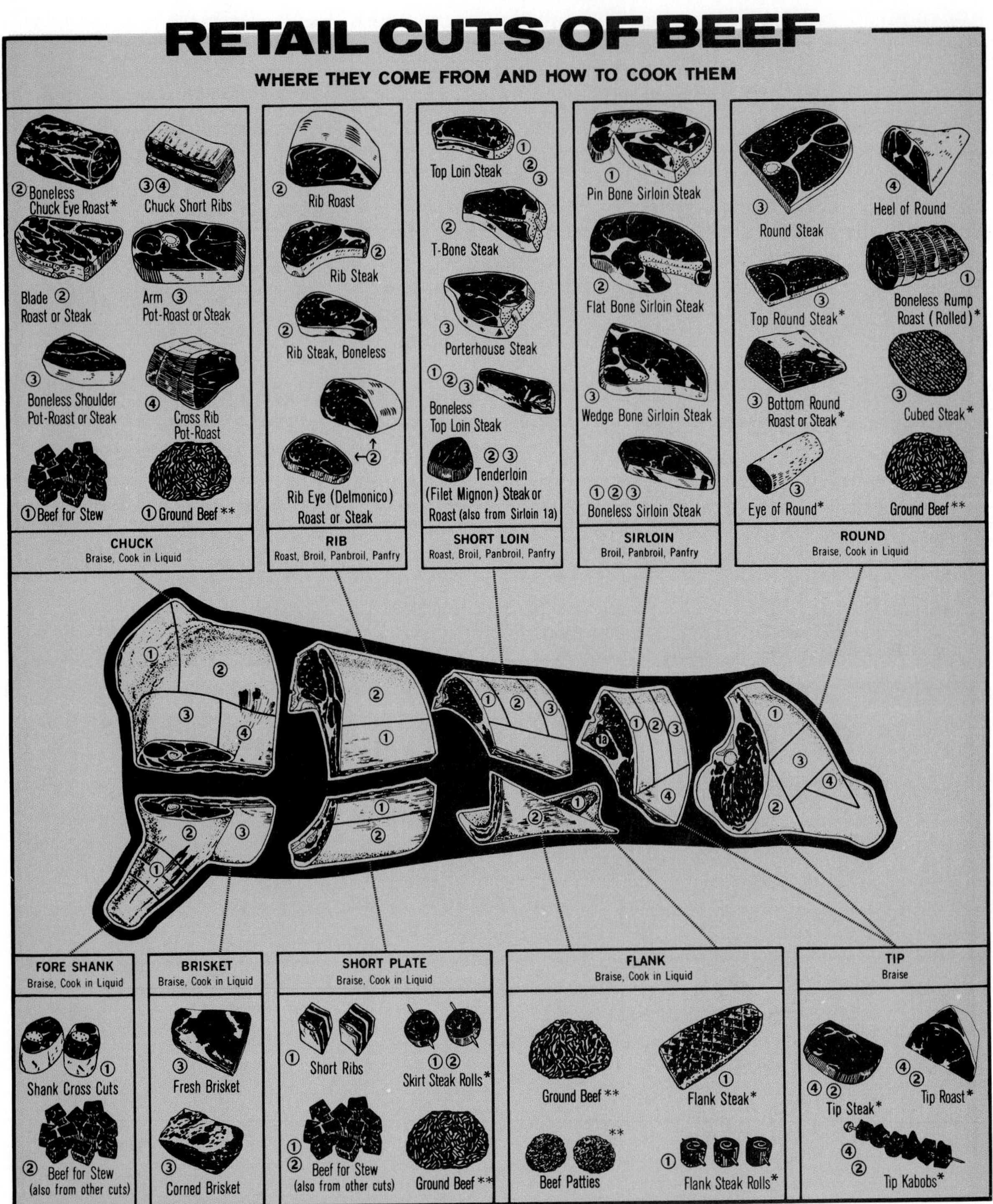

*May be Roasted, Broiled, Panbroiled or Panfried from high quality beef.

**May be Roasted, (Baked), Broiled, Panbroiled or Panfried.

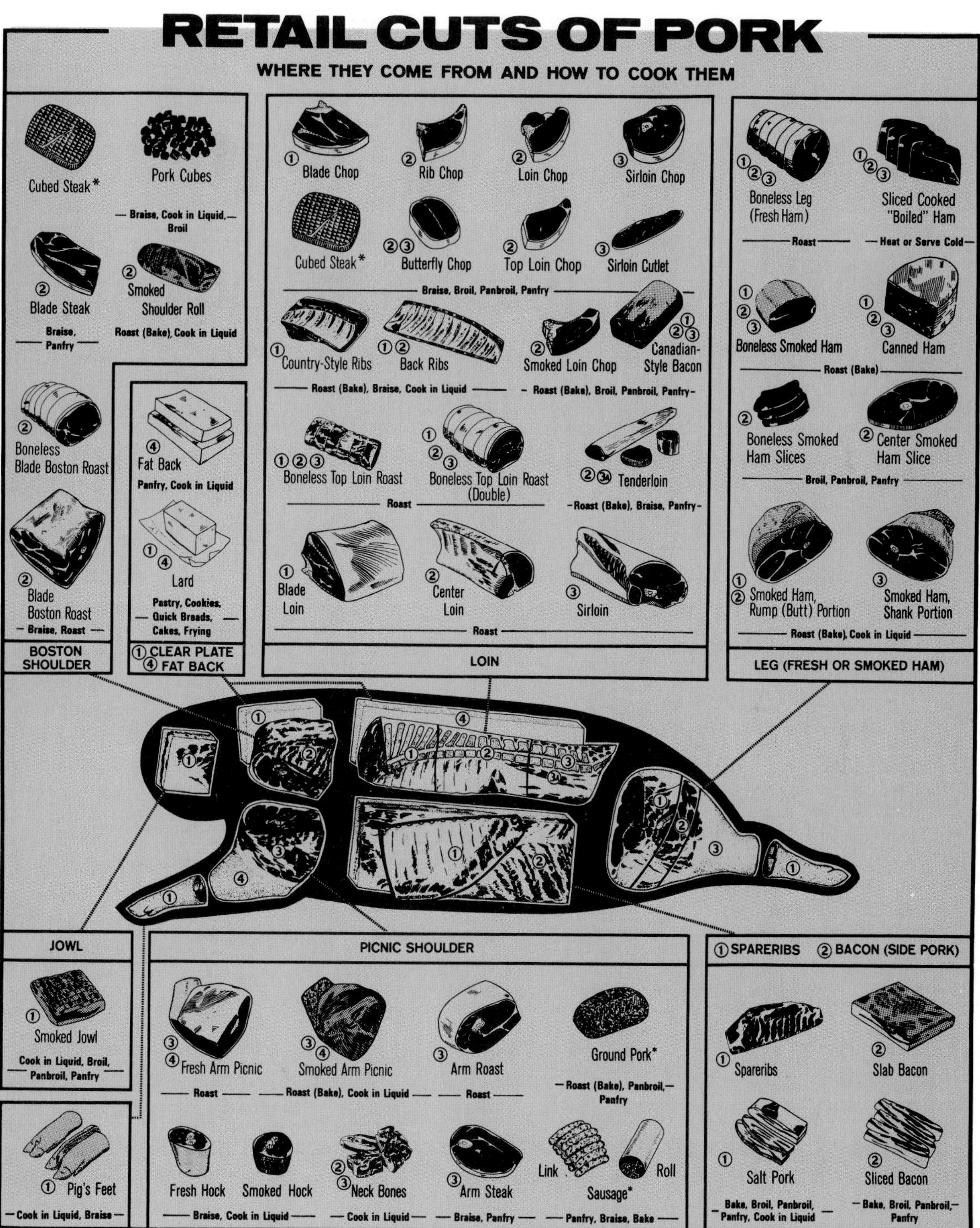

*May be made from Boston Shoulder, Picnic Shoulder, Loin or Leg.

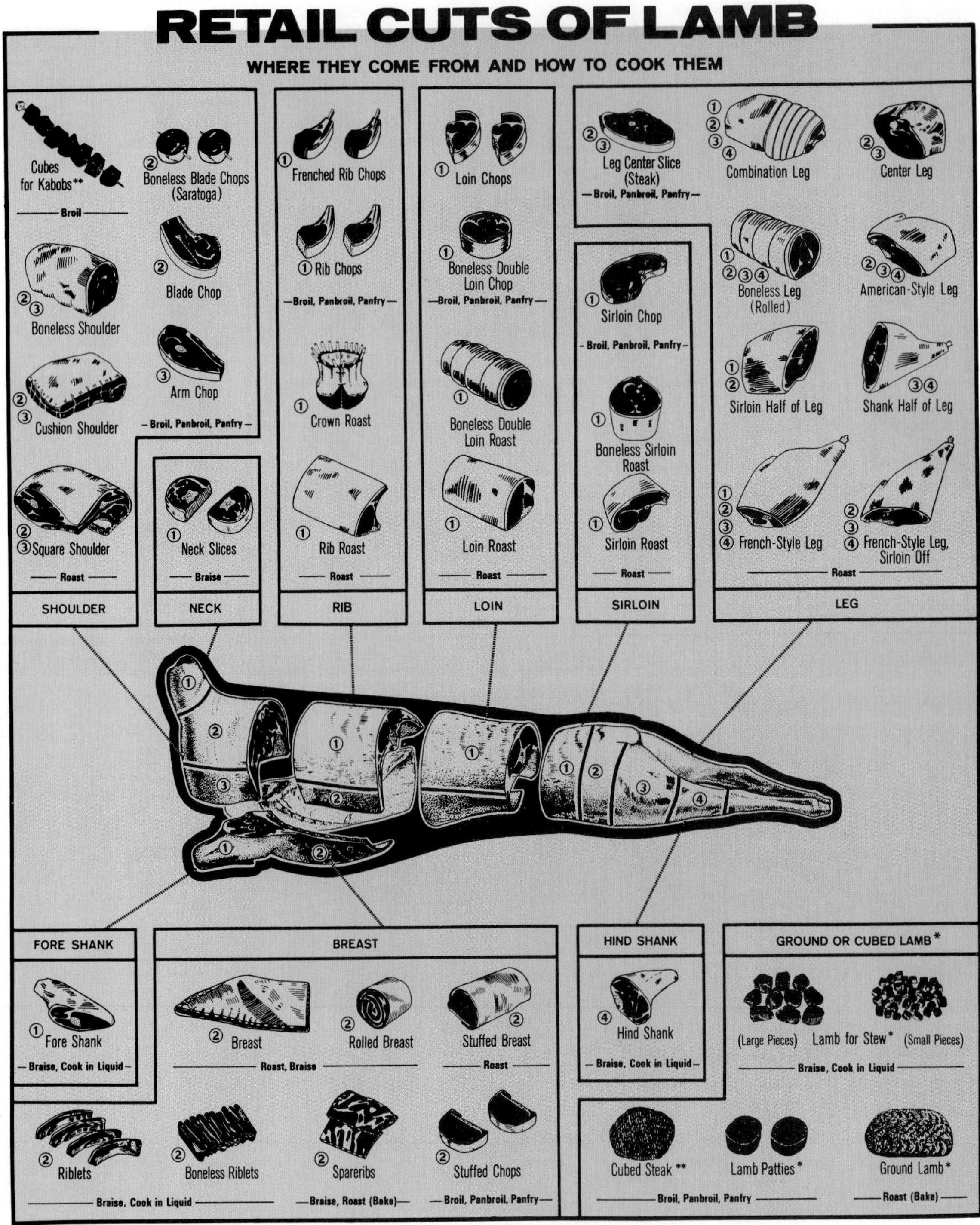

* Lamb for stew or grinding may be made from any cut.

**Kabobs or cubed steaks may be made from any thick solid piece of boneless Lamb.

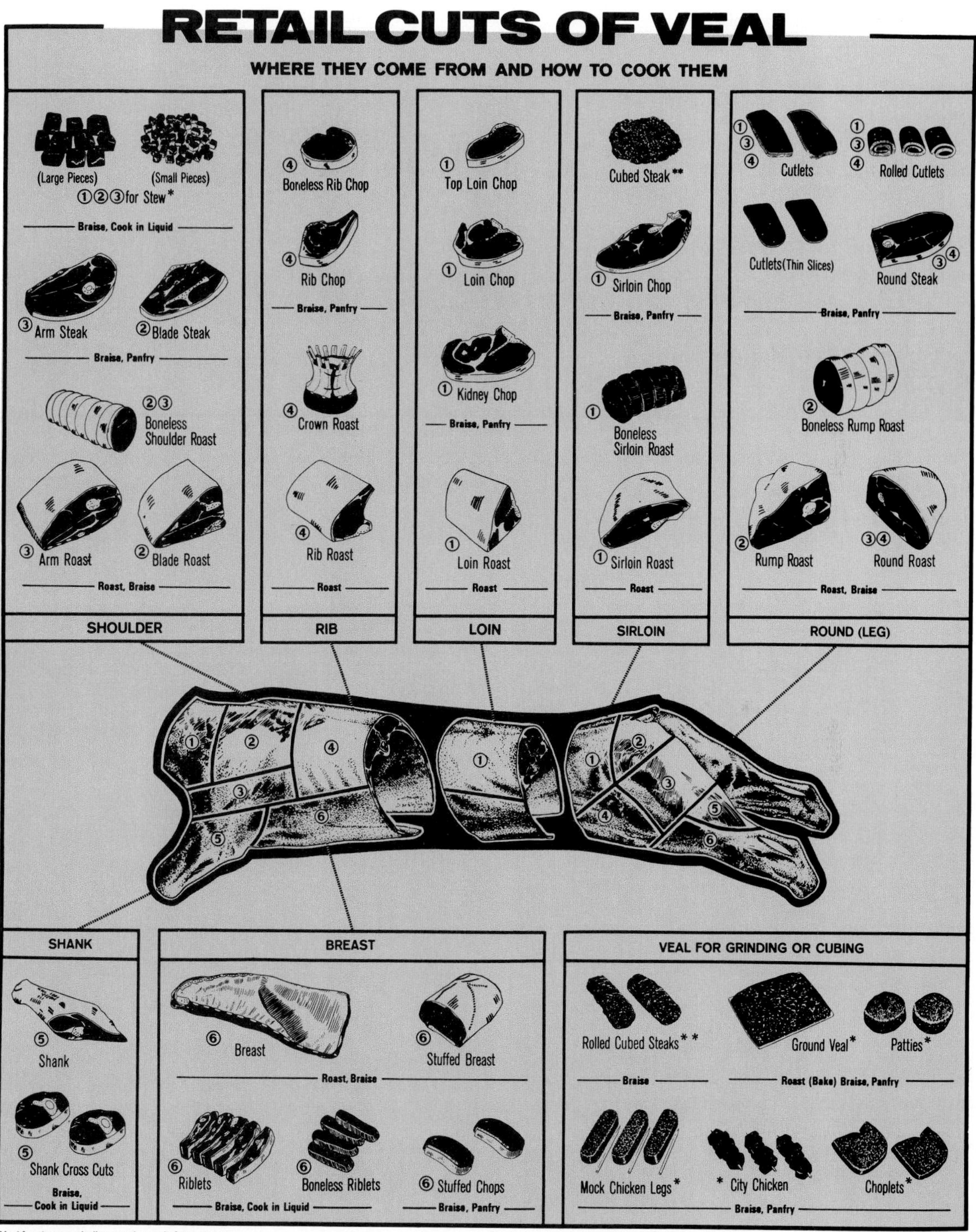

*Veal for stew or grinding may be made from any cut.

**Cubed steaks may be made from any thick solid piece of boneless veal.

Guide to Stuffing Poultry

Poultry/weight	*Stuffing*
Cornish game hen, 1 pound	¼ to ½ cup (50 to 125 mL)
(500 g)	1 tablespoon (15 mL) for neck
Broiler, 3 pounds	1 to 2 cups (250 to 500 mL)
(1.5 kg)	¼ cup (50 mL) for neck
Baking chicken, 4 to 5 pounds	3 to 5 cups (750 to 1250 mL)
(2 to 2.5 kg)	½ cup (125 mL) for neck.
Capon, 5 to 8 pounds	5 to 7 cups (1.25 to 1.75 L)
(2.5 to 4 kg)	1 cup (250 mL) for neck
Turkey, 9 to 12 pounds	4 to 6 cups (1 to 1.5 L)
(4.5 to 6 kg)	1 cup (250 mL) for neck
Turkey, 15 to 20 pounds	10 cups (2.5 L)
(7.5 to 10 kg)	1 to 2 cups (375 to 500 mL) for neck

Cooking Times for Whole Poultry

Size of bird	*Servings*	*Oven Temperature*	*Approximate Time in Hours*
2 to 3 pounds (1 to 1.5 kg)	2 to 4	375°F (190°C)	1
4 pounds (2 kg)	5 to 6	375°F (190°C)	1½
6 pounds (3 kg)	8 to 9	350°F (175°C)	2¼
9 to 12 pounds (4.5 to 6 kg)	8	325°F (165°C)	2½ to 3
12 to 15 pounds (6 to 7.5 kg)	12*	325°F (165°C)	4 to 5
17 to 20 pounds (8.5 to 10 kg)	15*	325°F (165°C)	5½ to 6
20 to 25 pounds (10 to 12.5 kg)	16*	325°F (165°C)	6 to 7½

*Servings planned to allow everyone a share of white meat. This number will undoubtedly serve more than the number specified for other types of meat. Note: To roast a bird that is stuffed in the neck and body cavity, add an extra 20 to 30 minutes to the times listed.

Nutritive Guide to Fast Foods

	Protein %	Vitamin A %	Vitamin C %	Riboflavin %	Niacin %	Calcium %	Iron %	Fat g	Sodium mg	Thiamin %	
Fish Fillet Sandwich and French Fries Calories: 660	25	4	20	15	25	10	15	38	908	—	
Hamburger and Vanilla Shake Calories: 770	60	10	6	60	35	40	25	25	830	30	
Double Hamburger with Mayonnaise-type Sauce, /Regular French Fries, Soft Drink Calories: 923	45	10	25	25	45	15	25	12	709	35	
Regular Cheeseburger Regular French Fries, 2% Milk Calories: 648	50	15	30	40	30	45	15	31	977	30	
Egg Sandwich with English Muffin, Orange Juice, Black Coffee Calories: 420	30	20	140	25	20	25	15	16	887	40	
Orange Juice, Scrambled Eggs, Sausage, Hash-browns, Buttered English Muffin, Black Coffee Calories : 780	60	25	150	60	30	20	30	46	1265	60	
Roast Beef Sandwich Calories: 353	35	*	2	25	38	8	20	15	590	15	

Continued on Next Page

	Protein %	Vitamin A %	Vitamin C %	Riboflavin %	Niacin %	Calcium %	Iron %	Fat g	Sodium mg	Thiamin %	
Pasta Seafood Salad **Calories: 394**	23	46	34	13	8	20	36	22	1570	25	
Boneless Chicken Chunks (6 pieces dipped in batter and fried) **Calories: 314**	30	*	*	10	40	*	6	17	546	8	
Beef Taco with Cheese **Calories: 463**	33	22	22	17	32	15	21	17	765	17	
Deep-Fried Chicken Breast **Calories: 257**	56	*	*	8	50	3	3	17	654	5	
Seafood Chowder **Calories: 112**	7	7	2	8	2	6	1	5	835	5	
Cole Slaw (⅓ cup) **Calories: 103**	1	5	31	1	1	2	1	6	171	2	
Hot Fudge Sundae **Calories: 310**	10	4	4	20	6	20	4	11	170	4	
Cherry Pie, (deep-fried) **Calories: 260**	4	2	*	2	2	2	4	14	427	2	
Box Chocolate Chip Cookies **Calories: 342**	6	2	2	15	8	2	8	16	313	8	

Continued on Next Page

	Protein %	Vitamin A %	Vitamin C %	Riboflavin %	Niacin %	Calcium %	Iron %	Fat g	Sodium mg	Thiamin %
Baked Potato with Broccoli and Cheddar Cheese **Calories: 340**	10	35	6	20	30	15	15	25	430	20
French Fried Onion Rings **Calories: 270**	4	*	*	*	*	*	2	16	655	4
Vegetarian D'Lite Pita (Whole-wheat pita bread stuffed with fresh garden salad and topped with alfalfa sprouts) **Calories: 270**	16	20	—	15	15	6	25	14	610	35
Salad Bar Offerings										
Alfalfa Sprouts **Calories: 20**	2	8	*	*	2	*	4	+	—	2
American Cheese-Imitation **Calories: 70**	15	10	*	*	*	20	*	6	—	*
Bacon Bits **Calories: 10**	2	—	*	*	*	*	*	5	—	*
Bell Peppers **Calories: 4**	*	*	40	*	*	*	*	+	5	*
Breadsticks **Calories: 20**	*	*	*	*	*	*	*	1	—	*

Continued on Next Page

	Protein %	Vitamin A %	Vitamin C %	Riboflavin %	Niacin %	Calcium %	Iron %	Fat g	Sodium mg	Thiamin %	
Broccoli Calories: 14	2	10	60	4	*	2	*	+	10	2	
Cantaloupe— Fresh Calories:4	*	5	4	*	*	*	*	+	0	*	
Carrots Calories: 12	*	60	4	*	*	*	*	+	15	*	
Cauliflower Calories: 14	*	*	60	2	*	*	*	+	5	2	
Cheddar Cheese- Imitation Calories: 90	15	8	*	2	*	20	*	6	450	*	
Chow Mein Noodles Calories: 60	*	*	*	2	4	*	2	3	80	6	
Cottage Cheese Calories: 110	30	4	*	10	*	6	*	5	425	*	
Croutons Calories: 30	*	*	*	*	*	*	*	1	90	3	
Cucumbers Calories: 4	*	*	6	*	*	*	*	+	0	*	
Eggs Calories: 14	2	*	*	*	*	*	*	1	10	*	
Green Peas Calories: 60	6	10	20	4	6	*	8	+	90	15	

Continued on Next Page

	Protein %	Vitamin A %	Vitamin C %	Riboflavin %	Niacin %	Calcium %	Iron %	Fat g	Sodium mg	Thiamin %	
Lettuce, Iceberg **Calories: 8**	*	4	4	*	*	*	*	+	5	2	
Lettuce, Romaine **Calories: 10**	*	20	15	2	*	*	4	+	5	2	
Mushrooms **Calories: 6**	*	*	*	4	2	*	*	+	5	*	
Oranges - Fresh **Calories: 10**	*	*	15	*	*	*	*	—	0	*	
Peaches - Packed in Syrup **Calories: 17**	*	2	20	*	*	*	*	+	0	*	
Pineapple Chunks - Packed in Juice **Calories: 80**	*	*	20	*	*	*	*	+	0	8	
Red Onions **Calories: 4**	*	*	*	*	*	*	*	+	0	*	
Saltine Crackers (4) **Calories: 45**	10	—	—	—	—	—	—	2	150	—	
Sunflower Seeds & Raisins **Calories: 180**	10	*	*	4	8	4	15	13	10	35	
Tomatoes **Calories: 6**	*	4	10	*	*	*	*	+	0	*	
Turkey Ham **Calories: 46**	10	—	—	—	—	—	—	2	—	—	

	Protein %	Vitamin A %	Vitamin C %	Riboflavin %	Niacin %	Calcium %	Iron %	Fat g	Sodium mg	Thiamin %	
Blue Cheese Dressing (1 tbsp.) Calories: 60	*	*	*	*	*	*	*	7	85	*	
Celery Seed Dressing (1 tbsp.) Calories: 70	*	*	*	*	*	*	*	6	65	*	
Golden Italian Dressing (1 tbsp.) Calories: 45	*	*	*	*	*	*	*	4	260	*	
Oil Dressing (1 tbsp.) Calories: 130	*	—	*	*	*	*	*	+	35	*	
Ranch Dressing (1 tbsp.) Calories: 80	*	*	*	*	*	*	*	9	155	*	
Red French Dressing (1 tbsp.) Calories: 70	*	*	*	*	*	*	*	5	130	*	
Reduced Calorie Dressing (1 tbsp.) Calories: 50	*	*	*	*	*	*	*	5	140	*	
Thousand Island (1 tbsp.) Calories: 70	*	*	*	*	*	*	*	7	115	*	

* = contains less than 2% of the U.S. RDA
\+ = contains less than 1 gram
— = data not available

Recipes

A

B

D

E

F

G

N

O

P

Q

R

S

T

U

V

W

Y

Z

Acknowledgments

We express our gratitude to the following professionals who were instrumental in creating *Foods:* Slater Studio (design, photography, and production), Alice Vernon (food styling), Lynn Lohman (food styling), Earl Slack (illustrations), Janell Fellrath (consultant), and Sheila Ashbrook (consultant). In addition, we would like to thank the following for their contributions.

Data from "North to the Pole." (Science Museum of Minnesota, St. Paul, MN),

Data from Mary McCann-Rugg, "Eating Right During Pregnancy." Circular 1215. (University of Illinois, Champaign-Urbana), "Feeding Your Baby During the First Year." Circular 1216. (University of Illinois, Champaign-Urbana), 83-88

Data from Robert Reber and Don Layman, "Don't Let Your Diet Let You Down—Guide for High School Athletes." Circular 1044. (University of Illinois, Champaign-Urbana), 78-81

Recipes

Betty Crocker's International Cookbook, General Mills, (Betty Crocker is a registered trademark of General Mills)
- African Sweet Potato Salad, 29
- Black Forest Cherry Cake, 150
- (Egg-and-Lemon Soup) Avgolemeno, 357
- Egg-Drop Soup (Tan Hua T'ang) 32
- Gazpacho, 123
- Gingered Pear Sorbet, 206
- Refried Beans, 24
- Spanish Crullers, 27
- Spicy Sausage Burritos, 137

Cooking Light '86, Oxmoor House, Inc.,
- Carrot Muffins, ©1986, 303
- Chocolate-Almond Fluff, ©1986, 74
- German Apple Pancake, ©1986, 25
- Grilled Sesame Chicken Breasts, ©1986, 329
- Oat Bran Muffins, ©1986, 45
- Mixed Vegetable Stir-fry, ©1986, 231
- Peanut-Butter Banana Muffins, ©1986, 291
- Spaghetti Squash Salad, ©1986, 229

Joan M. Clement
- Banana Ice Cream Pie, 413

Mary Ann Fugate,
- Company Chicken, 165
- Whole-Wheat Bread, 299

National Pork Producers,
- Javanese Pork Sate, 383
- Marinated Pork Salad, 324

Robert Reber,
Liquid Pregame Meal, 81
Science Museum of Minnesota,
Blue Cornbread, 272
Southern Heritage, Oxmoor House, Inc.,
Peanut Biscuits, ©1983, 215
Southern Living,
Crunchy Hot Chicken Salad, ©June 1980, 336
Individual Frozen Souffles, ©March 1980, 367
Sweet-and-Sour Fish, ©March 1980, 342

Photographs

Betty Crocker's International Cookbook (Betty Crocker is a registered trademark of General Mills), 13, 14, 20, 26, 28, 135, 298, 377
Bounty Microwave "Quick Cuisine", 57, 159, 313
California Strawberry Advisory Board, 177
Campbell Soup Company, 148
Cray Research, 406
Robert Fried, 69, 77, 89, 408
Gerber Products Company, 86
Jewel Companies, Inc., 374
Thomas J. Lipton, Inc., 384
Miller Flour Federation, 297
Minnesota Egg Council/American Egg Board, 361
National Dairy Council, 38, 39, 40, 41, 127
National Live Stock & Meat Board 444, 445, 446, 447
National Pork Producers Council, 43, 51, 317, 372, 383
Pillsbury Company, 23, 31, 169, 289
The Quaker Oats Company, 269
Rice Council, 413
Louis Rich, 331
Frank Schroder/Tanneblick Studio, 87
Will Steger/Firth Photography, 2
Tupperware® Home Parties, 185

Is there someone in your life who truly thrives on making opportunities "happen" for others? True teachers teach by inspiring others to stretch, grow, and "feel good about themselves" while they learn! My life has been blessed by several such mentors, and to one of them I dedicate this book-Edwin W. Vernon, Head of Instructional Design for the College of Agriculture at the University of Illinois. Dr. Vernon's own competence combined with his enthusiastic faith in my professional capabilities has kindled my yearning to share with others the daily excitement of learning to live a lifestyle that includes creative foods and nutritional updating.

And another heartfelt thank you is extended to Dr. Kathryn W. Smith, Professor of Home Economics and University Vocational Education Coordinator at Illinois State University, who has unselfishly shared her professional expertise and countless vocational opportunities with this grateful friend.

Alice Vernon
